Recent Developments in Urban and Regional Economics

The International Library of Critical Writings in Economics

Series Editor: Mark Blaug

Professor Emeritus, University of London, UK
Professor Emeritus, University of Buckingham, UK
Visiting Professor, University of Amsterdam, The Netherlands

This series is an essential reference source for students, researchers and lecturers in economics. It presents by theme a selection of the most important articles across the entire spectrum of economics. Each volume has been prepared by a leading specialist who has written an authoritative introduction to the literature included.

A full list of published and future titles in this series is printed at the end of this volume.

Wherever possible, the articles in these volumes have been reproduced as originally published using facsimile reproduction, inclusive of footnotes and pagination to facilitate ease of reference.

For a list of all Edward Elgar published titles visit our site on the World Wide Web at
www.e-elgar.com

Recent Developments in Urban and Regional Economics

Edited by

Paul C. Cheshire

Professor of Economic Geography
London School of Economics, UK

and

Gilles Duranton

Reader in Economic Geography
London School of Economics, UK

THE INTERNATIONAL LIBRARY OF CRITICAL WRITINGS IN ECONOMICS

An Elgar Reference Collection
Cheltenham, UK • Northampton, MA, USA

Published by
Edward Elgar Publishing Limited
Glensanda House
Montpellier Parade
Cheltenham
Glos GL50 1UA
UK

Edward Elgar Publishing, Inc.
136 West Street
Suite 202
Northampton
Massachusetts 01060
USA

A catalogue record for this book is available from the British Library

ISBN 1 84064 953 4

Printed and bound in Great Britain by MPG Books Ltd, Bodmin, Cornwall.

Contents

Acknowledgements

The editors and publishers wish to thank the authors and the following publishers who have kindly given permission for the use of copyright material.

American Economic Association for articles: Edward M. Gramlich (1994), 'Infrastructure Investment: A Review Essay', *Journal of Economic Literature*, **XXXII** (3), September, 1176–96; Antonio Ciccone and Robert E. Hall (1996), 'Productivity and the Density of Economic Activity', *American Economic Review*, **86** (1), March, 54–70; Gordon H. Hanson (1996), 'Localization Economies, Vertical Organization, and Trade', *American Economic Review*, **86** (5), December, 1266–78; Wallace E. Oates (1999), 'An Essay on Fiscal Federalism', *Journal of Economic Literature*, **XXXVII** (3), September, 1120–49; J. Peter Neary (2001), 'Of Hype and Hyperbolas: Introducing the New Economic Geography', *Journal of Economic Literature*, **XXXIX** (2), June, 536–61.

Blackwell Publishing Ltd for articles: Paul Cheshire and Stephen Sheppard (1995), 'On the Price of Land and the Value of Amenities', *Economica*, **62** (246), May, 247–67; Danny T. Quah (1996), 'Twin Peaks: Growth and Convergence in Models of Distribution Dynamics', *Economic Journal*, **106** (437), July, 1045–55.

Editions Dalloz for article: Jacques Crémer, Antonio Estache and Paul Seabright (1996), 'Decentralizing Public Services: What Can We Learn from the Theory of the Firm?', *Revue d'économie politique*, **106** (1), January–February, 37–60.

EIB Papers for article: Angel de la Fuente (2000), 'Convergence across Countries and Regions: Theory and Empirics', *EIB Papers*, **5** (2), 25–45.

Elsevier for articles: Dennis R. Capozza and Robert W. Helsley (1990), 'The Stochastic City', *Journal of Urban Economics*, **28** (2), September, 187–203; Keith R. Ihlanfeldt (1992), 'Intraurban Wage Gradients: Evidence by Race, Gender, Occupational Class, and Sector', *Journal of Urban Economics*, **32** (1), July, 70–91; Mitsuru Ota and Masahisa Fujita (1993), 'Communication Technologies and Spatial Organization of Multi-unit Firms in Metropolitan Areas', *Regional Science and Urban Economics*, **23** (6), 695–729; Lawrence Thurston and Anthony M.J. Yezer (1994), 'Causality in the Suburbanization of Population and Employment', *Journal of Urban Economics*, **35** (1), January, 105–18; Marlon G. Boarnet (1994), 'The Monocentric Model and Employment Location', *Journal of Urban Economics*, **36** (1), July, 79–97; Roland Bénabou (1994), 'Human Capital, Inequality, and Growth: A Local Perspective', *European Economic Review*, **38** (3–4), 817–26; Jan K. Brueckner, Jacques-François Thisse and Yves Zenou (1999), 'Why is Central Paris Rich and Downtown Detroit Poor? An Amenity-Based Theory', *European Economic Review*, **43** (1), 91–107; Donald R. Davis and

David E. Weinstein (1999), 'Economic Geography and Regional Production Structure: An Empirical Investigation', *European Economic Review*, **43** (2), 379–407; Pierre-Philippe Combes (2000), 'Economic Structure and Local Growth: France, 1984–1993', *Journal of Urban Economics*, **47**, 329–55; Vernon Henderson and Randy Becker (2000), 'Political Economy of City Sizes and Formation', *Journal of Urban Economics*, **48** (3), 453–84.

MIT Press Journals and the President and Fellows of Harvard College and the Massachusetts Institute of Technology for articles: Alberto F. Ades and Edward L. Glaeser (1995), 'Trade and Circuses: Explaining Urban Giants', *Quarterly Journal of Economics*, **CX** (1), February, 195–227; Dora L. Costa and Matthew E. Kahn (2000), 'Power Couples: Changes in the Locational Choice of the College Educated, 1940–1990', *Quarterly Journal of Economics*, **115** (4), November, 1287–315; Robert Dekle (2002), 'Industrial Concentration and Regional Growth: Evidence from the Prefectures', *Review of Economics and Statistics*, **84** (2), May, 310–15.

Oxford University Press for article: David B. Audretsch (1998), 'Agglomeration and the Location of Innovative Activity', *Oxford Review of Economic Policy*, **14** (2), 18–29.

Sage Publications, Inc. for article: Jan K. Brueckner (2000), 'Urban Sprawl: Diagnosis and Remedies', *International Regional Science Review*, **23** (2), April, 160–71.

Taylor and Francis Ltd (http://www.tandf.co.uk/journals/carfax/00343404.html) for articles: Sergio J. Rey and Brett D. Montouri (1999), 'US Regional Income Convergence: A Spatial Econometric Perspective', *Regional Studies*, **33** (2), 143–56; Gilles Duranton and Diego Puga (2000), 'Diversity and Specialisation in Cities: Why, Where and When Does it Matter?', *Urban Studies*, **37** (3), 533–55.

University of Chicago Press for articles: Paul Krugman (1991), 'Increasing Returns and Economic Geography', *Journal of Political Economy*, **99** (3), 483–99; Joseph Gyourko and Joseph Tracy (1991), 'The Structure of Local Public Finance and the Quality of Life', *Journal of Political Economy*, **99** (4), August, 774–806.

Every effort has been made to trace all the copyright holders but if any have been inadvertently overlooked the publishers will be pleased to make the necessary arrangement at the first opportunity.

In addition the publishers wish to thank the Library of Indiana University at Bloomington, USA for their assistance in obtaining these articles.

Introduction

Paul C. Cheshire and Gilles Duranton

The contrast between the literature available for the preparation of the first volume devoted to urban and regional economics in this series (Cheshire and Evans, 1991) and that available for this is of considerable interest. We have deliberately confined ourselves to papers published since 1990: the first volume covered 40 years. Since 1990, the divide between urban and regional economics as separate fields has all but disappeared. We have chosen not to have these separately represented here. Moreover, urban and regional – perhaps we should better call it spatial economics now[1] – has become in large measure a part of the mainstream. In the first volume, only 21 per cent of the articles selected first appeared in leading mainstream economics journals (and none of those had been published within the previous 10 years); 58 per cent were from interdisciplinary journals. In this volume, half the articles come from leading mainstream economics journals, all published over a period of only 12 years; only 11 per cent of the articles we have chosen are from interdisciplinary journals. In our view, this reflects the renewed interest of the economics profession in spatial economics, apparent over the past 15 years or so. Perhaps the convenient marker in this process was Krugman's 1991 classic (reproduced here as Chapter 21).

Why can Krugman's article be called a 'classic'? After all, in many ways it said nothing new. The foundation of Kaldor's (1970) analysis of regional growth was the existence of increasing returns to scale leading to economies of agglomeration, and this general idea can be traced back to Myrdal (1957) and probably beyond that. But Krugman – who deliberately made no reference to these earlier contributions – approached the issue in an entirely different way. His concern was to have a theory of regional growth processes, which grew in an entirely consistent way out of modern analysis resting on the rigorous Dixit and Stiglitz (1977) model of monopolistic competition with increasing returns and explicit microeconomic foundations. Conceptually the behaviour of Krugman's regional economies (pretty spaceless places, it must be acknowledged) was built up from individual consumers and firms. In terms of the phenomena that the model explained, one probably got a better understanding from the verbal analysis of Anas and Moses (1978), but Krugman's contribution was seminal because it reunited urban and regional economics with the mainstream. Of course there had been much work in urban economics, in particular, that we readily recognise as rigorous economic analysis sitting comfortably within the broader development of modern economics, but it remained a specialised sub-field which did not attract much attention from the big research departments. From 1991, although not getting the attention of international trade or labour economics, spatial economics was back on the research agenda of economists in major research departments. It had become, again, respectable.

Why did it largely disappear from the research agenda of mainstream economists from about 1970 to 1990? Perhaps part of the explanation is provided by the way in which the Introduction to the first volume (Cheshire and Evans, 1991) explained the 40-year intellectual development of urban and regional economics. The explanation was in terms of finding solutions to policy problems: the urban transport problem or problems associated with regional adjustment processes and unemployment disparities. These were – and continue to be – significant problems, but the research agenda of mainstream economics was not driven by them. Indeed it could be argued that for a long period economists were engaged in consolidating their new tools of mathematical analysis, which had become the dominant mode of analysis during the 1950s. In addition, mainstream economists were consolidating their discovery of micro-foundations and rethinking macroeconomics in an intellectual climate in which Keynes was a figure of the past.

In contrast, urban and regional economists were practical people whose motivation arose from wanting to do the best they could to investigate and provide solutions for the problems they thought to be important. Only the briefest exposure to the field showed that one could not ignore economies of scale or agglomeration. Space mattered, activities clustered and the consumption of many important goods was conditioned on precise location. Until new tools became available to allow economies of scale to be incorporated within the new formal neo-classical framework, mainstream economists preferred to assume them away. Urban and regional economics went down a practical policy-directed path, while mainstream economics consolidated its formal analytical frameworks. Of course, these had practical application but their development was not driven by practical needs. A further symbol of the divergence of urban and regional from mainstream economics was the continued dominance of Keynesian economics within urban and regional analysis. Partly this was because, as Kaldor had shown, neo-Keynesian growth models sat well with increasing returns to scale. But also simple tools such as the Keynesian income multiplier remained in practical use (just as the IS-LM framework remains widely used by central bankers).

In this mode of thought regions remained internally spaceless – they were modelled as subdivisions of national economies within which there was no spatial differentiation or competition for locations. But also 'regions' were in a sense themselves 'actors'. Regional economies were not conceived of as being the aggregate of a set of individual firms and households, which were simultaneously consumers, and suppliers of factors of production. Put differently, there were no explicit microeconomic foundations.

The growing theoretical concern in mainstream economics for explicit micro-foundations has been allied to vastly increased computing power and the availability of new data sets providing observations of individual households and firms. Most of the applied work represented in this volume fully reflects this development. The data sets analysed are composed of individual economic actors. Urban and regional economists have not lost their interest in understanding practical and policy-relevant problems, nor have they lost their motivation to understand important phenomena of the world we live in. But rejoining the mainstream has been intellectually invigorating and the ability to access and analyse new micro-level data sets has greatly enriched the empirical work in the subject. We hope these developments, which we ourselves have found stimulating and exciting, are reflected in this volume.

The collection is divided into six parts. The first three parts are devoted to the city and systems of cities. Part I is composed of four articles that have contributed to our theoretical understanding of urban structure, while Part II contains five papers devoted to its empirical analysis. Part III has four articles dealing with both theoretical and empirical analysis of systems of cities.

In Part IV, we have made a deliberate decision to unite both micro and macro based approaches to understanding the dynamics of cities, regions and their economies. It seems to us that growth performance differences between regions reflect underlying differences in the form, behaviour and interactions between the individual firms and households that live within them. Included within this broad generalisation will be differences deriving from agglomeration economies, resource and factor endowments (including, of course, endowment with human capital), infrastructure, climate and less tangible factors such as institutional arrangements, government and culture. Traditionally studies of the generation of innovation, the nature and extent of external economies between producers and regional economic performance have been regarded as separate branches of knowledge. It seems to us they are all aspects of one branch of knowledge and that combining articles representing developments in these fields underlines this point. Nevertheless we have a separate section, Part V, on the so-called New Economic Geography, to highlight this important development over the 1990s. We acknowledge, however, that if we took our argument to its logical extreme we might conclude that this approach should be included in an expanded Part IV. A theoretical piece, a recent survey of its contribution and two empirical articles represent the New Economic Geography. The final section, Part VI, contains four articles analysing aspects of local public finance and policy.

Part I: Inside the City (or Theoretically Inside the City . . .): Theoretical Analysis of City Structure

After the pioneering work of Alonso (1964), Mills (1967) and Muth (1969), the 1970s and 1980s saw a flourish of theoretical work about the internal structure of cities. This important strand of work came to be known as the 'New Urban Economics'. It is now part of the standard toolbox of all urban and regional economists. A simple summary of this work can be found in Brueckner (1987). Fujita (1989) provides an extensive summary of this literature prior to 1990. The past 15 years saw some further progress on the theoretical analysis of urban structures, albeit at a slower pace than before. We can distinguish four types of work.

A first stream of work has used insights and modelling tools from other fields of economics and incorporated them successfully in the standard paradigm. The article by Capozza and Helsley (Chapter 1) is illustrative of this type of work using insights from financial economics to look at the urban development process. They use a simple model of an isolated city in which household income, rents and prices for land follow stochastic processes. The key insight is that although investors are risk neutral, uncertainty affects both land rents and land prices in equilibrium. There is an option value for agricultural land, which occurs because the conversion of land from agricultural to urban use is irreversible. This model yields a rich set of predictions, which have been widely used by the empirical literature in urban and real estate economics. This paper, although very good, is only one example of a successful import of tools coming from other fields into urban modelling. In the same spirit but in a very different vein, Wasmer and Zenou (2002) provide an interesting analysis of how labour market imperfections affect urban structure. Without multiplying the examples, it is worth pointing out that modelling in urban and regional economics over the past ten years or so has become increasingly open to developments in other sub-fields of economic analysis. Hopefully, the thoughtful implementation of new technical developments from other sub-fields will keep providing us with new insights about cities.

To some extent, the article by Ota and Fujita (Chapter 2) can also be viewed as an import – a successful application of concepts drawn from industrial economics. However, this paper is more illustrative of a second important tendency. As time goes by, cities change in their shape and form. In this respect, the decentralisation of manufacturing activities to the outskirts of cities is a remarkable and empirically well-documented trend. At the same time, however, central business districts have prospered and maintained their advantage as favoured locations for command and control activities. Ota and Fujita propose the following explanation for these trends. They consider an isolated city in which production is generated by firms composed of multiple units that exchange information or services. More specifically, each firm consists of headquarters and a production plant. Each of the headquarters exchanges information with all other headquarters and with its production plant. In equilibrium firms face a standard trade-off between expensive but information-rich central locations and cheap but information-poor peripheral locations. They also face a trade-off between the gains from separating their units, locating their headquarters in the Central Business District (CBD) and their production plant in the periphery, and the costs of internal communication. Interestingly, under some circumstances, cheaper telecommunications can generate the type of decentralisation pattern that has been observed empirically.

Again, this paper, although quite remarkable, is only one example of this type of work. Another good example is provided by Henderson and Mitra (1996), who attempt to model the phenomenon of edge cities proliferating around large metro areas. It is our contention that cities will keep evolving and that these evolutions will present urban theory with new challenges calling for further work.

The third type of work in this literature is more classical. It consists in deepening the existing framework to explain phenomena hitherto not well understood. The article by Brueckner, Thisse and Zenou (Chapter 3) is a good example of this. For a long time, urban economists thought that patterns of location by income could be explained by a simple trade-off between commuting distance and the price of land. Provided the income elasticity of demand for land is large enough, the rich will demand more land and locate in the suburbs and the poor will live at high densities on more expensive land in central locations. However, the income elasticity of demand for land that would be needed for this to explain location patterns by income is implausibly large (Glaeser, Kahn and Rappaport, 2000). Brueckner, Thisse and Zenou propose instead an amenity-based explanation. In their model, when the centre has a strong amenity advantage over the suburbs, the rich are likely to live at central locations. When instead the centre's amenity advantage is weak or negative, the rich are likely to live in the suburbs. This argument naturally explains the contrast between many European cities and most US cities in location patterns by income; just as in the UK it explains differences between cities such as Oxford where the rich are concentrated in the centre, and nearby Reading where they are located in the ex-urbs (Cheshire, 1999). As with the previous two types of work, the paper we chose is a very good one but it is by no means the sole direction in which the monocentric framework has been pushed. Although developments of the basic monocentric model may have reached a region of decreasing returns, there are still some gaps in our knowledge to be filled. The most obvious one concerns, of course, the modelling of multicentric cities.

The last trend is very different from the previous three, in that it is a more radical departure from the standard monocentric framework. It is concerned with urban segregation, ghettos and neighbourhood effects. The understanding of these phenomena requires a precise modelling of the local externalities within neighbourhoods, as well as the possible linkages at the metropolitan level. The paper which pioneered this type of analysis is Bénabou (1993) (see also Fernandez and Rogerson, 1996). To keep the analysis tractable, the internal geography of cities was drastically simplified (usually by assuming just two districts). The article by Bénabou (Chapter 4) provides an accessible summary of this literature. It shows that strong patterns of stratification arise naturally from minor differences in education technologies, preferences, wealth or minor imperfections in capital markets. It also shows how such patterns of stratification can be very inefficient and self-reinforcing over time.

Part II: Inside the City (or . . . Actually Inside the City?): Empirical Analysis of City Structure

The monocentric model continues to dominate the intellectual landscape of urban analysis despite attempts to establish rigorous models of more 'realistic', polycentric, urban forms. White (1999) provides a survey of some of the work in this vein. A key assumption of the monocentric model is that employment is centrally located in the CBD and that at least its location is taken as given by households making their own location decisions. An outcome of the model is that particular zones – annular rings – in the urban area will be occupied exclusively by one class of user: households or businesses, or poor/rich households, commercial, retail or industrial employment, etc.

Our first selection in this applied section, Boarnet (Chapter 5), queries one of the central elements in the monocentric model: that the location of employment is exogenous with respect to the location of households. This uses geographically disaggregated data for 365 municipalities of the state of New Jersey (effectively part of the outer suburbs of the city of New York) over the period 1980 to 1988. The point of interest is the relationship between population growth and employment growth in the surrounding areas controlling for a range of variables (although not the sectoral composition). His main finding is that while population growth is not significantly determined by employment growth in the surrounding areas, it does significantly and positively influence employment growth. This study makes an interesting complement to the article by Thurston and Yezer (Chapter 7) which, because its analysis is disaggregated by sector, is able to show that this positive influence of population on employment growth may be specific to employment in population-serving sectors such as retail and personal services.

The article by Ihlanfeldt (Chapter 6) addresses another feature of the monocentric model, namely the wage gradient. Given the basic trade-off between commuting and housing/space costs, wages for given categories of workers should be expected to fall with distance from the CBD. Earlier work, for example, by Eberts (1981) had provided some evidence to support this hypothesis but the contribution of Ihlanfeldt is substantial. He uses micro-level data for three separated urban areas (Boston, Detroit and Philadelphia) in 1980, and so is effectively able to control for a wide range of worker and job characteristics. The approach adopted exploits the large size of the data set to estimate separate models for different groups. As predicted by the standard monocentric model of urban land use, the following results are obtained for most groups of white workers: negative and statistically significant wage gradients, steeper wage gradients for higher wage earners, and an increase in the steepness of wage gradients as the CBD is approached. Positive wage gradients are not found for black workers, despite the fact that suburban employers hire large numbers of these workers who reside within the central city. This result is taken as support for the hypothesis that blacks have been disadvantaged by job suburbanisation and continued housing market segregation.

Thurston and Yezer (Chapter 7) focus on an old chicken-and-egg question in urban economics: in the process of suburbanisation (or recentralisation), do people follow jobs or do jobs follow people? This came to particular prominence in the wake of the large-scale suburbanisation of large cities in advanced economies that was the dominant trend from the 1950s to about 1980. It is worth noting that the question features less obviously in the analysis of the initial phases of urbanisation associated with the Industrial Revolution and the growth of manufacturing cities. Indirectly, Thurston and Yezer return therefore to the issue explored by Boarnet (Chapter 5): is employment location exogenous?

The significant contribution of Thurston and Yezer's work is that they disaggregate employment movements by sector and use annual rather than decennial data. This allowed them not just to demonstrate that there were fundamental differences between sectors, but that there were also interesting interactions between movement of employment in one sector, subsequent population movement and then movement of employment in other sectors. Employment in construction and utilities decentralised ahead of population; decentralisation of retail and service sectors appeared to be significantly the result of population decentralisation; but the decentralisation of manufacturing employment appeared to reduce population decentralisation. They interpret this last finding as evidence of the localised negative externalities associated with manufacturing employment. Overall, however, the conclusion to be drawn from Thurston and Yezer is that simplistic questions, such as in suburbanisation do people follow jobs or vice versa, do not have simple answers.

Thurston and Yezer's finding that more manufacturing decentralisation was, other things held constant, associated with less decentralisation of people is consistent with the result reported in the next article by Cheshire and Sheppard (Chapter 8) that a significant price is paid for less industrial land use in a neighbourhood: that is, the proximity to industry is a 'bad' rather than a 'good'. That finding is only incidental to the article, however, which is both an application and an empirical test of the monocentric model, as well as an attempt to lay the groundwork for estimating the impacts of land use planning identified in Brueckner. In common with several of the empirical studies we have selected, Cheshire and Sheppard use disaggregated, individual data. The data set relates to individual houses sold in a particular community,[2] but these are precisely located and their structural characteristics are combined with very detailed data drawn from maps, aerial photographs, local education authorities and population censuses in order to estimate the hedonic prices not only of the physical attributes of the houses, but of the local amenities and public goods, and neighbourhood characteristics the location of each house endows its occupants with. Later studies (Cheshire and Sheppard, 1998, 2002) combined these estimates of the prices of housing attributes – including those of the goods (or amenities) provided by land use regulation – with data on the incomes of the households concerned. This made it possible to estimate the structure of demand for these attributes and the net impact of land use planning on economic welfare and the distribution of real incomes. But the article reprinted here is free-standing and provides striking evidence of the extent to which localised amenities and public goods are effectively capitalised into the market price of land and how, when their values are extracted, the underlying price of land as conceptualised in the monocentric model (the 'price of pure space with accessibility') emerges.

Given the importance of housing in consumers' budgets, the widespread use of land market regulation through systems of planning or zoning and the severity with which such controls are frequently applied, it can reasonably be argued that the economics of land market regulation have been neglected. One of the authors who has addressed the issue over a number of years is Brueckner (1990, 1995; Brueckner and Lai, 1996). Brueckner's piece selected for this volume (Chapter 9) is a non-technical synthesis of the economic issues that must be taken into account in any attempt to trace the welfare impacts of land use regulation. Because of potential problems of market failure and the interdependence of land uses, land use regulation has the capacity to generate public goods and enhance amenities and so contribute positively to economic welfare. At the same time, however, and especially if 'growth constraint' (or 'urban containment' as it is called in the UK) is a significant aim of land market regulation, it is likely that the price of space and so housing will be raised. Thus the task of the analyst is to attempt to unravel the positives from the negatives of any system of land market regulation. In addition to the effects on prices and the supply of public goods, because of necessity any impacts of land use regulation are associated with specific locations – the amenities and increased space prices are systematically distributed unevenly through space – the gains and losses associated with land market regulation will accrue to particular occupants of specific houses and differ as between owner-occupiers and non owner-occupiers. Thus there are potentially significant distributional effects of land market regulation, as well. These points are well discussed in Brueckner (2000), as is the potential to address problems of land market failure by means of taxes as opposed to direct regulation.

Part III: Systems of Cities

The economic modelling of urban systems was pioneered by Henderson (1974). However, this literature did not attract much attention during most of the 1970s and 1980s. Its main perceived weakness was an absence of solid micro-economic foundations. A second impetus was given by the work of Abdel-Rahman and Fujita (1990), building on the Dixit and Stiglitz (1977) model of monopolistic competition. Following these papers, the literature modelling urban systems developed very quickly during the 1990s.

The first two articles in this part, by Duranton and Puga (Chapter 10) and Henderson and Becker (Chapter 11), provide a complete overview of this literature. The survey by Duranton and Puga is concerned with the types of activities that cities perform. They first highlight a series of stylised facts about cities. Their empirical analysis is centred on the issue of the composition of economic activity in cities. Then they review the different strands in the theoretical literature on urban systems and assess how well they explain existing facts. The emphasis of Henderson and Becker is different. They focus on the political economy of city sizes and the formation of cities. They oppose the competitive model of large-scale land developers operating in national land markets and the self-organization model of agglomeration. They then analyse both types of framework and introduce local politics in them. This allows them to look at the rationale behind no-growth movements and megacities.

The next two chapters in this part are two provocative empirical articles looking at different aspects of urban systems. Ades and Glaeser (Chapter 12) assess empirically different possible explanations for megacities. Given that most of them are found in developing countries, they oppose an argument that relies on trade and the urban consequences of protectionist policies to a political-economy explanation whereby dictatorships lead to inefficient concentration in a primate city. Their main conclusion is that the political explanation dwarfs any effect of trade policies. The main city in a dictatorship is typically 50 per cent larger than the main city in a democracy and causality runs from the institutions to city size and not the other way round. This article is a good illustration of how much can be achieved by taking economic theory seriously and then going to the real world to test its implications in a creative way.

The last article in this part, by Costa and Khan (Chapter 13), looks at a very different problem. They first highlight the fact that college-educated workers are increasingly over-represented in large metropolitan areas in the USA. This could potentially point to a wide array of explanations, ranging from a change in the nature of agglomeration economies to an amenity explanation. In fact, they show that the primary cause of this phenomenon is the co-location problem faced by couples of college-educated workers. Despite higher housing costs, only the largest cities can provide sufficient alternatives in the labour market to satisfy both partners. This finding is of important practical interest since it suggests that smaller cities may experience reduced inflows of human capital relative to the past and thus become poorer.

Part IV: The Empirics of Agglomeration and Growth

Theory-informed empirical work came to the forefront of regional and urban analysis in the 1990s. This represents a key development in a field which was best characterised during most of its existence by an insurmountable divide between policy-driven and atheoretical applied work on the one hand, and elegant modelling detached from reality on the other. The article by Ades and Glaeser (Chapter 12), discussed above, is emblematic of this trend towards theory-informed empirical work. However, nowhere is this tendency as strong as in the empirical work on agglomeration and growth. In this respect it is interesting to note that urban agglomeration and regional growth were very much viewed as separate issues until the early 1990s. However, much of the work done over the past 10 to 15 years has contributed to making these boundaries fuzzier. By putting work on agglomeration economies and regional convergence together in the same section, we would like to take this trend forward and suggest that they are really complementary ways of analysing essentially the same phenomenon.

The article by Ciccone and Hall (Chapter 14) is exemplary of this renewal of empirical work and of the blending of regional and urban economics. Its goal is to understand large productivity differences between US states. To do so, the theoretical section of their paper uses modelling tools from urban economics to predict a relationship between the local density of employment and worker productivity. In doing this, they pursue the line of research pioneered by Sveikauskas (1975), which attempted to estimate agglomeration economies in cities, but they do that across the whole US territory. The first crucial difference is that previous work was using total employment at the city level (or total employment in the city and industry), whereas Ciccone and Hall motivate their new explanatory variable, employment density, with a theoretical argument. The urban literature estimating agglomeration economies was also plagued by a simultaneity problem. Is high density a cause or a consequence of high productivity? To answer this question, the second crucial input of this paper is to use modern econometric techniques, in particular, instrumental variables. The main result is that a doubling of employment density increases average labour productivity by around 6 per cent. More than half of the variance of output per worker across states can be explained by differences in the density of economic activity.

Most (if not all) of the work done on agglomeration economies before 1990 was static and looked at the relationship between a measure of local efficiency at a point in time and some explanatory variables at the same point in time. Following the pioneering work by Glaeser, Kallal, Scheinkman and Schleifer (1992), it can be argued that these externalities may be best viewed as dynamic. For instance, intense local competition may promote innovation locally and lead to increases in local employment in the industry. The next two articles by Deckle (Chapter 15) and Combes (Chapter 16) are important recent developments in this strand of literature. The chapter by Deckle has three crucial merits. Rather than local employment, it considers the evolution of productivity, which is arguably a better variable to look at. Like Combes, it also considers the entire spectrum of economic activity instead of focusing narrowly on manufacturing activity. Finally, and also like Combes, Deckle's analysis shows that good empirical work need not be done with US data. Their data, respectively from France and Japan, are of high quality and make it possible to explore in-depth issues that can be barely touched with US data. This healthy reminder should encourage non US-based researchers to use the comparative advantage of the data available in their country. Finally, the great advantage of the paper by Combes is that it contains a comprehensive discussion of methodological issues. This clarifies many of the misunderstandings which are common in this stream of work.

The paper by Audretsch (Chapter 17) is closely related to this literature, in that it provides a survey of the literature on innovation and location. Following the work by Jaffe (1989) and Feldman (1994), among others, the 1990s saw very interesting empirical developments underscoring the importance of location for innovative activities. This reading provides a nice survey of this burgeoning literature. It focuses on the way useful knowledge is transmitted and shows that proximity matters and matters enormously.

In research focusing conventionally on regional growth differences the huge concentration of published material falls into the 'convergence' mode associated with Barro (1991) and Barro and Sala-i-Martin (1991, 1992). This work is not directly represented in this volume. Although something can be learnt from this work about particular factors involved in differential urban and regional economic growth, it has been largely atheoretic and methodologically flawed. The article by de la Fuente (Chapter 18) is part survey and part synthesis. Its focus is convergence or divergence of 'economies': countries, regions or cities – it does not matter much which, given the level of abstraction of the argument. It pinpoints some of the methodological problems involved in the convergence literature and particularly those relating to a finding of an apparently significant negative relationship between the initial level of income and the growth rates in any set of economies.

The take of Quah (Chapter 19) is very different. His focus is on the meaning of 'convergence' and what happens to the cross-sectional distribution of economies' incomes rather than whether a single economy tends towards its steady state. In other words, he is interested in useful representations of the pattern of growth dynamics. In the previous article, de la Fuente has already alerted the reader to alternative concepts of convergence. Quah's contribution is to place the issue of convergence in the wider problem of the dynamics of income distribution: not only that, but to propose and apply a technique for representing these dynamics. The distribution of incomes might evolve over time, so that a group of rich economies was converging on a higher per capita income level and simultaneously getting richer, while another group of poorer economies was also converging on a common but lower level of per capita income. Such a development would be perfectly consistent with a falling standard deviation of the overall distribution and 'conditional' convergence but still be characterised by the emergence of an increasingly rich club of economies. The technique Quah proposes with which to analyse the dynamics of the distribution of incomes relies on a 'what-if?' procedure. One can look at the distribution of incomes at different points in time and estimate observed transition probabilities: given each economy has moved within the distribution between the start and end dates, what probability was there of any particular economy moving from one point in the distribution to any other? And then measure how the overall distribution would have evolved if the specific transition probabilities observed were replicated over successive periods. There are various ways in which this can be done. One, which applies the method with some refinements to the distribution of European regional incomes, is reported in Magrini (1999). He finds that the dynamics of the distribution were indeed characterised by Quah's 'twin-peakedness'.

The final selection in this part, by Rey and Montouri (Chapter 20), is representative of a body of work applying spatial econometric techniques to regional growth issues in order to test whether there are significant spatial patterns (in growth rates or in residuals from 'convergence' models). An important message of this piece, although not central to the authors' concerns, is the extent of long-term convergence of real per capita incomes in the USA. This very strong result for US states may unconsciously condition the approach of US researchers. The central point of the article, however, is the highly significant spatial dependence of both real incomes – rich states tend to border on other rich states and vice versa over the whole period 1929–94 – and growth rates. Part of this dependence may result from the borders of states sometimes dividing up larger metro-regional economies. For example, the rich state cluster is focused on the Boston–New York–Philadelphia corridor, including New York, New Jersey, Connecticut, Delaware, Rhode Island, Massachusetts and Pennsylvania; but some suggest underlying economic mechanisms are involved. In our judgement the measurement of spatial dependence is worthwhile but is, in the end, an essentially descriptive effort. On the one hand, it offers a warning that models which do not either offset for the effects by including spatial lags or include direct measures of the underlying mechanisms generating spatial dependence will be subject to estimation bias; on the other hand, spatial econometric approaches revealing spatial dependence tell us there is something interesting to investigate in the way of spatial economic mechanisms.[3]

Part V: The New Economic Geography

To the non-specialist in the field (and to many geographers), the work (and the heat) generated by Krugman's (Chapter 21) path-breaking work may seem to be the only significant evolution in urban and regional economics in the past 15 years. We hope the other articles in the volume will convince the reader that this is far from the case. However, as highlighted above, the paper by Krugman, which launched the so-called 'New Economic Geography', was a real breakthough. Single-handedly, Krugman was able to come up with a tractable framework to do regional analysis using the same rigorous modelling standards as in other fields of economic analysis. We felt that this seminal paper, although already widely known, had to be part of this volume.

The amount of theoretical work this paper has generated is enormous. There are literally hundreds of extensions and variations of this paper that have been produced so far. These extensions were partly driven by the fact that general results are difficult to obtain in this area of work. Consequently, the 'New Economic Geography' is to some extent a collection of specific examples. The robustness of the main results is mainly assessed through extensions and variations on a common theme. This state of affairs implies that a complete overview of this literature is difficult to get. To facilitate this, the following article in this part by Neary (Chapter 22) proposes a critical assessment of the New Economic Geography. Although originally written as a review of the book by Fujita, Krugman and Venables (1999), it proposes a very simplified exposition of the main effects at work in this literature. It also provides a thoughtful assessment of its strengths and weaknesses.

For a long time, the New Economic Geography was almost exclusively a theoretical enterprise. As such, its usefulness was going to be very limited. The New Economic Geography also ran the risk of running into a zone of sharply diminishing returns and disappearing like many other academic fads before. Fortunately, empirical research on trade and location has started to take seriously the New Economic Geography. Empirical work still lags way behind theory in this literature; however it is growing rapidly. In this volume, we particularly wanted to illustrate pioneering pieces of empirical analysis informed by the New Economic Geography.

The third article in this part, by Hanson (Chapter 23), looks at the Mexican apparel industry. Hanson uses a model much simpler than those developed by Krugman's followers. He considers an industry with two activities. The first one enjoys local external economies, whereas the other operates under constant returns. In the absence of trade (Mexico before trade liberalisation), the activity with external economies clusters in a centre. This bids up wages and thus leads the constant returns activity to disperse in peripheral regions. Introducing trade (Mexico after liberalisation), the same pattern is predicted to operate but this time internationally. Hanson finds that the Mexican apparel industry has indeed evolved in a way which was consistent with this simple application of the New Economic Geography.

The last article in this part, by Davis and Weinstein (Chapter 24), is a more ambitious enterprise, which attempts to test whether trade is best described by comparative advantage and constant returns or instead by the increasing returns favoured by New Economic Geography. To do so, they nest a comparative advantage model into a New Economic Geography framework. This framework is then used to account for the structure of regional production in Japan. Davis and Weinstein find support for the existence of economic geography effects in eight of 19 manufacturing sectors, including such important ones as transportation equipment, iron and steel, electrical machinery and chemicals. We believe this type of approach is an excellent exemplar of possible directions for future empirical work on the New Economic Geography. It is also interesting to note that the link with empirical work in international economics features prominently in the approach. To some extent, this type of work has given a new impetus to empirical work in international trade. This testifies to the success of regional and urban economics in economic analysis. Undoubtedly, the avenues of research opened by Hanson, and by Davis and Weinstein, will keep empirical researchers busy over the years to come.

Part VI: Public Finance and Policy

Since Tiebout's (1956) seminal paper, there has been a sustained interest from economists in the issues surrounding local public finances. These important questions keep generating a steady stream of research. To some extent, the literature of neighbourhood effects initiated by Bénabou (Chapter 4), with its focus on the financing of education, represents an interesting new development in this respect. The first article in this part, by Oates (Chapter 25), is a masterful survey of the traditional theoretical approaches to fiscal federalism. It assesses the welfare gains and costs of decentralisation. It also reviews more recent trends in this literature like the political economy of fiscal federalism, inter-jurisdictional competition and environmental federalism. It, finally, looks at how the traditional analysis can be appropriately modified to apply to developing and transitional economies.

The following article by Crémer, Estache and Seabright (Chapter 26) is a rare survey of recent work trying to use insights from modern contract theory to look at the internal organisation of powers within countries. Crémer et al. highlight a crucial paradox. The fiscal federalism literature was developed by authors who believed in the virtues of decentralisation. However, the main conclusion of this literature is that decentralisation entails some costs (externalities that are not internalised, imperfect competition, inappropriate instruments, etc.), whereas this literature fails to articulate the gains from decentralisation beyond a vague appeal to some informational benefits. Recent theoretical approaches used to analyse the issues surrounding the boundaries of firms make it possible to analyse precisely the informational gains and costs from decentralisation. The first key insight is that contracts between different levels of government are incomplete. This implies that different levels of government may face radically different incentives to provide some local public goods. In addition, the acquisition of information is also endogenous and the incentive to acquire it may depend on the level of government. We hope this new approach to local public finance (possibly blended with modern political economy as surveyed in Persson and Tabellini, 2000) will provide fresh insights on these long-standing concerns.

The next article, by Gyourko and Tracy (Chapter 27), is in some ways the culmination of a literature attempting to provide measures of how the quality of life varies between cities. Yet, at the same time, by introducing local public goods into the set of elements contributing to quality of life, it links in with the concerns of the previous two chapters and the continuing interest in the capitalisation of local public goods and amenities. A familiar assumption of US urban and regional economists is that people vote with their feet. This, at a local level, was central to Tiebout's (1956) model and has been applied at the interurban level in the analysis of migration (e.g. by Graves, 1976, 1980, 1983) and in the analysis of urban growth (Glaeser et al., 1995). The theoretical foundations for the quality of life literature were provided by Rosen (1979) and these ideas were applied by Roback (1982). The central idea was that if one can assume spatial/interregional equilibrium (or, pedantically, that the assumption is not so far off so that it is an acceptable approximation) and the main features of the neo-classical model apply, so that factors are paid the value of their marginal product, then differences in wages for given types of worker between cities/regions will be compensated with some combination of offsetting prices, amenities or – and this was the particular contribution of Gyourko and Tracy – differences in the quality of local public goods. The sheer volume of empirical analysis involved in making this simple-sounding idea reality is vast, quite aside from the technical skill involved. The bottom line seems to be that in an economy as integrated as that of the US, where migration is so responsive to spatial differences in net advantage, much can be gained from applying this idea. In more sticky environments such as Western Europe this is not so clear, but Gyourko and Tracy's article is a fine testament to theoretically informed, painstaking empirical research.

The final selection by Gramlich (Chapter 28) is a fine survey article on infrastructure. Infrastructure is central to the operation of urban and regional economies. In one of its most important forms – transport infrastructure – it provided one of the original catalysts for development of urban economics. Transport infrastructure also conditions urban form. How infrastructure should be paid for has provided one of the continuing topics of research in urban economics. Gramlich admirably surveys developments in the literature (with a strong US bias) from the late 1970s to the mid-1990s. It is a piece of its time however, even if a balanced and critical one, in that while it is interested in how infrastructure can be paid for, its central focus is on the contribution of infrastructure investment to (regional) economic growth. As a result of Aschauer's contributions (1989a, b, c), the role of infrastructure in contributing to economic growth was a sudden focus of attention. If Aschauer's early results were to be believed (and Gramlich's careful evaluation shows that they were not to be believed), then infrastructure investment seemed like the philosopher's stone: the answer to every policy-maker's prayer as to how to stimulate economic growth. This spurt of interest was catching and spread to Europe (e.g. Vickerman, 1991; Seitz, 1995), but as more thoughtful and careful analysis and techniques were brought to bear on the issue, so the interest began to fade.

We hope this selection of articles will stimulate students and lead them further into the field of spatial economics. Cities are as important to the development of humanity and to economic progress as the invention of the wheel or agriculture. They are arguably the most productive of all humanity's inventions, providing the essential basis for the development of specialisation and the division of labour; but also providing the basis for new ways of social living. The manufacturing city may be something of a short-term aberration in urban development, with cities increasingly reverting to their pre-industrial role as centres of government, commerce, finance and – in its broadest sense – culture. But cities have a future: these are the fastest-growing areas of economic activity in advanced economies and understanding better the ways in which cities work and generate dynamic agglomeration economies is an exciting prospect. At the same time, the decline of manufacturing as the basis for urban economies makes cities more attractive places to live.

We have chosen pieces of several kinds – original contributions, surveys and articles – which synthesise influential areas of work in accessible ways. Overall, while we have not avoided selecting quite technical pieces, where less technical articles were available we have preferred them, and we have always looked for a good rate of return for the reader's investment in understanding more technical arguments or presentation of evidence.

Notes

1. Since it extends to the economics of real estate now, perhaps even this is too confining.
2. Chosen partly to correspond to the assumptions of the monocentric model.
3. Or, of course, as Anselin and Rey (1991) or Magrini (2004) point out, warns us that our data is so structured that it includes 'nuisance spatial dependence'. The subdivision of large metro regions into separate regions for data reporting may provide just such an example of 'nuisance spatial dependence'.

References

Abdel-Rabman, H. and M. Fujita (1990), 'Product Variety, Marshallian Externalities, and City Sizes', *Journal of Regional Science*, **30** (2), 165–83.

Ades, A.F. and E.L. Glaeser (1995), 'Trade and Circuses: Explaining Urban Giants', *Quarterly Journal of Economics*, **110** (1), 195–227.

Alonso, W. (1964), *Location and Land Use*. Cambridge, MA: Harvard University Press.

Anas, A. and L. Moses (1978), 'Transportation and Land Use in the Mature Metropolis', in C.L. Leven (ed.), *The Mature Metropolis*. Cambridge, MA: Lexington Books.

Anselin, L. and S.J. Rey (1991), 'Properties for Tests for Spatial Dependence in Linear Regression Models', *Geographical Analysis*, **23** (1), 112–31.

Aschauer, D.A. (1989a), 'Is Public Expenditure Productive?', *Journal of Monetary Economics*, **23** (2), 177–200.

Aschauer, D.A. (1989b), 'Public Investment and Productive Growth in the Group of Seven', *Economic Perspectives*, **13** (5), 17–25.

Aschauer, D. A. (1989c), 'Does Public Capital Crowd Out Private Capital?' *Journal of Monetary Economics*, **24** (2), 171–88.

Audretsch, D.B. (1998), 'Agglomeration and the Location of Innovative Activity', *Oxford Review of Economic Policy*, **14** (2), 18–29.

Barro, R.J. (1991), 'Economic Growth in a Cross-section of Countries', *Quarterly Journal of Economics*, **106** (2), 407–501.

Barro, R.J. and X. Sala-i-Martin (1991), 'Convergence across States and Regions', *Brookings Papers on Economic Activity*, **0** (1), 107–82.

Barro, R.J. and X. Sala-i-Martin (1992), 'Convergence', *Journal of Political Economy*, **100** (2), 223–51.

Bénabou, R. (1993), 'Workings of a City: Location, Education and Production', *Quarterly Journal of Economics*, **108** (3), 619–52.

Bénabou, R. (1994), 'Human Capital, Inequality, and Growth: A Local Perspective', *European Economic Review*, **38** (3–4), 817–26.

Boarnet, M.G. (1994), 'The Monocentric Model and Employment Location', *Journal of Urban Economics*, **36** (1), 79–97.

Brueckner, J.K. (1987), 'The Structure of Urban Equilibria', in E.S. Mills (ed.), *Handbook of Regional and Urban Economics, Vol. 2*. Amsterdam: North Holland.

Brueckner, J.K. (1990), 'Growth Controls and Land Values in an Open City', *Land Economics*, **66** (2), 237–48.

Brueckner, J.K. (1995), 'Strategic Control of Growth in a System of Cities', *Journal of Public Economics*, **57** (3), 393–416.

Brueckner, J.K. (2000), 'Urban Sprawl: Diagnosis and Remedies', *International Regional Science Review*, **23** (2), 160–71.

Brueckner, J.K. and F.C. Lai (1996), 'Urban Growth Controls with Resident Landowners', *Regional Science and Urban Economics*, **26** (2), 125–43.

Brueckner, J.K., J.-F. Thisse and Y. Zenou (1999), 'Why is Central Paris Rich and Downtown Detroit Poor? An Amenity Based Theory', *European Economic Review*, **43** (1), 91–107.

Capozza, D.R. and R.W. Helsley (1990), 'The Stochastic City', *Journal of Urban Economics*, **28** (2), 187–203.

Cheshire, P. (1999), 'A Postscript: Ex-urbia or Islington?', in A. Summers, P. Cheshire and L. Senn (eds), *Urban Change in the United States and Western Europe: Comparative Analysis and Policy* (2nd edn). Washington, DC: The Urban Institute Press.

Cheshire, P.C. and A.W. Evans (eds) (1991), *Recent Developments in Regional and Urban Economics*. Aldershot: Edward Elgar.

Cheshire, P. and S. Sheppard (1995), 'On the Price of Land and the Value of Amenities', *Economica*, **62** (246), 247–67.

Cheshire P. and S. Sheppard (1998), 'Estimating the Demand for Housing, Land and Neighbourhood Characteristics', *Oxford Bulletin of Economics and Statistics*, **60** (3), 357–82.

Cheshire, P. and S. Sheppard (2002), 'Welfare Economics of Land Use Regulation', *Journal of Urban Economics*, **52** (2), 242–69.
Ciccone, A. and R.E. Hall (1996), 'Productivity and the Density of Economic Activity', *American Economic Review*, **86** (1), 54–70.
Combes, P.-P. (2000), 'Economic Structure and Local Growth: France, 1984–1993', *Journal of Urban Economics*, **47** (3), 329–55.
Costa, D.L. and M.E. Kahn (2000), 'Power Couples: Changes in the Locational Choice of the College Educated, 1940–1990', *Quarterly Journal of Economics*, **115** (4), 1287–315.
Crémer, J., A. Estache and P. Seabright (1996), 'Decentralizing Public Services: What Can We Learn from the Theory of the Firm?' *Revue d'Économie Politique*, **106** (1), 37–60.
Davis, D.R. and D.E. Weinstein (1999), 'Economic Geography and Regional Production Structure: An Empirical Investigation', *European Economic Review*, **43** (2), 379–407.
Deckle, R. (2002), 'Industrial Concentration and Regional Growth: Evidence from the Prefectures', *Review of Economics and Statistics*, **84** (2), 310–15.
Dixit, A.K. and J.E. Stiglitz (1977), 'Monopolistic Competition and Optimum Product Diversity', *American Economic Review*, **67** (3), 297–308.
Duranton, G. and D. Puga (2000), 'Diversity and Specialisation in Cities: Why, Where and When Does It Matter?', *Urban Studies*, **37** (7), 533–55.
Eberts, R.W. (1981), 'An Empirical Investigation of Intra-urban Wage Gradients', *Journal of Urban Economics*, **10** (1), 50–60.
Feldman, M.P. (1994), *The Geography of Innovation*. Boston, MA: Kluwer Academic Publishers.
Fernandez, R. and R. Rogerson (1996), 'Income Distribution, Communities, and the Quality of Public Education', *Quarterly Journal of Economics*, **111** (1), 135–64.
de la Fuente, A. (2000), 'Convergence across Countries and Regions: Theory and Empirics', *EIB Papers*, **5** (2), 25–45.
Fujita, M. (1989), *Urban Economic Theory: Land Use and City Size*. Cambridge: Cambridge University Press.
Fujita, M., P.R. Krugman and A.J. Venables (1999), *The Spatial Economy. Cities, Regions and International Trade*. Cambridge, MA: MIT Press.
Glaeser, E.L., M.E. Kahn and J. Rappaport (2000), *Why Do the Poor Live in Cities?*, National Bureau of Economic Research Working Paper No. 7636.
Glaeser, E.L., H.D. Kallal, J.A. Scheinkman and A. Shleifer (1992), 'Growth in Cities', *Journal of Political Economy*, **100** (6), 1126–52.
Glaeser, E.L., J.A. Scheinkman and A. Shleifer (1995), 'Economic Growth in a Cross-Section of Cities', *Journal of Monetary Economics*, **36** (1), 117–43.
Gramlich, E.M. (1994), 'Infrastructure Investment: A Review Essay', *Journal of Economic Literature*, **32** (3), 1176–96.
Graves, P.E. (1976), 'A Reexamination of Migration, Economic Opportunity, and the Quality of Life', *Journal of Regional Science*, **16** (1), 107–12.
Graves, P.E. (1980), 'Migration and Climate', *Journal of Regional Science*, **20** (2), 227–37.
Graves, P.E. (1983), 'Migration with a Composite Amenity: The Role of Rents', *Journal of Regional Science*, **23** (4), 541–6.
Gyourko J. and J. Tracy (1991), 'The Structure of Local Public Finance and the Quality of Life', *Journal of Political Economy*, **99** (4), 774–806.
Hanson, G.H. (1996), 'Localization Economies, Vertical Organization, and Trade', *American Economic Review*, **86** (5), 1266–78.
Henderson, J.V. (1974), 'The Sizes and Types of Cities', *American Economic Review*, **64** (4), 640–56.
Henderson, J.V. and R. Becker (2000), 'Political Economy of City Sizes and Formation', *Journal of Urban Economics*, **48** (3), 453–84.
Henderson, J.V. and A. Mitra (1996), 'The New Urban Landscape: Developers and Edge Cities', *Regional Science and Urban Economics*, **26** (6), 613–43.
Ihlanfeldt, K.R. (1992), 'Intraurban Wage Gradients: Evidence by Race, Gender, Occupational Class, and Sector', *Journal of Urban Economics*, **32** (1), 70–91.
Jaffe, A. (1989), 'Real Effects of Academic Research', *American Economic Review*, **79** (5), 957–70.

Kaldor, N. (1970), 'The Case for Regional Policies', *Scottish Journal of Political Economy*, **17** (3), 337–48.
Krugman, P.R. (1991), 'Increasing Returns and Economic Geography', *Journal of Political Economy*, **99** (3), 483–99.
Magrini, S. (1999), 'The Evolution of Income Disparities among the Regions of the European Union', *Regional Science and Urban Economics*, **29** (2), 257–81.
Magrini, S. (2004), 'Regional (Di)Convergence', in J.V. Henderson and J.F. Thisse (eds), *Handbook of Regional and Urban Economics, Vol. 4*. Amsterdam: North Holland.
Mills, E.S. (1967), 'An Aggregative Model of Resource Allocation in a Metropolitan Area', *American Economic Review Papers and Proceedings*, **57** (2), 197–210.
Muth, R.F. (1969), *Cities and Housing*, Chicago: University of Chicago Press.
Myrdal, G. (1957), *Economic Development and Underdeveloped Regions*. London: Methuen.
Neary, J.P. (2001), 'Of Hype and Hyperbolas: Introducing the New Economic Geography', *Journal of Economic Literature*, **39** (2), 536–61.
Oates, W.E. (1999), 'An Essay on Fiscal Federalism', *Journal of Economic Literature*, **37** (3), 1120–49.
Ota, M. and M. Fujita (1993), 'Communication Technologies and Spatial Organization of Multi-unit Firms in Metropolitan Areas', *Regional Science and Urban Economics*, **23** (6), 695–729.
Persson, T. and G. Tabellini (2000), *Political Economics: Explaining Economic Policy*, Cambridge, MA: MIT Press.
Quah, D.T. (1996), 'Twin Peaks: Growth and Convergence in Models of Distribution Dynamics', *Economic Journal*, **106** (437), 1045–55.
Rey, S.J. and B.D. Montouri (1999), 'US Regional Income Convergence: A Spatial Econometric Perspective', *Regional Studies*, **33** (2), 143–56.
Roback J. (1982), 'Wages, Rents and the Quality of Life', *Journal of Political Economy*, **90** (6), 1257–78.
Rosen, S. (1979), 'Wage-based Indexes of Urban Quality of Life', in P. Mieszkowski and M. Straszheim (eds), *Current Issues in Urban Economics*. Baltimore, MD: Johns Hopkins University Press.
Seitz, H. (1995), 'The Productivity and Supply of Urban Infrastructures', *Annals of Regional Science*, **29** (2), 121–41.
Sveikauskas, L.A. (1975), 'The Productivity of Cities', *Quarterly Journal of Economics*, **89** (3), 393–413.
Thurston, L. and A.M.J. Yezer (1994), 'Causality in the Suburbanization of Population and Employment', *Journal of Urban Economics*, **35** (1), 105–18.
Tiebout, C.M. (1956), 'A Pure Theory of Public Expenditures', *Journal of Political Economy*, **64** (5), 416–24.
Vickerman, R.W. (ed.) (1991), *Infrastructure and Regional Development*. London: Pion.
Wasmer, E. and Y. Zenou (2002), 'Does City Structure Affect Search and Welfare?' *Journal of Urban Economics*, **51** (3), 515–41.
White, M.J. (1999), 'Urban Areas with Decentralized Employment: Theory and Empirical Work', in P.C. Cheshire and E.S. Mills (eds), *Handbook of Regional and Urban Economics, Vol. 3: Applied Urban Economics*. Amsterdam: North Holland.

Part I
Inside the City (or Theoretically Inside the City . . .): Theoretical Analysis of City Structure

[1]

JOURNAL OF URBAN ECONOMICS 28, 187–203 (1990)

The Stochastic City*

DENNIS R. CAPOZZA

School of Business Administration, University of Michigan, Ann Arbor, Michigan 48109

AND

ROBERT W. HELSLEY

Faculty of Commerce and Business Administration, University of British Columbia, Vancouver, British Columbia, Canada V6T 1Y8

Received September 28, 1987; revised July 12, 1988

This paper analyzes a simple model of an urban area with growth and uncertainty. Household income, rents, and prices for land follow stochastic processes. Even though investors are risk neutral, uncertainty affects both land rents and land prices in equilibrium because the conversion of land from agricultural to urban use is irreversible. Growth, on the other hand, affects urban and agricultural land prices but not the level of rents. We show that uncertainty (i) delays the conversion of land from agricultural to urban use, (ii) imparts an option value to agricultural land, (iii) causes land at the boundary to sell for more than its opportunity cost in other uses, and (iv) reduces equilibrium city size. © 1990 Academic Press, Inc.

I. INTRODUCTION

This paper examines the effects of uncertainty on equilibrium land rents and prices in a simple model of a growing urban area. We apply the theory of continuous time stochastic processes to the timing of land conversion under uncertainty. Our analysis emphasizes the importance of a common, and seemingly innocuous, assumption in dynamic models of cities: the decision to convert land from agricultural to urban use is economically irreversible. When development is irreversible, uncertainty affects both land prices and land rents even when land owners are risk neutral. Growth, on the other hand, affects the value of urban and agricultural land but not the level of rents. We also show that uncertainty (i) delays the

*Earlier versions of this paper were presented at the ASSA meetings in New Orleans and at a workshop sponsored by the Lincoln Institute of Land Policy in Cambridge. We are grateful to participants in these sessions and in seminars at UBC and Simon Fraser University for helpful comments. Special thanks are extended to Richard Arnott, Shelby Brumelle, Bruce Hamilton, William Strange, and William Wheaton. Chris Mah and Bijan Zanganeh provided able research assistance. The financial support of the Real Estate Council of British Columbia is gratefully acknowledged.

0094-1190/90 $3.00

conversion of land from agricultural to urban use, (ii) imparts an option value to agricultural land, (iii) causes land at the boundary to sell for more than its opportunity cost in other uses, and (iv) reduces equilibrium city size.

The model developed in this paper is a synthesis of several strands of the economics literature. First, our analysis builds on existing models of urban growth, especially the durable capital, perfect foresight models of Arnott and Lewis [1], Arnott [2], and Wheaton [16]. Second, we draw on the literature dealing with optimal investment policy under uncertainty, for example, Bernanke [3], McDonald and Siegel [12], and Heaney and Jones [9]. Important papers by Mills [13] and Titman [15] examine how uncertainty affects the value and development of vacant urban land. More recently, Clarke and Reed [7] independently developed a model examining some of the issues discussed in this paper.

Including this introduction, the paper has six sections. Section II describes the model. In Section III the model is solved for the special case when future rents are known with certainty. Section IV describes the structure of equilibrium land rents and prices with uncertainty and risk neutrality. Section V outlines some of the implications of our analysis. Section VI summarizes and concludes the paper.

II. THE MODEL

This model is an extension of the simple dynamic model of a monocentric urban area developed in Capozza, *et al.* [4] and Capozza and Helsley [6]. We focus on the implications of uncertainty for the components of equilibrium land rents and prices. In the model household income, rents, prices, and city size follow stochastic processes.

Geography

A small, open urban area is located on a homogeneous plain. Employment and production are concentrated at the central business district (CBD), a point to which all households commute daily. Locations are indexed by their distance z from the CBD, where distance is measured so that the cost of commuting a unit of distance is \$1. The boundary of the urban area at time t, which is also the location of current development, is denoted by $z^*(t)$.

Households

Households are identical. They derive utility from land and a composite numeraire good x. Consumption of land is fixed at one unit per household. The budget constraint of a household living at location z is

$$y(t) = x + R(t, z) + z, \tag{1}$$

where $y(t)$ is exogenous household income at time t and $R(t, z)$ is land rent.

Household Equilibrium

Migration between urban areas is costless. Equilibrium for households is characterized by the single condition

$$V[R(t,z), y(t)] = \bar{V}, \tag{2}$$

where $V(\cdot)$ is the direct utility function and $\bar{V}$ is the national utility level. Since lot sizes are fixed, (2) implies that all households consume the same quantity of the numeraire good in equilibrium, $\bar{x}$, where

$$U(\bar{x}, 1) = \bar{V}, \tag{3}$$

and $U(\cdot)$ is the direct utility function. The bid rent function for land is

$$R(t,z) = y(t) - (\bar{x} + z). \tag{4}$$

Stochastic Assumptions

We assume that the urban area exports to an expanding world market. Shocks in world demand are transmitted through the labor market to household income and land rents as the export sector adjusts its output.[1] As a result household income rises over time in an uncertain fashion. More precisely, the sequence of random variables $\{y(t), t \geq 0\}$ is a Brownian motion process with drift $g > 0$ and variance σ^2. This implies that incomes follow (the infinitesimal analog of) a random walk that drifts upward by $\$g$ per unit of time. Formally, this assumption implies

(*a*) the stationary increments property, $y(t+s) - y(t) \sim N[gs, \sigma^2 s]$ for all t;

(*b*) the independent increments property, for all $t_0 < t_1 < \cdots < t_n$, $y(t_1) - y(t_0), y(t_2) - y(t_1), \ldots, y(t_n) - y(t_{n-1})$ are independent random variables with distributions given in (*a*);

(*c*) $y(0) = 0$; and

(*d*) $y(t) \equiv gt + \sigma B(t)$, where $\{B(t), t \geq 0\}$ is a standard Brownian motion process with drift 0 and variance 1.

From (4), bid rent is also a random variable. In fact, for every z, the sequence $\{R(t,z), t \geq 0\}$ has properties (*a*) and (*b*) above, with (*c*) replaced by

$$(c')\ R(0,z) = -(\bar{x} + z)$$

[1] Mills [13] describes more completely how shocks in export demand are transmitted to land rents in a simple general equilibrium model of a growing urban area.

and the equation in (d) replaced by

$$(d')\ R(t,z) \equiv R(0,z) + gt + \sigma B(t).$$[2]

(a), (b), and (d') imply

$$R(t+s,z) \overset{\mathrm{d}}{=} R(t,z) + gs + \sigma B(s), \tag{5}$$

where the random variables in (5) are equal "in distribution."

The Value of Urban Land

In a competitive market the price of land equals the expected present value of future land rents. We assume that land owners are risk neutral and share a common discount rate r. We also assume that land owners know current rents, $R(t, z)$, and the distribution of future rents, given by g and σ^2. The price at time t of a unit of urban land at location z is

$$P^u(t,z) = E\left\{\int_t^\infty R(\tau,z)e^{-r(\tau-t)}d\tau \middle| R(t,z)\right\}, \qquad z \le z^*(t). \tag{6}$$

The expectation in (6) is conditional on the information available at time t. Setting $\tau = t + s$ in (5) and substituting the resulting expression into (6) yields

$$\begin{aligned} P^u(t,z) &= E\left\{\int_0^\infty [R(t,z) + gs + \sigma B(s)]e^{-rs}ds \middle| R(t,z)\right\} \\ &= \frac{1}{r}\left[R(t,z) + \frac{g}{r}\right]. \end{aligned} \tag{7}$$

The Value of Agricultural Land

Land in agriculture earns rent A. The capital cost of converting a unit of land to urban use is C. Thus, urban land is produced from agricultural land by adding a fixed amount of capital per unit.[3] Once converted land

[2]Urban rent may be negative under some realizations. One curiosity of dynamic models of urban areas is that land rents (but not building rents) can be negative in equilibrium (see [13]). The model can also be solved when rents follow a log-normal diffusion which rules out negative rents (see [5]).

[3]The model is best viewed as a model of the land conversion process and not as a model of the decision to add structural capital to land. We have purposely kept the production and consumption decisions extremely simple to highlight the effects of uncertainty on prices. The central assumption is stochastic land rents. See Mills [13] for a more detailed articulation of the production and consumption sectors.

receives urban rents forever: the decision to convert land to urban use is irreversible. The capital used to convert land from agricultural to urban use does not depreciate. The value at time t of a unit of agricultural land at location $z > z^*(t)$ is

$$P^a(t, s, z)$$
$$\equiv E\left\{\int_t^{t+s} Ae^{-r(\tau-t)}d\tau + \int_{t+s}^{\infty} R(\tau, z)e^{-r(\tau-t)}d\tau - Ce^{-rs}\middle|R(t, z)\right\}, \quad (8)$$

where $t + s$ is the date the land is converted from agricultural to urban use and s is a stopping time. The first term in the expectation in (8) is the present value of agricultural rent up to the date of conversion. The second term is the present value of urban rent from the date of conversion onward. The last term is the present value of the cost of conversion at $t + s$. Using (5), (7), and the strong Markov property, (8) can be written

$$P^a(t, s, z) = \frac{A}{r} + \frac{1}{r}E\left\{\left[R(t + s, z) + \frac{g}{r} - A - rC\right]e^{-rs}\middle|R(t, z)\right\}. \quad (9)$$

Landowners choose the conversion time to maximize expected profits or the value of land. Formally, landowners solve the program

$$\max_s P^a(t, s, z). \quad (10)$$

Let t^* be the optimal time to convert. Then the price of land is $P^a(t, t^*, z) \equiv P^a(t, z)$.

III. RENTS AND PRICES WHEN THE FUTURE IS CERTAIN

The model is easy to solve when the future is certain. As σ approaches 0, (5) becomes

$$R(t + s, z) = R(t, z) + gs. \quad (11)$$

The optimal conversion time from (10) and (8) satisfies

$$R(t^*, z) = A + rC. \quad (12)$$

Under certainty land is converted when its rent in urban use equals the agricultural rent foregone plus the opportunity cost of the capital needed to convert the land. (12) implicitly defines the boundary of the urban area at time t.

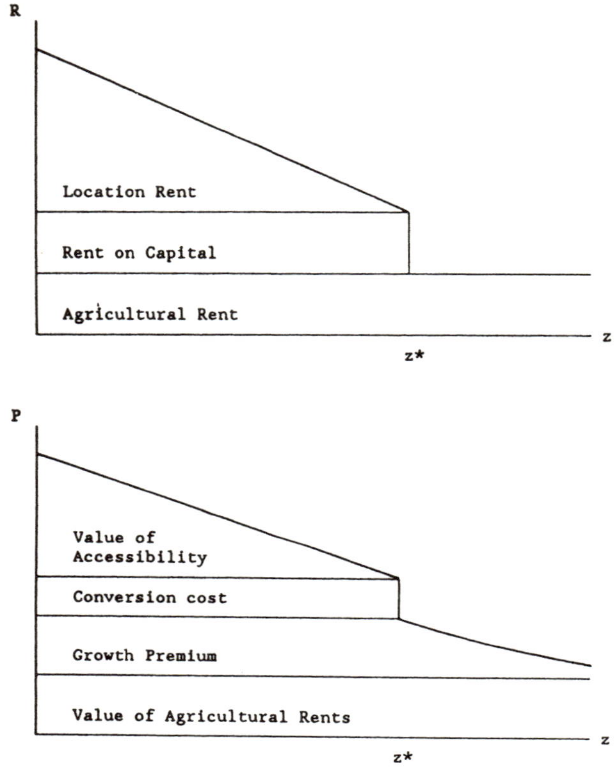

FIG. 1. Equilibrium land rents and prices under certainty.

From (4), the equilibrium rent function is

$$R(t,z) = \begin{cases} A + rC + z^*(t) - z & z \le z^*(t) \\ A & z > z^*(t). \end{cases} \tag{13}$$

From (7), the price of urban land is

$$P^u(t,z) = \frac{A}{r} + C + \frac{g}{r^2} + \frac{1}{r}[z^*(t) - z], \qquad z \le z^*(t). \tag{14}$$

Finally, the price of agricultural land from (10) is

$$P^a(t,z) = \frac{A}{r} + \frac{g}{r^2}e^{-r(t^*-t)}, \qquad z > z^*(t), \tag{15}$$

which may in turn be written[4]

$$P^a(t,z) = \frac{A}{r} + \frac{g}{r^2}e^{-r[z-z^*(t)]/g}, \qquad z > z^*(t). \tag{16}$$

Equilibrium land rents and prices have a simple structure in this model, especially when the future is certain. Figure 1 is a cross section of rents and prices inside and outside the city. Urban land rent consists of agricultural land rent, A, the opportunity cost of conversion capital, rC, and location rent, $z^*(t) - z$. Similarly, the price of urban land consists of the value of agricultural land rent, A/r, the cost of conversion, C, the value of accessibility, $(1/r)[z^*(t) - z]$, and a growth premium equal to the present value of anticipated increases in rents after development, $g/(r^2)$. The price of agricultural land equals the value of agricultural land rent, A/r, plus a growth premium that equals $g/(r^2)$ at the boundary of the urban area and decays as the distance from the boundary increases and the time of development moves further into the future.[5]

IV. RENTS AND PRICES WHEN THE FUTURE IS UNCERTAIN

First Hitting Time

To solve the model when the future is uncertain, we recast the landowner's problem into a hitting time problem. Let R^* represent the level of urban land rent at which is optimal to convert land from rural to urban use. We refer to R^* as the reservation rent level. The time of conversion, t^*, known as the first hitting time, is defined by[6]

$$t^* = \min_s \{t + s \geq t | R(t+s,z) \geq R^*\}. \tag{17}$$

The first hitting time is illustrated in Fig. 2.

Let $F(R^*)$ represent the expected price of agricultural land conditioned on R^*. From (9),

$$\begin{aligned} F(R^*) &= E\{P^a(t,t^*,z)|R(t,z),R^*\} \\ &= \frac{A}{r} + \frac{1}{r}\left[R^* + \frac{g}{r} - A - rC\right]E\{e^{-r(t^*-t)}|R(t,z),R^*\}. \end{aligned} \tag{18}$$

[4](4) and (12) imply $z^*(t) = gt - (A + rC + \bar{x})$.

[5]The effects of expected future growth on the price of land in a deterministic model are examined in detail in Capozza and Helsley [6].

[6]Problems like the one analyzed in this section can be found in the literature on investment under uncertainty. See, for example, McDonald and Siegal [12] and Heaney and Jones [9].

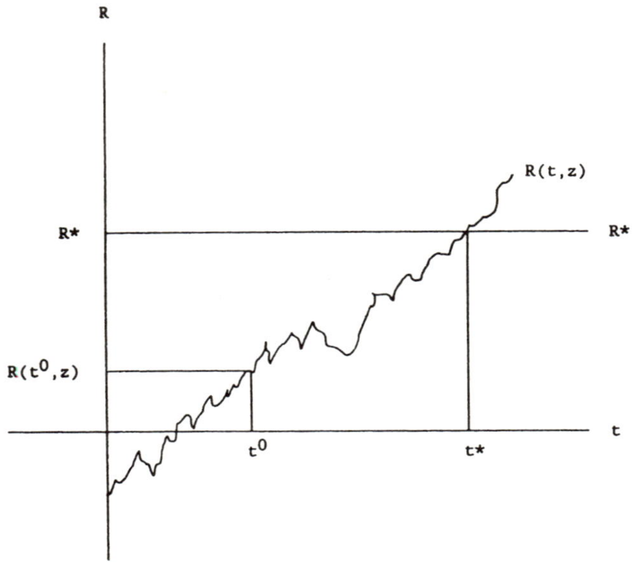

FIG. 2. The first hitting time.

Notice that the only random component of $F(R^*)$ is the first hitting time t^*.

The distribution of first hitting times under Brownian motion with drift is known. The moment generating function for t^* [11, p. 362] implies

$$E\{e^{-r(t^*-t)}|R(t,z),R^*\} = e^{-\alpha[R^*-R(t,z)]}, \tag{19}$$

where

$$\alpha = \frac{(g^2 + 2\sigma^2 r)^{1/2} - g}{\sigma^2}. \tag{20}$$

Hence, the expected price of agricultural land can be written

$$F(R^*) = \frac{A}{r} + \frac{1}{r}\left[R^* + \frac{g}{r} - A - rC\right]e^{-\alpha[R^*-R(t,z)]}. \tag{21}$$

Reservation Rent and Reservation Price

The optimal conversion value, or reservation rent level, R^* maximizes (21), which implies

$$R^* = A + rC + \frac{r - \alpha g}{\alpha r}, \tag{22}$$

where $\alpha \leq r/g$. Comparing (12) and (22), we see that the reservation rent, the rent level that triggers the conversion of agricultural land to urban use, is higher when the future is uncertain.[7] From (7), the corresponding reservation price is

$$P^* = \frac{A}{r} + C + \frac{g}{r^2} + \frac{r - \alpha g}{\alpha r^2}. \tag{23}$$

The Structure of Land Rents and Prices

The equilibrium land rent function is

$$R(t, z) = \begin{cases} A + rC + \dfrac{r - \alpha g}{\alpha r} + z^*(t) - z & z \leq z^*(t) \\ A & z > z^*(t). \end{cases} \tag{24}$$

From (4) and (22), the boundary of the urban area at time t is given by

$$z^*(t) = y(t) - (R^* + \bar{x}). \tag{25}$$

The price of urban land, from (7), is

$$P^u(t, z) = \frac{A}{r} + C + \frac{g}{r^2} + \frac{r - \alpha g}{\alpha r^2} + \frac{1}{r}[z^*(t) - z], \qquad z \leq z^*(t). \tag{26}$$

Finally, the price of agricultural land, from (23), is

$$P^a(t, z) = \frac{A}{r} + \frac{g}{r^2}e^{-\alpha[z - z^*(t)]} + \frac{r - \alpha g}{\alpha r^2}e^{-\alpha[z - z^*(t)]} \qquad z > z^*(t). \tag{27}$$

The key pricing results of the model can now be summarized in two pictures, as illustrated in Fig. 3. In addition to the components outlined for the certainty case, urban land rent now includes an uncertainty or irreversibility term, $(r - \alpha g)/\alpha r$, which is precisely the difference between

[7]For $\sigma^2 > 0$, $\partial\alpha/\partial\sigma^2 < 0$.

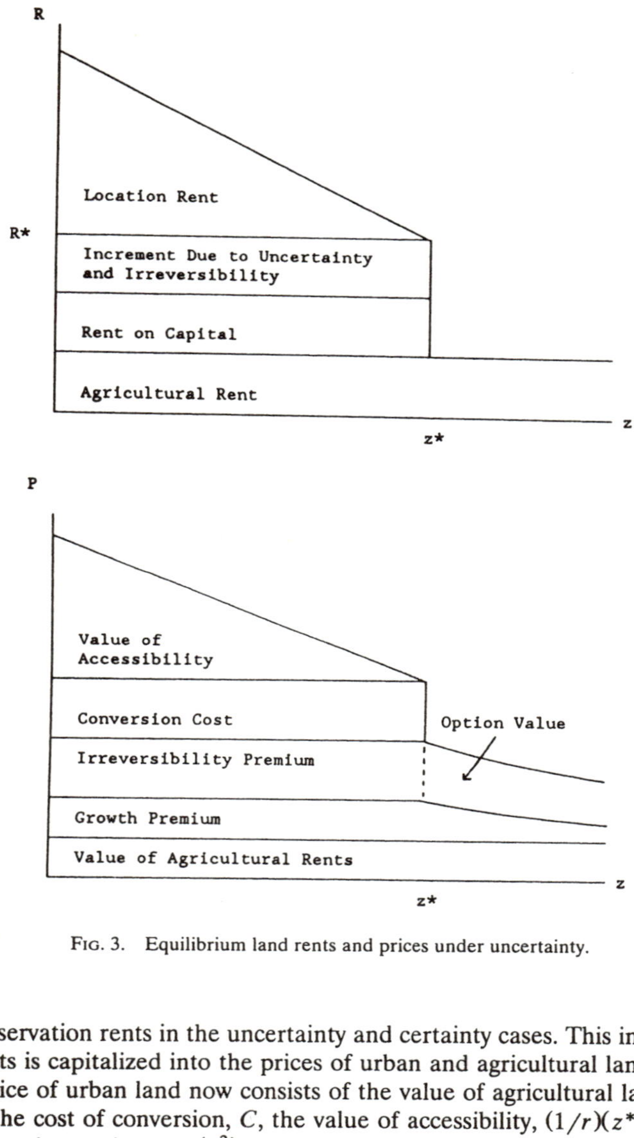

FIG. 3. Equilibrium land rents and prices under uncertainty.

the reservation rents in the uncertainty and certainty cases. This increment to rents is capitalized into the prices of urban and agricultural land. Thus, the price of urban land now consists of the value of agricultural land rent, A/r, the cost of conversion, C, the value of accessibility, $(1/r)(z^*(t) - z)$, the growth premium, $g/(r^2)$, and what we call an irreversibility premium, $(r - \alpha g)/(\alpha r^2)$. As before, the price of agricultural land includes a growth premium that decays as distance from the boundary increases.

However, the price of agricultural land now includes an option value as well, the counterpart of the irreversibility premium in the price of urban land.[8] This option value also grows smaller as the distance from the boundary of the urban area increases and the time of development moves further into the future.[9]

V. UNCERTAINTY, IRREVERSIBILITY, AND URBAN GROWTH

In this section we summarize the implications of our model for (a) development timing, (b) city size, (c) land prices and rents, (d) the gap between the price of land and the value of agricultural land rents at the urban boundary, and (e) the existence of vacant urban land in equilibrium.

Development Timing

In a deterministic model of a growing urban area, land is developed when rent in the urban use equals the opportunity cost of development—the sum of agricultural land rent and the opportunity cost of capital. How should the introduction of uncertainty about the future path of urban land rent affect this decision? Intuitively, we imagined that an optimal strategy would involve delaying development until urban land rent increased sufficiently to compensate investors for their aversion to risk. In other words, we imagined that development would occur when rent in the urban use equals the opportunity cost of development plus a risk premium.

While it is true in our model that conversion is delayed relative to the certainty case, the reasons for the delay differ from our intuitive expectations. The model implies that risk aversion is not the primitive cause of postponed development when future rents are uncertain. In fact, development is delayed even when investors are risk neutral. In the context of our model with risk neutral investors, development is postponed because the opportunity cost of development includes the option value of agricultural land—the value of the ability to avoid adverse outcomes in the risky urban land market while still retaining a claim on favorable outcomes. Development will not occur at the rent level that prompts conversion under certainty since investors know that rents may fall below this level in the immediate future. However, as conversion is postponed, and the level of urban land rent drifts upward, the probability that rents will fall below

[8]We have defined option value to be the net of the growth premium. This allows us to highlight the role of uncertainty. The finance literature usually includes the growth premium in option value.

[9]The growth premium in the price of agricultural land decays more quickly when the future is uncertain. Note that α approaches g/r as σ approaches 0, so the expressions for equilibrium rents and prices under certainty and uncertainty agree in the limit.

agricultural rents decreases. Thus, the present value of expected future returns is increased by delaying development, and even a risk neutral investor will adopt such a strategy.

With uncertainty and irreversibility, the rent level that triggers the conversion of land, the reservation rent, exceeds the sum of agricultural land rent and the opportunity cost of capital. Analogously, the reservation price of urban land exceeds the capitalized value of agricultural land rents plus the cost of conversion. Further, the reservation rent and the reservation price rise with the degree of uncertainty. From (22) and (23),

$$\frac{\partial R^*}{\partial \sigma^2} = -\frac{1}{\alpha^2}\frac{\partial \alpha}{\partial \sigma^2} > 0, \tag{28}$$

and

$$\frac{\partial P^*}{\partial \sigma^2} = -\frac{1}{r\alpha^2}\frac{\partial \alpha}{\partial \sigma^2} > 0. \tag{29}$$

City Size

In this open city model, uncertainty unambiguously reduces expected city size. Since rent at the boundary is higher the greater the degree of uncertainty about future land rents, at any point in time a greater fraction of income is devoted to land consumption and a smaller fraction to transportation in a "riskier" city. This can only be true if households at the boundary enjoy a shorter journey to work and the urban area with the greater variance of future rents is smaller. From (25), the expected boundary of the urban area at time t is

$$Ez^*(t) = gt - (R^* + \bar{x}), \tag{30}$$

where

$$\frac{\partial Ez^*(t)}{\partial \sigma^2} = -\frac{\partial R^*}{\partial \sigma^2} < 0. \tag{31}$$

Land Prices and Rents

The effects of uncertainty on land prices are closely related to its effects on city size and the timing of land development. A fundamental implication of our analysis is that equilibrium land prices in the agricultural area include an option value that increases with the variance of rents. This option value decreases as distance from the boundary of the urban area increases, implying a spatial gradient for agricultural land prices that is not directly related to the cost of transportation. Equilibrium land prices in the developed area include an irreversibility premium (equal to the option value at the boundary) that also rises with the variance of rents.

Our model implies that for a given city size, both urban and agricultural land prices should be higher in riskier urban areas. However, with the boundary of the urban area endogenously determined, the price of urban land is unaffected by uncertainty. From (26) and (27), the expected price of urban land can be written

$$EP^u(t, z) = \frac{g}{r^2} + \frac{1}{r}(gt - \bar{x} - z), \qquad z \leq z^*(t), \tag{32}$$

which is independent of σ^2.

The expected price of agricultural land depends on the degree of uncertainty when city size is endogenously determined. From (27), the expected price of agricultural land may be written

$$EP^a(t, z) = \frac{A}{r} + \frac{1}{\alpha r} e^{-\alpha[z - Ez^*(t)]} e^{(\sigma^2/2)t}, \qquad z > z^*(t). \tag{33}$$

The effect of greater uncertainty on agricultural land prices is ambiguous.[10] In particular, when two cities with different variances of expected future incomes are compared, agricultural land prices may be lower in the riskier city for some locations near the urban boundary. However, it can be shown that agricultural land prices are eventually higher in the high variance urban area. Figure 4 illustrates the effect of the degree of uncertainty on land prices and rents when city size is endogenous.

The effect of growth and uncertainty on equilibrium land rents is perhaps more surprising. Since rents are payments for the current use of land one might not expect future growth or uncertainty to influence the current payment. But here, because the option value increases the reservation rent, city size and therefore average equilibrium urban rents are affected by both the drift and the variance of the stochastic process for bid rents. For a given city size both rents and prices are higher in an uncertain city.

The Price Gap

Should the price of land at the boundary of an urban area equal the value of agricultural land rents plus the cost of converting land to urban use? Except in the context of very simple, static models, the answer is no. We have identified several factors that contribute to such a gap. In a

[10] The expression for $\partial P^a(t, z)/\partial \sigma^2$ is messy and its sign is ambiguous. Details are available on request.

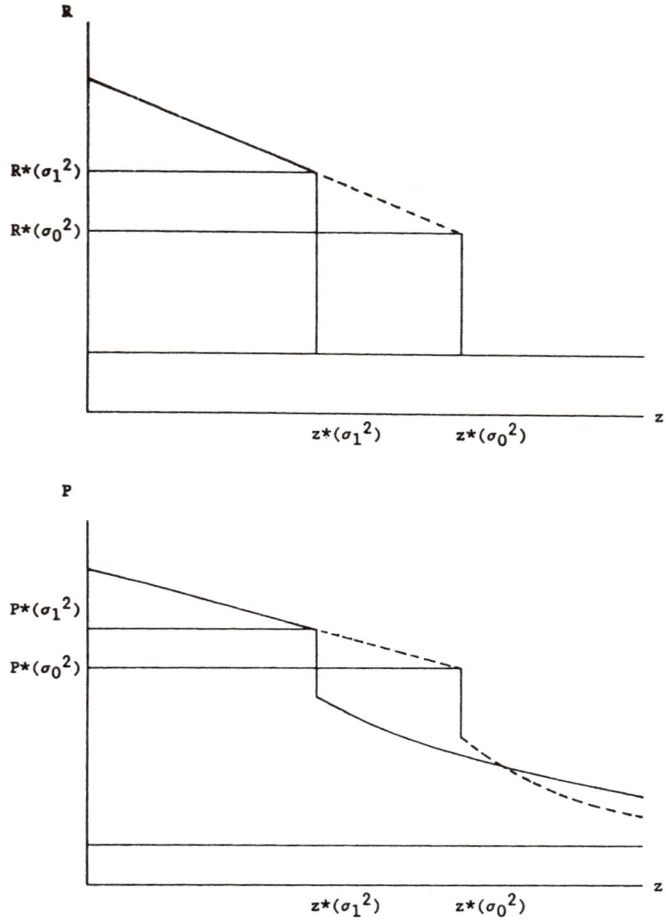

FIG. 4. Equilibrium land rents and prices and the degree of uncertainty ($\sigma_1^2 > \sigma_0^2$).

dynamic model where the future is certain, the price of land will include a growth premium equal to the value of expected future increases in urban land rents. When the future is uncertain and development is irreversible, the price of land will also include a premium caused by the option value in agricultural land. Economists sometimes appeal to government restrictions on land use and development to explain why the price of boundary land differs from the "static" opportunity cost of development. In fact, in all but the simplest of settings, such a differential is a characteristic of an efficient urban land market.

Leapfrogging

"Leapfrogging" is the discontinuous development of land in an urban area where vacant plots are surrounded by developed plots. There are two types of vacant plots—finished land that has been serviced and that is ready for development and raw land that has never been serviced.

Since a fixed amount of capital is applied to raw land, our model is best viewed as a model of the land conversion process, that is, as a model of the decision to convert raw land into finished land. The decision on the density of development is outside the scope of the model. As a result this model cannot address leapfrogging of the first kind. Vacant plots of finished land are not distinguishable from developed land.

However, the model can distinguish leapfrogging of the second kind—vacant raw land inside the urban boundary—and there is no leapfrogging of this kind in our model in equilibrium. There is vacant land awaiting conversion but it is all outside the urban boundary. Conversion takes place in a spatially continuous fashion.

Uncertainty about the future path of rents is neither necessary nor sufficient for the existence of vacant raw urban land in equilibrium. When the future is uncertain, it appears that an additional factor, such as variable densities [16, 15], competing land uses [8, 13], or heterogeneous expectations [13] is still required to generate vacant urban land in equilibrium.

VI. SUMMARY AND CONCLUSION

This paper analyzes a simple model of a growing urban area in which household income and land rent follow stochastic processes. Even though investors are risk neutral, uncertainty affects equilibrium land rents and prices, because the conversion of land from agricultural to urban use is irreversible.

In this model both rents and prices decompose into simple additive components with intuitive interpretations. Uncertainty affects the level of both rents and prices in the urban area. Growth affects the value of urban land and agricultural land but not the level of rents. We also show that uncertainty (i) delays the conversion of land from agricultural to urban use, (ii) reduces expected city size, and (iii) imparts an option value to agricultural land. The model suggests that land prices in two urban areas of equal size will be higher in a riskier urban area. Further, uncertainty and growth help explain why agricultural land near the boundary of an urban area sells for a large premium over the value of agricultural land rents.

The model developed in this paper is obviously highly simplified. To what degree do our results hinge on the assumptions we have made? Two of these assumptions seem especially important: (i) lot sizes are fixed, and (ii) migration is costless. Assuming fixed lot sizes simplifies the mathematics enormously, but, as noted above, it also predetermines the equilibrium spatial development pattern. We conjecture that uncertainty would encourage higher densities and discontinuous development in a more general model with variable lot sizes, but that prices and rents would no longer decompose in an additive fashion.

Assuming costless migration, or open cities, is common in long-run equilibrium models of city size. However, this is also an extreme assumption: in our model, it implies that unexpected growth in income is accompanied by unexpected growth in population to equalize utility levels. In a closed city, in which utility is endogenous, the effects of uncertain income growth might be very different. In fact, with population and hence the city boundary fixed in our model, income growth affects consumption of the composite good and utility in equilibrium, but it does not affect the level of land rents or prices. It would be more interesting and realistic to examine the effects of uncertain income growth in a partially closed model in which income changes in one period lead to migration in the next, and in which the adjustment to equilibrium is made explicit. This might illuminate precisely how our results depend on the open city assumption.

REFERENCES

1. R. Arnott and F. D. Lewis, The transition of land to urban use, *J. Polit. Econom.*, **87**, 161–169 (1979).
2. R. Arnott, A simple urban growth model with durable housing, *Reg. Sci. Urban Econom.*, **10**, 53–76 (1980).
3. B. Bernanke, Irreversibility, uncertainty, and cyclical investment, *Quart. J. Econom.*, **48**, 85–106 (1983).
4. D. R. Capozza, R. W. Helsley, and E. S. Mills, Urban growth and the price of land, *in* "Proceedings, Administrative Sciences Association of Canada" (1986).
5. D. R. Capozza and R. W. Helsley, "The Structure of Urban Prices and Rents with Growth and Uncertainty," Working Paper, Faculty of Commerce, University of British Columbia, Vancouver, BC (1986).
6. D. R. Capozza and R. W. Helsley, The fundamentals of land prices and urban growth, *J. Urban Econom.*, **26**, 295–306 (1989).
7. H. R. Clarke and W. J. Reed, "A Stochastic Analysis of Land Development Timing and Property Valuation," Manuscript, University of Victoria, Toronto, Ontario (1988).
8. M. Fujita, Spatial patterns of urban growth: Optimum and market, *J. Urban Econom.*, **3**, 209–241 (1976).
9. J. Heaney and R. Jones, "The Timing of Investment," Working Paper, Faculty of Commerce, University of British Columbia, Vancouver, BC (1984).

10. N. Ikeda and S. Watanabe, "Stochastic Differential Equations and Diffusion Processes," North-Holland, Amsterdam (1981).
11. S. Karlin and H. Taylor, "A First Course in Stochastic Processes," Academic Press, New York (1975).
12. R. McDonald and D. Siegal, The value of waiting to invest, *Quart. J. Econom.*, **101**, 707–728 (1986).
13. D. E. Mills, Growth, speculation, and sprawl in a monocentric city, *J. Urban Econom.*, **10**, 201–226 (1981).
14. S. Ross, "Stochastic Processes," Wiley, New York (1983).
15. S. Titman, Urban land prices under uncertainty, *Amer. Econom. Rev.*, **75**, 505–514 (1985).
16. W. C. Wheaton, Urban residential growth under perfect foresight, *J. Urban Econom.*, **12**, 1–21 (1982).

[2]

Regional Science and Urban Economics 23 (1993) 695–729. North-Holland

Communication technologies and spatial organization of multi-unit firms in metropolitan areas

Mitsuru Ota

Institute of Socio-Economic Planning, University of Tsukuba, Tsukuba 305, Japan

Masahisa Fujita*

Department of Regional Science, University of Pennsylvania, Philadelphia, PA 19104-6209, USA

Received October 1990, final version received June 1992

Departing from traditional location theory (which treats a firm as a single-unit entity), in this paper we consider that each firm consists of multiple units that exchange information or services. Specifically, we develop a general equilibrium model of the city, in which each firm consists of a front-unit (e.g. business office) and back-unit (e.g. plant or back-office). Each front-unit interacts with all other front-units for the purpose of business communications, while each back-unit exchanges information or management services only with the front-unit of the same firm. Each firm must choose the location of its front-unit and back-unit optimally. The equilibrium spatial configuration of the city is determined as an outcome of interactions among all firms and households through competitive land and labor markets. We show that, depending on parameters, a variety of interesting patterns of metropolitan spatial organization emerges.

JEL classification: R14; R30; L20

1. Introduction

In the traditional location theory, the firm has been treated as a single-unit entity.[1] In the context of urban location theory, this single-unit approach to a firm location might have been appropriate because, in the past, most firms

Correspondence to: Masahisa Fujita, Department of Regional Science, University of Pennsylvania, Philadelphia, PA 19104-6209, USA.

*Financial support of the Wharton Real Estate Center is gratefully acknowledged. The authors thank Mamoru Kaneko, Sung Woong Hong, Tony E. Smith, and two anonymous referees for their valuable comments on an earlier draft of this paper.

[1]We hasten to note that there are several papers on spatial pricing and spatial competition which consider location of multi-outlet firms [for a survey, see, for example, Gabszewicz and Thisse (1986)]. Here, however, our focus is on the *vertical division* of firm activities (in contrast to horizontal division). There also exist many papers which examine optimal location of multiple units having input–output linkages [for a survey, see, for example, Hansen et al. (1987)]. Here, our focus is on the general equilibrium aspects of cities with many firms having multiple units.

in a city conducted their main activities at a single location. Recently, however, many firms in large cities have started to conduct their activities at separate locations.

For example, many business firms (e.g. investment banks) in large cities of developed countries have recently moved a part of their office activities (such as billing, book-keeping, planning, research, and employee training) to the suburbs. A business firm typically conducts a part of its activities (such as face-to-face communication with other business firms) at the *front-office* located in the central business district (CBD), and the rest of its activities are carried out at the *back-office* located in the suburbs. As another example, many manufacturing firms in large cities conduct their business activities at their headquarters located in the CBD, while their manufacturing plants remain in the suburbs. This spatial segregation of firm activities is mainly due to the recent development of telecommunication technologies (including computer-related communication technologies).[2]

If a firm is located and conducts all of its activities in the CBD, both inter-communications (among its various units) and extra-communications (with other business offices) can be maintained most efficiently. However, by doing so, the firm must incur large floor-rents, while its workers must commute over long distances from the suburbs. On the other hand, if the firm moves all of its activities to the suburbs, it will incur a severe disadvantage in (face-to-face) communications with other business offices. Therefore, given recent developments in telecommunication technologies, a typical large firm (e.g. Merrill Lynch, the largest investment bank in the United States) may keep its front-office in the CBD (e.g. Manhattan) and build a spacious back-office (or production plant) in the far removed suburbs (e.g. Princeton), with the two offices connected by modern communication equipment such as inter-computer networks and facsimiles.

Given these innovations in the spatial reorganization of firm activities, in this paper we develop a multi-unit approach to the location of firms, and examine possible impacts of communication technologies on the spatial organization of large cities. Specifically, we develop a general equilibrium model of the city, in which each firm consists of a *front-unit* (e.g. business office) and a *back-unit* (e.g. plant, back-office, or R&D unit). Each front-unit is assumed to interact with all other front-units for the purpose of business communications, while each back-unit exchanges information or management services only with the front-unit of the same firm. Each firm must choose the location of its front-unit and back-unit optimally. The equilibrium

[2]There currently exists a large body of literature on information technologies and their impact on spatial and industrial organizations, which forms the background of this paper [for recent studies, see, for example, Estabrooks and Lamarche (1987) and Giaoutzi and Nijkamp (1988)]. Our purpose here is to develop a *formal model* for the study of interactions between the communication technologies and urban spatial organization.

spatial configuration of the city is determined as an outcome of interactions among all front-units, back-units, and households (i.e. workers) through competitive land and labor markets. Depending on parameter specifications (e.g. communication costs among front-units, communication costs between front-units and back-units, and commuting costs of workers), a variety of interesting patterns of metropolitan spatial organization emerges.

In section 2, we develop the model. Although our model is a multi-unit extension of the non-monocentric city model by Ogawa and Fujita (1980), the models differ in one essential aspect. That is, as was noted before, in our model each firm may occupy land at two different locations. This makes it difficult to apply the traditional concept of bid rent functions. We overcome this difficulty by reformulating the firm's behavior in a decentralized form. That is, in section 3 we introduce *shadow profit functions* of front-units and back-units, respectively, and propose to obtain the optimal location-pair (i.e. location of the front-unit and back-unit) of each firm as a *Nash location-equilibrium* in which each front-unit (back-unit) chooses its location optimally (so as to maximize its own shadow profit) while taking the location of the associated back-unit (front-unit) as given.

In section 4, first we describe the conditions for a *Nash equilibrium configuration* of the city, in which each front-unit and back-unit maximizes its own shadow profit function. A Nash equilibrium configuration, however, does not always represent a *global equilibrium configuration* in which each firm maximizes its (real) profit function by choosing the location of its front-unit and back-unit *simultaneously*. Hence, by introducing an additional requirement, we obtain the global equilibrium conditions. We also present a sufficient condition for a Nash equilibrium configuration to be a global equilibrium configuration (Theorem 4.1).

In section 5 we consider the case of the *linear city* with additional specifications of several parameter functions. In turns out that given each set of parameters, although there may exist more than one Nash equilibrium configuration, there exists one and only one global equilibrium configuration. We show that there exist, in total, eleven different (global) equilibrium configurations. We discuss which configuration is likely to be observed under what conditions. It is shown, in particular, that the advancement of intrafirm communication technology will eventually lead to a dichotomy of firm activities, where the front-unit activity (specialized in extrafirm communications) will concentrate in the city center, while the back-unit activity will locate in the far suburbs. Finally, in section 6 we discuss further research directions.

2. The model

Assume that a city develops in a given geographical space X. The city accommodates a continuum of homogeneous firms and a continuum of homogeneous households (i.e. workers). Each firm consists of two units, the *front-unit* and *back-unit*. Each front-unit interacts with all other front-units for the purpose of business communications, while each back-unit is assumed to interact (for the exchange of information or management services) with only the front-unit of the same firm. Each firm must choose the location of its front-unit and back-unit optimally. Households supply labor to firms by commuting, and receive wages. We assume that all land in the city is owned by absentee landlords, and that the land not occupied by households or firms is used for agriculture, yielding a constant rent, R_A. Everywhere in X, the density of land is assumed to be 1. Furthermore, both land and labor markets are assumed to be perfectly competitive. The equilibrium spatial configuration of the city is determined as an outcome of interactions among all firms and households through competitive land and labor markets. We describe below the behavior of each household and firm in detail.

2.1. Households

In the city, there exists a continuum of homogeneous households of size N. The utility function of each household is given by $U(S, Z)$, where S represents the consumption of land and Z the consumption of the composite (consumer) good. For simplicity, we assume that S is fixed for all households at some constant S_h. We also assume that each household supplies a unit of labor to a firm, and that the composite good is imported at a constant price of 1. Then, if a household chooses to reside at $x \in X$ and work at $x_w \in X$, its budget constraint is given by

$$Z + R(x)S_h + T(x, x_w) = W(x_w), \tag{2.1}$$

where $T(x, x_w)$ is the commuting cost from x to x_w, and $W(x_w)$ is the wage rate at x_w. Now, since the lot size is fixed at the constant S_h, the objective of each household is to choose a residential location x and working location x_w which maximize the amount of composite-good consumption given by

$$Z(x, x_w) = W(x_w) - R(x)S_h - T(x, x_w). \tag{2.2}$$

2.2. Firms

In the city, there is a continuum of homogeneous firms of size M.[3] Each firm produces some type of service or good which is exported outside the

[3]Note that all firms are assumed to be identical in *their location behavior*. They are, of course, different in other aspects such as the information or services they produce. Otherwise, no communication would be necessary among firms.

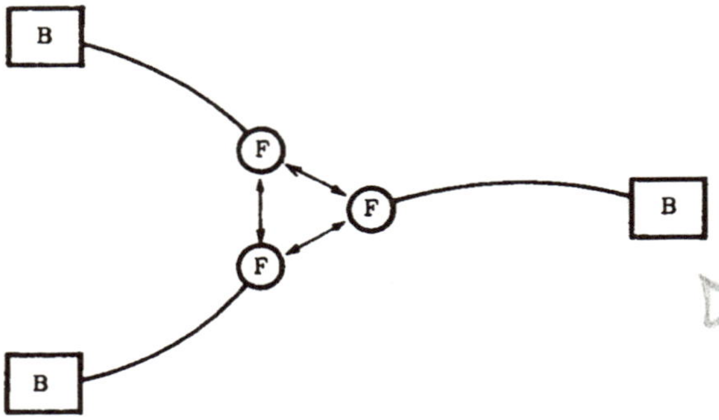

Fig. 1. Front-units (F) and back-units (B).

city at the constant (normalized) price of 1. As noted before, each firm consists of a front-unit and back-unit. The main task of the front-unit of a firm is to communicate with all other firms (through their front-units). The back-unit of a firm engages in the internal operation of the firm, and makes contact with the front-unit of the same firm only.[4] The relationship between front-units and back-units is depicted in fig. 1. If a firm chooses its front-unit at $x \in X$ and back-unit at $y \in X$, the firm incurs an *intrafirm communication cost*, $\Gamma(x, y)$, per unit of time. Here, we assume that such intrafirm communications can be attained through routine contacts between the two units, and hence the cost $\Gamma(x, y)$ depends only on the location pair, x and y. It is assumed that $\Gamma(x, x) = 0$ for all $x \in X$.

Each front-unit, however, actively engages in communication with other front-units. Here, it is postulated that communication itself is measurable in terms of some level of *contact activity*, q (e.g. the number of face-to-face contacts per unit of time), and that each front-unit is free to choose its optimal level of contact activity with other front-units.[5]

Each front-unit is assumed to require S_f units of land and L_f units of labor, while each back-unit requires S_b units of land and L_b units of labor. (Here, each S_f, L_f, S_b, and L_b is a given positive constant.) Let $f(x)$ and $b(x)$ denote, respectively, the density of front-units and that of back-units at each location $x \in X$, and $R(x)$ and $W(x)$ represent, respectively, the land rent and

[4]Although back-units may interact with other agents (in the city as well as outside the city), it is assumed in this paper that all such extrafirm interactions (by back-units as well as by front-units) are done through their front-units only. This assumption, however, represents an over-simplification of the reality. Explicit consideration of direct extrafirm interactions by back-units is left as an important extension of our model in the future.

[5]It is true that communications are two-way activities. Recall, however, that all firms are assumed to be identical in terms of their location behavior. Therefore, for any given pair of front-units, the optimal level of contact between the two units (which is chosen independently by each) becomes the same. Hence, no problem of asymmetric demand in contact arises. Here we assume implicitly that each pair of front-units splits equally their contact costs.

wage rate at each x. We assume that if a firm having the front-unit at x and back-unit at y chooses a level, $q(x,z)$, of communication with *every single front-unit* (of other firms) at location z (for all $z \in X$), the profit Π of the firm (per unit of time) is given by

$$\Pi(x,y,q(x,\cdot)) = \int_X V[q(x,z)]f(z)\,dz - \int_X c(x,z)q(x,z)f(z)\,dz$$

$$- R(x)S_f - W(x)L_f - R(y)S_b - W(y)L_b - \Gamma(x,y). \qquad (2.3)$$

Here, V is an appropriate numerical function and $V[q(x,z)]$ represents the contribution of contacts $q(x,z)$ (with a front-unit at z) to the revenue for the firm, and $c(x,z)$ represents the cost of communication per unit contact between locations x and z.[6] Hence, on the right-hand side of (2.3), the first and second terms represent, respectively, the total benefits and total costs of interfirm communications, the third and fourth terms represent the land cost and labor cost of the front-unit, the fifth and sixth terms those of the back-unit, and the last term represents the intrafirm communication cost.

Each firm chooses its front-unit location x, back-unit location y, and contact pattern $q(x,\cdot)$ so as to maximize the profit $\Pi(x,y,q(x,\cdot))$ [taking front-unit distribution $f(y)$ and other market variables as given]. To simplify expression (2.3), note that the first two terms on the right-hand side of (2.3) can be written as

$$\int_X V[q(x,z)]f(z)\,dz - \int_X c(x,z)q(x,z)f(z)\,dz$$

$$= \int_X \{V[q(x,z)] - c(x,z)q(x,z)\}f(z)\,dz.$$

Therefore, for each pair of x and $z \in X$, the optimal $q(x,z)$ can be determined independently of f. Namely, for each $c \in \Re_+$, let $q^*(c)$ be the solution to the following maximization problem:

$$\max_q V(q) - cq \quad \text{subject to } q \geqq 0. \qquad (2.4)$$

Then, the optimal $q(x,z)$ can be expressed as $q^*[c(x,y)]$. Hence, if we define the *accessibility measure*, $a(c)$, for each $c \in \Re_+$ by

$$a(c) \equiv V[q^*(c)] - cq^*(c), \qquad (2.5)$$

[6]Here, it is assumed that the contact activity $q(x,z)$ contributes to the enhancement of the (physical) productivity of the firm and also to the increase in the demand for the product of the firm. Hence, $V[q(x,z)]$ represents the total contribution of $q(x,z)$ to the increase in the revenue of the firm. In eq. (2.3), the benefits and costs of all activities of the firm other than those of communication, land, and labor are assumed to be fixed and suppressed.

then for each location pair, x and y, the maximum profit $\Pi(x,y) \equiv \Pi(x,y,q^*[c(x,\cdot)])$ is given by[7]

$$\Pi(x,y) = A(x) - R(x)S_f - W(x)L_f - R(y)S_b - W(y)L_b - \Gamma(x,y), \tag{2.6}$$

where

$$A(x) = \int_X a[c(x,z)]f(z)\,dz. \tag{2.7}$$

In (2.7) $A(x)$ represents the *aggregate accessibility measure* of each location $x \in X$.

From (2.6), given distributions $A(\cdot)$, $R(\cdot)$, and $W(\cdot)$, each firm chooses its front-unit location x and back-unit location y so as to maximize its profit $\Pi(x,y)$, while, from (2.2), each household chooses a residential location x and working location x_w so as to maximize the composite-good consumption $Z(x,x_w)$. An equilibrium is reached when all M firms achieve the same maximum profit, all N households the same maximum utility, and land and labor markets are cleared everywhere. Here, to ensure that a full employment prevails in the city at equilibrium, we assume that

$$N = (L_f + L_b)M. \tag{2.8}$$

3. Reformulation of the firm's behavior in a decentralized form

We wish to express the equilibrium conditions of the land-use model above by using the concept of *bid rent functions*. Our model, however, is fundamentally different from traditional models in one respect. Namely, as shown by (2.6), each firm occupies land at two different locations (provided $x \neq y$).[8] This makes it difficult to apply the traditional concept of bid rent functions. This is because how much rent the front-unit and back-unit of a firm can bid at each location depends on how the total revenue and cost of the firm are split between the two units; but we do not have any a priori knowledge on the equilibrium division of the total revenue and cost between them.

One way to overcome this difficulty, which we adopt in this paper, is to reformulate the firm's behavior in a decentralized form. Namely, suppose we can find a (*shadow*) *profit function*, $\Pi_f(x \mid y)$, of each front-unit and a (*shadow*) *profit function*, $\Pi_b(y \mid x)$, of each back-unit such that

[7]Notice that (2.3) represents a typical *communication model* (or *endogenous contact model*), while (2.6) represents a *spatial externality model* (or *accessibility model*). As we have seen, if we relate the accessibility function a and benefit function V by (2.5), the two models become mathematically equivalent. For further elaboration of this point, see Fujita and Smith (1990).

[8]This complication does not arise for households. Although each household must choose two locations, a residential location and working location, it consumes land at the residential location only.

$$\Pi(x^*, y^*) = \max_{x\in X, y\in X} \Pi(x, y) \Rightarrow \begin{cases} \Pi_f(x^* \mid y^*) = \max_{x\in X} \Pi_f(x \mid y^*), \\ \Pi_b(y^* \mid x^*) = \max_{y\in X} \Pi_b(y \mid x^*), \end{cases} \quad (3.1)$$

and

$$\left. \begin{aligned} \Pi_f(x^* \mid y^*) &= \max_{x\in X} \Pi_f(x \mid y^*) \\ \Pi_b(y^* \mid x^*) &= \max_{y\in X} \Pi_b(y \mid x^*) \end{aligned} \right\} \Rightarrow \Pi(x^*, y^*) = \max_{x\in X, y\in X} \Pi(x, y). \quad (3.2)$$

Condition (3.1) means that if (x^*, y^*) is an *optimal location-pair* of a firm, then it is also a *Nash equilibrium location-pair* for the front-unit and back-unit, where each unit maximizes its profit function independently (taking the location of the other as given). Conversely, condition (3.2) means that if (x^*, y^*) is a Nash equilibrium location-pair, then it is also an optimal location-pair.

If we can find such a pair of shadow profit functions, then the optimal location-pair of each firm will be obtained as a result of independent profit-maximization by each unit. It turns out that although it may not be easy to find a pair of shadow profit functions that always satisfy *both* conditions (3.1) and (3.2), we can readily find a pair of profit functions that always satisfy condition (3.1). For example, let us define

$$\Pi_f(x \mid y) = A(x) - R(x)S_f - W(x)L_f - \Gamma(x, y) - P(y), \quad (3.3)$$

$$\Pi_b(y \mid x) = P(x) - R(y)S_b - W(y)L_b - \Gamma(x, y), \quad (3.4)$$

where $P(\cdot)$ can be any function on X.[9] Recalling the original profit function (2.6), it can be readily verified that if we use (3.3) and (3.4), then conditions (3.1) are always satisfied.

Therefore, in what follows we adopt the shadow profit functions (3.3) and (3.4), and obtain equilibrium spatial configurations in two steps. In the first step, we obtain all *Nash equilibrium configurations* (of the city) in which the following Nash condition,

$$\begin{aligned} \Pi_f(x^* \mid y^*) &= \max_{x\in X} \Pi_f(x \mid y^*), \\ \Pi_b(y^* \mid x^*) &= \max_{y\in X} \Pi_b(y \mid x^*), \end{aligned} \quad (3.5)$$

is satisfied by the front-unit location x^* and back-unit location y^* of each firm. Then, in the second step, we choose the *global* (i.e. *real*) *equilibrium*

[9]More generally, in (3.3) we can replace $P(y)$ by $P_b(y)$ and in (3.4) we can replace $P(x)$ by $P_f(x)$, where $P_b(y)$ and $P_f(x)$ can be any function of y and x, respectively.

configurations (from all Nash equilibrium configurations) in which conditions (3.2) also are satisfied by the Nash location pair of every firm.

Note from (3.3) and (3.4) that the intrafirm communication cost, $\Gamma(x,y)$, appears in the shadow profit functions of both units. This double accounting of the intrafirm communication cost is an *accounting device* which is essential for conditions (3.1) to be satisfied, i.e for the optimal location pair of each firm to be sustained as a Nash equilibrium location pair.[10] To see the economic meaning of these profit functions, it would be sufficient to understand that $P(x)$ and $P(y)$ represent the *shadow* (i.e. *accounting*) *prices* of the *back-unit service* at the front location x and at the back-unit location y, respectively. In this context, (3.3) implies that the *shadow cost* (i.e. accounting cost) of the back-unit service for the front-unit locating at x equals $\Gamma(x,y)+P(y)$, i.e. the sum of the shadow price of the back-unit service at y and the transport cost of that service from y to x. Similarly, (3.4) implies that the *shadow net revenue* of the back-unit service (produced by the back-unit) at y equals $P(x)-\Gamma(x,y)$, i.e. the shadow price of that service at the front-unit location x minus the transport cost of that service. For the purpose of the determination of Nash equilibrium configurations, the choice of a shadow price function, $P(\cdot)$, is completely free. Hence, in the analysis below we specify this function in the most convenient manner so that the identification of global equilibrium configurations become easier.

Note also that our decentralized mechanism here is essentially different from any competitive price mechanism. From (3.3), a front-unit must take the location of the associated back-unit, y, as given; and y indeed affects the profit of the front-unit. Similarly, from (3.4), a back-unit must take the location of the associated front-unit, x, as given; and x indeed affects the profit of the back-unit. In a competitive price mechanism, each agent is assumed to respond to market prices only, hence no agent is concerned about the location of any other agent.

4. Equilibrium conditions

Given the context of decentralized locational choice of front-units and back-units, in this section we describe equilibrium conditions of land and labor markets in the city. To do so, first in subsection 4.1 below we

[10]Generalizing (3.3) and (3.4), let us consider the following pair of decentralized profit functions:

$$\pi_f(x\mid y)=A(x)-R(x)S_f-W(x)L_f-\alpha\Gamma(x,y)-P(y),$$
$$\pi_b(y\mid x)=P(x)-R(y)S_b-W(y)L_b-\beta\Gamma(x,y).$$

Then, it can be readily verified that condition (3.1) can be satisfied if and only if $\alpha=1=\beta$. In general, this suggests that if a firm adopts a division system (where each division becomes a profit center), then for the efficient decentralization of the firm's management the costs of communications and transportations between each pair of divisions must be double accounted by both divisions.

enumerate unknown variables and functions, and define urban configurations.

4.1. Urban configurations

For the first set of unknown functions, as before let $h(x)$, $f(x)$, and $b(x)$ represent, respectively, the household density, front-unit density, and back-unit density at each location $x \in X$. Similarly, $R(x)$ and $W(x)$ represent, respectively, the land rent and wage rate at each $x \in X$. Furthermore, $P(x)$ represents the shadow price of the back-unit service at each $x \in X$.[11]

Given density functions $h(x)$, $f(x)$, and $b(x)$ above, let their *positive supports* be defined, respectively, as

$$h_+ \equiv \{x \in X : h(x) > 0\}, \qquad f_+ \equiv \{x \in X : f(x) > 0\},$$
$$b_+ \equiv \{x \in X : b(x) > 0\}. \tag{4.1}$$

Then, as another set of unknown functions, we introduce *firm-location correspondences*, $x_f : b_+ \to f_+$, and $y_b : f_+ \to b_+$. Here, $x = x_f(y)$ means that those firms with their back-units at location y have their front-units at x; and $y = y_b(x)$ means that those firms with their front-units at location x have their back-units at y. It is always assumed that *both x_f and y_b are onto-functions (i.e. $x_f(b_+) = f_+$ and $y_b(f_+) = b_+$), and that x_f and y_b are inverse to each other almost everywhere (i.e. $x_f(y_b(x)) = x$ for almost all $x \in f_+$).*[12] We also introduce a *commuting correspondence, $C : h_+ \to f_+ \cup b_+$*; here $x_w = C(x)$ means that households at x commute to firms at x_w. *C is also assumed to be an onto-function (i.e. $C(h_+) = f_+ \cup b_+$).*

As the last set of unknowns, let $\pi_f(y)$ represent the (shadow) profit of a front-unit *whose associated back-unit is located at $y \in X$*, and $\pi_b(x)$ the (shadow) profit of a back-unit *whose associated front-unit is located at $x \in X$*.[13] Finally, let Z be the consumption level of the composite good per household, which must be the same for all households in equilibrium.

[11]As noted before, for the purpose of the determination of Nash equilibrium configurations, $P(x)$ can be any function of x. However, in the following analysis we treat it as an unknown function because we wish to choose such a function $P(x)$ that is most convenient for the identification of global equilibrium configurations.

[12]Here, we only require that x_f and y_b are inverse to each other *almost everywhere*. This is because in a symmetric configuration, for example, it may happen that $x_f(y) = x_f(-y)$ for some $y \in b_+$; thus the inverse of x_f does not exist. This difficulty, however, arises on a subset of b_+ having measure zero. Hence, this does not affect the following results in any essential way, and the reader may neglect the words 'almost everywhere'.

[13]The reason for the choice of notation $\pi_f(y)$ and $\pi_b(x)$ is as follows. Consider the front-unit and back-unit of any specific firm. Given the back-unit location, say y, the front-unit is free to choose its location. Therefore, the equilibrium (i.e. maximum) profit π_f of that front-unit should be a function of y (i.e. the location of the associated back-unit); hence we denote it by $\pi_f\ (y)$. Similarly, given the front-unit location, say x, the back-unit is free to choose its location. Therefore, the equilibrium profit π_b of that back-unit should be a function of x (i.e. the location of the associated front-line); hence we denote it by $\pi_b(x)$.

Now, we define an *urban configuration* by the system.

$$(h(x), f(x), b(x), R(x), W(x), P(x), C(x), x_f(y), y_b(x), \pi_f(y), \pi_b(x),$$
$$Z\colon x, y \in X).$$

4.2. Bid rent functions

As in the standard literature of urban economics, the equilibrium conditions of an urban configuration can be stated conveniently by utilizing the concept of bid rent functions. First, given the objective function of each household by (2.2), we define the *bid rent function of households* as

$$\Psi(x{:}\, x_w, Z, W(x_w)) = \frac{W(x_w) - T(x, x_w) - Z}{S_h}. \tag{4.2}$$

Next, given the profit function of each front-unit by (3.3), we define, the *bid rent function of front-units* as

$$\Phi_f(x{:}\, y, A(x), W(x), P(y), \pi_f) = \frac{A(x) - W(x)L_f - \Gamma(x, y) - P(y) - \pi_f}{S_f}. \tag{4.3}$$

Similarly, given the profit-function of each back-unit by (3.4), we define the *bid rent function of back-units as*

$$\Phi_b(y{:}\, x, W(y), P(x), \pi_b) = \frac{P(x) - W(y)L_b - \Gamma(x, y) - \pi_b}{S_b}. \tag{4.4}$$

By definition, $\Psi(x{:}\, x_w, Z, W(x_w))$ represents the maximum rent (per unit of land) which a household can bid at each residential location $x \in X$ (given its working location at x_w) while enjoying a consumption level, Z, of the composite good; here, the household also takes the wage rate $W(x_w)$ as given. Next, $\Phi_f(x{:}\, y, A(x), W(x), P(y), \pi_f)$ represents the maximum rent which a front-unit can bid at each location $x \in X$ (given the location of the associated back-unit at y) while enjoying a given profit level, π_f; here, the front-unit also takes $A(x)$, $W(x)$, and $P(y)$ as given. Similarly, $\Phi_b(y{:}\, x, W(y), P(x), \pi_b)$ represents the maximum rent which a back-unit can bid at each location $y \in X$ (given the location of the associated front-unit at x) while enjoying a given profit level, π_b; the back-unit takes $W(y)$ and $P(x)$ as given.

4.3. Equilibrium conditions

Now, let us consider a specific urban configuration represented by

$$(h^*(x), f^*(x), b^*(x), R^*(x), W^*(x), P^*(x), C^*(x), x_f^*(y), y_b^*(x),$$

$$\pi_f^*(y), \pi_b^*(x), Z^*: x, y \in X). \tag{4.5}$$

(As noted before, here x_f^* and y_b^* are inverse to each other almost everywhere.) To describe the equilibrium condition of this urban configuration, we introduce several additional functions. First, for each x, y, and $x_w \in X$ let us define

$$A^*(x) \equiv \int_X a[c(x,z)] f^*(z)\,dz, \tag{4.6}$$

$$\Psi^*(x \mid x_w) \equiv \Psi(x: x_w, Z^*, W^*(x_w)), \tag{4.7}$$

$$\Phi_f^*(x \mid y) \equiv \Phi_f^*(x: y, A^*(x), W^*(x), P^*(y), \pi_f^*(y)), \tag{4.8}$$

$$\Phi_b^*(y \mid x) \equiv \Phi_b(y: x, W^*(y), P^*(x), \pi_b^*(x)), \tag{4.9}$$

$$\Pi^*(x,y) \equiv A^*(x) - R^*(x)S_f - W^*(x)L_f - R^*(y)S_b - W^*(y)L_b - \Gamma(x,y). \tag{4.10}$$

In the context of the urban configuration (4.5), $A^*(x)$ represents the accessibility function of front-units. Furthermore, each Ψ^*, Φ_f^*, and Φ_b^* represents the bid rent function of households, front-units, and back-units, respectively, while Π^* represents the profit function of each firm. Next, let us define

$$h_+^* \equiv \{x \in X: h^*(x) > 0\}, \tag{4.11}$$

$$f_+^* \equiv \{x \in X: f^*(x) > 0\}, \tag{4.12}$$

$$b_+^* \equiv \{x \in X: b^*(x) > 0\}, \tag{4.13}$$

$$\Psi^*(x) \equiv \max_{x_w \in X} \Psi^*(x \mid x_w) \quad \text{for } x \in X, \tag{4.14}$$

$$\Phi_f^*(x) \equiv \max_{y \in b_+^*} \Phi_f^*(x \mid y) \quad \text{for } x \in X, \tag{4.15}$$

$$\Phi_b^*(y) \equiv \max_{x \in f_+^*} \Phi_b^*(y \mid x) \quad \text{for } y \in X. \tag{4.16}$$

In (4.14), $\Psi^*(x)$ represents the maximum value of household bid rent at x, which is attained by optimally choosing job location x_w. Next, by the definition of b_+^*, every one of M firms has its back-unit at some location in b_+^*. Therefore, in (4.15), $\Phi_f^*(x)$ represents the maximum of all front-unit bid rents at x which can be paid by front-units of M firms; here, by definition (4.8), a front-unit whose associated back-unit is located at y must retain the given shadow profit $\pi_f^*(y)$. Similarly, every one of M firms has its front-unit at some location $z \in f_+^*$. Hence, in (4.16), $\Phi_b^*(x)$ represents the maximum of all back-unit bid rents at x which can be paid by back-units of M firms; here, a back-unit whose associated front-units is located at z must retain the given shadow profit $\pi_b^*(z)$.

Now we are ready to state the equilibrium conditions. In short, an urban configuration is in equilibrium when each location of the city is occupied by the highest bidder, while the demand and supply of land and those of labor are balanced at every location in the city. To be precise, we say that (4.5) represents a *Nash equilibrium configuration* (of the city) if the following set of conditions are satisfied.

(i) For land market equilibrium: at each x and $y \in X$,

$$R^*(x) = \max\{\Psi^*(x), \Phi_f^*(x), \Phi_b^*(x), R_A\}, \tag{4.17}$$

$$h^*(x) > 0 \Rightarrow \Psi^*(x \mid C^*(x)) = R^*(x), \tag{4.18}$$

$$f^*(x) > 0 \Rightarrow \Phi_f^*(x \mid y_b^*(x)) = R^*(x), \tag{4.19}$$

$$b^*(x) > 0 \Rightarrow \Phi_b^*(x \mid x_f^*(x)) = R^*(x), \tag{4.20}$$

$$h^*(x)S_h + f^*(x)S_f + b^*(x)S_b \leq 1, \tag{4.21}$$

$$R^*(x) > R_A \Rightarrow h^*(x)S_h + f^*(x)S_f + b^*(x)S_b = 1. \tag{4.22}$$

(ii) For labor market equilibrium:

$$C^*(h_+^*) = f_+^* \cup b_+^*, \tag{4.23}$$

$$\int_B h^*(x)\,dx = \int_{C^*(B)} (f^*(x)L_f + b^*(x)L_b)\,dx \tag{4.24}$$

for every measurable subset B of h_+^*.

(iii) For equilibrium of firm-location correspondences:

$$x_f^*(b_+^*) = f_+^*, y_b^*(f_+^*) = b_+^* \quad \text{and} \quad x_f^*(y_b^*(x)) = x \quad \text{for almost all } x \in f_+^*, \tag{4.25}$$

$$\int_B f^*(x)\,dx = \int_{y_b^*(B)} b^*(x)\,dx \quad \text{for every measurable subset } B \text{ of } f_+^*. \tag{4.26}$$

(iv) For population equilibrium:

$$\int_X h^*(x)\,dx = N, \tag{4.27}$$

$$\int_X f^*(x)\,dx = M = \int_X b^*(x)\,dx, \quad \text{where } N = (L_f + L_b)M. \tag{4.28}$$

Furthermore, suppose that (4.5) is a Nash equilibrium configuration, and that it satisfies the following additional condition: there exists a constant π^* such that for each $x \in X$,

$$f^*(x) > 0 \Rightarrow \Pi^*(x, y_b^*(x)) = \pi^* = \max_{z \in X,\, y \in X} \Pi^*(z, y) \tag{4.29}$$

Then, we say that (4.5) represents a *(global) equilibrium configuration.*

Condition (4.17) means that at each location x, the market rent $R^*(x)$ equals the maximum of the highest bid rents by four types of agents (i.e. households, front-units, back-units, and agriculture). Condition (4.18) means that if some households reside at location x, then their bid rent must equal the market rent; their job location is specified by $C^*(x)$. Condition (4.19) means that if some front-units locate at x, then their bid rent must equal the market rent; here, the location of their associated back-units is specified by $y_b^*(x)$. Condition (4.20) has a similar meaning. Condition (4.21) represents an obvious physical land-constraint. Condition (4.22) means that if the market rent exceeds the agricultural rent, then the land must be occupied by either households or firms. Together, (4.17)–(4.22) ensure that each location is occupied by the highest bidder.

Condition (4.23) means that $C^*(x) > 0 \Leftrightarrow f^*(C^*(x)) + b^*(C^*(x)) > 0$, i.e. the commuting correspondence C^* indeed assigns a *job location* to each residential location. Condition (4.24) ensures that labor supply equals labor demand at each location. Next, (4.25) means that the firm-location correspondence x_f^* (and y_b^*) indeed assigns a front-unit location to a back-unit location (and vice versa). Condition (4.26) ensures that the firm-location correspondence x_f^* always assigns the same number of back-units to any given number of front-units. Finally, (4.27) and (4.28) represent obvious population constraints.

Finally, note that in (4.29), π^* represents the maximum profit that can be attained by a firm choosing optimally the location of its front-unit and back-unit simultaneously. Hence, condition (4.29) means that for each $x \in f_+^*$, $(x, y_b^*(x))$ forms a globally optimal location pair for firms. [Here, note by (4.25) that $y \in b_+^* \Leftrightarrow x_f^*(y) \in f_+^*$. Hence, (4.29) also implies that for each $y \in b_+^*$, $(x_f^*(y), y)$ forms a globally optimal location pair.]

4.4. Some additional implications of equilibrium conditions

First, let us examine the important implications of conditions (4.17)–(4.20). It can be readily verified that together (4.17) and (4.18) imply that

$$h^*(x) > 0 \Rightarrow Z^* = W(C^*(x)) - T(x, C^*(x)) - R^*(x)S_h$$

$$= \max_{x_w \in X}(W(x_w) - T(x, x_w) - R^*(x)S_h). \tag{4.30}$$

That is, the commuter correspondence C^* assigns an optimal working location to each household in the city so that all households attain the same maximum consumption, Z^*, of the composite good. Next, to see the additional implications of conditions (4.19) and (4.20), in the same manner as (3.3) and (3.4) let us define for each $x, y \in X$,

$$\Pi_f^*(x \mid y) \equiv A^*(x) - R^*(x)S_f - W^*(x)L_f - \Gamma(x, y) - P^*(y), \tag{4.31}$$

$$\Pi_b^*(y \mid x) \equiv P^*(x) - R^*(y)S_b - W^*(y)L_b - \Gamma(x, y). \tag{4.32}$$

Then, we can readily see that together (4.17) and (4.19) imply that

$$f^*(x) > 0 \Rightarrow \pi_f^*(y_b^*(x)) = \Pi_f^*(x \mid y_b^*(x)) = \max_{z \in X} \Pi_f^*(z \mid y_b^*(x)), \tag{4.33}$$

which means that given the back-unit location $y_b^*(x)$, x is indeed the optimal location of the associated front-unit; and $\pi_f^*(y_b^*(x))$ equals the maximum possible profit of that front-unit. Similarly, by (4.17) and (4.20), it follows that

$$b^*(y) > 0 \Rightarrow \pi_b^*(x_f^*(y)) = \Pi_b^*(y \mid x_f^*(y)) = \max_{z \in X} \Pi_b^*(z \mid x_f^*(y)), \tag{4.34}$$

which implies that given the front-unit location $x_f^*(y)$, y is indeed an optimal location of the associated back-unit; and $\pi_b^*(x_f^*(y))$ equals the maximum possible profit of that back-unit. Since $y = y_b^*(x)$ means $x = x_f^*(y)$, and since we have that $f^*(x) > 0 \Leftrightarrow b^*(y_b^*(x)) > 0$, we can conclude from (4.33) and (4.34) that for each $x \in f_+^*$, $(x, y_b^*(x))$ forms a Nash equilibrium location-pair, i.e. for each $y \in b_+^*$, $(x_f^*(y), y)$ forms a Nash equilibrium location-pair. That is, *the firm-location correspondence y_b^* (or x_f^*) assigns a Nash equilibrium location-pair to each firm, comprised of a front-unit and back-unit.*

Next, in order to ensure that the Nash equilibrium location-pair of each firm is indeed a (global) optimal location-pair, we must confirm that condition (4.29) is indeed satisfied for all $x \in f_+^*$. In general, such a confirmation may not be easy. However, under a realistic assumption of the intrafirm communication cost function $\Gamma(x, y)$, we can achieve the confirmation of condition (4.29) relatively easily. To explain this point, first let us introduce the following terminology.

Given any three locations, x', x, $y' \in X$, if we always have

$$\Gamma(x', y') \leq \Gamma(x', x) + \Gamma(x, y'), \tag{4.35}$$

then we say that the intrafirm communication cost function Γ has the property of *long-distance economies*. (Given the recent development in communication technologies, it is quite realistic to assume that Γ has the property of long-distance economies.) We can show the following result (see appendix A for a proof):

Lemma 4.1. Suppose (4.5) *represents a global equilibrium of the city. In addition, assume that the function Γ has the property of long-distance economies. Then, it holds that*

$$x \in f_+^* \cap b_+^* \Rightarrow \Pi^*(x, x) = \max_{z \in X,\, y \in X} \Pi^*(z, y). \tag{4.36}$$

In the lemma above, (4.36) means that in the global equilibrium, if some front-units and some back-units locate at the same point x, then (x, x) must be an optimal location pair of firms. Using this lemma, we can obtain the following result:

Lemma 4.2. Suppose (4.5) *represents a global equilibrium of the city, and let π^* be the associated maximum profit of firms defined in* (4.29). *In this case, let us arbitrarily choose two constants, $\tilde{\pi}_f$ and $\tilde{\pi}_b$,* such that

$$\tilde{\pi}_f + \tilde{\pi}_b = \pi^* \left(\equiv \max_{x \in X,\, y \in X} \Pi^*(x, y) \right), \tag{4.37}$$

and for each $x \in X$ define $\tilde{P}(x)$ by

$$\tilde{P}(x) = P^*(x) + \tilde{\pi}_b - \pi_b^*(x) \quad \textit{for } x \in f_+^*, \tag{4.38a}$$

$$\tilde{P}(x) = P^*(x) + \pi_f^*(x) - \tilde{\pi}_f \quad \textit{for } x \in b_+^*, \tag{4.38b}$$

$$\tilde{P}(x) = P^*(x) \quad \textit{for } x \in X - (f_+^* \cup b_+^*). \tag{4.38c}$$

Then, we have:

(i) *If the function Γ has the property of long-distance economies, then it holds that*

$$\pi_f^*(x) + \pi_b^*(x) = \pi^* \quad \textit{for } x \in f_+^* \cap b_+^*. \tag{4.39}$$

Hence, (4.38a)–(4.38c) *specify a well-defined function $\tilde{P}$ on X.*[14]

[14]Note that (4.38a)–(4.38c) specifies a well-defined function on X if and only if for each $x \in f_+^* \cap b_+^*$ we have $P^*(x) + \tilde{\pi}_b - \pi_b^*(x) = P^*(x) + \pi_f^*(x) - \pi_f^*$, or $\pi_f^*(x) + \pi_b^*(x) = \tilde{\pi}_f + \tilde{\pi}_b \equiv \pi^*$.

(ii) *Provided that $\tilde{P}$ above represents a well-defined function on X,*[15] *the new system of urban configuration,*

$$(h^*(x), f^*(x), b^*(x), R^*(x), W^*(x), \tilde{P}(x), C^*(x),$$

$$x_f^*(y), y_b^*(x), \tilde{\pi}_f, \tilde{\pi}_b, Z^*: x, y \in X), \tag{4.40}$$

also forms a global equilibrium having the same maximum profit π^* for all firms.

(iii) *In this global equilibrium, it also holds that*

$$\tilde{P}(x) = \tilde{P}(y_b^*(x)) + \Gamma(x, y_b^*(x)) \quad \text{for } x \in f_+^*. \tag{4.41}$$

Here we provide an intuitive explanation of Lemma 4.2(ii) above. [See appendix B for the proofs of Lemma 4.2(i) and (iii). Their meanings are also obvious.] Note that the two systems, (4.5) and (4.40), are different only in $(P^*(x), \pi_f^*(y), \pi_b^*(x))$ and $(\tilde{P}(x), \tilde{\pi}_f, \tilde{\pi}_b)$. Lemma 4.2(ii) means that if conditions (4.37) and (4.38) hold, this difference does not affect the rest of the equilibrium system at all. To see this result, first observe that by definitions (4.8) and (4.9) we have

$$\Phi_f^*(x \mid y) = \{A^*(x) - W^*(x)L_f - \Gamma(x, y) - P^*(y) - \pi_f^*(y)\}/S_f, \tag{4.42}$$

$$\Phi_b^*(y \mid x) = \{P^*(x) - W^*(y)L_b - \Gamma(x, y) - \pi_b^*(x)\}/S_b. \tag{4.43}$$

Hence, as long as relation (4.38a) holds, on $X \times f_+^*$ the function $\Phi_b^*(y \mid x)$ remains the same in the two systems. Similarly, if relation (4.38b) holds, on $X \times b_+^*$ the function $\Phi_f^*(x \mid y)$ remains the same in the two systems. Hence, by definitions (4.15) and (4.16), the functions $\Phi_f^*(x)$ and $\Phi_b^*(y)$ also remain the same on X. Hence, if conditions (4.17)–(4.20) hold for system (4.5), then they also hold for system (4.40). Therefore, since the rest of the equilibrium conditions, (4.21)–(4.29), are independent of $(P^*(x), \pi_f^*(y), \pi_b^*(x))$, if system (4.5) is in global equilibrium, then system (4.40) also must be in global equilibrium.

Lemma 4.2 implies that for the purpose of finding global equilibrium configurations of the city, it is sufficient to focus on those Nash equilibrium configurations which take the form of (4.40). For convenience of notation, let us newly denote each $\tilde{P}(x)$, $\tilde{\pi}_f$, and $\tilde{\pi}_b$ by $P^*(x)$, π_f^*, and π_b^*, respectively, and rewrite (4.40) as

$$(h^*(x), f^*(x), b^*(x), R^*(x), W^*(x), P^*(x), C^*(x),$$

$$x_f^*(y), y_b^*(x), \pi_f^*, \pi_b^*, Z^*: x, y \in X), \tag{4.44}$$

[15]Note that even without the assumption of function Γ having the property of long-haul economies, (4.38a)–(4.38c) may specify a well-defined function $\tilde{P}$ on X. For example, if $f_+^* \cap b_+^* = \varnothing$, then $\tilde{P}$ is always well-defined.

where each π_f^* and π_b^* is a constant. Since our objective in the rest of the paper is to find global equilibrium configurations, hereafter we focus on those Nash equilibrium configurations that take the form of (4.44) and satisfy the following additional condition:[16]

$$P^*(x) = P^*(y_b^*(x)) + \Gamma(x, y_b^*(x)) \quad \text{for } x \in f_+^*, \tag{4.45a}$$

or, equivalently,

$$P^*(y) = P^*(x_f^*(y)) - \Gamma(x_f^*(y), y) \quad \text{for } y \in b_+^*. \tag{4.45b}$$

The next theorem provides a sufficient condition for a Nash equilibrium configuration in the form of (4.44) to be a global equilibrium configuration [see appendix C for a proof].

Theorem 4.1. Suppose (4.44) *represents a Nash equilibrium configuration which satisfies condition* (4.45) [*in addition to* (4.17)–(4.28)]. *Assume also that the intrafirm communication cost function* Γ *has the property of long-distance economies. Then,* (4.44) *is also a global equilibrium if the following additional condition holds: for each* $x \in X$,

$$R^*(x) = \max\left\{ \Psi^*(x), \max_{y \in X} \Phi_f^*(x \mid y), \max_{z \in X} \Phi_b^*(x \mid z), R_A \right\}. \tag{4.46}$$

Note that by (4.15) and (4.16), condition (4.17) can be restated as

$$R^*(x) = \max\left\{ \Psi^*(x), \max_{y \in b_+^*} \Phi_f^*(x \mid y), \max_{z \in f_+^*} \Phi_b^*(x \mid z), R_A \right\}. \tag{4.47}$$

Thus condition (4.46) is a slightly stronger version of (4.17). Theorem 4.1 suggests that one way of finding global equilibrium configurations, which we follow in the next section, is first to find those Nash equilibrium configurations that take the form of (4.44) and satisfy the additional condition (4.45), and then to confirm that they also satisfy condition (4.46).

5. Equilibrium configurations for the linear model

In this section we intend to obtain explicit solutions to the equilibrium problem described. To do so, we consider a special case with the following simplifying assumption on parameters:

[16]Relation (4.45a) is the restatement of (4.41) in terms of new notations. Furthermore, (4.45b) is a restatement of (4.45a). That is, since $y_b^*(x_f^*(y)) = y$ and $x_f^*(y) \in f_+^*$ for each $y \in b_+^*$, by setting $x = x_f^*(y)$ in (4.45a) we can obtain (4.45b).

$$X = \Re, \tag{5.1}$$

$$T(x, x_w) = t|x - x_w| \quad \text{for all } x, x_w \in X, \tag{5.2}$$

$$\Gamma(x, y) = \tau|x - y| \quad \text{for all } x, y \in X, \tag{5.3}$$

$$a[c(x, y)] = \beta - \alpha|x - y| \quad \text{for all } x, y \in X, \tag{5.4}$$

where each t, τ, β, and α is a positive number. Eq. (5.1) represents a *linear location space* (i.e. a long-narrow city), while (5.2) and (5.3) represent, respectively, a linear commuting cost and a linear intrafirm communication cost. Similarly, (5.4) represents a *linear accessibility measure.*[17] Since each of (5.1)–(5.4) represents a linear function, we call this case the *linear model.* Note that since the linear function Γ given by (5.3) has the property of long-distance economies, Theorem 4.1 applies to this model.

For this linear model, we can show the following results. First, given any set of parameters, there always exists one and only one (global) equilibrium configuration for the city. Second, in total, there exist *eleven* different equilibrium configurations (which are depicted in fig. 3A–K below).

To show these results, we take the following procedure. [As noted above, in this section each urban configuration is generally represented by (4.44).] First, we consider a set of land use patterns (more precisely, eleven patterns) as candidates of (global) equilibrium land use patterns.[18] Second, given each specific candidate land use pattern, we specify the corresponding density distributions, $h^*(x)$, $f^*(x)$, and $b^*(x)$. Third, by utilizing some of the Nash equilibrium conditions [(4.17)–(4.28)] together with the additional condition

[17]One way to derive the linear accessibility measure (5.4) is as follows. In the profit function (2.3), assume that the communication benefit function V is given by the following entropy-type function:

$$V(q) = \begin{cases} (q/\gamma)(1 + \log\beta) - (q/\gamma)\log(q/\gamma) & \text{for } q < \gamma\beta, \\ \beta & \text{for } q \geq \gamma\beta. \end{cases}$$

Then solving the maximization problem (2.4), we obtain a *negative exponential contact function,* $q^*(c) = \gamma\beta\,\mathrm{e}^{-\gamma c}$. Substituting this relation into (2.5), we have a *negative exponential accessibility function,* $a(c) = \beta\,\mathrm{e}^{-\gamma c}$. Therefore, if we assume the following communication cost function,

$$c(x, y) = \log\left(1 - \frac{\gamma}{\beta}|x - y|\right)^{-1/\gamma},$$

then we obtain the linear accessibility measure (5.4). Notice that the communication cost function, $c(x, y)$, above is convex in distance $|x - y|$, which is a realistic specification for the case of a face-to-face communication under consideration. [For further explanations, see Fujita and Smith (1990).] Note also that in order to avoid the linear function (5.4) taking negative values in the city, the size of the city cannot be too large. Specifically, let $M(S_f + S_b) + NS_h \equiv 2l$, which gives the length of the city area (in equilibrium). Then, in order to assume that the function (5.4) always takes non-negative values in the city area $(-l, l)$, hereafter we assume that $\beta - \alpha 2l > 0$ or $M(S_f + S_b) + NS_h < \beta/\alpha$.

[18]In a manner similar to Ogawa and Fujita (1980), it can be shown that all other possible land patterns cannot be in equilibrium. Its verification, however, is very tedious, and hence in this paper we omit it.

(4.45), we determine the rest of the unknowns, $R^*(x)$ through Z^*, in (4.44). Fourth, we obtain the parameter region in which all Nash equilibrium conditions [(4.17)–(4.28)] are indeed satisfied. Fifth, by confirming that condition (4.46) is also satisfied by that Nash equilibrium configuration, we can conclude that it indeed represents a global equilibrium configuration. Finally, we confirm that the parameter regions of these eleven equilibrium configurations are mutually exclusive (except zero-measure areas) and exhaustive.

Several notes are in order. It turns out that either Z^* (equilibrium utility) or π^* ($\equiv \pi_f^* + \pi_b^*$, equilibrium profit) cannot be determined uniquely (i.e. we can choose any value for one of them).[19] Hence, in the subsequent analysis, we arbitrarily choose a positive number, $\bar{Z}$, and set[20]

$$Z^* = \bar{Z}. \tag{5.5}$$

Next, since the actual calculation for determination of each equilibrium configuration is tedious (and similar for many configurations), we demonstrate it for one configuration only in subsection 5.1 [See Ota (1991) for calculations for the rest of configurations.] In the subsequent analysis, we use the following definitions,

$$S \equiv S_f + S_b, \qquad L \equiv L_f + L_b, \tag{5.6}$$

and in figures the following notations:

F = a front-unit area, B = a back-unit area,

H = a residential area.

Each F, B, and H is a part (or the whole) of f_+^*, b_+^*, and h_+^*, respectively.

5.1. An example of calculations (for the case of pattern G)

Consider a symmetric land use pattern right half of which is depicted in fig. 2(a).[21] We examine under what conditions (on parameters) this land use pattern represents an equilibrium configuration.

As depicted in fig. 2(a), in this land use pattern all front-units are located together in the central area, $[-x_1, x_1]$, which forms the CBD. Workers for

[19] This is because each household consumes a fixed amount of land (S_h), and each firm has a fixed-coefficient technology.

[20] We can interpret (5.5) as follows. Although the number of firms in the city is fixed (at M), households are assumed to be able to move at no cost between the city and the rest of the national economy. Then, in equilibrium, the total number of households in the city is given by (2.8), and the utility of residents equals the national utility levels given by (5.2).

[21] In a manner similar to Ogawa and Fujita (1980), we can show that any (global) equilibrium configuration is symmetric with respect to the center of the city.

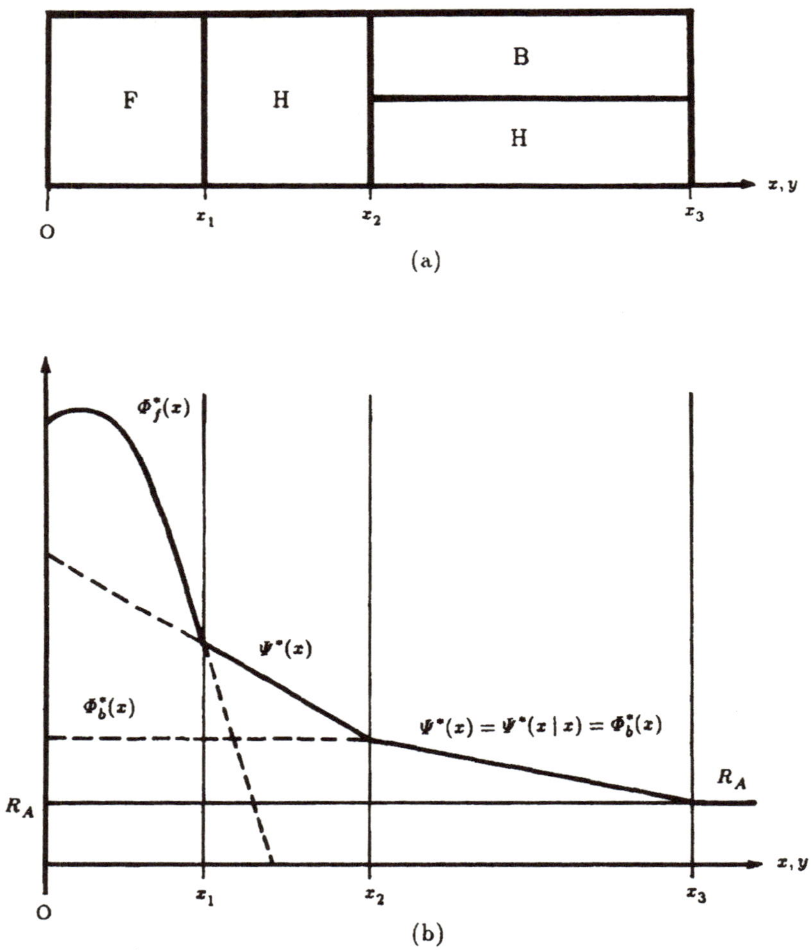

Fig. 2. Equilibrium configuration of pattern G.

the CBD commute from the surrounding residential areas, $[-x_2, -x_1]$ and $[x_1, x_2]$. All back-units, together with their workers, are located in the far suburbs, $[-x_3, -x_2]$ and $[x_2, x_3]$; no commuting occurs in these areas. Density distributions of agents are given by

$$h^*(x) = \begin{cases} 1/S_h & \text{for } x_1 \leqq |x| \leqq x_2, \\ L_b/(S_h L_b + S_b) & \text{for } x_2 \leqq |x| \leqq x_3, \\ 0 & \text{elsewhere,} \end{cases} \tag{5.7}$$

$$f^*(x)=\begin{cases}1/S_{\mathrm{f}} & \text{for } |x|\leqq x_1,\\ 0 & \text{elsewhere,}\end{cases} \tag{5.8}$$

$$b^*(x)=\begin{cases}1/(S_{\mathrm{h}}L_{\mathrm{b}}+S_{\mathrm{b}}) & \text{for } x_2\leqq|x|\leqq x_3\\ 0 & \text{elsewhere,}\end{cases} \tag{5.9}$$

where, by population constraints (4.27) and (4.28), we have

$$x_1=\frac{S_{\mathrm{f}}M}{2},\qquad x_2=\frac{(S_{\mathrm{f}}+S_{\mathrm{h}}L_{\mathrm{f}})M}{2},\qquad x_3=\frac{(S+S_{\mathrm{h}}L)M}{2}. \tag{5.10}$$

The land use pattern described by (5.7)–(5.10) is called *pattern G*. Using (4.6), (5.8), and (5.10), the accessibility function for this pattern can be obtained as

$$A^*(x)=\begin{cases}\beta M-\alpha M|x| & \text{for } |x|\geqq x_1,\\[2ex] \beta M-\dfrac{\alpha S_{\mathrm{f}}}{4}M^2-\dfrac{\alpha}{S_{\mathrm{f}}}x^2 & \text{for } |x|\leqq x_1,\end{cases} \tag{5.11}$$

Since front-units in area $[0,x_1]$ (in area $[-x_1,0)$) are associated with back-units in area $[x_2,x_3]$ (in area $[-x_3,-x_2]$), firm–location correspondences are given by[22]

$$x_{\mathrm{f}}^*(y)=\begin{cases}(y+x_2)x_1/(x_3-x_2) & \text{for } -x_3\leqq x\leqq -x_2,\\ (y-x_2)x_1/(x_3-x_2) & \text{for } x_2\leqq y\leqq x_3,\end{cases} \tag{5.12}$$

$$y_{\mathrm{b}}^*(x)=\begin{cases}(x_3-x_2)x/x_1-x_2 & \text{for } -x_1\leqq x<0,\\ (x_3-x_2)x/x_1+x_2 & \text{for } 0\leqq x<x_1.\end{cases} \tag{5.13}$$

The commuting correspondence is given by

$$C^*(x)=\begin{cases}(x+x_1)x_1/(x_2-x_1) & \text{for } -x_2<x\leqq -x_1,\\ (x-x_1)x_1/(x_2-x_1) & \text{for } x_1\leqq x<x_2,\\ x & \text{for } x_1\leqq|x|\leqq x_2.\end{cases} \tag{5.14}$$

Setting $Z^*=\bar{Z}$, $\pi_{\mathrm{f}}^*(y)=\pi_{\mathrm{f}}^*$, and $\pi_{\mathrm{b}}^*(y)=\pi_{\mathrm{b}}^*$ in eqs. (4.7), (4.8), and (4.9), we have the following bid rent functions:

[22]Again, correspondences (5.12) and (5.13) are just examples; there are infinitely many correspondences which are consistent with pattern G. The same note applies to the correspondence (5.14).

$$\Psi^*(x|x_w) = \frac{W^*(x_w) - t|x - x_w| - \bar{Z}}{S_h}, \tag{5.15}$$

$$\Phi_f^*(x \mid y) = \frac{A^*(x) - W^*(x)L_f - \tau|x - y| - P^*(y) - \pi_f^*}{S_f}, \tag{5.16}$$

$$\Phi_b^*(y \mid x) = \frac{P^*(x) - W^*(y)L_b - \tau|x - y| - \pi_b^*}{S_b}. \tag{5.17}$$

First, we determine the spatial structure of the shadow price function, $P^*(x)$. Since $f_+^* = [-x_1, x_1]$, it must hold by (4.16), (4.17), and (4.20) that

$$\Phi_b^*(x|x_f^*(x)) = \Phi_b^*(x) \equiv \max_{-x_1 \leqq z \leqq x_1} \Phi_b^*(x|z) \quad \text{for } x_2 \leqq |x| \leqq x_3, \tag{5.18}$$

which implies that

$$P^*(x_f^*(x)) - \tau|x_f^*(x) - x| = \max_{-x_1 \leqq z \leqq x_1} (P^*(z) - \tau|z - x|) \quad \text{for } x_2 \leqq |x| \leqq x_3. \tag{5.19}$$

Using the function $x_f^*(x)$ given by (5.12), we can readily see that for the relation (5.19) to hold for $x_2 \leqq |x| \leqq x_3$, $P^*(x)$ must be such that

$$P^*(x) = P^* - \tau|x| \quad \text{for } |x| \leqq x_1, \tag{5.20}$$

where P^* is an unknown constant. Next, together (4.15), (4.17), and (4.19) imply that

$$\Phi_f^*(x|y_b^*(x)) = \Phi_f^*(x) \equiv \max_{x_2 \leqq |y| \leqq x_3} \Phi_f^*(x|y) \quad \text{for } |x| \leqq x_1. \tag{5.21}$$

In a manner similar to the above, using (5.13) and (5.19), we can obtain the following relation:

$$P^*(x) = P^{**} - \tau|x| \quad \text{for } x_2 \leqq |x| \leqq x_3, \tag{5.22}$$

where P^{**} is another unknown constant. It is not difficult to see by the forms of bid rent functions (5.16) and (5.17) that by appropriately choosing π_f^* and π_b^*, we can require that $P^* = P^{**}$. Furthermore, the value of $P^*(x)$ in the area where no firm is located cannot be determined uniquely. Hence, for convenience, we assume that

$$P^*(x) = P^* - \tau|x| \quad \text{for all } x \in X. \tag{5.23}$$

Then, using (5.23) and definitions (4.15) and (4.16), we can obtain the following (*maximum*) *bid rent curves* of front-units and back-units, respectively:

$$\Phi_f^*(x) = \frac{A^*(x) - W^*(x)L_f - (P^* - \tau|x|) - \pi_f^*}{S_f} \quad \text{for } x \in X, \tag{5.24}$$

$$\Phi_b^*(x) = \frac{P^* - \tau|x| - W^*(x)L_b - \pi_b^*}{S_b} \quad \text{for } x \in X. \tag{5.25}$$

These curves are depicted in fig. 2(b).

Next, we define the spatial structure of the wage function, $W^*(x)$. In a manner similar to Ogawa and Fujita (1980), it can be readily verified that in order to sustain the commuting pattern given by (5.14), it must hold that

$$W^*(x) = W^* - t|x| \quad \text{for } |x| \leqq x_2, \tag{5.26}$$

and

$$\left|\frac{\mathrm{d}W^*(x)}{\mathrm{d}x}\right| \leqq t \quad \text{for all } x \in X. \tag{5.27}$$

Condition (5.27) implies that

$$\Psi^*(x) \equiv \max_{x_w \in X} \Psi^*(x \mid x_w) = \Psi^*(x \mid x) \quad \text{for all } x \in X. \tag{5.28}$$

Therefore, by (5.15) and (5.26),

$$\Psi^*(x) = \frac{W^* - t|x| - \bar{Z}}{S_h} \quad \text{for } |x| \leqq x_2, \tag{5.29}$$

which gives the houshold bid rent curve in the commuting area, $|x| < x_2$ [refer to fig. 2(b)]. Next, as depicted in fig. 2(b), in the *non-commuting area* where $x_2 \leqq |x| \leqq x_3$, households and back-units should have the same bid rent:

$$\Psi^*(x) = \Phi_b^*(x) \quad \text{for } x_2 \leqq |x| \leqq x_3. \tag{5.30}$$

Hence, using (5.28), we have that $\Psi^*(x \mid x) = \Phi_b^*(x)$ for $x_2 < |x| < x_3$, or

$$\frac{W^*(x) - \bar{Z}}{S_h} = \frac{P^* - \tau|x| - W^*(x)L_b - \pi_b^*}{S_b} \quad \text{for } x_2 \leqq |x| \leqq x_3,$$

which yields that

$$W^*(x) = \frac{(P^* - \pi_b^*)S_h + \bar{Z}S_b}{S_b + S_h L_b} - \frac{S_h}{S_b + S_h L_b}\tau|x| \quad \text{for } x_2 \leqq |x| \leqq x_3. \tag{5.31}$$

Setting $x=x_2$, by (5.25) and (5.30), we have

$$W^*=\frac{(P^*-\pi_b^*)S_h+\bar{Z}S_b}{S_b+S_hL_b}-\frac{(S_f+S_hL_f)MS_h}{2(S_b+S_hL_b)}\tau+\frac{(S_f+S_hL_f)M}{2}t. \tag{5.32}$$

Considering (5.27), without loss of generality we can set $W^*(x)=W^*(x_3)-t|x|$ for $|x|\geqq x_3$. In summary, we have

$$W^*(x)=\begin{cases} W^*-t|x| & \text{for } |x|\leqq x_2, \\ \dfrac{(P^*-\pi_b^*)S_h+\bar{Z}S_b}{S_b+S_hL_b}-\dfrac{S_h}{S_b+S_hL_b}\tau|x| & \text{for } x_2\leqq|x|\leqq x_3, \\ W^*(x_3)-t|x| & \text{for } |x|\geqq x_3, \end{cases} \tag{5.33}$$

where W^* is given by (5.32).

The value of $(P^*-\pi_b^*)$ in (5.32) and (5.33) can be determined as follows. By the boundary rent condition, $\Psi^*(x_3\,|\,x_3)=R_A$, we have that $W^*(x_3)=\bar{Z}+R_AS_h$. Hence, by (5.33), we have

$$P^*-\pi_b^*=R_AS_b+(\bar{Z}+R_AS_h)L_b+\frac{S+S_hL}{2}\tau M. \tag{5.34}$$

Finally, since the two bid rent curves, $\Phi_f^*(x)$ and $\Psi^*(x)$, must meet at $x=x_1$ [refer to fig. 2(b)], by setting $\Phi_f^*(x_1)=\Psi^*(x_1)$, we can obtain

$$P^*+\pi_f^*=\beta M-\frac{\alpha S_f}{2}M^2-W^*L_f-S_fR_A, \tag{5.35}$$

and hence[23]

$$\begin{aligned}\pi^* &= \pi_f^*+\pi_b^* \\ &= \beta M-\frac{\alpha S_f}{2}M^2-\left(W^*L_f+\frac{(P^*-\pi_b^*)S_h+\bar{Z}S_b}{S_b+S_hL_b}L_b\right) \\ &\quad -SR_A-\frac{S_b(S+S_hL)M}{2(S_b+S_hL_b)}\tau. \end{aligned} \tag{5.36}$$

Now, recalling condition (5.27) and referring to fig. 2(b), we can readily see

[23]Notice that since the equilibrium rent curve $R^*(x)$ is defined by (4.17), the only unknowns left are π_f^*, π_b^*, and P^*. It turns out that three unknowns cannot be determined uniquely. The indeterminacy of the three unknowns can be seen by (5.24) and (5.25). In the front-unit bid rent function (5.24), what matters is not the individual values of P^* and π_f^*, but the *sum*, $P^*+\pi_f^*$. Similarly, in (5.25), only the difference, $P^*-\pi_b^*$, matters.

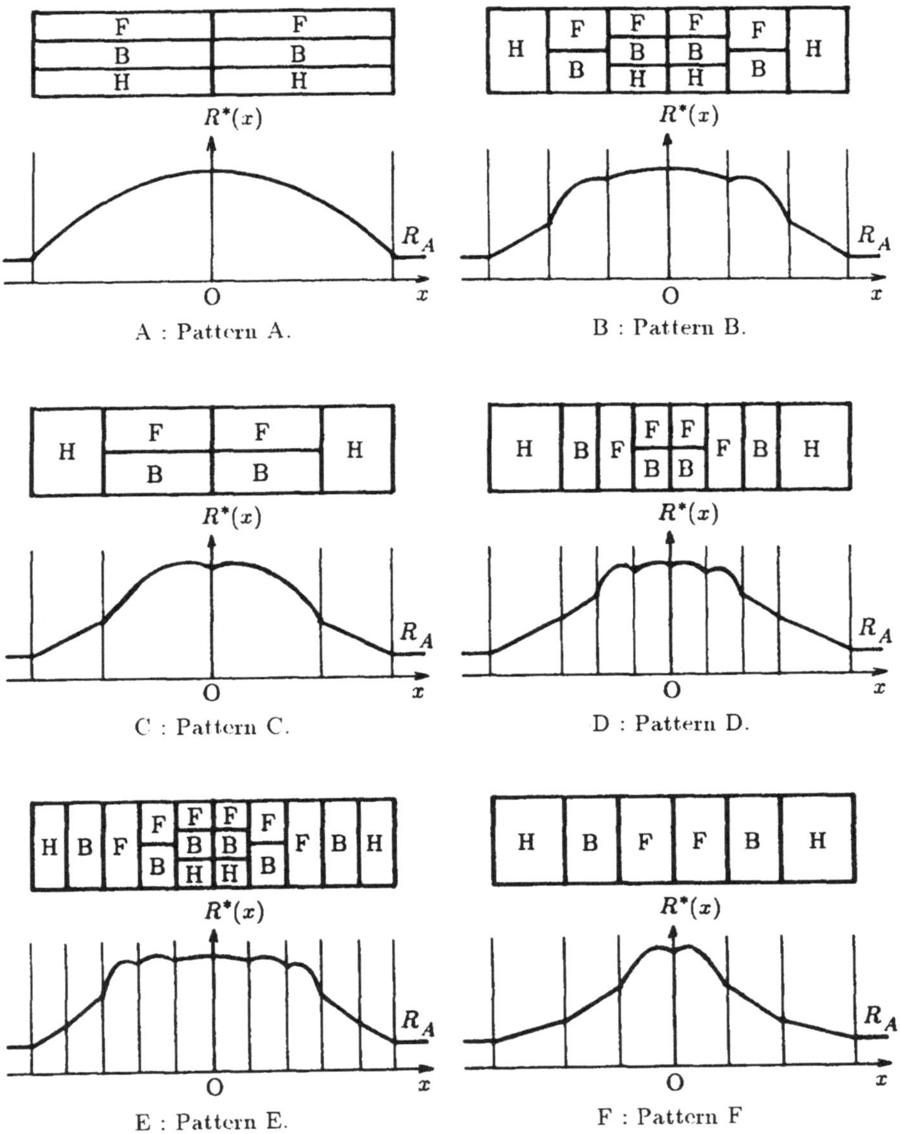

A : Pattern A.

B : Pattern B.

C : Pattern C.

D : Pattern D.

E : Pattern E.

F : Pattern F

Fig. 3. Equilibrium configurations.

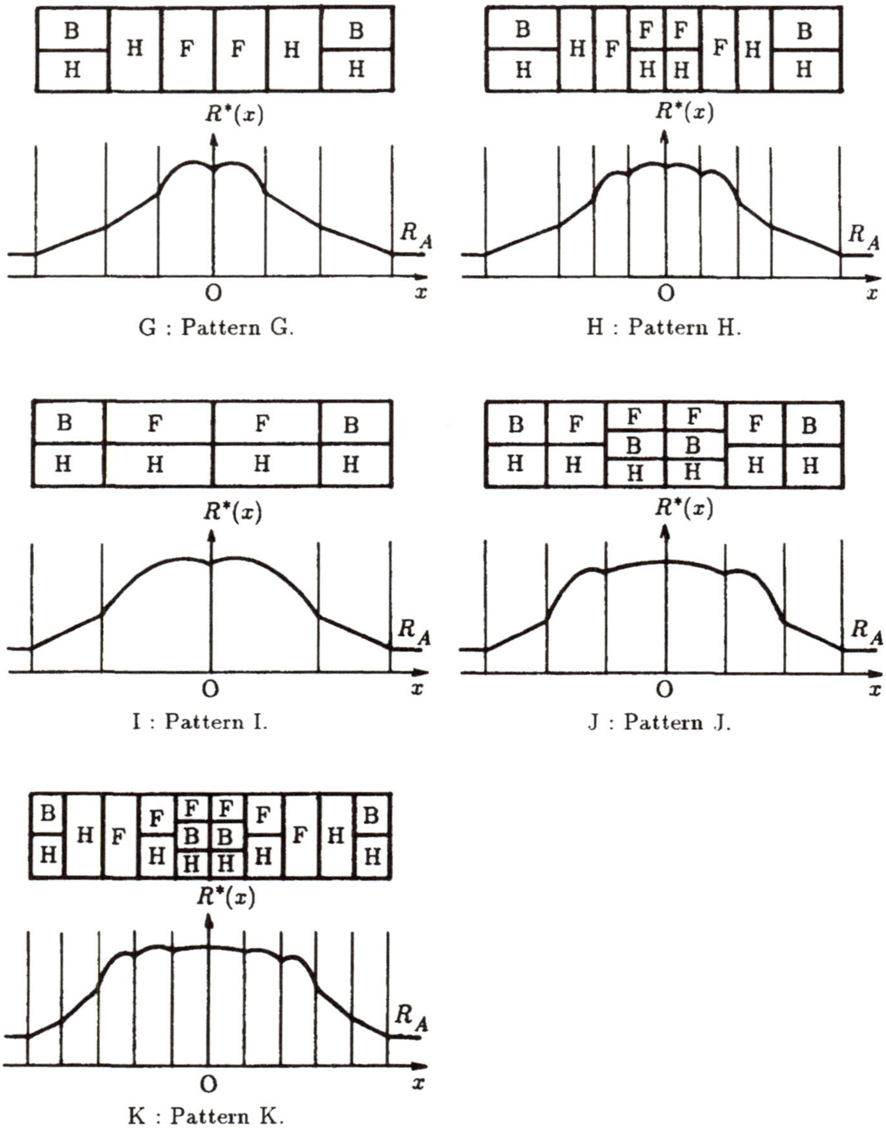

Fig. 3. Equilibrium configurations.

that for pattern G to represent a Nash equilibrium configuration, it is necessary and sufficient that the following three conditions be satisfied:

(a) $|\mathrm{d}W^*(x)/\mathrm{d}x| \leqq t$ for all $x \in X$,
(b) $\Phi_f^*(0) \geqq \Psi^*(0)$,
(c) $\Psi^*(x_1) \geqq \Phi_b^*(x_1)$.

By (5.32), condition (a) means that $S_h\tau/(S_b+S_hL_b) \leqq t$, or

$$\tau \leqq \frac{S_b+S_hL_b}{S_h}t. \tag{5.37}$$

Condition (b) leads to

$$\tau \leqq \frac{\alpha M}{2} - \frac{S_f+S_hL_f}{S_h}t. \tag{5.38}$$

It is not difficult to see that condition (c) is satisfied if and only if (5.37) holds.

Finally, utilizing fig. 2(b), we can readily verify that condition (4.46) is satisfied for pattern G above. Therefore, we can conclude that pattern G represents a global equilibrium land use configuration if and only if parameter condition (5.37) and (5.38) are satisfied. This parameter region for pattern G is denoted by area G in fig. 4 below.[24]

5.2. Comparison of equilibrium configurations

Fig. 3A–K depicts all possible equilibrium configurations. The upper part

[24]We would like to note that if we assume that all back-units supply a *homogeneous service*, called the *back-unit service*, to front-units, then the equilibrium configurations of pattern G can be supported by a competitive price system. To see this, suppose that [instead of shadow profit functions (3.3) and (3.4)] the (real) profit function of each front-unit is given by

$$\tilde{\Pi}_f(x) = A(x) - R(x)S_f - W(x)S_f - P(x), \tag{*}$$

and that of each back-unit by

$$\tilde{\Pi}_b(y,x) = P(x) - R(y)S_b - W(y)L_b - \Gamma(x,y). \tag{**}$$

In contrast to (3.3), we assume by the profit function (*) that each front-unit purchases the back-unit service at its location, x, at a given market price, $P(x)$. By (**), we assume that each back-unit (locating at y) is free to choose a location, x, for the sale of its back-unit service. It is not difficult to see that if we use $P^*(x)$ given by (5.23) as the market price of back-unit service at each location, then the land use configuration of pattern G can be attained as a competitive equilibrium [provided the parameter conditions (5.37) and (5.38) are satisfied]. More generally, it can be verified that any global equilibrium configuration can be obtained as a competitive equilibrium in this form. It must be emphasized, however, that in this paper we have been actually assuming that the contents of the services produced by each back-unit are unique to each firm. Therefore, competitive equilibria above are meaningful only mathematically, i.e. they are useful only as a mathematical device for obtaining global equilibrium solutions. In a subsequent paper, we plan to investigate systematically the mathematical relationship among global equilibria, Nash equilibria, and competitive equilibria.

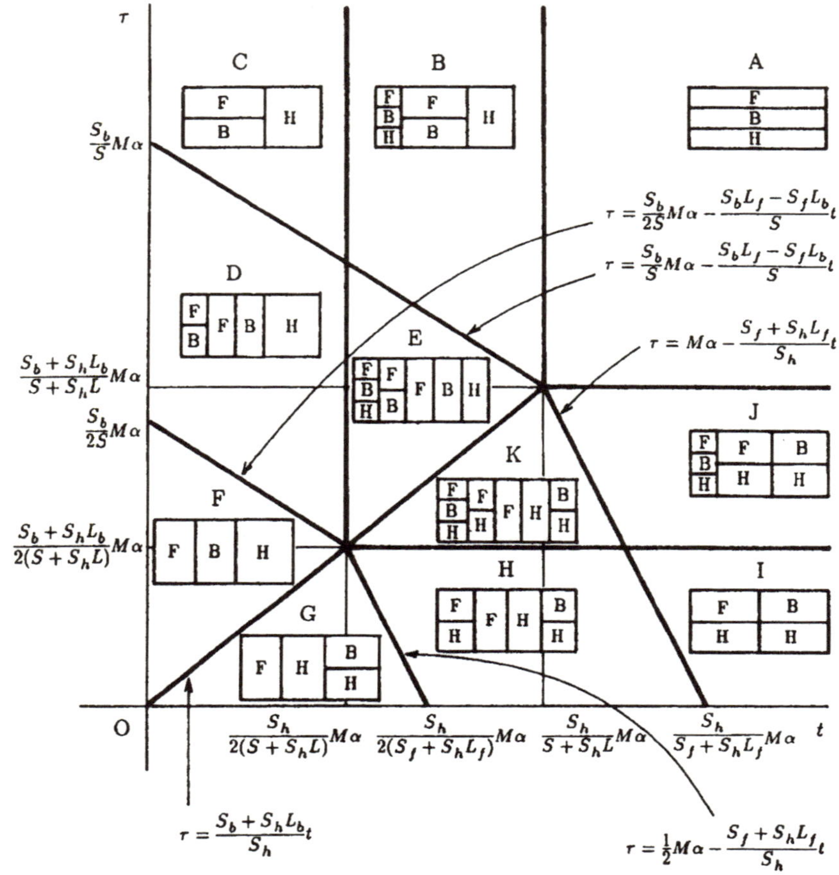

Fig. 4. Parameter regions for equilibrium configurations.

of each figure depicts a land use configuration, and the lower part shows the associated land rent configuration. The parameter region of each equilibrium configuration is denoted in fig. 4, where the horizontal axis, t, represents the commuting cost rate (per unit distance per worker), while the vertical axis, τ, represents the intrafirm communication cost rate (per unit distance per unit of time). (In fig. 4, each land use pattern describes the right half of the city.) We have these eleven different equilibrium configurations as the results of a combination of two basic effects: (i) as the commuting cost rate t becomes smaller, segregation of business and residential zones occurs, and (ii) as the intrafirm communication cost rate τ gets smaller, segregation of back-units from front-units occurs.

Pattern A represents a completely mixed configuration, in which all three types of agents (i.e. front-units, back-units, and households) are located in the same proportion everywhere in the city, that is, each front-unit is located together with its back-unit and its workers. As can be seen from fig. 4, this land use pattern occurs when both t and τ are very high. That is, when the commuting cost rate t is very high, households choose to reside at their job sites to save commuting costs; while when the communication cost rate τ is very high, front-units and back-units locate together to save their communication costs. Hence, if both t and τ are very high, all three types of activities locate together in a completely mixed manner. We can also see from fig. 4 that when the value of αM is very small (i.e. either the intrafirm communication cost rate α or the firm-number M is very small), then most of the $t-\tau$ space will be covered by the parameter region of pattern A. This is consistent with out casual observations of the real world in which most small cities take the form of mixed land use patterns. [Note that since M and N are proportional to each other in our model, small M implies a small N (population).]

In patterns B–F, the city is surrounded by pure residential areas on both sides of the furthest suburbs. Front-units and back-units always are located close together. As we can see from fig. 4, these five patterns occur when $\tau > ((S_b + S_h L_b)/S_h)t$, that is, when the intrafirm commuting cost rate, τ, is relatively high compared with the commuting cost rate, t. For example, pattern C occurs when t is very low in comparison with τ. That is, if τ is very high, front-units and back-units locate together to save communication costs; while if t is very low, households choose to locate in the suburbs to avoid high land rents at the center. Hence, we have the monocentric land use pattern C, which has been the dominant paradigm in the traditional urban economics. For another example, we have the land use pattern B when τ is very high while t is intermediate. That is, since τ is very high, front-units and back-units locate together; and when t is intermediate, households working at the city center reside there in order to avoid high commuting cost, while households working in the fringe firm-area commute from the surrounding suburbs.

In patterns G–K, both sides of the further suburbs consist of a back-unit area in which back-units are located together with their workers. As can be seen from fig. 4, these five patterns occur when $\tau < ((S_b + S_h L_b)/S_h)t$, i.e. when the intrafirm communication cost rate, τ, is relatively low compared with the commuting cost rate, t. For example, pattern H occurs when τ is very low while t is intermediate. Since τ is very low, back-units can locate in the far suburbs without losing the efficiency of intrafirm communications. Furthermore, since t is relatively high, households locate close to their job locations in three separate areas, i.e. at the city center (together with front-offices), in the middle suburbs (from which they commute to the front-offices inside), and in the far suburbs (together with back-offices). This land use pattern resembles that of the New York Metropolitan Area today.

We can also observe the following results from fig. 4:

(i) As we move towards the upper-right direction in fig. 4, i.e. as both the commuting cost rate t and intrafirm communication cost rate τ increase simultaneously, not surprisingly, more mixing of the three activities occurs.

(ii) Given any value of $M\alpha$ (= the firm population size multiplied by the interfirm communication cost rate), the (t, τ) parameter space is always divided into the same number (eleven) of regions (i.e. equilibrium configurations).

(iii) Furthermore, the parameter region of each equilibrium configuration expands towards the upper-right direction proportionally to $M\alpha$.

(iv) In turn, this implies that given any fixed combination of (t, τ), as $M\alpha$ continues to increase (e.g. the firm-population size M increases), the equilibrium configuration of the city becomes eventually either pattern F or G.

(v) Given any fixed combination of t and $M\alpha$, as τ keeps decreasing (i.e. as the intrafirm communication technology continues to improve), the equilibrium configuration of the city becomes eventually either pattern G, H, or I. In either one of these three patterns, the far suburbs are occupied by back-units and their workers. Therefore, *the advancement of intrafirm communication technologies provides a major cause of job suburbanization.*

6. Conclusion

In this paper we have developed a general equilibrium model of the city, in which each firm consists of a front-unit and back-unit. We have shown that, depending on the parameters, eleven different equilibrium configurations of a city emerge. In particular, it has been demonstrated that the advancement of intrafirm communication technology will eventually lead to a dichotomy of firm activities, where the front-unit activity (specialized in extrafirm communications) will concentrate in the city center, while the back-unit activity will be located in the far suburbs.

The model presented in this paper is relatively simple, and it is desirable to extend the model in the following directions. First, although we have assumed that there exists no fixed cost of intrafirm communications, this assumption is not very realistic, that is, intrafirm communications between a front-unit and back-unit may be hampered significantly even if the two units are located a block away. Hence, it is important to introduce the fixed cost of intrafirm communications. With such a fixed cost, some of the previous eleven configurations will not represent equilibrium solutions any more. Second, note that in any one of the eleven equilibrium configurations, all front-units are located contiguously (i.e. in each fig. 3A–K, the F-area is always connected). That is, in the context of the present paper, no subcenter emerges in the city. This result is due to the assumption of a linear accessibility measure [represented by (4.44)]. With the introduction of a non-linear accessibility measure, the formation of subcenters may become possible. For an extension in this direction, the work by Fujita and Ogawa (1982) will be useful. Third, although we neglected the direct interactions of back-units with other firms and households, a more general model should explicitly consider such interactions. Fourth, we need to replace fixed-coefficient functions with more general utility and production functions. Fifth, in this paper we have considered one type of labor and one type of firm only. With the introduction of multiple types of labor and firm, our model will become more useful for the explanation of actual spatial configurations of metropolitan areas. Finally, it would be interesting to extend the framework of the present model into a model of a system of cities in which firms can freely choose the locations of their front-units and back-units.

Appendix A: Proof of Lemma 4.1

Take any $x \in f^*_+ \cap b^*_+$. Then, since $x \in f^*_+$, if we define $y' \equiv y^*_b(x)$, then by (4.29) we have that

$$\Pi^*(x, y') = \pi^*. \tag{A.1}$$

Likewise, since $x \in b^*_+$, if we define $x' \equiv x^*_f(x)$, then $x' \in f^*_+$ and $y^*_b(x) = y^*_b(x^*_f(x)) = x$. Thus, by (4.29) we have that

$$\Pi^*(x', x) = \pi^*. \tag{A.2}$$

Now, recalling the definition of the function $\Pi^*(x, y)$ by (4.10), using (A.1) and (A.2) we can calculate as follows

$$\begin{aligned} 2\pi^* - \{\Pi^*(x, x) + \Pi^*(x', y')\} &= \{\Pi^*(x', x) + \Pi^*(x, y')\} \\ &\quad - \{\Pi^*(x, x) + \Pi^*(x', y')\} \\ &= \Gamma(x', y') - \Gamma(x', x) - \Gamma(x, y'). \end{aligned} \tag{A.3}$$

Since Γ is assumed to have the property of long-distance economies, by (4.35) and (A.3) we have that

$$2\pi^* - \{\Pi^*(x, x) + \Pi^*(x', y')\} \leqq 0. \tag{A.4}$$

While by (4.29), $\pi^* = \max\{\Pi^*(z, y) \mid z \in X,\ y \in X\}$ and hence

$$\pi^* \geqq \Pi^*(x, x), \qquad \pi^* \geqq \Pi(x', y'), \tag{A.5}$$

By (A.4) and (A.5) we have

$$\pi^* = \Pi^*(x,x), \qquad \pi^* = \Pi^*(x',y'), \tag{A.6}$$

and hence we can conclude as (4.36).

Appendix B: Proof of Lemma 4.2

(i) Take any $x \in f^*_+ \cap b^*_+$. Then, since $x \in f^*_+$, we have $y^*_b(x) \in b^*_+$. Thus, if we define $y' \equiv y^*_b(x)$, then $y' \in b^*_+$ and $x^*_f(y') = x^*_f(y^*_b(x)) = x$. Hence, setting $y = y'$ in (4.34), we have

$$\pi^*_b(x) = \Pi^*_b(y' \mid x) = \max_{z \in X} \Pi^*_b(z \mid x). \tag{B.1}$$

Likewise, since $x \in b^*_+$, we have $x^*_f(x) \in f^*_+$. Thus, if we define $x' \equiv x^*_f(x)$, then $x' \in f^*_+$ and $y^*_b(x') = y^*_b(x^*_f(x)) = x$. Hence, setting $x = x'$ in (4.33), we have

$$\pi^*_f(x) = \Pi^*_f(x' \mid x) = \max_{z \in X} \Pi^*_f(z \mid x). \tag{B.2}$$

Therefore, since $\pi^* = \Pi^*(x,x)$ [by (4.36)] $= \Pi^*_f(x \mid x) + \Pi^*_b(x \mid x)$ [by definition of functions Π^*, Π^*_f, and Π^*_b, and because $\Gamma(x,x) = 0$] $\leqq \max\{\Pi^*_f(z \mid x) : z \in X\} + \max\{\Pi^*_b(z \mid x) : z \in X\} = \pi^*_f(x) + \pi^*_b(x)$ [by (B.1) and (B.2)], we can conclude that

$$\pi^* \leqq \pi^*_f(x) + \pi^*_b(x). \tag{B.3}$$

Next, by (B.1) and (B.2) we have that

$$\pi^*_f(x) + \pi^*_b(x) = \Pi^*_f(x' \mid x) + \Pi^*_b(y' \mid x). \tag{B.4}$$

Furthermore, by the definition of functions Π^*, Π^*_f, and Π^*_b, we can obtain the following identity:

$$\Pi^*_f(x' \mid x) + \Pi^*_b(y' \mid x) \equiv \Pi(x',y') + \Gamma(x',y') - \{\Gamma(x',x) + \Gamma(x,y')\}. \tag{B.5}$$

Since Γ is assumed to have the property of long-distance economies, by (4.35) we have that $\Gamma(x',y') - \{\Gamma(x',x) + \Gamma(x,y')\} \geqq 0$. Hence, by (B.4) and (B.5), we have

$$\pi^*_f(x) + \pi^*_b(x) \leqq \Pi(x',y'). \tag{B.6}$$

Furthermore, by definition

$$\Pi(x',y') \leqq \max_{z \in X,\, y \in X} \Pi(z,y) = \pi^*. \tag{B.7}$$

Using (B.3), (B.6), and (B.7), we have that $\pi^* \leqq \pi^*_f(x) + \pi^*_b(x) \leqq \pi^*$, and hence $\pi^* = \pi^*_f(x) + \pi^*_b(x)$, which means (4.39).

(ii) For a proof of Lemma 4.2(ii), see the text.

(iii) By the definition of functions Π, Π^*_f, and Π^*_b, the following identity holds for all x, $y \in X$:

$$\Pi^*(x, y) \equiv \Pi_f^*(x \mid y) + \Pi_b^*(y \mid x) - P^*(x) + P^*(y) + \Gamma(x, y). \tag{B.8}$$

Take any $x \in f_+^*$. Then, we have

$$\begin{aligned}
\pi^* &= \Pi(x, y_b^*(x)) && \text{[by (4.29)]} \\
&= \Pi_f^*(x \mid y_b^*(x)) + \Pi_b^*(y_b^*(x) \mid x) - P^*(x) + P^*(y_b^*(x)) + \Gamma(x, y_b^*(x)) \\
& && \text{[by (B.8)]} \\
&= \pi_f^*(y_b^*(x)) + \pi_b^*(x) - P^*(x) + P^*(y_b^*(x)) + \Gamma(x, y_b^*(x)) \\
& && \text{[by (4.33) and (4.34)]} \\
&= \tilde{\pi}_f + \tilde{\pi}_b - \tilde{P}(x) + \tilde{P}(y_b^*(x)) + \Gamma(x, y_b^*(x)) && \text{[by (4.38a) and (4.38b)].}
\end{aligned}$$

Thus, by (4.37) we can conclude as (4.41).

Appendix C. Proof of Theorem 4.1

Suppose (4.46) represents a Nash equilibrium configuration which satisfies conditions (4.45) and (4.46) [in addition to (4.17)–(4.28)]. Condition (4.46) implies that

$$\Phi_f^*(x \mid y) \leqq R^*(x) \quad \text{for all } x, y \in X, \tag{C.1}$$

$$\Phi_b^*(x \mid z) \leqq R^*(x) \quad \text{for all } x, z \in X. \tag{C.2}$$

In the context of system (4.44), using definitions (4.2), (4.3), (4.8), (4.9), (4.31), and (4.32) we can see that relations (C.1) and (C.2) imply

$$\Pi_f^*(x \mid y) \leqq \pi_f^* \quad \text{for all } x, y \in X, \tag{C.3}$$

$$\Pi_b^*(x \mid z) \leqq \pi_b^* \quad \text{for all } x, z \in X. \tag{C.4}$$

Furthermore, in the context of system (4.44), by (4.33) and (4.34) we have that

$$\Pi_f^*(x \mid y_b^*(x)) = \pi_f^* \quad \text{for } x \in f_+^*, \tag{C.5}$$

$$\Pi_b^*(y \mid x_f^*(y)) = \pi_b^* \quad \text{for } y \in b_+^*. \tag{C.6}$$

Next, recall from (B.8) that the following identity holds for all $x, y \in X$:

$$\Pi^*(x, y) = \Pi_f^*(x \mid y) + \Pi_b^*(y \mid x) - P^*(x) + P^*(y) + \Gamma(x, y). \tag{C.7}$$

Given any $x \in f_+^*$, if we set $y = y_b^*(x)$ in (C.7), then by (C.7), (C.5), and (C.6) we have

$$\Pi^*(x, y_b^*(x)) = \pi_f^* + \pi_b^* \quad \text{for } x \in f_+^*. \tag{C.8}$$

Since $\Gamma(x,x)=0$, by (4.31) we have

$$\Pi_f^*(x\,|\,x)=A^*(x)-R^*(x)S_f-W^*(x)L_f-P^*(x). \tag{C.9}$$

Using (4.10), (4.32), and (C.9), we can obtain the following identity:

$$\Pi^*(x,y)\equiv\Pi_f^*(x\,|\,x)+\Pi_b^*(y\,|\,x) \quad \text{for all } x,y\in X.$$

Hence,

$$\begin{aligned}\max_{x\in X,y\in X}\Pi^*(x,y)&=\max_{x\in X,y\in X}\{\Pi_f^*(x\,|\,x)+\Pi_b^*(y\,|\,x)\}\\ &\leqq\max_{x\in X}\Pi_f^*(x\,|\,x)+\max_{x\in X,y\in X}\Pi_b^*(y\,|\,x)\\ &\leqq\pi_f^*+\pi_b^* \quad \text{[by (C.3) and (C.4)].}\end{aligned} \tag{C.10}$$

Then, since $\Pi^*(x,y_b^*(x))\leqq\max\{\Pi^*(x,y):x\in X,\ y\in X\}$, we can conclude from (C.8) and (C.10) that

$$\Pi^*(x,y_b^*(x))=\pi_f^*+\pi_b^*=\max_{x\in X,y\in X}\Pi^*(x,y) \quad \text{for } x\in f_+^*. \tag{C.11}$$

Thus, by setting $\pi^*\equiv\pi_f^*+\pi_b^*$ in (C.11), we can see that relation (4.29) holds for the system (4.44). Therefore, (4.44) must be a global equilibrium.

References

Estabrooks, M.F. and R.H. Lamarche, eds., 1987, Telecommunications: A strategic perspective on regional, economic and business development (Canadian Institute for Research on Regional Development, Moncton).

Fujita, M. and H. Ogawa, 1982, Multiple equilibria and structural transition of non-monocentric urban configurations, Regional Science and Urban Economics 12, 161–196.

Fujita, M. and T. Smith, 1990, Additive-interaction models of spatial agglomeration, Journal of Regional Science 30, 51–74.

Gabszewicz, J.J. and J.F. Thisse, 1986, Spatial competition and the location of firms, in J.J. Gabszewicz, J.F. Thisse, M. Fujita and U. Schweizer, eds., Location theory (Harwood, Chur, Switzerland).

Giaoutzi, M. and P. Nijkamp, eds., 1988, Information and regional development (Gower, Brookfield, VM).

Hansen, P., M. Labbe, D. Peeters, J.F. Thisse and J.V. Henderson, 1987, Systems of cities and facility location (Harwood, New York).

Ogawa, H. and M. Fujita, 1980, Equilibrium land use in a non-monocentric city, Journal of Regional Science 20, 455–475.

Ota, M., 1991, Communication technologies and urban spatial organization: A general equilibrium analysis, unpublished Ph.D. dissertation, Department of Regional Science, University of Pennsylvania, Philadelphia.

[3]

ELSEVIER European Economic Review 43 (1999) 91–107

EUROPEAN ECONOMIC REVIEW

Why is central Paris rich and downtown Detroit poor? An amenity-based theory

Jan K. Brueckner[a,*], Jacques-François Thisse[b,c], Yves Zenou[b,d]

[a] *Department of Economics, University of Illinois at Urbana-Champaign, Box 111, 1206 South Sixth Street, Champaign, IL 61820, USA*
[b] *CORE, Université Catholique de Louvain, Louvain-la-Neuve, Belgium*
[c] *CERAS, Ecole Nationale des Ponts et Chausées, Paris, France*
[d] *ERMES, Université Panthéon-Assas, Paris, France*

Received 1 April 1996; accepted 1 December 1997

Abstract

This paper presents an amenity-based theory of location by income. The theory shows that the relative location of different income groups depends on the spatial pattern of amenities in a city. When the center has a strong amenity advantage over the suburbs, the rich are likely to live at central locations. When the center's amenity advantage is weak or negative, the rich are likely to live in the suburbs. The virtue of the theory is that it ties location by income to a city's idiosyncratic characteristics. It thus predicts a multiplicity of location patterns across cities, consistent with real-world observation. © 1998 Elsevier Science B.V. All rights reserved.

JEL classification: R0; R1; R2; Z1

Keywords: Location; Income; Central-city

* Corresponding author. Fax: 217 244 6628.

0014-2921/98/$ – see front matter
PII: S0014-2921(98)00019-1

1. Introduction

Although some American central cities have rich enclaves, high-income residents in U.S. urban areas tend to live in the suburbs. This pattern is often reversed, however, outside the U.S. A prime example is the Paris metropolitan area, where the central city has higher average income than the surrounding suburbs. The contrast between the Parisian case and the case of Detroit, a major U.S. metropolitan area, is shown in Table 1. While the Table shows that Detroit's pattern of lower central-city income is repeated (although less dramatically) in other U.S. metropolitan areas, the average French provincial city does not resemble Paris, following the U.S. pattern instead. Notable exceptions, however, are Lyon (the second-largest city), Caen, and Nancy, where incomes are higher in the center.[1] The Parisian pattern is also repeated in other European cities outside France, as noted by Hohenberg and Lees (1986) in their monograph on European urban history. They state that 'incomes rose with distance to the city center in America, whereas they typically fell in Europe' (p. 299). Ingram and Carroll (1981) show that the Parisian pattern also exists in a number of Latin American cities. Location by income thus varies dramatically across countries, and these differences beg for a theoretical explanation.

One of the contributions of the monocentric-city model developed by Alonso (1964), Mills (1967) and Muth (1969) is to give insight into the effect of income on

Table 1
Central-city vs. suburban incomes in France and the US

Case	Household income[a]	
	Central-city	Suburbs
Ile de France (Paris metro area)	124 000 Fr.[b]	106 000 Fr.
Province (other metro areas)	76 000 Fr.	84 000 Fr.
France (all metro areas)	84 000 Fr.	82 000 Fr.
Detroit (metro area)	$20 207	$40 084
U.S. (all metro areas)	$26 727	$26 314

[a] Household incomes are the 1990 average value in France and the 1989 median value in the U.S. The French data are from Nicot (1996), and the U.S. data are from the 1990 Census.
[b] The current franc-dollar exchange rate is approximately 6 francs per dollar.

[1] See Nicot (1996). Tabard (1993) constructs an index measuring the extent to which highly skilled workers are represented in the work forces of French cities with populations over 50 000. All of the districts of central Paris (each treated as a separate city) are in the upper half of the distribution of this index when its values are ranked for cities in the Paris metropolitan area. This provides further indirect evidence of the concentration of high-income households in central Paris.

household location. Two opposing forces are identified by the model. First, the high housing consumption of the rich means that they are more strongly attracted than the poor by low housing prices in the suburbs. However, rich households also have a high opportunity cost of time and thus a high commuting cost per mile. Therefore, the rich value accessibility to the central business district (CBD) more than the poor. The theory shows that the net effect of these forces hinges on the behavior of the ratio of commuting cost per mile, t, and housing consumption, q. If t/q rises with income, then the accessibility effect dominates, and the rich tend to live at central locations. If t/q falls with income, then the effect of higher housing consumption dominates, and the rich tend to live in the suburbs.

Given this locational indeterminacy, the model is consistent with the variety of location patterns observed in real-world cities. For example, t/q might fall with income in the U.S. while rising with income in France, which would explain the location patterns in the two countries. However, it is unsatisfactory from a scientific point of view to explain real-world complexity by appeal to an ambiguous theory. Moreover, the required difference in the behavior of the t/q ratio across countries seems implausible.[2] Therefore, it is important to consider other explanations for the observed location patterns.[3]

The explanation proposed in the present paper links the location of different income groups to the spatial pattern of amenities in the city. To draw this link, the analysis adopts a key assumption, namely that the marginal valuation of amenities *rises sharply with income.* In addition, it is assumed that the conventional forces discussed above favor suburban location of the rich. Two cases are then considered: amenities fall rapidly with distance to the CBD; amenities fall slowly or even increase with distance to the CBD. In the first case, the amenity advantage of the center along with the high amenity demand of the rich generates a force that pulls the rich toward the center more strongly than the poor. If this force is powerful enough, it can dominate the conventional forces

[2] Wheaton (1977) found that t/q appears to be roughly constant across different income groups in the U.S. This suggests that observed location patterns cannot be explained by appealing to a difference in this ratio across income groups.

[3] LeRoy and Sonstelie (1983) introduce an important modification of the standard model by adding transportation mode choice. They assume that when rich and poor use the same transportation mode, t/q rises with income, so that the rich live in the center. However, if the rich switch to a faster commuting mode (i.e., auto) while the poor continue to use the slow mode (i.e., public transit), t falls for the rich but not for the poor. As a result, the mode switch can make t/q smaller for the rich, leading to a location reversal. While Gin and Sonstelie (1992) present historical evidence from Philadephia that supports this theory (the mode switch in this case was from walking to the streetcar), it is not clear that the theory is capable of explaining the worldwide variation in location patterns. Alternatively, Kern (1981) points to changes in taste as an explanation for reversals in the pattern of location by income.

that pull the rich outward, leading them to locate in the center. However, if the center's amenity advantage is weak or negative, then the amenity force will be insufficient to overcome the conventional forces, and the suburban location of the rich will be maintained.

The urban amenities that underlie this theory can be classified into three categories. *Natural amenities* are generated by an area's topographical features, including rivers, hills, coastline, etc. *Historical amenities* are generated by monuments, buildings, parks, and other urban infrastructure from past eras that are aesthetically pleasing to current residents of the city. While natural and historical amenities are largely exogenous, *modern amenities* are endogenous, with their levels depending on the current economic conditions in a neighborhood, especially the local income level. Such amenities might include restaurants, theaters, and modern public facilities such as swimming pools and tennis courts. Modern amenities may also be linked to historical amenities. This connection arises through the *renovation* of a central city's historical districts, which enhances historical amenities and may be responsive to the current level of income.

The theory sketched above focuses on natural and historical amenities. Since these amenities are *exogenous*, they can be viewed as a causal factor in determining the pattern of location by income. The first case discussed above, where exogenous amenities decline rapidly with distance to the center, might correspond to Paris. Its historical monuments, parks, boulevards, fine architecture, and river scenery give central Paris a large amenity advantage over the suburbs. If the amenity demand of the rich is strong enough, such an advantage might be sufficient to draw rich households to central locations, reversing the U.S. pattern. By contrast, since an American urban area like Detroit lacks the rich history of Paris, the central-city's infrastructure does not offer appreciable aesthetic benefits. This means that no amenity force is working to reverse the conventional forces that draw the rich to the suburbs. As a result, central Detroit is poor. The analysis developing this insight is presented in Section 2 of the paper.

While this theory claims that location by income depends on the city's amenity pattern, it ignores reverse causation. In other words, it overlooks the possibility that urban amenities are a *consequence* rather than a *cause* of the location patterns of different income groups. Amenities with this feature fall into the modern category discussed above, and in the case of Paris, they would include the concentration of excellent restaurants in the central city. While these restaurants constitute a major amenity, their presence is due in part to the high incomes of the local residents, and is not a causal factor explaining those incomes.

Section 3 shows that the major lessons of the exogenous-amenities model of Section 2 are mostly unaffected when endogenous, modern amenities are added to the analysis. This modification is carried out by assuming that neighborhood income also counts as an amenity, capturing the variety of ways in which income influences the quality of life in an area. It is shown that when the rich value the income amenity more highly than the poor, multiple equilibria may exist, with the rich living either in the center or the suburbs. In effect, the high income (and thus strong endogenous amenities) of their own neighborhood makes the rich reluctant to leave it wherever it might be located. However, the analysis shows that if the center has a strong exogenous-amenity advantage, then the *only* equilibrium has the rich living in the center. Therefore, to generate a location pattern with the rich in the suburbs, the center's exogenous-amenity advantage cannot be too great, as in previous model.

Regardless of whether or not endogenous amenities are present, the theory thus predicts that the pattern of exogenous amenities in a city has an important effect on location by income. But since the pattern of such amenities is highly idiosyncratic, varying across cities depending on their history and topography, the model predicts a variety of location patterns by income across cities. Given the variety of location patterns actually observed around the world, which seem to defy prediction by the standard model, this is a welcome implication.

The last step in the discussion is to consider why the pattern of exogenous amenities differs across cities. A central city's natural amenities are partly governed by transportation needs, which often dictate proximity to a body of water. On the other hand, historical amenities are determined mainly by past government decisions regarding investment in urban infrastructure. Section 4 presents a discussion of these factors, attempting to explain why exogenous amenities are more favorable in European than American central cities. Section 5 offers conclusions.

2. A model with exogenous amenities

To develop a formal model, let x denote distance to the CBD, and let the exogenous amenity level at distance x be given by $a(x)$. Consumer utility depends on amenities as well as on housing consumption, q, and consumption of a numeraire nonhousing good, denoted e, with the utility function given by $u(e, q, a)$. Assuming initially that the city has a single-income group, let income equal y and commuting cost per mile be given by t, so that disposable income at distance x is $y - tx$. The budget constraint is then $e + pq = y - tx$, where p is the price per unit of housing, and elimination of e allows utility to be written as $u(y - tx - pq, q, a)$.

The consumer maximizes this expression by choice of q taking p as parametric, which yields the first-order condition $u^q = pu^e$ (supercripts denote partial derivatives). But p must vary with x to ensure that utility is the same in all locations. Letting $\bar{u}$ denote the uniform utility level,[4] this requirement means

[4] The ensuing analysis applies regardless of whether the city is open or closed (i.e., whether $\bar{u}$ is exogenous or endogenous).

that $\max_{\{q\}} u(y - tx - pq, q, a) = \bar{u}$. Together, this equation and above first-order condition determine q and p as functions of location. These functions are $q(x)$ and $p(x)$, with the latter giving the 'bid-price' function for housing. To find the slope of the bid-price function, the uniform-utility condition is differentiated with respect to x, which yields

$$-[t + p'(x)q(x) + p(x)q'(x)]u^e + q'(x)u^q + a'(x)u^a = 0. \tag{1}$$

Since the $q'(x)$ terms in Eq. (1) cancel given $u^q = pu^e$, rearrangement gives the desired slope:

$$p'(x) = -\frac{t}{q(x)} + \frac{u^a}{q(x)u^e}a'(x) = -\frac{t}{q(x)} + \frac{v^a[y - tx, p(x), a(x)]}{q(x)}a'(x). \tag{2}$$

In the second part of Eq. (2), the marginal rate of substitution u^a/u^e is rewritten as the amenity derivative of the indirect utility function $v[y - tx, p(x), a(x)]$. Note that v^a gives the marginal valuation of amenities *after optimal adjustment of housing consumption.*

The standard urban model ignores amenities by assuming $v^a \equiv 0$. Eq. (2) shows that in this case, the housing price falls with distance to the CBD, compensating suburban consumers for their high commuting costs. This conclusion is reinforced if $a' < 0$, indicating that amenities decline with distance, because suburban housing prices must then compensate for inferior amenities as well as the high cost of commuting. However, if $a' > 0$, then the net advantage of the suburbs is ambiguous, and this is reflected in an ambiguous spatial behavior for p (i.e., Eq. (2) can take either sign). To simplify the discussion, the commuting-cost effect is assumed to dominate in this case, making p' negative at all locations regardless of the pattern of amenities.

Now, let the model be enlarged to include two income groups, poor and rich. Their incomes are y_0 and y_1, respectively, with $y_0 < y_1$, and their commuting cost parameters are t_0 and t_1. Since the value of time is higher for the rich, it follows that $t_1 > t_0$. The above analysis then generates two bid-price functions, one for each group, and these are denoted $p_0(x)$ and $p_1(x)$.

To develop the theory of location by income, observe that a given group will occupy the area of the city where it outbids the other group for housing. The boundary between the areas, denoted $\hat{x}$, is then the point where the groups' bid prices are equal, satisfying $p_0(\hat{x}) = p_1(\hat{x})$. Next, observe that the relative slopes of the bid-price curves at $\hat{x}$ determine where a given group's bid is maximal. If $p'_1(\hat{x}) > p'_0(\hat{x})$, so that the poor curve is steeper (more negatively sloped) at $\hat{x}$, then the poor outbid the rich for central housing while the rich outbid the poor for suburban housing. If $p'_1(\hat{x}) < p'_0(\hat{x})$, so that the rich curve is steeper, then the reverse pattern obtains.

Using Eq. (2), the difference between the bid-price slopes at $\hat{x}$ for the two groups can be written as

$$\Delta \equiv p_1'(\hat{x}) - p_0'(\hat{x}) = \frac{t_0}{q_0(\hat{x})} - \frac{t_1}{q_1(\hat{x})}$$

$$+ a'(\hat{x})\left(\frac{v^a[y_1 - t_1\hat{x}, p_1(\hat{x}), a(\hat{x})]}{q_1(\hat{x})} - \frac{v^a[y_0 - t_0\hat{x}, p_0(\hat{x}), a(\hat{x})]}{q_0(\hat{x})}\right), \quad (3)$$

where $q_0(x)$ and $q_1(x)$ give housing consumption for the two groups. Referring to Eq. (3), the rich locate in the suburbs (center) when $\Delta > (<)0$.

Using these principles, consider the standard analysis of location by income, which assumes $v^a \equiv 0$. Under this assumption, Eq. (3) yields $\Delta = t_0/q_0(\hat{x}) - t_1/q_1(\hat{x})$. To sign this expression, note that since the price of housing is the same for both groups at $\hat{x}$, the difference between $q_0(\hat{x})$ and $q_1(\hat{x})$ is solely a function of the difference in incomes. Since $y_1 - t_1\hat{x} > y_0 - t_0\hat{x}$ holds despite $t_1 > t_0$, it follows that $q_1(\hat{x}) > q_0(\hat{x})$. As noted in the introduction, this makes comparison of the t/q ratio across groups ambiguous. If t rises *less rapidly* than q as income increases, then $t_0/q_0(\hat{x}) > t_1/q_1(\hat{x})$ holds and $\Delta > 0$, implying that the rich live in the suburbs. If t rises *faster* than q as income increases, $t_0/q_0(\hat{x}) < t_1/q_1(\hat{x})$ holds and $\Delta < 0$, implying that the rich live in the center.

To formalize the main argument of the paper, let the amenity effect be reintroduced. To evaluate the sign of Δ, which now depends on the amenity term in Eq. (3), two assumptions are made. First, conventional locational effects, as embodied in the t/q ratio, are assumed to favor suburban location of the rich. The difference in the t/q ratios in Eq. (3) is then positive. Second, v^a is assumed to rise with income, and its rise is assumed to be more rapid than the increase of housing consumption. Thus, the marginal valuation of amenities (after adjustment of q) rises faster than housing consumption itself. This assumption means that the difference between the v^a/q ratios in Eq. (3) is positive (note that this conclusion uses the fact that the v^a terms have equal price arguments). To show that the assumed behavior of v^a/q is not unreasonable, the appendix presents an example showing that this ratio, indeed, rises with income under CES preferences, provided that a mild parameter restriction holds.

Under these assumptions, consider the effect of the amenity pattern on the sign of Eq. (4). If $a'(\hat{x})$ is negative but small in absolute value, then the entire amenity term in Eq. (4) is similarly negative but close to zero. The positive sign of the first part of Eq. (4) will then dominate, yielding $\Delta > 0$. Thus, if the center's amenity advantage over the suburbs is weak, the U.S. location pattern holds: the poor live in the center and the rich live in the suburbs. The same conclusion holds if the amenity function is upward sloping, so that $a'(\hat{x}) > 0$.

On the other hand, if $a'(\hat{x})$ is negative and large in absolute value, then the amenity term will dominate the conventional forces in determining the sign of

Eq. (4). The sign is then negative, so that $\Delta < 0$. Thus, if the center has a large amenity advantage, so that amenities fall rapidly with distance, then the U.S. pattern is reversed: the rich live in the center and the poor live in the suburbs. As noted above, this corresponds to the case of Paris, which has a steep amenity gradient and central location of the rich.

Thus, under the maintained assumptions, the pattern of location by income *can be reversed by steepening the city's exogenous amenity gradient.* Superior amenities make the central city rich, while weak amenities make it poor. Since location by income is then linked to a city's idiosyncratic features, the multiplicity of observed location patterns around the world becomes explicable.

Unfortunately, the above argument is imprecise. The reason is that the other variables in Eq. (3) are held fixed as the magnitude of $a'(\hat{x})$ is altered, and this is done without proper justification. To supply the required justification, let the analysis be carried out by comparing two cities: a *reference* city and a *comparison* city. The reference city has the location pattern of the first city considered above, where the rich live in the suburbs. Its $\hat{x}$ value is denoted $\hat{x}_r$, and its amenity function is $a_r(x)$. The comparison city satisfies a number of requirements. For each group, income, commuting cost, and utility are the same as in the reference city. In addition, the comparison city's amenity function, denoted $a_c(x)$, has the property that $a_c(\hat{x}_r) = a_r(\hat{x}_r)$. Thus, the two amenity functions intersect at $\hat{x}_r$, the group boundary in the reference city.

This assumption has a number of implications. First, it implies that the poor's bid-price at distance $\hat{x}_r$ in the comparison city equals their bid-price at $\hat{x}_r$ in the reference city.[5] The rich bid-prices are similarly equal at $\hat{x}_r$. Since the rich and poor bid-price curves intersect at $\hat{x}_r$ in the reference city, it follows that the comparison city's curves also intersect at $\hat{x}_r$. This in turn implies that the group boundaries are the same in the two cities (i.e., $\hat{x}_c = \hat{x}_r$). Finally, with prices and amenities equal at the common boundary distance, housing consumption for a given group must be the same at this distance in both cities.

Let the common group boundary in the two cities be denoted $\hat{x}$, and let the common amenity level at this location be denoted $\hat{a}$. In addition, let the common housing price level at $\hat{x}$ be $\hat{p}$, and let the common levels of poor and rich housing consumption be denoted $\hat{q}_0$ and $\hat{q}_1$. The only variable whose value is different at $\hat{x}$ in the two cities is then the *slope* of the amenity function, which equals $a_r'(\hat{x})$ in the reference city and $a_c'(\hat{x})$ in the comparison city. To emphasize this difference,

[5] To see why both cities must have the same poor bid-prices at $\hat{x}_r$, recall that incomes and commuting costs are the same and that amenities at $\hat{x}_r$ are the same by assumption. Thus, for the utilities of the poor to be equal across cities, bid-prices at distance $\hat{x}_r$ must be the same. The same argument applies to the rich.

the Δ expression in Eq. (3) can be written twice, once for the reference city and once for the comparison city. This yields

$$\Delta_r = \frac{t_0}{\hat{q}_0} - \frac{t_1}{\hat{q}_1} + a_r'(\hat{x})\left(\frac{v^a[y_1 - t_1\hat{x}, \hat{p}, \hat{a}]}{\hat{q}_1} - \frac{v^a[y_0 - t_0\hat{x}, \hat{p}, \hat{a}]}{\hat{q}_0}\right), \tag{4}$$

$$\Delta_c = \frac{t_0}{\hat{q}_0} - \frac{t_1}{\hat{q}_1} + a_c'(\hat{x})\left(\frac{v^a[y_1 - t_1\hat{x}, \hat{p}, \hat{a}]}{\hat{q}_1} - \frac{v^a[y_0 - t_0\hat{x}, \hat{p}, \hat{a}]}{\hat{q}_0}\right). \tag{5}$$

Under this formulation, the procedure of holding the other elements of the Δ expression fixed as the amenity gradient changes is proper. The key constraint is that the amenity function continues to intersect the original function at the fixed $\hat{x}$ as it steepens, as shown in Fig. 1. As above, such steepening ultimately generates a reversal of the U.S. location pattern. This conclusion is summarized as follows:

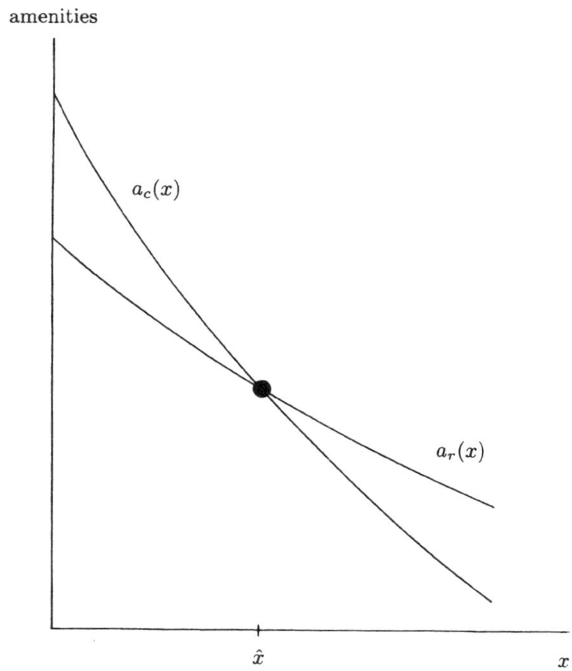

Fig. 1. Amenity functions.

Proposition. Suppose that the conventional locational forces dominate in the reference city, so that $\Delta_r > 0$ holds and the rich live in the suburbs. Suppose further that the marginal amenity valuation v^a rises faster than housing consumption as income increases. Then, the location pattern will be reversed in the comparison city, with $\Delta_c < 0$ holding and the rich living in the center, whenever $a_c'(\hat{x})$ is negative and sufficiently large in absolute value.

3. A model with endogenous amenities

The analysis up to this point has assumed that amenities are exogenous. However, as explained in the introduction, the modern amenities available at a given location depend in part on the local income level. Such amenities are therefore a by-product rather than a determinant of the location patterns of different income groups. In this section, the analysis is broadened to include endogenous amenities. The modified model involves a number of simplifying assumptions and is meant only to be suggestive.

The utility function is now written $u(e, q, a, z)$, where a again represents exogenous amenities and z represents the income of the consumer's neighborhood. Modern amenities are assumed to be an increasing function of neighborhood income. To simplify the characterization of neighborhoods, the continuous distance measure is dropped and replaced by a discrete measure that recognizes just two locations: center and suburbs. The z value in a given location then depends on which income group lives there. Commuting costs at the center are equal to zero, while total commuting costs from the suburbs equal t_0 and t_1 for the poor and rich (suburban distance is normalized to one).

For simplicity, it is also assumed that dwellings at any location are available in two fixed sizes, q_0 and $q_1 > q_0$, with the rich choosing the larger size. Finally, the poor are assumed to be indifferent to the level of exogenous amenities and neighborhood income, while the rich value both. This assumption, which mirrors the one made in Section 2, means that $u^a = u^z = 0$ holds when e and q are small while $u^a, u^z > 0$ holds when e and q are large.

Let $\tilde{p}_0$ denote the poor's bid-price for housing in the center and $\bar{p}_0$ denote their bid-price in the suburbs. Since these prices must equalize the utility of the poor in the two locations, it follows that

$$u(y_0 - \tilde{p}_0 q_0, q_0, \tilde{a}, \tilde{z}) = u(y_0 - t_0 - \bar{p}_0 q_0, q_0, \bar{a}, \bar{z}), \tag{6}$$

where $\tilde{a}$ and $\tilde{z}$ give exogenous amenities and neighborhood income in the center and $\bar{a}$ and $\bar{z}$ give the suburban values. Because the poor are unaffected by a and z, the difference in these variables between center and suburbs has no effect on the bid prices in Eq. (6). Satisfaction of Eq. (6) requires only that nonhousing consumption be equal in the two locations, which implies $\tilde{p}_0 q_0 = t_0 + \bar{p}_0 q_0$.

Rearranging, the bid-price differential for the poor between center and suburbs then equals

$$\tilde{p}_0 - \bar{p}_0 = \frac{t_0}{q_0}. \tag{7}$$

Since the rich care about neighborhood income, their bid prices at the different locations depend on the residential pattern. To see this, let the pattern which has the rich in the center and the poor in the suburbs be denoted A, with B denoting the reverse pattern. The rich bid-prices under pattern A, denoted $\tilde{p}_1^A$ and $\bar{p}_1^A$, must then satisfy

$$u(y_1 - \tilde{p}_1^A q_1, q_1, \tilde{a}, y_1) = u(y_1 - t_1 - \bar{p}_1^A q_1, q_1, \bar{a}, y_0). \tag{8}$$

Note that under pattern A, $\tilde{z} = y_1$ and $\bar{z} = y_0$. Observe also that $\bar{p}_1^A$ gives the price that a rich person would pay to live amidst the poor in the suburbs, a movement that would upset the assumed residential pattern. Assuming that $\tilde{a} > \bar{a}$, the center has better exogenous amenities than the suburbs and offers better modern amenities, a consequence of its higher income. Therefore, utility equalization for the rich requires *lower* nonhousing consumption in the center, which means $\tilde{p}_1^A q_1 > t_1 + \bar{p}_1^A q_1$. Rearranging, the rich's bid-price differential between suburbs and center under pattern A satisfies

$$\tilde{p}_1^A - \bar{p}_1^A > \frac{t_1}{q_1}. \tag{9}$$

As in the model with continuous distance, the group with the larger bid-price differential lives in the center.[6] Using this principle, the bid-price differentials for the rich and poor must be compared to decide whether pattern A is an equilibrium. Assuming $t_0/q_0 > t_1/q_1$ as before, a comparison of Eqs. (7) and (9) shows that pattern A may, indeed, satisfy the requirements of equilibrium. In other words, $\tilde{p}_1^A - \bar{p}_1^A > t_0/q_0 = \tilde{p}_0 - \bar{p}_0$ may hold, indicating that the rich have the larger bid-price differential, provided that $\tilde{p}_1^A - \bar{p}_1^A$ is much larger than t_1/q_1. In this case, $\tilde{p}_1^A - \bar{p}_1^A$ will exceed t_0/q_0 even though $t_0/q_0 > t_1/q_1$. For this outcome to occur, the center's exogenous amenity advantage must be sufficiently large.

The intuitive explanation follows the argument of Section 2. A rich person moving to the suburbs would forsake exogenous amenities and would also enter a lower-income area, with a consequent loss of modern amenities. If center has

[6] In equilibrium, the value of p in the suburbs would equal a constant δ that depends on the opportunity cost of urban land. The p value in the center would then equal δ plus the *smaller* of the bid-price differentials. Because the group living in the center has the larger differential, its bid for suburban housing would then be less than δ, ensuring that the residential pattern is an equilibrium.

a large amenity advantage, these losses will overwhelm the conventional forces that draw the rich to the suburbs, assuring that pattern A is an equilibrium.

Observe that if the endogenous, modern amenities are dropped from the model, the above argument is unaffected and the conclusion mirrors that of Section 2. More noteworthy is the fact that pattern A can be an equilibrium when exogenous amenities are *absent*, with the endogeneous component operating by itself. In this case, central location of the rich generates an endogenous amenity in the center that is sufficient to maintain the location pattern despite the lure of cheaper housing in the suburbs (and the absence of exogenous amenities).

Pattern B, where the rich locate in the suburbs, can also be an equilibrium with endogenous amenities. The bid-prices for the rich under this pattern, denoted $\tilde{p}_1^B$ and $\bar{p}_1^B$, must satisfy

$$u(y_1 - \tilde{p}_1^B q_1, q_1, \tilde{a}, y_0) = u(y_1 - t_1 - \bar{p}_1^B q_1, q_1, \bar{a}, y_1). \tag{10}$$

Since $\tilde{a} > \bar{a}$ while modern amenities are worse in the center, the center's net advantage over the suburbs is ambiguous. As a result, nonhousing consumption could be either smaller or larger in the center, implying that the bid-price differential $\tilde{p}_1^B - \bar{p}_1^B$ could be larger or smaller than t_1/q_1. However, as long as $\tilde{p}_1^B - \bar{p}_1^B$ is less than the poor differential t_0/q_0, pattern B is an equilibrium. Note that this outcome is assured if exogenous amenities are absent, which implies $\tilde{p}_1^B - \bar{p}_1^B < t_1/q_1 < t_0/q_0$.

This discussion shows that endogenous amenities introduce the possibility of multiple equilibria. In particular, patterns A and B are both equilibria when

$$\tilde{p}_1^A - \bar{p}_1^A > t_0/q_0 > \tilde{p}_1^B - \bar{p}_1^B. \tag{11}$$

For the first inequality in Eq. (11) to be satisfied, $\tilde{a}$ must be large enough relative to $\bar{a}$ so that the combined exogenous and endogenous amenity advantage of the center under pattern A is large enough to offset the pull of the conventional forces, keeping the rich in the center. For the second inequality in Eq. (11) to hold, $\tilde{a}$ must not be so large as to offset the combined pull of the conventional forces and endogenous suburban amenities under pattern B, keeping the rich in the suburbs.

The intuitive reason for the existence of multiple equilibria is that endogenous amenities make the existing location of the rich attractive to them wherever it might be. Moving into the poor area requires a sacrifice of endogenous amenities, which depresses the bid-price of the rich and tends to maintain the existing location pattern, whether it is A or B. Note that the possibility of multiple equilibria may help explain the puzzling variety of location patterns by income. However, this explanation is not as compelling as in the exogenous-amenities case because it requires one to argue that different equilibria are somehow selected in different cities.

Despite this ambiguity, the clearcut implications of the Section 2's analysis, namely that strong exogenous amenities in the center ensure central location of the rich, also emerges in the presence of endogenous amenities. This follows because both bid-price differentials in Eq. (11) are increasing in $\tilde{a}$, the level of central amenities. As a result, once $\tilde{a}$ becomes sufficiently large, the second inequality in Eq. (11) is violated, ruling out pattern B as an equilibrium. Thus, as in Section 2, the rich must live in the center whenever its exogenous amenity advantage is sufficiently large.

4. Why exogenous-amenity patterns differ across cities

Because the theory says that location by income depends on the spatial pattern of exogenous amenities, it is important to ask why such amenity patterns differ across cities. To start, consider the pattern of natural amenities, focusing on water access. Since the need for cheap transportation often caused urban areas to develop on seacoasts, rivers or lakes, many European and U.S. central cities enjoy the natural amenity of proximity to a body of water. Given this common outcome, differential access to water appears not to be an important source of amenity differences between European and U.S. central cities. In the case of Paris, however, the Seine river seems to play a larger role in the life of the city than do water-related amenities in many other urban areas. As a result, this particular natural amenity may be an important factor in generating central Paris's advantage over its suburbs.

Turning to historical amenities, Europe's longer history provides an obvious reason why its central cities contain more buildings and monuments of historical significance than do their U.S. counterparts. Many European cities were major metropolises at a time when much of the U.S. had not even been settled, and the legacy of urban development from this distant past provides an atmosphere in European city centers that appears to be highly valued by the residents.

In addition to the effect of a longer history, government investment in central-city infrastructure appears in many cases to have been more extensive in European cities than in the U.S. This in turn may reflect different political arrangements, as argued in the literature on urban 'primacy.' This literature, which attempts to explain why many countries contain a single, dominant city, argues that an important factor is a highly-centralized national government. When a country has such a government, tax resources are heavily invested in developing the capital city, which then tends to become dominant (see Henderson, 1988). Ades and Glaeser (1995) offer a similar argument, claiming that when the residents of given city amass political power (as when the city is the capital of a centralized country), government resources flow toward that city, making it large. Even though these arguments are directed toward explaining primacy in a centralized nation, they also imply that lavish government investment in buildings, monuments, parks, and other infrastructure is likely to occur over the capital city's history in such a country, generating a foundation for the historical amenities enjoyed by present-day residents.

Being the capital city of country with a strong central government, Paris clearly fits the above description. In addition, it is apparent that many of the historical amenities in central Paris are the result of substantial investment of national tax revenues over the city's history, as the above argument would predict. The same phenomenon is obviously at work in other European cities such as London, whose abundance of historical amenities can be traced in part to a dominant role in the life of its country.[7] By contrast, the greater degree of political decentralization in the U.S. means that the capital city, Washington, DC, benefits less from national tax revenue than would otherwise be the case. Indeed, the fiscal crisis currently underway in the District of Columbia would be unimaginable in a country like France or Britain. As a result, although Washington offers historical amenities, their effect is not strong enough to generate a Parisian-style pattern of location by income.

Although the previous discussion might suggest otherwise, historical amenities actually depreciate over time, which means that their maintenance requires ongoing investment. If such expenditures were withheld, the central city's amenities would decay, and high-income residents would be increasingly drawn to the suburbs. In the case of Paris, it is obvious to any visitor that substantial expenditures of this type are devoted to maintaining the stock of historical amenities.[8]

One could argue that such expenditures arise for the same political reasons as the original investment in historical infrastructure, namely the dominance of the capital city. In addition, in the case of Paris, it is clear that spending on amenity restoration and maintenance is also designed to preserve the city's appeal for tourism, which generates large benefits for the local economy. But, as noted in the introduction, such spending also has the features of an endogenous, modern amenity that responds to the local income level in the same way as the number of restaurants or theaters. In other words, amenity maintenance is a local public good whose allocation may be skewed toward politically important,

[7] In Brussels, a substantial part of the historical center has been demolished and replaced by office buildings, a phenomenon that has been dubbed 'Brusselization' by disapproving Europeans. Moreover, location by income in that city follows the U.S. pattern, which is consistent with the present theory (see Thomas and Zenou, 1997, for evidence).

[8] One highly visible expenditure supports the fabled corps of Paris street cleaners, who maintain an immaculate central-city environment. According to Nicot (1996), other French urban areas have stimulated the movement of high-income households to their central cities by following Paris' example, using tax revenues to restore historical districts.

high-income neighborhoods.[9] This argument predicts that if the rich were somehow to relocate to the suburbs, the central city's historical amenities might wither through lack of maintenance.

This view, which suggests that historical amenities are themselves partly endogenous, may contain an element of truth. Nevertheless, the historical amenities in European central cities are best viewed as exogenously determined. Their presence, which arises from a long European history and the lavish past investments of strong central governments, constitutes an important difference between the U.S. and European cities. This difference may in turn help explain the different patterns of location by income in the two cases.

5. Conclusion

Despite substantial progress in urban economic theory since the 1960s, the absence of a convincing and robust explanation of location by income represents a significant failure of the standard model. This paper has attempted to remedy that failure by presenting an amenity-based theory. The theory demonstrates that the relative location of different income groups depends on the spatial pattern of exogenous amenities in a city. The analysis shows that when the center has a strong advantage over the suburbs in exogenous amenities, and when valuation of these amenities rises rapidly with income, the rich are likely to live at central locations. This conclusion applies regardless of whether or not endogenous amenities, which depend an area's income level, are present. The virtue of the theory is that it ties location by income to a city's idiosyncratic characteristics. It thus predicts a multiplicity of location patterns across cities, consistent with real-world observation.

Acknowledgements

This work was initiated while the first author was a visitor at CERAS-ENPC in Paris. The authors thank PIR-Villes for financial support and a referee for helpful suggestions.

Appendix A

The argument in Section 2 hinges on the assumption that v^a/q is increasing in income, and it is important to know whether this assumption is consistent with

[9] Empirical evidence is scarce on the extent to which government spending within jurisdictions is skewed in favor of high-income residents. For one study, see Behrman and Craig (1987), who investigate the allocation of police across neighborhoods in Baltimore.

familiar specifications of preferences. The following discussion shows that the assumption is, in fact, consistent with CES preferences under a particular parameter restriction.

Suppose the utility function takes the CES form

$$u(e, q, a) \equiv [\alpha e^{-\theta} + \beta q^{-\theta} + (1 - \alpha - \beta)a^{-\theta}]^{-1/\theta}. \tag{A.1}$$

Differentiation then establishes

$$\frac{u^a}{u^e} = \frac{(1 - \alpha - \beta)}{\alpha}\left(\frac{e}{a}\right)^{1/\sigma}, \tag{A.2}$$

where $\sigma = 1/(1 + \theta)$ is the elasticity of substitution. The demand functions for e and q are given by $e(x) = (y - tx)\,[\Omega(x) / (\Omega(x) + p(x))]$ and $q(x) = (y - tx) / (\Omega(x) + p(x))$, where $\Omega(x) = (\alpha p(x) / \beta)^{\sigma}$. Substituting the expression for $e(x)$ into Eq. (A.2), and then dividing the result by the expression for $q(x)$ yields

$$\frac{v^a[y - tx, p(x), a(x)]}{q(x)} = \frac{(1 - \alpha - \beta)}{\beta} p(x)\, a(x)^{-1/\sigma}(y - tx)^{(1-\sigma)/\sigma}[\Omega(x) + p(x)]^{-(1-\sigma)/\sigma}. \tag{A.3}$$

Inspection of Eq. (A.3) shows that v^a/q is increasing in income, as assumed in the above proposition, provided that the elasticity of substitution is less than one (the exponent of $y - tx$ is then positive). A low elasticity of substitution means that the indifference curves are strongly bowed toward the origin, and this property in turn implies that their absolute slope $|\partial e/\partial a|$ in (a, e) space increases rapidly as e rises in response to an increase in income. When $\sigma > 1$, the absolute slope rises faster than q, so that v^a/q increases. Thus, the key assumption of the theory presented in Section 2 is validated under a common specification of preferences.[10]

References

Ades, A.F., Glaeser, E.L., 1995. Trade and circuses: Explaining urban giants. Quarterly Journal of Economics 110, 195–227.

Alonso, W., 1964. Location and land use. Harvard University Press, Cambridge, MA.

Behrman, J.R., Craig, S.G., 1987. The distribution of public services: An exploration of local government preferences. American Economic Review 77, 37–49.

[10] Note that with Cobb–Douglas preferences, $\sigma = 1$ and v^a/q is independent of income.

Gin, A., Sonstelie, J., 1992. The streetcar and residential location in nineteenth century Philadelphia. Journal of Urban Economics 32, 92–107.
Henderson, J.V., 1988. Urban Development: Theory, Fact and Illusion. Oxford University Press, New York.
Hohenberg, P.M., Lees, L.H., 1986. The Making of Urban Europe 1000–1950. Harvard University Press, Cambridge, MA.
Ingram, G.K., Carroll, A., 1981. The spatial structure of Latin American cities. Journal of Urban Economics 9, 257–273.
Kern, C.R., 1981. Upper-income renaissance in the city: Its sources and implications for the city's future. Journal of Urban Economics 9, 106–124.
Leroy, S.F., Sonstelie, J., 1983. Paradise lost and regained: Transportation innovation, income, and residential location. Journal of Urban Economics 13, 67–89.
Mills, E.S., 1967. An aggregative model of resource allocation in a metropolitan area. American Economic Review 57, 197–210.
Muth, R.F., 1969. Cities and Housing. University of Chicago Press, Chicago.
Nicot, B.H., 1996. La répartition du revenu des foyers fiscaux. In: Pumain, D., Godard, F. (Eds.), Données Urbaines. Anthropos, Paris.
Tabard, N., 1993. Des quartiers pauvres aux banlieues aisées: une représentation sociale du territoire. Economie et Statistique 270, 5–22.
Thomas, I., Zenou, Y., 1997. Segregation and labor discrimination in Brussels: Theory and evidence. ERMES Working Paper, Université Panthéon-Assas.
Wheaton, W.C., 1977. Income and urban residence: An analysis of consumer demand for location. American Economic Review 67, 620–631.

[4]

ELSEVIER European Economic Review 38 (1994) 817–826

EUROPEAN
ECONOMIC
REVIEW

Theories of Persistent Inequalities

Human capital, inequality, and growth: A local perspective

Roland Bénabou [a,b,c,*]

[a] *MIT, Dept. of Economics, 50 Memorial Drive, Cambridge, MA 02139-4307, USA*
[b] *NBER, Cambridge MA, USA*
[c] *CEPR, London, UK*

Abstract

A recent body of work has demonstrated the crucial role played by local human capital externalities and local school funding in generating socio-economic segregation, persistent poverty, and low aggregate income or productivity growth. We present a simple model which captures the main insights from this literature, and prove three general propositions. First, minor differences in education technologies, preferences, wealth, or minor imperfections in capital markets, can lead to a high degree of stratification. Second, stratification makes inequality in education and income more persistent across generations; the same is true for total wealth, provided the rich succeed in capturing the rents created by their secession. Finally, this polarization or urban areas can be very inefficient, especially in the long run.

Key words: Inequality; Education; Growth; Stratification

JEL classification: D31; O40; I22

1. Introduction

A recent body of work, both theoretical and empirical, has demonstrated the potentially crucial role played by local human capital externalities in generating socio-economic segregation, persistent income inequality across generations, and inefficiently low levels of aggregate income or productivity growth. These local interactions may operate through direct spillovers such as those documented by educators and sociologists (peer or neighborhood

* I am grateful to Olivier Blanchard, Peter Diamond, Michael Kremer and Julio Rotemberg for useful comments. Financial support from the NSF is gratefully acknowledged.

SSDI 0014-2921(93)E0073-T

effects, role models, norms, etc.) and often gathered under the heading of 'social capital', or through the effects of a community's financial resources and political equilibrium on the funding of its schools. In either case, education takes on the features of a club or local public good, and the manner in which society stratifies becomes a key determinant of both income distribution and aggregate performance.

Rather than survey the literature, which the space available here would not allow us to do adequately, we present instead a very simple model in which the main issues and insights are easily demonstrated and related to some of the relevant papers. These include Loury (1977, 1987), De Bartolome (1990), Borjas (1992a, b), Bénabou (1993a, 1992), Durlauf (1992, 1993), Lundberg and Startz (1992) and Fernandez and Rogerson (1992, 1993), among others. The model is a stripped-down version of Bénabou (1993b). That paper also contains more general versions of the results reported here (with the proofs, which we omit), a more complete review of the literature (especially empirical), and some policy implications.

2. A basic model

There is a continuum of families, with unit measure. Parents are of two types, A and B (rich and poor, White and Black, etc.), in proportions n and $1-n$, and endowed with human capital $h_A > h_B$. They all reside in a metropolitan area composed of two towns or communities, $j=1,2$, each of which holds a fixed number 1/2 of land plots or housing units; all land belongs to absentee landowners, a neutrality assumption. The proportion of A agents in community j is denoted x^j, and community 1 is defined as the richer one: $x^1 \geqslant 2n - x^1 = x^2$. There are two periods. A parent with type $h \in \{h_A, h_B\}$ living in a community with percentage x of rich households and paying ρ in land rent enjoys utility:

$$V(h,x,\rho) \equiv \max_d \{U(c,c',h') = U(\omega(h)+d-\rho,\, y(h)-P(h,d),\, F(h,L(x))\} \tag{1}$$

In the first period, she consumes c and pays rent ρ out of her initial resources $\omega(h)$, plus borrowing d. The interest rate $r(h,d)$ may depend on her type and on the amount borrowed or saved. In the second period, the amount c' available for consumption or bequest (both interpretations are possible) equals second period income $y(h)$, minus debt repayment $P(h,d) \equiv d(1+r(h,d))$. Finally, the child's human capital h' is determined by that of the parent (through at-home learning), and by the quality of education in the chosen community, measured some increasing function $L(x)$ of the local distribution of human capital.

There are two channels through which this distribution can matter. The first and simplest one is pure 'social capital' spillovers, of the type mentioned earlier. We assume $L'(x) \geqslant 0$, $L(0)=h_B$ and $L(1)=h_A$, so that $L(x)$ can be interpreted as an average (not necessarily arithmetic) of local residents' human capital levels; its value $L(n)$ over a representative sample of the population will be denoted $\bar{L}$. A key issue is whether, in a mixed school or neighborhood, it is the stronger individuals who tend to 'pull up' the average to their level, or the weaker ones who 'drag it down' to theirs. These benefits or costs from heterogeneity are reflected in the concavity or convexity of $L(x)$, which will be an important determinant of the efficiency of equilibrium. The second channel through which community composition matters is decentralized school expenditures $E(x)$. We do not model here local spending and taxation decisions; see the full model in Bénabou (1993b). We point out instead a simple way in which (1) can incorporate the effect of community resources on local public goods spending. Let $h'=F(h, E(x))$, and let each town finance its school by taxing residents on their labor income (say, $y(h)=h$) at the same fixed rate τ^*. This can be derived as the unanimous outcome of voting when preferences are logarithmic (Glomm and Ravikumar, 1992). Per pupil expenditures are then $E(x)=\tau^* L(x)$, where $L(x) \equiv xh_A+(1-x)h_B$ is mean income in the community, and $\omega(h)$ is then simply replaced by $\omega(h)-\tau^* h$ in (1); hence the result. Note that in contrast to the pure spillover model, this one necessarily relies on capital market imperfections, since schools must be financed out of parents' income.

3. Causes of stratification

In period 1, parents choose a community $C^j, j=1,2$, so as to maximize the resulting utility $V(h, x^j, \rho^j)$. When will equilibrium in the land market result in stratification? Intuitively, whenever the (human capital) *rich are willing or able to bid more than the poor for land in a richer community.* Formally, this is a standard single-crossing condition of iso-utility-curves, or bid-rents, in the space of community quality and price:

$$R_x(h, x, \rho) \equiv \left.\frac{\mathrm{d}\rho'}{\mathrm{d}x'}\right|_{V(x', \rho')=V(x, \rho)} = \frac{V_x(h, x, \rho)}{-V_\rho(h, x, \rho)} \quad \textit{increases with } h. \tag{2}$$

In that case, the slightest divergence from the symmetric equilibrium $x^1=x^2=n$ triggers a cumulative process: rich agents outbid poor ones for land in community 1, thereby further raising x^1, ρ^1 and lowering x^2, ρ^2. This leads to further migration of the rich to C^1 and concentration of the poor in C^2, until at least one community is completely homogeneous.

Proposition 1. (1). *If* $R_{hx}(h, x, \rho)>0$ *for all* (x, ρ), *the unique stable equilibrium is stratified: if* $n \leqslant 1/2$, *all the rich live in community 1* ($x^1=2n$, $x^2=0$); *if*

$n \geqslant 1/2$, all the poor live in community 2 ($x^1=1$, $x^2=2n-1$). The symmetric equilibrium $x^1=x^2=n$ is unstable. (2). *If $R_{hx}(h,x,\rho)<0$ for all (x,ρ), the unique equilibrium is completely integrated (i.e. symmetric), and it is stable.*

We therefore examine the marginal rate of substitution between first-period consumption and child education. Using the Euler equation for the optimal level of borrowing d, we have

$$R_x(h,x,\rho)=\frac{U_3(c,c',h')}{U_2(c,c',h')}\cdot\frac{F_L(h,L(x))}{P_d(h,d)}\cdot L'(x). \tag{3}$$

Inspection of (3) yields the following, intuitive results (see Bénabou (1993b) for proofs):

Proposition 2. *Stratification can result from even the smallest degree of:*
1. *Complementarity between parental education and community quality: $F_{hL}(h,L)>0$.*
2. *Imperfections in credit markets, resulting in a higher opportunity cost of funds for poor families ($\partial P_{hd}(h,d)/\partial h<0$), when better educated families have higher financial resources ($\omega'(h)>0$, $y'(h)>0$).*
3. *Differences in lifetime wealth ($z'(h)\equiv\omega'(h)+y'(h)/(1+r)>0$), given that education is a normal good (U_3/U_2 increasing in z).*

The simplest case is by far the first one, with linear utility and perfect capital markets: $U=c+(c'+h')/(1+r)$. The bid-rent then simplifies to $R_x(h,x,\rho)=F_L(h,L)L'(x)/(1+r)$, and stratification occurs if families with higher human capital are more sensitive to neighborhood or school quality than those with lower human wealth. If $n<1/2$, there are B agents in both communities, and the equilibrium rent differential is $\rho^1-\rho^2=(F(h_B,L(2n))-F(h_B,L(0)))/(1+r)$; if $n>1/2$, here are A agents in both communities, and $\rho^1-\rho^2=(F(h_A,L(1))-F(h_A,L(2n-1)))/(1+r)$. When $n=1/2$, perfect segregation is sustained by any differential between these two values. Note that the result is *independent of the distribution of financial resources* (ω, y). Thus, in contrast to most of the inequality literature, *redistributive policies have no effect* on either the distribution of educational attainment or the efficiency of equilibrium.

The second result shows how differences in families' 'ability' to pay complement those in 'willingness' to pay for school or community quality. There are a variety of imperfections in loan markets, due to asymmetric information or tax distortions, which raise the opportunity cost of funds for the poor. These include: (a) increasing marginal cost of borrowing $P(d)=d(1+r(d))$, $P', P''>0$, such as a wedge between lending and borrowing rates; (b) borrowing constraints, $d\leqslant\bar{d}$, which make the Euler condition underlying (3) an inequality at low levels of wealth; (c) tax subsidies to home ownership relative to renting (interest deductions), when only wealthy families can afford a down payment.

The second channel through which financial resources matter, and this even with perfect credit markets, is by changing parents' relative preferences for education relative to old age consumption or financial bequest. If education is a normal good, the marginal rate of substitution $(U_3/U_2)(c, c', h')$ which results from optimal borrowing decisions tends to increase with lifetime wealth $z(h) \equiv \omega(h) + y(h)/(1+r)$, leading again to segregation if $z'(h) > 0$. It should be emphasized that no matter how small wealth differences and credit market imperfections are, they can lead to stratification.

Two other important sorting mechanisms were omitted for brevity. The first one is the standard 'voting with one's feet' of Tiebout (1956): agents flock to communities with a higher proportion of their own type, since decisions over taxation and spending on public goods (e.g. schools) are closest there to their preferred choices. The second one, particularly relevant when poor and rich belong to different ethnic groups, includes any practices (from discrimination in the housing market to outright harassment) which raise the cost to a poor family, relative to a rich one, of moving into a rich community. Having identified these multiple sources of stratification, we shall from here on focus mostly on the simplest case: $V(h, x, \rho) = z(h) - \rho + F(h, L(x))/(1+r)$, with $F_{hL} > 0$. This is only for expositional purposes, as the points made under these assumptions are quite general (see Bénabou, 1993b).

4. Implications for aggregate productivity

Is it efficient for different classes to segregate in education? Leaving distributional issues to the next section, we focus here on aggregate productivity of the whole metropolitan area. A community with a fraction x of rich households generates a net surplus equal to $S(x)/2$, where

$$S(x) \equiv xF(h_A, L(x)) + (1-x)F(h_B, L(x)). \tag{4}$$

When the city stratifies, the net output of community 1 increases by $S(x^1) - S(n)$, while that of community 2 declines by $S(n) - S(2n - x^1)$, where $x^1 = \min\{2n, 1\}$. Gains in the rich community therefore dominate losses in the poor one if S is convex; the reverse is true if S is concave. We therefore compute:

$$2S' = F(h_A, L) - F(h_B, L) + (xF_L(h_A, L) + (1-x)F_L(h_B, L))L';$$

$$2S'' = 2(F_L(h_A, L) - F_L(h_B, L)L' + (xF_{LL}(h_A, L) + (1-x)F_{LL}(h_B, L))(L')^2 + (xF_L(h_A, L) + (1-x)F_L(h_B, L))L'', \tag{5}$$

where $L = L(x)$, etc. The first term in S'' is positive, reflecting an efficiency gain from stratification, if a well-educated family benefits more than a less educated one from an increase in community or school quality: $F_{hL} > 0$.[1] The second term measures how the marginal productivity of community quality (for the average resident) varies with its level: when $F_{LL} < 0$, there are decreasing returns, hence an efficiency loss from stratification. The last term measures where a marginal well-educated family contributes most to raising the quality of the community: if $L'' < 0$, such a family is much less valuable in the already well-educated community which it joins than it was in the education-poor community which it abandons; hence another loss from stratification.

Proposition 3. Agents segregate or integrate depending on $F_{hL} \gtrless 0$, no matter how small. The equilibrium can be very inefficient, if F_{LL} or L'' are large in absolute value and have the opposite sign of F_{hL}.

Note that the potential for inefficiently low output is even greater when $F_{hL} < 0$ and stratification results from credit market imperfections, wealth effects or discrimination, which are unrelated to the productivity of education. On the other hand, standard local public goods (e.g. purchased school inputs $E(x)$) will lead to efficient sorting, in the absence of other externalities or imperfections (Tiebout, 1956). When both $E(x)$ and $L(x)$ affect education, stratification therefore involves a tradeoff, which is examined in De Bartolome (1990) and Bénabou (1993b). Finally, while we are mostly interested in the case where the city becomes polarized, Proposition 3 also shows how inefficient mixing can occur.

5. Implications for inequality

We now turn to the distribution of gains and losses from stratification. A recurrent theme in the literature, starting with Loury (1977, 1987), is that racial or socio-economic segregation makes inequality more persistent, by compounding disparities in educational inputs at the family and community levels. A proper analysis of persistence requires a dynamic setting. In Bénabou (1993b) we extend the model presented here to overlapping generations, and prove Claims 1 and 2 below; but the underlying intuitions can already be outlined in the present two-period model. Assuming $n = 1/2$ for simplicity, we see that inequality in children's attainment and income is indeed larger than if families had remained integrated:

[1] One half of $2(F_L(h_A, L) - F_L(h_B, L))L'(x)\mathrm{d}x$ represents the private gains from trade accruing to a pair of A and B agents which trade places between communities with compositions x and $x + \mathrm{d}x$. The other half is external: a marginal rise in L is more valuable, ceteris paribus, in the community with more L-sensitive agents; see the expression for S'.

$$h_A'/h_B' = F(h_A, h_A)/F(h_B, h_B) > F(h_A, \bar{L})/F(h_B, \bar{L}). \tag{6}$$

We explain below how this can give rise to ghettos or poverty traps. But first we make clear that the general argument about increased persistence rests on plausible but often *implicit* assumptions about the appropriate measure of inequality, and the net cost to the rich of separating themselves from the poor. Indeed, better communities and schools come at the cost of higher rents or taxes. Comparing the *total* wealth of children (human capital plus bequest), or more generally the utility levels of parents, may therefore not lead to the same answer as the standard comparison of educational achievements or earnings:

Proposition 4. Stratification need not increase inequality between rich and poor families' total wealth $c'+h'$ *or utility levels. When* $n<1/2$, *it is indeed the case that* $F(h_A, L^1) - F(h_B, L^2) - (1+r)(\rho^1 - \rho^2) > F(h_A, \bar{L}) - F(h_B, \bar{L})$. *But when* $n>1/2$, *the inequality is reversed, and when* $n=1/2$, *the ranking is ambiguous.*

The result follows directly from the values of the equilibrium differential $\rho^1 - \rho^2$ described below Proposition 2, together with $F_{hL}>0$ and $L^1 > \bar{L} > L^2$. In the absence of bequests, i.e. if all of c' is consumed in old age, the costs of education are absorbed into parental consumption. But it is then debatable whether one should focus on *child inequality* or on *family inequality*. The more fundamental question, however, becomes more apparent if we do interpret c' as a financial bequest, and compare children's total wealth $c'+h'$, which incorporates the difference between the rents paid and received by their parents. What is the net cost paid by the rich to separate themselves from the poor? Who owns the assets or property rights which make segregation possible, and appropriate the rents which it may create? In Proposition 4, the capital gains $\rho^1 - \bar{\rho}$ and losses $\rho^2 - \bar{\rho}$ accrue to outside landowners, or equivalently to all city residents in equal proportions. It is essentially through less neutral allocations (the *A*'s own relatively more of community 1, the *B*'s of community 2) that stratification will increase inequality in *total* wealth.

In practice, the rich do appear successful in capturing the capital gains which their secession creates, leaving the corresponding losses to the poor. This may be because they hold the relevant scarce factors (e.g. prime real estate), or because the poor are latecomers (immigrants), or through various collective practices which raise, even temporarily, the relative cost to the poor of joining or remaining in a community which is appreciating. Prime among these – at least historically – is racial segregation. More recent devices such as zoning regulations discriminate instead on the basis of income (Durlauf, 1992, 1993; Wheaton, 1993; Fernandez and Rogerson, 1993). We shall therefore make from here on the standard assumption that human wealth inequality translates into total wealth inequality, without any rent dissipation.

A shown by (6) and confirmed empirically by Borjas (1992a, b), segregation tends to slow down convergence in education and income levels. But it can even magnify small initial disparities, leading to very unequal long-run outcomes. This is the case when $F(h, L)$ has decreasing returns in h alone, but increasing returns in (h, L) jointly over some range. Clearly, if h_A and h_B lie on opposite sides of an unstable fixed point of the equation $h^* = F(h^*, h^*)$, then under perfect segregation $h_A' > h_A$ but $h_B' < h_B$. Under integration, inequality is always reduced (see (6)), but what happens to the levels of human capital depends on the sensitivity of L to heterogeneity.

Claim 1. Stratification can trap poorer families in a steady-state of low human capital and income, while for richer families these variables keep growing. Under the same conditions, integration would have lead to convergence (eliminating inequality) and sustained growth for all families.

The idea that local increasing returns, *realized only through segregation*, constitute the mechanism through which ghettos or local poverty traps arise and persist, is one of the main insights of the literature (Bénabou, 1993a, 1992; Durlauf, 1992, 1993; Lundberg and Startz, 1992).[2] Another important idea is that stratification can even hurt the productivity and income of richer dynasties, when, in addition to local interactions in education, the different classes interact at the *global*, or economy-wide level in the production of goods or knowledge. This may result from technological spillovers (Tamura, 1991a, b), complementarities in the labor market (e.g., some are managers, others workers – no market failure is required; Bénabou (1993a, 1992)), or inter-community externalities (Cooper, 1992). A simple way of capturing such this interdependence (see the papers for micro models) is to write individual output or marginal product as

$$y(h) = G(h, H), \tag{7}$$

where H is an economy-wide index of human capital and G some aggregator. Clearly, one can now have $h_A' > h_A$ and $h_B' < h_B$ and yet $y(h_A') < y(h_A)$ and $y(h_B') < y(h_B)$. Intuitively, the combination of highly trained managers and workers with low levels of literacy and numeracy may not be very efficient. More generally, in a dynamic setting, the secession of managerial dynasties can prevent worker dynasties from acquiring the skills necessary to keep up, so that productivity growth slows down and may even die out. When

[2] Tamura (1991b) and Galor and Tsiddon (1992) present models which combine increasing returns at the *individual* (country or family) level with an economy-wide technological externality, through which the rich eventually lift the poor out of poverty. The implicit assumption is that the rich do not segregate (i.e., limit interactions to their own group), as they do when given the opportunity in our model.

education uses real resources, this also feeds back on the accumulation of human capital.

Claim 2. Stratification can lead to a long-run level – or even growth rate – of human capital and income which is lower, for all dynasties, than under integration.

As intuition suggests, the relative sensitivity to heterogeneity of the local and aggregate indices L and H is a key determinant of the costs and benefits of stratification and so is the degree of complementarity in G; see Bénabou (1992). But the potential for '*self-defeating secession*' is a very robust and general feature of models with multi-level interactions and mobility (Bénabou, 1993a). It implies that society may face an intertemporal tradeoff. In the short run, stratification can lead to gains for the rich in excess of the losses of the poor, so that overall growth increases ($S''>0$ in Section 4). Over time, however, the greater heterogeneity of the segregated economy can act as a drag on growth and hurt all dynasties.

6. Conclusion

We used a simple model to demonstrate three very general propositions. First, even minor differences in education technologies, preferences, or wealth, as well as minor imperfections in capital markets, can lead to a high degree of stratification. Second, stratification makes inequality in education and income more persistent across generations; the same is true for total wealth, provided the rich are able to capture the rents created by their secession. Finally, the social polarization of urban areas can be very inefficient, both from the point of view of aggregate growth and in the Pareto sense, especially in the long run.

References

Bénabou, R., 1992, Heterogeneity, stratification, and growth, Working paper 93-4 (MIT, Cambridge, MA) Dec.

Bénabou, R., 1993a, Workings of a city: Location, education and production, Quarterly Journal of Economics 108, 619–652.

Bénabou, R., 1993b, Education, poverty and growth: The local connection, Mimeo. (MIT, Cambridge, MA) Sep.

Borjas, G., 1992a, Ethnic capital and intergenerational mobility, Quarterly Journal of Economics 108, 123–150.

Borjas, G., 1992b, Ethnicity, neighborhoods, and human capital externalities, Mimeo. (University of California, San Diego, CA) Sep.

Cooper, S., 1992, A positive theory of income redistribution, Mimeo. (Stanford University, Stanford, CA) July.

De Bartolome, C., 1990, Equilibrium and inefficiency in a community model with peer group effects, Journal of Political Economy 98, 110–133.

Durlauf, S., 1992, A theory of persistent income inequality, Working paper 4056 (NBER, Cambridge, MA) April.

Durlauf, S., 1993, Neighborhood feedbacks, endogenous stratification, and income inequality, Mimeo. (University of Wisconsin, Madison, WI) April.

Fernandez, R. and R. Rogerson, 1992, Income distribution, communities and the quality of public education: A policy analysis, Mimeo. (Boston University, Boston, MA) July.

Fernandez, R. and R. Rogerson, 1993, Keeping people out: Income distribution, zoning and the quality of public education (Boston University, Boston, MA) July.

Galor, O. and D. Tsiddon, 1992, Income distribution and output growth: The Kuznets hypothesis revisited, Mimeo. (Brown University, Providence, RI). November.

Glomm, E. and B. Ravikumar, 1992, Public versus private investment in human capital: Endogenous growth and income inequality, Journal of Political Economy 100, 818–834.

Loury, G., 1977, A dynamic theory of racial income differences, in: A. Le Mond, eds., Women, minorities and employment discrimination (Lexington Books, Lexington, MA).

Loury, G., 1987, Why should we care about group inequality?, Social Philosophy and Policy 5, 249–271.

Montgomery, J., 1991, Social networks and persistent inequality in the labor market: Toward an economic analysis, American Economic Review 81, 1408–1418.

Lundberg, S. and R. Startz, 1993, On the persistence of racial inequality, Mimeo. (University of Washington, Seattle, WA) Aug.

Streufert, P., 1991, The effect of underclass social isolation on schooling choice, Working paper DP 954-91 (University of Wisconsin, Madison, WI) Aug.

Tamura, R., 1991a, Income convergence in an endogenous growth model, Journal of Political Economy 99, 522–540.

Tamura, R., 1991b, From decay to growth: A dynamic equilibrium model of income distribution, Mimeo. (University of Iowa, Iowa City, IA) Nov.

Tiebout, C., 1956, A pure theory of local expenditures, Journal of Political Economy 64, 416–424.

Wheaton, W., 1993, Land capitalization, Tiebout mobility and the role of zoning regulations, Journal of Urban Economics, forthcoming.

Part II
Inside the City (or . . . Actually Inside the City?): Empirical Analysis of City Structure

[5]

JOURNAL OF URBAN ECONOMICS 36, 79–97 (1994)

The Monocentric Model and Employment Location

MARLON G. BOARNET*

Department of Urban and Regional Planning, School of Social Ecology, University of California at Irvine, Irvine, California 92717-5150

Received August 18, 1992; revised July 1, 1993

The monocentric urban model highlights the important link between transportation access and urban form. Yet as metropolitan areas have become increasingly multicentric, the monocentric model has been criticized on several levels. This paper tests an important assumption used in many monocentric models—namely that employment location is exogenous to population location within an urban area. Using data on population and employment changes in a group of New Jersey municipalities, this work shows that employment changes are endogenous to the population change in a surrounding labor market. This suggests that urban models should give more attention to the problem of employment location within metropolitan areas. © 1994 Academic Press, Inc.

1. INTRODUCTION

There is a growing concern about the validity of the monocentric urban model. The criticisms of that model are largely of three types. First, many authors have noted that employment is not concentrated in a central business district. (See, e.g., Garreau [11], Giuliano and Small [12], McDonald [17], and Wheaton [26]. For models of non-central employment, see, e.g., White [28], Wieand [30], and Yinger [31].) Second, starting with Hamilton, there has been a debate about whether urban commuters engage in "wasteful commuting" in their journey to work (Cropper and Gordon [9], Hamilton [14] and [15], Small and Song [23], White [29]). This debate can be interpreted as questioning whether the distribution of jobs and residences is the primary determinant of the journey to work. Third,

*I have benefited from discussions with James R. Hines, Jr., Mark Alan Hughes, and Julian Wolpert. I am also grateful to Jan Brueckner, Randall Crane, Katherine O'Regan, and two anonymous referees for comments on an earlier draft. Seminar participants at the University of California at Irvine also provided helpful suggestions. Support for some of the initial data collection was provided by the U.S. Department of Transportation and the New Jersey Department of Transportation. This research was also supported in part by the University of California through an allocation of computer time. Of course, I alone am responsible for the analysis that is presented here.

0094-1190/94 $6.00

some authors have questioned the monocentric assumption of exogenous employment location (Steinnes [24], Steinnes and Fisher [25]).

In comparing these criticisms, it is useful to consider what the monocentric model means and what would constitute a damaging contradiction of that model. I suggest that the meaningful insight of the monocentric model, as developed by Alonso [1], Mills [19], and Muth [21], was not that employment is concentrated in the central business district. That was a simplifying assumption. Instead, the meaningful insight was that transportation access to employment is an important determinant of urban form. For most monocentric models, an important part of the analysis was to assume that employment location is exogenous to population location. Thus a fair interpretation of the monocentric tradition is that access to fixed (or exogenous) employment is an important factor in explaining residential settlement patterns. To that extent, multicentric models that assume exogenous suburban employment nodes are really in the monocentric tradition. Many such models are strikingly similar to monocentric models in terms of the analytical approach and the nature of the theoretical predictions (White [28], Wieand [30], and Yinger [31]).

Given that, two criticisms of the monocentric model would be most damaging. The first would be the wasteful commuting issue. If persons do not choose their residential location to minimize their commute to work, this suggests that, at a minimum, there are non-transportation factors which are also influential in residential location (Hamilton [14], Small and Song [23]). While this is an interesting issue, it has been discussed elsewhere (Cropper and Gordon [9], Hamilton [14] and [15], Small and Song [23], White [29]) and is not the focus of this paper. Instead, this paper focuses on the other distinguishing theoretical characteristic of the monocentric model—the assumption of exogenous employment location. In particular, this paper tests the monocentric idea that residential location is endogenous to employment location, but that employment location is largely exogenous to residential location. Given the large number of theoretical and empirical models that rely to some extent on exogenous employment location, this is an important question. If employment location is endogenous to residential location, the partial equilibrium approach of most monocentric models is inappropriate.

The test reported here is based on a simultaneous regression model of population and employment changes in a sample of 365 municipalities in northern New Jersey. The dependent variables in the model are the changes in municipal population and employment from 1980 to 1988. The results of the model show that municipal employment growth is endogenous to population growth in a surrounding labor market area, but municipal population growth is not affected by employment growth in the surrounding labor market area. While this is consistent with past research on causality in urban development (Steinnes [24], Mills [18]), it turns the usual monocentric story on its head. Before the empirical model is developed, the basic structure of the test will be described.

2. DESCRIPTION OF THE EMPIRICAL TEST

While the technique here is similar in spirit to previous research on causality in population and employment location (Steinnes [24], Mills [18]), this research has the following advantages. First, the availability of data for the 1980s allows this test to focus on a recent time period. The growth of suburban employment centers was especially pronounced during the 1980s (Garreau [11]). To that extent, earlier data might misrepresent current conditions. Second, these data provide more geographic detail than the data used in most other tests. Previous research (Steinnes [24], Mills [18]) has compared the growth of population and employment within central cities to growth in a suburban ring. This does not allow any differentiation within large and varied suburban areas. Since suburban areas are clearly not homogeneous, especially in terms of their employment density (Giuliano and Small [12]), it is more interesting to examine growth patterns for several locations within an urban area. This research does that.

Since the municipalities are geographically small (over 100 of the 365 are less than two square miles) and contiguous, the spatial interaction of the municipalities cannot be ignored. In particular, population and employment theoretically interact at the level of a labor market which presumably bears no relationship to arbitrarily drawn municipal borders. Given that labor markets in the northern New Jersey study region are most likely larger than municipalities, those labor markets were measured with potential variables. (The exact form of those variables is discussed in Section 4.) This makes the regressions similar to those used in Steinnes and Fisher [25]. In fact, this paper can be viewed as contrasting the usual monocentric model with the simultaneous model developed by Steinnes and Fisher [25].[1]

Unlike Steinnes and Fisher [25], the model in this paper uses spatial econometric techniques. This is necessary both because spatial lags of dependent variables appear as independent variables in the regressions and because there is spatial autoregression in the error in the population growth equation. These issues are also discussed more fully in Section 4.

3. THE DATA

The data in this study are from observations on the 365 municipalities in the northern 13 counties of the state of New Jersey. Eleven of the 13

[1]This point was suggested by an anonymous referee and Jan Brueckner.

counties are part of the New York metropolitan area, and New York City has a large influence on all parts of the study region.

The dependent variables in this study are the population and employment changes in the municipalities from 1980 to 1988. The independent variables measure the transportation access characteristics of a municipality and other local municipal characteristics that might affect residential and firm location choices. In the empirical model, those variables are referred to as vectors, denoted by T and τ, for transportation access characteristics valued by residents and firms, respectively, and E for the other local characteristics valued by residents and ε for other local characteristics valued by firms. In this section, the specific variables that constitute the T, τ, E, and ε vectors will be discussed. These variables are listed in the Appendix. A complete discussion of the variables, and their expected signs, is given in Boarnet [4, Chaps. 4 and 7].

Local transportation access is measured by dummy variables that are equal to one if a municipality is on a major highway (ANYHIWAY) or contains a commuter rail station (NJTRNSIT). The local characteristics for population growth include measures of municipal demographic characteristics (PRBLCK80, PRHISP80, and POVRAT80), crime rates (VIORAT80 and PRPRAT80), housing stock age (HOUPRE40), fiscal policy (PCNECEXP and PCTAX80), and distance from New York City (NYCDIST and NYCDSTSQ). New York City is the center of the metropolitan area that contains northern New Jersey, so that the distance variables (NYCDIST and NYCDSTSQ) measure development patterns related to distance from the urban core. The effect of distance is measured quadratically to allow for the possibility that growth will occur on the urban fringe, as predicted by some dynamic monocentric urban models (Fujita [10], Wheaton [27]).

The local characteristics for employment growth include municipal crime rates (VIORAT80 and PRPRAT80), land available for development (proxied by FRMPAR80), fiscal policy (PEBUSEXP and EQZDTX80), agglomeration economies (TOTMAN82 and TOTRET82), and distance from New York City (NYCDIST and NYCDSTSQ). Both regressions include municipal land area as an independent variable to control for differences in the size of municipalities.[2]

Some of the independent variables described above clearly belong in only one of the population or employment growth regressions. For exam-

[2]The regressions were also fit with densities as the dependent variable. The results of those regressions verify that the change in municipal employment density depends on the change in population density in a surrounding labor market, although that result is statistically significant at the 10% level, rather than the much smaller significance levels reported in Table 1 of this paper.

ple, industrial mix (manufacturing and retail employment, measured by TOTMAN82 and TOTRET82) is important for employment location, but presumably can be excluded from a population growth regression. Likewise, demographic characteristics that might influence residential location (such as PRBLCK80 and PRHISP80) might be much less of a factor in firm location. Added to these initial exclusion restrictions, some variables were insignificant in one equation and were dropped from the final specifications. For example, the amount of land available for development (proxied by the number of farm parcels in the municipality, FRMPAR80) was originally included in both the population and the employment growth regressions, but was statistically insignificant in the population growth model. Further note that the NJTRNSIT variable was originally included in both the population and the employment growth regressions, but it was highly insignificant in the population growth regression and was dropped from the population growth models reported in this paper. For a full discussion of the theoretical basis of the choice of independent variables and the resulting exclusion restrictions, see Boarnet [4, Chap. 4].

Some of the variables above, most notably the fiscal variables and the agglomeration economy variables, were constructed from existing data. The fiscal variables, PCNECEXP, PCTAX80, PEBUSEXP, and EQZDTX80, measure, respectively, per capita municipal spending on a class of common or necessary services, per capita tax burdens (including the municipality and all overlying jurisdictions below the state level), per employee expenditures on basic infrastructure categories presumed to be important for firms, and the equalized tax rate in the municipality. These variables were constructed, following Grubb [13], to capture the effect of both the tax and the spending sides of the local fisc. See Boarnet [6] or the Appendix of this paper for more detailed information on the spending categories in the expenditure variables (PCNECEXP and PEBUSEXP).[3]

TOTMAN82 and TOTRET82 are potential variables that measure agglomeration benefits in particular locations. The variables measure, respectively, access to manufacturing and retail employment in 1982. The form of these potential variables is similar to that used for labor markets, shown in Eq. (11) and (12) below, except that the potential variables are assumed to damp quadratically with distance (Boarnet [6]).

[3]Note that PEBUSEXP, per employee business expenditures, is, to some extent, problematic. It is not clear whether firms care about the aggregate level of expenditures in this category, a per capita measure of those expenditures, or the per employee level that was used here. All those variables and others were tried in the empirical research. The results do not differ according to which variable is used, and no variable performed appreciably better than the variable PEBUSEXP that is reported here. For a further discussion, see Boarnet [4, Chap. 7; 6].

Lastly, the number of farm parcels in a municipality is intended to measure the amount of land that is available for development. For evidence that farm parcels are a good proxy for developable land, see Boarnet [4], Chap. 7, pp. 5–6.

4. EMPIRICAL MODEL

This section addresses the key issues in the modeling effort. Readers who want a more complete description of the empirical model are referred to Boarnet [4, 6].

Equilibrium Relationships

A regression specification for municipal population and employment changes can be based on the equilibrium relationships shown below. Those relationships can be derived from simple bid-rent models of household and firm location (Boarnet [4, Chap. 3; 5]),[4]

$$\mathrm{POP}^*_{i,t} = f\left(T_{i,t}, E_{i,t}, \overline{\mathrm{EMP}}^*_{i,t}\right) \tag{1}$$

$$\mathrm{EMP}^*_{i,t} = g\left(\tau_{i,t}, \varepsilon_{i,t}, \overline{\mathrm{POP}}^*_{i,t}\right), \tag{2}$$

where

$\mathrm{POP}^*_{i,t}$ = equilibrium population
$\mathrm{EMP}^*_{i,t}$ = equilibrium employment
$T_{i,t}$ = measures of transportation access for residents
$\tau_{i,t}$ = measures of transportation access for firms
$E_{i,t}$ = measures of local environmental amenities for residents
$\varepsilon_{i,t}$ = measures of local environmental amenities for firms
$\overline{\mathrm{POP}}^*_{i,t}$ = equilibrium population in the labor market centered on municipality i in time t
$\overline{\mathrm{EMP}}^*_{i,t}$ = equilibrium employment in the labor market centered on municipality i in time t

i subscripts refer to municipalities
t subscripts refer to time.

The equilibrium relationships assume that the simultaneity between population and employment works at the level of a labor market that may not be coterminous with municipalities. Since persons might commute

[4]Note that, since (1) and (2) are derived from bid-rent models, location-specific characteristics are capitalized into land prices. This suggests that land prices could potentially be omitted from the empirical model, if the locational characteristics that drive land prices (and thus population and employment movements) are included in the model. This research did not have land price information, but did have a wealth of locational characteristics which were included in the model. For a further discussion of this, see Boarnet [6].

across municipal boundaries, equilibrium population in a municipality depends on job opportunities in a surrounding labor market, $\overline{\text{EMP}}^*_{i,t}$, and likewise equilibrium municipal employment depends on the surrounding labor market population, $\overline{\text{POP}}^*_{i,t}$. These labor market variables are measured using potential variables, as is discussed later.

A Lagged Adjustment Model of Intrametropolitan Growth

Changes in municipal population and employment levels are assumed to be adjustments toward equilibria. Following work done by Mills and Price [20] and by Carlino and Mills [7], the changes in population and employment are assumed to follow a lagged adjustment model,

$$\text{POP}\Delta_{i,t} = \text{POP}_{i,t} - \text{POP}_{i,t-1} = \lambda_{\text{p}}(\text{POP}^*_{i,t} - \text{POP}_{i,t-1}) \tag{3}$$

$$\text{EMP}\Delta_{i,t} = \text{EMP}_{i,t} - \text{EMP}_{i,t-1} = \lambda_{\text{e}}(\text{EMP}^*_{i,t} - \text{EMP}_{i,t-1}), \tag{4}$$

where

$\text{POP}_{i,t}$ = actual population at i in time period t
$\text{EMP}_{i,t}$ = actual employment at i in time period t
$\text{POP}^*_{i,t}$ = equilibrium population at i in time period t
$\text{EMP}^*_{i,t}$ = equilibrium employment at i in time period t

$\lambda_{\text{p}} \in [0, 1]$, $\lambda_{\text{e}} \in [0, 1]$.

Assuming that equilibrium relationships (1) and (2) are linear, with normally distributed error terms, and substituting those equilibrium relationships into (3) and (4) give the model

$$\text{POP}\Delta_{i,t} = \alpha_0 + T_{i,t}\alpha_1 + E_{i,t}\alpha_2 + \alpha_3\overline{\text{EMP}}^*_{i,t} - \lambda_{\text{p}}\text{POP}_{i,t-1} + u_{i,t} \tag{5}$$

$$\text{EMP}\Delta_{i,t} = \beta_0 + \tau_{i,t}\beta_1 + \varepsilon_{i,t}\beta_2 + \beta_3\overline{\text{POP}}^*_{i,t} - \lambda_{\text{e}}\text{EMP}_{i,t-1} + v_{i,t}, \tag{6}$$

where

$T_{i,t}$ = a vector of transportation access variables for residents
$\tau_{i,t}$ = a vector of transportation access variables for firms
$E_{i,t}$ = a vector of local environmental amenity variables for residents
$\varepsilon_{i,t}$ = a vector of local environmental amenity variables for firms

u and v are normally distributed error terms.

The unobservable equilibrium quantities in (5) and (6), $\overline{\text{POP}}^*_{i,t}$ and $\overline{\text{EMP}}^*_{i,t}$, are related to observable quantities by assuming that the lagged adjustment model given in (3) and (4) also operates at the level of labor markets. This gives the relationships

$$\overline{\mathrm{POP}}^*_{i,t} = \overline{\mathrm{POP}}_{i,t-1} + \frac{1}{\lambda_\mathrm{p}}(\overline{\mathrm{POP}}_{i,t} - \overline{\mathrm{POP}}_{i,t-1}) \tag{7}$$

$$\overline{\mathrm{EMP}}^*_{i,t} = \overline{\mathrm{EMP}}_{i,t-1} + \frac{1}{\lambda_\mathrm{e}}(\overline{\mathrm{EMP}}_{i,t} - \overline{\mathrm{EMP}}_{i,t-1}), \tag{8}$$

where overbars denote labor market values, * denotes an equilibrium value, and other values are actual values.

Substituting (7) and (8) into (5) and (6) gives the model

$$\begin{aligned}\mathrm{POP}\Delta_{i,t} = {}& \alpha_0 + T_{i,t}\alpha_1 + E_{i,t}\alpha_2 + \alpha_3\overline{\mathrm{EMP}}_{i,t-1} \\ &+ \frac{\alpha_3}{\lambda_\mathrm{e}}(\overline{\mathrm{EMP}}_{i,t} - \overline{\mathrm{EMP}}_{i,t-1}) - \lambda_\mathrm{p}\mathrm{POP}_{i,t-1} + u_{i,t}\end{aligned} \tag{9}$$

$$\begin{aligned}\mathrm{EMP}\Delta_{i,t} = {}& \beta_0 + \tau_{i,t}\beta_1 + \varepsilon_{i,t}\beta_2 + \beta_3\overline{\mathrm{POP}}_{i,t-1} \\ &+ \frac{\beta_3}{\lambda_\mathrm{p}}(\overline{\mathrm{POP}}_{i,t} - \overline{\mathrm{POP}}_{i,t-1}) - \lambda_\mathrm{e}\mathrm{EMP}_{i,t-1} + v_{i,t}.\end{aligned} \tag{10}$$

Measurement of the Labor Market Variables

The labor market variables in (9) and (10), $\overline{\mathrm{POP}}_{i,t}$, $\overline{\mathrm{POP}}_{i,t-1}$, $\overline{\mathrm{EMP}}_{i,t}$, and $\overline{EMP}_{i,t-1}$, correspond to commuting relationships. They are measured using potential variables

$$\overline{\mathrm{POP}}_i = \sum_{j\neq i} \frac{\mathrm{POP}_j}{(d_{i,j})^\alpha} + \mathrm{POP}_i \tag{11}$$

$$\overline{\mathrm{EMP}}_i = \sum_{j\neq i} \frac{\mathrm{EMP}_j}{(d_{i,j})^\alpha} + \mathrm{EMP}_i, \tag{12}$$

where $d_{i,j}$ = the distance between municipalities i and j.[5]

The parameter α in (11) and (12) describes how labor market relationships damp with distance. That parameter was estimated from commuting data before the regression analysis for population and employment changes was performed. The technique interprets the potential variables in (11) and (12) as defining commuter sheds and then estimates α from 1979 census journey-to-work data. That technique is described in Boarnet [6].

[5]For municipalities that were less than one mile apart, $d_{i,j}$ was set equal to one to avoid inflating the influence of those municipalities in the potential variable.

Model Identification

The model in (9) and (10) contains independent variables that are possibly endogenous. The labor market population and employment variables are constructed in such a way that municipal values of population and employment change are both endogenous in the estimation. This amounts to using a technique which is similar to two-stage least squares (2SLS), but which allows for the spatial structure of the model, as discussed below. Yet many other independent variables, most notably local fiscal policy and demographic characteristics, are also endogenous to municipal population and employment changes. Thus (9) and (10) cannot be estimated as shown.

For that reason, the T, τ, E, and ε variables in (9) and (10) were lagged to a prior time period to lessen simultaneity problems. This technique was originally suggested by Carlino and Mills [7] and has become common in later work (Palumbo *et al.* [22], Luce [16]). Thus the empirical model regresses population and employment changes from 1980 to 1988 on independent variables measured in 1980:

$$\begin{aligned}\text{POP}\Delta_{i,t} &= \alpha_0 + T_{i,t-1}\alpha_1 + E_{i,t-1}\alpha_2 + \alpha_3\overline{\text{EMP}}_{i,t-1}\\ &\quad + \frac{\alpha_3}{\lambda_e}(\overline{\text{EMP}}_{i,t} - \overline{\text{EMP}}_{i,t-1}) - \lambda_p\text{POP}_{i,t-1} + u_{i,t} \qquad (13)\end{aligned}$$

$$\begin{aligned}\text{EMP}\Delta_{i,t} &= \beta_0 + \tau_{i,t-1}\beta_1 + \varepsilon_{i,t-1}\beta_2 + \beta_3\overline{\text{POP}}_{i,t-1}\\ &\quad + \frac{\beta_3}{\lambda_p}(\overline{\text{POP}}_{i,t} - \overline{\text{POP}}_{i,t-1}) - \lambda_e\text{EMP}_{i,t-1} + v_{i,t}. \qquad (14)\end{aligned}$$

Since lagging the T, E, τ, and ε vectors of independent variables does not guarantee that simultaneity bias has been eliminated, a method of moments test was conducted to examine whether the instruments for the endogenous variables (population and employment change) were orthogonal to the error in the reduced forms (Boarnet [6]). While one rejects the hypothesis of orthogonality for both regressions at the 0.05 level, the test statistic for the employment growth regression is extremely close to the 5% value. (The p value for that statistic is 0.046.) For population growth, the hypothesis of orthogonality is rejected at a much higher level (p value = 0.004.) While one may not be overly concerned about covariance between the instruments for population growth and the regression error in the employment regression, the similar concern in the population growth regression is a more troubling issue.

Still, one should note that the results reported here appear consistently throughout a detailed data analysis that tested many different specifications (Boarnet [5]). Even given the difficulties discussed above, this work provides evidence for the endogeneity of employment changes in a simultaneous model of intrametropolitan population and employment growth.

Spatial Structure of Model

One implication of the potential variables in (11) and (12) is that the model in (13) and (14) can be expressed in matrix notation as[6]

$$\text{POP8880} = \alpha_0 + T_{80}\alpha_1 + E_{80}\alpha_2 + + \alpha_3(\mathbf{I} + \mathbf{W})\text{EMP80} + \frac{\alpha_3}{\lambda_e}(\mathbf{I} + \mathbf{W})\text{EMP8880} + \lambda_p\text{POP80} + u \quad (15)$$

$$\text{EMP8880} = \beta_0 + \tau_{80}\beta_1 + \varepsilon_{80}\beta_2 + \beta_3(\mathbf{I} + \mathbf{W})\text{POP80} + \frac{\beta_3}{\lambda_p}(\mathbf{I} + \mathbf{W})\text{POP8880} - \lambda_e\text{EMP80} + \upsilon, \quad (16)$$

where

POP8880 is a (365 × 1) vector of observations of $\text{POP8880}_i = (\text{POP88}_i - \text{POP80}_i) = \text{POP}\Delta_i$;

EMP8880 is a (365 × 1) vector of observations of $\text{EMP8880}_i = (\text{EMP88}_i - \text{EMP80}_i) = \text{EMP}\Delta_i$;

I is a (365 × 365) identity matrix;

W is a (365 × 365) matrix of weights, where each element is $1/(d_{ij})^\alpha$, as was used to derive the potential variables;

POP80 is a (365 × 1) vector of observations of POP80_i, which is municipal population in 1980;

EMP80 is a (365 × 1) vector of observations of EMP80_i, which is municipal employment in 1980;

POP88_i and EMP88_i are, respectively, population and employment in municipality i in 1988;

the subscript i refers to municipalities and the subscript $t - 1$ is denoted by 80 for the year 1980.

For simplicity, note that (15) and (16) can be written as[7]

$$\text{POP8880} = \rho_1(\mathbf{I} + \mathbf{W})\text{EMP8880} + X_1\beta_1 + u_1 \quad (17)$$

$$\text{EMP8880} = \rho_2(\mathbf{I} + \mathbf{W})\text{POP8880} + X_2\beta_2 + u_2, \quad (18)$$

[6]Note that the spatial lag of a variable does not include the municipality's own value of that variable, since $d_{i,i} = 0$. Thus variables that are summed over all municipalities must be written as the municipal value plus the spatial lag. For example, $\overline{\text{EMP}}_{i,80} = \mathbf{W}(\text{EMP80}) + \text{EMP80}_i$.

[7]All the variables measured in 1980, including municipal population and employment (POP80 and EMP80), are assumed to be either exogenous or predetermined. Thus all 1980 variables appear in x_1 or x_2 below.

where X_1 and X_2 are matrices of the exogenous variables in (15) and (16), u_1 and u_2 are normally distributed errors, $\rho_1 = \alpha_3/\lambda_e$, and $\rho_2 = \beta_3/\lambda_p$.

The variables **WPOP8880** and **WEMP8880** are spatial lags of the dependent variables. (For a definition and discussion of the concept of a spatial lag, see Anselin [3, Chap. 3].) Since least squares yields biased and inconsistent estimates when spatial lags of dependent variables appear on the right-hand side (Anselin [2, 3]), traditional two-stage least squares was not used to estimate (17) and (18). Instead, an instrumental variables technique was used that treats POP8880, EMP8880, and the spatial lags of both those variables as endogenous. (This technique was suggested by Anselin [3].) In particular, POP8880 and EMP8880 were instrumented by the exogenous variables in X_1 and X_2. Following Anselin [2, pp. 83–86; and 3, pp. 81–86], the resulting instrumental variable (IV) estimator is

$$\hat{\delta}_1 = (Z_1^{*\prime} Z_1)^{-1}(Z_1^{*\prime}\text{POP8880}), \tag{19}$$

where

$$\begin{aligned}
\delta_1' &= (\rho_1 | \beta_1') \\
Z_1 &= ((\mathbf{I} + \mathbf{W})\text{EMP8880} | X_1) \\
Z_1^* &= \left((\mathbf{I} + \mathbf{W})\widehat{\text{EMP8880}} | X_1\right) = ((\mathbf{I} + \mathbf{W}) P_x \text{EMP8880} | X_1) \\
P_X &= X(X'X)^{-1}X' \\
X &= (X_1 | X_2),
\end{aligned}$$

and

$$\hat{\delta}_2 = (Z_2^{*\prime} Z_2)^{-1}(Z_2^{*\prime}\text{EMP8880}), \tag{20}$$

where

$$\begin{aligned}
\delta_2' &= (\rho_2 | \beta_2') \\
Z_2 &= ((\mathbf{I} + \mathbf{W})\text{POP8880} | X_2) \\
Z_2^* &= \left((\mathbf{I} + \mathbf{W})\widehat{\text{POP8880}} | X_2\right) = ((\mathbf{I} + \mathbf{W}) P_x \text{POP8880} | X_2) \\
P_X &= X(X'X)^{-1}X' \\
X &= (X_1 | X_2).
\end{aligned}$$

After (19) and (20) were used to estimate the parameters in (17) and (18), a Moran's I test using the regression residuals showed that the errors in (17) and (18) are spatially correlated (Boarnet [5]). Under these conditions, the standard errors for the estimators shown in (19) and (20) will be biased and inconsistent (Anselin [2, pp. 120–122; 3, p. 59]). For that reason, the model in (17) and (18) was estimated with first-order spatially autoregressive errors.

Considering just the equation in (17), the error term was assumed to be

$$u_1 = \theta_1 \mathbf{W} u_1 + \varepsilon_1 \tag{21}$$

or

$$u_1 = (I - \theta_1 \mathbf{W})^{-1} \varepsilon_1 \tag{22}$$

with $\varepsilon_1 \sim N(0, \sigma_1^2 I)$.

Premultiplying (17) by the matrix $\mathbf{A}_1$, where $\mathbf{A}_1 = (\mathbf{I} - \theta_1 \mathbf{W})$, gives an equation with spherical errors,

$$\mathbf{A}_1 \text{POP8880} = \mathbf{A}_1 Z_1 \delta_1 + \varepsilon_1 \tag{23}$$

where POP8880, Z_1, and δ_1 are as defined above.

As before, EMP8880 was instrumented in $(\mathbf{I} + \mathbf{W})$ EMP8880. An instrumental variables estimator for (23) is

$$\hat{\delta}_1 = (Z_1^{*\prime} \mathbf{A}_1' \mathbf{A}_1 Z_1)^{-1} (Z_1^{*\prime} \mathbf{A}_1' \mathbf{A}_1 \text{POP8880}), \tag{24}$$

where

$$Z_1^* = \left((\mathbf{I} + \mathbf{W})\widehat{\text{EMP8880}} | X_1\right) = \left((\mathbf{I} + \mathbf{W}) P_x \text{EMP8880} | X_1\right)$$

$$X = (X_1 | X_2)$$

$$P_x = X(X'X)^{-1} X'$$

$$\mathbf{A}_1 = (I + \theta_1 \mathbf{W}).$$

Since the matrix $\mathbf{A}_1$ contains the parameter θ_1, the parameters must be estimated using maximum likelihood (Anselin [2, pp. 41–44 and pp. 142–144]). A grid search over the allowable values of θ_1 (from -1 to 1) was used. The log-likelihood function for (23) is derived, and the grid search is described in more detail in Boarnet [5].

The employment growth regression shown in (18) also is assumed to have a first-order spatially autoregressive error. The maximum likelihood estimator for the employment growth equation is analogous to the population growth estimator shown in (24). The asymptotic variance of the estimator in (24) is

$$\text{avar}(\hat{\delta}_1) = \sigma_1^2 (Z_1^{*\prime} \mathbf{A}_1' \mathbf{A}_1 Z_1)^{-1} (Z_1^{*\prime} \mathbf{A}_1' \mathbf{A}_1 Z_1^*) (Z_1' \mathbf{A}_1' \mathbf{A}_1 Z_1^*)^{-1}, \quad (25)$$

which is obtained by simplifying the expression for $E[(\delta_1 - \hat{\delta}_1)(\delta_1 - \hat{\delta}_1)']$. The asymptotic variance for the employment growth estimator is analogous.

5. RESULTS

The results of the maximum likelihood estimation are shown in Table 1. The population growth estimator is as defined in (24), with asymptotic variance given by (25), and analogously for employment growth. While this paper does not focus on all the coefficient estimates, readers might note that the signs of most of the significant coefficients in Table 1 are in agreement with theory. The notable exception in the employment growth regression is the PRPRAT80 variable, which is significantly positive in the employment growth regression. Elsewhere (Boarnet [6]), I discuss that the coefficient on that variable should not be interpreted to mean that higher property crime rates cause municipal employment growth. Instead, that coefficient probably represents some of the simultaneity between economic activity and property crime rates. Further note that the opposite signs on the agglomeration economy variables, TOTMAN82 and TOTRET82, are consistent with the shift out of manufacturing and into service sector employment in this region. In such a situation, municipalities with agglomeration benefits for manufacturing (measured by TOTMAN82) might actually lose jobs to municipalities with agglomeration benefits in faster growing retail and related sectors (measured by TOTRET82). For a further discussion of the expected signs of the coefficients and the overall performance of the empirical model, see Boarnet [6].

Municipal population and employment changes are simultaneous at the level of labor markets. To examine the simultaneity of those variables, one should examine the coefficients on $(\mathbf{I} + \mathbf{W})$ EMP8880 in the population growth regression and $(\mathbf{I} + \mathbf{W})$ POP8880 in the employment growth

TABLE 1
Results of the Empirical Model

	POP8880		EMP8880
NYCDIST	88.64	NYCDIST	−102.45
	(1.38)		(−1.94)
NYCDSTSQ	−1.65	NYCDSTSQ	0.99
	(−1.90)		(1.46)
ANYHIWAY	643.56†	ANYHIWAY	789.43†
	(3.22)		(3.24)
LANDAR80	72.05†	NJTRNSIT	753.69†
	(8.36)		(2.84)
PRBLCK80	2646.38	LANDAR80	52.04†
	(1.79)		(3.47)
PRHISP80	4322.04*	VIORAT80	−266.73†
	(2.30)		(−5.01)
POVRAT80	−7725.97	PRPRAT80	17.24†
	(−1.89)		(2.59)
VIORAT80	−115.99*	FRMPAR80	−2.60*
	(−2.11)		(−2.19)
PRPRAT80	10.01	PEBUSEXP	−0.23
	(1.86)		(−0.88)
HOUPRE40	−1541.88*	EQZDTX80	45.69
	(−2.37)		(0.30)
PCNECEXP	2.92	TOTMAN82	−0.25†
	(1.33)		(−5.16)
PCTAX80	−0.99	TOTRET82	0.61†
	(−1.88)		(6.65)
TOTEMP80	−0.006	TOTPOP80	−0.001
	(−0.85)		(−0.86)
(**I** + **W**) EMP8880[a]	0.01	(**I** + **W**) POP8880[a]	0.10†
	(0.34)		(3.91)
POP80	−0.02†	EMP80	0.02
	(−4.40)		(0.81)
INTERCEPT	699.95	INTERCEPT	789.31
	(0.29)		(0.54)
N	358	N	358
log L	−2819.54	log L	−2913.63
θ_1	0.13	θ_2	−0.05

Note. θ_1 and θ_2 are the parameters of spatial autoregression in the error term. t statistics in parentheses. *Significant at the 0.5 level. †Significant at the 0.01 level. [a]Instrumented.

regression. (**I** + **W**) EMP8880 is the spatial lag of EMP8880, which is the change in municipal employment from 1980 to 1988. Stated equivalently, (**I** + **W**) EMP8880 is a vector whose elements are the change in employment in the labor market that is centered on each municipality. Likewise, the vector (**I** + **W**) POP8880 gives the change in population in the labor market that is centered on each municipality.

From examining the coefficients on (**I** + **W**) EMP8880 and (**I** + **W**) POP8880 in Table 1, we can see that municipal population changes do not depend on changes in employment in the surrounding labor market, but municipal employment changes depend on changes in population in the surrounding labor market. This reproduces Steinnes' [24] finding that employment follows population more than vice versa. Furthermore, it reproduces that finding using detailed observations on locations within one urban area.

This suggests that, during the 1980s, employment changes within the northern New Jersey area were endogenous to labor market population changes, but population changes were relatively independent of surrounding labor market employment changes. Given these results, the assumption that employment location is exogenous to residential location might be inappropriate.

6. CONCLUSION

This paper has presented a test of the monocentric assumption that intrametropolitan employment location is largely exogenous to intrametropolitan population location. The results, based on data from northern New Jersey in the 1980s, suggest that employment changes within an urban area depend on population changes in a surrounding labor market. This suggests that the evolving pattern of metropolitan employment location is endogenous to population changes within an urban area.

This is broadly consistent the findings of other authors who have studied modern urban development. Many of those authors have discussed how the urban form appeared to markedly change during 1980s (See, e.g., Cervero [8], Garreau [11], Giuliano and Small [12].) The common thread in all these writings is the focus on suburban employment centers. Many persons, including those cited just above, have suggested that the trend toward large employment centers in suburban areas constitutes an important departure from past patterns of urban development. To the extent that is true, a focus on employment location is vital in understanding American urban areas. For reasons already stated, the monocentric assumption of exogenous employment location leaves that tradition poorly suited to study endogenous employment location. This suggests that urban economic models should give redoubled attention to the problem of employment location within metropolitan areas.

APPENDIX: VARIABLE NAMES

Dependent Variables

Variable name	Description	Source
POP8880	Change in municipal population from 1980 to 1988 (POP88-POP80)	NJ Department of Community Affairs (NJDCA) Annual Reports
EMP8880	Change in municipal private sector employment, 1980 to 1988 (EMP88-EMP80)	NJ Department of Labor Covered Employment by Municipality, 1980 and 1988

Independent Variables

Variable name	Description	Source
	Accessibility variables for population and employment, T and τ	
ANYHIWAY	Dummy variable = 1 if municipality lies on any one of I78, I80, I195, I287, I280, limited access portion of I95, New Jersey Turnpike, Garden State Parkway, US1, US9, US46, US202, US206	Various New Jersey roadmaps
NJTRNSIT	Dummy variable = 1 if municipality has a New Jersey Transit commuter rail station	New Jersey Transit schedules
	Amenity variables for population, E	
PRBLCK80	Proportion of municipal population that is Black, 1980	1980 Census of Population
PRHISP80	Proportion of municipal population that is Hispanic, 1980	1980 Census of Population
POVRAT80	Municipal poverty rate (as a proportion), 1980	1980 Census of Population
PCTAX80	per capital local tax payments, 1980 (includes all overlying jurisdictions other than state and federal)	NJDCA 1980 Annual Report
PCNECEXP	1980 per capita municipal expenditures on fire departments, police, streets and drainage, sewage, garbage collection, and courts	NJDCA 1980 Annual Report
VIORAT80	violent crimes per 1000 municipality residents, 1980	New Jersey Uniform Crime Reporting Program, 1980
PRPRAT80	property crimes per 1000 munipality residents, 1980	New Jersey Uniform Crime Reporting Program, 1980
HOUPRE40	proportion of 1980 municipality housing stock built before 1940	1980 Census of Population and Housing
NYCDIST	distance in miles from the municipality to the geographic centroid of Manhattan Island	Calculated using Atlas Draw mapping software
NYCDSTSQ	NYCDIST squared	

Independent Variables—Continued

Variable name	Description	Source
	Amenity variables for employment, ε	
TOTMAN82	Potential variable measuring manufacturing employment agglomeration in 1982 (formula shown below):	New Jersey Employment and Wages, Annual Municipality Report, New Jersey Department of Labor (NJDOL)

$$\text{TOTMAN82}_i = \sum_{j \neq i} \frac{\text{MANU}_{j,1982}}{(d_{i,j})^2} + \text{MANU}_{i,82},$$

where MANU_i = manufacturing employment in municipality i
$d_{i,j}$ = distance in miles from i to j

Variable name	Description	Source
TOTRET82	Potential variable measuring retail employment agglomeration, 1982 (same form as for TOTMAN82)	NJDOL 1982 Annual Municipality Report
EQZDTX80	Equalized property tax rate, 1980 (includes all overlying jurisdictions other than state and federal)	NJDCA 1980 Annual Report
PEBUSEXP	Per employee expenditures on streets and drainage and sewage	NJDCA 1980 Annual Report
FRMPAR80	Number of farm property parcels in the municipality, 1980	NJDCA 1980 Annual Report
NYCDIST, NYCDSTSQ, VIORAT80, and PRPRAT80 as defined above		
	Labor market variables	
TOTPOP80	Potential variable for population, 1980	NJDCA 1980 Annual Report

$$\sum_{j \neq i} \frac{\text{POP}_{j,1980}}{(d_{i,j})^{\alpha}} + \text{POP}_{i,1980}$$

Variable name	Description	Source
TOTEMP80	Potential variable for employment,	NJDOL covered employment by municipality 1980

$$\sum_{j \neq i} \frac{\text{EMP}_{j,1980}}{(d_{i,j})^{\alpha}} + \text{EMP}_{i,1980}$$

Variable name	Description	Source
	Other variables	
POP80	Municipal population in 1980	NJDCA 1980 Annual Report
EMP80	Municipal private sector employment in 1980	NJDOL covered employment by municipality, 1980
LANDAR80	Municipality land area in square miles, 1980	NJDCA 1980 Annual Report

REFERENCES

1. W. Alonso, "Location and Land Use: Toward a General Theory of Land Rent," Harvard Univ. Press, Cambridge, MA (1964).
2. L. Anselin, "Estimation Methods for Spatial Autoregressive Structures: A Study in Spatial Econometrics," Cornell University Program in Urban and Regional Studies, Ithaca, NY (1980).
3. L. Anselin, "Spatial Econometrics: Methods and Models," Kluwer Academic, Dordrecht, The Netherlands (1988).
4. M. G. Boarnet, Intra-metropolitan growth patterns: The nature and causes of population and employment changes within an urban area, unpublished Ph.D. dissertation, Princeton University (1992).
5. M. G. Boarnet, An empirical model of intrametropolitan population and employment growth, working paper, University of California, Irvine (1992).
6. M. G. Boarnet, An empirical model of intrametropolitan population and employment growth, *Papers in Regional Science: The Journal of the RSAI*, **73**, forthcoming (1994).
7. G. A. Carlino and E. S. Mills, The determinants of county growth, *Journal of Regional Science*, **27**, 39–54 (1987).
8. R. Cervero, Jobs–housing balancing and regional mobility, *Journal of the American Planning Association*, **55**, 136–150 (1989).
9. M. L. Cropper and P. L. Gordon, Wasteful commuting: A reexamination, *Journal of Urban Economics*, **29**, 2–13 (1991).
10. M. Fujita, Spatial patterns of residential development, *Journal of Urban Economics*, **12**, 22–52 (1982).
11. J. Garreau, "Edge City: Life on the New Frontier," Doubleday, New York (1991).
12. G. Giuliano and K. A. Small, Subcenters in the Los Angeles region, *Regional Science and Urban Economics*, **21**, 163–182 (1991).
13. W. N. Grubb, The flight to the suburbs of population and employment, 1960–1970, *Journal of Urban Economics*, **11**, 348–367 (1982).
14. B. W. Hamilton, Wasteful commuting, *Journal of Political Economy*, **90**, 1035–1053 (1982).
15. B. W. Hamilton, Wasteful commuting, again, *Journal of Political Economy*, **97**, 1497–1504 (1989).
16. T. F. Luce, Jr., Local taxes, public services, and the intrametropolitan location of firms and households, working paper, University of Minnesota (1990).
17. J. F. McDonald, The identification of urban employment subcenters, *Journal of Urban Economics*, **21**, 242–258 (1987).
18. E. S. Mills, Urban density functions, *Urban Studies*, **7**, 5–20 (1970).
19. E. S. Mills, "Studies in the Structure of the Urban Economy," Johns Hopkins Univ. Press, Baltimore, MD (1972).
20. E. S. Mills and R. Price, Metropolitan suburbanization and central city problems, *Journal of Urban Economics*, **15**, 1–17.
21. R. Muth, "Cities and Housing," Univ. of Chicago Press, Chicago, IL (1969).
22. G. Palumbo, S. Sacks, and M. Wasylenko, Population decentralization within metropolitan areas: 1970–1980, *Journal of Urban Economics*, **27**, 151–167 (1990).
23. K. A. Small and S. Song, "Wasteful" commuting: A resolution, *Journal of Political Economy*, **100**, 888–898 (1992).
24. D. N. Steinnes, Causality and intraurban location, *Journal of Urban Economics*, **4**, 69–79 (1977).
25. D. N. Steinnes and W. D. Fisher, An econometric model of intraurban location, *Journal of Regional Science*, **14**, 65–80 (1974).

26. W. C. Wheaton, Monocentric models of urban land use, *in* "Current Issues in Urban Economics" (P. Mieszkowski and M. Straszheim, Eds.), Johns Hopkins Univ. Press, Baltimore, MD (1979).
27. W. C. Wheaton, Urban residential growth under perfect foresight, *Journal of Urban Economics*, **12**, 1–21 (1982).
28. M. J. White, Firm suburbanization and urban subcenters, *Journal of Urban Economics*, **3**, 323–343 (1976).
29. M. J. White, Urban commuting journeys are not "wasteful", *Journal of Political Economy*, **96**, 1097–1110 (1988).
30. K. F. Wieand, An extension of the monocentric urban spatial equilibrium model to a multicenter setting: The case of the two-center city, *Journal of Urban Economics*, **21**, 259–271 (1987).
31. J. Yinger, City and suburb: Urban models with more than one employment center, *Journal of Urban Economics*, **31**, 181–205 (1992).

[6]

JOURNAL OF URBAN ECONOMICS **32**, 70–91 (1992)

Intraurban Wage Gradients: Evidence by Race, Gender, Occupational Class, and Sector

KEITH R. IHLANFELDT*

Policy Research Center, Georgia State University, Atlanta, Georgia 30303

Received April 19, 1990; revised December 17, 1990

A general functional form is used to estimate intraurban wage gradients for various groups of workers with 1980 data from the Philadelphia, Detroit, and Boston metropolitan areas. As predicted by the standard monocentric model of urban land use, the following results are obtained for most groups of white workers: negative and statistically significant wage gradients, steeper wage gradients for higher wage earners, and an increase in the steepness of wage gradients as the CBD is approached. Positive wage gradients are not found for black workers, despite the fact that suburban employers hire large numbers of these workers who reside within the central city. This result is taken as support for the hypothesis that blacks have been disadvantaged by job suburbanization and continued housing market segregation. © 1992 Academic Press, Inc.

I. INTRODUCTION

The existence of intraurban wage gradients is of interest for several reasons. First, systematic spatial variation in wage rates within urban areas will influence the location of economic activity and the commuting patterns and transportation demands of urban workers. Second, because negative wage gradients are predicted by the standard monocentric model of urban land use, the existence of such gradients is a confirmation of this model. Third, the decentralization of lower-skilled jobs, combined with the surburban residential exclusion of low-income households, may cause a positive wage gradient for these jobs. If this is the case, and if housing market discrimination restricts the relative ability of blacks to offer their labor supply to surburban employers, then at least part of the racial difference in earnings can be attributed to housing segregation. Finally, the existence of wage gradients has important implications for studies that make earnings comparisons among different groups of workers. With few exceptions, these studies have treated intraurban variation in wage rates as part of the residual. However, this will lead to biased estimates if wage gradients exist, because the work locations of different groups of workers,

*The author thanks the Research Committee, College of Business Administration, Georgia State University, for partial support for this project. Comments from Julie Hotchkiss, Jorge Martinez, David Sjoquist, and an anonymous referee improved the manuscript.

0094-1190/92 $5.00

for which earnings comparisons are frequently made, are not randomly distributed within urban areas [13].

A number of studies have investigated differences in the average wage paid across large intraurban work areas, where these areas are most frequently the central city and the surburban ring [3, 6, 13, 27, 29–31, 34].[1] Other studies, while not actually estimating wage gradients, have theoretically derived and empirically implemented methodologies which test whether or not wage gradients exist [20, 21]. The only study that has estimated intraurban wage gradients is by Eberts [4]. He found negative and statistically significant relationships between the wage rate and the airline distance between the location of the job and the CBD for four or five groups of municipal public employees. Eberts believes that his results for public sector labor markets can be used to infer characteristics of intraurban private sector labor markets, since evidence he cites suggests that there is considerable mobility between public and private sector jobs. However, the pattern of unionization, and the laws governing collective bargaining, dispute resolution, and wage determination may be sufficiently different between the public and private labor markets to cause wage gradients to differ. It is, therefore, important to estimate separate gradients for private and public employees. An additional limitation of Eberts' analysis is that his data did not enable him to include any worker productivity variables in his equations other than the number of hours worked per week. There is, therefore, a real possibility that the omission of relevant variables biased his results.

The purpose of this paper is to present evidence obtained from the 1980 Public-Use Microdata Sample (PUMS) for the Philadelphia, Detroit, and Boston MSAs on the existence, shape, and slope of intraurban wage gradients. The PUMS contains a sufficient number of observations to estimate separate gradients for groups of workers categorized by occupation, gender, race, and sector (private vs public). It was therefore possible to investigate for the first time a number of hypotheses regarding differences in wage gradients between blacks and whites, men and women, and among different occupational groups.

In the following section, hypotheses regarding intraurban wage gradients are reviewed. Section III contains a comparison for each of the three metropolitan areas of work site and workers' residential locations for various occupational classes. These comparisons set the stage for the empirical work presented in Sections IV and V, which provide a descrip-

[1]These studies should not be confused with those that have made earnings comparisons between central-city and suburban residents [26, 28, 33]. The purpose of the latter studies has been to investigate the effect of residential location on earnings and not to provide evidence on the spatial variation in wage rates within urban areas.

tion of the estimated equations and a discussion of the results, respectively. The conclusions of the paper are stated in Section VI.

II. HYPOTHESES

A negative relationship between the price per unit of housing services and distance from the CBD (i.e., a declining housing price gradient) is predicted by the standard urban land use model. This prediction has generally been supported by studies that have carefully controlled for other determinants of the price of housing (e.g., [14, 22, 25]), including one that used data from the Philadelphia metropolitan area [5], which is one of the areas studied in the present paper. If the metropolitan labor market conforms to the conditions required for perfect competition, in particular perfect mobility, a declining housing price gradient implies that the wage gradient must also be negative. Wage rates must be higher at work sites closer to the CBD to compensate workers for the higher cost of closer-in housing or for the higher transportation cost incurred by commuting from more distant residential locations where housing costs are lower. Formally, the condition that must be satisfied in order for workers to be indifferent to their work location is that the decline in the wage rate from working one mile farther from the CBD must be equal to the savings in commuting costs, i.e.,

$$\frac{\partial w(k)}{\partial k} = -0.125t(k), \tag{1}$$

where w is the hourly wage rate, k is the number of miles that the job is located from the CBD, and t is the cost of one-mile of round-trip commuting.[2] The multiplication of $t(k)$ by 0.125 assumes that the cost of commuting is amortized over an eight-hour workday.

In addition to the prediction that wage gradients have negative slope, additional hypotheses can be deduced by making reasonable assumptions regarding the components of $t(k)$. Assume that commuting speed is $1/s$ miles per hour and that speed declines as the CBD is approached because congestion increases [24]. Also assume that the value of one hour of travel time is equal to some constant fraction, a, of the hourly wage rate [1, 16]. The value of $t(k)$ can therefore be expressed as

$$t(k) = 2(s(k) \cdot a \cdot w(k) + m), \tag{2}$$

where out-of-pocket commuting cost is m dollars per mile. Women may value their travel time at a different fraction of the wage rate than men.

[2] For a formal derivation of this condition, see White [35].

While reliable empirical evidence on this issue does not exist, Madden [19] has shown that if market goods and household-produced goods are not easily substitutable and if women produce more household goods than men, women will value their travel time at a higher fraction of the wage rate. This will cause wage gradients to be steeper for women than for men if a finite elasticity of substitution exists between equally skilled men and women workers.

To determine the rate of change in the wage gradient as distance to the CBD increases, (2) is substituted into (1) and then differentiated with respect to k,

$$\frac{\partial w_k(k)}{\partial k} = -0.25 \cdot s(k) \cdot w_k - 0.25 \cdot s_k \cdot a \cdot w(k), \tag{3}$$

where a subscript indicates a partial derivative. Since the sign of (3) is positive, wage gradients will increase at an increasing rate as the CBD is approached. There are two reasons for this: (1) the first term on the right-hand side of (3) indicates that the wage rate increase per mile is larger closer in because travel time is more valuable for workers with higher-paying jobs working closer to the CBD, and (2) the second term on the right-hand side of (3) indicates that the increase is also larger closer in because the time necessary to travel another mile is higher because of greater traffic congestion.

Finally, substituting (2) into (1) and differentiating with respect to the wage rate indicates that gradients will be steeper for higher-wage workers:

$$\frac{\partial w_k(k)}{\partial w(k)} = -0.25 \cdot a \cdot s(k). \tag{4}$$

Equation (4) states that the increase in the steepness of the wage gradient as the wage rate increases at a particular distance from the CBD is directly related to the opportunity cost of traveling an additional mile.[3]

[3]The prediction that the wage gradient will be steeper for higher-wage workers can also be obtained by assuming that higher-wage workers have a stronger preference to live farther from the city center. To illustrate, let the random variable D_i represent the monetary equivalent of the disutility from commuting by the ith worker. For simplicity assume that there are only two work locations, namely, the central city and the suburbs. As the wage rate in the central city rises relative to the wage rate in the suburbs, workers with the lowest D_i will be the first to commute from the suburbs to the central city. As the number of workers who commute from the suburbs to the central city rises, a higher D_i value on the distribution function $[F(D_i)]$ is reached. In equilibrium, the marginal worker is indifferent to working in either the central city or the suburbs. Hence, the city wage (W_c) and the suburban wage (W_s) will differ by the D_i of the marginal worker (D_m): $W_s + D_m(F(D_i), M) = W_c$. The magnitude of D_m will depend on the distribution function and the level of import demand (M) for

In summary, four testable hypotheses regarding intraurban wage gradients are obtained from the standard urban land use model: (1) wage gradients will be negatively sloped; (2) wage gradients will be steeper for women than for men; (3) wage gradients will not be linear, but will instead increase in steepness as the distance to the CBD declines; and (4) wage gradients will be steeper for higher-wage workers.

The urban land use model assumes that locational choices are unconstrained. Workers therefore maximize their utility by selecting a residential location that is farther from the CBD than their job location and commute inward toward the CBD. The assumption of unconstrained residential location may be untenable in the case of unskilled or low-skilled workers or in the case of black workers. These workers are frequently excluded from suburban neighborhoods as the result of fiscal zoning, the racial or class prejudice of housing suppliers, and the necessity for lower income households to purchase less expensive, filtered-down housing within the central city. If these exclusions are sufficiently strong, as White [35–37] has noted, a suburban firm located at some distance, k', may find an insufficient labor supply farther out than the firm itself that is willing to work for the $w(k')$ implied by the standard model. At this wage, the firm's labor demand exceeds supply. To satisfy its labor requirements, this firm will have to raise wages in order to induce workers who live beyond a distance k_L to outcommute, where $k_L < k'$. Firms at distances greater than k' will have to pay correspondingly higher wage rates to compensate outcommuters for their longer commutes. Hence, beyond k_L the wage gradient changes in slope from negative to positive. Straszheim [30, 31] has suggested that for black workers the wage gradient may be positive throughout the metropolitan area because these workers remain concentrated in ghettos located within or close to the CBD. In the context of White's model, this equates to a k' that is equal to zero. Straszheim's model predicts that wage gradients for blacks will rise and those for whites will decline. These predictions are based on the assumption that black workers outcommute and white workers incommute. It is also necessary to assume that a finite elasticity of substitution exists between equally skilled black and white workers. Wage gradients can differ only between blacks and whites if race is a factor in hiring decisions.

---

suburban workers by central city employers. If higher-wage workers have a stronger preference to live in the suburbs, M will be larger for them, *ceteris paribus*, which implies a steeper wage gradient. The assumption that higher-wage workers place a higher value on their commuting time implies that for them $F(D_i)$ is flatter. Hence, differences in both M and $F(D_i)$ between higher- and lower-wage workers suggest that the slope of the wage gradient will be inversely related to the wage rate.

In summary, in the absence of outcommuting caused by labor shortages that may arise at some distance from the CBD, we would expect the negative wage gradients predicted by the standard urban land use model. However, if labor shortages for certain groups of workers do exist, the models of White and Straszheim suggest that positive gradients will prevail, at least beyond some distance from the CBD. In the next section, evidence is presented on whether or not there are shortages of resident labor for particular types of jobs within the suburbs of Philadelphia, Detroit, and Boston.

III. AN OVERVIEW OF THE SPATIAL CHARACTERISTICS OF THE PHILADELPHIA, DETROIT, AND BOSTON LABOR MARKETS

For a small number of large metropolitan areas, the 1980 PUMS identifies the job and residential locations of individual workers for sub-county areas. The three metropolitan areas selected for this study are those for which at least 15 work areas are identified on the Sample A (2.5%) tapes. Wage gradients for MSAs with less than 15 work areas could not be reliably estimated using the technique described below, while Sample B (0.5%) provided too few observations to study differences in wage gradients among the various groups.[4]

Twenty-seven work areas are identified for Philadelphia, 25 for Detroit, and 18 for Boston. For each MSA, the CBD and the rest of the central city constitute separate work locations. Residential location is identified for the same areas as work location, except the CBD is not separately identified within the central city. A unique characteristic of the Philadelphia PUMS is that the same work areas and residential areas are identified for both the A and B samples. Since these samples are independently drawn, there is a negligible overlap between them [32]. They were therefore combined to form a 3% sample.

The areas identified were used to divide each MSA into the central city, inner suburban ring, middle suburban ring, and outer suburban ring. For each of these divisions, the number of jobs within a particular occupational class located there was divided by the number of workers within that occupational class who reside there to form the "import ratio." For Philadelphia and Detroit, separate import ratios were computed for blacks and whites. Because of the relatively small number of blacks living in

[4]The A and B samples of the PUMS are actually 5 and 1% samples, respectively. However, as a cost-saving measure the Census Bureau only recorded work location for one-half of these samples. Observations including work location information constitute random subsamples of the total files.

Boston, import ratios (and wage gradients) for this MSA were computed only for white workers. An import ratio greater than (less than) one indicates that the area is a net importer (net exporter) of workers within the designated occupational/racial class.

In the context of the standard urban land use model, worker's residential locations are more decentralized than their job locations. That is, the employment density gradient is steeper than the population density gradient. This implies that the magnitude of the import ratio will systematically decline for the four rings identified as the distance from the CBD increases.

As indicated in Table 1, for all three MSAs, the import ratios for white workers are lower in the suburbs than within the central city and also tend to be lower in the outer than in the inner suburbs. Import ratios are greater than one for the central city, and generally smaller than one for each of the suburban rings. The central city is therefore a net importer of suburban workers and the basic commuting direction is toward the CBD. In light of this evidence, the expectation is that negative wage gradients exist for white workers in all seven occupational classes working in all three metropolitan areas.

The import ratios for blacks strongly contrast to those computed for whites. In Philadelphia, black import ratios are highest within the inner suburban ring for all seven occupational classes. For the professional and managerial, sales, and administrative support occupational classes, import ratios are larger than one for both the central city and the inner suburban ring and less than one for the middle and outer suburban rings. This indicates that for these groups, commuting tends to be toward the CBD as implied by the standard model. Hence, for these groups, negative wage gradients are also expected. For the remaining four occupations—craftsmen, service workers, operatives, and laborers—central city import ratios for Philadelphia blacks are less than one, which indicates that the central city is a net exporter of these workers to the suburbs. This is further illustrated by the residential locations of black workers in these occupations who work within the inner suburban ring: 44% live within the inner ring, 41% live within the central city, and the other 15% are located in the middle and outer suburban rings. Since for these groups, suburban employers rely heavily on outcommuters from the central city, positive wage gradients are expected.

As was true for Philadelphia, import ratios for Detroit blacks are highest within the inner suburban ring for all seven occupational classes. However, in the case of Detroit, import ratios are less than one within the central city for blacks in both white-collar and blue-collar occupations. For all of the suburban rings and for all occupational classes, import ratios are greater than one. This indicates that in Detroit, the basic commuting

TABLE 1
Import Ratios (Jobs ÷ Workers) by Area, Race, and Occupation

	Central city	Inner ring	Middle ring	Outer ring
Philadelphia				
Whites				
Professional and managerial	1.61	0.70	0.61	0.50
Sales	1.11	0.84	0.68	0.52
Administrative support	1.33	0.94	0.78	0.65
Craftsmen	1.36	0.94	0.77	0.73
Service	1.06	1.03	0.98	0.77
Operatives	1.19	0.97	0.85	0.77
Laborers	1.09	1.13	0.88	0.75
Blacks				
Professional and managerial	1.08	1.38	0.52	0.45
Sales	1.00	1.15	0.93	0.53
Administrative support	1.01	1.16	0.65	0.86
Craftsmen	0.86	1.91	0.82	0.80
Service	0.87	1.63	1.00	0.98
Operatives	0.86	1.58	0.85	1.27
Laborers	0.87	1.29	1.08	1.00
Detroit				
Whites				
Professional and managerial	2.07	1.12	0.62	0.78
Sales	1.47	1.00	0.90	0.86
Administrative support	1.80	0.97	0.76	0.81
Craftsmen	2.17	0.99	0.74	0.81
Service	1.18	0.97	0.92	1.01
Operatives	1.59	0.84	0.97	0.91
Laborers	1.31	0.88	0.93	1.04
Blacks				
Professional and managerial	0.89	1.64	1.15	2.26
Sales	0.76	3.22	1.76	1.92
Administrative support	0.85	3.04	1.31	1.70
Craftsmen	0.67	4.90	1.70	1.83
Service	0.79	4.90	1.57	1.90
Operatives	0.60	9.33	2.90	2.01
Laborers	0.71	5.66	1.23	2.57
Boston				
Whites				
Professional and managerial	2.39	0.80	0.77	0.57
Sales	1.97	0.90	0.82	0.81
Administrative support	2.19	0.69	0.82	0.74
Craftsmen	2.04	0.95	0.75	0.82
Service	1.34	0.89	0.93	0.94
Operatives	1.61	0.91	0.89	0.87
Laborers	1.69	0.82	1.00	0.88

direction of blacks is outward from the central city regardless of their occupational class. Only positive wage gradients are therefore expected for blacks living in the Detroit metropolitan area.

In this section, the locations of jobs relative to the locations of worker residences were described for three metropolitan areas using the concept of the import ratio. The evidence presented suggested that negative wage gradients should apply for white workers in all occupational classes in each of the three MSAs. Negative wage gradients are also expected for white-collar black workers living in Philadelphia. However, Philadelphia blacks working in blue-collar and service occupations are observed to be net outcommuters from the central city to the suburbs. This is also true for blacks living in Detroit across all occupational classes. For these groups, at least some portion of the wage gradient is expected to be positively sloped. We now turn to the methods that were employed to estimate the wage gradients for the various groups.

IV. ESTIMATED EQUATIONS

The relationship between the wage rate paid to the worker and the distance his job is located from the CBD was investigated by using the 1980 PUMS data for the selected metropolitan areas to estimate wage equations of the general functional form

$$W_i^{(\lambda_1)} = \beta_0 + \sum_{j=1}^{J} \beta_j X_{ij} + \alpha D_i^{(\lambda_2)} + \varepsilon_i, \qquad (5)$$

where W_i is the hourly wage rate of the ith individual, X_{ij} is the jth characteristic variable for the ith individual, D_i is the distance in miles between the CBD and the ith worker's job location, and ε_i captures the unobserved variables and is assumed to be $N(O, \sigma_\varepsilon^2)$.

D_i was estimated by assigning each worker the airline distance between the CBD and the center of the largest city or town within the work area that his or her job was located.[5] Because intraarea differences in work locations are not captured, D_i contains an unknown amount of measurement error. However, because of the large number of work areas identified for each of the three MSAs, these errors are not expected to cause

[5]For central city workers whose jobs were located outside the CBD, D_i equaled one-half of the mean of the north, south, east, and west radial distances between the edge of the CBD and the city limits.

unreliable results. Evidence in support of this expectation was obtained by conducting Hausman's [9] specification test on errors in variables.[6]

The X_{ij} variables included age, age squared, years of schooling, schooling squared, age times years of schooling, whether a disability limits work, past unemployment, veteran status, marital status, and sex. These variables represent a union of the sets of variables found significant in a number of earlier earnings studies employing PUMS data [7, 11, 18].[7]

The transformations of the wage rate and distance variables are those proposed by Box and Cox [2], namely,

$$\begin{aligned} W_i^{(\lambda_1)} &= (W_i^{\lambda_1} - 1)/\lambda_1, && \lambda_l \neq 0 \\ &= \ln W_i, && \lambda_1 = 0 \\ D_i^{(\lambda_2)} &= (D_i^{\lambda_2} - 1)/\lambda_2, && \lambda_2 \neq 0 \\ &= \ln D_i, && \lambda_2 = 0. \end{aligned}$$

[6]This test involves comparing OLS and instrumental variable (IV) estimates. An IV estimator is asymptotically unbiased, but also inefficient. The OLS estimator is efficient but possibly biased if measurement errors are present. A test of the difference between IV and OLS estimates is a test of the null hypothesis of no misspecification. To construct the IV, all workers who reported that they used private motorized transportation to get to a job located within the CBD were extracted from the metropolitan sample. This subsample was used to compute for each work area the mean travel time to the CBD. Non-CBD workers were assigned the time for that area within which their job was located. This variable was judged to be an acceptable instrument since it is highly correlated with the distance the worker's job is located from the CBD and is expected to be uncorrelated with the disturbance. The OLS and IV estimates were compared for selected groups of workers and were not found to be statistically different. The null hypothesis of no misspecification therefore could not be rejected.

[7]A number of variables known to affect earnings (e.g., achievement motivation) are not provided by the PUMS data. This may bias estimates of the wage gradient if workers processing more of a particular unobservable earnings characteristic tend to select jobs that are located at only certain distances from the CBD. For example, if more motivated workers self-select jobs located within the central city, the estimated coefficient on D_i will be biased downward. Some evidence on this issue has been provided by Ihlanfeldt [13], which suggests that this type of potential bias is not a major concern. PUMS data for the Atlanta metropolitan area were employed to test for selectivity bias using the two-step procedure outlined by Heckman [10]. In the first step, maximum likelihood probit models were estimated for each race, where the dependent variable equaled one if the individual worked in the central city and zero if the work location was the suburbs. In the second step, the sample was stratified by race, occupational class, and work location to form 12 subsamples. For each subsample, a separate earnings equation was estimated, which included a selectivity variable predicted from the probit results. If the estimated coefficient on this variable is not significantly different from zero, the null hypothesis that sample selection is an unimportant phenomenon can be accepted. In 10 of the 12 regressions, the results indicated that self-selection of work location is an unimportant phenomenon. In the other two cases the results suggested that self-selection may cause the steepness of the wage gradient to be underestimated.

The λ_1 and λ_2 parameters were permitted to take on values that resulted in the following alternative functional forms: linear, log–log, semi-log, reverse semi-log, reciprocal, logarithmic reciprocal, and exponential.[8] Also tested but not expressed by (5) were quadratic and cubic forms.

V. RESULTS

For the Philadelphia and Boston samples, in those cases where a statistically significant wage gradient is found, the Box–Cox log-likelihood function is maximized when $\lambda_1 = \lambda_2 = 0$, which is the double-log functional form. For Detroit, the double-log and semi-log ($\lambda_1 = 0$, $\lambda_2 = 1$) forms yield maximum and indistinguishable fits. To facilitate comparisons across MSAs, only gradients estimated with double-log equations are presented. For all three MSAs, the null hypothesis that the wage–distance relationship is linear, H: $\lambda_1 = \lambda_2 = 1$, is consistently rejected at the 5% level of significance. The results therefore support the hypothesis that wage rates increase at an increasing rate as the CBD is approached.

Table 2 reports distance elasticities for white and black private sector workers in Philadelphia and Detroit and for white private sector workers in Boston. (Also reported are mean wage rates for each occupational group.)[9] The results are similar for white workers across the MSAs and provide strong evidence that wage gradients exist. Negative and statistically significant (at the 5% level by a one-tailed test) distance elasticities are found in all three MSAs for the following occupational classes: professional and managerial, sales, administrative support, and craftsmen.[10] Another consistent finding is that estimated distance elasticities are statistically insignificant for laborers. An explanation for the absence of a wage gradient for laborers is that roughly a third of these workers are employed in construction and therefore do not have a fixed work location. Alternatively, the opportunity cost of travel time of these workers may be below the threshold necessary to generate an observable wage gradient. Only for operatives and service workers do the results differ among the MSAs. The

[8]To allow those functional forms that logarithmically transform D_i, one mile was added to all estimated values of D_i.

[9]The estimated coefficients on the X_{ij} variables were generally significant and of the anticipated sign in the equations estimated for the many different groups. To conserve space, these results are not reported.

[10]The "too-large sample size problem" may exist in the case of white private sector workers, since many of the samples contained over 3000 observations. Leamer [17] has suggested that the significance level be adjusted downward as the sample size grows to improve the interpretation of the data against a null hypothesis. When a 1% rather than the 5% level of significance is used for the larger samples, none of the conclusions regarding statistical significance are changed.

TABLE 2
Estimated Wage Gradients for Private Sector Employees
(Double-Log Equations)

	Whites				Blacks			
	Mean wage	Estimated coefficient	*t*-statistic	Observations	Mean wage	Estimated coefficient	t-statistic	Observations
Philadelphia								
Professional and managerial	$9.43	−0.050	−9.68	8265	$7.81	−0.061	−3.19	677
Sales	6.69	−0.037	−3.74	3638	5.80	0.023	0.26	246
Administrative support	5.68	−0.030	−6.18	6733	5.85	−0.042	−2.68	867
Craftsmen	8.33	−0.021	−2.32	4230	7.85	−0.006	−0.36	446
Service	4.47	0.010	0.84	3058	5.07	−0.025	−1.17	895
Operatives	6.90	−0.025	−2.58	4308	6.83	0.031	1.18	982
Laborers	6.10	0.034	1.45	1055	7.18	0.023	0.42	319
Detroit								
Professional and managerial	10.75	−0.041	−5.21	5920	8.70	0.002	0.08	479
Sales	7.04	−0.027	−1.76	2784	6.07	0.007	0.17	233
Administrative support	6.62	−0.029	−3.81	4729	6.58	0.011	0.70	660
Craftsmen	10.41	−0.032	−2.78	3699	10.20	0.030	0.70	341
Service	4.91	−0.079	−4.92	2750	5.50	0.005	0.18	602
Operatives	8.54	−0.032	−2.51	3941	8.86	0.104	3.20	967
Laborers	6.46	−0.020	−0.62	923	7.86	0.110	1.50	166
Boston								
Professional and managerial	$9.28	−0.042	−4.82	6033	—	—	—	—
Sales	6.54	−0.047	−2.71	1997	—	—	—	—
Administrative support	5.63	−0.036	−4.51	4370	—	—	—	—
Craftsmen	7.80	−0.040	−2.20	1954	—	—	—	—
Service	4.56	−0.008	−0.40	2198	—	—	—	—
Operatives	6.03	0.006	0.32	1902	—	—	—	—
Laborers	5.24	−0.057	−1.37	636	—	—	—	—

distance elasticity for operatives is negative and significant for Philadelphia and Detroit, but positive and insignificant for Boston. For service workers, the distance elasticity is not significantly different from zero for Philadelphia and Boston, but it is negative and significant for Detroit. The finding of an insignificant wage gradient for white service workers in Philadelphia and Boston may be partially attributable to the fact that these workers earn, by far, the lowest wage rates of any occupational class and therefore have the lowest opportunity cost of commuting time. In addition, the import ratios of Table 1 suggest that job and worker gradients have similar slopes in the case of white service workers, which indicates that they tend to live relatively close to where they work.[11] Since white service workers are not required to make long commutes (and place a low value on travel time), employers need not provide much of a compensating differential for travel costs.

In the case of the Detroit MSA, the distance elasticity for service workers is not only highly significant but is larger in absolute magnitude than for any other occupational class. Considerable experimentation, which included estimating equations for the individual occupations that make up the class of service workers, failed to shed light on this anomalous result.

In those cases where the distance elasticity was not found to be significantly different from zero, the hypothesis that there is no spatial variation in wage rates was tested. This involved estimating a wage equation that included the X_{ij} variables and dummy variables for $(n - 1)$ of the identified work areas. The joint significance of the area dummies was determined to test the null hypothesis

$$H_0: \gamma_1 = \gamma_2 = \cdots = \gamma_{n-1} = 0.$$

The F-statistics for this test indicate that, in all cases, the null hypothesis of insignifance cannot be rejected.

The estimates presented in Table 2 are based on the assumption that wage gradients do not differ between men and women workers. To investigate this, the dummy variable representing a female worker was interacted with all of the other independent variables, including the natural logarithm of distance from the CBD. The t-statistic on the estimated coefficient for the latter interaction variable indicates whether the distance elasticity is significantly different between women and men. In all

[11]This was confirmed by computing mean travel to work times for each of the occupational classes. For example, for white service workers living in Philadelphia, the mean one-way commute is only 18.8 minutes. In comparison, Philadelphia white workers in the other occupational classes had mean travel times ranging from 22.7 to 27.3 minutes. Similar differences in mean times were found for white service workers in Detroit and Boston.

TABLE 3
Male and Female Wage Gradients for White Private Sector Workers
(Double-Log Equations)

	Philadelphia		Detroit		Boston	
	Males	Females	Males	Females	Males	Females
Professional and	−0.036	−0.061	−0.022	−0.063	−0.020	−0.067
managerial	(−5.72)	(−7.01)	(−2.40)	(−4.50)	(−1.76)	(−5.00)
Administrative	−0.013	−0.034	0.002	−0.035	0.019	−0.044
support	(−1.30)	(−6.40)	(0.16)	(−4.10)	(0.94)	(−5.00)

Note. The numbers in parentheses are *t*-statistics.

cases, the distance elasticity is not found to differ between black women and black men. For whites, the sign on the distance–female interaction variable is consistently negative, but only for the professional and managerial occupational class and the administrative support occupational class are gender differences in distance elasticities significantly different (by a one-tailed test at the 5% level). This is true across all three MSAs. Possible reasons for these mixed results are that the gender difference in the value of travel time and the substitutability of male for female labor varies among occupational classes. The data do not permit the resolution of this issue.

Table 3 reports the results obtained from estimating separate equations for men and women for the two occupational classes where distance elasticities are found to vary by gender. The results are very similar across the MSAs. In the case of professional and managerial workers, distance elasticities are significantly different from zero for both men and women, but they are roughly two to three times larger in absolute magnitude for women. All of the distance elasticities are statistically significant for female administrative support workers, while none are significant for men. The results in Table 3 are therefore consistent with the hypothesis that wage gradients are steeper for women than for men because women value their travel time at a higher fraction of the wage rate.

To investigate the hypothesis that wage gradients are steeper for higher-wage workers, zero-order (Pearsonian) correlations were computed between the mean wage rates for each occupational class and the appropriate distance elasticities are reported in Tables 2 and 3. Correlation coefficients were based on 21 observations (seven occupational classes times three MSAs) and computed separately for white men and women. The correlation coefficient for women is −0.56 and is significant at the 1% level, while the correlation coefficient for men is −0.30 and is significant at the 19% level. The results therefore provide limited support for the hypothesis.

Turning to the results obtained for blacks, negative and statisticallv significant distance elasticities are found for only two of the seven occupational groups in Philadelphia, namely, professional and managerial workers and administrative support workers. For these two groups, the Box–Cox log-likelihood function was again maximized for the double-log functional form. For the other five groups, estimated distance elasticities are not statistically significant for any of the various functional forms. Once again, joint significance tests using area dummy variables were performed and the null hypothesis of no spatial wage rate variation for these occupational groups is confirmed.

The negative gradients found for black professional and managerial workers and administrative support workers living in Philadelphia are consistent with the import ratios presented in Table 1, since these workers commute toward the CBD. The relative magnitudes of the distance elasticities estimated for these groups are also consistent with the hypothesis that wage gradients are steeper for higher-wage earners. However, since sales workers are also found on net to be incommuters, the insignificant gradient observed for them was unexpected. This contrary result may reflect the fact that, for this group, the sample size may have been too small to pick up the wage gradient effect.

In Philadelphia, the central city in a net exporter and the inner suburban ring is a net importer of black blue-collar and service workers. Positively sloped wage gradients are expected, but are not found. These results suggest that extra compensation is not required in order to induce lower-skilled black workers to reverse commute between the central city and the inner suburbs. There are two possible explanations for this finding: (1) employers located within the inner suburban ring may not be required to offer much of a wage inducement to workers imported from the central city if jobs within the inner ring are easily accessible to these workers; and (2) a wage inducement may also be unnecessary if imported workers are unable to find alternative employment within the central city at a competitive wage. To investigate the first explanation, mean one-way commuting times broken down by mode of transportation were computed for black blue-collar and service workers who resided in the central city and worked within the inner suburban ring. Seventy percent of these workers are found to commute by automobile and the mean one-way commuting time is 35 minutes. For 26% percent of these automobile commuters, the commute takes at least 45 minutes. Twenty-five percent of the workers use public transportation and on average take over 60 minutes to get to work. Clearly, jobs within the inner suburbs are not easily accessible to black central city residents. Black lower-skilled workers who outcommute to the inner suburbs and beyond, which the PUMS data indicate exceeds 15,000 individuals, are obviously suffering declines in their earnings, net of commuting costs, as the result of their long commutes. The only reasonable explanation for this behavior is that these workers cannot find alternative employment within the central city at a competitive wage, and therefore suburban employers do not have to pay them a compensating differential to cover their commuting costs.

The results for blacks working in the Detroit MSA are consistent with those obtained for Philadelphia. The import ratios for Detroit indicate that the central city is a net exporter and each of the suburban rings is a net importer of black workers in all seven occupational classes. However, only for the operatives occupational class is there a positively sloped wage gradient that is statistically different from zero. These results were again confirmed by joint significance tests using area dummy variables. As is true for Philadelphia, black outcommuters from the central city of Detroit have considerable commutes. Ninety-one percent of these workers travel by automobile and the mean one-way commuting time is 31 minutes. Twenty percent of these automobile travelers have commutes that take at least 45 minutes. The 9% of outcommuters who rely on public transit take on average over 50 minutes to get to work. The number of outcommuters is considerably greater in Detroit in comparison to Philadelphia. Roughly 40,000 blacks living in the central city of Detroit commute to the suburbs for employment. Approximately 15,000 of these workers are in the operatives occupational class. This leaves 25,000 workers who reverse commute who do not receive a compensating differential to cover their commuting costs.

The import ratio, commuting time, and wage evidence presented for Philadelphia and Detroit black workers are all consistent with John Kain's [15] spatial mismatch hypothesis. According to this hypothesis, the suburbanization of jobs and continued housing market segregation have acted together to reduce the economic welfare of central city blacks.

Distance elasticities were also estimated for selected categories of public sector employees. Due to small sample sizes and the concentration of state and federal government jobs within the central city, many of the cells created from stratifying the sample contained insufficient variation in work distance from the CBD to reliably estimate a wage gradient. However, it was possible to estimate wage gradients for three of the occupational classes (namely, professional and managerial, administrative support, and service) for local government workers in each of the MSAs. A number of gradients were also estimated for federal government workers in Philadelphia.

The results for local government workers are reported in Table 4. Separate distance elasticities are reported for men and women where the

TABLE 4
Estimated Wage Gradients for Local Government Workers
(Double-Log Equations)

	Mean wage	Estimated coefficient	*t*-statistic	Observations
Philadelphia				
Whites				
Professional and managerial, men	$10.58	−0.039	−2.68	795
Professional and managerial, women	9.13	−0.079	−3.38	981
Administrative support, women	5.15	−0.083	−3.74	476
Service	6.93	−0.098	−5.55	834
Blacks				
Professional and managerial	8.37	−0.039	−1.01	344
Administrative support	6.64	−0.049	−1.20	179
Service	6.62	−0.047	−1.14	268
Detroit				
Whites				
Professional and managerial, men	11.91	−0.025	−1.30	519
Professional and managerial, women	10.43	−0.049	−1.65	730
Administrative support, women	5.58	−0.064	−2.51	356
Service	7.71	−0.089	−4.50	634
Blacks				
Professional and managerial	10.80	−0.049	−1.50	297
Administrative support	7.18	−0.115	−3.70	171
Service	7.66	−0.073	−1.65	229
Boston				
Whites				
Professional and managerial	9.19	−0.035	−1.73	1175
Administrative support, women	5.04	−0.091	−2.72	310
Service	7.27	−0.091	−2.94	623

gender difference is found to be statistically significant. Distance elasticities were estimated for white women but not for white men in the administrative support occupational class. This decision was based upon the large gender differences observed for this class in the case of private sector workers and the fact that the sample sizes for men are very small (i.e., less than 100 observations). Distance elasticities are significantly different from zero with the expected negative sign for white workers in all three occupational classes in all three MSAs. The elasticities estimated for white local government workers in the professional and managerial class are very similar to those obtained for private sector workers. However, the elasticities estimated for administrative support and service workers are larger than those estimated for the private sector. Service workers employed by local government have better-paying jobs than service workers in the private sector because of occupational differences. Service workers employed by local government are most frequently policemen and firemen, while service workers in the private sector are most frequently employed in private household, food preparation, or personal service occupations. Therefore, the higher estimated distance elasticities for local government workers are consistent with the expectation that higher-wage workers have steeper wage gradients. However, the absolute magnitude of the elasticities estimated for both local government service workers and local government administrative support workers are generally greater than those obtained for any other group, public or private. These high elasticities may reflect the fact that there is an inverse relationship between distance from the CBD and the population size of the local government unit. Larger governments may have the budgeting wherewithal to hire employees with more specialized skills and therefore may tend to pay higher average wage rates. Unfortunately, the data did not permit an investigation of this hypothesis.

The distance elasticities estimated for black local government workers are all negative. However, although the distance coefficients in all six estimated equations have associated *t*-statistics greater than one, only two of the coefficients are statistically significant at the 5% level. Small samples may account for these results.

The wage gradients estimated for federal government workers in Philadelphia are for three groups: white professional and managerial workers, white administrative support workers, and black administrative support workers. These elasticities are all highly significant and equal −0.048, −0.036, and −0.086, respectively. Elasticities are not significantly different between men and women workers.

Thus far the discussion has focused on the existence of wage gradients and not much has been said regarding their quantitative importance. To study this, the implied percentage decline in wages between working at the CBD and working at various distances from the CBD was computed for white private sector workers where a statistically significant wage gradient was found. Table 5 reports the total percentage wage decline at 5, 10, and 20 miles from the CBD, respectively. Working 10 miles from the CBD reduces the earnings of private sector workers by 4.8 to 18.9% depending on the group considered. Working 20 miles from the CBD reduces earnings by 6.1 to 24.0%. The results, therefore, indicate that the wage gradient phenomenon is an important source of wage variation within metropolitan areas.

One way to judge the reasonableness of these estimates is to assume realistic values of the operating and time costs involved in commuting and calculate an implied percentage wage decline per mile. Based upon such

TABLE 5
Total Percentage Decline in Wages at Various Distances from the CBD in Comparison to a CBD Work Location for White Private Sector Workers

	Five miles from CBD	Ten miles from CBD	Twenty miles from CBD
Philadelphia			
Professional and managerial, men	6.5	8.6	11.0
Professional and managerial, women	10.9	14.6	18.6
Sales	6.6	8.9	11.3
Administrative support, women	6.5	8.6	11.0
Craftsmen	3.8	5.0	6.4
Operatives	4.5	6.0	7.6
Detroit			
Professional and managerial, men	3.9	5.3	6.7
Professional and managerial, women	11.3	15.1	19.2
Sales	4.8	6.5	8.2
Administrative support, women	6.3	8.4	10.6
Craftsmen	5.7	7.7	9.7
Service	14.1	18.9	24.0
Operatives	5.7	7.7	9.7
Boston			
Professional and managerial, men	3.6	4.8	6.1
Professional and managerial, women	12.0	16.1	20.3
Sales	8.4	11.3	14.3
Administrative support, women	7.9	10.5	13.3
Craftsmen	7.2	9.6	12.2

assumptions for a typical worker and the assumption of a linear wage gradient, Mills and Hamilton [23] have estimated that wages should decline about 1% for each additional mile the job is located from the CBD. The numbers in Table 4 are roughly consistent with this expectation for jobs located at distances of 10 miles or less from the CBD. Beyond 10 miles, the estimated gradients become relatively flat implying wage declines of much less than 1% per mile.

VI. CONCLUSIONS

This paper has provided some rare evidence on intraurban wage gradients. The negative slope and curvilinear shape of the gradients found for most white workers living in Philadelphia, Detroit, and Boston and for white-collar black workers living in Philadelphia are consistent with the predictions obtained from the standard monocentric model of urban land use. The model is appropriate for these groups because they are observed to commute toward the CBD.

In contrast to the above groups, black blue-collar and service workers living in Philadelphia and blacks in all occupational classes living in Detroit are found to be net outcommuters from the central city. The models of White and Straszheim predict that outcommuting will result in positive wage gradients. These models assume that workers can find alternative employment with the central city, and therefore suburban employers must pay imported workers a compensating differential to cover their commuting costs. The results of this study are generally contrary to this prediction and indicate that black workers do not earn more outside the central city, despite the long average commute associated with a suburban job. The only exception to this finding are workers in the operatives occupational class living in the Detroit MSA, for which a positively sloped wage gradient is observed. The uniqueness of this result likely reflects the concentration of automobile manufacturing in Detroit. The findings are consistent with the hypothesis that there exists a surplus of resident black labor within the central city. Policies for improving the accessibility of suburban jobs to black workers are strongly recommended by this study.

Hughes and Madden [12] have also used the 1980 PUMS data to study the relationship between housing segregation and the economic status of blacks. They focused on two of the three MSAs used in the present study —Philadelphia and Detroit—and the Cleveland–Lorain MSA. Their approach involved evaluating the economic welfare of individuals at each possible work and residential location and then comparing the actual distribution of work and residential location by race with the welfare-maximizing distribution. They find that restrictions on the residential locations of blacks contribute to their lower economic status by increasing housing and/or commuting costs. This finding is consistent with those of the present study. They also find that the relative economic status of employed blacks can be improved by changing their job locations. The reasons stated for this are that blacks tend to work at employment locations that offer relatively low wages and/or involve high commuting costs. The results of the present study suggest that most blacks would not receive higher wages from changing their job locations. But the welfare of many blacks would improve if they could eliminate their suburban commute by finding employment within the central city.

REFERENCES

1. M. E. Beesley, "Urban Transport: Studies in Economic Policy," Butterworths, London (1973).
2. G. E. P. Box and D. R. Cox, An analysis of transformations, *Journal of the Royal Statistical Society Service B*, **26**, 211–243 (1964).
3. S. Danziger and M. Weinstein, Employment location and wage rates of poverty-area residents, *Journal of Urban Economics*, **3**, 127–145 (1976).

4. R. W. Eberts, An empirical investigation of intraurban wage gradients, *Journal of Urban Economics*, **10**, 50–60 (1981).
5. R. Edelstein, The determinants of value in the Philadelphia housing market: A case study of the main line 1967–1969, *Review of Economic Statistics*, Aug, 319–328 (1974).
6. R. G. Ehrenberg and G. S. Goldstein, A model of public sector wage determination, *Journal of Urban Economics*, **2**, 223–245 (1975).
7. J. D. Gwartney and J. E. Long, The relative earnings of blacks and other minorities, *Industrial and Labor Relations Review*, Apr, 336–346 (1978).
8. B. Harrison, The intrametropolitan distribution of minority economic welfare," *Journal of Regional Science*, **12**, 23–43 (1972).
9. J. A. Hausman, Specification tests in econometrics, *Econometrica*, **46**, 1251–1271 (1978).
10. J. J. Heckman, The common structure of statistical models of truncation, sample selection and limited dependent variables and a simple estimator for such models, *Annals of Economic and Social Measurement*, Fall, 475–492 (1976).
11. H. W. Herzog, R. A. Hofler, and A. M. Schlottmann, Life on the frontier: Migrant information, earnings and past mobility," *Review of Economic Statistics*, Aug, 373–382 (1985).
12. M. A. Hughes and J. F. Madden, Residential segregation and the economic status of black workers: New evidence for an old debate, forthcoming.
13. K. R. Ihlanfeldt, Intra-metropolitan variation in earnings and labor market discrimination: An econometric analysis of the Atlanta labor market, *Southern Economics Journal*, July, 123–140 (1988).
14. J. R. Jackson, Intraurban variation in the price of housing, *Journal of Urban Economics*, **6**, 464–479 (1979).
15. J. F. Kain, Housing segregation, negro employment, and metropolitan decentralization," *Quarterly Journal of Economics*, **82**, 175–197 (1968).
16. T. Keeler, *et al.*, "The Full Costs of Urban Transit," Part 3, Monograph 21, Institute of Urban and Regional Development, University of California, Berkeley, CA, (July 1975).
17. E. E. Leamer, "Specification Searches: Ad Hoc Inference with Non Experimental Data," Wiley, New York (1978).
18. J. E. Long, Public-private sectoral differences in employment discrimination, *Southern Economics Journal*, July, 89–96 (1975).
19. J. E. Madden, A spatial theory of sex discrimination," *Journal of Regional Science*, **17**, 369–380 (1977).
20. J. E. Madden, Urban wage gradients: Empirical evidence, *Journal of Urban Economics*, **18**, 291–301 (1985).
21. D. P. McMillen and L. D. Singell, Jr., "Work Location, Residence Location, and the Intraurban Wage Gradient," working paper, University of Oregon (1990).
22. E. S. Mills, The value of urban land, *in* "The Quality of the Urban Environment" (H. Perloff, Ed.), Resources for the Future, Washington, DC, (1969).
23. E. S. Mills and B. W. Hamilton, "Urban Economics," Scott, Foresman, Glenview, IL (1989).
24. L. N. Moses, "Towards a Theory of Intraurban Wage Differentials and Their Influence on Travel Patterns," *Proceedings of the Regional Science Association*, **9**, 52–63 (1962).
25. R. F. Muth, "Cities and Housing," University of Chicago Press, Chicago (1969).
26. R. Price and E. Mills, Race and residence in earnings determination, *Journal of Urban Economics*, **17**, 1–18 (1985).
27. A. Rees and G. Schultz, "Workers and Wages in an Urban Labor Market," The University of Chicago Press, Chicago (1970).

28. C. E. Reid, The effect of residential location on the wages of black women and white women, *Journal of Urban Economics*, **18**, 350–363 (1985).
29. M. Segal, "Wages in the Metropolis," Harvard University Press, Cambridge, MA (1960).
30. M. R. Straszheim, Discrimination and the spatial characteristics of the urban labor market for black workers, *Journal of Urban Economics*, **7**, 119–140 (1980).
31. M. R. Straszheim, "Urban Labor Markets and Their Consequences for Black Employment," *Annual Housing Survey Study*, No. 11, U.S. Department of Housing and Urban Development, Office of Policy Development and Research (1980).
32. U.S. Department of Commerce, Public-Use Microdata Samples Technical Documentation, Washington, DC (1983).
33. J. Vrooman and S. Greenfield, Are blacks making it in the suburbs? Some new evidence on intra-metropolitan spatial segmentation, *Journal of Urban Economics*, **7**, 155–167 (1980).
34. M. L. Wachter, Wage determination in a local labor market: A case study of the Boston labor market, *Journal of Human Resources*, **7**, 87–103 (1972).
35. M. J. White, Firm suburbanization and urban subcenters," *Journal of Urban Economics*, **3**, 232–243 (1976).
36. M. J. White, Job suburbanization, zoning and the welfare of urban minority groups, *Journal of Urban Economics*, **5**, 219–240 (1978).
37. M. J. White, Locational choice and commuting behavior in cities with decentralized employment, *Journal of Urban Economics*, **24**, 129–152 (1988).
38. F. D. Wilson, "Residential Consumption, Economic Opportunity, and Race," Academic Press, New York (1979).

[7]

JOURNAL OF URBAN ECONOMICS **35**, 105–118 (1994)

Causality in the Suburbanization of Population and Employment

LAWRENCE THURSTON

District of Columbia Office of People's Council, Washington, DC 20007

AND

ANTHONY M. J. YEZER

Department of Economics, The George Washington University, Washington, DC 20052

Received July 11, 1991; revised November 25, 1992

Using the slope of the density function as a measure of centralization, we find that suburbanization of the residential population is enhanced by rising income and suburbanization of employment in the transportation, communication, and public utilities and service sectors and by the failure of manufacturing to decentralize. Suburbanization of population is only a positive force in promoting decentralization of the service and retail sectors. However, there are a number of interesting interactions between decentralization of some industrial sectors and suburbanization of other sectors. Overall, our results differ significantly from those of previous studies which failed to disaggregate employment by industry and which aggregated change over decennial rather than annual time intervals.

I. INTRODUCTION

Decentralization of both population and employment has proceeded steadily in U.S. cities. Inevitably the possible causal relations between decentralization in one industrial sector and movement of other sectors and between decentralization of population and suburbanization of employment have attracted significant popular attention and a modest level of academic inquiry. Urban economic theory, stemming from the models of Muth [14] and Mills [11], provides strong a priori expectations for the causes of changing residential population density across the city. However, there is no comparable theoretical result for the spatial distribution of employment across the urban area. Given that the distribution of population depends on the location of employment and residential population provides both labor inputs and markets for firms, it is possible that suburbanization of population is both a cause and an effect of employment decentralization.

Given the theoretical ambiguity regarding causes of industrial decentralization and the fundamental importance of the question, it is surprising that only a few empirical studies have attempted to evaluate the causal

0094-1190/94 $6.00

structure relating suburbanization of employment in different sectors and suburbanization of residential population. Seminal work by Steinnes [17] formulated the problem in terms of a simple causality test based on a series of reduced-form difference equations in which measures of current suburbanization of employment or population were related to past rates of suburbanization. Subsequent papers have extended this approach by measuring suburbanization as the decline in the density gradient of a particular activity and by examining the effects of a variety of factors such as crime, taxes, and amenity on the pace of decentralization.

There are three aspects of this paper which differ from previous empirical literature on the relation among decentralization of employment by sector and decentralization of population. First, estimates are based on a detailed and inclusive disaggregation of industrial sectors. Such disaggregation of industrial sectors is consistent with the prior presumptions that intraurban location decisions should vary by type of industry. Second, there is a more detailed time disaggregation, using annual changes rather than changes over 5- or 10-year periods. Third, transportation improvements are made endogenous to the model. Overall, our results differ significantly from those of other studies. We find very little support for the contention that jobs follow population into the suburbs. Also it appears that failure of previous models to disaggregate by industrial sector has concealed interesting interindustry effects and hidden some details of the interaction of population decentralization with suburbanization of particular sectors.

II. THEORY AND LITERATURE REVIEW

As reviewed in detail by Brueckner [3], standard models of population distribution given concentrated exogenous employment provide a theoretical rationale for the exponential population density function. The density function for a city with employment concentrated at its center, which had proved so promising in empirical studies beginning with Clark [4], is written as

$$D(k) = D_0 e^{-gk}, \tag{1}$$

where $D(k)$ is population density k miles from the city center, D_0 is population density at $k = 0$, and g is the population density gradient. The value of the density gradient, g, should vary inversely with both household income and the quality of transportation facilities. Subsequent dynamic versions of this model by Wheaton [20] and others demonstrate that, if the housing capital stock is putty-clay, then the exact form of the density function should vary by city depending on the specific history of changes in income and transportation costs.

Empirical studies of the population density gradient in Eq. (1) have been reviewed in great detail by Kau *et al.* [8] and McDonald [10]. Many studies using time-series and cross section data have established the secular decline in the population density gradient as a stylized fact. Generally the results agree with the basic implications of theory that rising income lowers the density gradient, but effects of improved transportation facilities are less clear. Other factors, such as crime, tax, race, or amenity differences associated with distance from the center city, have been investigated, most recently by Mills [12], and found to be of marginal significance in accounting for changing density gradients. Curiously, these studies consistently treat the location of employment as exogenous.

Under the generic title "the flight to the suburbs," a variety of papers have examined suburbanization of residential population with tests based on functional forms other than the population density gradient. Perhaps the best known is the study by Bradford and Kelejian [2] which relates the fraction of total population living in the central city to the fraction of land area in the center city. Unfortunately this functional form does not correspond to the reduced form of any general urban model. Many other papers have examined various implications of residential population decentralization. However, these studies do not consider the causal relations among decentralizing population and total employment or among employment in different sectors.

While empirical analysis of changes in population density gradients has become common, application of the density gradient to output or employment has been more limited. Schmenner [15], among others, has demonstrated that a negative exponential density function is a useful descriptive device for the spatial distribution of urban employment. However, a review by Stahl [16] concluded that the intraurban analysis of business location decisions has not reached a mature state.

A small literature has attempted to relate changes in the density gradient of population to changes in the density gradients for various types of employment. The goal of these studies is to evaluate the structure of causal relations between movement of population and employment. Initial attempts at testing the causal linkage between decentralization of population and employment were due to Steinnes [17], building on a model by Steinnes and Fisher [19] in which employment and population were simultaneously determined. The reduced form of the Steinnes–Fisher model implies that the proportion of city population living in the central city depends on lagged values of itself, lagged values of the proportion of employment in the central city, and various exogenous variables. Thus the process of decentralization of housing and industry could be described by a reduced-form difference equation in which the percentage of an economic activity in the central city was a function of prior values of the percentage of that activity in the central city and of the lagged values of the central city percentages of other activities.

Steinnes estimated separate equations for residential population and for employment in the manufacturing, retail, and service sectors. Overall, his results suggested that causality ran from decentralization of population to movement of jobs in the manufacturing and service sectors, i.e, that "jobs follow people." In sharp contrast to expectations based on the Muth–Mills model, Steinnes found that manufacturing employment decentralization decreased the suburbanization of population. Steinnes suggested that households might be repelled by externalities related to the suburbanization of manufacturing employment, whereas the standard assumption is that employment should attract population. In a subsequent paper considering only manufacturing employment and population over different time intervals, Steinnes [18] used both lagged and leading values of the right-hand side variables and confirmed his earlier finding that manufacturing jobs follow population and that suburbanization of manufacturing retards population decentralization.

Cooke [5] reformulated Steinnes' test to conform to the reduced form suggested by the Muth–Mills model. Specifically, he used measures of population and employment density gradients rather than simple proportions of population and employment in the center city as measures of suburbanization. Thus the estimated equation system related the current level of density gradients for population and three industrial sectors, manufacturing, retail, and services, to lagged values of these variables and a vector of exogenous variables,

$$
\begin{aligned}
\mathrm{GP}_{it} &= f_1(X_{it}, \mathrm{GP}_{it-1}, \mathrm{GM}_{it-1}, \mathrm{GR}_{it-1}, \mathrm{GS}_{it-1}, u_i + v_{it})\\
\mathrm{GM}_{it} &= f_2(X_{it}, \mathrm{GP}_{it-1}, \mathrm{GM}_{it-1}, \mathrm{GR}_{it1}, \mathrm{GS}_{it-1}, r_i + q_{it})\\
\mathrm{GR}_{it} &= f_3(X_{it}, \mathrm{GP}_{it-1}, \mathrm{GM}_{it-1}, \mathrm{GR}_{it-1}, \mathrm{GS}_{it-1}, k_i + m_{it})\\
\mathrm{GS}_{it} &= f_4(X_{it}, \mathrm{GP}_{it-1}, \mathrm{GM}_{it-1}, \mathrm{GR}_{it-1}, \mathrm{GS}_{it-1}, s_i + w_{it}),
\end{aligned}
\qquad (2)
$$

where i is a city subscript, t is a time subscript, GP, GM, GR, and GS are density gradients for population, manufacturing, retail, and services, and X is a vector of exogenous variables including time, total population, median income per capita, percentage of the city population which is white, and vector of city dummy variables. The variables u, r, k, and s are cross section fixed effects error components, and v, q, m, and w are identically and independently distributed random error terms. The coefficient of the lagged endogenous variable in each equation is interpreted as a reflection of a lagged adjustment process, i.e., one minus the estimated coefficient is the degree of partial adjustment of the actual density gradient to its long-run equilibrium in one time period.

Cooke estimated equation system (2) using data from 18 cities from the Census of Business and Manufacturing for 1948, 1954, 1958, and 1963. In contrast with Steinnes, there was no evidence that population decentralization was retarded by suburbanization of manufacturing. Indeed the only significant determinant of population decentralization was increases in household income. For both retail and manufacturing employment, Cooke concluded that jobs follow population. While his results are far more favorable to the Muth–Mills model than those obtained earlier by Steinnes, a number of strange interindustry employment effects were largely ignored. For example, Cooke found that the lagged service density gradient had a negative and significant effect on the manufacturing gradient but that the lagged manufacturing density gradient had a positive and significant effect on the service gradient. Taken together, the Steinnes and Cooke papers raise more interesting questions than they settle, and yet further work on intraurban causality models with industry disaggregation has not, to our knowledge, been published in the literature.

Since the Steinnes–Cooke exchange, a few papers have attempted to estimate the causal relation between employment and population decentralization, but interindustry employment effects have not been considered. For example, Mills and Price [13] estimated a system similar to Eq. (2) adding a richer array of relative amenity variables but aggregating all employment as single regressor. The sample was a cross section of cities with population and employment changes over the 1960 to 1970 period used to compute the changes in gradients. The results provide strong support for the hypothesis that aggregate employment decentralization follows population, but the lagged employment gradient has a non-significant relation to the population density gradient. The estimated coefficient of the lagged population density gradient was positive and significant in the equations for employment density gradients in construction, retail and services, and public administration. Only for public services was the effect of population on employment non-significant. Relative urban amenity variables were also non-significant in both the employment and the population equations. These results agree with the proposition that jobs follow population taken by Cooke.

III. A DISAGGREGATED CAUSALITY TEST

This paper extends previous work on causality in movement of employment and population by disaggregating both employment sectors and the time period under study. Steinnes [17] and Cooke [5] have demonstrated that the relation between population and employment decentralization varies by industrial sector. We have increased the sectoral disaggregation from three to seven sectors, and the time period of analysis has been disaggregated from 5- or 10-year periods to annual changes. This enhances the opportunity to detect the causal structure of relations between changes in the density gradient of one specific activity and lagged changes in density gradients of other activities.

Employment is disaggregated into construction; manufacturing; wholesale trade; retail trade; finance, insurance and real estate; transportation, communications, and public utilities; and service sectors. This extended disaggregation has the obvious advantage of creating more homogenous categories of activity in terms of locational preferences. It also accounts for virtually all urban employment and hence eliminates problems of omitted variable bias that could exist when only a fraction of employment is included among the regressors. For example, if there are N land uses, and one conducts a Steinnes–Cooke-type test on $N - 1$ of them, then the effects of the residual category which reside in the error term may not be independent of the regressors. Estimates presented in the next section indicate that the additional sectoral and temporal disaggregation along with inclusion of all employment sectors produced different results than previous studies.

Time disaggregation into annual periods both produces far more observations than other studies and provides a greater opportunity to observe causality in cases where the response of one sector to changes in another is rapid. Time aggregation problems arise when the reaction interval between variables is smaller than the time interval at which there are observations. The possibility of testing for causal structure in the sense of improving forecasts of a conditional mean discussed in Granger [6] depends on the periodicity of the data. If there is a recursive structure, e.g., from decentralization of population to decentralization of jobs, time-series data whose periodicity is lengthy may only reveal a simultaneous relation.

The causality model also allows us to examine the effects of various exogenous variables on suburbanization. Given the particular interest in effects of total population growth, racial composition, income, and transportation facilities in the literature, variables reflecting all four of these aspects of the urban area are included in the specification. Of these four variables, income and transportation costs have a specific theoretical significance in the standard urban model. Anas and Kim [1] have recently affirmed that rising income lowers the population density gradient even with heterogenous population. We give special attention to the measurement of transportation effects which have tended to have the "wrong" sign in previous studies. Herrin and Kern [7] have noted that tests of the role of transportation cost generally imply testing a joint hypothesis involving both the fundamental trade-off of transportation cost for housing price and a number of auxiliary hypotheses. The measure of transportation cost used in this paper is the percentage change in transportation investment. Clearly there is an auxiliary hypothesis that these investments lower transportation cost. Given that transportation investment is often announced long before it is implemented, there is some question as to the econometric exogeneity of even lagged values of transportation investment changes, particularly when the lag is only one year. Therefore estimation was performed using instrumental variables estimation techniques.[1]

The specific estimation equation for the population density gradient is

$$\begin{aligned} \text{GPOP}_{it} = f_p(&\text{GPOP}_{it-1}, \text{GCONST}_{it-1}, \text{GMFG}_{it-1}, \\ &\text{GTCPU}_{it-1}, \text{GWHL}_{it-1}, \text{GRET}_{it-1}, \\ &\text{GSER}_{it-1}, \text{INC}_{it}, \text{TRANS}_{it-1}, \text{TPOP}_{it}, \text{WPOP}_{it}, \text{TIME}_t, v_i + u_{it}). \end{aligned} \quad (3)$$

i is an index of city, t is a time index, GPOP is the population density gradient, GCONST, GMFG, GTCPU, GWHL, GRET, and GSER are employment density gradients for construction; manufacturing; transportation, communications, and public utilities; wholesale trade; retail trade; and services, respectively. INC is the annual percentage change in income per capita. TRANS is the annual percentage change in transportation investments. TPOP is the annual percentage change in total population. WPOP is the percentage of the white population in the central city. TIME is a time trend which has also had the wrong (positive) sign in previous studies. The random variables v_i and u_{it} are identically and independently distributed error terms, with v_i uniquely associated with each city. City-specific effects are eliminated by adding a vector of city dummy variables.

IV. DATA AND ESTIMATION RESULTS

Unlike previous studies which have used the Census of Population and the Census of Business and Manufacturing to estimate density gradients, the density functions estimated here are based on data from the Local Personal Income Series produced by the U.S. Department of Commerce, Bureau of Economic Analysis. This series provides annual observations on

[1]Transportation investment is the percentage change in dollar investments in highways and roads, deflated by the fixed investment price deflator for non-residential structures, for the years 1966 to 1980. The instrumental variables used in this study include total federal expenditure on highways, federal highway revenues, federal highway balances, total state expenditure on transportation (for the state(s) in which the cities were located), and the state/local and federal/state matching ratios for highway construction. All highway expenditure variables were deflated by the non-residential investment price index. It is possible that further investigation could detect even better instrumental variables which could improve final results. Our approach was to select a set of instruments and estimate the model once rather than to add further instruments when results proved to be of marginal significance.

TABLE 1
Instrumental Variable Estimates of the Relation among Population and Employment Gradients

Independent variables	Population gradient	Construction gradient	Manufacturing gradient	Transportation, Communication, and public utility gradient	Wholesale gradient	Retail gradient	Finance insurance, and real estate gradient	Services gradient
Intercept	0.115**	0.411	0.037	0.467	0.337	0.002	0.415*	−0.115
	(2.76)	(1.29)	(0.32)	(1.06)	(1.11)	(0.01)	(1.89)	(0.76)
$GPOP_{t-1}$	0.759**	0.167	0.148	−0.726	0.109	0.438**	−0.107	0.530**
	(12.7)	(0.36)	(0.90)	(1.15)	(0.25)	(2.68)	(0.34)	(2.46)
$GCONST_{t-1}$	0.003	0.290**	0.042	0.290**	−0.018	−0.006	−0.025	−0.006
	(0.23)	(2.76)	(1.12)	(2.02)	(0.18)	(0.15)	(0.34)	(0.13)
$GMFG_{t-1}$	−0.097**	−0.570**	0.609**	0.248	0.065	0.040	−0.272**	−0.107
	(4.04)	(3.08)	(9.30)	(0.98)	(0.37)	(0.61)	(2.15)	(1.23)
$GTCPU_{t-1}$	0.020*	0.241**	0.053*	0.387**	0.128	0.023	0.019	0.039
	(1.82)	(2.78)	(1.72)	(3.25)	(1.56)	(0.73)	(0.32)	(0.96)
$GWHL_{t-1}$	−0.001	−0.018	−0.011	−0.249	−0.005	−0.069	−0.078	−0.082
	(0.01)	(0.15)	(0.26)	(1.52)	(0.04)	(1.61)	(0.95)	(1.50)
$GRETAIL_{t-1}$	0.021	0.255	−0.032	0.611	1.324**	0.831**	0.344*	0.110
	(0.55)	(0.88)	(0.31)	(1.54)	(4.84)	(8.11)	(1.74)	(0.81)
$GFIRE_{t-1}$	−0.020	−0.161	−0.008	−0.021	−0.249*	−0.002	0.574**	0.017
	(1.11)	(1.16)	(0.17)	(0.11)	(1.89)	(0.04)	(6.03)	(0.26)
$GSER_{t-1}$	0.063**	0.205	0.029	−0.081	−0.011	−0.120*	0.123	0.697**
	(2.57)	(1.08)	(0.43)	(0.31)	(0.06)	(1.79)	(0.95)	(7.86)
INCOME	−0.015**	0.017	−0.003	0.401	0.033	−0.007	−0.004	−0.007
	(2.03)	(0.30)	(0.12)	(0.51)	(0.61)	(0.33)	(0.10)	(0.27)
TPOP	−0.040	0.113	0.136	0.424	0.065	0.048	0.235	0.104
	(1.27)	(0.47)	(1.59)	(1.28)	(0.28)	(0.56)	(1.42)	(0.92)

continued over

TRANS	−0.003	−0.007	0.010	0.036	0.018	0.015**	0.004	0.015
	(0.95)	(0.34)	(1.40)	(1.25)	(0.89)	(1.99)	(0.30)	(1.52)
WPOP	−0.007	−0.004	0.057	−0.069	0.055	0.010	−0.045	0.048
	(0.54)	(0.03)	(1.53)	(0.48)	(0.56)	(0.27)	(0.63)	(0.97)
TIME	−0.001**	−0.004	−0.001	−0.002	−0.004*	−0.000	−0.002	0.008
	(2.28)	(1.62)	(0.48)	(0.59)	(1.81)	(0.44)	(1.63)	(0.75)
R^2	0.999	0.980	0.998	0.969	0.991	0.998	0.995	0.995

Note. Absolute values of *t* statistics are in parenthesis.
* Significant at 5% level for a two-tail test.
** Significant at 10% level for a two-tail test.

industry employment, per capita income, and population for central cities and counties. Transportation investment is estimated based on total expenditures for roads and highways by SMSA taken from "Highway Statistics," an annual publication of the Department of Transportation. The population and employment density gradients are computed using Mills' "two-point" approach, an iterative technique based on the Newton–Raphson method.[2] The sample consists of a cross section of 11 cities observed over 14 years, yielding a total of 143 observations. City selection was based on data availability. The final sample size is significantly larger than that used in previous studies, but it is not large enough to permit the investivation of second-order lags in the relation between population and employment decentralization.[3]

Table 1 presents estimation results for all variables except the city dummy variables, which are of no particular importance. The estimated coefficients of the fully exogenous variables on the population density gradient generally follow expectations based on both theory and past studies as reviewed by McDonald [10]. Increasing income per capita has a significant negative effect on the density gradient as expected based on theory and recent empirical work by Margo [9]. While Steinnes and Cooke found non-significant and positive and significant time trends, respectively, our estimates indicate a significant decline in the population density

[2]The population and employment density gradients were estimated using the standard two-point method described by Mills [11]. Assuming that the density function is a negative exponential as in Eq. (1), it follows that

$$\frac{\mathrm{POP_c}}{\mathrm{POP_m}} = \frac{1 - (1 + gr)e^{r}}{1 - (1 + gR)e^{R}},$$

where $\mathrm{POP_c}$ and $\mathrm{POP_m}$ are the population of the central city and metropolitan area, respectively, g is the density gradient, and r and R are the radius of the central city and metropolitan area, respectively. Given annual data on population or industry employment for the central city and suburbs, this becomes a single equation in unknown g. The value of g was estimated using iterative Newton–Raphson techniques.

[3]The 11 SMSA's included in the sample were Boston, Hartford, Buffalo, Philadelphia, Washington, DC, Baltimore, Columbus, St. Louis, Portland, and Sacramento. Annual observations were from 1966 to 1980, so that the total sample size generated was 143 observations. There were 15 annual observations for 11 cities, but 1 annual observation per city was lost to create lagged values of the dependent variables. Because data series from a number of sources, some of which have been altered or discontinued, were combined in this study, it was not possible to extend either the time period or the cross section of cities covered. The estimation consumed 24 degrees of freedom, the 14 variables listed in Table 1 and the 10 city dummy variables. Thus the estimates are based on 119 degrees of freedom. Adding a second-order lag would have consumed 1 additional degree of freedom for each city and 8 degrees of freedom for the second-order lags of the eight endogenous variables for a total of 19 additional degrees of freedom, leaving only 100 degrees of freedom for the estimates.

gradient over time. In contrast to most of the studies reviewed above, the estimated coefficient of transportation investment has the expected negative sign but it is non-significant.[4] As suggested by theory, findings by Mills and Price [13] or more recently by Mills [12], the rate of population growth has no effect on the gradient and the changing percentage of the white population in the center city is also non-significant.

In contrast to the results reported in both Cooke and Mills and Price, there is evidence that decentralization of some employment sectors significantly affects subsequent population decentralization. The estimates indicate that lagged values of the services gradient, GSER, and the transportation, communication, and public utility gradient, GTCPU, both have positive and significant effects on the population gradient. Taken together with the result that GTCPU also has a positive and significant estimated coefficient in the construction gradient equation, this suggests that the falling TCPU gradient reflects suburban infrastructure development that allows decentralization of other sectors.

The negative and significant estimated coefficient of GMFG, also found by Steinnes [17, 18], indicates that decentralizing manufacturing employment retards population decentralization. An equivalent way to state this last effect is that increased concentration of manufacturing employment in the central city may speed the suburbanization of the residential population. Steinnes argued that manufacturing could generate local negative externalities that account for the negative effect on population.

The effect of lagged retail employment density, GRET, on population decentralization, reported to be positive and significant by Steinnes and non-significant by Cooke, is non-significant in these results. The failure of Mills and price to observe any significant relation between changes in the aggregate employment gradient and population decentralization may be due to aggregation across sectors which have different effects on the population gradient.

Estimation results for the effects of changes in the population gradient on job decentralization in the seven industrial sectors appear plausible. The lagged value of the population density gradient, GPOP, is non-significant in all employment equations except for the retail trade and services sectors where it is positive and significant. This presumably reflects a demand side linkage between consumers and industries selling consumption goods. The finding in both Steinnes and Mills and Price of a significant effect of population suburbanization on manufacturing decen-

[4]Theory suggests that travel cost rather than transportation investment is the appropriate measure to be used in these estimates. Failure to obtain a statistically significant coefficient for TRANS is likely due to a combination of our inability to observe transportation cost and to the limited choice of instrumental variables used in the two-stage least-squares estimates.

tralization is not supported. Indeed, beyond retail and services, there is little support for the jobs follow population argument made by Steinnes, Cooke, and Mills and Price.

The variables included in the employment density gradient equations based on their possible role in population decentralization, income change, total population growth, and the percentage of whites in the center city, are all non-significant in the industry gradient equations as expected. Transportation investment is non-significant except for a positive effect on the retail gradient.

Relatively little is known about the relation among intraurban location decisions of different industrial sectors in an urban area. The estimation results indicate that there are a modest number of significant interactions among the density gradients of the disaggregated industrial sectors. Changes in the construction density gradient have a positive and significant effect on transportation and public utilities. This may reflect the demand for utilities that follows suburbanization of construction. Manufacturing decentralization has a negative and significant effect on construction and finance, insurance, and real estate, as well as its previously noted negative effect on population decentralization. Taken together, our results suggest the rather surprising conclusion that manufacturing decentralization may retard suburbanization of residential population, finance, insurance, and real estate.

The density gradient for retail trade has a positive and significant effect on changes in the wholesale trade and finance, insurance, and real estate gradients. The least plausible estimated coefficients are the negative and significant effect of the density gradients of finance, insurance, and real estate on wholesale trade and the negative and significant effect of the density gradient of services on retail employment.

V. SUMMARY AND CONCLUSIONS

The empirical analysis of determinants of variation in density gradients for both population and industrial sectors described in this paper builds on Steinnes' [17] attempt to explore causal relations between suburbanization of employment and population. Using greater disaggregation, both by time and by sector, produces different results.

The importance of sectoral disaggregation of employment is illustrated by the estimated parameters of the population density gradient equation. We find both a significant negative effect of the manufacturing gradient on the population gradient and significant positive effects of the service and public utility gradients on the population gradient. Clearly aggregation across such employment sectors could conceal important detail on relations between individual sectors and population decentralization.

The effect of the population density gradient on the gradient for the retail and service sectors is positive and significant. But for other sectors the estimated effect of population decentralization is non-significant. Thus we find that only a limited amount of employment decentralization is caused by the suburbanization of population. This contrasts with previous findings and with the general perception that population decentralization, driven by forces that are well understood, determines employment decentralization, which is otherwise rather difficult to model. We find a variety of interesting interactions among the density gradients of various industrial sectors but must conclude that Stahl [16] was correct in remarking that we have much to learn about intraurban location of employment by sector.

Overall, the results reported here suggest that the answer to the popular questions, "Do people follow jobs?" and "Do jobs follow people?", is, generally, "no" to both.

REFERENCES

1. A. Anas and I. Kim, Income distribution and the residential density gradient, *Journal of Urban Economics*, **31**, 145–163 (1992).
2. D. Bradford and H. Kelejian, An econometric model of flight to the suburbs, *Journal of Political Economy*, **81**, 566–589 (1973).
3. J. Brueckner, The structure of urban equilibria: A unified treatment of the Muth–Mills model, *in* "Handbook of Regional and Urban Economics" (E. Mills, Ed.), Vol. 2, Chap. 20, North-Holland, New York (1987).
4. C. Clark, Urban population densities, *Journal of the Royal Statistical Society*, **114A**, 490–496 (1951).
5. T. Cooke, Causality reconsidered: A note, *Journal of Urban Economics*, **5**, 538–542 (1978).
6. C. W. J. Granger, Some recent developments in a concept of causality, *Journal of Econometrics*, **39**, 199–212 (1988).
7. W. E. Herrin and C. R. Kern, Testing the standard urban model of residential choice: An implicit markets approach, *Journal of Urban Economics*, **31**, 145–163 (1992).
8. J. Kau, C. Lee, and C. F. Sirmans, "Urban Econometrics: Model Developments and Empirical Results," JAI Press, London (1986).
9. R. A. Margo, Explaining the postwar suburbanization of population in the United States: The role of income, *Journal of Urban Economics*, **31**, 300–310 (1992).
10. J. F. McDonald, Econometric studies of urban population density: A survey, *Journal of Urban Economics*, **26**, 361–385 (1989).
11. E. S. Mills, "Studies in the Structure of the Metropolitan Economy," Johns Hopkins Univ. Press, Baltimore (1972).
12. E. S. Mills, The measurement and determinants of suburbanization, *Journal of Urban Economics*, **32**, 377–387 (1992).
13. E. S. Mills and R. Price, Metropolitan suburbanization and central city problems, *Journal of Urban Economics*, **15**, 1–17 (1984).
14. R. F. Muth, "Cities and Housing," University of Chicago Press, Chicago (1969).
15. R. Schmenner, The rent gradient for manufacturing, *Journal of Urban Economics*, **9**, 90–96 (1981).

16. K. Stahl, Theories of urban business location, *in* "Handbook of Regional and Urban Economics" (E. Mills, Ed.), Chap. 19, North-Holland, New York (1987).
17. D. Steinnes, Causality and intraurban location, *Journal of Urban Economics*, **4**, 69–79 (1977).
18. D. Steinnes, Do "people follow jobs" or "do jobs follow people"?: A causality issue in urban economics, *Urban Studies*, **19**, 187–192 (1982).
19. D. Steinnes and W. Fisher, An econometric model of intraurban location, *Journal of Regional Science*, **16**, 65–80 (1974).
20. W. C. Wheaton, Urban spatial development with durable but replaceable capital, *Journal of Urban Economics*, **12**, 1–21 (1982).

[8]

Economica (1995) **62**, 247–67

On the Price of Land and the Value of Amenities

By Paul Cheshire and Stephen Sheppard

University of Reading and Oberlin College, Ohio.

Final version received 5 October 1993.

A house represents not only a bundle of structural characteristics but also a set of location specific characteristics. Adding locational coordinates and site area to other house characteristics makes it possible to estimate a land rent surface as well as the hedonic prices attached to local patterns of land use and other neighbourhood characteristics. One can then estimate how the value of such location-specific characteristics are capitalized into land prices. This analysis, illustrated with estimates based on data from two British towns, has a number of wider implications. It generates a more parsimonious method of estimating amenity values. It also reveals likely systematic biases produced by conventional hedonic studies which exclude land and location. Finally, it clarifies the conceptual definition of land and suggests that monocentric models can perform well despite recent criticism.

Introduction

There have been comparatively few detailed studies of local housing markets in Britain using micro data and employing a hedonic approach, and even fewer that include as housing characteristics land consumption, location, neighbourhood and local environmental factors. Studies that combine at least some of these ingredients have been comparatively common in the United States, at least since Kain and Quigley (1970a, b).[1] Though less frequently applied in the British context, there have been some studies, notably Awan *et al.* (1982), Rosenthal (1989) and Pennington *et al.* (1990).

It is now widely accepted that housing is a composite and heterogeneous good. Housing, however, is composed not only of characteristics relating to the structure itself—such as type of house, size, number of rooms or the existence of central heating—but also of characteristics determined by location. These latter include the classic element of urban economic models, accessibility. There are additional location-determined characteristics, however, such as the character of neighbouring houses and households, localized traffic effects and the quality of the micro environment and local public goods such as schools. Different authors have grouped these characteristics in different ways, but the distinction made by Wilkinson (1973), between dwelling-specific and location-specific factors, seems the most fundamental. To date, far more econometric attention has been paid in the literature to dwelling-specific factors than to location-specific ones, although, as the results reported in this paper suggest, the location-specific characteristics are of significant interest.

Attention has begun to turn to the location-specific characteristics as attempts to value environmental quality have intensified[2] and as labour and housing market models have been combined in attempts to quantify urban quality-of-life differences.[3] In this paper we aim to show that it is necessary to include both the accessibility aspect of location and a full range of the neighbourhood characteristics if one is to get stable and reliable estimates of the effects of either. We also outline a technique which, under appropriate conditions, can provide estimates of the marginal value of neighbourhood characteristics: value that will be capitalized into, and is often confused with, the value of land.

The analytical approach presented in this paper has several novel features. Urban rent theory suggests that land values result from a trade-off between transport costs and accessibility. Transport systems, and so transport costs, however, are not necessarily symmetric, so the rent function employed here allows for multiple asymmetries in the urban system. The analysis utilizes a more complete specification of neighbourhood characteristics than is usual, including measures of the patterns of land use. These latter prove to be important explanatory factors in their own right, but have been formulated in ways designed directly to reflect the 'outputs' of the British land use planning system. These outputs are simplified but are defined as the separation of land uses, 'containment',[4] the provision of unbuilt, accessible urban space and the provision of areas for new housing.

This model is fitted to data for the town of Reading in the UK, but is shown to be at least to a degree generalizable; it is also fitted to data for Darlington in the UK, and the differences in estimated parameters are shown directly to reflect physical differences between the cities and differences in their land use planning regimes and transport systems.

Hedonic models are often estimated using incomplete data, and local amenities are perhaps most frequently excluded. By successively adding sets of location-specific characteristics to the model, it is possible econometrically to simulate the capitalization of these characteristics into land values. This suggests an alternative method of estimating the value to be allocated to neighbourhood and environmental characteristics, and an application of this technique is then developed. This analysis helps to clarify important debates in urban economics. Urban rent theory as developed by authors such as Alonso (1964), Muth (1969) or Evans (1973) implies that land values essentially arise from the trade-off between accessibility and transport costs. These results are derived on the basis of monocentric models, however, and the applicability of such models to modern cities has been increasingly questioned (see e.g. Brueckner 1987; Straszheim 1987; Yinger 1992).

The results reported here suggest that, if location-specific characteristics of housing are appropriately measured, monocentric models *can* perform well. This in turn draws attention to the fact that land itself is a composite good. The price of land as conceptually treated in urban rent theory is the price of pure land, as space at a location, but independent of the bundle of neighbourhood, environmental characteristics and local public goods embodied in land. This implies that, contrary to some recent suggestions (see e.g. Helsley and Rosenthal 1991), observed prices of vacant or recently redeveloped plots of urban land *cannot* be used to estimate land rent surfaces in the sense in which such surfaces exist in urban rent models. Vacant plots of urban land are seething with location-specific and valuable characteristics, in addition to their area of 'pure' land.

Finally, the measures that have been devised to value the outputs of the land use planning system provide a means of examining the benefits created by that system as well as its costs (see Cheshire and Sheppard 1989).

I. Estimation: Functional Form and Structure

Before proceeding to obtain estimates, two issues must be dealt with. The form for the hedonic price function must be chosen, and the characteristics or variables to be included in the estimates must be decided upon. This latter decision may involve recognition of relevant variables which are omitted from the analysis. We first present and discuss the functional form used in the estimates, and then discuss issues that arise because of omitted variables.

Functional form

Although some earlier writers (e.g. Linneman 1980) had employed the Box–Cox functional form, it is since Halvorsen and Pollakowski's (1981) contribution that this form has become widely employed in hedonic studies. The results reported here would justify the choice of the Box–Cox form on the technical grounds for which it was originally developed (Box and Cox 1964): there is evidence that linear forms of the model are confronted with non-normal errors. The results obtained using the Box–Cox form so dominated the linear version that these latter results are not reported here.[5]

Because theory suggests that land values will vary with accessibility, the hedonic price function should permit the spatial structure of land values to be estimated from the observations. Conventional urban economic theory has been developed on the basis of a monocentric city, with land values declining with distance from the centre. Such models, however, have been criticized as lacking realism as decentralized employment subcentres have emerged. The most complex estimated land rent functions of which we are aware are those presented in Jackson *et al.* (1984). Their completely free form approach is not used here, however, partly because of the smaller size of the available data-sets and partly because experience strongly suggests that the use of very flexible land rent functions, when combined with an attempt separately to estimate the value of location-specific amenities, results in estimates that are not robust.

The land rent function used here is given by:

$$(1) \qquad r(d, \theta) = \beta_1 \exp\{d[\beta_2 + \beta_3 \sin(n\theta - \beta_4)]\},$$

where

d = distance from town centre
θ = angle of deflection from East
β_i = parameters to be estimated
n = an integer, the value of which is to be determined by investigation

Note that this form allows for multiple radial asymmetries in land rents to emerge via the estimated parameters β_3 and β_4 and the chosen structure of the land rent function which depends, in part, upon n. This function does not impose downward-sloping land rents or monocentricity; nor does it impose simple symmetry. Asymmetries can emerge reflecting, for example, transport networks or topography. The form is, however, 'monocentric' in the limited sense that, along any linear path from the city centre, land rents will increase or decrease at a constant rate.

The basic hedonic model to be estimated, incorporating the land rent function, is as follows:

$$\text{(2)} \qquad \frac{p^{\psi}-1}{\psi}=K+\sum_{i\in D}\beta_i x_i+\sum_{j\in C}\beta_j\frac{x_j^{\lambda}-1}{\lambda}+r(d,\theta)\frac{L^{\xi}-1}{\xi},$$

where:

p = rentalized price of structure
x_i, x_j = structure or location-specific characteristics
K, β_i, β_j, λ, ψ, ξ = parameters to be estimated
L = quantity of land included with structure
D = set of indices of characteristics that are dichotomous
C = set of indices of characteristics that are continuously variable
$r(d, \theta)$ = land rent function defined above
ψ, λ, ξ are the standard parameters of the Box–Cox functional form

It should be noted that this form contains the additional innovation that separate Box–Cox transformation parameters are estimated for continuously variable structure and neighbourhood characteristics, and for land. There is no reason in theory why the same non-linearities should apply to land as apply to housing characteristics.[6]

Estimation and the problem of omitted variables

Parameter estimates for the hedonic functions were obtained using standard maximum likelihood techniques.[7] Obtaining robust estimates of individual characteristic values, as distinct from attempting to forecast the market value of structures, also meant that the resolution of problems of colinearity between characteristics was particularly important. There is frequently joint variation between structure or neighbourhood characteristics, for example between the number of bathrooms and the number of WCs, or between the socioeconomic characteristics of a neighbourhood and the rate of owner occupation. The approach adopted here, where two or more variables were closely correlated, was to subsume the effect of that class of variables within one variable.[8]

Data measuring, as appropriately as possible, the maximum practicable number of relevant variables were collected. At least one from each 'class' of variable is included, but judgment—on the basis of comparing many different model estimates—has been exercised to exclude those variables that seem to add little additional insight into the underlying market processes and which, by their exclusion, lessen the problems of colinearity. In the final model reported here (see Table 1), all included variables had relatively stable parameter estimates, in the sense that no comparable models that had been estimated had generated parameter values of different sign or with absolute values differing by more than about one standard error.[9] The result of this process is that the value of bathrooms, for example, is included in the value of WCs, and socioeconomic and ethnic composition of the neighbourhood is reflected in just two variables. The variables finally used are defined in Table A1.

In hedonic studies it is most common to omit or have inappropriate measures of neighbourhood characteristics. This is both because such data are more difficult to collect and because it is less obvious, *a priori*, which are relevant in determining prices. The potential set of structure characteristics is by comparison limited and well researched. In fact, non-structure characteristics can themselves be subdivided into two groups based on the congestibility of consumption. There are general background amenities such as proximity to major metropolitan centres, key infrastructure or climate. These latter may be properly regarded as pure public goods consumed at the same level by all local residents. The larger class of neighbourhood amenities, however, will be subject to congestion and correlated with the amount of land consumed by a household. Neighbourhoods in which land consumption is, on average, larger will of necessity have lower density of occupation and hence less crowding of the local amenities. In this sense we depart from the world considered by Parsons (1990), in which all amenities are pure public goods and as a result the hedonic function must have such attributes weighted by land area. We assume that local amenities are fundamentally subject to congestion and hence such weighting is not appropriate.

While consumption of congestible amenities will be correlated with land consumption, the 'neighbourhood' nature of these characteristics implies that in general they will not be correlated with structure characteristics. This simple observation allows us to characterize more precisely the bias that results in hedonic estimation when these amenities are unobserved.

The expected value of the jth unobserved characteristic is given by

$$\hat{x}_j = \alpha_{1j} + \alpha_{2j} L. \tag{3}$$

The parameters have a clear interpretation, with α_{1j} representing the constant or 'background' level of the amenity associated with any structure located in the area, and α_{2j} being the marginal increase in amenity associated with the reduced congestion brought about by consumption of an additional unit of land area, L.

In this case, with unobserved amenity variables whose consumption is correlated with land consumption, it can be formally shown that the estimation of the hedonic function yields unbiased estimates of hedonic prices for all observed characteristics except land area (see Cheshire and Sheppard 1993). Characterization of the bias in estimating land prices leads to the idea that an approximate measure of the aggregate value of a neighbourhood amenity can be obtained by summing the change in estimated land rents that results when that amenity is excluded from the model.

II. The Data

The data for this study were collected in Reading and Darlington in the summer of 1984 towards the end of a period of comparative stability in the British housing market. Details of approximately 350 properties in Darlington and 490 properties in Reading were obtained by taking a 15% sample of all houses being offered for sale by local estate agents. The geographic area that was sampled was delimited by the boundaries of the contiguous built-up area

Each property was identified on large-scale Ordnance Survey maps showing property boundaries. The location was recorded, and the exact amount of land measured. The price of the structure was taken to be the listed asking price. The actual transaction price for structures would be the usual variable to include in hedonic analysis, but this variable was not directly available, and indeed is rarely made available for English housing markets. Because of the stability of the market during the time when this information was collected, it might be argued that the asking price offered a good approximation of the actual transaction price. To test this, and to collect additional information about the households, surveys were sent to each address approximately three months after the samples had been selected. The response rate (after follow-up) was 47% and 31% gross respectively for Reading and Darlington; but a number of houses were vacant, so this represents a somewhat higher response rate for potential responders. For houses that had actually sold, the mean transaction price was within 1% of the mean asking price.

A wide range of data on neighbourhood characteristics was collected. This included a full set of ward-level data from the 1981 Census of Population. To this was added information on the secondary school catchment area in which the house was located. For particular schools this was the only local amenity information included on estate agents' particulars, and a reasonable view of the competitive process might therefore imply that it was a locational characteristic of a house that affected its price.

In addition, information on the accessibility of each house to the bus network and the class of road on which the house was located was generated. Roads were divided into five categories from culs-de-sac to main roads using the Ordnance Survey's classification. The aim was to reflect the level of both traffic disturbance and pollution to which a house was subject[10] and—more speculatively—the localized crime rate. Location on larger roads might also provide an increased level of accessibility and the possibility of conversion to commercial use, and so might increase a house's value. The actual observed effect would be the net outcome of these two effects, so that in general the road classification variable might take either positive or negative values.

Finally, each structure was located in a kilometre square and the pattern of land uses and measures of the local topography were calculated for that square from Ordnance Survey maps and aerial photographs, and assigned to the structure. The measures of land use were formulated to reflect, in a simplified way, the goals of land use planning policy. Table A1 presents a list of the variables selected for the analysis along with brief descriptions.

Table A2 presents some descriptive statistics of the variables (in the first two columns following the variable names) and (in the remaining columns) correlations between the local amenity and neighbourhood variables and the other variables used. All continuous variables have been formulated in a way that implies that more of them is 'better'.

No variables reflecting variation in local air quality were included. This decision was partly practical—data were not readily available—but also it was thought unlikely that there would be sufficient variation, independently of local traffic density, which would be reflected in the street classification, to yield any result. Although the contiguous built-up area of Reading is considerably larger than the political district of Reading (it has about 250,000 inhabitants compared with 135,000 in the borough itself), it is still quite small in absolute terms and there are no obvious sources of localized pollution.

III. The Results

The analysis reported below has three principal objectives. First, we report estimates of hedonic price functions based on the data collected, and explore the consequences of alternative specifications. In particular, we examine the effects of excluding local amenity variables for goodness of fit and stability of parameter estimates. Second, we present calculations based on the estimated hedonic functions of the hedonic prices of structure and neighbourhood characteristics and the value of residential land. These are examined for consistency with local urban structure and transport infrastructure. Finally, we derive a technique for obtaining estimates of the capitalized value of local amenities, or groups of amenities.

Hedonic function estimates

Table 1 presents hedonic function estimates for seven models fitted to the data for Reading. Model 1, in the rightmost column, is the simplest of all reported: it excludes land and location altogether. Model 2 is similar to many that are estimated and reported in the literature: it includes land area but not structure location. The next five models have increasingly complete specifications of local amenities. The eighth column reports the results of fitting a model that is essentially the same as the most complete Reading model to the Darlington data.

The final four rows of the table present information concerning the estimation of each model and some statistical tests that facilitate comparison and analysis of each specification. The rows labelled 'Observations' and 'Log likelihood' require no explanation.[11] The final two rows of the table present likelihood ratio statistics to test two hypotheses concerning each model. The penultimate row tests the hypothesis that the model for that column does not represent a significant restriction compared with the most complete specification reported as model 7. The statistic cannot always be calculatd based on the reported likelihood values in each column. Rather, it is based on likelihood values achieved in estimates restricted to the observations for which all variables used in the most complete model are available. Values marked with a double asterisk indicate rejection of the null hypothesis at the 1% level; those rejected at the 5% level are marked with a single asterisk. It is apparent from the penultimate row that dropping any set of amenity variables results in a model that performs significantly less well.

The statistics presented in the last row test each model with the model that precedes it (to the left). That is, the hypothesis is that the elimination of the variables added in the model to the left does not constitute a significant restriction. Levels of significance are indicated as in the previous row. From these tests it will be seen that any restriction from the full specification is statistically significant. In addition, omitting any group of variables results in a restriction that is statistically significant.

Another question relates to the stability of parameter estimates: are changes observed as the models estimated become increasingly complete, statistically significant? Although it does not represent a precise test, changes in parameter estimates that are greater than one standard error provide a good indication of significant shifts. On this criterion—ignoring the constant term—only the

TABLE 1
HEDONIC FUNCTION ESTIMATES[a]

Variable	Estimates for Darlington	All variables: model 7	Add social & ethnic: model 6	Add streets: model 5	Add schools: model 4	Land and location: model 3	No location: model 2	No land: model 1
Constant	−1·174491	−0·437801	−0·594678	−0·566182	−0·710626	−0·959410	−0·729530	−0·777317
	(−4·995)	(−3·351)	(−7·324)	(−6·989)	(−7·048)	(−9·212)	(−1·551)	(−1·395)
Bedrooms	0·299203	0·071472	0·064125	0·058385	0·063012	0·061127	0·053402	0·040457
	(5·249)	(4·277)	(3·579)	(3·034)	(3·250)	(2·293)	(2·556)	(1·946)
WCs	0·105324	0·075433	0·071710	0·074240	0·076084	0·090055	0·082569	0·066626
	(1·715)	(4·690)	(4·467)	(4·440)	(4·566)	(5·031)	(4·756)	(4·027)
Terrace	−0·476244	−0·087253	−0·079594	−0·088716	−0·102989	−0·113737	−0·109585	−0·113742
	(−8·278)	(−4·256)	(−3·929)	(−4·163)	(−4·625)	(−4·821)	(−4·578)	(−4·627)
Semi	−0·265631	−0·082580	−0·077908	−0·081802	−0·094010	−0·097954	−0·095283	−0·089928
	(−5·821)	(−5·069)	(−4·863)	(−5·017)	(−5·510)	(−5·673)	(−5·391)	(−5·131)
Flat	−0·547298	−0·114750	−0·101039	−0·104322	−0·110082	−0·119533	−0·108817	−0·146778
	(−3·861)	(−4·934)	(−4·581)	(−4·575)	(−4·747)	(−4·957)	(−4·295)	(−5·524)
Parking	0·018019	0·020847	0·023584	0·038669	0·039480	0·050720	0·042643	0·039313
	(0·621)	(1·432)	(1·641)	(2·553)	(2·547)	(3·068)	(2·635)	(2·468)
Garage	0·072521	0·054970	0·053862	0·070244	0·072197	0·083190	0·069596	0·069478
	(2·023)	(3·382)	(3·346)	(4·036)	(4·030)	(4·405)	(3·774)	(3·811)
Central heating	0·116745	0·049574	0·048599	0·050052	0·045687	0·046967	0·048926	0·044805
	(4·776)	(4·170)	(4·127)	(4·086)	(3·736)	(3·674)	(3·729)	(3·497)
Floors	0·418049	0·077741	0·079254	0·072809	0·088885	0·068230	0·064479	0·096429
	(4·342)	(2·718)	(2·103)	(1·788)	(2·107)	(1·256)	(1·642)	(2·579)
Plot width	0·011508	0·009989	0·020703	0·030109	0·029272	0·041272	0·030089	0·084845
	(0·688)	(1·642)	(1·932)	(2·302)	(2·250)	(2·300)	(1·568)	(2·217)
Square feet	0·009364	0·032946	0·086691	0·112926	0·138355	0·230749	0·149617	0·167241
	(0·560)	(3·995)	(4·065)	(4·410)	(3·860)	(3·880)	(1·378)	(1·345)
λ	0·334236	0·240681	0·110559	0·069006	0·059605	−0·012685	0·057107	0·059509
(transformation for RHS)	(1·753)	(6·249)	(1·915)	(1·204)	(0·976)	(−0·171)	(0·485)	(0·533)

continued over

TABLE 1—continued

Variable	Estimates for Darlington	All variables: model 7	Add social & ethnic: model 6	Add streets: model 5	Add schools: model 4	Land and location: model 3	No location: model 2	No land: model 1
Ψ	0·242562	−0·315410	−0·345799	−0·333964	−0·296199	−0·281266	−0·291849	−0·335842
(transformation for LHS)	(3·244)	(−3·423)	(−3·595)	(−3·535)	(−3·268)	(−3·613)	(−3·200)	(−3·638)
ξ	0·996934	0·186003	0·145476	0·116929	0·127366	0·203249	0·147468	
(transformation for land)	(33·972)	(4·604)	(3·487)	(3·007)	(3·136)	(7·250)	(1·241)	
$\beta 1$	0·000080	0·020580	0·023047	0·028862	0·025811	0·015781	0·023132	
	(7·179)	(3·299)	(3·067)	(3·110)	(2·902)	(3·554)	(0·994)	
$\beta 2$	−0·157455	−0·153300	−0·056985	−0·013993	−0·000507	−0·039435		
	(−0·882)	(−3·674)	(−2·196)	(−0·724)	(−0·031)	(−1·867)		
$\beta 3$	−0·049834	0·070557	0·030564	0·017152	0·011587	−0·013950		
	(−0·493)	(3·431)	(2·233)	(1·588)	(1·220)	(−1·286)		
$\beta 4$	4·079206	4·323855	4·403086	4·252557	4·181550	5·968773		
	(2·760)	(28·160)	(14·194)	(9·189)	(6·417)	(7·887)		
School 1	0·116754	0·084157	0·071125	0·085485	0·090087			
	(2·296)	(4·639)	(4·394)	(5·076)	(5·298)			
School 2	0·108617	0·061509	0·043120	0·039428	0·034087			
	(3·232)	(3·425)	(2·729)	(2·561)	(2·175)			
School 3		0·027228	0·001817	0·000372	−0·002204			
		(1·456)	(0·120)	(0·024)	(−0·137)			
Street 1	−0·036657	−0·003028	−0·006576	−0·009486				
	(−1·434)	(−0·294)	(−0·649)	(−0·916)				
Street 2	−0·052320	−0·005415	−0·004569	−0·010576				
	(−1·167)	(−0·401)	(−0·344)	(−0·764)				
Street 3	0·140230	−0·054976	−0·062174	−0·085600				
	(1·474)	(−1·606)	(−1·808)	(−2·359)				
Street 4	−0·000608	0·023645	0·019449	0·020353				
	(−0·008)	(1·231)	(1·030)	(1·029)				
Bus		0·006856	0·001032	0·001956				
		(0·849)	(0·133)	(0·242)				

TABLE 1—continued

Variable	Estimates for Darlington	All variables: model 7	Add social & ethnic: model 6	Add streets: model 5	Add schools: model 4	Land and location: model 3	No location: model 2	No land: model 1
Blue collar	0·058055	0·007029	0·031092					
	(1·493)	(0·887)	(2·833)					
Ethnic	0·042708	0·022653	0·019128					
	(1·958)	(2·957)	(2·492)					
Altitude		0·005692						
		(0·739)						
Industrial land	0·004198	0·028713						
	(0·312)	(1·580)						
New construction	0·158051	−0·022332						
	(2·595)	(−1·895)						
Open land amenity	0·017486	0·005600						
	(2·710)	(1·710)						
Closed land amenity	0·000002	0·005962						
	(0·000)	(3·605)						
Observations	309	432	432	434	461	461	461	461
Log likelihood	−25·5733	−297·29	−312·48	−326·92	−349·60	−372·75	−376·68	−401·93
χ^2: model compared with full specification			30·38**	56·88**	66·38**	109·55**	116·69**	165·53**
χ^2: model compared with preceding			30·38**	26·50**	9·53**	46·30**	7·86*	50·50**

[a]Beneath each parameter estimate is given the t-statistic for the parameter in parentheses.

estimates for the parameters for square feet, the transformation parameter for land (ζ) and some location-related components of the rent function (β_2, β_3) show more than one such change. We may thus conclude that with one important exception the estimates of the structure variables are robust. The effects of the exclusion of the amenity or location-specific variables are reflected primarily in changes in the land-related parameter estimates.

Nevertheless, since total floor area of the structure is an important motor in the results obtained from many models fitted without land and location, the observation that its estimated value is sensitive to the exclusion of location-specific characteristics is significant. Its estimated value changes by more than one standard error when schools are included, again when the social and ethnic variables are added, and again when the planning and land-related variables are included. The explanation for this sensitivity to the inclusion of location-specific characteristics is likely to be the high correlation (see Table A2) between internal area of the structure and land area. That the land and location-related parameter estimates are sensitive to location-specific characteristics is consistent with the underlying hypothesis of this paper.

Estimated hedonic prices

It is straightforward to differentiate equation (2) to obtain the hedonic prices for each characteristic. Evaluating the resulting expressions at sample mean values for the independent variables presented in Table A2 provides estimates of the hedonic prices derived from each model. These are presented in Table 2 for all characteristics except land area.

TABLE 2

HEDONIC PRICES FOR AN AVERAGE STRUCTURE

Variable	Darlington	All variables: model 7	Add ethnic: model 6	Add Streets: model 5	Add schools: model 4	Land and location: model 3	No location: model 2	No land: model 1
Bedrooms	0·2604	0·2144	0·1738	0·1483	0·1497	0·1309	0·1257	0·1020
WCs	0·1699	0·3967	0·3750	0·3753	0·3622	0·4076	0·3902	0·3365
Terrace	−0·8250	−0·6177	−0·5895	−0·6456	−0·7085	−0·7653	−0·7491	−0·8301
Semi	−0·4602	−0·5846	−0·5770	−0·5953	−0·6468	−0·6591	−0·6513	−0·6563
Flat	−0·9481	−0·8123	−0·7484	−0·7592	−0·7573	−0·8043	−0·7438	−1·0711
Parking	0·0831	0·4776	0·6913	1·1876	1·1631	1·6342	1·2530	1·2287
Garage	0·2191	0·5499	0·5981	0·7810	0·7621	0·8876	0·7308	0·7780
Central heating	0·3034	0·4163	0·4397	0·4491	0·3883	0·3968	0·4134	0·4040
Floors	0·3480	0·2347	0·2163	0·1864	0·2128	0·1473	0·1530	0·2449
Plot width	0·0022	0·0047	0·0064	0·0079	0·0071	0·0075	0·0071	0·0217
Square feet	0·0002	0·0014	0·0016	0·0016	0·0017	0·0017	0·0018	0·0022
School 1	0·2023	0·5958	0·5268	0·6221	0·6198			
School 2	0·1882	0·4354	0·3194	0·2869	0·2345			
School 3		0·1928	0·0135	0·0027	−0·0152			
Street 1	−0·0635	−0·0214	−0·0487	−0·0690				
Street 2	−0·0906	−0·0383	−0·0338	−0·0770				
Street 3	0·2429	−0·3892	−0·4605	−0·6229				
Street 4	−0·0011	0·1674	0·1441	0·1481				
Bus		0·0485	0·0076	0·0142				
Blue collar	0·0087	0·0024	0·0065					
Ethnic	0·0127	0·0265	0·0172					
Altitude		0·0016						
Ind. land	0·0004	0·0064						
New const.	0·2738	−0·1581						
Open land	0·0073	0·0044						
Closed land	8×10^{-7}	0·0089						

It is apparent that calculated hedonic prices exhibit reasonable stability over alternative specifications including different local amenity variables. It is also worth noting that, capitalizing at then current after-tax interest rates,[12] the estimated parameters imply values that are sensible. Central heating, for example, adds about £4700 to the value of an average structure. An additional square foot of internal space added about £16 to the value. Of particular interest for planning policy are the estimated values of open amenity land (open space to which public access is explicitly or implicitly provided) and closed amenity land (open space with no provision for public access) and the comparison between Reading and Darlington. Both are measured as the percentage of the kilometre square containing the property devoted to each land type.

Reading has abundant open space to which there is formal or informal access. Not only are there extensive park areas, but there are large areas of unbuilt land penetrating nearly to the centre of the town in the Thames and Kennett valleys. The mean percentage of open land per kilometre square was 18·1% compared with 8·5% in Darlington. Closed land—that is, intensively farmed land and woodland—was scarce in Reading relative to Darlington: 7·8% compared with 9·1%. The estimated hedonic prices accurately reflect this. In Reading the capitalized hedonic price of open access land was £50 per percentage point on the margin, while in Darlington—despite lower incomes—it was £83; closed land was, however, £101 in Reading compared with effectively a zero price in Darlington. (The capitalized value was 1p per percentage point.) This is consistent with the observation of lobbying efforts to prevent the extension of urban areas on to agricultural land in South East England. Both communities revealed a positive valuation of the separation of industrial from residential land, although the implied price was considerably higher in the richer town of Reading.

When it came to areas of new construction, however, there was a clear-cut difference between the two communities; there was a substantial—larger than any other land-related variable—negative hedonic price in Reading but a strongly positive one in Darlington. There would seem to be two possible but not mutually exclusive explanations for this result, both related to the operation of the local planning system.[13] The variable in principle provides an indicator of neighbourhood characteristics where new housing is being constructed, but may also capture some structure-specific characteristics of new houses. It could be that developers who are able to make a free choice of locations for new housing are able to select areas that have positive local amenities that are only partially included in the models presented here. In Darlington this is then reflected in a positive price associated with the new construction variable.

In Reading, however, with its highly restrictive planning system (see Cheshire and Sheppard 1989), developers are constrained by the system to build in areas with negative unmeasured local amenities; the Gloomy Place phenomenon explored by Evans (1991). Two of the main areas of new construction in Reading were, in fact, adjacent to the M4 motorway, which might have been characterized by high noise levels. The alternative explanation might be that the higher price of land in Reading, induced by a supply restriction operating through the local planning system, caused developers to substitute land cost for construction cost so that new houses in Reading tended to be inferior to older houses.

The estimated hedonic value of land exhibits considerable change between alternative specifications. Since land rents are estimated spatially, they are presented in the form of plots of estimated land rent surfaces. The hedonic estimates are capitalized and scaled to get a land price per acre in residential use. Estimated land prices depend not only upon location, but also on the values of the other independent variables. For the plots the values of non-location variables have been fixed at the mean for the sample.

Figure 1(a) shows the estimated land prices based on the fourth model, which includes only school variables. As indicated in the figure, the rent surface is not monotonically declining from the centre. It generally declines moving north or south from the Central Business District (CBD), but movements east or west are associated with increases in land prices.

Introduction of additional amenity variables has a pronounced effect on the estimated pattern of land prices, as indicated in Figure 1(b). Here the land price estimates are based on the model that includes schools, street and bus, ethnic and social variables. Although the land price surface is not steeply sloped, a generally monocentric pattern emerges. A pronounced change is evident, however, on moving to the complete specification by adding the land use variables. The resulting estimates are presented in Figure 1(c), which also shows land price contours projected on to a plane on which the main transport network is indicated. There is a strong monocentric pattern with land prices falling rapidly with distance from the CBD.

Of further interest is the fact that the land price contours generated by the full model reflect very closely the transport routes in a way consistent with standard urban economic theory. Land prices are stretched along the main east–west transport route formed by the A329(M), the A4 and M4. The north–south routes are far more congested and also less significant in terms of access to out-of-town destinations. The main bottleneck is generated by the Thames crossing going north. To test whether the symmetric north–south rapid fall-off of land prices was emerging from the form of the land rent function, a north-of-the-Thames dummy variable was tested. This did not improve the performance of the rent function reported here.

The influence of transport networks on land prices is strongly supported by the results obtained from fitting this same underlying model to the data for Darlington. The estimates for the underlying hedonic model are reported in column (8) of Table 1. The model is as close as possible to the most complete Reading model in order to facilitate comparison. The bus variable could not be included because bus route data were not available for Darlington for 1984; in Reading, however, this variable was of only minor importance. There was considerable experimentation with the altitude variable but no significant or stable estimates resulted. This is perhaps to be expected, since topographically Darlington is essentially flat while Reading has hills to the north of the Thames and in the west of the built-up area. Thus, for this variable the statistical results reflect essential differences in topography between the two communities.

The differences in the planning variables have been discussed above. The most interesting difference in the present context, however, relates to the form of the land price surface.[14] Considerable experimentation showed that results obtained with $n=1$ (see land rent functional form defined in equation (1)) dominated any other value and the resulting land price surface, while exhibiting

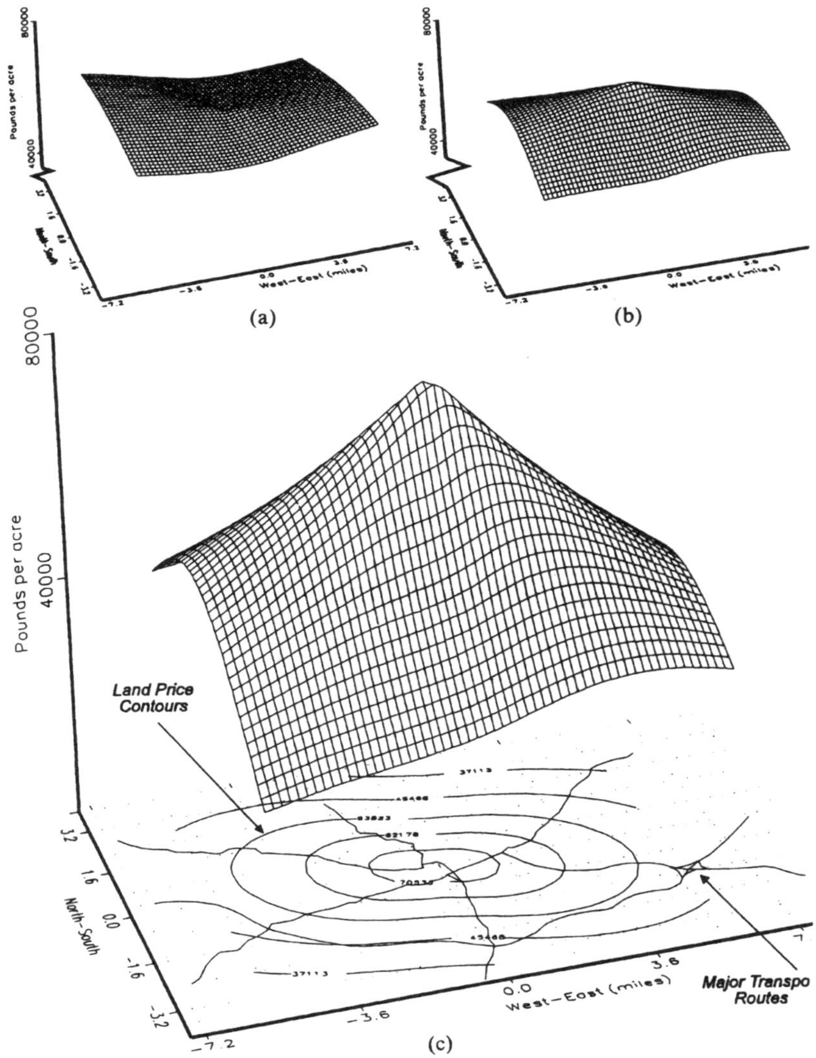

FIGURE 1. Estimated Reading land prices: (a) School variables; (b) schools, street, ethnic and social variables; (c) complete model.

declining values in all directions from the city centre shows them to be falling most slowly to the north-west approximating the line of the improved access route to the A1(M) along the A68 (B6279). Thus, in Darlington as in Reading, the pattern of observed land prices in the fully specified model shows a strong monocentricity with the asymmetries reflecting differential accessibility.

Analysis of amenities

Results presented above have documented the importance of both land and neighbourhood amenities in hedonic analysis of housing markets. Equation (3), if satisfied, implies the possibility of estimation of hedonic prices and absorption of the values of omitted amenities or other characteristics into land values. This suggests a possible technique for examining the aggregate value of neighbourhood amenities or local public goods.

The theoretically preferred approach for valuing an amenity is to estimate the structure of demand, and then calculate the equivalent variation in income associated with the presence of the amenity (Blomquist and Worley 1981). Their analysis suggested that significant errors may be made if the structure of amenity demand is not estimated. Further refinements and techniques for using hedonic price models to approximate the value of local amenities are presented in Bartik (1988).

As is often the case with good advice, however, following the theoretically correct approach may be very difficult. The data-set required to estimate the structure of amenity demand is considerably larger than the information needed to estimate the hedonic prices of the characteristics,[15] but analysts may still wish to provide some estimate of the benefits derived from amenities, however qualified.

Under the assumptions introduced above, the value of amenities omitted from the hedonic analysis will be absorbed into the estimated value of land. This suggests that the aggregate value of some amenity or group of amenities can be obtained by estimating two hedonic functions, one with and one without the amenities of interest. Given two estimated land value functions $r_i(d, \gamma)$ and $r_j(d, \gamma)$, suppose that the function j is estimated excluding some amenity. Then we calculate the marginal value of the amenity as

$$\int_{-\pi}^{\pi}\int_{a}^{b} d\,[r_j(d,\theta)-r_i(d,\theta)]\,\mathrm{d}d\,\mathrm{d}\theta, \tag{4}$$

where the limits of integration a and b are to be chosen so that a reflects the innermost extent of residential property and b reflects the maximum extent of the built-up area in the city.

TABLE 3

ESTIMATED AGGREGATE MARGINAL VALUE OF AMENITIES: READING

Row model minus column model	Minus model 4 (add schools)	Minus model 5 (add streets)	Minus model 6 (add ethnic/social)	Minus model 7 (add land use)
Model 3 (no amenities)	43,430	−37,770	81,820	137,900
Model 4 (schools)		−81,200	38,390	94,490
Model 5 (streets)			119,600	175,700
Model 6 (ethnic/social)				56,100

Table 3 presents the difference in the aggregate value of land between the rent surfaces. These have all been obtained integrating over an elliptical area with major axis oriented east–west having length 9·89 miles, and minor axis having length 8·80 miles. A very small central area was excluded: a circular area having diameter of 0·57 miles. These dimensions were chosen to encompass all the observations in the sample. It should be noted that, as constructed, the street variable represents a 'negative' amenity. This represents a problem that is necessarily encountered when any characteristic is represented as a dichotomous variable; *a priori* a zero value of the characteristic cannot be assigned. Although the street variable could have been respecified with street class 3 acting as datum, this is not necessary for the purpose of demonstrating the technique.

The structure of the table is as follows. Each cell is the aggregate difference in estimated land prices between the model in the far left column (row label) and the model indicated in the column header. The variables in the models are cumulative with movement in the table from left to right or top to bottom. Thus, for example, the 'Ethnic/Social' model includes not only the ethnic composition and social variables but also the schools and street variables. The difference between aggregate land prices estimated in the completely specified model and those in a model with no amenity variables is indicated in the upper right-hand corner, i.e. £137,900. The caveat noted above with respect to the negative measured value of the street group of amenities should be borne in mind, however, in interpreting this aggregate.

The capitalization effect is illustrated by the fact that, as we move left to right, the values increase in any row. Row 3 values are higher because they are obtained by comparison with the depressed values obtained from a model having only schools and streets. The entries along the principal diagonal of the table are then the decreases in aggregate land price estimated as a result of adding the variable indicated at the top of the column. This is the amount that might be said to represent the marginal value of the amenities.

In applying this technique and interpreting the values it may generate, it is however important not to forget the assumptions that are embodied in equation (3). If the value of the amenities that are the focus of interest does not depend on the consumption of land, then the amenities will not be capitalized into land values. In addition, to the extent that land consumption is effectively correlated with other characteristics, the aggregate valuation of amenities will be biased.

IV. Concluding Remarks

The salient conclusion from the results reported in this paper is that they demonstrate the importance of having as fully specified an hedonic model as possible if robust estimates of the effects of any housing characteristics—but particularly of land prices and to a lesser extent internal space—are to be derived. This might be thought to be a self-evident point, yet the reality is that the inclusion of land, location and a realistic and relatively full range of location-specific characteristics is virtually unknown in the literature.[16] Furthermore, it has been shown that amenities—location-specific characteristics—are systematically reflected in land prices and that, on certain assumptions, this fact can be turned to advantage to generate estimates of the aggregate value of amenities, or of groups of amenities, from a comparatively restricted set of data.

The derivation of these results in turn clarifies the conceptual definition of land in the context of the urban economy. It is important to distinguish between the 'hedonic price of land' and the amount for which vacant land might sell in an actual market. The price of vacant land observed in actual markets may indeed be free of the complicating effects of built structure, but it is rarely free of the presence of local amenities or public goods. A parcel of land is capable of yielding utility to a consumer or output for a producer even when the localized effects of other agents in the economy are totally absent. It would therefore typically command a positive price even when the level of local amenities or public goods is zero. Theories of the urban land market typically focus on this intrinsic usefulness of land (as reflected by the utility function of residents or the production functions of housing suppliers) and on the differential accessibility of land at various locations. The combination of these two forces determines an equilibrium price for land, and it is this price that is defined here as the hedonic price of land. In normal circumstances such a price will be less than the observed sales price of vacant land since the latter would include the value of local amenities.

The market price of land reflects not only the price of land as space with a particular level of accessibility to the CBD, but also the net value of neighbourhood characteristics, local public goods and all the other non-structure-specific characteristics of houses. Thus, land price surfaces as they exist for the purposes of economic theory cannot be directly estimated from observed market transactions in vacant land. With the clarification of land prices that comes with filtering out amenity values, the conventional monocentric urban model, despite recent criticism, can perform very well, and the results generalize to the only other British city for which the appropriate data are available.

The analysis also generates a new technique for, and specific insight into, the economic evaluation of the British land use planning system. Measures of local land use designed to reflect specific planning policies show that, besides having costs, there are benefits associated with some outputs of the planning system. However, these benefits appear to vary in systematic ways between the cities analysed depending on the relative supply of different types of amenity land. Apart from the costs associated with the supply-restricting effects of planning policies, there can also be costs associated with new housing. From the evidence available, it is not possible to be certain as to the precise mechanism giving rise to these costs, although it seems most plausible to attribute them to the operation of the planning system.

APPENDIX

TABLE A1

DESCRIPTION OF VARIABLES USED

Variable name	Description
Price[a]	Rentalized after-tax annual cost of structure in thousands of pounds
Bedrooms[a]	Number of bedrooms in the structure
WCs[a]	Number of WCs in the structure
Terrace[a]	Dummy variable, 1 if property is terrace style
Semi[a]	Dummy variable, 1 if property is semi-detached
Flat[a]	Dummy variable, 1 if property is a flat
Parking[a]	Dummy variable, 1 if property has off-street parking
Garage[a]	Dummy variable, 1 if property has a garage
Central heat[a]	Dummy variable, 1 if structure has central heating
Floors[a]	Defined as: (5—number of floors in structure)
Plot width[b]	Width of plot in feet
Sq. feet[a]	Square feet of living area in structure
Land (L)[b]	Area of land in square feet associated with the structure
Distance[b]	Distance in miles from city centre
Theta[b]	Angle in radians from East
School 1[c]	Dummy variable, 1 if property is located in Highdown area
School 2[c]	Dummy variable, 1 if property is located in Maiden Erleigh area
School 3[c]	Dummy variable, 1 if property is located in Waingels Copse area
Street 1[b]	Dummy variable, 1 if property is located on minor road
Street 2[b]	Dummy variable, 1 if property is located on road with >4·3 metres metalling
Street 3[b]	Dummy variable, 1 if property is located on a 'B-class' roadway
Street 4[b]	Dummy variable, 1 if property is located on an 'A-class' roadway
Bus[b,d]	Dummy variable, 1 if property within $\frac{1}{4}$ mile of local bus route
Blue collar[e]	Defined as: (100—fraction of ward labour force in blue-collar occupations)
Ethnic[e]	Defined as: (15—fraction of urban area Afro-Caribbean population located in ward)
Altitude[b]	Maximum altitude (metres) in 1 km OS square containing address
Industrial land[b,f]	Defined as: (100—percentage of land in Industrial use within 1 km OS square containing address)
New construction[b,f]	Dummy variable, 1 if majority of observations in 1 km OS square are new construction
Open land amenity[b,f]	Percent of land in accessible open space in 1 km OS square
Closed land amenity[b,f]	Percent of land in inaccessible open space 1 km OS square

Sources: [a]Estate agents' particulars; [b]Ordnance Survey; [c]Local education authority; [d]Reading Transport; [e]1981 Population Census, ward data; [f]Aerial photographs.

TABLE A2

DESCRIPTIVE STATISTICS AND CORRELATIONS FOR VARIABLES USED

	Descriptive statistics		Bivariate correlations							
Variable	Mean	Std. dev.	Floors	Sq. feet	Ethnic	Blue-collar	Open land	Closed land	Alt.	Ind. land
Price	4·428	1·790	−0·21	0·75	0·29	0·34	0·03	0·15	0·14	0·28
Bedrooms	3·097	0·946	−0·52	0·75	0·14	0·13	0·00	0·07	0·08	0·20
WC	1·479	0·657	−0·24	0·51	0·18	0·17	0·03	0·05	0·03	0·17
Terrace	0·137	0·344	−0·13	−0·15	0·43	−0·29	−0·08	−0·11	−0·11	−0·30
Semi	0·347	0·477	−0·24	−0·11	0·13	−0·09	0·10	−0·07	0·13	0·08
Flat	0·100	0·300	0·56	−0·30	0·15	−0·08	−0·11	−0·05	−0·11	−0·15
Parking	0·213	0·410	0·08	−0·11	0·03	−0·03	−0·01	−0·02	−0·07	−0·03
Garage	0·634	0·482	−0·06	0·22	0·44	0·31	0·13	0·16	0·17	0·31
Heat	0·799	0·402	−0·05	0·23	0·26	0·20	0·10	0·06	0·08	0·23
Floors	3·072	0·444	1·00	−0·48	0·02	0·01	0·03	0·01	0·00	−0·08
Plot width	35·327	26·901	−0·07	0·60	0·26	0·29	−0·01	0·12	0·10	0·24
Sq ft	826·662	350·474	−0·48	1·00	0·06	0·13	−0·09	0·08	0·07	0·17
School 1	0·153	0·360	−0·10	0·20	0·10	0·28	−0·06	−0·10	0·12	0·11
School 2	0·095	0·293	−0·07	0·04	0·14	0·11	−0·05	−0·12	−0·08	0·13
School 3	0·083	0·277	−0·01	0·01	0·01	0·10	0·11	−0·10	−0·33	0·00
Street 1	0·296	0·457	−0·11	0·07	0·34	−0·03	−0·19	−0·10	−0·03	−0·09
Street 2	0·116	0·320	0·09	0·03	0·06	−0·05	0·02	−0·08	0·11	0·00
Street 3	0·014	0·117	−0·02	−0·01	0·05	−0·06	−0·01	−0·05	0·04	0·07
Street 4	0·051	0·220	−0·09	0·18	0·02	0·03	−0·13	0·05	−0·04	0·01
Bus	0·556	0·497	0·07	−0·06	0·10	−0·02	−0·22	−0·04	−0·04	−0·04
Ethnic	10·694	3·659	0·02	0·06	1·00	0·58	0·26	0·29	0·34	0·41
Blue collar	54·979	15·142	0·01	0·13	0·58	1·00	0·14	0·31	0·03	0·30
Open land	18·100	12·527	0·03	−0·09	0·26	0·14	1·00	0·15	−0·02	0·16
Closed land	7·813	16·057	0·01	0·08	0·29	0·31	0·15	1·00	0·17	0·12
Altitude	69·363	16·077	0·00	0·06	0·34	0·03	−0·02	0·17	1·00	0·35
Industrial	95·558	7·136	−0·08	0·17	0·41	0·30	0·16	0·12	0·35	1·00
New constr.	0·188	0·391	0·00	−0·10	0·23	0·19	0·11	0·08	−0·13	0·11
Distance	2·152	0·985	−0·05	−0·00	0·52	0·27	0·33	0·29	0·14	0·33
θ (direction)	−0·157	1·993	−0·09	0·15	0·13	0·27	−0·10	0·14	0·29	0·19
Land area	4,214·275	4,291·651	−0·08	0·56	0·24	0·22	−0·01	0·09	0·14	0·25

ACKNOWLEDGEMENTS

This paper draws upon research funded by the Economic and Social Research Council under award no. D00232044. This support is gratefully acknowledged, as is the support and advice of numerous colleagues. These are too many to list individually, but particular thanks must be offered to Charles Leven, Elia Werczberger and Christine Whitehead. Finally the comments of the anonymous referees of an earlier version of this paper were particularly helpful. Despite this support, errors and shortcomings remain. For these the authors take full responsibility.

NOTES

1. Other US studies focusing on amenities include Linneman (1980, 1981) and Cobb (1984): that by Jackson *et al.* (1984) includes, in addition, land consumption.
2. For recent British examples see Garrod and Willis (1992a, b).
3. See e.g. Roback (1982), Blomquist *et al.* (1988), Gyourko and Tracy (1991).
4. That is, the definition of a physical boundary for urban development and the protection of agricultural land.
5. Some provisional results using a simple linear model and focusing on the effects of planning restrictions on house and land prices were reported in Cheshire and Sheppard (1989). A brief comparison of the results discussed here with those obtained using OLS is provided in the Cheshire and Sheppard (1993). Full results from the present model can be obtained from the authors.
6. It may be objected that each continuously variable characteristic should have a separately estimated associated transformation parameter. Experiments estimating different transformation parameters for structure characteristics and neighbourhood amenities showed that the problem identified above in the context of totally flexible land rent functions appeared. It became difficult to obtain robust estimates of individual characeristics.

7. These were obtained using the GaussX routines running under Gauss386i.
8. This involved extensive experimentation. For example, all the variables for wards from the 1981 Census of Population were available. Over 40 formulations of the social class variables alone were tried. It is of interest that the formulation of variables that proved most robust in Reading was very similar to that which performed best in Darlington.
9. Although, as local amenity variables were added, the estimated parameters of the land rent function changed—often by more than one standard error—the only structural parameter to exhibit changes much larger than a standard error was the internal area of the structure. The analysis below examines these changes in more detail.
10. One reason for constructing the accessibility of the bus network variable was to try to capture separately the enhanced accessibility value of main roads.
11. Alternative measures of goodness of fit are, of course, possible. The log likelihood measures goodness of fit in terms of transformed values of variables. Since interest here is on hedonic prices, it is appropriate to select models on the basis of goodness of parameter estimation. In other contexts interest might focus on the predictive power of the model. This would imply other techniques and measures. Some consequences that flow from this observation are explored in Cheshire and Sheppard (1993).
12. Taken to be 8·75%.
13. The most obvious explanation for a negative value—localized supply shocks—is not consistent with the significant positive value in Darlington.
14. The appropriate figure is available from the authors.
15. If the structure of demand is to be identified, it is necessary to have reliable data concerning the income and identifying the characteristics of consumers. In addition, in the case of dichotomous characteristics it is likely that data from several housing markets will be necessary and more restrictive assumptions will have to be imposed.
16. Of the hedonic studies cited in this paper, only that by Jackson *et al.* (1984) includes all of these.

REFERENCES

ALONSO, W. (1964). *Location and land use: towards a general theory of land rent.* Cambridge, Mass.: Harvard University Press.

AWAN, K., ODLING-SMEE, J. C. and WHITEHEAD, C. (1982). Household attributes and the demand for private rental housing. *Economica*, **49**, 183–200.

BARTIK, T. J. (1988). Measuring the benefits of amenity improvements in hedonic price models. *Land Economics*, **64**, 172–83.

BLOMQUIST, G. C. and WORLEY, L. (1981). Hedonic prices, demand for urban housing amenities, and benefit estimates. *Journal of Urban Economics*, **9**, 212–21.

——, BERGER, M. C. and HOEHN, J. P. (1988). New estimates of the quality of life in urban areas. *American Economic Review*, **78**, 89–107.

BOX, G. and COX, D. (1964). An analysis of transformations. *Journal of the Royal Statistical Society, Series B*, **26**, 211–52.

BRUECKNER, J. (1987). The structure of urban equilibria: a unified treatment of the Muth–Mills model. In E. S. Mills (ed.), *Handbook of Regional and Urban Economixs*, Vol. II, 821–45. Amsterdam: North-Holland.

CHESHIRE, P. and SHEPPARD, S. (1989). British planning policy and access to housing: some empirical estimates. *Urban Studies*, **26**, 469–85.

—— and —— (1993). *Evaluating the Impact of Neighbourhood Effects and Land Use Planning on House Prices and Land Rents: Results from an Extended Model.* University of Reading Discussion Papers in Economics, Series C, no. 86.

COBB, S. (1984). The impact of site characteristics on housing cost estimates. *Journal of Urban Economics*, **15**, 26–45.

EVANS, A. W. (1973). *The economics of residential location.* London: Macmillan.

—— (1991). Rabbit hutches on postage stamps. *Urban Studies*, **28**, 853–70.

GARROD, G. D. and WILLIS, K. G. (1992a). Valuing goods' characteristics: an application of the hedonic price method of environmental attributes. *Journal of Environmental Management*, **34**, 59–76.

—— and —— (1992b). The environmental economic impact of woodland: a two-stage hedonic price model of the amenity value of forestry in Britain. *Applied Economics*, **24**, 715–28.

GYOURKO, J. and TRACY, J. (1991). The structure of local public finance and the quality of life. *Journal of Political Economy*, **99**, 774–805.

HALVORSEN, R. and POLLAKOWSKI, H. (1981). Choice of functional form for hedonic price equations. *Journal of Urban Economics*, **10**, 37–49.

HELSLEY, R. and ROSENTHAL, S. (1991). Redevelopment and the urban land price gradient. Mimeo, University of British Colombia.

JACKSON, J., JOHNSON, R. and KASERMAN, D. (1984). The measurement of land prices and the elasticity of substitution in housing production. *Journal of Urban Economics*, **16**, 1–12.

KAIN, J. F. and QUIGLEY, J. N. (1970a). Measuring the value of housing quality. *Journal of the American Statistical Association*, **65**, 330.

—— and —— (1970b). Evaluating the quality of residential environment. *Environment and Planning*, **2**(2), 23–32.

LINNEMAN, P. (1980). Some empirical results on the nature of the hedonic price function for the urban housing market. *Journal of Urban Economics*, **8**, 47–6.

—— (1981). The demand for residence site characteristics. *Journal of Urban Economics*, **13**, 129–48.

MUTH, R. F. (1969). *Cities and housing*. Chicago: University of Chicago Press.

PARSONS, G. R. (1990). Hedonic prices and public goods: an argument for weighting locational attributes in hedonic regressions by lot size. *Journal of Urban Economics*, **27**, 308–21.

PENNINGTON, G., TOPHAM, N. and WARD, R. (1990). Aircraft noise and residential property values adjacent to Manchester International Airport. *Journal of Transport Economics and Policy*, **24**, 49–59.

ROBACK, J. (1982) Wages, rents and the quality of life. *Journal of Political Economy*, **90**, 1257–8.

ROSENTHAL, L. (1989). Income and price elasticities of demand for owner-occupied housing in the UK: evidence from pooled cross-sectional and time-series data. *Applied Economics*, **21**, 761–75.

STRASZHEIM, M. (1987). The theory of residential structure. In E S. Mills (ed.), *Handbook of Regional and Urban Economics*, Vol. II, 717–57. Amsterdam: North-Holland.

WILKINSON, R. K. (1973). House prices and the measurement of externalities. *Economic Journal*, **83**, 72–86.

YINGER, J. (1992). City and suburb: urban models with more than one employment center. *Journal of Urban Economics*, **31**, 181–205.

[9]

INTERNATIONAL REGIONAL SCIENCE REVIEW 23, 2: 160–171 (April 2000)

URBAN SPRAWL: DIAGNOSIS AND REMEDIES

JAN K. BRUECKNER
Department of Economics and Institute of Government and Public Affairs,
University of Illinois at Urbana–Champaign,
jbrueckn@uiuc.edu

This article argues that urban spatial expansion results mainly from three powerful forces: a growing population, rising incomes, and falling commuting costs. Urban growth occurring purely in response to these fundamental forces cannot be faulted as socially undesirable, but three market failures may distort their operation, upsetting the allocation of land between agricultural and urban uses and justifying criticism of urban sprawl. These are the failure to account for the benefits of open space, excessive commuting because of a failure to account for the social costs of congestion, and failure to make new development pay for the infrastructure costs it generates. Precise remedies for these market failures are two types of development taxes and congestion tolls levied on commuters. Each of these remedies leads to a reduction in the spatial size of the city.

Strong sentiment against the phenomenon known as urban sprawl has developed over the last few years in the United States. Many local governments and several states have adopted policies designed to deal with sprawl. The issue has even been placed on the national agenda, with the Clinton administration proposing to use federal money for the preservation of open space. At the root of this effort is a perception that the process of urban growth in the United States has gone awry.

This perception involves a number of interlocking complaints. Cities, it is claimed, take up too much space, encroaching excessively on agricultural land. Aesthetic benefits from the presence of open space are lost, and an allegedly scarce resource, namely farmland, is depleted. Excessive urban expansion also means overly long commutes, which generate traffic congestion while contributing to air pollution. Unfettered suburban growth is also thought to reduce the incentive for redevelopment of land closer to city centers, contributing to the decay of downtown areas. Finally, by spreading people out, low-density suburban development may reduce social interaction, weakening the bonds that underpin a healthy society. Twelve articles in the fall 1998 issue of *Brookings Review* (vol. 16) provide an excellent overview of the sprawl debate.

Are these complaints justified? If so, which remedies can policy makers apply? To answer these questions, a definition of the issue at hand is essential. Urban

I thank Andrew Isserman for helpful expository suggestions. I am grateful to J. Fred Giertz, Scott Koeneman, Gerrit Knaap, Elizabeth Powers, and Paul Quirk for helpful feedback.

sprawl means different things to different people, and this dispersion of views can impede useful discussion. Here, the term *urban sprawl* will refer to excessive spatial growth of cities. The key word in this definition is excessive. Although cities must grow spatially to accommodate an expanding population, the claim is that too much spatial growth occurs. If this allegation is correct, current public policies should be altered to restrict the spatial expansion of cities.

The stakes in this policy debate are substantial. Policy measures designed to attack urban sprawl will ultimately affect a key element of the American lifestyle, the consumption of large amounts of living space at affordable prices. A simple supply-and-demand argument establishes this conclusion. Restricting urban spatial growth means limiting the supply of land for residential development. With supply limited, urban land prices and ultimately the price of housing (measured on a per square foot basis) must rise. In response to such price escalation, consumers would reduce their consumption of housing space, making new homes smaller than they would have been otherwise. Therefore, an attack on urban sprawl would lead ultimately to denser cities containing smaller dwellings.

If the criticisms of urban sprawl are correct, then the loss from lower housing consumption would be offset by other gains such as improved access to open space and lower traffic congestion, and consumers on balance would be better off. But if the attack on sprawl is misguided, with few benefits arising from restricted city sizes, people would be packed into denser cities for no good reason, leading to a reduction in the American standard of living. The same conclusion would arise if some limitation of city sizes is desirable but policy makers are overzealous. If only mild measures are needed to restrict urban growth that is slightly excessive, but draconian measures are used instead, consumers are likely to end up worse off.

Because the stakes are high in the debate on sprawl, it is important to gain an understanding of the forces that might lead to excessive spatial growth of cities and to understand the nature of appropriate remedies. In working toward this understanding, the ensuing discussion does not address an issue frequently raised in criticisms of urban sprawl, namely, the proliferation of unattractive land uses such as strip malls and fast food outlets. Because this complaint concerns the character of development rather than its spatial extent, it lies outside the definition of urban sprawl used here. Although ugly development cannot be banned, a remedy for this problem lies in the use of zoning regulations and other tools of urban planning, which allow land use to be channeled toward more aesthetic outcomes. These tools can complement the policies discussed below, which are designed to limit the extent, rather than the character, of development.

Why Growth Is Mostly Benign: The Forces Underlying Urban Expansion

Competition for land between real estate developers and nonurban users (mainly farmers and other agricultural users) helps to determine the spatial sizes of cities.

For a city to grow spatially, developers must be able to bid away additional land from agricultural users. A successful bid by developers means the land is worth more in urban use than in agriculture, reflecting a greater economic contribution in its developed state. In this sense, land conversion is guided by the economist's "invisible hand," which directs resources to their highest and best use.

The key implication of this principle is that urban growth is not an indiscriminate process, devouring agricultural land without regard to its worth. Although many critics of urban sprawl seem to hold this unfavorable view of the growth process, the view is not consistent with the operation of a free market economy, where resources find their most productive uses. Buttressing this claim, evidence has shown that in regions where agricultural land is productive and its value high, cities are more spatially compact than in regions where agricultural land is unproductive and therefore cheap (Brueckner and Fansler 1983). Productive agricultural land is thus more resistant to urban expansion than unproductive land, reflecting the operation of the invisible hand.

Concerns about loss of "scarce" farmland are also misplaced. Because the value of farm output is fully reflected in the amount that agricultural users are willing to pay for the land, a successful bid by developers means that society values the houses and other structures built on the land more than the farm output that is forgone. If farmland became truly scarce and in need of preservation, its selling price would be high, making the land resistant to urban encroachment. With only a tiny fraction of the U.S. land area occupied by cities, farmland scarcity is not a problem currently, nor is it likely to become a problem in the future.

Although the allocation of land is governed by competition between urban and agricultural uses, the outcome has increasingly tipped in favor of urban use, leading to substantial spatial growth of cities and prompting criticism of urban sprawl. Economists believe that three underlying forces—population growth, rising household incomes, and transportation improvements—are responsible for this spatial growth (see Mieszkowski and Mills 1993). As the nation's population expands, cities must grow spatially to accommodate more people. In addition, rising incomes affect urban growth because residents of the city demand more living space as they become richer over time. By itself, the greater demand for space causes the city to expand spatially as dwelling sizes increase. This effect is reinforced by the residents' desire to carry out their greater housing consumption in a location where housing is cheap, namely the suburbs. So the spatial expansion due to rising incomes is strengthened by a price incentive favoring suburbanization.

A similar phenomenon occurs in response to investment in freeways and other transportation infrastructure. Because such investment makes travel faster and more convenient, thus reducing the cost of commuting, consumers can enjoy cheap housing in the suburbs while paying smaller commuting-cost penalties. As a result, suburban locations look increasingly attractive as commuting costs fall, which spurs suburbanization and leads to spatial growth of the city.

Job suburbanization has also occurred as cities have grown spatially. This relocation of jobs to the suburbs has been due in part to changes in the transport orientation of businesses. Rather than shipping their output through centrally located rail depots and port facilities, firms increasingly rely on truck transport and, thus, prefer the easy highway access (as well as the low cost) of suburban locations. However, the evidence shows that jobs also follow people. In other words, job suburbanization is partly a response to the suburbanization of the population, which occurs for the reasons discussed above. Thus, unlike the fundamental forces driving urban expansion, job suburbanization is partly an effect rather than a cause of this growth. Thurston and Yezer (1994) provide a useful empirical analysis of the interaction between job and population decentralization.

The confluence of an expanding national population, rising incomes, and falling commuting costs makes the rapid expansion of cities in recent decades unsurprising. The real question is whether this expansion has been too rapid. In other words, does the invisible hand, which guides the conversion of land to urban use, push too hard in the direction of bigger cities?

Economists use the term *market failure* to describe a situation in which the invisible hand fails to allocate resources in a socially desirable manner, so as to maximize aggregate economic well-being. Market failure arises when economic agents face incentives that are distorted because of institutional failings or some other reason, leading to economic outcomes that are bad from society's point of view. The classic example of a market failure is air and water pollution, where a factory has little incentive to take account of the environmental damage it causes and, thus, ends up polluting too much. Is a similar market failure involved in the spatial expansion of cities? If so, the criticism of urban sprawl is justified, and measures are needed to restrict urban expansion. Economists have, in fact, identified several market failures that may affect the urban growth process.

SOURCES OF MARKET FAILURE IN URBAN GROWTH AND POTENTIAL REMEDIES

Three market failures may lead to excessive spatial growth of cities. The first arises from a failure to take into account the social value of open space when land is converted to urban use. The second arises from a failure on the part of individual commuters to recognize the social costs of congestion created by their use of the road network, which leads to excessive commuting and cities that are too large. The third market failure arises from the failure of real estate developers to take into account all of the public infrastructure costs generated by their projects. Thus, development appears artificially cheap from the developer's point of view, encouraging excessive urban growth. These market failures, and the steps that can be taken to correct them, are discussed sequentially.

Failure to Account for the Social Value of Open Space

Ready access to open space is important for society's well-being. Open space provides city dwellers with an easy escape from the frenetic urban scene and a chance to enjoy nature. Such open-space benefits, however, are not taken into account when land is converted to urban use. As noted above, conversion depends solely on the land's productivity in urban use (which depends on the value of the houses built) relative to the land's productivity in agriculture (as reflected in the value of farm output). The problem is that since intangible open-space benefits do not constitute part of the income earned by the land when it is in agricultural use, the disappearance of these benefits does not show up as a dollar loss when the land is sold to a real estate developer. The invisible hand thus ignores open-space benefits, causing too much land to be converted to urban use and leading to excessive spatial growth of cities.

A simple form of government intervention can remedy this problem: charging a development tax on each acre of land converted from agricultural to urban use (this tax is added to any fees already levied). The magnitude of the tax is set equal to the value of the open-space benefits that are lost when the land is converted. By raising the cost of conversion, the tax retards the development process and slows the rate of urban expansion.

The subjective nature of open-space benefits makes crafting a public policy to preserve them very difficult and potentially counterproductive. The problem is that implementing such a policy requires assigning a dollar value to the open-space benefits provided by an acre of land. Although economists have tried to estimate such values, the results are not sufficiently credible to be a reliable basis for policy (for an overview of the methods used by economists to measure the value of environmental amenities, see Blomquist and Whitehead 1995). This estimation problem puts the policy maker in the position of having to guess the correct magnitude for a development tax. The proper tax could be quite small (even zero) if most consumers are not very concerned about the availability of open space around their cities. However, a well-meaning policy maker, perhaps swayed by the arguments of a vocal interest group, might charge a high development tax because of a gross overestimate of open-space benefits, with harmful results. Such a tax would needlessly restrict expansion of the city, raising housing prices and shrinking housing consumption.

Failure to Account for the Social Costs of Freeway Congestion

The second market failure affecting the spatial sizes of cities arises through the activity of commuting. Commuters incur substantial costs, which include the out-of-pocket expenses of vehicle operation as well as the "time cost" of commuting.

The latter cost measures the dollar value to the commuter of the time consumed while in transit, which is mostly wasted. Together, these out-of-pocket and time costs represent the "private cost" of commuting, the cost that the commuter himself bears.

When the commuter drives on congested roadways to get to work, another cost is generated above and beyond the private cost. This cost is due to the extra congestion caused by the commuter's presence on the road. Such congestion arises because slight increases in traffic on a crowded roadway can lead to a substantial drop in traffic speed. The lower speed prolongs everyone's trip, raising the time cost of travel for all commuters. Thus, on congested roads, the true social cost of commuting for an individual includes the costs imposed on other commuters through that extra congestion. Although this extra congestion is slight, its impact is significant because many other commuters are affected.

Because these congestion costs are borne by others, the commuter himself has no incentive to take them into account. This missing incentive constitutes a market failure, and it means that commuting on congested roadways looks artificially cheap to individual commuters. Therefore, congested roads are overused from society's point of view.

To correct this problem, reducing road usage to socially optimal levels, several steps are appropriate. Some traffic should be diverted to off-peak hours, when roads are less congested, and some car commuters should switch to public transit. In addition, because of the overlooked social costs of commuting, the average commute distance is too long from society's point of view and should be shortened. But an excessively long average commute means that cities are too spread out. Therefore, by causing people to commute too far, the market failure associated with freeway congestion can lead indirectly to urban sprawl. Wheaton (1998) provides a clear theoretical demonstration of this point.

Because the source of the problem is the individual's false perception of the costs of commuting, the remedy is to raise commuting costs by imposing a "congestion toll." Such a toll charges each commuter for the congestion damage imposed on others. When a toll is levied, the out-of-pocket cost of rush-hour commuting rises, and individuals have an incentive to shorten their commutes. Because this means living closer to one's job location, the ultimate effect is a spatial shrinkage of the city. The city becomes denser, just as if a development tax had been imposed. With people driving shorter distances to work, total traffic volume (as measured by vehicle miles) falls, as does the amount of auto-related air pollution, addressing key complaints of the critics of urban sprawl. All these effects would emerge, of course, only over a very long time period as land use adjusts to the higher cost of commuting.

Unlike the development tax, the proper magnitude of congestion tolls can be computed reliably, drawing on the wealth of accumulated knowledge about commuting behavior (for a discussion of toll computation and the practicality of tolls, see Small 1992). Yet, although economists and transportation engineers uniformly endorse congestion tolls, they are seldom levied in practice. One problem is political: even though the revenue earned from tolls would allow other taxes to be reduced, commuters view tolls as a net tax increase, which creates opposition.

Another problem is the daunting logistics of collecting tolls in a manner that does not impede traffic flow. In principle, technological advances can remove this obstacle by allowing toll charges to be tallied by electronic meters installed in the automobiles. Low-tech solutions such as downtown parking taxes and costly bumper stickers that permit rush-hour usage of central roadways are also feasible. The latter approach was implemented in Singapore, whereas cities in Norway have experimented with more high-tech methods of collecting tolls (for details of these schemes, see Small and Gomez-Ibanez 1999).

Congestion tolls may also reduce road usage in the other ways mentioned above, which do not affect urban sprawl. Some commuters may give up their cars, switching to public transit to get to work. Also, businesses might alter work schedules to allow their employees to commute at off-peak hours when no toll is charged.

Failure to Fully Account for the Infrastructure Costs of New Development

The infrastructure costs generated by new development are another source of market failure that affects urban growth. When a new housing development is built, roads and sewers must be constructed, and facilities such as schools, parks, and recreation areas are needed. Homeowners, through the property tax system, pay for this infrastructure.

The market failure arises because, under current financing arrangements, the infrastructure-related tax burden on new homeowners is typically less than the actual infrastructure costs they generate. The reason is that the cost of new sewers and schools is shared among all of the city's residents rather than charged directly to those who require the new infrastructure. In effect, infrastructure is priced approximately at average cost rather than marginal cost. Because the property tax burden on new homeowners is lower than if they fully paid for their infrastructure costs, these homeowners are able to pay a higher purchase price for their houses than if the correct tax were levied. With their houses selling for more, developers are then able to offer more for agricultural land than would be possible if the correct tax burden were levied on new homeowners. Higher bids for agricultural land in turn mean more conversion of land to urban use, leading to too much development and excessive spatial sizes for cities. Thus, by undercharging new homeowners for the infrastructure costs they generate, the current system of public finance leads to urban sprawl.

The way to correct this problem is to alter the system of infrastructure financing so that new development pays for its infrastructure costs. In fact, many communities have undertaken such an alteration by adopting a system of "impact fees." Under this system, infrastructure costs are paid up front in a lump sum fashion rather than being spread over many years of property tax payments. The impact fees are calculated exactly to offset the infrastructure costs from the new development, so that no additional financing is required. The fees are paid directly by housing developers instead of by homeowners. The dollar amounts can be substantial, reflecting the high per house cost of sewers, school facilities, and other infrastructure. Altshuler and Gomez-Ibanez (1993) provide an excellent overview of the use of impact fees in the United States.

Because impact fees correctly charge for infrastructure costs, the burden they impose is higher than under traditional property tax financing. As a result, impact fees depress the amount that housing developers are able to pay for agricultural land relative to the traditional case. This in turn slows the development process, limiting the pace of urban spatial growth. Theoretical analysis by Brueckner (1997) demonstrates the need for impact fees and characterizes their effects.

Impact fees are widely used in many parts of the United States. Many Chicago-area communities charge school impact fees, for example, which defray the cost of new school construction. These fees often amount to several thousand dollars per house. Historically, impact fees have been challenged in the courts by real estate developers, who have contested the rights of communities to levy the fees or the methods used to calculate them. In some cases, the fee computations have in fact been flawed, so that the magnitudes do not properly reflect infrastructure costs. Correct impact fees can be computed, however, and their use can lead to better development decisions.

USE OF GROWTH BOUNDARIES TO CONTAIN URBAN SPRAWL

The three remedies (development taxes, congestion tolls, and impact fees) prescribed for the market failures leading to urban sprawl each involve use of the price mechanism. Policy makers, however, often favor a much blunter instrument, usually called an urban growth boundary (UGB). A UGB is a zoning tool that slows urban growth by banning development in designated areas on the urban fringe. In effect, imposition of such a boundary involves drawing a polygon around a city and prohibiting development outside it. Ding, Knaap, and Hopkins (1999) provide an analysis of the operation of UGBs.

A UGB is easy to implement but has great potential for misuse. The problem is similar to the one that arises in taxing development to preserve open space, namely, the need for guesswork. In particular, without a careful inquiry into the sources of market failure, policy makers cannot gauge the exact extent of urban overexpansion. As a result, a UGB may be much too stringent, needlessly restricting the size of the city and leading to an inappropriate escalation in housing costs and unwarranted increases in density.

The way to avoid such errors is to attack urban sprawl at its source by imposing the specific remedies outlined above. Proper congestion tolls and impact fees can be computed with a high degree of reliability, ensuring that the resulting adjustments in urban spatial size are correct from society's point of view. A development tax designed to preserve open space works well also, provided that a proper measure of open-space benefits can be computed.

Portland, Oregon, has the best-known example of a UGB (for a discussion of land use planning in Oregon, see Knaap and Nelson 1992). Some commentators claim that Portland's UGB is responsible for excessive house price escalation in that city, whereas others argue that the boundary is so loose that its price effects are negligible. This controversy illustrates an important point, namely, that there is no way to tell whether a UGB is set properly without focusing on the underlying market failures that lead to urban sprawl. Regardless of which view of the Portland case is correct, UGBs retain the potential for excessively restricting city sizes and should be used with great care.

"Voting with One's Feet" and Urban Sprawl

In addition to population growth, rising incomes, and falling commuting costs, another fiscal force has contributed to the suburbanization process in U.S. cities. This is the desire of high-income consumers to form separate jurisdictions for the provision of public goods such as education, public safety, and parks. When households of different incomes are intermixed, high-income households pay more than an equal share of the cost of public goods, a consequence of their larger property tax bills. In addition, high-income households may end up with lower public spending than they would prefer, a consequence of the lesser ability to pay of low-income voters. However, when high-income households "vote with their feet," forming their own jurisdictions for provision of public goods, both of these drawbacks are avoided. Separate jurisdictions eliminate the need to subsidize low-income households, so that taxes can be lowered at the same time that public good provision is increased. The location for such new jurisdictions is on the suburban fringe. Thus, spatial expansion of cities is partly driven by the fiscal incentive of high-income households to separate themselves from the less well off. Tiebout (1956) provided the seminal analysis of the fiscal incentives leading to such homogeneous communities, and Wildasin (1986) provides an overview of more recent studies.

This force cannot be categorized as a market failure like those discussed above. It is an outgrowth of the U.S. system of public finance, which gives local governments great autonomy in choosing spending levels. This autonomy spurs the process of voting with one's feet, which allows high-income households to insulate themselves fiscally from their low-income counterparts. To undo the urban spatial expansion created by this impulse for fiscal segregation, a change in the underlying structure of fiscal incentives is required. For example, the current system of autonomous jurisdictions could be modified by adding a higher level metropolitan-area government with the power to tax suburban residents and to spend the proceeds in the central city. Alternatively, a more restricted type of tax base sharing among municipalities could be implemented. Because either change would limit the ability of high-income households to escape redistributive taxation that benefits low-income consumers, the incentive to form separate communities on the suburban fringe would be weakened, curbing the spatial expansion of cities.

Any proposal for a metropolitan-area government, however, is likely to encounter fierce political opposition from well-off households, making such a change impractical. An account of such opposition is provided by the Orfield (1998) article in the Brookings symposium, which documents the political struggle over metropolitan government in Minneapolis. In addition, such proposals have the drawback of interfering with freedom of choice in the public sector, which comes from a household's ability to select a place of residence from among a host of fully autonomous jurisdictions offering different amounts of public spending.

BY-PRODUCTS OF AN ATTACK ON URBAN SPRAWL

Suburbanization contributes to the decay of central cities by reducing the incentive to redevelop land near the center. The reason is that the suburbanization forces generated by rising incomes and falling commuting costs end up reducing the demand for aging central-city housing, depressing its price and diminishing the incentive for upgrading and redevelopment. Although central decay is therefore a likely outcome even if the spatial growth of cities is not excessive, the problem is exacerbated when cities overexpand. By inappropriately increasing the supply of developed land, overexpansion puts downward pressure on housing prices throughout the city. With central-city prices lower than they would be if city size were not excessive, the incentive for upgrading and redevelopment of aging dwellings is further reduced.

If, however, sprawl is attacked with an instrument such as a development tax, then the city ultimately shrinks, and housing prices rise everywhere, as noted above. By raising the return to real estate investment, this price escalation is likely to spur redevelopment efforts in central neighborhoods. Thus, one by-product of an attack on sprawl at the urban fringe may be upgrading and redevelopment in decaying central neighborhoods (for an empirical analysis of the redevelopment process, see Rosenthal and Helsley 1994).

Many commentators criticize the process of suburbanization, and its attendant "car culture," as weakening the nation's social bonds by spreading residences out in low-density patterns that discourage interaction. These critics wish to return to a previous type of urban existence, one characterized by the interactive street life that results from high densities and intermixing of residences and commercial establishments. Hayward (1998) presents a clear statement of this position.

Yet, by opting for the suburban lifestyle, with its promise of spacious houses and its segregation of residential and commercial land uses, consumers have apparently rejected this earlier pattern in favor of something different. Despite this choice, some commentators in effect argue that people may not really know what is good for them, concluding that a return to an earlier urban lifestyle may actually make society better off. If these critics are correct, then an attack on urban sprawl, by partly dismantling the offending suburban lifestyle, may produce benefits via greater social interaction in cities.

CONCLUSION: TAKE A CAUTIOUS APPROACH

When crafting policies to address sprawl, policy makers must recognize that the potential market failures involved in urban expansion are of secondary importance compared to the powerful, fundamental forces that underlie this expansion. For example, although the failure to fully charge for infrastructure costs may impart a slight upward bias to urban expansion, the bulk of the substantial spatial growth that has occurred across the United States cannot be ascribed to such a cause. Instead, this growth mostly reflects fundamentals such as the nation's growing population and the higher incomes of its citizens. Because of the secondary role of market failure, a draconian attack on urban sprawl is probably not warranted. By greatly restricting urban expansion, such an attack might needlessly limit the consumption of housing space, depressing the standard of living of American consumers. Instead, a more cautious approach, which recognizes the damage done by unwarranted restriction of urban growth, should be adopted.

Such caution is a built-in feature of the development taxes and congestion tolls discussed above, which attack sprawl at its source by correcting specific market failures. UGBs, by contrast, can easily yield undesirably draconian outcomes because they are not directly linked to the underlying market failures responsible for sprawl. However, because UGBs simply require an extension of existing zoning powers, local policy makers may find them more convenient to use than taxes or tolls. UGBs may therefore end up as the instrument of choice for attacking urban sprawl. Policy makers should resist the temptation to impose stringent UGBs, recognizing that a substantial restriction of urban growth is likely to do more harm than good.

REFERENCES

Altshuler, A. A., and J. A. Gomez-Ibanez. 1993. *Regulation for revenue: The political economy of land-use exactions*. Washington, DC: Brookings Institution.

Blomquist, G. C., and J. C. Whitehead. 1995. Existence value, contingent valuation, and natural resources damage assessment. *Growth and Change* 26: 573-89.

Brueckner, J. K. 1997. Infrastructure financing and urban development: The economics of impact fees. *Journal of Public Economics* 66: 383-407.

Brueckner, J. K., and D. Fansler. 1983. The economics of urban sprawl: Theory and evidence on the spatial sizes of cities. *Review of Economics and Statistics* 55: 479-82.

Ding, C., G. J. Knaap, and L. D. Hopkins. 1999. Managing urban growth with urban growth boundaries: A theoretical analysis. *Journal of Urban Economics* 46: 53-68.

Hayward, S. 1998. Legends of the sprawl. *Policy Review*, September-October (no. 91).

Knaap, G., and A. C. Nelson. 1992. *The regulated landscape: Lessons on state land use planning from Oregon*. Cambridge, MA: Lincoln Institute of Land Policy.

Mieszkowski, P., and E. S. Mills. 1993. The causes of metropolitan suburbanization. *Journal of Economic Perspectives* 7: 135-47.

Orfield, M. 1998. Conflict or consensus: Forty years of Minnesota metropolitan politics. *Brookings Review* 16: 31-34.

Rosenthal, S. S., and R. W. Helsley. 1994. Redevelopment and the urban land price gradient. *Journal of Urban Economics* 35: 182-200.

Small, K. A. 1992. *Urban transportation economics*. Chur, Switzerland: Harwood Academic.

Small, K. A., and J. A. Gomez-Ibanez. 1999. Urban transportation. In *Handbook of regional and urban economics*, vol. 3, edited by E. S. Mills and P. Cheshire. Amsterdam: North-Holland.

Thurston, L., and A.M.J. Yezer. 1994. Causality in the suburbanization of population and employment. *Journal of Urban Economics* 35: 105-18.

Tiebout, C. M. 1956. A pure theory of local expenditures. *Journal of Political Economy* 64: 416-24.

Wheaton, W. C. 1998. Land use and density in cities with congestion. *Journal of Urban Economics* 43: 258-72.

Wildasin, D. E. 1986. *Urban public finance*. Chur, Switzerland: Harwood Academic.

Part III
Systems of Cities

[10]

Urban Studies, Vol. 37, No. 3, 533–555, 2000

Diversity and Specialisation in Cities: Why, Where and When Does it Matter?

Gilles Duranton and Diego Puga

[Paper received in final form, August 1999]

Summary. Why are some cities specialised and others diversified? What are the advantages and disadvantages of urban specialisation and diversity? To what extent do the structure of cities and the activities of firms and people in them change over time? How does the sectoral composition of cities influence their evolution? To answer these and related questions, we first distil some key stylised facts from the empirical literature on cities and the composition of their activities. We then turn to a review of different theories looking at such issues, and study the extent to which these theories contribute to the understanding of the empirical regularities.

1. Introduction

At a time when most central governments, at least in developed economies, have abandoned the idea of a strongly interventionist industrial policy, a new economic activism seems to be on the rise at the local level. Local authorities frequently strive for specific patterns of economic activities in their jurisdictions. Specific models of industrial organisations are explicitly targeted, with the industrial districts of the Third Italy or Silicon Valley as prime models to be followed (Bartik, 1996, gives a broad review of these issues). While not all of these interventions are necessarily misguided, many seem to lack a clear rationale or even to be based on common misconceptions.[1]

The issues relating to the composition of cities are necessarily complex. Why are some cities specialised and others diversified? What are the advantages and disadvantages of urban specialisation and diversity? To what extent do the structure of cities and the activities of firms and people within them change over time? How does the sectoral composition of cities influence their evolution? To answer these and related questions, this paper starts by distilling some key stylised facts from the empirical literature on cities and the composition of their activities. We then turn to a review of different theories concerned with such issues, and study the extent to which these contribute to our understanding of empirical regularities. We structure these theories into three groups. First, those that are static in nature and focus on the geography within cities rather than on their spatial location with respect to each other. Secondly, static theories that look

Gilles Duranton is in the Department of Geography and Environment, London School of Economics, Houghton Street, London WC2A 2AE, UK. Fax: 0171 955 7412. E-mail: G.Duranton@lse.ac.uk. Diego Puga is in the Department of Economics, University of Toronto, 150 St George Street, Toronto, Ontario M5S 3G7, Canada. Fax: 416 946 5312. E-mail: dpuga@chass.utoronto.ca. *The authors are very grateful to Duncan Black for giving them access to data on US cities, as well as for his comments. They also greatly benefited from comments by Henry Overman and Andrés Rodrĝuez-Pose. The paper was partly written when the first author was visiting CESURE, Université de Lille 1, and while the second author was visiting the Institut d'Anàlisi Econòmica, Barcelona. The hospitality of both institutions is gratefully acknowledged.*

0042-0980 Print/1360-063X On-line/00/030533-23

more carefully at the spatial relations across cities. And, finally, theories that incorporate an explicit intertemporal dimension in the study of urban systems. A final section gathers some additional thoughts.

While concerned with policy issues, this survey does not aim to offer easy prescriptions. Instead, it highlights and discusses some of the complexities involved. But an additional motivation is present. There is a large body of extremely interesting empirical work on the structure of urban systems, but this often lacks an adequate theoretical base that could help to structure it. At the same time, related theoretical developments are not regularly subject to the discipline of assessing their correspondence with known empirical regularities. And both the empirical and theoretical research on the structure of cities is rarely well known to those not working in the field. Our main objective in this exercise of gathering, structuring and relating different empirical and theoretical approaches is to help build a common understanding of the nature and structure of cities.

2. Some Facts about Diversity and Specialisation in Cities

A large recent empirical literature has established a number of stylised facts about the composition of cities, their sizes and locations. In this context, note that gathering data on economic activity in cities is difficult. Since most of the recent research comes from the US, our exposition of the facts in this section is thus biased towards that country. Whenever possible, evidence about other countries is also given. US data and available data from the rest of the world often tend to go in the same direction as far as the issues examined here are concerned. However, it should be the task of future research to go into more depth and to corroborate or invalidate US findings. Another difficulty in exploring patterns of activities in cities involves the problems of definition raised by the concept of cities. In order to overcome these, to circumvent data limitations and to limit the scope of this paper, we shall focus mostly on cities with more than 50 000 inhabitants. This is not neutral with respect to the theories that we examine in sections 3–5, since our stylised facts in this section ignore small cities and concentrate on medium-sized and large cities, which may be of a nature different from smaller cities. In this section, we summarise and structure facts about the composition of economic activity in cities under five headings.

Stylised fact 1. Specialised and diversified cities co-exist.

In nearly all countries, cities largely specialised in a few activities co-exist with much more diversified cities. To start looking at diversity and specialisation in cities in some detail, one needs to specify measures of specialisation and diversity. The simplest way to measure a city's specialisation in a given sector is to quantify the share of this sector in local employment. Since different cities are specialised in different sectors, one useful measure of specialisation for comparisons across cities is the employment share of each city's largest sector. If we denote s_{ij} as the share of industry j in city i, we can define the following specialisation index:

$$ZI_i = \underset{j}{Max}(s_{ij}) \tag{1}$$

Of course, certain sectors account for a larger share of overall (say, national) employment than others. To correct for this, it is helpful to look at a city's relative (rather than absolute) specialisation, which can be measured as above, but dividing the share of each sector in local employment by its share in national employment. This leads naturally to the following relative-specialisation index:

$$RZI_i = \underset{j}{Max}(s_{ij}/s_j) \tag{2}$$

where, s_j is the share of industry j in national employment.

Table 1 lists, for selected US cities, the local relative-specialisation index for two-digit manufacturing sectors in 1992 (with the corresponding sector in parentheses).[2] Black and Henderson (1998) provide a detailed description of the data set. Among the most

Table 1. Most and least specialised and diversified US cities in 1992

	Specialisation		Diversity	
Rank	City (sector)	RZI	City	RDI
1	Richmond, VA (tobacco)	64.4	Cincinnati, OH	166.6
2	Macon, GA (tobacco)	55.0	Oakland, CA	161.2
3	Lewiston, ME (leather)	49.6	Atlanta, GA	159.4
4	Galveston, TX (petroleum)	49.1	Philadelphia, PA	151.4
5	Bangor, ME (leather)	45.6	Salt Lake City, UT	120.8
6	Owensboro, KY (tobacco)	44.4	Buffalo, NY	110.1
7	Corpus Christi, TX (petroleum)	37.6	Columbus, OH	108.3
8	Cheyenne, WY (petroleum)	33.4	Portland, OR	94.1
315	Buffalo, NY (rubber and plastics)	1.6	Lawton, OK	2.4
316	Cincinnati, OH (chemicals)	1.5	Richland, WA	2.4
317	Chicago, IL (metal products)	1.5	Steubenville, OH	2.4

Source: Black and Henderson data set.

specialised cities, there are those specialised in sectors largely dependent on natural resources such as tobacco (Richmond, Macon, Owensboro), petroleum products (Galveston, Corpus Christi, Cheyenne) and leather (Laredo, Bangor, Lewiston). These are extreme cases for which the relative-specialisation index is often above 30, indicating the presence of a sector with a share in local employment 30 times larger than its share in national employment. We also find cities highly specialised in manufacturing sectors, which are less dependent upon local resources, such as textiles (Burlington, Danville, Anderson), industrial machinery and equipment (Rochester) or transport equipment (Flint). At the other extreme, we find cities with a very low relative-specialisation index (Cincinnati, Buffalo, Chicago), with no sector having a share of manufacturing employment larger than 1.6 times its national share.

Turning to diversity, a common measure is the inverse of a Hirshman–Herfindahl index. For each city i this sums over all sectors the square of each sector's share in local employment. Formally, the inverse Hirshman–Herfindahl index or diversity index is given by

$$DI_i = 1/\sum_j s_{ij}^2 \quad (3)$$

If economic activity in the city under consideration is fully concentrated in a sector, we find $DI_i = 1$, and this index increases as activities in the city become more diverse.

Again, it is important to correct this measure for differences in sectoral employment shares at the national level. One possible way of making such a correction is to compute a relative-diversity index by summing for each city, over all sectors, the absolute value of the difference between each sector's share in local employment and its share in national employment. Formally, this leads to

$$RDI_i = 1/\sum_j |s_{ij} - s_j| \quad (4)$$

This index increases the more the composition of activities in city i mirrors the diversity of the national economy. Table 1 lists, for selected US cities, the relative-diversity index based on two-digit manufacturing sectors in 1992. Note that, when measured in this way, diversity and specialisation are not exact opposites. A city with a main industry and a broad base of other industries can be both diversified and specialised. Nevertheless, the most diverse cities (Atlanta, Philadelphia and Salt Lake City) are also not very specialised in any particular sector.

One interpretation of the co-existence of diverse and specialised cities is that patterns of specialisation and diversity are purely random. However, in their careful study of the agglomeration of industries in the US, Ellison and Glaeser (1997) show that this is highly unlikely: the distribution of economic activity in the US is too concentrated geographically at the level of most four-digit sectors for this to be the result of a random allocation. A second interpretation is that patterns of specialisation and diversification in cities merely mirror the spatial distribution of resources. For instance, cities in the French Alps or on the French Riviera tend to specialise in recreational activities for obvious topological and climatic reasons. This second possible explanation is more difficult to dismiss. Nevertheless, using panel-data econometrics, Henderson (1997a) is able to separate externalities from local fixed effects (i.e. persistent comparative advantage). He shows that even when fixed effects are accounted for, externalities are important. Thus, specialisation in cities is partly the result of economic interactions within a given sector (often called localisation economies), whereas diversity in cities is fostered by economic interactions across sectors (urbanisation economies).

Stylised fact 2. Larger cities tend to be more diversified. Cities of similar specialisation are of similar size.

We now turn to the relationship between city size and specialisation/diversity. It is widely believed that larger cities are more diversified. This assertion, while justified, needs some qualifications. First, there is a positive correlation between city size and the relative-diversity index described above, calculated on the basis of all private employment at the two-digit level in 1992, as shown in the plot of Figure 1. Note, however, that this link is not especially strong, partly because all cities have a large component of employment in non-tradeable activities. However, there is more to it than that. There are cases of specialised large cities, such as Los Angeles, which is a fairly specialised city (in entertainment) relative to its size. At this level of sectoral disaggregation, New York is also quite specialised in business services, although this sector comprises very heterogeneous activities. At the same time, smaller cities such as Buffalo, Columbus and Portland are very diversified.

Henderson (1997b) goes into more depth on this issue of diversity and size, and distinguishes between medium-sized cities

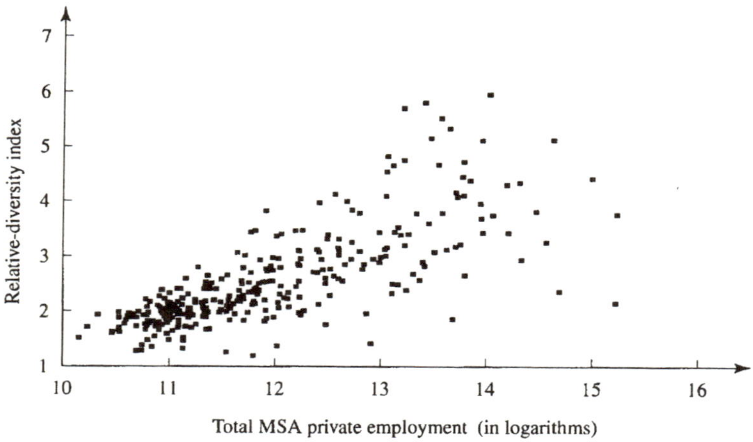

Figure 1. The size–diversity relation for US cities in 1992. *Source:* Black and Henderson (1998) data set.

(50 000–500 000 population) and large cities (over 500 000). He shows that large cities are, on average, more specialised in services (finance, insurance and real estate sectors) and less in manufacturing, than medium-sized cities. Looking at the industrial detail, medium-sized cities are more specialised in mature industries (such as textiles, food, pulp and paper) and less in new industries (such as electronic components and instruments). The contrast between instruments and textiles, which are sectors of comparable size, is particularly striking. In 1987, none of the 45 largest US metropolitan areas had more than 1 per cent of its workforce working in textiles, whereas 19 cities with a population of over 500 000 had between 1 and 5 per cent of their workforce in the instrument sector. Focusing on the size of specialised cities and distinguishing types of specialisation, Henderson (1988) shows that cities specialised in similar activities also tended to be of similar size. However, the evidence on this point is not very strong, given that standard deviations are often fairly high. Black and Henderson (1998), in their more comprehensive investigation of US cities for 1900–90, show that cities can be classified into groups of similar size/specialisation.

> *Stylised fact 3.* The distribution of relative city sizes, individual city-size rankings and individual city specialisations are stable over time.

An examination of the distribution of city size in various countries reveals that this is very stable. This is all the more remarkable, given the growth of the average size of cities. However, as always in the analysis of the dynamics of distributions, looking at the shape of the distribution is not enough.[3] One needs to examine movements within this distribution—the ups and downs in the size of individual cities. Over the past 30 years in the US there are contrasting examples. For example, the size of the City of Phoenix increased by a factor of nearly 10 between 1950 and 1990, while the cities of Detroit and Pittsburgh both lost nearly half their population over the same period.[4] But the systematic analysis by Black and Henderson (1998) of all US cities between 1900 and 1990 shows that Phoenix, Detroit and Pittsburgh are the exception, not the rule; in general, the relative sizes of US cities changed very little. Further, the current distribution of city size is very close to the ergodic (limiting) distribution, which we can interpret as evidence that the US urban system might be close to a 'steady state'. The general pattern is thus one of parallel urban growth, even though some cities gain more population than others. According to Eaton and Eckstein (1997), this pattern of overall stability is even stronger in France and Japan.

Not only are relative city sizes very stable, but there is also strong persistence of the same activities in the same cities. As with city size, there are some historical exceptions involving major overhauls at the sector level. These include the flight of textiles during the 18th century from the cities of Leiden and Haarlem in Holland to Manchester and Sheffield in the UK. Brezis and Krugman (1997) discuss these examples in further detail. More recent examples would include the successful economic restructuring of certain European cities formerly specialised in declining traditional activities, such as Cholet in France. The general pattern is, nonetheless, one of stability. Kim (1995) shows that the correlation of the coefficient of regional localisation for two-digit industries in the US between 1860 and 1987 at the state level is 0.64, which is surprisingly high, given the length of the period. Dumais *et al.* (1997) provide further evidence, showing that for US industries at the three-digit level, patterns of agglomeration have been rather stable over time. They show that industrial concentration in the US went up until 1947 and then down slightly until 1992 (which is consistent with the relative growth of larger cities, which are less heavily specialised). For most industries, the stability in their agglomeration patterns over 1972–92 is striking. The same picture of relative stability emerges from Henderson (1998) who studied in great detail 9 3-digit industries (4 high-tech industries and 5 machinery industries) over 30 years. Even though, in the leading city, 7 out of 9 industries has changed between 1963 and 1992, specialisation patterns have tended to persist over time in these 9 industries.[5] Henderson (1997b) gives broader evidence of the stability of specialisation patterns for medium-sized cities in the US.

Stylised fact 4. Individual city growth is related to specialisation and diversity, and to relative location.

Despite this overall picture of stability, some cities prosper, whereas others decay. A large part of the recent empirical literature has focused on trying to understand what characteristics of cities may contribute to their growth or decline. Glaeser *et al.* (1992) tackle this issue by asking whether diversity spurs further growth. Looking at employment growth in US cities, they find that diversity and local competition foster urban employment growth, whereas specialisation reduces urban employment growth. However, this finding could in part be a reflection of the recent relative decline in traditional manufacturing employment in the US, which tends to be more geographically concentrated (Black and Henderson, 1998). Some US and European cities specialised in traditional manufacturing activities were hit very hard by the decline of such activities. This suggests that distinguishing among sectors may be important. In fact, Henderson *et al.* (1995) find that, while urban diversity is, indeed, important for attracting new and innovative sectors, a history of similar past specialisation appears to matter more for mature industries. Furthermore, production of less-standardised or non-traditional items tends to be more concentrated in diversified metropolitan areas. On the other hand, production of traditional standardised items tends to be more heavily concentrated in cities which are often quite specialised in terms of the goods that are exported to other cities (Henderson, 1997a).

Urban growth also seems to be related to the relative locations of cities. Harris-Dobkins and Ioannides (1998), using US data beginning in 1900, find that larger cities tend to grow at a slower pace. Larger cities also favour the development of adjacent cities as well of those located far away, but hinder the development of cities located at a medium distance (80–500 km). Black and Henderson (1998), using a different data set on US cities, find that the effect of lagged own-city size on growth is negative, but they find that the external market potential has a positive effect.[6] However, the positive effect of external market potential disappears if lagged own-city size is not considered (Ioannides and Overman, 1999). One possible interpretation of this is that cities tend to grow more when their market potential is large relative to their size, and that growth slows down as city size catches up. In any case, all these results are relatively weak.

While stylised facts about the effects on urban growth of relative location do not directly say anything about specialisation and diversity, these are nonetheless useful for discriminating between theories that do consider specialisation and diversity, but have different predictions regarding the link between urban growth and relative location. However, it must be said that the evidence to date remains very patchy and more work is needed on these issues.

Stylised fact 5. There is a high rate of plant turnover. Most innovations take place in particularly diversified cities and most new plants are created there. Most relocations are from diversified to specialised cities.

The strong persistence of individual city specialisation discussed above is all the more surprising since data from several countries show that about 1 in 10 establishments closes down every year, to be replaced by new establishments (Dunne *et al.*, 1989a, 1989b; Davis and Haltiwanger, 1992). According to Dumais *et al.* (1997) more than one-half of all US manufacturing employees in 1992 worked in firms that did not exist in 1972, and nearly three-quarters of the plants existing in 1972 were closed by 1992. Even for surviving plants, changes have been dramatic. Among all plants still in operation in

1992 which had between 950 and 1050 employees in 1972, the mean for 1992 was 793 and the standard deviation 678. This would not be too surprising if new plants just replaced older plants, but Dumais *et al.* (1997) show that the birth process for new plants and the closure process are spatially very biased. The birth of new plants (in particular for new firms) tends to reduce the degree of agglomeration of particular sectors, suggesting that new plants are created in locations with below-average specialisation in the corresponding sector. On the other hand, the closure of existing plants tends to increase it. Unfortunately, the data set used by Dumais *et al.* (1997) does not distinguish the real death of plants from changes in the property rights or their relocation.

More details are available from data on French establishments. This data set, which traces all relocations of establishments between employment areas (defined according to commuting patterns), allows for changes in property rights and separates relocations from new plant creations. A complete description of the data is given by Delisle and Lainé (1998). These data have been studied by Duranton and Puga (1999) for the period 1993–96. Over those 4 years, 258 305 new plants were created in continental France (representing 27.8 per cent of the average stock over this period). At the same time, 23 281 establishments relocated to another employment area (2.5 per cent of the average stock over this period).[7] Of all new plants, 58.6 per cent were created in an employment area with above-median diversity (as measured by the inverse of a Herfindahl index of local employment shares of different sectors). Those numbers confirm that most creations take place in diversified cities. Regarding plant relocations, 93.9 per cent of all relocations across employment areas departed from an employment area with above-median diversity. Two-thirds of those went to locations with above-median specialisation (as measured by the share of the corresponding sector in local employment). This implies that 61.6 per cent of all relocations across employment areas both departed from an employment area with above-median diversity and arrived in an employment area with above-median specialisation, while less than 3 per cent of all relocations across employment areas were from an employment area with below-median diversity to an employment area with below-median specialisation. Note that this spatial bias in the movement of firms is necessary to make the bias in the creation of new plants towards larger and more diversified cities consistent with the stability in city size and specialisation described under Stylised fact 3. If new firms and new sectors were born in larger and more diversified cities without any posterior differences, those cities would come to dominate the urban landscape, whereas specialised cities should disappear, and we have seen that this is not the case.

Not only is the creation of new plants biased towards larger and more diverse cities, but so is the location of innovative activities that lead to new products. Jacobs (1960) was the first to argue forcefully that localised diversity may favour innovation. Nonetheless, it is only recently that hard evidence on this issue has been gathered. Feldman and Audrescht (1999) use a data set of 3969 US product innovations in 1982 for which the address of the innovating establishment can be identified. They first find that a staggering 96 per cent of the innovations were made in those metropolitan areas, which accounted for only 30 per cent of the US population. Cities are thus the places where innovations occur. But it is important to establish what is the main force driving the innovative process: pure city size, urban diversity or urban specialisation. To investigate this issue, Feldman and Audrescht (1999) relate each four-digit industry to an underlying scientific base (using previous scientific surveys), and group together industries sharing a common scientific base.[8] Using this information, they first show that industries sharing a common scientific base tend to cluster together. Then for each city-industry, they regress the innovative output on an index of relative specialisation in the sector, an index of diversity across industries with a common science base, city size and other controls. They find that own-industry specialisation has a negative effect on innovative output, whereas diversity across industries with a common science base and city size both have a positive and highly significant effect on innovative output. Similar results are obtained when the same analysis is carried on at the level of the firm. Using data for nine major Japanese electronic firms, Fujita and Ishii (1998) show that their R&D activities are located solely in the major metropolitan areas of Tokyo, Kyoto and Boston. When looking at production, they distinguish between trial plants and mass-production plants, and show that trial plants are also overwhelmingly located in major metropolitan areas, whereas mass-production plants are almost always located in smaller cities or rural areas.

Having outlined the main stylised facts about diversity and specialisation in cities, we now turn to theories looking at these issues.

3. Static Theoretical Approaches with No Trading Costs for Final Goods

Most theories of urban systems dealing with issues of size, diversity and specialisation, have some common structure, even if this is not always apparent. To make comparisons easier, we shall describe each theoretical approach starting from a statement about four basic assumptions. First of all, it is useful to view cities as an equilibrium outcome, whether static or dynamic, which balances agglomeration forces (that create benefits for people and firms locating close to each other) and dispersion forces (that create costs from such closeness). Hence, every consistent theory needs to make an explicit assumption about agglomeration forces (Assumption 1) and an explicit assumption about dispersion forces (Assumption 2). Agglomeration forces give a rationale for the existence of cities, while dispersion forces place limits on city size. With respect to agglomeration and following Hoover (1936), we distinguish between localisation economies (agglomeration forces within individual sectors) and urbanisation economies (agglomeration forces across different sectors). We think of both agglomeration (also called centripetal) forces and dispersion (centrifugal) forces as arising from economic interactions. Non-economic interactions, even if important in explaining early cities, are probably not strong enough to sustain today's larger cities. The limits placed by congestion costs on city size imply that not everyone concentrates in a single location. This calls for two additional assumptions. One of these spells out the relationships between cities in an urban system, which requires making assumptions about the mobility of goods and households (Assumption 3). Finally, the structure of the urban landscape needs to be made explicit. Either the number and locations of cities are taken as exogenous, or some mechanism for city formation needs to be proposed (Assumption 4).

The starting-point of the first thread of the literature is Henderson (1974). Building on the Alonso–Muth framework (Alonso, 1964; Muth, 1969), which models the internal structure of cities, he extends it to a system of cities in general equilibrium with a finite number of sectors. The following is a simplified description of his model. He makes four main assumptions.

> *Assumption 1a (Marshallian agglomeration).* Existence of own-sector externalities.

In Henderson (1974), localisation economies take the form of pure Marshallian externalities, whereby the productivity of labour in any given sector in any given city is assumed to increase with total employment in that sector in that city. The strength of local externalities is also assumed to vary, so that these are stronger in some sectors and weaker in others.

> *Assumption 2a (dispersion through crowding).* Cities are subject to congestion costs, which increase with their population.

This can be easily justified with reasonable assumptions about commuting costs and land rents. Consider the simple case of a city with a single central business district. An extra worker added at the edge of a city will face higher commuting costs than the worker previously furthest from the city centre. This will make closeness to the city centre more valuable, and lead to higher land rents. The combination of commuting costs and land rents is a congestion effect that increases with population.

Assumption 3a (perfect product and labour mobility). Inter-city trade is free for all final goods and labour is perfectly mobile across cities.

The first part of this assumption, the possibility of transporting between cities at no cost, is most important. Relaxing it, as we shall see later in section 4, can qualitatively change the results. By contrast, the extreme assumption of perfect mobility of labour across cities will not play a very big role in this context. In a static framework, some form of labour mobility is necessary for the final landscape not to be fully determined by the initial conditions. At the same time, the degree of this mobility is not crucial.

Assumption 4a (large agents). Large agents can create new cities.

In Henderson (1974), large agents take the form of urban developers. These developers are competitive in the sense that they maximise their profits, taking as given the product and labour-market implications of the behaviour of other developers.

Note that under Assumptions 1a, 2a and 3a, no developer is willing to open more than one sector in a given city. The reason is simple: by segregating sectors across cities, congestion is reduced without affecting productivity, since positive externalities take place only within sectors. Alternatively, by keeping city size constant and specialising the activities of a city, a developer keeps congestion at the same level and increases the productivity in this city. Thus productive efficiency calls for complete urban specialisation, which is implemented by profit-maximising developers. Free entry of developers drives these profits to zero, which ensures that cities are of optimal size. This equilibrium/optimal city size is the result of a tension between localisation economies, which act as an agglomeration force, and urban crowding, which tends to disperse the population. Equilibrium/optimal city size is increasing with the degree of localisation economies and decreasing with the extent of crowding. Since cities specialised in different sectors experience economies of localisation with a different intensity, they are of different sizes, but cities with the same specialisation are of the same size.

Result 1. Under Assumptions 1a, 2a and 3a, the urban system is only composed of fully specialised cities, provided that the initial number of cities is large enough. Furthermore, imposing Assumption 4a results in an efficient urban system with cities of optimal size.

Here we have presented Assumptions 1a–4a in their most extreme forms for expositional clarity, so that the lack of realism need not be of concern. A more relevant shortcoming is the lack of microeconomic foundations for localisation economies under Assumption 1a. These foundations have a theoretical importance in understanding what localisation economies precisely are, and how these may vary as other features of the urban system change. Such foundations are also important empirically when one tries to measure those externalities. Finally, the precise understanding of local externalities is also crucial from a policy perspective, particularly since the latter often call for corrective policies; one can hardly evaluate the need for, and design of, such corrective policies without an adequate understanding of the nature of the externalities.

Regarding its predictive ability, this model is consistent with the existence of specialised cities of similar size having the same specialisation (Stylised fact 2). However, this model also implies that all cities are fully specialised cities and rules out diversified cities, which contradicts Stylised fact 1. In this framework, provided that cities do not overlap, their relative locations do not matter, and this can be related to some of the features described under Stylised fact 4. Finally, the model predicts the emergence of a market for cities with active land developers on the supply side. This is a useful construct and one that is very relevant for understanding the formation of many edge cities in the US (Garreau, 1991). It also suggests that restrictions on the ability of land developers to operate may be a contributing factor to the large (often to the extent of being considered inefficient) size of the typical metropolis in less-developed economies. At the same time, it may be less applicable to other geographical areas such as Europe, where land developers play less of a role. Nonetheless, it can be shown that under certain conditions the more plausible assumption of active local governments leads to similar results.[9] Furthermore, Assumption 4a just ensures the optimal city-size result. Even without any large agent, specialisation will occur provided the initial number of cities is large enough.[10]

Overall, this model remains a true landmark in the understanding of urban systems, allowing us to capture in a simple framework a general equilibrium of a system of cities, where the cities arise endogenously from a tension between economies of agglomeration and urban crowding, and interact with each other through trade. A large fraction of the subsequent literature takes this model as its starting-point. In the rest of this section, we shall examine models that try to amend Assumption 1a. Theories dealing with departures from Assumptions 3a and 4a are presented in section 4, whereas more complicated dynamic structures are introduced in section 5.

A number of authors have provided adequate microeconomic foundations for Assumption 1a. Abdel-Rahman (1988), Fujita (1988) and Rivera-Batiz (1988) took this step around the same time, by introducing Chamberlinian monopolistic competition in the standard urban framework. The extension of this line of research to a general-equilibrium model of urban systems can be found in Abdel-Rahman and Fujita (1990). Assumption 1a is replaced by

Assumption 1b (Chamberlinian agglomeration). Final goods are produced by using non-tradeable differentiated services, and a larger range of locally available services lowers the costs of production for final goods.

The details of the assumption are as follows. Final goods are produced in a two-stage process. First, labour is used by monopolistically competitive service firms to produce differentiated producer services under increasing returns to scale. These firms are monopolist producers of their own variety and thus choose prices to maximise profits. However, free entry and exit drive their profits to zero. These services are, in turn, used by competitive final-good producers who have a production function where the different varieties enter with a constant elasticity of substitution. The larger a sector in a city, the larger is the range of service producers that it can support, and the higher the final output that can be produced from the same labour supply. Thus the replacement of Assumption 1a by 1b leads to Result 1 again.

Yet the contribution of Abdel-Rahman and Fujita (1990) is important beyond this equivalence result, in that it suggests a different source for the increasing returns: Chamberlinian economies of agglomeration instead of the pure Marshallian economies in Henderson (1974). Even though the aggregate implications of Marshallian and Chamberlinian economies of agglomeration are the same, Abdel-Rahman and Fujita (1990) show that the policy implications can be very different. Under Assumption 1a (Marshallian agglomeration), the production of each good is subject to constant returns to scale, and firms are perfectly competitive, yet there is a city-wide externality. By contrast, under Assumption 1b (Chamberlinian agglomeration) the production of each intermediate service is subject to increasing returns to scale at the level of each imperfectly competitive firm, and economies of agglomeration stem from price interactions between firms. In their particular model, Abdel-Rahman and Fujita (1990) show that optimal city size can be reached without much intervention under Assumption 1a. Under Assumption 1b, however, a production subsidy is required to reach optimal city size.

Helsley and Strange (1990) propose an alternative microeconomic foundation for urban externalities, using a labour-market argument. They rely on the general idea that cities may offer specialised workers more employment opportunities and that, conversely, a larger pool of workers makes it easier for employers to find specialised labour. Consequently, the matching between employers and specialised employees is easier in larger cities. Furthermore, cities can also be thought of as fostering the specialisation of labour in the first place. Duranton (1998) shows how the specialisation of labour implies economic agglomeration, which helps to sustain a high degree of labour specialisation (Smithian agglomeration). The main assumption is one of increasing marginal productivity when the time spent on a given range of tasks increases. When final goods are produced using localised specialised services, this again leads to a reduced form similar to those obtained by Henderson (1974) and Abdel-Rahman and Fujita (1990) at the city level. However, Smithian agglomeration economies can be thought to be different in nature from both Marshallian and Chamberlinian agglomeration economies. Smithian agglomeration economies stem from interactions at the level of the labour market and are likely to result, yet again, in different prescriptions in terms of economic policy.[11]

Providing microeconomic foundations for the production function, however useful, still does not allow us to generate both diversified and specialised cities—complete urban specialisation is still the only possible outcome in this thread of literature. Abdel-Rahman (1990a, 1990b), Abdel-Rahman and Fujita (1993) and Abdel-Rahman (1994) provide the four main static models which introduce the possibility that some cities specialise and others diversify. Abdel-Rahman (1990a) amends Assumption 1b slightly by including non-tradeable final goods.

Assumption 1b′ (Chamberlinian agglomeration with non-tradeable sector). Final goods are produced by using non-tradeable differentiated services, and a larger range of locally available services lowers the costs of production for final goods. There is a non-tradeable and essential final-good sector that can engage in production using the same differentiated services as any of the tradeable sectors.

The main result of Abdel-Rahman (1990a) is:

Result 2. Under Assumptions 1b′, 2a, 3a and 4a, all cities manufacture the non-tradeable final good and one of the tradeable final goods. In equilibrium, larger cities are more specialised in the production of one of the tradeable goods.

The first part of the result is easy to understand. Since the non-tradeable good is essential in the utility function, all cities will produce it in equilibrium. The existence of this non-tradeable sector will tend to limit urban specialisation. This is a desirable property of the model, since we saw earlier that most cities had a large part of their labour force employed in sectors such as retail or health services. The other important aspect of the model is that tradeable and non-tradeable final goods can make use of the same intermediate goods. This aims to capture the idea of diversification arising from cost-saving due to shared inputs. The second part of the result is less intuitive. To understand it, consider the following thought experiment. Starting with a city of small size, imagine an increase in its population. Then, due to the economies of agglomeration, production will become more efficient. Thanks to this increase in efficiency of the city, the population will be richer and thus will demand more imported goods. The only way that this can be paid for is by specialising more in the production of the tradeable good. This prediction can be meaningful when distinguishing very small cities, which are often dominated by the production of non-tradeable goods to a greater extent than medium-sized and large cities. But if our focus is on medium-sized and large cities, as it is here, this result contradicts Stylised fact 2.

An alternative way of generating diversified cities is to introduce cross-sector externalities. This leads to a tension between localisation and urbanisation economies. Abdel-Rahman (1990b) develops this idea in a partial-equilibrium framework. His main assumption is the following.

> *Assumption 1a′ (Marshallian agglomeration plus cross-sector externalities).* Existence of own-sector externalities and of cross-sector externalities.

The simplest way to represent this assumption is to consider only two sectors, with positive own-sector externalities in each sector, and also with a positive cross-sector externality from sector 2 to sector 1. In this partial-equilibrium analysis, the number of cities is fixed (and their location is irrelevant given the absence of trading costs).

> *Assumption 4b (set landscape).* The number and location of cities is fixed.

If the two products are essential in the utility function, we reach the following result.

> *Result 3.* Under Assumptions 1a′, 2a, 3a and 4b, three configurations are possible in equilibrium: only specialised cities (good-1 cities and good-2 cities); only diversified cities; and mixed configurations with both good-2 cities and diversified cities. Under a mixed configuration, diversified cities are smaller than specialised cities.

Regarding the first part of the result, note that if cross-sector externalities are very weak, these can actually be ignored. This drives us back to Assumption 1a, and we obtain Result 1 again, with only specialised cities. In the opposite case, when cross-sector externalities are very strong and own-sector externalities very weak in sector 1, this sector will always be attached to sector 2, and the equilibrium configuration will always imply either only diversified cities or a mixed configuration. The last part of the result is more subtle. Diversified and specialised cities cannot be of the same size. If they were, diversified cities would have the same urban crowding with weaker localisation economies in sector 2. This would make the net wage of labour employed in sector 2 lower in diversified cities. But, with labour mobility, workers in sector 2 must receive the same net wage in both types of city. Potentially, wage equalisation across cities could be ensured by having sector 2 larger in diversified cities than in specialised cities. But this situation is unstable as individual workers gain by relocating from diversified to specialised cities, where there is less crowding. This would reinforce the economies of agglomeration in specialised cities. Thus diversified cities cannot remain larger than specialised cities. It can be shown formally that the only possible stable equilibrium is to have specialised cities being larger than diversified cities. This, again, is in contradiction with Stylised fact 2. The other empirical limit to the model is that it precludes the co-existence of diversified cities and specialised cities of both types (i.e. good-1 cities, good-2 cities and diversified cities). This type of co-existence, however, seems relatively common. In France, for instance, Sochaux is specialised in the car industry and Toulouse in the aircraft industry, whereas Paris is diversified with both industries being (non-trivially) represented.

Abdel-Rahman and Fujita (1993) attempt to tackle the same problem differently, by taking a general equilibrium approach. They start from the idea that diversification may stem from economies of scope. In their model, they consider again two sectors, 1 and 2, producing homogeneous goods, and three possible technologies for factory cities.

> *Assumption 1c (agglomeration through fixed costs).* Three technologies are available. The first technology involves a labour overhead and a rising marginal cost to produce good 1. The second technology also involves a labour overhead and a rising marginal cost to produce good 2. Finally, the third technology involves a

labour overhead and a rising marginal cost to produce jointly both goods.

Clearly, the use of the first two technologies leads to specialised cities, whereas the last one results in diversified cities. Regarding dispersion, Abdel-Rahman and Fujita (1993) impose Assumption 2a. Perfect mobility is also assumed for final goods (Assumption 3a). Finally, their general equilibrium framework leads to the reintroduction of Assumption 4a. Their main result is:

Result 4. Under Assumptions 1c, 2a, 3a and 4a, three configurations are possible in equilibrium: only specialised cities; only diversified cities; and mixed configurations with both diversified cities and specialised cities of one type. Under a mixed configuration, diversified cities are larger than specialised cities.

Thus, the three types of configuration that emerge in equilibrium are very similar to those in Abdel-Rahman (1990b). However, unlike this latter paper, Abdel-Rahman and Fujita (1993) find that when specialised cities exist, they are smaller in equilibrium than diversified cities. This is easy to understand. If the labour overhead associated with the mixed technology 3 is relatively small, only diversified cities will exist. For a mixed configuration (and thus specialised cities) to be sustainable, a relatively large labour overhead is needed in the diversified city. This will result in diversified cities being of a larger size. This is an attractive result in that it is consistent with Stylised fact 2. What is not so appealing is that, together with the other results from this model, it is driven by large city-specific fixed costs. As a consequence, cities are taken to be factory towns, which are not very common nowadays.

Abdel-Rahman (1994) pursues this line of investigation further, and tries to provide some microeconomic foundations for the previous model. He does so by introducing a production structure with two stages. Service producers manufacture differentiated intermediate goods, which are later aggregated into final goods as under Assumption 1b. The twist here is that service producers have the choice between different technologies as with Assumption 1c (so that large city-specific fixed costs are replaced by the more plausible assumption of small firm-specific fixed costs). Intermediate goods producers can thus choose whether to produce intermediates for any one sector or for both. As before, the same three types of configuration are possible. However, this model brings back the counterfactual result that in the mixed configuration specialised cities are larger than diversified cities. This occurs for the same reason as in Abdel-Rahman (1990b).

All the papers described in this section propose very intuitive explanations as to why there might be a tension between localisation and urbanisation economies, leading cities to diversify or specialise depending on the circumstances. The models used to carry through the analysis are clean and tractable. Nonetheless, this type of approach has some important limits since it seems difficult to take the consistency with stylised facts much beyond the co-existence of diversified and specialised cities of Stylised fact 1.

4. Approaches with Trading Costs for Final Goods

The second strand of literature can be traced back to Christaller (1933) and central-place theory. Christaller starts from the observation that goods are bought with different frequencies, and argues that this may justify the existence of an urban hierarchy. For instance, imagine that good A is bought on a daily basis, whereas good B is bought on a monthly basis. He argues that this should give rise to a hierarchical system of cities, with some cities selling only good A (central places of level 1), and other cities selling both good A and good B (central places of level 2). In a two-dimensional space (and using a specific metric), this gives rise to the famous contiguous hexagonal market areas for central places of level 2. The market areas for the higher-frequency goods are successively built on the market areas of the lower-frequency goods. Christaller justified this structure on the basis that it would minimise transport costs. The strength of this approach is that the postulated configuration matches real urban landscapes in certain important respects and can be related to Stylised facts 1, 2 and 4 (see Berry and Parr, 1988, for a more detailed review). However, there is no explanation as to why such a configuration would emerge as an equilibrium outcome of decentralised actions by economic agents. The urban system postulated by central-place theory is such that transport costs are minimised, but no one explicitly performs this minimisation, nor does it result from the microeconomic behaviour of firms and consumers. Eaton and Lipsey (1982) were the first to propose an equilibrium model of central places in which they try to deduce the propositions of central-place theory from rigorously stated assumptions. Given the enormous difficulty of the problem, they were only able to present a very stylised model in partial equilibrium. The main assumptions are the following.

> *Assumption 1c′ (agglomeration through fixed costs with cities as shops)*. Profit-maximising retailers, facing a fixed cost for each new shop, sell two homogeneous goods, A and B. Prices are exogenously determined.

Compared with Assumptions 1a and 1b, the primary source of agglomeration is the fixed cost faced by retailers, which prevents them from spreading continuously across space. While treating prices as parametric is not very satisfactory, having price competition makes the model of Eaton and Lipsey (1982) intractable.

> *Assumption 2b (direct dispersion)*. Households are uniformly distributed over the real line. They consume good A and good B at constant unitary rates.

Note that this assumption is much more extreme than Assumption 2a, since here the dispersion of demand is assumed directly (and in such a way that cities are 'empty' of people) and not derived within the theory. The focus of the model is solely on shopping issues.

> *Assumption 3b (shopping costs)*. Households are allowed to shop at regular intervals. When they shop, they can buy at most one bundle of fixed size of each good. Households shop so as to minimise shopping costs.

Here, the free-trade Assumption 3a is replaced by an assumption of strictly positive trading costs. These trading costs take the specific form of shopping costs, capturing the indivisibilities of shopping (goods are bought in bundles at regular intervals).

Overall Assumptions 1c, 2b, 3b and 4a can be seen as the rigorous statement of the implicit assumptions in the informal story given at the beginning of this section. Beyond this formal statement of the assumptions of traditional central-place theory, Eaton and Lipsey (1982) also make explicit the decision to locate cities. Households choose their shopping strategy so as to minimise shopping costs, while retailers choose their location so as to maximise their profits, taking the action of other retailers as given (using the concept of a Nash equilibrium). From this set of assumptions they derive the following result.

> *Result 5*. Under Assumptions 1c′, 2b, 3b and 4a, at least one central place of level 2 exists in equilibrium. If central places of levels 1 and 2 co-exist, then all central places of level 1 offer the same good.

The first part of the result requires the following thought experiment. Imagine that a central place of level 1 which sells good A is located to the left of a central place of level 1, which sells good B. Then the retailer selling good A would gain by shifting rightwards and relocating closer to the retailer selling good B. By so doing, the retailer would benefit from the 'lump' of demand which went to the shop selling good B (these benefits are often called 'economies of multi-purpose shopping'). Similarly, the retailer selling good B will benefit from a leftwards move. The benefits from the two retailers locating closer to each other will only be exhausted once a central place of level 2, selling both goods, is created. This central place of level 2 allows each retailer to take advantage of shoppers going to the other retailer. In short, each store creates a positive demand externality for stores selling the other good.

The previous reasoning implies that a central place of level 1 selling good A cannot locate next to a central place of level 1 selling good B. Thus, the equilibrium must have either only central places of level 2, or central places of level 2 alternating with central places of level 1 all selling the same good. This result confirms some of Christaller's intuitions and provides justifications for aspects of Stylised facts 1, 2 and 4. In particular, the physical location of cities can now be considered in the model, albeit in a very stylised way. However, it also shows that the typical central-place pattern need not emerge in equilibrium, and that the regular geography proposed by Christaller does not generally arise. In terms of the economic underpinnings, the insights of a central-place theory driven by shopping costs can help to illuminate many issues surrounding small cities, but they are probably of much less relevance for larger cities producing goods sold everywhere in the economy. This suggests replacing the assumption of shopping costs by one of shipping costs.

> *Assumption 3c (shipping costs).* Shipping goods to consumers involves costs that increase with distance and differ across goods.

This then leads simply to:

> *Result 6.* Under Assumptions 1c′, 2b, 3c and 4a, there is no tendency for producers to cluster.

The tendency of producers to cluster disappears because, without shopping costs, there are no economies of multipurpose shopping. The derivation of the equilibrium market area of firms depends on the pricing mechanism. But it can be shown that in each sector, competition will lead to an equilibrium market area where producers make zero profits. The equilibrium market area differs from sector to sector, but there is no reason for the ratio of the size of market areas in different sectors to be exactly an integer, so that central places can only arise by chance (Anderson *et al.*, 1992). The difficulty of dealing with physical distance using well-specified models, along with the negative results derived by Eaton and Lipsey (1982), drastically limited the amount of research using this type of approach. The replication of the regular geometry of central-place theory started to be viewed as a nearly impossible task. It is only in the very recent past that new models have been developed, in which physical space is considered explicitly.

Coming from a radically different perspective from that of Eaton and Lipsey (1982), Abdel-Rahman (1996) develops a model similar in spirit to Henderson (1974). The initial framework is the same, but he introduces trading costs and fixes the initial location of cities (Assumption 4b). In his setting, there are two sectors in which final goods are produced by using labour and differentiated intermediate goods (Assumption 1b). Cities are monocentric with congestion due to crowding (Assumption 2a). Finally, the costs of shipping goods between any two cities are the same.

> *Assumption 3c′ (shipping costs and perfect labour mobility).* Shipping goods to consumers involves costs that increase with distance. Labour is perfectly mobile.

This assumption is very close to Assumption 3c. It can also be thought of as Assumption 3a, but with shipping costs being strictly positive. This allows Abdel-Rahman to study the conditions under which cities specialise or diversify. His main result is:

> *Result 7.* Under Assumptions 1b, 2a, 3c′ and 4b, two configurations are possible in equilibrium: pure specialisation and pure diversification. Pure specialisation arises for low shipping costs, while pure diversification arises for high shipping costs.

It is useful to compare this result with Result 1. Without shipping costs, cities specialise as in Henderson (1974). Again, diversification is costly since it reduces the economies of localisation while holding urban crowding constant. Here, however, positive shipping costs also make specialisation costly, since it is expensive to import from other cities. As a result, when shipping costs are high, cities will diversify. This result can be thought of as capturing the evolution of cities in the past. During the Industrial Revolution, lower shipping costs coincided with the rise of more specialised cities (Bairoch, 1988). However, in the more recent past, the decline in shipping costs does not seem to have promoted more specialised cities. On the contrary, large diversified cities seem to have done particularly well (Black and Henderson, 1998; Glaeser *et al.*, 1992). Note also that the model does not predict the co-existence of diversified and specialised cities (in contradiction with Stylised fact 1). Finally, the modelling of physical space remains 'incomplete', since the model considers only the impact of spatial frictions on the composition of cities with their location exogenously given.

The next step towards a better modelling of physical distance in urban systems was taken by Fujita and Krugman (2000) and Fujita *et al.* (1999), who adapted the approach developed by Krugman (1991) for regional systems to a more specifically urban framework. Their approach represents a significant departure from central-place theory in that they do not try to generate a regular urban system. According to Christaller, existing urban systems are irregular because of physical features and other distortions. Remove the distortions and urban systems should tend towards geometric regularity. By contrast, Fujita and Krugman (2000) show that lack of perfect regularity in the spatial distribution of cities may be a fundamental property of urban systems, which would arise even without any unevenness in physical space. The general-equilibrium model built by Fujita and Krugman (2000) relies on the following assumptions.

> *Assumption 1b″ (Chamberlinian agglomeration from consumer tastes).* There is a single manufacturing sector producing differentiated consumer goods. Consumers have a taste for variety.

Note that this assumption is very close to Assumption 1b, except that the differentiated goods are directly consumed instead of being used to produce another good. The important aspect of consumer preferences regarding manufactured goods is the taste for variety.

> *Assumption 2c (dispersion through fixed factors).* Agricultural land is represented by a line. The agricultural good is essential. Agricultural income is spent where it is generated.

This assumption introduces a second type of good: a homogeneous agricultural product, to which consumers devote a fraction of their income. Unlike the differentiated goods that give rise to localised increasing returns, the agricultural good is produced under constant returns to scale. Another crucial difference between agricultural and manufactured goods is that the production of the former requires not only labour but also an immobile factor (land), and returns to this factor follow the spatial distribution of land.

Regarding mobility, Fujita and Krugman (2000) assume again that shipping final goods is costly and that labour is mobile (Assumption 3c′). City formation is now the aggregate outcome of individual decisions by firms and workers.

> *Assumption 4c (self-organisation).* Cities can form endogenously from the optimising behaviour of individual firms and workers.

An equilibrium is a situation in which the following obtain: workers maximise their utility and firms their profits, subject (respectively) to the relevant budget and technological constraints; individual workers are unwilling to relocate; it is unprofitable for more firms to begin production; and no existing firm wants to relocate or cease production. These assumptions lead to the following result:

> *Result 8.* Under Assumptions 1b″, 2c, 3c′ and 4c, there are many possible equilibrium configurations. In particular, a system of cities with cities of different sizes can arise endogenously.

Consider first how the propensity of firms and workers to agglomerate arises in this context. As is usual with Chamberlinian monopolistic competition, each variety will be produced by a single firm. A larger number of locally produced varieties of manufactures will make a location more attractive to consumers (all goods can be consumed everywhere, but it is less costly to buy them closer to the place of production). Migration will increase market size, making the location more attractive to firms. This creates a mechanism of circular causation, by which more firms attract more workers/consumers and more workers/consumers attract more firms. Note that the intuition is similar to Abdel-Rahman and Fujita (1990) which is discussed above, the main difference being that here the model deals with imperfectly tradeable final goods instead of non-tradeable intermediate goods.

However, it is not always the case that all firms agglomerate at one location. When the economy is large enough, a unique city may not be sustainable in equilibrium. Since manufactured goods are substitutes, some firms may find it profitable to relocate away from the city and serve mainly farmers located in the agricultural fringe. This quite naturally generates a system of cities, with cities of different size but with smaller cities being miniature replicas of the larger cities. To show this result, the analytical tool used by Fujita and Krugman (2000) is the market-potential function. This tool has a long tradition in economic geography. However, they provide a microeconomic basis for it, regarding it as the profit at every possible location for a firm considering relocation. They further refine it by taking into account substitution effects between goods. This market potential has two main components: demand from the city and demand from the farmers. As a firm moves away from the city, the first component declines while the second increases. The sum of these two components of the market potential does not change monotonically as distance to the city increases. Close to the city, the negative effect of losing urban demand is stronger; but, further away, the positive effect of stronger agricultural demand may dominate. Thus, typically, there will be a large city in the centre of the economy and smaller cities close to the fringes.

When Fujita and Krugman (2000) introduce the possibility of multiple sectors with goods having different shipping costs, they can generate hierarchical systems of cities as in traditional central-place theory. Starting from an economy with a single city, a growth in population will expand the agricultural hinterland and lead sectors with higher shipping costs to spread out. The original city will keep all sectors, but new peripheral cities will form, initially based on those goods with high shipping costs and importing the rest from the original city. Thus, in equilibrium, it is possible to obtain a system of cities with large and diversified cities along with small and specialised cities. This modelling framework is quite attractive although analytical complexity and multiplicity of equilibria emerge as two important drawbacks. To deal with these issues, Fujita *et al.* (1999) propose a refinement of the previous approach. They use an evolutionary framework in which population grows over time and they assume a set of simple and plausible rules for equilibrium selection. Using numerical simulations for a three-sector economy, they show that population growth leads to the formation of a hierarchical system of cities with large and diversified cities and small specialised cities, as in Fujita and Krugman (2000). They also show that typically central places of level 1 will be located between central places of higher levels which offer a broader range of goods.

The work of Fujita *et al.* (1999) represents a landmark in the modelling of urban systems, since this is the first paper able to deal with central-place theory in a general-equilibrium framework with well-specified microeconomic foundations. Empirically, it can again replicate well Stylised facts 1 and 2. It also provides some spatial predictions related to Stylised fact 4. Nonetheless, this approach has certain drawbacks. First, the model yields very few testable results. Compared to Fujita and Krugman (2000), it can tackle the multiplicity of equilibria reasonably well. However, it still relies on numerical results, and it would appear that almost any observed urban system can be seen to be a possible outcome of their model. The second undesirable property of their model is the constant creation and destruction of new cities. When a new city is formed or when transport costs decline, the whole urban system is often reshuffled. Perhaps this excessive urban turbulence would be mitigated in a more realistic framework, with mobility costs for labour and sunk capital investments. The third problem is that the entire model relies on the differences in market potential between a continuum of locations. This introduces physical space into the model in a meaningful way, but the approach may be too extreme since, as discussed under Stylised fact 4, the evidence on market potential driving urban growth is relatively weak. Finally, this approach relies purely on self-organisation. While Assumption 4a assigns too strong a role to land developers, here large agents (including central or local government) are ignored completely. More work in the middle ground is clearly needed.

5. Dynamic Approaches

So far, we have discussed essentially static theoretical approaches to the study of urban systems. These necessarily ignore some of the most important stylised facts reviewed in section 2—those describing the dynamics of urban systems and of economic agents in such systems. There is a significant tradition of dynamic urban modelling, surveyed by Miyao (1987), but the focus of most of this literature rests solely on issues of urban size and residential investment. It is only very recently that dynamic theoretical models have been proposed to try to understand better some of the stylised facts about specialisation and diversity in cities.

Brezis and Krugman (1997) attempt to explain why particular sectors may rise and fall in some cities (and, in certain cases, where the city is heavily specialised, draw the city along in this rise and fall). While we saw that the overall picture is one of stability in the production structure of cities (Stylised fact 3), this does not preclude significant changes from time to time. Brezis and Krugman (1997) propose a simple partial-equilibrium model of a region with one initial city, and focus on the dynamics of localisation economies.

> *Assumption 1d (learning-by-doing and localised knowledge leading to agglomeration).* Production technologies are localised. New technologies in a given sector arise randomly. Social learning-by-doing implies that a new technology may initially be less productive than the old one but will eventually become more productive.

Brezis and Krugman (1997) assume an initial state of the world where a dominant technology is available to manufacture a given good. This dominant technology is localised in an established city which specialises in the manufacture of the good. Since knowledge is localised, the good cannot be profitably produced elsewhere using the dominant technology. There is also social (in the sense that no firm or worker is large enough to internalise its effects) learning-by-doing. This increases the productivity of labour with the amount of accumulated production in the city where the dominant technology is used. Brezis and Krugman (1997) also assume that cities are subject to crowding (Assumption 2a). Finally, for the sake of simplicity, they also make Assumption 3a about the perfect mobility of goods and labour. Their main conclusion is Result 9.

> *Result 9.* Under Assumptions 1d, 2a, 3a and 4c, the arrival of a new technology can lead to the gradual emergence of a new

city and the fall of the established city using the old technology.

This urban leapfrogging arises because, when a new technology is introduced, firms in the established city find it preferable to keep using the old technology at a higher level on the learning curve. Since learning-by-doing is collective, no firm in the established city is willing to start using it and pay the cost of a learning-by-doing process, the benefits of which will be freely available to all. However, urban crowding in the established city may make it profitable for some workers to break away and form a new city. There, the lower initial productivity of the new technology may be offset by the absence of urban crowding. In equilibrium, the allocation of workers across the new and the established city is such that wages are equalised across locations. This implies that the new city is initially much smaller than the established city since, with its less-productive technology, it cannot support crowding costs as large as those for the established city. However, the potential for learning-by-doing in the new technology is more important. Over time, the productivity of labour in the new city will rise relative to that in the established city. This will induce workers to migrate to the new city and reinforce learning by doing until the production of the good is entirely concentrated in the new city. Brezis and Krugman (1997) provide an elegant formalisation justifying the episodes of changing urban fortunes described as exceptions to Stylised fact 3. While the assumptions about learning by doing are rather special and extreme, Amiti (1998) shows that a similar leapfrogging result holds with Chamberlinian economies of agglomeration.

Duranton and Puga (1999) take a broader view about the dynamics of firms and products within urban systems. Their framework is related to those of Henderson (1974) and Abdel-Rahman and Fujita (1990), but introduces an explicit dynamic dimension related to the process of firms learning how best to produce new goods.

Assumption 1b‴ (Chamberlinian agglomeration and imperfect initial knowledge). A firm making a new good does not know what the best production process is. It can produce prototypes with processes drawn from existing local sectors. A firm recognises its ideal process after producing a prototype with it, and is then able to begin mass production. A larger number of firms using the same type of process lowers production costs associated with that type of process due to Chamberlinian agglomeration economies. Firms have some probability of closing down in any period.

As in most models reviewed, cities are subject to urban crowding (Assumption 2a). Assumption 3d summarises mobility issues.

Assumption 3d (imperfect firm and labour mobility and perfect product mobility). Firms can change location at a cost. Final goods are freely tradeable. At every period, a small proportion of workers can freely relocate.

When it is costly for firms to relocate, the presence of a learning process that draws from local processes creates dynamic advantages based on diversity. This is because a city with a wider range of local sectors using different processes allows firms producing new products to try more processes in search of their ideal one without incurring relocation costs. At the same time, there are advantages to specialisation stemming from more traditional Chamberlinian agglomeration economies. Urban crowding places a limit on city size and makes the choice between diversity and specialisation a meaningful one. Result 10 summarises the solution to this trade-off.

Result 10. Under Assumptions 1b‴, 2a and 3d, three configurations are possible in equilibrium: specialised cities only; diversified cities only; and a mixed configuration with both specialised and diversified cities. The mixed configuration arises when learning is moderately difficult. In the mixed configuration, firms begin producing prototypes in a diversified

> city and relocate to a city of the relevant specialisation to begin mass production when they learn their ideal process. Further imposing Assumption 4a results in an efficient urban system with cities of optimal size. When all three configurations are possible, the mixed configuration dominates the other two in terms of welfare.

In the mixed equilibrium with both diversified and specialised cities, locating in a diversified city can be seen as an investment. It implies higher production costs but also faster learning, which makes possible an earlier transition to more efficient mass production. Production costs are higher in a diversified city because, for a firm using a given production process, the presence of producers using different processes causes urban crowding without creating stronger static localisation economies. However, bearing these higher costs can be worthwhile for new firms because they expect to have to try a variety of processes before finding their ideal one, and a diversified city allows them to do so, without relocating after each trial. Once a firm finds its ideal production process, there are no further benefits from being in a diverse environment. The firm avoids the congestion imposed by the presence of other sectors by relocating to a city where all other firms share its specialisation.

The mixed configuration arises for moderately difficult learning, because if learning is too difficult the investment of initial location in diversified cities does not pay off. On the other hand, if learning is very easy, firms expect not to have to try too many different processes, and prefer to exploit static localisation economies from the beginning. In this dynamic steady state, diversified and specialised cities co-exist. Cities are stable in their size and sectoral composition, but there is a constant turnover of firms. Some existing firms close down during every period, and new firms enter to replace them with new products. This turnover follows a life-cycle pattern. New products are created and developed in diversified cities, but production eventually relocates to specialised cities.[12] All of this is consistent with Stylised facts 1, 3 and 5. At the same time, the model has less to say about Stylised facts 2 and 4. The optimal size of diversified and specialised cities is the same, and whether specialised or diversified cities are larger in equilibrium depends on the ability of large agents to operate in each type of city. The simplifying assumption of goods being freely traded also ignores the issue of the relative location of cities.

6. Policy Implications and Conclusions

Two main issues arise time and again in the empirical and theoretical work on the structure of systems of cities reviewed in this paper. The first major issue is the efficiency of the urban system as a whole. Existing theories are divided on this point. Models in the spirit of Henderson (1974) tend to suggest that urban systems without central regulation will be efficient in terms of size and number of cities of each type. This is true, provided that some mechanism enabling the creation and development of new cities is present. The two usual mechanisms are autonomous local governments or the market, with land developers. Of course, there are likely to be distortions such as imperfect competition between developers or political-economy issues, making the interests of local communities not perfectly aligned with those of the ruling politicians. Nevertheless, these two mechanisms should bring urban systems reasonably close to efficiency. In contrast, theories where distance matters tend to have a more reserved judgement about the overall efficiency of the urban system. Unfortunately, detailed welfare analysis has not yet been carried out in this type of framework. Despite this division, a few policy prescriptions emerge. For instance, anything that hinders the creation and development of new cities, such as poorly defined property rights, is likely to result in inefficient urban systems. The desirability of other policy actions is less clear. For instance, the need for (and the type of) intervention in the presence of localisation and urbanisation economies depends delicately on the source of these economies—something that is far from well understood.

The second major issue is about the composition of economic activity in individual cities. From our review, it seems that specialisation has both advantages and disadvantages. The advantages are less urban crowding and stronger localisation economies arising from the proximity of closely related producers. The disadvantages are less innovation and more exposure to risk as the fortunes of specific sectors and technologies rise or fall. Overall, there appears to be a need for both large and diversified cities and smaller and more specialised cities. The main problem with this dichotomy of diversified and specialised cities is that the latter are exposed to a greater risk with the rise and fall of specific sectors and technologies. To limit the risks of urban specialisation, policy may want to curb this. But limiting specialisation may forego important present benefits for the sake of avoiding a possible future downturn. Insurance by the central government may be a good alternative. However, this is costly, and complete insurance may lead to complacency. Another alternative is to give local governments the power to restructure. The disadvantage here is the involvement of local government in excessively ambitious economic-development policies. In particular, not every community can create the next Silicon Valley in its backyard. Moreover, the link between innovation and diversity seems fairly robust, so that highly innovative clusters cannot be bred in previously highly specialised environments. An alternative solution is to encourage labour-force mobility—but in Europe this awakens fears about lost regional identities.

In the end, there will always be a need for large diversified cities like London, New York or Paris, and for more specialised cities like Sheffield or Clermont-Ferrand. The likes of London may always be more dynamic than the likes of Clermont-Ferrand, but this does not imply that one type of city is economically more desirable than the other. For manufacturing and services, unlike for agriculture, 'sowing' and 'reaping' can take place in different locations. Some cities specialise in churning new ideas and new products; this requires a diversified base, as some of the theories reviewed suggest—and which the evidence appears to confirm. However, other cities specialise in more standardised production; this in turn, is better carried out in a more specialised environment. Urban systems may thus have an innate tendency to create this type of imbalance.

Notes

1. For instance, narrow specialisation is often seen as a means to spur innovation. Yet empirical evidence and some of the theoretical approaches reviewed in this paper show that, in general, narrow specialisation hinders innovation, while diversity across a range of related activities promotes it.
2. Considering all private employment would give similar results, but would lead to the inclusion among the top places of cities specialised in mining such as Duluth, and 'leisure cities' such as Las Vegas and Atlantic City.
3. Since the primary focus of the review is on the patterns of economic activities in cities, we will not deal here with issues that have mostly to do with size such as the rank–size distribution and the growth of average city size, even though we feel that many of these issues are ultimately related to the composition of economic activity.
4. In 1950, Detroit was more than 17 times bigger than Phoenix, but was overtaken by the latter shortly after 1990. Note that we use here population estimates for the 'urban places'. Using a broader definition of cities, such as metropolitan area, would nonetheless yield comparable results, indicating an even stronger growth for Phoenix and a less dramatic decline for Detroit and Pittsburgh.
5. The detailed results of Henderson (1998) are of particular interest. He shows that high-tech industries tend to be more concentrated than machinery-related industries and that they also tend to be more mobile.
6. In Black and Henderson (1998), the market potential of a given city is defined as the sum over each other city of its population divided by its distance to the city under consideration. This is discussed further in section 4.
7. This, of course, underestimates the number of goods whose production relocated, since it

ignores the opening of new establishments that coincide with the gradual phasing out of old ones. Furthermore, many multi-establishment firms do relocate the production of some of their products without actually opening new plants or closing down existing ones. Fujita and Ishii (1998) provide evidence of this from the electronics industry.

8. For instance, the agro-business cluster has 21 industries, and the critical knowledge for this cluster comes from chemistry, agricultural science, computer science and biology.
9. Henderson and Becker (2000) offer an extended comparison of land developers and active autonomous local governments. Helsley and Strange (1997, 1998) provide an in-depth discussion of private land developers and the impact of market imperfections upon land development and urban efficiency.
10. It can be shown formally that if the economy is not constrained by the number of cities, then in the absence of land developers, equilibria with incomplete urban specialisation are unstable.
11. Note that our three categories of agglomeration economies (Marshallian, Chamberlinian and Smithian) reproduce the categories employed by Marshall (1890), since he spoke about the circulation of ideas, the availability of intermediate goods and labour-market pooling. However, a detailed discussion about the nature of externalities is beyond the scope of this paper.
12. Note that the idea of diversified cities being nurseries for new firms and new products is different from the traditional 'incubator hypothesis', which highlights differences between the inner city and its periphery. The traditional focus is on firm creations and movements of firms within a given city and not between cities. The literature on this is discussed by Fagg (1980).

References

ABDEL-RAHMAN, H. (1988) Product differentiation, monopolistic competition and city size, *Regional Science and Urban Economics*, 18, pp. 69–86.

ABDEL-RAHMAN, H. (1990a) Sharable inputs, product variety, and city sizes, *Journal of Regional Science*, 30, pp. 359–374.

ABDEL-RAHMAN, H. (1990b) Agglomeration economies, types, and sizes of cities, *Journal of Urban Economics*, 27, pp. 25–45.

ABDEL-RAHMAN, H. (1994) Economies of scope in intermediate goods and a system of cities, *Regional Science and Urban Economics*, 4, pp. 497–524.

ABDEL-RAHMAN, H. (1996) When do cities specialize in production?, *Regional Science and Urban Economics*, 26, pp. 1–22.

ABDEL-RAHMAN, H. and FUJITA, M. (1990) Product variety, Marshallian externalities, and city sizes, *Journal of Regional Science*, 30, pp. 165–183.

ABDEL-RAHMAN, H. and FUJITA, M. (1993) Specialization and diversification in a system of cities, *Journal of Urban Economics*, 33, pp. 159–184.

ALONSO, W. (1964) *Location and Land-use: Towards a General Theory of Land Rent.* Cambridge, MA: Harvard University Press.

AMITI, M. (1998) *Regional specialisation and technological leapfrogging*. Department of Economics, La Trobe University (mimeograph).

ANDERSON, S., DE PALMA, A. and THISSE, J.-F. (1992) *Discrete Choice Theory of Product Differentiation*. Cambridge, MA: MIT Press.

BAIROCH, P. (1988) *Cities and Economic Development: From the Dawn of History to the Present.* Chicago, IL: University of Chicago Press.

BARTIK, T. (1996) Strategies for economic development, in: R. ARONSON and E. SCHWARTZ (Eds) *Management Policies in Local Government Finance*, pp. 287–311. Washington, DC: International City/County Management Association for the ICMA University.

BERRY, B. J. L. and PARR, J. B. with EPSTEIN, G., GHOSH, A. and SMITH, R. (1988) *Market Centers and Retail Location: Theory and Applications*. Englewood Cliffs, NJ: Prentice Hall.

BLACK, D. and HENDERSON, J. V. (1998) *Urban evolution in the US.* Department of Economics, London School of Economics (mimeograph).

BREZIS, E. and KRUGMAN, P. (1997) Technology and the life-cycle of cities, *Journal of Economic Growth*, 2, pp. 369–383.

CHRISTALLER, W. (1933/1966) *Die Zentralen Orte in Süddeutschland [Central Places in Southern Germany]*, trans. by C. W. BASKIN. Englewood Cliffs, NJ: Prentice-Hall.

DAVIS, S. and HALTIWANGER, J. (1992) Gross job creation, gross job destruction, and employment reallocation, *Quarterly Journal of Economics*, 107, pp. 819–863.

DELISLE, J.-P. and LAINÉ, F. (1998) Les transferts d'établissements contribuent au desserrement urbain, *Economie et Statistique*, 311, pp. 91–106.

DUMAIS, G., ELLISON, G. and GLAESER, E. (1997) *Geographic concentration as a dynamic process.* Working Paper 6270, NBER.

DUNNE, T., ROBERTS, M. and SAMUELSON, L. (1989a) The growth and failure of U.S. manufacturing plants, *Quarterly Journal of Economics*, 104, pp. 671–698.

DUNNE, T., ROBERTS, M. and SAMUELSON, L. (1989b) Plant turnover and gross employment flows in the U.S. manufacturing sector, *Journal of Labor Economics*, 7, pp. 48–71.

DURANTON, G. (1998) Labor specialization, transport costs, and city size, *Journal of Regional Science*, 38, pp. 553–573.

DURANTON, G. and PUGA, D. (1999) *Nursery cities: urban diversity, process innovation and the life-cycle of products*. Department of Economics, University of Toronto (mimeograph).

EATON, C. and LIPSEY, R. (1982) An economic theory of central places, *Economic Journal*, 92, pp. 56–72.

EATON, J. and ECKSTEIN, Z. (1997) Cities and growth: theory and evidence from France and Japan, *Regional Science and Urban Economics*, 27, pp. 443–474.

ELLISON, G. and GLAESER, E. (1997) Geographic concentration in US manufacturing industries: a dartboard approach, *Journal of Political Economy*, 105, pp. 889–927.

FAGG, J. (1980), A re-examination of the incubator hypothesis: a case study of Greater Leicester, *Urban Studies*, 17, pp. 35–44.

FELDMAN, M. and AUDRETSCH, D. (1999) Innovation in cities: science-based diversity, specialization and localized competition, *European Economic Review*, 43, pp. 409–429.

FUJITA, M. (1988), A monopolistic competition model of spatial agglomeration, *Regional Science and Urban Economics*, 8, pp. 87–124.

FUJITA, M. and ISHII, R. (1998) Global location behavior and organizational dynamics of Japanese electronics firms and their impact on regional economies, in: A. CHANDLER, P. HAGSTRÖM, and O. SÖLVELL (Eds) *The Dynamic Firm: The Role of Technology, Strategy, Organization and Regions*, pp. 343–383. Oxford: Oxford University Press.

FUJITA, M. and KRUGMAN, P. (2000), A monopolistic competition model of urban systems and trade, in: J. M. HURIOT and J. THISSE (Eds) *Economics of Cities*. Cambridge: Cambridge University Press (forthcoming).

FUJITA, M., KRUGMAN, P. and MORI, T. (1999) On the evolution of hierarchical urban systems, *European Economic Review*, 43, pp. 209–251.

GARREAU, J. (1991) *Edge city: Life on the New Frontier*. New York: Doubleday.

GLAESER, E., KALLAL, H., SCHEINKMAN, J. and SCHLEIFER, A. (1992) Growth in cities, *Journal of Political Economy*, 100, pp. 1126–1152.

HARRIS-DOBKINS, L. and IOANNIDES, Y. (1998) *Spatial interactions among US cities*. Department of Economics, Tufts University (mimeograph).

HELSLEY, R. and STRANGE, W. (1990) Matching and agglomeration economies in a system of cities, *Regional Science and Urban Economics*, 20, pp. 189–212.

HELSLEY, R. and STRANGE, W. (1997) Limited developers, *Canadian Journal of Economics*, 30, pp. 329–348.

HELSLEY, R. and STRANGE, W. (1998) Private government, *Journal of Public Economics*, 69, pp. 281–304.

HENDERSON, J. V. (1974) The sizes and types of cities, *American Economic Review*, 64, pp. 640–656.

HENDERSON, J. V. (1988) *Urban Development: Theory, Fact and Illusion*. Oxford: Oxford University Press.

HENDERSON, J. V. (1997a) Externalities and industrial development, *Journal of Urban Economics*, 42, pp. 449–470.

HENDERSON, J. V. (1997b) Medium size cities, *Regional Science and Urban Economics*, 27, pp. 583–612.

HENDERSON, J. V. (1999) *Marshall's economies*. Working Paper 7358, NBER.

HENDERSON, J. V. and BECKER, R. (2000) Political economy of city sizes and formation, in: J. M. HURIOT and J. THISSE (Eds) *Economics of Cities*. Cambridge: Cambridge University Press (forthcoming).

HENDERSON, V., KUNCORO, A. and TURNER, M. (1995) Industrial development in cities, *Journal of Political Economy*, 103, pp. 1067–1090.

HOOVER, E. (1936) *Location Theory and the Shoe and Leather Industries*. Cambridge, MA: Harvard University Press.

IOANNIDES, Y. and OVERMAN, H. G. (1998) *Spatial evolution of US cities*. Department of Geography, London School of Economics (mimeograph).

JACOBS, J. (1960) *The Economy of Cities*. New York: Random House.

KIM, S. (1995) Expansion of markets and the geographic distribution of economic activities: the trends in US regional manufacturing structure 1860–1987, *Quarterly Journal of Economics*, 110, p. 881–908.

KRUGMAN, P. (1991) Increasing returns and economic geography, *Journal of Political Economy*, 99, pp. 483–499.

MARSHALL, A. (1890) *The Principles of Economics*. New York: Macmillan.

MIYAO, T. (1987) Dynamic urban models, in: E. MILLS (Ed.) *Handbook of Regional and Urban Economics, Vol. II*, pp. 877–925. Amsterdam: Elsevier Science Publishers (North-Holland).

MUTH, R. (1969) *Cities and Housing*. Chicago, IL: University of Chicago Press.

RIVERA-BATIZ, F. (1988) Increasing return, monopolistic competition and agglomeration economies in consumption and production, *Regional Science and Urban Economics*, 8, pp. 125–153.

[11]

Journal of Urban Economics **48,** 453–484 (2000)
doi:10.1006/juec.2000.2176, available online at http://www.idealibrary.com on IDEAL®

Political Economy of City Sizes and Formation*

Vernon Henderson

Department of Economics, Brown University, Providence, Rhode Island 02912

and

Randy Becker

CES, U.S. Bureau of Census, 4700 Silver Hill Road, Room 211 WP11, Washington, DC 20233-6300

Received July 20, 1999; revised February 4, 2000

There are two paradigms of city formation and size—the competitive model of large-scale land developers operating in national land markets and the self-organization model of agglomeration. This paper examines the effects of local politics, urban classes, and restrictions in national land markets on city size and formation. It starts by introducing local politics into the two paradigms. Then it turns to a growth situation, where land developers initiate new settlements, but existing cities are either self-organized or governed locally. The paper also examines the politics of local no-growth movements and of governance of specially favored mega-cities.

Social scientists and social commentators have struggled with the question of whether cities are too big or too small.[1] The question is also very much in the public policy area. International agencies take the position that the urban agglomeration benefits heralded by Marshall a century ago do not justify the sizes of today's major metropolitan areas, or mega-cities. In noting that in 1950 there were only 2 metro areas in the world with over 10 million people, but today there are 14 with that number projected to double within 20 years, the United Nations [35] asks how bad "the negative factors associated with very large cities" need to get "before [it is in the]

* The paper has benefited from comments of participants in seminars at VPI and Boston University and a CEPR conference in Switzerland. Elhanan Helpman and Harl Ryder provided insightful comments on defining the core. We also acknowledge the helpful comments of Will Strange and Jim Rauch on an earlier draft of this (retitled) paper and Giles Duranton on a later draft. Finally, we acknowledge helpful comments of the editor and very detailed, helpful comments of two referees.

[1] For an overview of the debate, see "A Survey of Cities," *The Economist*, 7/29/95.

0094-1190/00 $35.00

self-interest of those in control to encourage development of alternative centers." The same report warns of "unbalanced urban hierarchies," the crime, congestion, and social inequality in mega-cities, and the social upheavals involved in draining hinterland villages and cities to populate metro areas. Similarly, these issues have been part of the World Bank's agenda since Renaud's [30] book, which examined national policies and institutional structures that lead to over-concentration in the urban sector, and they are a subject of the World Development Report for 1999/00.

On a more everyday scale, there is a very different debate in some developed countries about whether, in essence, certain communities are too small and should be forced to grow (see Scott [32] and Fischel [10]). A variety of "no-growth" instruments exist so communities may restrict population size and composition, including large lot zoning, moratoria on site services (e.g., sewer and water connections), restrictions on the number of building permits issued, and open space zoning and provision for greenbelts. There is a corresponding urban economics literature on growth controls (Helsley and Strange [16]). A basic question is Why do such situations arise where people are attempting to enter particular communities from which they are excluded?

In this paper we will specify a common framework to analyze the political economy of situations in which the international agency and no-growth controls perspectives are relevant. To do so, and more generally, to evaluate and answer the question about when cities are too big, we need to understand the fundamentals of city formation and local politics. What are the key market and institutional mechanisms? What are the political conflicts and the roles of land developers, local governments, national land markets, property rights specifications, instruments such as local zoning and subsidies to local businesses, and the like? We will develop limit cases, where in free national land markets, the fundamentals of city formation lead to efficient outcomes. However, we will suggest that restrictions in national land markets on city formation and autonomy in local governance in many countries lead to situations where cities tend to be oversized, as suggested by international agencies. In such contexts there is also an incentive for citizens of pro-active cities to attempt to limit their sizes, but conflicts among groups within cities about the limits to impose.

Sections 1–3 of this paper develop the relevant limit cases. Section 1 presents the standard general equilibrium model (from the urban and local public finance literature of city formation and size), in an economy where agents such as land developers operate freely in competitive national land markets (e.g., Henderson [18], Hamilton [15]). The model is restricted to the symmetric case with one type of city, to focus on the issues of city formation. Results generalize directly to an economy with many types of cities (Henderson [18]). While Section 1 synthesizes known results, it contains a new critical result on coalition-proofness of equilibrium. Also, as a new feature, the model contains two types of urban residents who own local businesses and workers who labor for them. Having two classes of people enriches the context, setting the stage to study the political economy for resolving the conflict between classes of people in the determination of city size and allocation of local property rights and tax burdens, as discussed in later sections of the paper.

Section 2 turns to the other extreme case in the literature. This is city formation through "self-organization" (e.g., Henderson [18], Krugman [24, 25], and Krugman and Venables [26]). Under self-organization no agents act in national land markets to form cities because either such agents do not exist or political institutions prohibit their proper functioning. Cities form through unorganized clustering of workers and firms, which can generate enormously oversized cities. Section 2 explains a limiting case to self-organization, where once clusters form they become governed by autonomous local governments, raising issues of how such governments operate. In whose interests (workers or entrepreneurs) do they act and what are their inducements to tax local property and subsidize local businesses?

Section 3 characterizes how we think cities actually form and achieve equilibrium sizes in freely functioning national land markets. Our context is a growing economy, where land developers may set up new cities but do not control existing cities. Existing cities are self-organized through migration of workers and firms and may be governed by more or less pro-active local governments. A fundamental result will be that unconstrained developer formation of new cities can be sufficient to force existing self-organized cities to efficient sizes.

In Section 4, we turn to typical situations in many countries, both developed (e.g., the United States and UK) and undeveloped (e.g., Indonesia), where institutional restrictions in national land markets inhibit city formation and inefficiently limit the number of cities. This context will bring the paper full circle to the mega-city size and no-growth control debates and link the two. In institutionally restricted situations, pro-active local governments have incentives to act to limit size and composition—i.e., to exclude people or impose "no-growth" controls. This extends to the mega-city context. As we will explain, the context of mega-cities typically involves a city favored by the national government with special amenities (e.g., capital cities such as Paris, Bangkok, and Jakarta). While such cities grow to relatively large sizes, residents still have strong incentives to limit growth and alter composition. Outcomes depend critically on whether such cities are ruled by democratic local governments or ruled by local oligarchies. They also explain the reasons for the battles in local communities, in courts, or among national planners in developing countries over city sizes, composition, and land tenure and ownership rights.

1. COMPETITIVE MODEL OF CITY FORMATION

In this section we present the traditional model of city formation in the literature, integrating a variety of existing results and presenting new results on uniqueness and coalition-proofness. This section serves as a *benchmark* and platform from which to proceed to subsequent sections. This section is broken into three parts: (i) the internal structure of cities, (ii) the economy-wide equilibrium with agents such as land developers who "own" and operate cities in competitive national labor and land development markets, and (iii) the required local instruments of control to achieve the specified equilibrium. Throughout the paper specific functional forms are used. While the qualitative results hold for a variety of specifications, use of particular functional forms allows us to be specific about existence conditions.

The Internal Structure of Cities

To have multiple, noninfinitesimal size cities in an economy requires each city to experience centripetal forces of "attraction" so as to have agglomeration and centrifugal forces of "repulsion" to limit each city's size. Forces of attraction are based on the technology of production and those of repulsion on the internal spatial structure of cities.

Technology. The two types of atomistic agents in an economy, workers and entrepreneurs, both live in cities and are perfectly mobile nationally. Each entrepreneur owns and operates one firm and workers labor for the entrepreneur. For simplicity, we model agglomeration benefits as involving information spillovers, where entrepreneurs in the city communicate information to each other about production and market conditions. For each firm, this is a positive externality (Marshall [27]), involving information spillovers, where "mysteries of the trade" are learned "unconsciously" and each idea becomes "the source of yet more ideas." Kim [22] building on Fujita and Ogawa [12] shows the problem can be modeled also as endogenous information exchange based on firms' decisions to purchase/exchange costly information. In our particular formulation, firm output is

$$y = Em^{\epsilon}\tilde{n}^{\delta}, \quad 0 < \delta < 1, 0 < \epsilon, \tag{1}$$

where $\tilde{n}$ is firm employment of labor and m is total entrepreneurs in the city, m^{ϵ} represents the external spillover benefits to the firm of having more firms locally, ϵ is the elasticity of firm output with respect to the number of local firms, and $\delta < 1$ ensures limited firm sizes.

Given identical technologies in (1) total city output $Y = my$ and total city employment/population $n = m \cdot \tilde{n}$. The city production function is

$$Y = Em^{\gamma}n^{\delta}$$
$$0 < \gamma \equiv 1 + \epsilon - \delta < 1. \tag{2}$$

Note that, given $\gamma + \delta > 1$, there are joint economies of scale to city population. $\gamma < 1$ ensures regularity conditions (in particular stability and second-order conditions). Later (Proposition 1), we will require $\epsilon < 1/2$ in order to have multiple cities in the economy. Entrepreneurs, in maximizing profits, hire labor according to the value of its marginal product (MP_n) and earn a residual return (RR). From (2), the social marginal product (SMP_m) of entrepreneurs exceeds their private residual return, given that entrepreneurs generate an information spillover externality. These relationships are

$$MP_n = \delta y/\tilde{n} = \delta Y/n$$
$$SMP_m = \gamma Y/m \tag{3}$$
$$RR = (1 - \delta)y = (1 - \delta)Y/m.$$

Urban Structure. The internal spatial structure of cities is the simplest standard version (Mohring [28]), demonstrating that costs of living rise with city size, as average commuting costs rise. All production in a city occurs at a point, defined as the Central Business District, or CBD. Surrounding the CBD in a circle are residences, where each resident, whether an entrepreneur or worker, lives on a lot of fixed size, 1, and commutes to the CBD (and back) at cost per unit distance of t (paid in units of city output). Equilibrium in the land market is characterized by a rent gradient, extending from the CBD at zero to the city edge at u_1. Rents at the city edge (in the best alternative use) are normalized to zero, and rent at distance u from the city center can be shown to be $R(u) = t(u_1 - u)$.[2] From this, we calculate total rents in the city to be $\int_0^{u_1} 2\pi u R(u)\,du = \frac{1}{3}\pi t u_1^3$ (given lot sizes of 1, the population at any distance is $2\pi u\,du$). Commuting costs are $\int_0^{u_1} 2\pi u(tu)\,du = \frac{2}{3}\pi t u_1^3$.

[2] An equilibrium in residential markets requires all residents (living on equal size lots) to spend the same amount on rent plus commuting costs; so for each consumer group, any member then has the same amount left over to spend on all other goods, so as to equalize utility levels of group members. At the city edge, rent plus commuting costs are tu_1 since $R(u_1) = 0$; and elsewhere they are $R(u) + tu$. Equating total rent plus commuting cost expenditures at the city edge with those amounts elsewhere yields the rent gradient $R(u) = t(u_1 - u)$.

City population is

$$\text{pop} = n + m, \tag{4}$$

consisting of all workers and entrepreneurs. Given a circular city with lot sizes of 1, $n + m = \pi u_1^2$ or $u_1 = \pi^{-1/2}(n + m)^{1/2}$. We may then write

$$\text{total commuting costs} = B(n + m)^{3/2} \tag{5}$$

$$\text{total land rents} = \frac{1}{2}B(n + m)^{3/2} \tag{6}$$

$$B \equiv \frac{2}{3}\pi^{-1/2}t.$$

Note that average commuting costs and rents rise with city size $(n + m)$, representing scale diseconomies to the city, or the centrifugal forces. The elasticity of *per person* commuting resource costs with respect to population is 1/2. Equation (6) gives rental income, for distribution.

City Formation

In the benchmark case, land development companies ("developers") compete in national land markets to "own" and operate cities. Cities form on identical sites, in an unspecified national geography, where there is an unexhausted supply of potential sites, each operated by a different developer. Each development company is owned by Arrow–Debreu shareholders and seeks to maximize land rents net of any costs in its city. Each developer offers a "contract" to local workers and entrepreneurs who enter its city. The contract is $\{n, m, T_n, T_m\}$, where n and m are the workers and entrepreneurs in the city, and T_n and T_m are per person subsidies (which may be zero) to workers and entrepreneurs who locate there. The reasons the contract is specified to contain quantity and price items are analyzed in the next section. Within the city, the company allows free labor and residential land markets. From Eq. (3), entrepreneurs pay workers their MP_n, and entrepreneurs collect residual firm profits. Workers and entrepreneurs pay their own commuting costs and rents, and as Arrow–Debreu shareholders, collect dividends, if any, from development companies in which they hold shares. Workers and entrepreneurs are freely mobile across cities.

The developer's problem in any city is to maximize profits subject to constraints that workers and entrepreneurs earn their going returns in national markets. Thus we have

$$\max_{n,m,T_n,T_m} \Pi = \frac{1}{2}B(n+m)^{3/2} - T_n n - T_m m \tag{7a}$$

$$\text{s.t.} \qquad T_n + E\delta n^{\delta-1}m^{\gamma} - \frac{3}{2}B(n+m)^{1/2} - \overline{V} = 0 \tag{7b}$$

$$T_m + E(1-\delta)n^{\delta}m^{\gamma-1} - \frac{3}{2}B(n+m)^{1/2} - \overline{R} = 0 \tag{7c}$$

In the objective function, the company collects total local land rents (Eq. (6)) and pays workers (n) and entrepreneurs (m) any subsidies (T_n or T_m). In the constraints, subsidies are set so local factor compensation (Eqs. (3)), less per person rents plus commuting costs (Eqs. (5) and (6)), equals the going compensation rate, respectively $\overline{V}$ or $\overline{R}$, in national markets (including any perceptually fixed dividend payments). Solving (7) we get

$$\overline{R} = E\gamma m^{\gamma-1}n^{\delta} - \frac{3}{2}B(n+m)^{1/2} \tag{8a}$$

$$\overline{V} = E\delta m^{\gamma}n^{\delta-1} - \frac{3}{2}B(n+m)^{1/2}. \tag{8b}$$

Substituting (8a) and (8b) back into (7a) we solve

$$\begin{aligned} T_n &= 0 \\ T_m &= E\epsilon m^{\gamma-1}n^{\delta}, \end{aligned} \tag{9}$$

where $\epsilon = (\gamma + \delta - 1)$. Land development companies allow market compensation for workers in Eq. (8b), but intervene to subsidize entrepreneurs in (8a) according to the externality they generate in (1). The residual market return of $(1-\delta)y$ is augmented by ϵy to raise the total to γy, which is an entrepreneur's social marginal product (Eq. (3)).

In national markets, land developers compete for residents. Given a large enough number of cities, we utilize standard folk theorem entry solutions from the industrial organization literature, with their attendant problems discussed below. Developers enter the city formation business until profits in (7) are driven to zero. Substituting in (7) for T_m from (9), $\Pi = 0$ implies

$$E\epsilon m^{\gamma}n^{\delta} = \frac{1}{2}B(m+n)^{3/2}. \tag{10}$$

To determine city sizes and numbers nationally, we impose full employment, presuming that cities are identical in equilibrium (see Proposition 2).

The national factor ratio is

$$m/n = A, \tag{11}$$

assuming people types are immutable. Substituting (11) into (10), we get worker population in the representative city $\overset{*}{n}$, where

$$\overset{*}{n} = \left\{\epsilon 2B^{-1}E(1+A)^{-3/2}A^{\gamma}\right\}^{1/(1/2-\epsilon)}. \tag{12}$$

We loosely call this $\overset{*}{n}$, city size. Obviously, true city size is $\overset{*}{n} + \overset{*}{m}$ ($= \overset{*}{n}(1 + A)$). In (12), the expression in brackets is a parameter collection. $1/2 - \epsilon > 0$ is required to have multiple cities in an economy (see Proposition 1). City size increases as the degree of scale economies, the forces of attraction, ϵ, rises toward the degree of scale diseconomies, 1/2, in commuting costs.

The nature of the equilibrium nationally is characterized by the following proposition.

PROPOSITION 1. *Given $E, B, A > 0$ and $0 < \gamma, \delta < 1$, necessary and sufficient conditions for the existence of a unique competitive equilibrium with multiple cities of noninfinitesimal sizes are*

$$\gamma\frac{(1+A)}{A}, \delta(1+A) > 3\epsilon$$

$$0 < \epsilon < \frac{1}{2}$$

Such an equilibrium has the following characteristics:

(a) *All local land rents are transferred to entrepreneurs/firms.*

(b) *Equilibrium city size is given by*

$$\overset{*}{n} = \left[2\epsilon B^{-1}E(1+A)^{-3/2}A^{\gamma}\right]^{1/(1/2-\epsilon)}$$

and is increasing in the degree of scale economies, ϵ, and with advances in technology such as increases in E or declines in unit commuting costs, t, reflected in lower values of B.

(c) *The number of cities in the economy is $\overset{*}{S}$, where $\overset{*}{S} = N/\overset{*}{n}$ for $N \gg \overset{*}{n}$, where N is national worker population.*

(d) *The equilibrium is a free mobility one, where in the contract $[\overset{*}{n}, \overset{*}{m}, \overset{*}{T}_n, \overset{*}{T}_m]$ offered by each developer $\overset{*}{n}$ and $\overset{*}{m}$ are self-enforcing.*

Proposition 1 summarizes the standard results in the literature. Item (a) follows given free entry of developers in national land markets drives profits to zero. Note, from (9), that the LHS of (10) is mT_m and, from (6), that the RHS of (10) is total local rents. This is the "golden rule" in Flatters et al. [11], aptly renamed the Henry George theorem by Stiglitz [33]. Local urban land rents fill the gap between the social and the private marginal product of entrepreneurs. Later in the paper these notions will provide an economic basis for assigning ownership of urban lands to entrepreneurs in a growth context.

Item (b) in Proposition 1 follows by inspection of Eq. (12) and suggests that city sizes increase with technological change, whether exogenous or in an endogenous growth context as in Black and Henderson [4]. Item (c) is obvious, as a folk theorem result, ignoring integer problems (in defining $\mathring{S} = N/\mathring{n}$ or in defining $\mathring{n}$ and $\mathring{m}$).[3] However, folk theorems are potentially problematic. When we divide the national population into an intended $\mathring{S}$ integer number of cities, city sizes will be $\mathring{n}$ plus a fraction of $\mathring{n}$, where the fraction only goes to zero as national scale becomes infinitely large (Henderson [18]). These fractions can present problems in finding equilibria in the core of an economy, as discussed momentarily. For item (d), once $\mathring{n}$ and $\mathring{m}$ are achieved, the developer does not need to enforce them. No resident worker or entrepreneur acting on his or her own would want to move and deviate from this equilibrium. From (8), $\partial \mathring{R}/\partial m|_{\mathring{n}} < 0$ and $\partial \mathring{V}/\partial n|_{\mathring{m}} < 0$,[4] so if, say, a worker leaves one city (lowering its n) and goes to another (raising its n), the worker will be worse off.

Continuing with Proposition 1, given the inherent nonconvexities in agglomeration models, well-behaved solutions are confined to particular regions of parameter space. First, factor consumptions must be positive, or $V, R > 0$ (otherwise, economic agents will choose to "consume their endowments," yielding a normalized utility of zero.) The net returns to entrepreneurs and workers, by substitution into (8), are

$$\mathring{R} = Z\{\gamma(A + 1) - 3A\epsilon\} > 0 \qquad (13a)$$

$$\mathring{V} = ZA\{\delta(A + 1) - 3\epsilon\} > 0, \qquad (13b)$$

[3] More formally, $\mathring{S}$ could be realized in a sequential game (see Helsley and Strange [16]) where there are $\bar{S}(\gg \mathring{S})$ potential developers. In a staged game, each city-developer enters in a (arbitrary) predetermined sequence. Given the one-time option to enter, developers enter as long as potential profits are positive. Entry stops at $\mathring{S}$, which then defines the number of cities. In the penultimate stage of the game, workers and entrepreneurs each choose a contract $\{n, m, T_n, T_m\}$ offered by a city. In the final stage, internal local and land markets clear.

[4] Even at the equilibrium $\mathring{T}_m$ in the second city, with entry both the residual return to an entrepreneur falls and rents plus commuting costs rise.

where $Z \equiv \mathring{n}^{1/2}(1/2)B\epsilon^{-1}A^{-1}(1+A)^{1/2}$. As indicated in the proposition, positive factor returns require $\gamma(A+1)/A$, $\delta(A+1) > 3\epsilon$.[5] In terms of other restrictions, $\epsilon > 0$ is required for urban agglomeration, or $\mathring{n} > 0$ in (12). Additionally $\epsilon < 1/2$ is required. Total city compensation, $\mathring{n}\mathring{V} - \mathring{m}\mathring{R}$, is positive only if $\epsilon < 1/2$ and $\epsilon \geq 1/2$ violates a social planner's second-order conditions in this context (see Proposition 2). Why? If $\epsilon \geq 1/2$, $\mathring{n}$ is not defined because we want only one city in the economy. Scale effects are so large as to always outweigh the disadvantages of increased commuting costs as city size increases. Finally in Proposition 1, there remains uniqueness. Uniqueness can be proved by showing that, in a competitive equilibrium, cities which are of efficient size for their A cannot operate with different A's and pay the same utility levels.[6]

Comment 1. If entrepreneurs can choose to be workers instead of entrepreneurs (but not vice versa), then (13) requires A such that $\mathring{R} \geq \mathring{V}$, or

$$\gamma \geq \delta A.$$

For competitive equilibria, this would place an upper bound on A $(A \leq \gamma/\delta)$. If A starts at a higher value, entrepreneurs would convert to workers until $A(\equiv m/n)$ falls to γ/δ.

The equilibrium characterized in Proposition 1 has two desirable properties, which are summarized in the next proposition. The second property forms the conceptual foundation for later results.

PROPOSITION 2. *(a) The only allocation of factors which is efficient requires all cities to be size* $\mathring{n}$. *(b) Cities of size* $\mathring{n}$ *constitute the only coalition-proof equilibrium.*

From (7) $\mathring{n}$ is a Pareto efficient equilibrium for $m/n = A$, since it maximizes developer profits, for V and R fixed. However, $m/n = A$ imposes symmetry. That asymmetric allocations are inefficient can be determined by showing that the national isoquants for this one good

[5] If the restrictions in (13) are met, the complete second-order conditions to the maximization problem in (8) are also satisfied.

[6] Consider, say, m_i and n_i for a particular city type (A_i). At that m_i and n_i, with optimizing behavior and entry so $\Pi_i = 0$, we have an equilibrium city size in (12) $\mathring{n}(A_i)$. Equilibrium in national factor markets still requires that factor returns be equalized for different cities, i and j, when $A_i \neq A_j$. However $\mathring{V}$ is a monotonic increasing function of A so $\mathring{V}(A_i) = \mathring{V}(A_j)$ iff $A_i = A_j$. (Evaluating $\partial\mathring{V}/\partial A$ reduces to signing $(1/2)\gamma[\delta(1+A) - 3\epsilon] + (1/2)\delta A[\gamma(1+A) - 3\epsilon A]$, which is positive if $V, R > 0$ from Eq. (13).)

economy are convex in N, M space.[7] With convexity, efficiency requires that all cities operate at the full employment A, the national endowment ratio. Thus part (a) tells us that having cities of size $\overset{*}{n}$ is the only candidate for the core of the economy. Part (b) states that the equilibrium $\overset{*}{n}$ is in the core. We can show that there is no deviating "coalition" with a city of a different size, which can attract factors away from cities of size $\overset{*}{n}$.[8] However, this is where our folk theorem and integer issues for $\overset{*}{S}$ present a problem. In a finite-sized economy, as noted above, if we think of $\overset{*}{S}$ as an integer, then equilibrium city size will be $\overset{*}{n}$ plus a fraction of $\overset{*}{n}$. Scotchmer and Wooders [31] point out that these fractions present problems in finding equilibria in the core of an economy. However, Henderson [20] and Conley and Konishi [5] suggest that we may want to redefine coalition-proofness, given that equilibrium coalitions should be subject to free mobility (cannot restrict their membership). That is, the assumption of the mobility in urban economics is at odds with usual coalition proofness requirements that permit exclusionary objecting coalitions in defining whether equilibria are in the core.

Coalition-proofness is fundamental to the paper. $\overset{*}{n}$ is the only allocation that is impervious to "large (or small) deviations" by coalitions of any type,

[7] Consider an isoquant for an arbitrary large national output $\overline{Y}_0$. Along any factor ray in national N and M space, where $A = M/N, \overline{Y}_0$ is produced in $S(A)$ cities where $S(A) = \overline{Y}_0/Y(A)$. $Y(A)$ is the net output $(Y - B(n+m)^{3/2} = E\overset{*}{n}^{\gamma+\delta}A^{\gamma} - B\overset{*}{n}^{3/2}(1+A)^{3/2})$ produced in a city of efficient size, $\overset{*}{n}(A)$, from (12). Then nationally to produce $\overline{Y}_0$, for any A, we need $N(A)$ workers where $N(A) = S(A) \cdot \overset{*}{n}(A) = \overline{Y}_0\overset{*}{n}(A)/Y(A)$. Substituting in for $Y(A)$ and $\overset{*}{n}(A)$ we get $N(A) = C_1 A^{-(1/2)\gamma/(1/2-\epsilon)}(1+A)^{(3/2)\epsilon/(1/2-\epsilon)}$. Rewriting this, substituting in $A = M/N$, we get

$$N^{\delta}M^{\gamma}(N+M)^{-3\epsilon} = C_2^{(1/2-\epsilon)/(1/2)}, \quad \text{(a)}$$

where C_1 and C_2 are collections of parameters. This equation defines N, M combinations nationally needed to produce $\overline{Y}_0$ in cities of efficient sizes. Differentiating this and then evaluating for $A = M/N$ we get $\frac{dN}{dM} = -A^{-1}\left(\frac{\gamma(1+A) - 3\epsilon A}{\delta(1+A) - 3\epsilon}\right)$ and $\frac{d^2N}{dM^2} > 0$ if $\frac{dN}{dM} < 0$. As long as isoquants are downward sloping (and it is never efficient to operate where they are positively sloped), they are strictly convex. Based on (a), if we define the isoquant function $N_i = N(M_i, \overline{Y}_0)$ in N, M space, strict convexity means $N(\lambda M_1 + (1-\lambda)M_2; \overline{Y}_0) < \lambda N(M_1; \overline{Y}_0) + (1-\lambda)N(M_2; \overline{Y}_0) = \overline{N}$, for any λ where $\lambda M_1 + (1-\lambda)M_2 = \overline{M}$. If $\overline{N}$ and $\overline{M}$ are national endowments of labor and entrepreneurs, the inequality means that, relative to having cities with different A_i, the same output can be produced with less labor, if cities operate at the same A.

[8] In particular, $m(A_i)R(A_i) + n(A_i)V(A_i) < m(A_i)R(A) + n(A_i)V(A)$ for all $A \neq A_i$. $R(A)$ and $V(A)$ are the returns in Eq. (13). $m(A_i)$, $n(A_i)$, $R(A_i)$ and $V(A_i)$ are employments and returns (for $\Pi_i = 0$) in a city of efficient size for factor ratio A_i. To see this, we maximize $[m(A_i)R(A_i) + n(A_i)V(A_i)]/[m(A_i)R(A) + n(A_i)V(A)]$ with respect to A_i and show that the unique maximum occurs where $A = A_i$.

whether land developers exist or not. Land developers can be viewed as constructs, or agents, facilitating the formation of efficient size coalitions.

Instruments of Control

For future reference in analyzing the political economy of more realistic situations, it is helpful to understand the actual instruments of control and extent of ownership agents need in order to achieve the equilibrium just presented. What instruments do developers need to specify contracts of the form $\langle \overset{*}{n}, \overset{*}{m}, \overset{*}{T}_n, \overset{*}{T}_m \rangle$? We start by stating why $\overset{*}{n}$ and $\overset{*}{m}$ need to be specified at all, since equilibria are self-enforcing in $\overset{*}{n}$ and $\overset{*}{m}$. Suppose just $\overset{*}{T}_n, \overset{*}{T}_m$ are announced, and workers and entrepreneurs mill around choosing potential cities. The problem is that $\overset{*}{S}$ cities may not be filled. In particular, suppose residents choose to flow into $\hat{S}$ cities, where $\hat{S} < \overset{*}{S}$ and $\hat{n} > \overset{*}{n}$. Generally, as the next section on self-organization shows, there will be no incentive for residents to go to announced but unoccupied sites (where there is no scale of operation), given $\overset{*}{T}_n = 0$ and $\overset{*}{T}_m > 0$ in those unoccupied sites. Specifying $\overset{*}{n}$ and $\overset{*}{m}$ ensures that an efficient number of cities will form.[9] In a large, mixed-use commercial development (e.g., a new edge city), the developer can specify the number of businesses $\overset{*}{m}$ and the density of employment (giving $\overset{*}{n}$). More traditionally, the developer specifies the total residential population and number of businesses through a land use plan, indicating the number of lots for residential and commercial development and their density (e.g., the number of dwelling units per lot). Reichman [29], Ellickson [9], and Fischel [10] argue persuasively that land use plans, which are submitted to higher level governmental boards, are effectively binding in the community formation stage.

The other portion of the developers' contracts concerns factor rewards. Developers need to offer a lump-sum subsidy of $\overset{*}{T}_m$ to entrepreneurs. Local subsidies to new business are almost universal and include underpriced land, holidays from local taxes and fees, and subsidized loans. A general analysis of choice of fiscal instruments is beyond the scope of this paper. There remains a potential issue concerning the developer's access to the income specified in Eqs. (7), in order to pay subsidies. It might appear as if the developer must own all local lands in order to collect the specified land rent income, which can raise questions of a developer's ability to assemble such large pieces of land (Helsley and Strange [17]). However, the objective function does *not* require developer ownership of residential land, per se. To see this, by substituting constraints (b) and (c) into the objective function (a) in Eq. (7), we can rewrite the problem as a

[9] Of course, if only $\hat{S}$ cities were filled, that would not be a coalition-proof equilibrium. But for new developers to move residents into more cities would still require specification of a contract such as $\langle \overset{*}{n}, \overset{*}{m}, \overset{*}{T}_n, \overset{*}{T}_m \rangle$.

command one where the developer's objective function is $Y - \bar{V}n - \bar{R}m - B(n + m)^{3/2}$. Here if the developer owns and controls the commercial district of the city, to optimize, he needs "access" to local residential land rents so he may pay entrepreneurs a lump-sum transfer. If workers own their residential local lands, in theory, the developer can access implicit rents by taxing workers in the commercial district and remitting proceeds to entrepreneurs. If entrepreneurs already own the local land, no transfers are necessary.

2. SELF-ORGANIZATION

If there are no developers operating in national land markets, city formation occurs by workers and entrepreneurs milling around on the urban landscape, self-organizing, and forming "natural" clusters, or cities, given the joint scale economies from agglomerating together. In Krugman [25] and Krugman and Venables [26], this problem is given more structure by imposing a national geography and, in growth contexts, a specific history (initial allocation). However, those analyses do not examine efficiency or comparisons with city formation when there are developers. Here the self-organization context is simpler, but suggests an important problem in city formation.

Before we proceed to examine equilibria under self-organization, there is an issue of who gets urban land rents. In general, following the Arrow–Debreu tradition, land rents could go out of each city to national shareholders, where each person in the economy would own an equal share of rents in every city. We will note the key feature of this case in this section because it is arguably the most general: under self-organization, land rent income for an individual is then independent of location decisions. However, the urban literature often assumes land rent income of a city is redistributed within a city, and we adopt a specific version as our base case. We assume that only the local entrepreneurs in a city share in the land rental income in that city. This assumption allows us to isolate the key source of market failure under self-organization—absence of a market for city formation—from the issue of the effect on city size of marginal pricing of entrepreneurs' entry to cities. Because local entrepreneurs get all local land rents, at an efficient city size from the previous section, they will receive the social marginal product of their entry to the city. Under any other rent distribution scheme they would get less than their social marginal product, introducing a distortion in micro-location decisions. Consistent with this logic, a mechanism by which entrepreneurs would be assigned these rents is the existence of a local government which taxes land rents to redistribute to entrepreneurs, in order to subsidize their location given the positive externalities they generate. Such a local government does not otherwise participate in self-organization solutions. In particular, it does not act to restrict populations, unlike what we will allow pro-active governments to do later in the paper.

The assumption has two other advantages. First, it simplifies the number of cases to be considered without affecting qualitative results, by having bounds on city sizes correspond to previously calculated expressions. Second, in the next section, we will provide a basis for the assumption that local entrepreneurs claim local land rents, in an enhanced self-organization context.

To solve for equilibria under self-organization we start by looking at returns to our two types of factors in any natural cluster, or city, which happens to exist. Then we determine the set of possible equilibrium cluster configurations nationally. In any city, workers are paid their MP from Eq. (3) and pay rent plus commuting costs. Each entrepreneur gets residual firm income, pays commuting plus rent costs, and receives a share of total local land rents. In a representative city, worker utility, V, and entrepreneur utility, R are

$$V = E\delta n^{\delta-1}m^{\gamma} - \frac{3}{2}B(n+m)^{1/2} \tag{14a}$$

$$R = E(1-\delta)n^{\delta}m^{\gamma-1} - \frac{3}{2}B(n+m)^{1/2} + \frac{1}{2}B(n+m)^{3/2}m^{-1}. \tag{14b}$$

In this section, for the benchmark case, we consider only symmetrical self-organization equilibria, in which all cities end up being identical in size. Asymmetrical Nash equilibria may also exist and, in some regions of parameter space, they may be "stable."[10] The analysis in subsequent sections will hold for asymmetric equilibria as well, and asymmetry is not the focus of this paper. Symmetrical self-organization equilibria provide a sufficient benchmark.

There are three parts to characterizing self-organization equilibria. First, as in Section 1, real incomes of factors must exceed the alternative of "consuming endowments," as before, normalized to yield zero. Given $m = An$, $V > 0$ and $R > 0$ define two different maximal, n's, $n^V_{\max}$ and $n^R_{\max}$, which the representative city must be less than.[11] Maximum city size

[10] This is particularly the case when national $A < 1/2$. In relevant regions for A constant, V is decreasing in city size while R is increasing.

[11] These are

$$n^V_{\max} = \left[\frac{2}{3}B^{-1}A^{\gamma}(1+A)^{-1/2}E\delta\right]^{1/(1/2-\epsilon)}$$

$$n^R_{\max} = \left[2B^{-1}A^{\gamma}(1+A)^{-1/2}E(1-\delta)(2A-1)^{-1}\right]^{1/(1/2-\epsilon)} \text{ for } A > 0.5.$$

$n^R_{\max}$ is defined only for $A > 0.5$, because for $A \le 0.5$, R rises indefinitely as n rises.

is therefore less than

$$n_{\max} = \min\left[n^V_{\max}, n^R_{\max}\right]. \tag{15}$$

At $n_{\max}$ the agglomeration benefits to at least one factor are totally dissipated. The second part in determining equilibrium is to specify Nash allocations. Any city smaller than $n_{\max}$ is a Nash equilibrium because in (14) $\partial V/\partial n|_m < 0$ and $\partial R/\partial m|_n < 0$ (given $0 < \gamma, \delta < 1$). Nash requirements do not narrow the scope of potential equilibria. In order to narrow the scope of potential equilibria, the final part imposes robustness to pairwise deviations or other perturbations to equilibria. This is traditional local "dynamic" stability.[12] Robustness holds only if

$$n \geq \left\{\epsilon 2B^{-1}E(1+A)^{-3/2}A^{\gamma}\right\}^{1/(1/2-\epsilon)} = \overset{*}{n}, \tag{16}$$

where $\overset{*}{n}$ is efficient city size in Eq. (12).

Equations (15) and (16) define upper and lower bounds on equilibrium city sizes. From (16) robust city sizes are at least as large as $\overset{*}{n}$, and from (15) sizes must be less than $n_{\max}$. For existence of equilibrium, $n_{\max} > \overset{*}{n}$, which reduces to the parametric restrictions of Proposition 1. In summary:

PROPOSITION 3. *In a self-organizing economy, equilibrium city size lies between the efficient size, $\overset{*}{n}$ and $n_{\max}$. Existence requires the same parametric restrictions as in Proposition* 1.

[12] The simplest criterion examines the "partial equilibrium" for any one city. Consider an equilibrium $\bar{V}$ and $\bar{R}$ in national labor markets, where each city has $\bar{n}$ entrepreneurs. Perturb the equilibrium populations in one city, where internal markets adjust instantanteously to yield new values of V and R for that city, for national $\bar{V}$ and $\bar{R}$ unchanged (the partial equilibrium assumption). Given the adjusting V and R there must be further factor movements to or from the city so as to return the city to the original equilibrium. The dynamic adjustment equations are $dn/ds \equiv \dot{n} = d_n(V - \bar{V})$ and $dm/ds \equiv \dot{m} = d_m(R - \bar{R})$, where s is time and d_n and d_m are speeds of migration flows to the city from national markets. Doing a first-order Taylor series expansion about $\bar{n}$ and $\bar{m}$ yields

$$\begin{bmatrix} \dot{n} \\ \dot{m} \end{bmatrix} = \begin{bmatrix} d_n\, \partial V(\bar{n},\bar{m})/\partial n & d_n\, \partial V(\bar{n},\bar{m})/\partial m \\ d_m\, \partial R(\bar{n},\bar{m})/\partial n & d_m\, \partial R(\bar{n},\bar{m})/\partial m \end{bmatrix} \begin{bmatrix} n - \bar{n} \\ m - \bar{m} \end{bmatrix}.$$

A necessary and sufficient condition for convergence is that the matrix be "stable" or have negative characteristic roots. This requires its trace to be negative (which it is) and its determinant to be positive. Evaluating the determinant at $m = An$ results in Eq. (16). This condition for stability is the same for a two-city national labor market with workers and entrepreneurs. In this case, the factor adjustment equations are $\dot{n}_1 = d_n(V_1 - V_2)$ and $\dot{m}_1 = d_m(R_1 - R_2)$. Doing a Taylor series expansion about, say, V_2 and R_2, results in equations such as $\dot{n}_1 = d_n(\frac{\partial V}{\partial n} \cdot (n_1 - n_2) + \frac{\partial V}{\partial m} \cdot (m_1 - m_2))$. Proceeding as above, again, yields (16).

To help motivate this result, consider a model with just one factor of production. $\mathring{n}$ would be at the maximum of the inverted U-shaped curve defining utility for that factor as a function of city size. Stability would require that city size not lie to the left of that maximum. Similarly the upper bound size in a one-factor model would be at an enormous city size so far to the right of the peak of the utility curve that a person would be off in autarky—living in no city. Here, with two factors of production, as elaborated in Becker and Henderson [3] in a different but related model, the peak of the utility curve for workers (as it varies with city size, for A fixed) may lie to the left ($A > 0.5$, $\delta(1 + A) < 3/2$) or to right ($A > 0.5$, $\delta(1 + A) > 3/2$) of that for entrepreneurs (with $\mathring{n}$ in between the two peaks), or the curve for entrepreneurs may rise indefinitely ($A \leq 0.5$).

Given existence, any city size in the interval $(\mathring{n}, n_{\max})$ constitutes a robust equilibrium. To determine the size of the interval, we form the ratio $n_{\max}/\mathring{n}$.

$$\frac{n_{\max}}{\mathring{n}} = \left[\frac{1}{3}\delta\frac{(1+A)}{\epsilon}\right]^{1/(1/2-\epsilon)} \quad \text{for } A \leq 0.5$$

$$= \min\left[\left(\frac{1}{3}\delta\frac{(1+A)}{\epsilon}\right)^{1/(1/2-\epsilon)}, \left(\frac{(1-\delta)(1+A)}{\epsilon(2A-1)}\right)^{1/(1/2-\epsilon)}\right] \quad \text{for } A > 0.5.$$

Consider "typical" parameter values from the scale externality literature (Henderson [19]) and national proportions of workers to extrepreneurs and their compensations. We use $\delta = 0.80$, $A = 0.30$, and $\gamma = 0.25\text{–}0.35$ (so $\epsilon = 0.05\text{–}0.15$). Then $n_{\max}$ is 10–75 times $\mathring{n}$.[13] In general self-organizing city sizes are not efficient. Here they are oversized, potentially enormously so.

If, instead of local land rents going just to local entrepreneurs, they are more widely distributed, the lower bound on city size will be less than $\mathring{n}$, but the potential to be enormously oversized remains. For example, with Arrow–Debreu ownership, the lower bound will be $\mathring{n}(2/3)^{1/(1/2-\epsilon)}$ which is less than $\mathring{n}$. As noted earlier, if local entrepreneurs do not collect local rents, their entry to the city is priced at less than social marginal product, which is a force reducing city sizes. Here, by assigning local rents to local entrepreneurs, we have isolated the key problem with self-organization, that being the lack of a national market for city formation which leads cities to be too big.

[13] Note $(n_{\max}/\mathring{n}) \to 1$ as $\gamma + \delta \equiv 1 + \epsilon$ gets "large." For $\epsilon \geq 1/2$, only one city in the economy is desired and $n_{\max}$ and $\mathring{n}$ coincide. Second $(n_{\max}/\mathring{n})$ gets arbitrarily large as $\epsilon \to 0$ and hence, $\mathring{n} \to 0$ (i.e., no cities are desired).

Narrowing the set of equilibria: *Growth*. The literature sometimes puts self-organization in the context of an economy experiencing population growth (only), as a way of trying to specify what equilibria are likely to emerge over time (Henderson [18]; Fujita et al. [13]). Suppose we grow population N and M such that A remains constant. Starting with an arbitrary given number of cities, population will grow in each city until the n_{max} limit is hit, causing "bifurcation," where some workers or entrepreneurs deviate and form new cities. The number of new cities may not be deterministic with bifurcation. Population growth then continues in the new set of cities until the n_{max} bound is again reached, and then more cities form. This depressing "growth" process of repeatedly hitting a Malthusian upper-bound on city sizes (where worker or entrepreneur utility approaches zero), continues indefinitely. As a solace, in the United States, there is little evidence of a bifurcation process, which implies large drops and cycles in individual city populations. In Dobkins and Ioannides [6], virtually all cities increase in size every decade. Population losses, when they occur, are small.

Local Governments in Self-Organized Cities

Suppose to the self-organization model we add a national constitution which requires that each natural cluster, or self-organized city, have a local government. While, unlike developers, local governments cannot form cities, the assumption is that, once a natural cluster forms, a local government evolves. Further, let us assume that *all* such governments are pro-active in maximizing the welfare of either local workers or entrepreneurs. Both assumptions are extreme, and certainly introduce mischief into simple self-organized worlds. But they tell us about self-organization with local politics, and they provide a useful framework and benchmark for thinking about the "real world" scenarios presented in Sections 3 and 4 to follow.

Under these assumptions, self-organization can be consistent with efficient outcomes. First, we state and prove the proposition and then comment on our exercise.

PROPOSITION 4. *If every self-organized city is governed by an autonomous local government acting to maximize the welfare of the representative member of the majority population and if such governments can operate unconstrained by free mobility* (*i.e., can exclude residents*), *all self-organized cities will be of identical, efficient size.*

To prove this, we examine the behavior of the local government in any city. Assume for now that workers are the majority ($A < 1$) and that local lands are owned locally by entrepreneurs. Both assumptions are noncritical. The government then seeks to maximize the return to workers, subject to the city's ability to attract entrepreneurs, or

$$\max_{n,m,T_m} E\delta n^{\delta-1}m^{\gamma} - \frac{3}{2}B(n+m)^{1/2} - T_m m/n \tag{17}$$

$$\text{s.t. } T_m + E(1-\delta)n^{\delta}m^{\gamma-1} - \frac{3}{2}B(n+m)^{1/2}$$

$$+\frac{1}{2}B(n+m)^{3/2}m^{-1} - \bar{R} = 0.$$

In the objective function, the first two terms are wages net of per-worker rents plus commuting costs. $T_m \gtrless 0$ is a transfer payment, where each entrepreneur gets T_m and each worker $-T_m m/n$. In the constraint, besides collecting T_m, firm profits, and paying rents plus commuting costs ($\frac{3}{2}B(n+m)^{1/2}$), each entrepreneur collects a dividend—his or her share of land rents ($\frac{1}{2}B(n+m)^{3/2}/m$) which the local government recognizes as endogenous. The local government sees a fixed return to entrepreneurs, $\bar{R}$, which we will show in equilibrium will equal the R in Eq. (13a) above. By substituting the constraint into the objective function for T_m, it is apparent that the optimization problem (in n, m) is unchanged if workers, rather than developers, own local lands. Thus the initial ownership assignment is not relevant. Optimizing in (17) yields Eq. (10) for the Henry George theorem. Because entrepreneurs own local lands, $T_m = 0$; but the existence of T_m functions as a mechanism for potential entrepreneur–worker transfers, so workers choose to satisfy Eq. (10). Optimization also yields Eq. (8a) (or (14b)) which defines a relationship among R, m, and n in the city. How do we know that, with pro-active governments, the equilibrium R ($= \bar{R}$ perceived by any city government) and city size are the same as those in Section 1?

If all self-organized agglomerations are governed by pro-active local governments, then all cities satisfy Eq. (10), and Eq. (8a) (or (14b)) defines R as a function of the national A, given that with symmetry m/n in each city equals A. We then get Eqs. (12) and (13) for, respectively, efficient city size and corresponding factor returns.[14] That is, the imposition of symmetry across cities means each $m/n = A$ and optimizing with respect to size forces $\overset{*}{n}$. That leaves us with R as defined in Eq. (13a). Proposition 1 established uniqueness, where if Eq. (10) is satisfied in every city and factor returns are equalized across cities, all cities must operate at the

[14] Equation (13b) for V is satisfied, given that, into the objective, or welfare function of workers in (16), Eqs. (10) and (8b) are substituted for R (given T_m) and land rent income terms.)

same composition, A, the national factor ratio and Proposition 2 gave us efficiency. This establishes Proposition 4.

How did we get this slight-of-hand outcome—self-organization with efficient outcomes? We did it by imposing the requirement that as people mill around on the nation's surface, every time they coalesce, a local government forms. Then we assumed that every such government is pro-active and limits city size toward $\overset{*}{n}$, "excluding" residents from the oversize self-organization cities of Proposition 3. This exclusion forces "new" agglomerations to form which also "by definition" have local governments that optimize with respect to size and composition, forcing all city sizes toward $\overset{*}{n}$ (where sizes below $\overset{*}{n}$ are not robust). Moreover, in this context of all pro-active governments, control issues in local politics are irrelevant. Whether governments maximize the welfare of workers or entrepreneurs and which group nominally owns land rents have no effect on the final outcome.

This is a nice benchmark. But it is not the reality of national land markets and constitutional institutions. Not all agglomerations have single local pro-active autonomous local governments. Local autonomy may not be part of the national constitution; many local governments may not or cannot be pro-active; and not all agglomerations are governed by a single local government or by a set of township governments that coordinate well. In the next two sections, we try to model aspects of more complex situations.

3. THE ROLE OF DEVELOPERS AND SELF-ORGANIZATION IN AN EXPANDING ECONOMY

In considering the first two extreme cases presented—a world with competitive profit-maximizing land development companies governing each city in Section 1 and a world with no agents organizing cities in Section 2—one might react that the Section 1 world appears to apply to new cities and the Section 2 world to existing cities. Specifically, many new towns are started by large agents controlling the entire city at the time of formation. Historically, these can be cities founded by railway companies (e.g., the Canadian Pacific Railway in Vancouver, Canada), by commercial enterprises (e.g., the British East India Company in Calcutta), or by the church (e.g., Mannheim, Germany), quite apart from land developers. In the United States the role of land developers in the formation of "new towns" has been recognized (e.g., Reichman [29]). Joel Garreau's [14] book on edge cities provides an overarching survey of new city formation in the United States. Garreau identifies 130 established edge cities, all formed between the late 1960s and late 1980s, which generally are each the work of a single land development company (Henderson and Mitra [21]). However, once formed, developers relinquish control of such cities and they are taken over by a public or private governance process by the occupants (Knapp [23]). Existing cities certainly offer subsidies, but absent exclusionary zoning may do little to specify n or m. In this section, we generally consider existing cities to be self-organized—not subject to a developer or local governance process setting city size.

Coexistence of Self-Organized and Developer Cities

The basic point of this section can be made in the static model utilized in Sections 1 and 2. Then we exposit the result in the context of an economy experiencing population growth and provide a justification for the assignment of land ownership in self-organized cities.

Suppose, at any instant, the economy is composed of just self-organized cities, which are all inefficiently sized, or too large. While we will generally assume there is a symmetrical equilibrium in the self-organized sector, the basic proposition will apply directly to asymmetric starting points as well. Within self-organized cities, we assume, as in Section 2, that land rental income is assigned to local entrepreneurs. Suppose we now allow there to be free entry of developers into city formation activity. With the introduction of developers, we have the following proposition.

PROPOSITION 5. *If to an economy with just self-organized cities, free entry of competitive land developers who can set up and operate cities is introduced the only equilibrium is characterized by all cities being of identical and efficient size and composition.*

There are two instructive ways to prove this proposition. The first is to apply Proposition 2 directly. Since having cities of size $\mathring{n}$ at the national factor ratio A is the only point in the core, a developer can make profits (increase total output for a given factor allocation) by setting up such a city, if all other cities are not at $\mathring{n}(A)$ and operating at the national factor ratio A. Note that Proposition 2 explicitly considered asymmetric cities, as points outside the core.

The second method of proof looks at the nature of the final equilibrium itself. Such an equilibrium must be characterized by three conditions. First, utility levels of workers must be equalized across self-organized and developer cities so $\bar{V}$ in (8b) equals V in (14a). The same applies to entrepreneurs, so $\bar{R}$ in (8a) equals R in (14b). Finally with free entry of developers, profits for land development firms (cities) must be zero, so Eq. (10) is satisfied. If we specify (equilibrium) city size and composition in the developer sector as n_d and A_d, and in the self-organized sector as n_s and A_s (not ruling out potentially multiple A_s's under asymmetry) and manipulate the three equations to solve out n_d and n_s, we get an implicit function

$g(A_d, A_s) = 0$ which can only be satisfied at $A_s = A_d$.[15] $A_s = A_d$ requires developer and self-organization cities to have the same composition. Given that, equality of factor returns across cities requires identical sizes, which are hence efficient given developer behavior.[16]

Given this, we note

Comment 2. If self-organized cities are governed by local governments pro-active in regulating size and composition, Proposition 5 also holds.

With optimizing local governments, Eq. (10) is satisfied, which means given the objective function and constraint in (17), the welfare of workers and entrepreneurs in local government cities is described by Eqs. (14)

15

$$g(A_d, A_S) = A_d^{(-1/2\gamma)/(\epsilon-1/2)}\left[E\delta\left(\frac{1}{2}\epsilon^{-1}BE^{-1}(1+A_d)^{3/2}\right)^{\epsilon/(\epsilon-1/2)} - \frac{3}{2}B(1+A_d)^{(1/2(1+\epsilon))/(\epsilon-1/2)}\left(\frac{1}{2}\epsilon^{-1}BE^{-1}\right)^{(1/2)/(\epsilon-1/2)}\right]$$

$$-\left(\frac{1}{2}E^{-1}B\right)^{\epsilon/(\epsilon-1/2)} A_s^{(-1/2\gamma)/(\epsilon-1/2)}(1+A_s)^{(1/2\epsilon)/(\epsilon-1/2)}$$

$$\times\left\{\delta E\left[\frac{(1+A_d)\epsilon^{-1}F_1 + 3/2(A_s - A_d)}{F_2 + (1/2)\epsilon^{-1}(1-\delta)\delta(A_s - A_d)(1+A_d)}\right]^{\epsilon/(\epsilon-1/2)} - \frac{3}{2}B\left[\frac{(1+A_d)\epsilon^{-1}F_1 + \frac{3}{2}(A_s - A_d)}{F_2 + (1/2)\epsilon^{-1}(1-\delta)\delta(A_s - A_d)(1+A_d)}\right]^{(1/2)/(\epsilon-1/2)}\right\} = 0,$$

where

$$F_1 \equiv \frac{3}{2}(1-\delta)A_s + A_d\delta\left(\frac{1}{2} - A_s\right)$$

$$F_2 = \frac{3}{2}(1-\delta)A_d + A_2\delta\left(\frac{1}{2} - A_d\right).$$

Tedious calculations show $\frac{\partial g(\cdot)}{\partial A_s} = 0$ at $A_s = A_d$, indicating that the condition for the implicit function to define other A_s, A_d pairs in the neighborhood of $A_s = A_d$ is not satisfied. In particular, for any A_d, $g(\cdot)$ takes a maximum at $A_s = A_d$, where at that tangency $g(\cdot)$ just equals zero.

16 We can give more structure to the problem by having a developer entry game outlined in footnote 3. Perfect foresight developers enter in an arbitrary sequence, where the last developer to enter is the one who drives profits of all developers to zero, forcing all developers to run cities of efficient size and composition and forcing all self-organized cities to the identical position in order to survive.

under self-organization. With free entry of developers setting up cities competing with local government cities, Proposition 4 can be applied directly. But, in fact, the result is stronger. Local government action generates Eqs. (8) and (10), given (14) and (10) both apply. Given that, uniqueness in Proposition 1 requires all cities operating under Eqs. (8) and (10) be identical.

Population Growth

We now turn to an explicit growth context, where an economy experiences continuous population growth. It is possible to embed the problem in an endogenous growth model, where individuals invest in human capital and there are local "knowledge" spillovers within cities.[17] While in such a model competitive city sizes are efficient for the human capital accumulated at any point in time, equilibrium human capital investments may be inefficient. That issue is beyond the scope of this paper. Here we focus on accommodating national population growth through city formation, so we specify a simple growth context without economic growth. The city formation results generalize to a richer growth context.

Suppose an economy's population grows at a rate g, maintaining the same national composition A. Then, if S is the number of cities and n

[17] We would adapt the model in Black and Henderson [4] where there is one factor of production and two goods and types of cities (see also Eaton and Eckstein [8]). Here there is one type of city and two factors of production. To introduce growth we write the firm production function in (1) as $y_i = (E_0 h^{\psi}(t) h_i^{\theta}(t) m^{\epsilon} \tilde{n}^{\delta}$ where $h(t)$ is the average level of human capital in the city and $h_i(t)$ is the firm entrepreneur's own human capital. Human capital is the only capital in the model and only entrepreneurs gain by accumulating it. The firm optimizes as above with respect to $\tilde{n}$ to get the entrepreneur's per period residual return

$$RR_i(t) = \left(E_0 h(t)^{\psi/(1-\delta)} h_i(t)^{\theta/(1-\delta)}\right)(1-\delta)\delta^{\delta/(1-\delta)} m(t)^{\epsilon/(1-\delta)} w(t)^{\delta/(1-\delta)},$$

where $w(t)$ is worker wage. For an equilibrium solution the land developer faces a succession of static optimization problems as in (7), where for example $\overset{**}{n} = \mathring{n} h(t)^{(\psi+\theta)/(1/2-\epsilon)}$ in a symmetrical equilibrium (in choices of $h_i(t)$), with $\mathring{n}$ given in (12). Dynastic families who grow at a rate g and discount at rate $\rho(\rho > g)$ have preferences $\frac{C_i(t)^{1-\sigma} - 1}{1-\sigma}$ where $C_i(t)$ is per person consumption. They face an equation of motion where $\dot{h}_i(t) = RR_i(t) + T_m(t) - \frac{3}{2} b n(t)^{1/2} - C_i(t) - g h_i(t)$. On the RHS the first three terms are real income, $C_i(t)$ is consumption, and $g h_i(t)$ is capital allocated to new family members to maintain equal human capital per member. Growth solutions are standard. There is steady-state growth (with no transition path) if $(\psi + \theta)/(1 - 2\epsilon) = 1$ and we converge to steady-state levels of $(\psi + \theta)/(1 - 2\epsilon) < 1$. The key results are that city sizes grow at twice the rate of human capital or at $2\gamma^h$ where $\gamma^h \equiv \dot{h}/h$. With steady-state levels, where $\dot{h}/h = 0$, $\dot{n}/n = 0$ so $\dot{S}/S = g$, as in Eq. (18).

their worker population,

$$\frac{\dot{S}}{S} + \frac{\dot{n}}{n} = g.$$

Assume for now that technology is time invariant. At time zero, developers set up cities for the initial population, satisfying Eqs. (8)–(13). Assume for the moment that developers retain control of their formed cities. At the next instant the new popualtion needs to be housed in cities, but in this stationary context Eqs. (8)–(13) still describe the situation for any city. Thus city sizes remain the same and the new population is accommodated in new cities also of size $\overset{*}{n}$, so

$$\dot{S}/S = g. \tag{18}$$

At every instant Eq. (18) holds, as long as there is no technological change altering city sizes (see Proposition 1).

So far, in this context, there is no distinction between new and old cities, and, in fact, we could simply reshuffle the deck at each instant, having all cities be "new." It is simple to adjust the model to have cities once established stay in existence. A one time sunk cost, C, for setting up a city will be sufficient, so that a developer's objective function becomes

$$\int_0^\infty \left(\frac{1}{2} B(n(t) + m(t))^{3/2} - T_n(t)n(t) - T_m(t)m(t) \right) e^{-rt}\, dt - C,$$

where the discount factor, r, is from outside the specification.[18] In a stationary context where $\dot{n} = \dot{m} = \dot{T}_n = \dot{T}_m = 0$, given the Henry George theorem, $T_m = (1/2)B(n+m)^{3/2}/m - rC/m$. Developers reduce subsidies to entrepreneurs, to recover their initial capital costs, C.

Now for the key part. The same efficient outcome with cities being of efficient size $\overset{*}{n}$ and numbers growing at the rate g can be achieved if developers dissociate themselves from their cities once they have formed, leaving the cities as self-organized entities. In showing this, let us presume that developers turn urban lands over to local entrepreneurs, offering each an equal share in ownership of local lands, a presumption we will justify momentarily. If they were to retain control of the city, competitive developers would indefinitely turn all rents over to entrepreneurs. Now they simply turn over all local lands for free to local entrepreneurs. (If there is a sunk cost, C, to setting up a city, local entrepreneurs must reimburse the

[18] For example, r can be defined as the opportunity return on capital in the model in footnote 17, which is explicitly defined if we introduce national capital markets (see Black and Henderson [4]). Here it can also be a personal discount factor.

developer for this cost in return for ownership of lands.) With ownership of urban lands, entrepreneurs collect rents; and factor returns are given by Eqs. (14). We may then apply Proposition 5 directly. With new cities always ready to be formed by competitive developers (to accommodate not just new, but potentially existing people), existing cities must be of efficient size in order to survive.

So, if the developers dissociate themselves, why turn lands over to entrepreneurs as we presumed, rather than to workers? From Proposition 2, the only point in the core at an instant involves cities where all rents go to entrepreneurs. So a city where rents go to workers could not survive developer formation of new cities. Moreover if, when the developer dissociates himself from the city, an autonomous local public government forms (the institutional reality in the United States (Knapp [23])) and is pro-active, from Section 2 we know that who is assigned land ownership is not relevant. Efficient local tax policy will ensure all rental income ends up in the pockets of entrepreneurs, in order to internalize scale externalities.

4. POLITICAL ECONOMY OF INDIVIDUAL CITY SIZE

In this section, we examine two nonlimit cases which we characterized as the mega-city and the no-growth controls problems in the introduction. These describe common situations in national land development markets. The solutions in prior sections assume: (i) Agglomerations, whether developer inspired or self-organized, may form freely on the national landscape. (ii) Developers or local governments have autonomy to set local taxes and to restrict size and composition through zoning. (iii) All cities have identical environments, or production and consumption conditions.

Land markets in most countries differ from other markets in a fundamental way. Land markets are highly planned and regulated, with a high degree of public ownership. To undertake a development or for a development to self-organize in many countries requires building permits, environmental permits, and regulation by zoning, whether within existing cities or outside cities and hence regulation by county, state, or national agencies. Formation of new cities is restricted by regulation. Planned development also requires assemblage of relatively unencumbered land with clear title. In many Asian countries, for example, land tenure and titles are unclear, greatly inhibiting transactions and alteration of land usage from, say, agriculture to urban use (see Dowell and Leaf [7] and Struyk et al. [34]). But even if an agglomeration forms, the autonomy of developers or local governments is very limited, in terms of the ability to impose taxes and the ability to regulate composition through industrial zoning. For example, in Indonesia and Chile, the property tax is more a national than local tax. In some countries local zoning is more a national than local responsibility as well, or is unenforceable, or both. Use of these instruments also requires local officials who have some degree of sophistication, a major problem in Indonesia, for example (see Aksoro [2]).

These comments suggest that a "partial" self-organization situation may exist in many countries, where the number of cities is limited, where cities are generally oversized, and where most do not regulate their sizes. Within that context, suppose one or a few cities are sufficiently sophisticated in governance and sufficiently pro-active to optimize by restricting city size and composition through zoning and tax-subsidy policy. How does a pro-active exclusionary city then compare to the mass of self-organized and/or nonactive cities? We explore that question first in this section, analyzing what we call the exclusionary city case.

The third condition listed above requires all cities to have identical environments. In general, that condition will not be met for one of two reasons and suggests our second special case of this section. First, natural geography differs, so one city may be on a site with better port facilities, access to water, terrain for building, climate, etc., than other potential sites in the country. Second, and more critically, in many countries, especially nonfederal ones or ones with limited political freedoms, the national government may either favor one city, such as the national capital with better infrastructure and public services, or restrict other cities in their transport and communication linkages to national and international markets. Ades and Glaeser [1] suggest such conditions enhance urban primacy of national capitals in a country, which accords with earlier empirical work (e.g., Henderson [19]). The motivation is fairly straightforward. National rulers seek to enhance the quality of life in the city in which they live and with which they are familiar (and where they also own property). Earlier we noted examples such as Bangkok, Paris, and Jakarta, to which we would add Cairo, Buenos Aires, Dacca, Karachi, and even Tokyo.

Our second special case attempts to characterize this favored city situation. To isolate the impact of one city having special conditions from issues of restrictions in national land markets, we revert to assuming that national land markets function perfectly with free formation of cities. It is just that one city is favored with special production (or consumption) conditions, but all cities are pro-active in restricting size and composition. We call this the mega-city case. In the mega-city case, political economy plays a strong role in determining city composition.

We solve the two cases analytically. However, given the complexity of the model, both to get analytical results and to limit the number of situations to be considered, we impose one restriction. We assume that not only are workers the majority but that they outnumber entrepreneurs by more than two to one. That is, we assume

$$A < \frac{1}{2}.$$

Restricting $A < 0.5$ puts us in one of three general regions of parameter space in this model.[19] But it seems a reasonable assumption, given that in the United States, the average number of workers per enterprise for all private enterprises generates an A of about 0.07.

The Exclusionary City

For this case we assume that, apart from the one exclusionary city, all other cities in the economy operate as self-organized entities. Their equilibrium factor returns are described by Eqs. (14) from Section 2 on self-organization. They operate identically at, effectively, the national factor ratio A (i.e., the exclusionary city is "small" relative to the nation). Their sizes are greater than $\mathring{n}$ in (12) and less than $n_{\max}$ in (16), given their composition A. We label their size and composition n and A. Whatever size they attain, they pay factor returns from (14) denoted by $\bar{V}$ and $\bar{R}$.

The pro-active government in the exclusionary city chooses its size and composition, n_e and A_e, and taxes to maximize the welfare of the local representative member of the majority population, workers. The city takes as given $\bar{R}$, the cost of entrepreneurs in national markets. And any solution must satisfy $V_e \geq \bar{V}$, the going return for workers in national markets. The optimization problem for the local government is given in Section 2 in Eq. (17), except we replace n by n_e and m by m_e (for A by $A_e \equiv m_e/n_e$). Optimizing in (17), as before, yields two conditions. To optimize, we substitute the constraint into the objective function for T_m and maximize with respect to n_e and m_e. Combining the two first-order conditions yields

$$n_e = \left[E\epsilon 2B^{-1}A_e^{\gamma}(1 + A_e)^{-3/2}\right]^{1/(1/2-\epsilon)}. \tag{12'}$$

Equation (12′) is the same as for $\mathring{n}$, except it is defined for the exclusionary city's A_e, not the national A. Second, from the first-order condition for n_e alone, after rearrangement, we obtain an expression for R_e,

$$R_e = E(1 - \delta)A_e^{\gamma-1}n_e^{\epsilon} + Bn_e^{1/2}(1 + A_e)^{1/2}A_e^{-1}\left(\frac{1}{2} - A_e\right). \tag{19}$$

Note we are just considering the case where $A < 1/2$.

[19] For $A < 1/2$, V holding A constant in (8b) as a function of individual city size rises and reaches a maximum before $\mathring{n}$, while R in (8a) rises indefinitely as noted earlier.

With this framework we can prove

PROPOSITION 6. *In an otherwise self-organized economy, the pro-active autonomous local government in an exclusionary city, in maximizing the welfare of a representative member of the majority worker population, will reduce city population and alter composition to reduce A, or increase the relative number of workers to entrepreneurs relative to other cities.*

The proposition is proved by showing that R_e in (19) can equal $\bar{R}$ from (14) as required in equilibrium, iff $A_e < A$ and $n_e < n$ (so $n_e + m_e < n + m$ also).[20] So an exclusionary city, which acts to maximize the welfare of workers, increases their relative numbers but decreases their absolute numbers (and hence total city population, $n_e + m_e$).

The key result here is the reduction in city population. Relative to the oversized self-organized sector, a pro-active government restricts size to

[20] In equilibrium R_e in (19) must equal $\bar{R}$, where by rearranging (14) $\bar{R} = E(1 - \delta)A^{\gamma-1}n^{\epsilon} + Bn^{1/2}(1 + A)^{1/2}A^{-1}(\frac{1}{2} - A)$. If we start with $A = A_e$, then $R_e < \bar{R}$, given $n_e = \mathring{n}$ for $A = A_e$ from (12) and (12′) and $\mathring{n} < n$, by definition of the experiment, with $\partial R_e/\partial n_e > 0$ in (19). Then, to bring R_e into equality with $\bar{R}$, we can show that we must lower A_e relative to A, given in (19) $dR_e/dA_e < 0$, accounting (from (12′)) for the impact of A_e on n_e. Thus we know $A_e < A$. But by inspection of $\bar{R}$ and (19), given $R = R_e$ at $A = A_e$ and $n = n_e$, but $\partial R/\partial A, \partial R_e/\partial A_e < 0$ and $\partial R_e/\partial n_e, \partial R/\partial n > 0$, if $A_e < A$ then equality of R and R_e requires $n_e < n$. For properties of R_e by combining (12′) with (19) we get

$$R_e = \left(\frac{1}{2}B\epsilon^{-1}\right)n_e^{1/2}A_e^{-1}(1 + A_e)^{1/2}[\gamma(1 + A_e) - 3\epsilon A_e] \tag{a}$$

or

$$R_e = \left[E\gamma 2B^{-1}A_e^{\gamma}(1 + A_e)^{-3/2}\right]^{(1/2)/(1/2-\epsilon)} \times\left(\frac{1}{2}B\epsilon^{-1}\right)A_e^{-1}(1 + A_e)^{1/2}[\gamma(1 + A_e) - 3\epsilon A_e]. \tag{b}$$

Then we can show

$$\text{Sign}[dR_e/dA_e] = \text{sign}\left[\frac{(-\gamma A(1 + \epsilon - \gamma))}{2} + \epsilon\gamma - \frac{1}{2}\gamma(1 - \gamma) + \frac{1}{2}A(1 + \epsilon - \gamma)(-\gamma(1 + A) + 3\epsilon A)\right].$$

All terms on the RHS are negative given $\delta(1 + A) > 3\epsilon$ and $\gamma(1 + A) > 3\epsilon A$ from Proposition 1. Note $\frac{-A(1 + \epsilon - \gamma)}{2} - \frac{1}{2}(1 - \gamma) + \epsilon = -\frac{-\delta(1 + A)}{2} + \frac{3}{2}\epsilon$, for $\delta = \epsilon + 1 - \gamma$. Note in (a) $dR_e/dA_e = \partial R_e/\partial A_e + (\partial R_e/\partial n_e)(\partial n_e/\partial A_e)$.

benefit the majority population.[21] The alteration in composition towards more workers reflects what is needed to equilibrate factor markets. (In fact, if the city is ruled by an oligarchy of entrepreneurs, examples indicate they will set also $n_e < n$ and $A_e < A$, accentuating the drop in the latter.) The situation can be interpreted as describing a key aspect of U.S. no-growth communities. They act to restrict their sizes, benefiting their residents. In fact, no-growth controls usually apply exclusively to residential populations, not numbers of businesses, m_e. In Proposition 6, m_e is a self-enforcing outcome given $R_e = \bar{R}$. Naturally, excluded residents who are worse off ($V < V_e$) want to get in (and may sue to attempt to do so).

The Mega-City

For this case, we assume there is free formation of cities, to isolate the impact of one city having favored conditions. All but the favored city have identical production and consumption conditions. However, the favored city has special features, either natural ones or, more critically, ones endowed by the national government. Here we simply represent that favoritism as a shift factor for firms so, in production functions, $E_e > E$ (but the story works equally well with $B_e < B$ in commuting), where we continue to use subscript e to denote the special city. Besides having special features, the special city is pro-active in zoning and taxation to regulate population and composition.

We consider two cases, one where the special city is governed by a local democracy acting to maximize the welfare of the representative worker and the other where the special city is governed by an oligarchy of local entrepreneurs. Both specifications lead the special city to become a mega-city. But the implications for population composition are rather different. In particular we can show

PROPOSITION 7. *If there is a city endowed with special advantage (higher E or lower B), this city will be larger than other cities in the economy, but is still restricted in size. That is, $n_e > n$ $(= \mathring{n})$. If the city is governed by a local democracy, workers will act to restrict their numbers absolutely, and relative to entrepreneurs, so $A_e > A$. Conversely, an oligarchy of local entrepreneurs will seek to restrict the relative and absolute number of entrepreneurs, so $A_e < A$.*

To prove the proposition we start by noting that, for all other cities, assuming the special city is small relative to the rest, sizes and factor returns are described by Eqs. (12) and (13), given that these are all

[21] Note $V_e > \bar{V}$, given $\bar{V}$ is obtainable by duplicating self-organized cities and we optimized relative to that.

pro-active government developer run cities. For the special city, let us start with the case where it is governed by a pro-active local democracy. In that case, size and returns to entrepreneurs are described by the same equations as for the exclusionary city, or (12′) and (19). To show that for a local democracy $n_e > n(=\mathring{n})$ and $A_e > A$, we equate $\bar{R}$ in all other cities, given by (13a), with R_e in the special city.[22] The result in Proposition 7 that in a mega-city workers want to increase A_e relative to A but in an exclusionary city in Proposition 6 they want to decrease A_e relative to A may seem contradictory. It is not. Exclusionary cities are smaller than other cities in the economy, so to pay an equilibrium R with less scale they must lower A to increase the return to capital. Mega-cities are larger than other cities so with greater scale (and greater E or lower B) to pay an equilibrium R they raise A.

If the city is governed by a local oligarchy of entrepreneurs in the second part of the proposition, it acts to maximize the welfare of a representative entrepreneur. Local entrepreneurs collect residual returns in their firms, pay rent plus commuting costs, collect local land rents, and can tax workers. But workers must earn the going return in national markets, $\bar{V}$. The maximization problem is

$$\max_{n_e, m_e, T_n} E(1-\delta)n_e^{\delta}m_e^{\gamma-1} - \frac{3}{2}B(n_e+m_e)^{1/2} + \frac{1}{2}B(n_e+m_e)^{3/2}m_e^{-1} + T_n n_e/m_e \tag{20}$$

$$\text{s.t.}\ \bar{V} - E\gamma n_e^{\delta-1}m_e^{\gamma} + \frac{3}{2}B(n_e+m_e)^{1/2} + T_n = 0.$$

Optimizing in (20) yields an expression for city size given by (12′) and an expression for V_e as a function of E_e, n_e and A_e, corresponding to (13b). To prove the rest of the proposition, we show that equating this V_e to an

[22] By substituting (12) into (13a) for $\mathring{n}$, we get an expression $\bar{R} = R(A, E)$. The same expression for R_e is given in Eq. (b) in footnote 20. From footnote 20, we know $\partial R(\cdot)/\partial A_e < 0$ and $\partial R(\cdot)/\partial E > 0$ by inspection. Thus if $E_e > E$, then $A_e \geq A$ for $R_e = \bar{R}$. From (13a) and Eq. (a) in footnote 20, where E does not appear explicitly (only implicitly in n), we know $\partial R/\partial A|_n < 0$. The sign of $\partial R/\partial A|_n$ is given by the sign $[\gamma(1+A)(\frac{1}{2}\epsilon A - 1) - \frac{3}{2}\epsilon A^2]$. It is sufficient that $A < 2$ and we have assumed $A < \frac{1}{2}$. Thus if $A_e > A$ for $R_e = \bar{R}$, we require also $n_e > n$. If the special circumstances of the city have $B_e < B$ (rather than $E_e > E$), the same statement applies. To prove that we would rewrite (13a) replacing $n^{1/2}$ by n^{ϵ} in evaluating Eq. (8a) to get new forms to (13a) or (a) in footnote 20.

expression for $\bar{V}$ for all other cities requires $A_e < A$, if $E_e > E$ and that $n_e > n$.[23]

In summary, in the mega-city democratic case, as opposed to the exclusionary city case, workers want their mega-city to be larger than other cities and to have relatively more entrepreneurs (or "high skill" people, given Comment 1). The term mega-city seems appropriate because small differences in E generate big differences in n. Note the elasticity of n_e or $\dot{n}$ in (12′) or (12) with respect to E is around 2.5 for "typical" empirical values of ϵ of 0.1. The outcome accords with the image of mega-cities—unusually large and endowed with relatively more high-skill people. The relative abundance of high-skill entrepreneurs benefits workers, through factor proportion effects on factor returns. But even still the city is smaller than it would be with free migration. Having been endowed with special features, residents want to preserve their benefits, as opposed to having them dissipated by free migration of workers into the city. Favored cities run by local oligarchies will also be mega-cities. But now the oligarchy will want to enhance the relative number of workers, augmenting factor proportions in their favor. While city size will be relatively large, it will be also restricted. The enforced restriction is on the number of businesses or entrepreneurs, given now $R_e > \bar{R}$, while the equilibrium worker population will be self-enforcing. In viewing real world mega-cities, the issue is the ability of these cities to limit in-migration. While legal residents and population may be well regulated by zoning and licensing, squatter settlements are another issue.

5. CONCLUSIONS

In this paper we showed that, with freely functioning national land markets, either city formation by competitive land developers or having pro-active autonomous local governments in every self-organized agglomeration leads to efficient resource allocation. That result generalizes to a growth context, where new cities are formed by developers. Once a city is formed, developers dissociate from their cities, leaving existing cities as

[23] Optimizing in (20) yields

$$V_e = \left(\frac{1}{2}B\epsilon^{-1}\right)n_e^{1/2}(1 + A_e)^{1/2}[\delta(1 + A) - 3\epsilon] \quad \text{(a)}$$

$$V_e = \left(\frac{1}{2}B\epsilon^{-1}\right)\left[2B^{-1}\epsilon E A_e^{\gamma}(1 + A_e)^{-3/2}\right]^{(1/2)/(1/2-\epsilon)}(1 + A_e)^{1/2}[\delta(1 + A_e) - 3\epsilon]. \quad \text{(b)}$$

For all other cities, the expressions for $\bar{V}$ as functions of A, n, and E are identical to (a) and (b). If $E_e > E, V_e > \bar{V}$, for $A = A_e$. This is based on substituting for $\dot{n}$ and n_e from (12) and (12′) in the relevant equation from (13b) to get $V = V(A, E)$. Evaluating $V_e = \bar{V}$ for $E_e > E$, we can show $A_e < A$ (using the same methodology in footnote 20). Then from (13b), because $\partial V/\partial A|_n > 0$, $n_e > n$.

potentially ungoverned (at least with respect to size and composition policy). The growth context with formation of new cities by developers is sufficient both to efficiently limit sizes of existing cities and to provide an economic basis for assignment of ownership of urban lands to entrepreneurs rather than workers.

If there are not freely functioning national land markets with developers and autonomous local governments, in general, self-organized cities tend to be oversized. In that context, any single city has an incentive to restrict its size and alter its composition. If a city such as a national capital has special advantages relative to other cities, with freely functioning national land markets, its size will be larger than other cities (although still restricted). If governed by a local democracy, its composition will be altered in favor of increasing the relative number of entrepreneurs. This is consistent with notions of mega-cities—large cities with relatively many high-skill people. However, if governed by an oligarchy of entrepreneurs, its composition will be altered in favor of more (low-skill) workers.

REFERENCES

1. A. F. Ades and E. L. Glaeser, Trade and circuses: Explaining urban giants, *Quarterly Journal of Economics*, **110,** 195–227 (1995).
2. L. W. Aksoro, "The Effects of the Location Permit in Urban Land Markets," Master's Thesis, MIT (1994).
3. R. Becker and J. V. Henderson, Intra-industry specialization and urban development, *in* "The Economics of Cities" (J. Thisse *et al.*, Eds.), Cambridge Univ. Press, Cambridge, UK, 2000.
4. D. Black and J. V. Henderson, A theory of urban growth, *Journal of Political Economy*, **107,** 252–284 (1999).
5. J. Conley and H. Konichi, "Migration-Proof Tiebout Equilibrium: Existence and Asymptotic Efficiency," Paper presented at RSAI meetings, November 1999.
6. L. H. Dobkins and Y. Ioannides, "Evolution of the USA Size Distribution of Cities," mimeo, Tufts University (1995).
7. D. Dowell and M. Leaf, The price of land for housing in Jakarta, *Urban Studies*, **28,** 707–722 (1991).
8. J. Eaton and Z. Eckstein, Cities and growth: Theory and evidence from France and Japan, *Regional Science and Urban Economics*, **27,** 443–474 (1997).
9. R. Ellickson, Suburban growth controls: An economic and legal analysis, *Yale Law Review*, **86,** 385–511 (1977).
10. W. A. Fischel, "The Economics of Zoning Laws," Johns Hopkins Univ. Press, Baltimore (1985).
11. F. Flatters, V. Henderson, and P. Mieszkowski, Public goods, efficiency, and regional equalization, *Journal of Public Economics*, **3,** 99–112 (1974).
12. M. Fujita and M. Ogawa, Multiple equilibria and structural transition of non-monocentric urban configurations, *Regional Science and Urban Economics*, **12,** 161–196 (1982).
13. M. Fujita, P. Krugman, and T. Mori, "On the Evolution of Hierarchical Urban Systems," mimeo (1995).
14. J. Garreau, "Edge City," Doubleday, New York (1991).

15. W. Hamilton, Zoning and property taxation in a system of local governments, *Urban Studies*, **12,** 205–211 (1975).
16. R. W. Helsley and W. C. Strange, Matching and agglomeration economies in a system of cities, *Regional Science and Urban Economics*, 189–212 (1990).
17. R. W. Helsley and W. C. Strange, Strategic growth controls, *Regional Science and Urban Economics*, **25,** 435–460 (1995).
18. J. V. Henderson, The sizes and types of cities, *American Economic Review*, **64,** 640–656 (1974).
19. J. V. Henderson, "Urban Development: Theory Fact and Illusion," Oxford Univ. Press, New York (1988).
20. J. V. Henderson, Separating Tiebout equilibrium, *Journal of Urban Economics*, **29,** 128–152 (1991).
21. J. V. Henderson and A. Mitra, The new urban landscape: Developers and edge cities, *Regional Science and Urban Economics*, **26,** 613–643 (1996).
22. H. S. Kim, "Optimal and Equilibrium Land Use Pattern in a City: A Non-monocentric Approach," Ph.D. dissertation, Brown University (1998).
23. K. Knapp, Private contracts for durable local public good provision, *Journal of Urban Economics*, **29,** 380–402 (1991).
24. P. Krugman, Increasing returns and economic geography, *Journal of Political Economy*, **99,** 483–499 (1991).
25. P. Krugman, On the number of location of cities, *European Economic Review*, **37,** 293–308 (1993).
26. P. Krugman and A. Venables, "The Seamless World: A Spatial Model of International Specialization," NBER Working Paper No. 5220 (1995).
27. A. Marshall, "Principles of Economics," MacMillan, London (1890) (see p. 332 for quotes).
28. H. Mohring, Land values and measurement of highway benefits, *Journal of Political Economy*, **49,** 236–249 (1961).
29. U. Reichman, Residential private governments, *University of Chicago Law Review*, **43,** 253–306 (1976).
30. B. Renaud, "National Urbanization Policy in Developing Countries," Oxford Univ. Press, New York (1981).
31. S. Scotchmer and M. Wooders, Competitive equilibrium and the core in club economies with anonymous crowding, *Journal of Public Economics*, **34,** 159–173 (1987).
32. R. W. Scott, "Management and Control of Growth," Urban Land Institute, Washington, DC, Vol. 11, Chapter 12, pp. 355–487 (1975).
33. J. Stiglitz, The theory of local public goods, *in* "The Economics of Public Services" (M. S. Feldstein and R. P. Inman, Eds.), MacMillan, New York (1977).
34. R. Struyk, M. Hoffman, and H. Katsura, "The Market for Shelter in Indonesian Cities," Urban Institute, Washington, DC (1990).
35. United Nations, "World Urbanization Prospects: 1992 Revision," New York (1993).

[12]

TRADE AND CIRCUSES: EXPLAINING URBAN GIANTS*

ALBERTO F. ADES AND EDWARD L. GLAESER

Using theory, case studies, and cross-country evidence, we investigate the factors behind the concentration of a nation's urban population in a single city. High tariffs, high costs of internal trade, and low levels of international trade increase the degree of concentration. Even more clearly, politics (such as the degree of instability) determines urban primacy. Dictatorships have central cities that are, on average, 50 percent larger than their democratic counterparts. Using information about the timing of city growth, and a series of instruments, we conclude that the predominant causality is from political factors to urban concentration, not from concentration to political change.

I. INTRODUCTION

Over 35 percent of Argentina's population is concentrated in Buenos Aires, a city of 12 million inhabitants. What is it about countries such as Argentina, Japan, and Mexico that justifies their urban concentration when the United States' largest city contains only 6 percent of its population? We investigate the causes of urban primacy using evidence from a cross section of 85 modern countries and five case studies (classical Rome, 1650 London, 1700 Edo, Buenos Aires in 1900, and Mexico City today). We find that concentration in the nation's largest city falls with total population and with the share of labor employed in agriculture. As predicted by Krugman and Livas [1992], countries with high shares of trade in GDP or low tariff barriers (even holding trade levels constant) rarely have their population concentrated in a single city. Urban centralization also falls with the development of transportation networks.

But political forces, even more than economic factors, drive urban centralization: dictatorships cause concentration in a single metropolis. Political instability also increases central city size. Figure I summarizes our findings that both political weakness and centralized power lead to centralized urban populations. One

*We are grateful to Alberto Alesina, Olivier Blanchard, Glenn Ellison, Antonio Fatás, Eric Hanushek, Vernon Henderson, Paul Krugman, Norman Loayza, Aarón Tornell, and seminar participants at Harvard University; the University of Rochester; the Graduate School of Business, Columbia University; the Graduate School of Business, University of Chicago; the Wharton School, University of Pennsylvania; and the World Bank for helpful suggestions. We are particularly grateful to Andrei Shleifer for his advice and encouragement. Greg Aldrete provided extremely useful insights on Roman history. Both authors gratefully acknowledge financial support from the National Science Foundation.

The Quarterly Journal of Economics, February 1995

STABLE DEMOCRACIES Urban Concentration = 0.23 (0.032) Number of Observations = 24	STABLE DICTATORSHIPS Urban Concentration = 0.3 (0.03) Number of Observations = 16
UNSTABLE DEMOCRACIES Urban Concentration = 0.35 (0.07) Number of Observations = 6	UNSTABLE DICTATORSHIPS Urban Concentration = 0.37 (0.02) Number of Observations = 39

FIGURE I
Politics and Urban Concentration

Urban concentration is defined as the average share of urbanized population living in the main city from 1970 to 1985. Stable countries are defined as those whose average number of revolutions and coups is below the worldwide median. Dictatorships are countries whose average Gastil index for the period is higher than 3. Standard errors are in parentheses.

interpretation of these results is that unstable regimes must cater to mobs near the center of power and dictatorships freely exploit the wealth of the hinterland.

Our work has some significant predecessors: Wheaton and Shishido [1981] and Rosen and Resnick [1980] show that urban concentration is negatively associated with the country's population. They also find that concentration is first increasing and then decreasing in per capita GDP. Henderson [1986] and Wheaton and Shishido show across a small sample of countries that both concentration of government expenditures and nonfederalist governments lead to urban concentration.[1] Using data on Western

1. These three authors' evidence differs from ours because of the following: (1) their use of self-constructed political variables, (2) their emphasis on explicitly spatial government characteristics (i.e., degree of local spending or autonomy), and (3) their small sample size (less than 40) and restrictive time period (Henderson

European cities from 1000 to 1800 C.E., De Long and Shleifer [1993] demonstrate that urban growth (not urban concentration) is the product of nonabsolutist regimes that respect property rights. Our next section presents our basic hypotheses. Section III describes the data, and Section IV presents the results. Section V presents our case studies of megalopolises. Section VI concludes.

II. Alternative Theories of Urban Giants

In this section we discuss three forces driving the concentration of urban population in a single city: trade and commerce, industry, and government. We also set up our estimation strategy.

II.1. Trade and Commerce

Urban theorists from von Thünen [1826] to Krugman [1991] have argued that when transportation is expensive activities will group together to save on travel costs. This theory predicts that urban concentration will be higher when transportation is more costly.[2] Krugman and Livas [1992] use this idea to suggest a link between protectionism and the growth of Mexico City. In their model, international firms supply the main city and the hinterland equally well. Domestic firms pay lower transport costs when serving their own location. Thus, domestic prices, net of travel, are lower where domestic firms are concentrated.

When tariffs are low, imported goods are a large part of consumption. Imports are not cheaper in the central city, so workers spread over space to save on congestion costs. With protection, domestic suppliers take over the market. Prices, net of transport costs, are lower for domestic goods in the central city because firms are located in that city. Workers then come to the city to pay lower prices for domestic goods.[3] This theory predicts that protectionism generates larger central cities.

---

uses only 1974–1976). In addition to this, endogeneity problems are much more serious for their political variables. As one measure of government centralization, these authors use the share of local governments in total government expenditures. This variable is clearly a function of the distribution of population in space. A further difference with our work is that we only look at the nation's largest city. This change was necessary to increase sample size.

2. The relationship between trade and concentration can be nonmonotonic. When foods deteriorate rapidly in transit, people must live near food supplies, as they did before the domestication of pack animals [Bairoch 1988].

3. Protectionist policies might also encourage urban concentration by promoting the growth of import-competing activities that are dependent on essential inputs found only in the capital; central cities might be good places for avoiding tariffs (New York City and Buenos Aires were both centers of smuggling). Proximity to central government might also be particularly important when exemptions to tariffs are being handed out or the spoils of protection are being distributed.

Of course, free trade does not always decrease urban concentration. Among our case studies, London and Buenos Aires are trade cities that grew through commerce. We can therefore test Krugman and Livas' hypothesis of a negative correlation between trade and concentration against an alternative hypothesis that central cities have a comparative advantage in commerce and grow with the volume of trade.

II.2. Industry

Activities such as agriculture, which depend on immobile natural resources, will not be able to relocate to reap the benefits from being in the capital. The extent to which an economy is agricultural thus limits the extent to which that economy can centralize in one location. This basic argument suggests that any movement away from agriculture will raise urban centralization.

Centralizing population lowers transport costs and raises effective aggregate demand for a fixed level of GDP. If the level of demand is important for the growth of industry (because of fixed costs in manufacturing), then urban centralization may be correlated with industrial expansion. Industrialization creates a further incentive for firms to congregate if industrialization increases the need for physical infrastructure and infrastructure costs can be shared by firms located in the same city. Manufacturing may also increase the need for intellectual spillovers that are only available in the central city (perhaps those caused by diversity as in Glaeser et al. [1992] or from access to the pool of international human capital). Large cities also allow firms to specialize in a thinner range of products, as they provide larger markets for these specialized products. We test the positive relationship between manufacturing and concentration predicted by the above theories against an alternative hypothesis in which manufacturing only affects urbanization and not concentration.

II.3. Government and Politics, Including a Model

Politics affects urban concentration because spatial proximity to power increases political influence. Political actors from revolutionaries in 1789 to lobbyists in 1994 have increased their clout by working in the capital. Distance can lessen influence in many ways: (1) when influence comes from the threat of violence, distance makes that violence less direct; (2) distance makes illegal political actions (e.g., bribes) harder to conceal; (3) political agents living in the hinterland have less access to information; and (4) distance hurts communication between political agents and government. The political power of the capital's population should induce the government to transfer resources to the capital, and these transfers will attract migrants. Rent-seekers coming to the capital to renk-seek may also raise the city's population.[4] The political power of the capital's residents is most important when governments have the following characteristics: (1) they are weak and respond easily to local pressure; (2) they have large rents to dispense; and (3) they do not respect the political rights of the hinterland. Effect (1) predicts that instability will create urban concentration since buying off local agitators is most important in susceptible regimes. Instability may also create concentration if weak governments are unable or unwilling to protect life and property outside of the capital. Effects (2) and (3) suggest that dictatorships will have more concentration since they are willing to ignore the wishes of the politically weak hinterland. Dictators may also have more rents to dispense. We test the positive connection of dictatorship and instability with urban concentration against an alternative hypothesis where dictatorship and instability lead governments to protect themselves by moving the seat of power away from the central city (and thus lessening concentration), or by controlling migration (as in Stalinist Russia or Communist China) to disperse population across space.

The model of government and politics formally connects the type of political regime (dictatorships versus democracy) and the degree of political instability with the size of the central city. We examine the spatial structure of taxation chosen by a government facing legal political pressure from the electorate and revolutionary political pressure from mobs in the capital city. Our main results are that more dictatorial regimes have higher taxes in the hinterland (because dictators ignore the rights of the median voter who resides in the hinterland), and that more unstable regimes lower

4. Hoselitz [1955] argued that there were a class of "parasitic" cities involved in rent-seeking. Olson [1982] emphasizes the role of government distribution policies in determining the size of cities. He suggests that the capital will grow when transportation and communication networks are poorly developed in rural areas. This, he claims, "makes it more costly and difficult for those in rural areas to mobilize political power. . . ." Williamson [1991] gives an elegant description of the policies put in place for transferring resources from the hinterland to the capital. Technically, these theories are all about the nation's capital not the nation's largest city. Since the nation's largest city is its capital in more than 90 percent of the countries in our sample, we have decided to gloss over this distinction.

taxes in the capital (because unstable regimes are vulnerable to agitation by mobs near the seat of power).[5]

We divide each country into two locations: the main city and the hinterland. Migration between locations is assumed to be costless. Total population in the country is normalized to one. Wages in each location (including amenities, psychic income, and income from household production) are assumed to be locally declining in that location's population because of congestion. Taxes are lump sum and may vary across space.

The assumption of costless migration implies that after-tax wages will be equalized across locations, or

$$W_1(N) - \tau_1 = W_2(1 - N) - \tau_2, \tag{1}$$

where N is the population of the central city, τ_i is the tax level (net of benefits) in region i (for $i = 1,2$), where region 1 is the central city, and $W_i(.)$ are location-specific continuously differentiable wage functions, with $W_i' < 0$ due to congestion. Equation (1) defines a population function:

$$N = N(\tau_2 - \tau_1), \tag{2}$$

where $N'(.) < 0$, from $W_i'(.) < 0$. The population of the central city depends on the difference in the tax rates across space.

The government takes (2) as given, and chooses τ_1 and τ_2 to maximize

$$(1 - rR(\tau_1) - eE(\tau_2))V + \tau_1 N(\tau_2 - \tau_1) + \tau_2(1 - N(\tau_2 - \tau_1)), \tag{3}$$

where V is a parameter measuring the value of survival, and $1 - rR(\tau_1) - eE(\tau_2)$ describes the probability of surviving to the period. $rR(\tau_1)$ is the probability of a violent or illegal revolt, where r is a shift parameter capturing the propensity of the country to revolt or the level of instability. The probability of a revolt starting and succeeding is assumed to be a function of the degree of exploitation in the central city (τ_1), because we assume that only revolts in the capital can be successful.[6] $eE(\tau_2)$ is the probability of a successful legal or electoral change of government.[7] The election function is based on the taxes facing the median voter τ_2 (as long as

5. We would get identical results if the degree of dictatorship measured the size of the rents to be allocated and the degree of instability measured the ability of local political actors to access those rents.

6. Our results could be generalized to allow revolts starting in both areas as long as the capital has a comparative advantage in unseating the government.

7. Both probabilities are conditional on the other change of government not occurring.

we assume that at least 50 percent of the population lives in the hinterland). e is a shift parameter measuring the power of the electorate, with low e's indicating dictatorship. In equation (3) the government faces a trade-off between current rents and future survival when choosing the levels of taxes in each location.

The government maximizes (3) over τ_1 and τ_2 subject to (2). The first-order conditions (FOC) are given by

$$(4) \qquad -Vr\frac{\partial R}{\partial \tau_1} + N(\tau_2 - \tau_1) + \frac{\partial N}{\partial(\tau_2 - \tau_1)}(\tau_2 - \tau_1) = 0$$

and

$$(5) \qquad -Ve\frac{\partial E}{\partial \tau_2} + 1 - N(\tau_2 - \tau_1) - \frac{\partial N}{\partial(\tau_2 - \tau_1)}(\tau_2 - \tau_1) = 0.$$

We assume that the second-order conditions hold. Our interest here is how the difference between the tax rates ($\tau_2 - \tau_1$, which determines N, the size of the central city) responds to democracy (e) and revolutionary instability (r).

Figure II shows the loci of city taxes and countryside taxes that satisfy each FOC. The City Tax schedule shows equation (4), the FOC with respect to τ_1. The Countryside Tax schedule shows equation (5), the FOC with respect to τ_2. We are using a linearized version of the model for which we have assumed that

$$(6) \qquad N = \tfrac{1}{4} + \tfrac{1}{4}(\tau_2 - \tau_1)$$

and

$$(7) \qquad 1 - rR(\tau_1) - eE(\tau_2) = k - \frac{r\tau_1^2}{2} - \frac{e\tau_2^2}{2}.$$

The initial equilibrium is given at point A.

It is simple to show that the gap between the level of taxes in the countryside and those in the central city increases when the degree of democracy falls and the degree of instability rises. Indeed, Figure II shows that a fall in e (lower democracy) induces an upward shift in the Countryside Tax schedule; the tax schedule shifts up because the marginal cost of taxing the countryside, which comes from the ability of the countryside to hurt the government, has fallen. The new equilibrium is given by B, where while both city and country taxes are higher, countryside taxes have risen relatively more than city taxes. Taxing the hinterland is

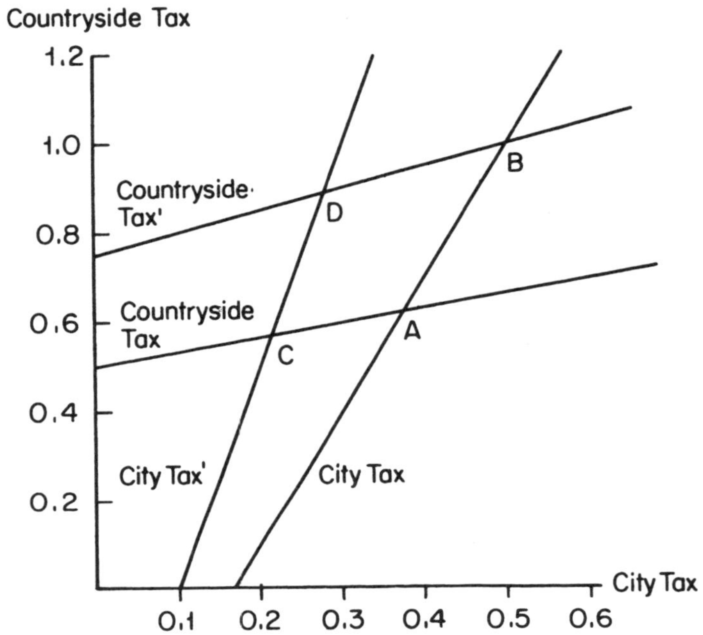

FIGURE II
Stability, Dictatorship, and Taxes across Space

a cheaper activity for the government when an absence of democratic representation leaves voters in the hinterland powerless.

Starting again from *A*, an increase in instability (a higher *r*) raises again the exploitation gap between the country and the central city. In Figure II this is shown by a shift to the left of the City Tax schedule that brings the economy to an equilibrium at *C*. While both tax rates fall, the reduction is more important for the City. Essentially, instability makes it more dangerous to tax the capital city, since the capital becomes more prone to violence. Since democracy and stability both lower the tax differences over space, they will also lower the central city's population. Point *D* shows the effect of both dictatorship and instability.

It is also straightforward to prove algebraically that instability is more important in democracies than in dictatorships (i.e., $d^2N/drde < 0$). The intuition for this effect is that there are two forces limiting taxation of the hinterland: democracy, and the movement of population in the hinterland to the capital. When democracy is strong, the tax rate on the hinterland is initially low so new taxes on the hinterland (created by more instability) will have a smaller migration effect than they would if the tax rate on the hinterland were initially high.

II.4. Estimation Strategy

Our empirical strategy is basically an estimation of equation (1), the indifference relationship across locations. A larger urban population in a country will be our indicator that features of that country attract people to the central city. This inference requires that there be some freedom to migrate and that utility in each location is locally decreasing in the number of people in that location. Our regressions actually assume an indifference relationship across locations where congestion effects are power functions (i.e., wages in each location are a function of national characteristics times the population of that region raised to some power). We thus estimate

$$\ln (N_c) = \alpha + \beta_1 \ln (N_u) + \beta_2 \ln (N_h) + \sum_{j=1}^{j=n} \delta_j x_j, \tag{8}$$

where the x_j's are national characteristics that change the incentives to live in different locations. Equation (8) is justified by a model, but it also has intuitive appeal. This estimation can be interpreted as finding the factors determining the size of the main city holding the population of the other urbanized areas and the hinterland constant. By moving $\ln (N_u)$ or $\ln (N_h)$ over to the other side of (8), one can think of this equation as estimating the ratio of population in the central city to that of other urbanized areas, or the ratio of population in the central city to nonurbanized population.

III. The Data

III.1. Construction of the Data Set

We collected the 1970, 1975, 1980, and 1985 observations for 85 countries to make our data set. The list of countries included in this sample is shown in the Appendix. The data on urbanization and population in the main urban agglomeration come from the 1988 edition of the *Prospects of World Urbanization,* which has data for countries or areas with two million or more inhabitants in

1985.[8] We used the country's largest city, not its capital, as the capital city is *only* appropriate for testing political theories. Our choice is irrelevant, since 77 of the 85 large cities in our sample are capitals and no results change if we drop the noncapital cities. The data on each country's land area were taken from the 1986 edition of the *FAO Production Yearbook*. Data on the share of the labor force outside of agriculture, nominal GDP measured in units of national currency, and merchandise imports and exports are from the World Bank's *World Tables*. The share of the labor force outside of agriculture is defined as the percentage of the labor force not in farming, forestry, hunting, and fishing.

Data on total population, political rights, and instability are from the Barro and Wolf [1989] database. GDP numbers are compiled by Summers and Heston [1991]. The Gastil index of political rights annually ranks countries in seven categories according to a checklist of political rights. The data on political instability measure the number of revolutions, coups, or strikes per year in each country. The data on import duties and government expenditures on transportation and communications are from the IMF's *Government Finance Statistics*.

Our basic sample has 85 countries, but we lose several observations in dealing with import duties and government transportation expenditures. We used averages of the 1970, 1975, 1980, and 1985 observations when feasible except for the data directly taken from the Barro-Wolf data set.[9]

III.2. Description of the Data

The 1988 *Prospects of World Urbanization* reports 100 urban agglomerations with two million or more inhabitants in 1985 (compared with 62 in 1970). These cities account for 487 million inhabitants, which represents 10 percent of the world's total population and 24 percent of the world's urban population. Of those 100 largest urban agglomerations, 40 are in the more developed regions of the world. In 1985, 46 of them contained between 2 and 2.9 million persons; 24 contained between 3.0 and

8. An urban agglomeration is an area comprising a central city or cities surrounded by an urbanized area, and is close to the U. S. definition of "consolidated metropolitan statistical area."

9. Averages were used rather than running all four observations as a panel, primarily because appropriate panel techniques are only usable if we put some structure on how lagged values of country characteristics change current urban concentration. We were unwilling to make the assumptions needed for that structure.

4.9 million; and 30 had more than 5 million inhabitants. In this last group eleven agglomerations contained ten million or more persons, with seven of them in the less developed regions of the world. During the fifteen-year period of 1970–1985 that we analyze, agglomerations that in 1985 had two million or more inhabitants grew faster than the world's total population. While large agglomerations in the developed world grew at an average of 1.0 percent per year, their counterparts in the less developed world grew at an average rate of 3.3 percent per year.

Table I shows the five largest and five smallest main cities of the world first ranked by absolute population and then ranked by share of their country's population. Ranking by either measure, three of the five largest main cities in the world are in less developed countries. All of the smaller cities are in less developed countries. The correlation between absolute population and share of country's population is far from perfect. Shanghai is one of the world's most populated main cities when ranked by its raw population and one of the world's least populated main cities when ranked by its share of China's population. The southern cone of South America seems particularly prone to urban concentration; three of the five most concentrated countries in the world are there.

IV. Results

Table II gives the means and standard deviations for the sample that we use in our regressions. Table III shows the raw correlations of our variables. Higher levels of central city population were positively associated with larger and more populated countries, high levels of per capita GDP, and high shares of the labor force outside of agriculture. Central city population is negatively correlated with the presence of dictatorships, the share of trade in GDP, and the share of government transportation and communication expenditures in GDP. The growth rate of main city population is positively associated with dictatorships, revolutions and coups, and high tariff barriers. The raw data also show some correlation between trade and politics, suggesting that trade and political effects might be confused empirically.

We use the log of average population in the main city as the dependent variable in most of our regressions. All regressions include the same set of controls; a capital city dummy that takes a

TABLE I
DESCRIPTION OF THE DATA

City	Population	Share of country's population
	Five biggest main cities by 1985 population	
Tokyo, Japan	19,037,361	15.76%
Mexico City, Mexico	16,465,487	20.97%
New York, United States	15,627,553	6.53%
Sao Paulo, Brazil	15,538,682	11.46%
Shanghai, China	11,843,669	1.14%
	Five smallest main cities by 1985 population	
Pt. Moresby, Papua N.G.	156,850	4.47%
Porto Novo, Benin	182,653	4.52%
Kigali, Rwanda	198,915	3.30%
Bujumbura, Burundi	261,098	5.56%
Kathmandu, Nepal	277,539	1.66%
	Five biggest main cities by share of country's population in 1985	
Singapore, Singapore	2,558,000	100%
Hong Kong, Hong Kong	5,044,073	92.5%
Montevideo, Uruguay	1,157,450	39.36%
Buenos Aires, Argentina	10,759,291	35.47%
Santiago, Chile	4,227,049	34.87%
	Five smallest main cities by share of country's population in 1985	
Shanghai, China	11,843,669	1.14%
Calcutta, India	10,227,890	1.34%
Kathmandu, Nepal	277,539	1.66%
Kigali, Rwanda	198,915	3.30%
Sana, Yemen	284,561	3.57%

value of one if the main city in question is a capital city and zero otherwise, the log of average nonurbanized population, the log of average urbanized population outside of the main city, the log of average real per capita GDP, and the log of land area. Unless otherwise specified, all of our regressions report OLS results, with

TABLE II
SUMMARY STATISTICS

Variable	Obs	Mean	Std. dev.	Minimum	Maximum
Population	85	30,000,000	77,000,000	1,748,250	655,000,000
Main city size	85	2,489,953	3,511,807	120,404	16,900,000
Main city growth	85	0.039	0.028	−0.011	0.139
Land area	85	974	1,912	11	9,976
Per capita GDP in 1980 US$	85	3,005	3,122	287	10,898
Share of labor outside of agriculture	85	0.51	0.28	0.067	0.97
Share of trade in GDP	85	0.43	0.21	0.0	1.18
Dictatorship dummy	85	0.65	0.48	0	1
Revolution and coups	85	0.23	0.25	0	1.15
Import duties/imports	70	0.086	0.058	.0000267	0.297
Gov. transp. expen-dit./GDP	50	0.02	0.01	.0000075	0.061

Note. All variables are averages of their 1970, 1975, 1980, and 1985 observations. The 1985 observation is missing for the Share of labor outside of agriculture. The 1970 observation is missing for Import duties and Government transportation and communication expenditures. The data on Land area is in thousands of hectares. The Dictatorship dummy takes a value of one for countries with an average Gastil index larger than three.

standard errors based on White's heteroskedasticity-consistent covariance matrix in parentheses.[10]

In Table IV regression (1) includes our standard set of controls and the share of the labor force outside of agriculture. The regression explains 81 percent of the total variation in the dependent variable. In regression (1) the capital city dummy is positive and significant. The coefficient on this variable indicates that main cities are, on average, 42 percent larger if they are also capital cities. This fact may mean that power attracts population, but it may also mean that capitals are located in larger cities. Both population controls also take positive values, but only the log of nonurbanized population is large and significant. This coefficient is typically well below one so that urban areas grow with their countries but less than proportionately. The coefficient on the log of land area is also positive and usually close to 0.12, implying that a 10 percent increase in the size of the country increases population in the main city by about 1.2 percent. An increase in the size of the

10. These standard errors do not differ greatly, however, from those obtained by OLS. We also tried running the regressions weighing them by population.

TABLE III
SAMPLE CORRELATIONS

	Population	Main city size	Main city growth	Land area	Per capita GDP	Non-agricultural labor share	Share of trade in GDP	Dictatorship dummy	Revolutions and coups	Import duties/ imports	Govt. transp. exp./GDP
Population											
Main city size	0.537										
	(.000)										
Main city growth	−0.139	−0.290									
	(0.206)	(0.007)									
Land area	0.353	0.462	−0.098								
	(0.001)	(0.000)	(0.370)								
Per capita GDP (1980 US$)	0.045	0.334	−0.596	0.301							
	(0.684)	(0.002)	(0.000)	(0.005)							
Nonagricultural labor share	0.024	0.367	−0.697	0.200	0.849						
	(0.825)	(0.001)	(0.000)	(0.067)	(0.000)						
Share of trade in GDP	−0.313	−0.392	0.105	−0.269	0.065	0.118					
	(0.004)	(0.000)	(0.337)	(0.013)	(0.554)	(0.281)					
Dictatorship dummy	−0.192	−0.217	0.582	−0.107	−0.720	−0.691	−0.011				
	(0.077)	(0.046)	(0.000)	(0.328)	(0.000)	(0.000)	(0.919)				
Revolutions and coups	−0.071	−0.106	0.232	−0.064	−0.441	−0.358	−0.197	0.469			
	(0.517)	(0.334)	(0.033)	(0.561)	(0.000)	(0.001)	(0.071)	(0.000)			
Import duties/ imports	0.309	−0.119	0.416	−0.100	−0.660	−0.567	−0.141	0.460	0.350		
	(0.009)	(0.327)	(0.000)	(0.408)	(0.000)	(0.000)	(0.245)	(0.000)	(0.003)		
Govt. transp. exp./GDP	−0.244	−0.353	0.252	−0.288	−0.119	−0.027	0.395	−0.016	−0.216	−0.008	
	(0.088)	(0.012)	(0.078)	(0.042)	(0.411)	(0.852)	(0.005)	(0.911)	(0.132)	(0.960)	

Note. Sample used is that of Table II. The significance probability of the correlation under the null hypothesis that the statistic is zero is shown in parentheses.

TABLE IV

Dependent variable: log of average population in main city (1970–1985)	(1)	(2)	(3)	(4)	(5)	(6)
Intercept	1.136	2.014	1.156	0.651	0.808	0.297
	(0.878)	(0.934)	(0.942)	(1.109)	(1.082)	(1.063)
Capital city dummy	0.424	0.465	0.374	0.336	0.283	0.408
	(0.204)	(0.196)	(0.181)	(0.200)	(0.180)	(0.188)
Log of average nonurbanized population	0.595	0.553	0.583	0.640	0.623	0.641
	(0.068)	(0.066)	(0.063)	(0.073)	(0.072)	(0.071)
Log of average urbanized population outside the main city	0.059	0.066	0.063	0.058	0.054	0.045
	(0.050)	(0.045)	(0.042)	(0.042)	(0.040)	(0.038)
Log of land area	0.167	0.155	0.115	0.109	0.113	0.120
	(0.051)	(0.049)	(0.049)	(0.054)	(0.053)	(0.055)
Log of average real GDP per capita	0.034	0.058	0.165	0.193	0.149	0.166
	(0.129)	(0.131)	(0.127)	(0.146)	(0.149)	(0.148)
Average share of the labor force outside of agriculture	2.656	2.556	2.704	2.623	2.782	3.071
	(0.554)	(0.567)	(0.549)	(0.547)	(0.518)	(0.516)
Share of trade in GDP		−0.609	−0.676	−0.463	−0.404	−0.519
		(0.225)	(0.204)	(0.228)	(0.240)	(0.244)
Dictatorship dummy based on Gastil's index of political rights			0.444	0.324	0.442	0.705
			(0.154)	(0.156)	(0.148)	(0.181)
Africa dummy				0.160	0.127	0.172
				(0.263)	(0.260)	(0.257)
Latin America dummy				0.390	0.342	0.295
				(0.159)	(0.158)	(0.162)
New democracy					0.428	
					(0.177)	
Revolution and coups						2.372
						(0.772)
Dictatorship dummy × revolution and coups						−2.705
						(0.803)
Number of observations	85	85	85	85	85	85
Adjusted R^2	0.81	0.81	0.82	0.83	0.83	0.84

Note. All variables are averages of their 1970, 1975, 1980, and 1985 observations. The 1985 observation is missing for the Share of labor outside of agriculture. The Dictatorship dummy takes a value of one for countries with an average Gastil index larger than three. White-corrected standard errors in parentheses.

country (holding population constant) represents a decrease in population density, which might indicate an increase in the transportation costs of supplying the hinterland. This result thus provides our first support for the Krugman hypothesis.

Our income control usually takes positive values, but the coefficient loses size and significance whenever we also control for the share of labor outside of agriculture. The share of labor outside agriculture is meant to capture the country's state of industrial development and the fraction of the population that is not tied to natural resources.[11] This last variable has a large and significant effect on the size of the main city. We find that a 1 percent increase in the share of the labor force outside of agriculture increases the size of the largest city by about 2.5 percent. Both the agriculture and GDP results suggest that large cities require some economic development.

Regression (2) adds the share of trade in GDP to our first regression. This variable is negatively related to the size of the largest city. An increase of 10 percent in the share of trade in GDP leads to a reduction of 6 percent in the size of the main city. Alternatively, a one-standard-deviation increase in the share of trade in GDP reduces the size of the main city by about 13 percent. This result supports Krugman and Livas' [1992] theory against the alternative hypothesis that big cities grow as a result of commerce and trade.

The third regression in Table IV shows our first political variable. This dictatorship dummy (based on Gastil's index of political rights) assigns a value of one to countries that do not protect political rights. Since our predictions about dictatorship occur because dictatorships ignore the political rights of their citizens, this measure is good for our purposes. Adding this dictatorship dummy to our list of controls, we find that dictatorships have main cities that are about 45 percent larger than main cities in countries with nondictatorial regimes.[12] We deal with the possible endogeneity of the trade and dictatorship variables in Tables VI and VII.

Region dummies are generally excluded from our regressions because we want to include the information contained in interregional variation, but to check robustness, we include region dummies in regression (4). Our three main variables of interest remain significant and large, although the coefficients on trade and

11. This variable was chosen instead of the share of the population in manufacturing to increase sample size. Using a pure manufacturing variable for a smaller subsample of countries did not change the results.

12. Our results are not particularly sensitive to the choice of the cutoff point in the Gastil index for deciding whether a country is a democracy or a dictatorship. More detailed examination of the data suggests a slightly nonlinear relationship between city size and political rights, where countries in the [4,5) interval have, other things equal, the largest central cities. While our results do not change if we use a nonlinear continuous dictatorship variable, we find our dummy variable easier to interpret. Our cutoff of three follows Perotti [1991].

politics fall by about a quarter. The coefficient on the Latin American dummy is positive and indicates that countries in this region have main cities that are 40 percent larger than those of other countries.

In regression (5) we add a second political variable to regression (4). The New democracy dummy was constructed using data from Banks [1973], which contains data for a wide cross-section of countries going back to 1815. This variable takes a value of one if the country in question did not have a well-functioning and efficient Parliament at the time it became independent, but was a democracy between 1970 and 1985.[13] This New democracy dummy is intended to capture the effect of political history on the size of the central city. Regression (5) shows that among the democracies in our sample, those that were dictatorships in the past have central cities that are 40 percent larger than those of countries that were always democracies.

The final regression in Table IV includes the average number of revolutions and coups as a regressor, and an interaction between this variable and the dictatorship dummy to the previous set of regressors. We find that political instability substantially increases city size in democracies. In those regimes one extra revolution or coup per year increases the average size of the central city by 2.4 percent. In dictatorial regimes political instability does not change the main city size.

The first three regressions in Table V examine the trade-city size connection more closely. Regression (7) includes a tariff variable: the ratio of import duties to total imports.[14] We find that imports duties do indeed expand the size of the primary city. A 1 percent increase in the ratio of import duties to imports raises the size of the central city by almost 3 percent. The import duty effect remains important when we control for the quantity of trade and dictatorship in regressions (8) and (9).

Regression (10) includes the share of government expenditures spent on transportation and communications for a small subset of our sample (50 countries). A 1 percent increase in the share of GDP spent on government transportation reduces main city size by 10 percent. This evidence supports Krugman [1991]:

13. For those countries that were never a colony or that became independent before 1815, we used the 1850 observation if available or the 1900 one.

14. We also used an alternative measure provided in Lee [1992], who uses the actual average tariff rate on imported inputs, intermediate, and capital goods in or around 1980. This variable (which was available for a subsample of 67 countries) also entered strongly positive and significant in our regressions.

TABLE V

Dependent variable: log of average population in main city (1970–1985)	(7)	(8)	(9)	(10)	(11)	(12)
Intercept	3.015	3.768	3.128	2.475	2.2792	1.752
	(0.927)	(1.059)	(0.992)	(0.823)	(0.8010)	(0.8224)
Dummy for capital city	0.445	0.460	0.375	0.566	0.5190	0.4592
	(0.214)	(0.209)	(0.180)	(0.244)	(0.2151)	(0.2146)
Log of average nonurbanized population	0.491	0.456	0.498	0.191	0.1547	0.2259
	(0.075)	(0.075)	(0.072)	(0.112)	(0.1160)	(0.1064)
Log of average urbanized population outside the main city	0.091	0.097	0.092	0.504	0.6071	0.5312
	(0.056)	(0.051)	(0.049)	(0.110)	(0.1228)	(0.1154)
Log of land area	0.176	0.162	0.124	0.115	0.0039	0.0228
	(0.063)	(0.060)	(0.061)	(0.070)	(0.0778)	(0.0734)
Log of average real GDP per capita	0.686	0.676	0.825	0.217	0.2478	0.4488
	(0.114)	(0.112)	(0.129)	(0.129)	(0.1342)	(0.1418)
Import duties/imports	2.942	2.909	2.733			
	(1.424)	(1.415)	(1.212)			
Share of trade in GDP		−0.535	−0.512			
		(0.342)	(0.303)			
Dictatorship dummy based on Gastil's index of political rights			0.444			0.4581
			(0.177)			(0.2206)
Share of government transportation and communication expenditures to GDP				−10.481	−10.320	−8.624
				(5.717)	(4.8250)	(4.293)
Roads density in 1970					−0.00036	−0.00023
					(0.00016)	(0.00015)
Number of observations	70	70	70	50	50	50
Adjusted R^2	0.77	0.78	0.79	0.84	0.85	0.86

Note. See Table IV. The 1970 observation is missing for Import duties and Government transportation and communication expenditures.

high internal transport costs create an incentive for the concentration of economic activity in space. Regression (11) further examines the role of transportation costs using the density of roads in 1970 (from Canning and Fay [1993]). The coefficient on the initial density of roads in the country is negative (and the coefficient on government spending stays negative) further indicating that well-developed transport facilities lower the size of central cities. The last regression in Table V controls for possibly omitted political effects and shows that the transportation expenditures are robust to controlling for political effects.

Tests for Causality

Like most of our variables, transport spending is endogenous. Similar caveats apply to our trade and dictatorship variables. Concentration of population in a single city might give local firms a transport cost advantage over foreign suppliers and thus lower the amount of foreign trade. Dictators' coups might be easier in spatially concentrated countries.

To examine the results of Table IV more closely, Table VI reproduces regression (3) but allows for the possibility that trade and the dictatorship dummy are endogenously determined. We use three sets of instruments to examine how exogenous changes in the share of trade in GDP and the type of political regime alter the size of the main city.

(1) Regional Political Characteristics: following Ades and Chua [1993] we use the average number of revolutions and coups in neighboring countries, the average number of per capita political assassinations in neighboring countries, and a dummy variable that takes a value of one if the average Gastil index of political rights in neighboring countries is higher than three.

(2) Predetermined Political Characteristics: we use the 1960 value of an index of ethnolinguistic fractionalization in the country (from Taylor and Hudson [1972]), and a dummy variable that takes a value of one if the country became independent after the end of World War II.

(3) Regional Infrastructure: we use the average road density in neighboring countries (from Canning and Fay [1993]).

Our identifying assumptions are that these variables affect politics and trade but do not change urban structure directly. We test these assumptions using a Wu-Hausman test of the overidentifying restrictions for the system of equations and find that our assumptions pass these tests.

Regression (13) repeats regression (3) using our instrumental-variables approach. The coefficient on the dictatorship dummy remains significant and large. A 1 percent increase in the probability of having a dictatorship increases the size of the central city by about 1.8 percent. The coefficient on the share of trade in GDP is

TABLE VI

Dependent variable: log of average population in main city (1970–1985)	(13) 2SLS	(14) 2SLS
Intercept	−0.738	1.919
	(2.607)	(1.512)
Dummy for capital city	0.065	0.383
	(0.366)	(0.233)
Log of average nonurbanized population	0.710	0.565
	(0.146)	(0.086)
Log of average urbanized population outside the main city	0.047	0.066
	(0.056)	(0.042)
Log of land area	0.003	0.051
	(0.103)	(0.031)
Log of average real GDP per capita	0.472	0.194
	(0.289)	(0.175)
Share of labor outside of agriculture	3.240	2.672
	(0.909)	(0.638)
Share of trade in GDP	−0.361	−1.017
	(1.197)	(0.857)
Dictatorship dummy based on Gastil's index of political rights	1.788	0.511
	(0.901)	(0.291)
Number of observations	85	85
Adjusted R^2	0.69	0.82
R^2 of regression of residuals on instruments	+0.063	+0.02
p-value of restrictions	0.75	0.75

Note. See Table IV. In regressions (13) and (14) the Dictatorship dummy and the Share of trade in GDP are treated as endogenous. The instruments that we used are the average number of revolutions and coups in neighboring countries, the average number of per capita political assassinations in neighboring countries, a dummy variable that takes a value of one if the average Gastil index of political rights in neighboring countries is higher than three and zero otherwise, the 1960 value of the ethnic heterogeneity index, a dummy variable that takes a value of one if the country became independent after the end of World War II and zero otherwise, and the average road density in neighboring countries. In regression (14) we add two generated instruments to our list of controls: these are the fitted values obtained from running a PROBIT for the Dictatorship dummy and a TOBIT for the Share of trade on all the exogenous variables in the system. The p-values for the test of the overidentifying restrictions are obtained by running the residuals from the second stage regression on all the instruments. The obtained R^2 multiplied by the number of observations is distributed as a χ^2 with j degrees of freedom, where j is the number of instruments minus the number of instrumented variables.

negative and smaller than the estimates obtained with OLS. Regression (14) adds to our list of instruments the fitted values obtained from running a PROBIT for the Dictatorship Dummy and a TOBIT for the Share of Trade on all the exogenous variables in the system. This specification improves the precision of the first stage regression by improving the functional form. The coefficient on the dictatorship dummy now falls to a level consistent with our previous OLS estimates. The coefficient on trade, while negative and large, is still not estimated precisely.

Instrumental variables provide one approach to causality. Timing provides another approach. The first three regressions in Table VII examine causality using the correlation of initial variables with later changes. This test for causality is imperfect, but at

TABLE VII

Dependent variable:	Change in the share of trade to GDP 1970–1985 (15)	Dictatorship dummy in 1985 (PROBIT) (16)	Growth of population in main city 1970–1985 (17)	Per capita GDP growth 1970–1985 (18)
Intercept	0.380	−0.532	0.0687	−0.046
	(0.292)	(3.496)	(0.0293)	(0.042)
Log of population in main city in 1970	−0.012	0.310	−0.008	
	(0.025)	(0.373)	(0.005)	
Log of nonurbanized population in 1970	−0.007	−0.275	0.0059	
	(0.025)	(0.317)	(0.0036)	
Log of urbanized population outside the main city in 1970	−0.001	−0.0007	−0.0004	
	(0.007)	(0.116)	(0.0006)	
Log real per capita GDP in 1970	−0.054	−1.178	0.0060	−0.005
	(0.052)	(0.481)	(0.0057)	(0.006)
Share of the labor force outside of agriculture in 1970	0.306	−0.545	−0.044	0.071
	(0.174)	(1.910)	(0.025)	(0.028)
Dictatorship dummy in 1970	−0.009	1.103	0.0133	0.004
	(0.046)	(0.436)	(0.0051)	(0.005)
Share of trade in GDP in 1970	−0.425	1.599	0.0615	−0.0137
	(0.205)	(1.397)	(0.0140)	(0.014)
Growth of urbanized population outside of main city 1970–1985			0.035	
			(0.093)	
Share of total population in main city in 1970				−0.083
				(0.034)
Urbanization outside main city in 1970				−0.055
				(0.023)
Log of total population in 1970				0.003
				(0.002)
Secondary school enrollment in 1970				0.028
				(0.015)
Number of observations	85	85	85	85
Adjusted R^2	0.10	0.49	0.55	0.23

Note. White-corrected standard errors are in parentheses.

least we can see whether large central cities push countries into dictatorship or whether dictatorships expand central cities. The timing of the relationship between country variables and urban concentration shows what predates what (if not what causes what).

Regression (15) looks at the effect of the spatial distribution of population on the change in the share of trade in GDP. We find no effect of main city size on trade growth. In regression (16) the dependent variable is the dictatorship dummy for 1985, controlling for the dictatorship dummy in 1970. This regression captures the effect of initial urban concentration on the probability of being a dictatorship in 1985, conditional on being a dictatorship in 1970. We find no evidence for large central cities causing a switch to dictatorship or preventing a switch away from dictatorship. Regression (17) makes the growth rate of population in the main city between 1970 and 1985 the dependent variable. The role of dictatorships here is critical: the presence of a dictatorship increased the growth rate of population in the main city by 1.3 percent a year. Trade has a weak or nonexistent effect.

Regression (18) suggests that concentration in a single city also has strong effects on growth. A 1 percent increase in the share of total population living in the central city reduces the growth rate by 0.08 percent per year. Large cities generate rent-seeking and instability, not long-term economic growth.

The results of this section support the idea that dictatorship causes urban centralization. Tests based on both instrumental variables and the timing of growth indicate that dictatorship influences urban development. Our evidence does not confirm any causal relationship between trade and city size.

V. Short Case Studies

V.1. Rome, 50 B.C.E.

At its height, Rome's population probably stood at over 1,000,000 inhabitants, or approximately 2 percent of the empire's population. Earlier cities had been large, but none had never grown to one half that size.[15] While there is dispute over Rome's popula-

15. Ur reached a population of approximately 24,000 around 2800 B.C. Babylon may have had as many as 300,000 inhabitants under Hammurabi in 1700 B.C. According to Bairoch [1988], Alexandria (the largest Hellenic city) never exceeded a population of 320,000. India and China had big population centers several centuries before the common era. All of these centers were associated with extremely powerful empires. Bairoch stresses the role of international trade in supporting these cities. However, as much as Babylon was a trading city, it was even

tion and over the period of Rome's greatest growth, in this discussion we accept Garnsey's [1988] population figures and his claim that the period 130–50 B.C.E. is the period of Rome's greatest expansion, when its population grew from 375,000 to 1,000,000.[16] During this period, five distinct political events directly and indirectly increased the incentives to come to Rome: (1) the empire expanded into Gaul and the eastern provinces of Asia: Bithynia, Pontus, Cilicia, and Syria; (2) Pompey declared that all conquered land was the property of the city's government; (3) the Gracchis' Sempronian law and then the Clodian law extended the grain distribution to a large number of the citizens as long as they came to Rome; (4) Sulla extended Roman citizenship to all of the inhabitants of Italy; and (5) internecine warfare made the hinterland fundamentally unsafe. As a result of events (3) and (4), by 46 B.C. E. 320,000 people were in Rome receiving grain handouts.

The first two events mentioned above were the result of successful Roman military leadership, impressive military technology, and the remarkable incentives (ranging from great wealth to control over the world's largest empire) offered to reward military success. Events (3)–(5) are related to internal Roman weakness. The traditional aristocracy was forced during this period, first by the Gracchis and later by popular uprisings, to distribute grain more liberally to Roman citizens.[17] The expansion of citizenship throughout the Italian peninsula was the result of the Roman failure (under the leadership of Gaius Marius) to reject the demands of the Italian rebels in 90 B.C.E., despite these rebels' defeat in the Social Wars. Weak control over local mobs and local revolts coupled with strong control over distant empires enabled Roman mobs to extract rents (indirectly via the legions) from

more a center of taxation and tribute. Herodotus estimates that two-thirds of Babylon's revenues came from non-Assyrian provinces. Babylon's main function was as a base for military force and political stability, not as a center for trade.

16. Rome's population is disputed. Bairoch estimates the population at about 800,000 by the second century A.D. based (in part) on the list of recipients of state grain (Garnsey also uses this source to get estimates at over one million). In contrast, using structural densities as an estimation device, Russell [1985] provides us with a lower bound of approximately 200,000 at the height of Imperial Rome. While there are problems with any estimate, the mass of evidence (ranging from the structural expansion of Rome in this period to the eyewitness discussions of overcrowding during the 130–50 B.C.E. period) suggest that Rome was growing rapidly during the late Republic.

17. The grain distributions were not completely egalitarian. Some fee was required for the distribution (under the earlier Sempronian Law but not under the later Clodian Law), and slaves and others of the poor were excluded. But the grain was essentially a dole meant to appease the politically active elements of Rome. See Scullard [1959].

distant Egypt and Spain. The Roman empire delivered rents not just to the Proconsuls of the territories but also to the general population of the capital. Most visible of all these rents being transferred from the conquered province to the masses of Rome were the circuses (and other games) which cost fortunes to produce and were put on (at their height) more than 50 times per year.

Eventually, Julius Caesar restored stability and reduced the grain distribution around 45 B.C.E. The growth of Rome then began to slow. Rome's growth illustrates how an ability to extract from the hinterland and an inability to quell revolts at home together lead toward overconcentration in the capital. While other factors also played an important role (Rome had both trade and industry), Rome's huge unemployment and underemployment levels, and the overwhelming size of the state's bureaucratic, military, and redistributional systems make it clear that Rome's size was, ultimately, a result of government size and transfers. The timing of Rome's expansion suggests that liberal grain distributions funded by foreign conquests fueled Rome's growth.

V.2. London, 1670 C.E.

For almost 1200 years after Rome's disintegration in the fifth century C.E., Europe had only two cities with 400,000 or more inhabitants: Byzantium, with a population of between 400,000 and 600,000 from 600–1000 C.E., and Cordoba with a population of approximately 400,000 in 1000 C.E. [Bairoch 1988]. The first strictly European metropolises to come close to 500,000 inhabitants were London and Paris around 1700. While the first British population census with data for London is in 1801 (giving London a population of 960,000), Wrigley [1986] has earlier estimates that seem consistent with the numbers given by Bairoch, Braudel [1979], and others. His estimates for London's population are 55,000 in 1520 (or 2.25 percent of England's population), 200,000 in 1600 (or 5 percent), and 475,000 in 1670 (or 9.5 percent). London's population continued to rise after 1670, and as a share of England's population it peaked at 11 percent in 1700.[18]

While the rise of textile production in London in the late sixteenth century did coincide with the period of the city's growth,

18. A particularly striking feature of London's growth between 1600 and 1670 is the dominance of deaths over births. Wrigley and Schofield [1981] report that London had 600,000 more burials than baptisms between 1600 and 1675. Given a natural deficit of this magnitude, net migration to the capital must have been more than 875,000 people.

it seems that London's rising control over these goods indicates the increasing importance of trade, not any causal role play by textile technology. This rise in trade is one explanation of London's growth. The late sixteenth century saw innovations in both internal and external trade. Kerridge [1988] argues that the four-wheel cart (a major innovation introduced in 1558) made transport much cheaper within England and increased London's role as a center of internal commerce. International trade grew because of military victories against the Spanish, improvement in shipping technology, the discovery of vast new markets in Asia and the Americas, and rising government support for trade. The London transport industry also benefited from the massive emigration to the New World [Borer 1977].

Some of the trade-related factors were actually political. The ability of England to subdue Spain and acquire goods from the hinterland reflects political strength outside the capital. The allocation of rents to local trade monopolies represents Stuart weakness at home. London's growth was also closely related to political factors. Despite the unusual English system of local justice, the centralization of military power and financial strength in the hands of Parliament and the King in the city of London made England the European nation with the most centralized political structure and the most control over its provinces [Brewer 1990].

Several Tudor monarchs, (Henry VII, Henry VIII and Elizabeth I) were strong and semidictatorial, but Stuart (James I and Charles I) disregard for the rights of Parliament, which represented the hinterland, was particularly blatant. Stuart instability is also easily seen: Charles I lost his throne and his head in the Civil War. As in our model, these dictators responded to instability by collecting more income from the weak provincial areas and relatively less from the dangerous capital. Examples of Stuart redistribution from provinces to capital include James I's novel imposition of naval taxes (ship moneys) on the hinterland. James I also re-created trade monopolies (which had been eliminated by Elizabeth I) and allocated them to the great London merchants. Stuart mercantilism can be seen as a policy of enriching the capital's traders and producers at the expense of the hinterland's consumers [Ekelund and Tollison 1981]. Instability also increased London's size because the mid-seventeenth century civil war made much of the hinterland unsafe. It is unclear whether London's growth was more strongly based on trade or politics. We believe that the evidence points to the importance of both factors.

V.3. Edo, 1700 C.E.

While both Paris and London appeared like colossi upon the map of Europe in 1700, neither city was nearly as big as the Asian capitals of China and Japan. Peking had reached a population of 600,000 by 1500, and was the largest city in the world until London surpassed it in 1830. Japan's capital, Edo (modern Tokyo), was almost as large as Peking in 1700 in absolute population and much larger relative to Japan's much smaller population. Excluding military personnel, Edo's population in 1700 lay between 500,000 [Sansom 1963] and one million [Seidensticker 1980], or between 2 and 4 percent of Japan's population. The high productivity of rice economies has been the traditional explanation of Asian urbanization, but while this nutritional edge might explain urbanization in general, it does not explain concentration in a single city. The period of Edo's greatest growth was between 1580, when Edo was a castle surrounded by a village, and 1700, when it was the second largest city in the world.

Edo's growth derives from its establishment as the Shogunal capital by Tokugawa Ieyasu. Ieyasu (along with Odo Nobunaga and Hideyoshi) unified Japan in the late sixteenth century. Over the seventeenth century Ieyasu's descendants amassed a monopoly of political and economic power far beyond that of any European king. By 1690 the Shogun had rice revenues of 14.68 million *koku*, approximately half of the country's produce and more than six times the Shogun's revenues in 1598.[19] The Tokugawa shoguns stripped rival chieftains of their authority and limited the power of the samurai (following the path of Hideyoshi and his great sword hunt). At the end of the civil war, 100,000 *ronin* (unemployed soldiers) were left lordless; many of these were induced to come to the military capital. The *daimyo* (local lords) and the shogunate cut soldiers off from their local power bases and encouraged samurai to take their feudal dues as annuities and move elsewhere (mainly to the capital) [Sansom 1963]. Despite the power of the Shogun, some instability (such as the Shimabara uprisings of 1638–1639) remained in the hinterland and further encouraged people to move to the safety of the capital.

There is some support for the Krugman-Livas trade hypothesis in the story of Edo. The Tokugawa shoguns excluded Christians

19. This should be compared with a national production of 25 million *koku* and with the nutritional needs of one Japanese of one *koku* per year. This means that 2.56 million people could be fed by the rice revenues owed to Ieyasu alone.

from Japan in 1638, lowered the importance of foreign trade and thus damaged Edo's rival, the international trade center of Nagasaki. Anticommercial attitudes of the *Bakufu* (the Shogunate) also limited the rise of Osaka (the leading commercial center). The anti-industrial bias of the leadership further prevented any other cities growing from the development of local industries. Japan does not display the Roman combination of strength abroad and weakness in the capital—the Shogunate was strong everywhere. However, the sheer power of the central Japanese government created such a disproportionate amount of employment, safety, and wealth in Edo that the city became an urban giant.

V.4. Buenos Aires, 1900 C.E.

Latin American nations, such as Chile, Mexico, Peru, and Uruguay are often heavily concentrated in their central cities. The first of these Latin American urban giants was Buenos Aires. By 1914 Buenos Aires was the largest urban agglomeration south of New York City with 1.6 million inhabitants (20 percent of Argentina's population). Although Buenos Aires had been growing for 250 years before 1887 (and has not stopped during the 80 years since 1914), the 27 years between 1887 and 1914 mark the period when the city grew most. Over those 25 years the city grew by more than 1.1 million people (an increase of 265 percent).

Industry did not play a prominent role in the rise of Buenos Aires. In 1914 less then 15 percent of the Argentine labor force was involved in manufacturing activities. The Argentine government displayed hostility toward manufacturing and innovation (examples include heavy tariffs on manufactured exports and the absence of effective patent protection). By comparison, trade expanded heavily over this period. Total exports rose 400 percent between 1887 and 1914 (measured in gold pesos, cattle, or sheep). Approximately 20 percent of Argentina's population (and a much higher percentage of Buenos Aires' population) was involved in commerical activities.

The growth of Buenos Aires came from its role as a commercial center and from its role as a center for migration. The city expanded with almost even increases in native population and immigrants. The share of immigrants in Buenos Aires' population (mostly of Italian and Spanish origin) was 52.4 percent in 1887 and 49.6 percent in 1914. From 1905 to 1909 immigrants to Argentina, almost entirely coming through Buenos Aires, totaled around one million. Between 1887 and 1914 approximately 550,000 out of three million immigrants to Argentina stayed in Buenos Aires. Buenos Aires retained a larger proportion of its immigrants than its new world rival, New York, possibly because of: (1) undeveloped transportation facilities within the hinterland; (2) the absence of any other important pre-existing urban centers or industry in the hinterland; (3) a decline in the demand for labor in the hinterland as agriculture was consolidated into large firms that replaced labor with capital; and (4) instability in the hinterland coming from wars and unfriendly relations with the native Americans.

Politics also played a role in Buenos Aires' growth. In 1914, 95 percent of government revenues came from tariffs. Scobie [1974] suggests that this heavy dependence on port-related income induced the government to keep its activities in Buenos Aires, the source of its wealth. The heavy dependence on tariffs created an incentive for the government to support trade and Buenos Aires at the expense of industry and the hinterland. The large share of government revenues that came from tariffs also created a stunning array of regulations open to interpretation by local officials. Unsurprisingly, this created tremendous opportunities for bribery or *coima*. An estimate by Scobie puts bribery in Argentina at about 25 percent of government revenues. This kind of personalized corruption greatly increased the need to be close to the officials administering the tariffs.[20] Like London, Buenos Aires was a center for international movements of goods and capital (both human and physical), but the concentration of government and bureaucratic corruption also played a prominent role.

V.5. Mexico City, Today

Mexico City (*née* Tenochtitlan) dates from the fourteenth and fifteenth centuries, when it was built as the center for the Aztec empire. Both the Aztecs and later the Spaniards extracted as much wealth as possible from surrounding provinces and spent that wealth either in the city or sent it elsewhere (i.e., Spain). Despite a limited role as a center for trade (e.g., the Manila Galleons), premodern Mexico was ultimately a collector of rents. Mexico City remained a small rent-seeking capital until after World War II. In 1900 when Buenos Aires had already reached preeminence, Mexico

20. Along with this concentration around revenues, came other governmental actions that increased the size of Buenos Aires. Massive public works programs were associated with the celebration of the one-hundredth anniversary of Argentina's independence from Spain in 1910. Streetcar mileage increased fourfold between 1887 and 1914. There was no corresponding increase in public investment in the hinterland.

City had 470,000 inhabitants. By 1940 the city had 1.5 million people. By 1970 this number had swelled to 8.5 million (in the metropolitan area), and today Mexico City's population has reached 18 million.

As Krugman and Livas argue, trade did not play a role in the growth of Mexico City. The city grew as a center for manufacturing. Mexico's industrial expansion was heady in the 1945–1970 period. Industrial real wages increased by 250 percent over this period. Manufacturing employment expanded by 2.3 million (120 percent). The federal district's (Mexico City and its environs) share of manufacturing employment grew from 25 percent in 1950 to over 40 percent in 1960 and back down to 30 percent in 1970. Employment in the service sector expanded by 1.2 million (600 percent). Agricultural employment actually declined over the 1960–1970 period.

Industrial growth was concentrated in Mexico City because the capital was the major market for most goods as well as the major supplier (Krugman and Livas' thesis). Mexico's industrialization followed the big-push-type pattern [Murphy, Shleifer, and Vishny 1989]; urban concentration facilitated the coordination of demand and supply. Import-substitution policies made it more necessary for consumers (especially firms consuming intermediate inputs) to locate in Mexico City close to domestic suppliers because foreign suppliers were excluded from the country. Industrial growth also thrived in the capital because Mexico City was the center for foreign capital and ideas.

Political factors behind Mexico's concentration were also quite strong. Mexico has a nominally federal government, but all real power is concentrated in the capital. Even regional governors spend most of their time within the capital out of fear of losing political influence [Kandell 1988]. The Mexican government is also particularly susceptible to unrest in the capital. Kandell describes a typical episode of rural-urban migrants coming to the outskirts of the central city and beginning as squatters on the land. These migrants then choose a political leader or *cacique* who agitates against the leading party (the PRI). The government responds by giving the migrants title to the land and providing them with some kind of minimal infrastructure (paid for with taxes levied on the country as a whole). The migrants then become loyal supporters of the PRI. This model of an oligarchic regime paying off local rioters with transfers seized from remote regions of the country is highly reminiscent of Rome. It suggests that politics, as well as trade, contributed to Mexico City's size.

VI. Conclusion

Krugman and Livas' [1992] hypothesis that urban concentration is negatively related to international trade is borne out in the data. Good internal transportation infrastructure also decreases urban concentration. However, our time series and instrumental-variables results cast doubt on the causality in these correlations. Trade and cities are connected, but it may be that urban concentration is causing low levels of trade, not that low levels of trade induce concentration.

Our political results are stronger than our results on trade. They display a robust causality running from dictatorship to urban centralization. Urban giants ultimately stem from the concentration of power in the hands of a small cadre of agents living in the capital. This power allows the leaders to extract wealth out of the hinterland and distribute it in the capital. Migrants come to the city because of the demand created by the concentration of wealth, the desire to influence the leadership, the transfers given by the leadership to quell local unrest, and the safety of the capital. This pattern was true in Rome, 50 B.C.E., and it is still true in many countries today.

Appendix

In the 85-country sample	Not in 70-sample	Not in 50-sample
Algeria	*	*
Benin	*	*
Burundi		*
Cameroon		*
Central African Republic	*	*
Chad	*	*
Egypt		
Ethiopia		
Ghana		
Ivory Coast	*	*
Kenya		
Liberia		
Madagascar	*	*
Malawi		
Mali		**

APPENDIX
(CONTINUED)

In the 85-country sample	Not in 70-sample	Not in 50-sample
Morocco		
Niger	*	
Nigeria	*	
Rwanda		
Senegal	*	*
Sierra Leone		*
Somalia	*	*
Sudan		*
Tanzania		*
Togo	*	*
Tunisia		
Uganda		
Zaire		*
Zambia		
India		*
Israel		*
Japan		*
Jordan		
Korea		
Malaysia		*
Nepal		
Pakistan		
Philippines		
Saudi Arabia	*	*
Sri Lanka		
Syria		*
Thailand		
Austria		
Belgium		
Denmark		
Finland		
France		
Germany		
Greece		
Ireland		*
Italy		
Netherlands	*	
Norway		
Portugal		*
Spain		
Switzerland		*
Turkey		
United Kingdom	*	
Canada		
Costa Rica		
Dominican Republic		*

APPENDIX
(CONTINUED)

In the 85-country sample	Not in 70-sample	Not in 50-sample
El Salvador		
Guatemala		
Haiti		*
Honduras		
Jamaica		*
Mexico		
Nicaragua		
Panama		
United States		
Argentina		*
Bolivia		*
Brazil		*
Chile		
Colombia		*
Ecuador		
Paraguay		
Peru		*
Uruguay		
Venezuela		
Australia		*
Burkina Faso		
Yemen	*	
Indonesia		

GOLDMAN, SACHS, & CO.
HARVARD UNIVERSITY

REFERENCES

Ades, Alberto, and Hak Bin Chua, "Thy Neighbor's Curse: Regional Instability and Economic Growth," Harvard mimeo, 1993.

Bairoch, P., *Cities and Economic Development* (Chicago: University of Chicago Press, 1988).

Banks, A. S., *Cross-National Time Series, 1815–1973* (Ann Arbor, MI: Inter-University Consortium for Political and Social Research, 1976).

Barro, Robert, and H. Wolf, "Data for Economic Growth in a Cross-Section of Countries," NBER working paper, 1989.

Borer, M., *The City of London* (London: Constable, 1977).

Braudel, F., *Civilization and Capitalism* (New York: Harper & Row, 1979).

Brewer, J. *The Sinews of Power* (Cambridge: Harvard University Press, 1990).

Canning, David, and Marianne Fay, "The Effect of Transportation Networks on Economic Growth," Discussion Paper, Columbia University, 1993.

De Long, B., and A. Shleifer, "Princes and Merchants: European City Growth before the Industrial Revolution, *Journal of Law and Economics* XXXVI (1993), 671–702.

Ekelund, R., and R. Tollison, *Mercantilism as a Rent-Seeking Society* (College Station: Texas A & M University Press, 1981).

Garnsey, P., *Famine and Food Supply in the Graeco-Roman World* (Cambridge: Cambridge University Press, 1988).
Gastil, R., *Freedom in the World* (Westport, CT: Greenwood Press, 1987).
Glaeser, E. L., H. D. Kallal, J. A. Scheinkman, and A. Shleifer, "Growth in Cities," *Journal of Political Economy*, C (1992), 1126–53.
Henderson, J. V., "A Framework for International Comparisons of Systems of Cities," *Urban and Regional Report* No. 80-3 (Washington, DC: World Bank, 1980).
____, *Economic Theory and the Cities* (New York: Academic Press, 1986).
Hoselitz, B., "Generative and Parasitic Cities," *Economic Development and Cultural Change*, III (1955), 278–94.
Kandell, J., *La Capital: The Biography of Mexico City* (New York: Henry Holt, 1988).
Kerridge, E., *Trade and Banking in Early Modern England* (Manchester, England: Manchester University Press, 1988).
Krugman, P., "Increasing Returns and Economic Geography," *Journal of Political Economy*, XCIX (1991), 483–99.
Krugman, P., and R. Livas, "Trade Policy and the Third World Metropolis," NBER working paper No. 4238, 1992.
Lee, Jong-Wha, "International Trade, Distortions and Long-Run Economic Growth," Harvard mimeo, 1992.
Murphy, K., A. Shleifer, and R. Vishny, "Industralization and the Big Push," *Journal of Political Economy*, XCVII (1989) 1003–26.
Olson, Mancur, *The Rise and Decline of Nations: Economic Growth, Stagnation and Social Rigidities* (New Haven, CT: Yale University Press, 1982).
Perotti, Roberto, "Income Distribution and Growth: Theory and Evidence," mimeographed, 1991.
Rosen, K., and M. Resnick, "The Size Distribution of Cities: An Examination of the Pareto Law and Primacy," *Journal of Urban Economics*, VIII (1980), 165–86.
Russell, J. C., *Late Ancient and Medieval Population Control* (Philadelphia: American Philosophical Society, 1985).
Sansom, Sir George Bailey, *A History of Japan* (Stanford: Stanford University Press, 1963).
Scobie, James, *Buenos Aires: Plaza to Suburb, 1870–1910* (New York: Oxford University Press, 1974).
Scullard, H. H., *From the Gracchi to Nero: A History of Rome 133 BC to AD 68* (London, England: Routledge, 1959).
Seidensticker, E., *Low City, High City: Tokyo from Edo to the Great Earthquake* (New York: Knopf, 1981).
Summers, Robert, and Alan Heston, "The Penn World Table (Mark 5): An Expanded Set of International Comparisons, 1950–1988," *Quarterly Journal of Economics*, CVI (1991), 327–68.
Taylor, Charles L., and Michael C. Hudson, *World Handbook of Political and Social Indicators* (Ann Arbor MI: ICPSR, 1972).
von Thünen, Johann Heinrich, *The Isolated State* (Hamburg: Perthes, English translation, 1826; Oxford: Pergamon, 1966).
Wheaton, W., and H. Shishido, "Urban Concentration, Agglomeration Economies and the Level of Economic Development," *Economic Development and Cultural Change*, L (1981), 17–30.
Williamson, Jeffrey, G., "Migration and Urbanization," in Hollis Chenery and T. N. Srinivasan, eds., *Handbook of Development Economics* (Amsterdam, The Netherlands: North-Holland, 1991).
Wrigley, E., "Urban Growth and Agricultural Change: England and the Continent in the Early Modern Period," in R. I. Rotberg and T. K. Rabb, eds., *Population and Economy* (Cambridge: Cambridge University Press, 1986).
Wrigley, E., and R. Schofield, *The Population History of England, 1541–1871: A Reconstruction* (Cambridge: Harvard University Press, 1981).

[13]

POWER COUPLES: CHANGES IN THE LOCATIONAL CHOICE OF THE COLLEGE EDUCATED, 1940–1990*

DORA L. COSTA AND MATTHEW E. KAHN

College educated couples are increasingly located in large metropolitan areas. These areas were home to 32 percent of all college educated couples in 1940, 39 percent in 1970, and 50 percent in 1990. We investigate whether this trend can be explained by increasing urbanization of the college educated or the growth of dual career households and the resulting severity of the colocation problem. We argue that the latter explanation is the primary one. Smaller cities may therefore experience reduced inflows of human capital relative to the past and thus become poorer.

I. INTRODUCTION

Couples in which both husband and wife have at least a college education are increasingly, and disproportionately, located in large metropolitan areas. In 1940 32 percent of all college educated couples were located in metropolitan areas of at least 2 million. By 1970 this figure was 39 percent and by 1990 50 percent. In contrast, there has been little change in the proportion of couples in which neither spouse has a college education in large cities. In 1940 27 percent of these couples were located in large metropolitan areas, and in 1970 30 percent were. By 1990 only 34 percent were.[1]

Two main factors may account for the disproportionate increase in college educated couples' propensity to be in a large city. The college educated, regardless of marital status, may be becoming more urbanized, perhaps because the returns to education in large cities are rising relative to those in small cities or because such urban amenities as access to cultural activities are normal goods.[2] In addition, more of the college educated may now be

* We have benefited from the comments of Edward Glaeser, Claudia Goldin, Lawrence Katz, Michael Kremer, Steven Levitt, Erzo Luttmer, Sendhil Mullainathan, Jörn-Steffen Pischke, James Poterba, Peter Temin, and two anonymous referees and of workshop participants at the University of Chicago, Boston College, Princeton University, Stanford University, and the April 1999 NBER Labor Studies meeting. Dora Costa gratefully acknowledges the support of NIH grant AG12658.

1. Estimated from the integrated public use census samples [Ruggles and Sobeck 1997].

2. Of course, the cost of living in a large metropolitan area is higher rents and, for those living in central cities, such urban disamenities as crime and pollution. However, since 1970 these disamenity costs have been falling [Glaeser 1998; Kahn 1997].

The Quarterly Journal of Economics, November 2000

meeting and marrying in large cities because fewer of their marriages are now formed in high school or college and because more of the single college educated are moving to large cities. If they remain in large cities, the proportion of college educated couples in large cities will increase.

Second, as more households become dual career households, more of them face a colocation problem. All dual career households are more likely to be joint decision makers, and they face the difficulty of finding two jobs commensurate with the skills of each spouse within a reasonable commute from home. In 1940, among couples in which the husband was 25 to 39 and the wife 23 to 37 and in which both had at least a four-year college education, only 20 percent of wives worked. By 1990 73 percent of them were in the labor force.[3] The colocation problem is likely to be particularly severe for the college educated. As documented by Goldin [1997], by 1990 college educated women aspired to careers, not to the jobs held by their counterparts in the 1970s. The resulting colocation problem should lead to the greater concentration of college educated couples in large metropolitan areas because such areas offer many more potential job matches. Furthermore, if the returns to education are greater in larger cities because large cities permit specialization, the financial sacrifice of living in a small relative to a large metropolitan area would be greater for a dual career family than for other household types.

This paper documents trends in locational choice since 1940 between large, midsize, and small cities by household type. We examine whether the long-run trends are most consistent with a worsening of the colocation problem or with the growing urbanization of the college educated. We predict that if colocation is a plausible explanation then dual career households will be disproportionately represented in large cities relative to other couple types. In contrast, if urbanization were the primary explanation, then we should not observe a disproportionate increase in college educated couples in large metropolitan areas relative to college educated singles. We find that colocation is the most likely explanation for the observed trend in locational choice.

Our findings have implications for city growth and for family economics. As skilled professionals are increasingly bundled with an equally skilled spouse, their demand for large cities will

3. Estimated from the integrated public use census samples [Ruggles and Sobeck 1997].

increase. The presence of large numbers of highly skilled workers within a concentrated geographic area may in turn provide positive growth externalities.[4] Smaller cities, particularly those located in low amenity areas, may experience reduced inflows of human capital relative to the past and therefore become poorer. We present some suggestive evidence on the ability of firms in small cities to attract highly skilled workers by examining how the relationship between city size and the quality of university graduate programs has changed since 1970. Colocation increases inequality not only across city size but also among households. Because large cities facilitate the matching of the highly educated and because they enable professional couples to solve their joint location problem, large cities magnify household income inequality. Large cities may also preserve the marriages of dual career households because living in large metropolitan areas with diversified labor markets reduces the degree to which both husband and wife must compromise their individual gains from marriage [Mincer 1978].

II. Trends

We view all households as one of five types: "power" couples in which both spouses have a college education, "part-power" couples in which only one spouse has a college education, "low-power" couples in which neither spouse has a college education, and single households of the college educated and the noncollege educated. We define the college educated as those who have completed four or more years of college in 1940, 1970, and 1980 and those who hold a bachelor's or graduate degree in 1990 (see the Appendix for details). We distinguish between college and noncollege rather than postcollege (more than four years of college completed in 1940, 1970, and 1980 and a graduate degree in 1990), college, and noncollege because the postcollege represent a small proportion of the population and because college educated women experienced greater career growth.[5] We define two individu-

4. This insight has been incorporated in theoretical models [Lucas 1988; Acemoglu 1996] and is supported by empirical investigations of the relationship between wages and average human capital [Heckman, Layne-Farrar, and Todd 1996; Rauch 1993] and local growth and average human capital within a city [Simon 1998; Glaeser, Shleifer, and Scheinkman 1995].

5. The postcollege educated were more likely to have careers in 1970 whereas the college educated were more likely to have "jobs." In 1970 and 1990 couples in which both husband and wife had a postcollege education were more likely to be in a larger rather than a smaller metropolitan area. The growth in power couple

TABLE I
PERCENTAGE OF MARRIAGES BY COUPLE TYPE

	1940	1960	1970	1980	1990
Low-power	90.3	82.5	76.8	67.6	66.2
Part-power	7.3	12.3	14.6	18.4	18.5
Power	2.4	5.2	8.6	14.0	15.3

A power couple is defined as one in which both husband and wife are college graduates, a part-power couple as one in which only one spouse is a college graduate, and a low-power couple as one in which neither spouse is a college graduate. All numbers are estimated from the integrated public use census samples [Ruggles and Sobek 1997] and are for households in which the husband was age 25 to 39 and the wife 23 to 37.

als to be a couple if they are married to each other and are both in the same household. Singles can be either never married, divorced, or widowed. Both couples and singles may be in multifamily households. We examine couples in which the husband was 25 to 39 years of age and the wife 23 to 37. This age restriction allows us to examine couples in the early stages of their careers and also allows us to create a comparable group of singles. We impose the same age restrictions on singles.

II.1. Trends: Power Couple Formation

The proportion of married couples in which both husband and wife have at least a college education has increased from 2 percent in 1940 to 15 percent in 1990 (see Table I). The percentage increase in the proportion of couples in which only one spouse has a college education has been smaller, rising from 7 percent in 1940 to 18 percent in 1990.[6] These increases in the relative proportion of power couples arose largely from greater college attendance rates, which in turn were spurred both by the growth of public universities and of high schools and by the rising economic returns to college.[7]

Rising wives' labor force participation rates have turned couples into true dual career households and increased the fraction of couples with a colocation problem. This is particularly true for power couples because increases in wives' labor force

concentration in large metropolitan areas was slightly more pronounced among the college educated compared with the postcollege educated.

6. Among part-power couples in 1940, the husband was the college educated spouse in 76 percent of all cases. In 1990 he was the college educated spouse in 63 percent of all cases.

7. Although prime-aged women in 1970 gained little direct economic return from their degrees, their indirect gains were considerable because for them college was a marriage market [Goldin 1992].

TABLE II
EMPLOYMENT AND FERTILITY TRENDS BY EDUCATION OF COUPLE

	1940	1960	1970	1980	1990
Wife works (%)					
Low-power	18.1	27.0	36.6	52.3	64.2
Part-power	18.3	22.7	34.5	57.4	70.4
Power	20.1	29.6	43.4	64.8	73.3
Have child (%)					
Low-power	73.1	89.9	90.2	85.9	83.4
Part-power	60.9	86.8	82.7	74.6	72.6
Power	58.0	81.3	72.9	64.4	62.7
Wife works and works full-time (%)					
Low-power	73.6	68.0	64.8	66.8	68.5
Part-power	73.4	65.7	60.5	65.6	68.7
Power	68.1	62.7	58.1	68.1	70.2
Wife works and in traditionally female job (%)					
Power	71.5	71.4	73.2	59.4	42.7

A full-time job is defined as 35 hours or more per week. A traditionally female occupation is defined as one in which women were overrepresented relative to men in 1970; that is, one in which more than 50 percent of all employees age 18 to 64 were women in 1970. All couples are restricted to those in which the husband was 25 to 39 years of age and the wife 23 to 37. All numbers are estimated from the integrated public use census samples [Ruggles and Sobek 1997]. A power couple is defined as one in which both husband and wife are college graduates, a part-power couple as one in which only one spouse is a college graduate, and a low-power couple as one in which neither spouse is a college graduate.

participation rates have been larger among power than among low-power couples (see Table II).[8] The labor force participation rate of power couple wives rose from 20 to 73 percent between 1940 and 1990, whereas the increase for low-power wives was from 18 to 64 percent. Since 1970 the increase in full-time work was greatest among power wives.

Other fundamental economic changes have also increased the costs to a household of picking a city size in which the wife earns relatively little. The proportion of working power couple wives in such traditional female occupations as schoolteacher, nurse, librarian, or social worker fell from 72 to 43 percent between 1940 and 1990. The percentage with at least one child rose to 81 percent in 1960 from 58 percent in 1940, but by 1980 had fallen to 64 percent. Prime-aged college educated women in 1940 generally became schoolteachers upon graduation, leaving the labor force because of

8. Some of the growth in wives' labor force participation rates may arise from the increased propensity of women who aspire to careers to marry [Goldin 1997].

marriage bars. Goldin [1997] describes their experience as "first jobs then family." In contrast the experience of their 1970 counterparts was "first family then jobs." The majority majored in such fields as education and nursing where few men got degrees and upon graduation had been tracked into traditionally female sectors, regardless of their majors. They left the labor force when their first child was born and only reentered when all children were in school. By 1990, and to a lesser extent by 1980, college educated women aspired to "career then family" or "career and family" [Goldin 1997]. Their college majors were similar to men's, and in terms of labor supply parameters they began to resemble men as well, with small wage and income elasticities [Goldin 1990, pp 119–158].

II.2. Trends: Locational Choice

We study trends in household locational choice conditional on marital status and on the education of both spouses. That is, for every year, we estimate

(1) Prob (lives in big city|household type).

Our data come from the 1940 and 1970–1990 integrated public use census samples. We classify the suburbs of central cities as part of the labor market of the central city and create three city size categories: large metropolitan areas (those with populations of at least 2 million), midsize metropolitan areas (those with populations of between 2 million and 250,000), and small and nonmetropolitan areas (metropolitan areas with populations of less than 250,000 and nonmetropolitan areas). Although we document trends from 1940 to 1990, our discussion will emphasize the 1970 to 1990 trends because this was the period of growth in wives' careers. An additional advantage of focusing on this period is that the definition of a metropolitan area was most comparable from 1970 to 1990 and because there is likely to be less measurement error in our classifications of households by educational levels.[9] Details about variable construction and comparability are provided in the Appendix.

Table III illustrates trends in locational choice between large and midsize metropolitan areas and small localities. Note that the

9. College graduation rates are overstated in the 1940 census in part because individuals who went to the preparatory department within a college were enumerated as having gone to college. We thank Claudia Goldin for pointing this out to us.

TABLE III

PROBABILITY OF LOCATIONAL CHOICE BY HOUSEHOLD TYPE

	1940	1970	1980	1990
Conditional on power couple				
Large metropolitan area	0.321	0.391	0.414	0.495
Midsize metropolitan area	0.254	0.313	0.325	0.295
Small and nonmetropolitan area	0.426	0.296	0.261	0.210
Conditional on part-power couple				
Large metropolitan area	0.319	0.362	0.371	0.421
Midsize metropolitan area	0.268	0.326	0.334	0.308
Small and nonmetropolitan area	0.413	0.312	0.295	0.271
Conditional on low-power couple				
Large metropolitan area	0.266	0.301	0.308	0.339
Midsize metropolitan area	0.240	0.299	0.312	0.292
Small and nonmetropolitan area	0.494	0.399	0.380	0.369
Conditional on single, power man				
Large metropolitan area	0.383	0.523	0.512	0.569
Midsize metropolitan area	0.258	0.291	0.295	0.266
Small and nonmetropolitan area	0.358	0.186	0.193	0.165
Conditional on single, power woman				
Large metropolitan area	0.286	0.507	0.499	0.555
Midsize metropolitan area	0.223	0.309	0.308	0.281
Small and nonmetropolitan area	0.491	0.184	0.193	0.164
Conditional on single, low-power man				
Large metropolitan area	0.299	0.442	0.415	0.441
Midsize metropolitan area	0.225	0.297	0.305	0.278
Small and nonmetropolitan area	0.476	0.260	0.280	0.281
Conditional on single, low-power woman				
Large metropolitan area	0.307	0.455	0.430	0.444
Midsize metropolitan area	0.245	0.305	0.313	0.297
Small and nonmetropolitan area	0.448	0.240	0.257	0.260

A power couple is defined as one in which both husband and wife are college graduates, a part-power couple as one in which only one spouse is a college graduate, and a low-power couple as one in which neither spouse is a college graduate. Couples were restricted to those in which the husband was 25 to 39 years of age and the wife 23 to 37. All singles were also in that age range. A power single is a college graduate, while a low-power single is not. Large metropolitan areas are those in which the population was at least 2 million, midsize metropolitan areas as those between 2 million and 250,000, and small as those less than 250,000. Within each year for each household type, the probabilities should sum to one. Estimated from the integrated public use census samples [Ruggles and Sobeck 1997].

probability of a power couple being in a large city rose by 0.174 between 1940 and 1990 and by 0.104 between 1970 and 1990. In contrast, the increase in these probabilities for part-power couples was only 0.102 and 0.059, respectively. For college educated singles the probability of being in a large city rose sharply between 1940 and 1970, but only changed by 0.040 for men and 0.048 for women between 1970 and 1990.

III. Hypotheses and Empirical Methodology

Are power couples urbanizing because they are college educated or because they have a colocation problem? We begin by considering the benefits of being in a large city for different couple types within a single year and whether changes in these factors might account for the trend.

Consider first the advantages of urbanization by couple type. If large metropolitan areas offer higher returns to education and if urban amenities are normal goods, then large metropolitan areas will appeal to the college educated, regardless of marital status. If urban areas offer such singles' amenities as marriage markets, then singles will be more concentrated in large metropolitan areas than couples of the same educational level. The concentration of power couples in large cities will increase if the returns to city size for the college educated are rising, if urban amenities continue to be normal goods, or if more college educated singles are moving to large cities because cities are becoming better marriage markets and are staying there upon marriage. We will run wage regressions to test whether the returns to city size have been rising for the college educated. We find that most of the increasing urbanization of the college educated is explained by increasing returns to city size and not because urban amenities are normal goods. We cannot directly test whether large cities are attracting more college educated singles because they are becoming better marriage markets for the college educated. But, we can provide some evidence on the marriage propensities of the college educated relative to the noncollege educated.

Second, consider the colocation problem. Large metropolitan areas offer both spouses the opportunity to pursue careers. The diversified labor markets of larger cities also insure against health and unemployment shocks to one spouse. All couples face a colocation problem. Because the college educated are more versatile (and can take jobs for which they are overqualified), the colocation problem may be less severe for the college educated. But, because the college educated may be more career oriented or may have more specialized skills, the colocation problem may be severer for the college educated.[10] Large cities offer more potential job matches, so the probability of drawing a good initial match is higher. The probability of drawing good subsequent matches is also higher, and this increased job mobility will lead to greater lifetime wage growth [Topel and Ward 1992]. Furthermore, if the initial match was a poor one, then the probability of drawing a good match on the second try will be higher than in a smaller city. A spouse who knows that the other spouse has these options in a large city can make firm-specific career investments. The long-run financial sacrifice to being in a large city is therefore likely to be smaller. A worsening colocation problem should therefore increase the proportion of couples, particularly power couples, in large cities, but not affect the proportion of singles.

We test whether the increase in the proportion of power couples in large cities is determined by colocation by comparing power couples with other couple types and to singles. Our comparisons with singles are based upon "coincidental" couples. We refer to a coincidental couple as two individuals (one male and one female) coincidentally living in a large metropolitan area. Trends in coincidental couple concentration allow us to analyze trends in the urbanization of the college educated independent of colocation. Suppose that there are 100 single power men and women and that 40 of the men are in large cities and 60 are in small cities and that 60 of the women are in large cities and 40 are in small cities. At most 80 "marriages" could form—40 in large cities and 40 in small cities. The probability of a coincidental couple being in a large city is therefore 0.5. We therefore take our estimates of the probability of a single power man living in city size $s(p_s^{M,P})$ and our estimates of the probability of a single power woman living in city size $s(p_s^{F,P})$ and take the minimum of these probabilities (min $(p_s^{M,P},p_s^{F,P})$). We then estimate the probability that a coincidental couple will be living in a given city size (min $(p_s^{M,P},p_s^{F,P})/\Sigma_s$ min $(p_s^{M,P},p_s^{F,P})$).[11]

Table IV provides a schematic illustration of our strategy to identify the colocation problem of power and low-power couples and the differential colocation problem of power relative to

10. Baumgardner [1988] documents the greater specialization among physicians found in large cities. See Kim [1989] for a model of labor specialization and the size of the labor market.

11. Note that this method assumes that the numbers of single power men and single power women are the same. Although this is a reasonable assumption in most years, in 1940 there were more single unmarried power women because of the low marriage propensities of college educated women.

TABLE IV
CHANGE IN BENEFITS OF LIVING IN A LARGE CITY BY COUPLE TYPE

Couple type	Benefits of living in a large city
1 Power couple	colocation power urbanization power (urban amenities, education)
2 Coincidental power couple	urbanization power singles' amenities (e.g., marriage markets)
3 Double difference (1–2)	colocation power, singles' amenities
4 Low-power couple	colocation low-power urbanization low power (urban amenities)
5 Coincidental low-power couple	urbanization low power singles' amenities
6 Double difference (4–5)	colocation low-power, singles' amenities
7 Triple difference (3–6)	colocation power relative to low-power

A power couple is defined as one in which both husband and wife are college graduates, and a low-power couple as one in which neither spouse is a college graduate. A coincidental power couple consists of two single college educated individuals (one male and one female) coincidentally living in the same city size. A coincidental low-power couple consists of two single noncollege educated individuals (one male and one female) coincidentally living in the same city size.

low-power couples. The increase in power couple concentration in large metropolitan areas could be driven by a worsening colocation problem and the growing urbanization of the college educated. The increase in the concentration of coincidental couples could be driven by the urbanization of power couples or the increased value of singles' amenities (including changes in the value of large urban areas as marriage markets). If the value of singles' amenities has not changed and if urban amenities are of the same value to singles as they are to married couples, then the double difference (the increase in power couple concentration minus the increase in coincidental couples concentration) measures the differential effect of colocation. Note that any differences in the valuation of urban amenities of married couples and singles will not be differenced out. Therefore, an alternative explanation for the increase in power couple relative to power single concentration in large metropolitan areas is the increased amenity value of metropolitan areas to couples. Now consider the case of low-power couples. The increased concentration of low-power couples in large metropolitan areas could arise either from growing urbanization or from colocation. The growing concentration of low-power singles could arise either from growing urbanization or from the growing value of such singles' amenities as a marriage market. If the value of singles' amenities has not changed and if urban amenities are of the same value to singles as they are to married couples, then the double difference (the increase in low-power couple concentration minus the increase in coincidental low-power couple concentration) yields the effect of colocation for low-power couples. Again, differences in the valuation of urban amenities to married couples and to singles will not be differenced out. The triple difference yields the differential effect of colocation for power relative to low-power couples, assuming either that there are no differences in the valuation of urban amenities between married couples and singles or, if there are, that these differences are the same for the college educated as for the noncollege educated.

The triple difference estimate of the differential effect of colocation for power relative to low-power couples can be further refined. Because labor force participation rates of single women are higher than those of married women and because only couples in which the wife works have a colocation problem, we also compare power and low-power couples in which the wife works with coincidental couples in which the woman works and calculate the triple difference. Larger double and triple differences for couples in which the wife works than for all couples would suggest that colocation, not differences in amenity values, determines the concentration of power couples in large metropolitan areas.

IV. Basic Results

Testing the theories requires us to examine differential trends in locational choice by couple type. We present these trends in this section, standardized on race and age. That is, we estimate

(2) Prob (lives in city size s and wife works|household ltype)

(3) Prob (lives in city size s and wife does not work|household type)

for couples and

(4) Prob (lives in city size s and works|household type)

(5) Prob (lives in city size s and does not work|household type)

for singles. For couples these probabilities can be thought of as the outcome of a joint decision between city size and wife's labor force participation. Because of data limitations we cannot unravel whether the low labor force participation rate of wives in smaller cities arises from the choice of these areas by wives with little attachment to the labor force or whether it arises from wife's wage effects of being in a small city.

We estimate the probabilities in equations (2) through (5) by means of a multinomial logit choice model. We use information on what city size category a couple chooses to live in and whether the wife works to create six groups, one each for wife's labor force participation status and the city size category. We then estimate a multinomial logit of the choice of wife's labor force participation and city size as a function of the husband's age and race and the educational attainment of the husband and wife (dummies for less than high school graduate, high school graduate, college graduate, and postcollege graduate with less than high school graduate as the omitted dummy). Thus, defining $P_{s,ww}$ as the probability of being in one of three city sizes s and ww as an indicator equal to one if the wife works, we estimate

$$\log\left(\frac{P_{s,ww}}{P_{s=0,ww=1}}\right) = \beta' X \tag{6}$$

for $s = 1$ to 2 and $ww = 0, 1$ and $s = 0$ and $ww = 0$. We calculate robust standard errors clustering on metropolitan areas (or on the state in the case of nonmetropolitan areas). Finally, we predict the choice of location and wife's labor force participation, $P_{s,ww}$, for a white household in which the husband is 35 years of age and the wife 33 conditional on being a power, part-power, or low-power couple. For single individuals we estimate similar multinomial logit specifications (separately for men and women) except that labor force status is own labor force status and we control only for own characteristics. We then predict locational choice for single, white men age 35 and single, white women age 33 conditional on being a power or a low-power individual and estimate locational choice for coincidental couples.[12] Recall that a coincidental couple consists of two single individuals (one male and one female) coincidentally living in a large metropolitan area.

Table V shows the predicted probabilities, conditional on being a power, part-power, or low-power couple, of locational choice across city sizes and the wife's labor force participation status for a white couple in which the husband was 35 years old and the wife 33. Power couples are leaving nonmetropolitan areas

12. The base group is small or nonmetropolitan area and wife out of the labor force. Our results are robust to the choice of base group.

TABLE V
PREDICTED PROBABILITIES OF LOCATIONAL CHOICE AND WIFE'S LABOR FORCE PARTICIPATION (LFP) STATUS CONDITIONAL ON HOUSEHOLD TYPE

	1940	1970	1980	1990
Conditional on power				
Large metropolitan area, LFP = 1	0.083	0.146	0.255	0.348
Large metropolitan area, LFP = 0	0.264	0.240	0.157	0.141
Midsize metropolitan area, LFP = 1	0.045	0.136	0.206	0.218
Midsize metropolitan area, LFP = 0	0.217	0.183	0.121	0.080
Small and nonmetropolitan area, LFP = 1	0.067	0.142	0.179	0.165
Small and nonmetropolitan area, LFP = 0	0.325	0.152	0.082	0.049
Conditional on part-power				
Large metropolitan area, LFP = 1	0.058	0.092	0.187	0.262
Large metropolitan area, LFP = 0	0.276	0.258	0.179	0.142
Midsize metropolitan area, LFP = 1	0.043	0.101	0.176	0.210
Midsize metropolitan area, LFP = 0	0.226	0.222	0.152	0.097
Small and nonmetropolitan area, LFP = 1	0.064	0.116	0.174	0.205
Small and nonmetropolitan area, LFP = 0	0.333	0.210	0.132	0.084
Conditional on low-power				
Large metropolitan area, LFP = 1	0.048	0.083	0.145	0.200
Large metropolitan area, LFP = 0	0.246	0.205	0.157	0.132
Midsize metropolitan area, LFP = 1	0.044	0.106	0.159	0.191
Midsize metropolitan area, LFP = 0	0.200	0.196	0.152	0.100
Small and nonmetropolitan area, LFP = 1	0.070	0.153	0.196	0.245
Small and nonmetropolitan area, LFP = 0	0.392	0.258	0.190	0.133

All predictions are from a multinomial logit model in which the outcome variables were city size and labor force participation rate. The independent variables were husband's age, age squared, and race; wife's age and age squared, and dummy variables for educational levels (less than high school, high school, college, college plus) of the husband and of the wife. The predictions are for a white couple in which the husband was 35 years old and the wife 33. Robust standard errors ranged from 0.001 to 0.006. Conditional on couple type, the rows should sum to one. Estimated from the integrated public use census samples.

and moving to the largest metropolitan areas. In 1940 39 percent were in nonmetropolitan areas whereas by 1970 the figure was 29 percent and by 1990 21 percent. In 1940 35 percent were in the largest metropolitan areas, and in 1970 39 percent were; whereas in 1990 49 percent were. Power wives' labor force participation rates are lower in larger metropolitan areas in 1970, 1980, and 1990, suggesting that higher returns to city size for college educated husbands are inducing them to leave the labor force.

Power couples are increasingly concentrating in large metropolitan areas relative to part-power or low-power couples. Between 1970 and 1990 the predicted proportion of low-power couples located in nonmetropolitan areas fell only slightly from 41 to 38 percent, and their share in the largest metropolitan areas increased from 29 to 33 percent. The predicted percentage of part-power couples in the largest metropolitan areas rose from 35 to 40 percent.

Table VI presents predictions of locational choice from multinomial logit models for unmarried men and women conditional on their education. Note that between 1940 and 1970 the probability of singles being in a large metropolitan area increased substantially, rising from 29 to 49 percent among power women. Between

TABLE VI
PREDICTED PROBABILITIES OF LOCATIONAL CHOICE, UNMARRIED MEN AND WOMEN, CONDITIONAL ON EDUCATION

	1940	1970	1980	1990
Single, power man				
Large metropolitan area	0.394	0.526	0.518	0.542
Midsize metropolitan area	0.267	0.294	0.291	0.273
Small and nonmetropolitan area	0.339	0.180	0.191	0.185
Single, power woman				
Large metropolitan area	0.289	0.489	0.501	0.534
Midsize metropolitan area	0.230	0.319	0.305	0.291
Small and nonmetropolitan area	0.482	0.192	0.193	0.175
Coincidental power couple				
Large metropolitan area	0.337	0.508	0.510	0.544
Midsize metropolitan area	0.268	0.305	0.296	0.278
Small and nonmetropolitan area	0.395	0.187	0.194	0.178
Single, low-power man				
Large metropolitan area	0.313	0.432	0.406	0.411
Midsize metropolitan area	0.232	0.304	0.305	0.282
Small and nonmetropolitan area	0.454	0.264	0.290	0.308
Single, low-power woman				
Large metropolitan area	0.323	0.420	0.415	0.413
Midsize metropolitan area	0.250	0.316	0.317	0.304
Small and nonmetropolitan area	0.428	0.264	0.269	0.283
Coincidental low-power couple				
Large metropolitan area	0.322	0.425	0.414	0.421
Midsize metropolitan area	0.238	0.308	0.311	0.289
Small and nonmetropolitan area	0.440	0.267	0.274	0.290

All predictions are derived from a multinomial logit model and are for white 35 year old men and white 33 year old women. Within each year for each group the predicted probabilities for singles and coincidental couples should sum to one. The independent variables used in the multinomial logit were age, age squared, race, and educational level. The outcome variables were city size and labor force participation. With the exception of 1940, relatively few individuals were out of the labor force. The results that are presented are the predicted probabilities summed over city size. Robust standard errors ranged from 0.002 to 0.006. Estimated from the integrated public use census samples [Ruggles and Sobeck 1997].

1970 and 1990 changes were much more modest. Among power men the probability of being in a large city rose from 53 to 54 percent. The increase among coincidental couples was from 51 to 54 percent. The probability of low-power men and women being in a large city decreased somewhat, with a decline from 43 to 42 percent among coincidental couples.

We summarize standardized trends in locational choice by couple type, including coincidental couples (see Table VII). Between 1970 and 1990 the probability of power couples being in a

TABLE VII
TRENDS IN PROPENSITY TO LIVE IN GIVEN CITY SIZE, 1970–1990, BY COUPLE TYPE (BASED UPON PREDICTED PROBABILITIES)

	City size		
	Large	Midsize	Small
Differences, 1990–1970			
Power couples (Δ^{P})	0.103	−0.022	−0.081
	(0.007)	(0.006)	(0.006)
Part-power couples (Δ^{PP})	0.054	−0.016	−0.038
	(0.006)	(0.006)	(0.006)
Low-power couples (Δ^{LP})	0.043	−0.011	−0.033
	(0.003)	(0.002)	(0.004)
Coincidental power couple (Δ^{CP})	0.036	−0.027	−0.009
	(0.005)	(0.010)	(0.005)
Coincidental low-power couple (Δ^{CLP})	−0.004	−0.019	0.023
	(0.005)	(0.004)	(0.004)
Power, wife works ($\Delta^{P,W}$)	0.202	0.082	0.023
	(0.004)	(0.004)	(0.005)
Part-power, wife works ($\Delta^{PP,W}$)	0.170	0.109	0.089
	(0.004)	(0.004)	(0.004)
Low-power, wife works ($\Delta^{LP,W}$)	0.117	0.085	0.092
	(0.002)	(0.002)	(0.003)
Power, wife does not work ($\Delta^{P,NW}$)	−0.099	−0.103	−0.103
	(0.005)	(0.005)	(0.006)
Part-power, wife does not work ($\Delta^{PP,NW}$)	−0.116	−0.125	−0.126
	(0.004)	(0.004)	(0.004)
Low-power wife does not work ($\Delta^{LP,NW}$)	−0.073	−0.096	−0.125
	(0.003)	(0.003)	(0.004)
Coincidental power, woman works ($\Delta^{CP,W}$)	0.037	−0.031	−0.006
	(0.007)	(0.007)	(0.006)
Coincidental low-power, woman works ($\Delta^{CLP,W}$)	−0.011	−0.029	0.040
	(0.004)	(0.005)	(0.004)

Differences are in probability units. Probabilities are calculated from Tables V and VI, except for coincidental couples in which the woman works. These were calculated by using the multinomial logit predictions for working women only.

large metropolitan area rose by 0.103, whereas that of part-power, low-power, and coincidental power couples being in a large city rose by 0.054, 0.043, and 0.036, respectively. The increase in coincidental couple concentration suggests that at most 35 percent of the increase in power couple concentration in large cities is attributable to the growing urbanization of the college educated. Among power couples in which the wife works, the probability of being in a large city rose by 0.202; whereas among power couples in which the wife does not work, this probability fell by 0.099. Among coincidental power couples the probability of being in a large city rose by only 0.036, and among low-power coincidental couples it fell by −0.004. Urbanization of the noncollege educated therefore cannot explain the rise in low-power concentration in large cities.

The differential trend for power couples' probability of being in a large metropolitan area was 0.049 relative to part-power couples, 0.060 relative to low-power couples, and 0.067 relative to coincidental couples (see Table VIII). The latter figure implies that at least 65 percent of the 0.103 rise in power couple concentration in large cities is attributable to colocation. The differential trend of 0.047 in low-power relative to coincidental low-power couple concentration implies that all of the 0.043 increase in low-power couple concentration in large cities is attributable to colocation. The triple difference shows that 0.020 (19 percent) of the increase in power couple concentration is accounted for by the unique colocation problems of the college educated relative to the noncollege educated.

Recall that we can further refine our triple difference estimate by restricting ourselves to couples (including coincidental couples) in which the woman works. We would only expect a colocation problem among working couples. Among couples in which the woman works, the differential trend in power couples' probability of being in a large city was 0.032 relative to part-power couples, 0.085 relative to low-power couples, and 0.165 relative to coincidental couples. The comparison with coincidental couples implies that 87 percent of the rise in working power couple concentration can be explained by colocation. The differential trend in low-power couples' probability of being in a large city relative to coincidental couples was 0.128, conditional on the woman being in the labor force. This figure implies that all of the increase in working low-power couple concentration in large cities can be explained by colocation. The triple difference estimate of

TABLE VIII
DIFFERENTIAL TRENDS IN PROPENSITY TO LIVE IN GIVEN CITY SIZE, 1970–1990, BY COUPLE TYPE (BASED UPON PREDICTED PROBABILITIES)

	City size		
	Large	Midsize	Small
Double differences, 1990–1970			
$\Delta^{P} - \Delta^{PP}$	0.049	−0.006	−0.043
	(0.009)	(0.008)	(0.008)
$\Delta^{P} - \Delta^{LP}$	0.060	−0.011	−0.048
	(0.008)	(0.006)	(0.007)
$\Delta^{P} - \Delta^{CP}$	0.067	0.005	−0.072
	(0.009)	(0.007)	(0.008)
$\Delta^{LP} - \Delta^{CLP}$	0.047	0.008	−0.056
	(0.006)	(0.004)	(0.006)
$\Delta^{P,W} - \Delta^{CP,W}$	0.165	0.113	0.029
	(0.008)	(0.008)	(.007)
$\Delta^{LP,W} - \Delta^{CLP,W}$	0.128	0.114	0.052
	(0.004)	(0.005)	(0.005)
Triple differences, 1990–1970			
$[\Delta^{P} - \Delta^{CP}] - [\Delta^{LP} - \Delta^{CLP}]$	0.020	−0.003	−0.016
	(0.010)	(0.008)	(0.010)
$[\Delta^{P,W} - \Delta^{CP,W}]] - [\Delta^{LP,W} - \Delta^{CLP,W}]$	0.037	−0.001	−0.023
	(0.009)	(0.009)	(0.009)

Δ^{P}, Δ^{PP}, Δ^{LP}, and Δ^{CP} represent the change from 1970 to 1990 of the probability of being in a given sized metropolitan area for power, part-power, low-power, and coincidental power couples, respectively. $\Delta^{P,W}$, $\Delta^{LP,W}$, $\Delta^{CP,W}$, and $\Delta^{CLP,W}$ represent the probability of being in a given sized metropolitan area for power and low-power couples in which the wife works and this probability for coincidental power and low-power couples in the woman works, respectively. Probabilities are calculated from Tables V and VI.

0.037 suggests that 36 percent of the increase in power couple concentration is accounted for by the unique colocation problems of the college relative to the noncollege educated.

V. URBANIZATION AND THE COLLEGE EDUCATED

Two factors could account for the increasing urbanization of the college educated: increasing returns to city size by education and the increasing value of urban amenities to the college educated (including marriage markets). To test the labor market incentives of moving to large metropolitan areas, we estimate the returns to city size by education in every decade. We therefore estimate wage regressions of the form

$$\ln(w) = \beta_0 + \beta_1 \ln(d) + \beta_2 X + u \qquad (7)$$

for white, full-time, and full-year wage and salary workers for every decade and every education level, where w is the hourly wage in 1997 dollars, d is metropolitan area population, X is a vector consisting of age and age squared, and u is an error term. We include both married and unmarried men and women in our sample.[13] Because we cannot observe population in area of residence for individuals living in nonmetropolitan areas, we omit these individuals from our regressions. For ease of exposition we estimate separate equations by educational attainment. When income is topcoded, we multiply the topcode by 1.45. The 1970 census reported weeks and hours of work only as intervals. We take the midpoint of the interval. We drop all individuals whose hourly earnings are less than half of the minimum wage. We also drop individuals earnings more than $500 per hour.

Table IX shows the returns to city size by education for individuals living in a metropolitan area (β_1). Note that returns to city size are greater for the highly educated. For each increase in the logarithm of population in 1970 the logarithm of a man's wage increases by 0.065 for those with a graduate degree and by 0.060 for those with a college degree in 1970 whereas for those with a high school education it only increases by 0.049 and for those with less than a high school education by 0.034. Only the returns to city size for those with a graduate school education are statistically significantly different from the returns for those with less than a high school education (at the 5 percent level). By 1990 the logarithm of the husband's wage increases by 0.101 for those with a graduate education, by 0.078 for those with a college education, by 0.076 for those with a high school education, and by 0.023 for those with less than a high school education. The returns to city size for those with a graduate, college, and high school education are statistically significantly different from the returns to those with less than a high school education, at the 1, 10, and 1 percent level, respectively. Returns to city size by education barely changed between 1970 and 1980, a period characterized by falling returns to education [Katz and Murphy 1992].

Women's returns to city size by educational attainment exhibit similar patterns as those of men, but only in 1990 are the returns to city size for those with a graduate education statistically significantly different from the returns to those with less than a high school education. One possible explanation is that

13. The results are very similar when we restrict the sample to the married.

TABLE IX
RETURNS TO CITY SIZE BY EDUCATION

	1940	1970	1980	1990
Men				
Less than high school	0.045	0.034	0.007	0.023
	(0.008)	(0.014)	(0.019)	(0.015)
High school	0.053	0.049	0.041	0.076
	(0.005)	(0.006)	(0.010)	(0.006)
College	0.044	0.060	0.051	0.078
	(0.010)	(0.007)	(0.005)	(0.010)
Graduate degree	−0.002	0.065	0.061	0.101
	(0.019)	(0.005)	(0.007)	(0.014)
Women				
Less than high school	0.065	0.062	0.040	0.065
	(0.007)	(0.011)	(0.012)	(0.014)
High school	0.060	0.066	0.058	0.075
	(0.012)	(0.006)	(0.007)	(0.009)
College	0.085	0.069	0.055	0.071
	(0.018)	(0.007)	(0.006)	(0.009)
Graduate degree	0.072	0.038	0.056	0.091
	(0.028)	(0.011)	(0.010)	(0.013)

Estimated returns are for individuals living in a metropolitan area only. We estimated regressions by educational attainment in which the logarithm of the hourly wage was the dependent variable and the independent variables were the logarithm of metropolitan area population and age and age squared. Robust standard errors are in parentheses. Estimated from the integrated public use census samples.

many women work in the nonprofit sector and in this sector wage differences across city size may be smaller and may have grown more so over time. In the case of schoolteachers this may have been spurred by the move away from direct local funding to state and federal funding and the move toward collective bargaining agreements [Flyer and Rosen 1997]. In fact, when we exclude schoolteachers, those in government jobs, or those in traditionally female jobs (a job in which women were overrepresented relative to men in 1970), we find that in 1990 the returns to city size were 0.058, 0.093, 0.089, 0.123 for those with less than a high school education, a high school education, a college education, and a graduate education, respectively. The returns to city size for those with a high school education or greater were statistically significantly different from the returns for those with less than a high school education.

Table IX shows that the returns to city size for the college educated rose between 1970 and 1990, with most of the increase taking place between 1980 and 1990. We predict that when the returns to city size for the college educated are rising then the college educated should move to large cities and that they should leave large cities when these returns are falling. Between 1970 and 1980, when the returns to city size by education were stagnant or falling, coincidental couples migrated to large cities at a slower rate (0.002) than between 1980 and 1990, when the returns to city size by education were rising (0.034). These figures suggest that most of the 0.036 increase (0.032 = 0.034 − 0.002) in coincidental power concentration in large cities between 1970 and 1990 can be explained by increasing returns to city size for the college educated. Note also that between 1970 and 1980, when the returns to city size were stagnant, power couples still migrated to large cities at a faster rate (0.026) than coincidental couples (0.002), implying that the immediate pecuniary gains to city size are not the sole motivation for power couple migration.[14]

Our final hypothesis for the urbanization of the college educated was that power singles may be more likely to migrate to large cities because cities may be becoming better marriage markets. Most power singles are in a large metropolitan area (see Table VI) and, because fewer marriages are now formed in high school or college, the value to being in an area with a large concentration of singles may be rising. It is also conceivable that a forward looking highly educated single will foresee a future colocation problem and will therefore prefer to meet someone who already has invested in a large city. But, if there is value to being in an area with a large concentration of singles, this has not increased the probability of marriage. Power singles in large cities are now less likely to marry relative to low-power singles.[15]

We therefore conclude that 35 percent of the increased concentration of power couples in large cities can be explained by the increasing urbanization of the college educated and that virtually all of this 35 percent was due to increasing returns to city size for the college educated.

14. Such couples, however, may recognize long-term pecuniary gains. Glaeser and Maré [forthcoming] show that there are returns to city experience. Large cities allow for greater job mobility and hence for greater lifetime wage growth and for insurance against job loss.

15. Among individuals living in a large city 5 years ago and less than 30 years of age, marriage rates among power men fell from 55 to 54 percent between 1980 and 1990, whereas those of low-power men rose from 58 to 63 percent. Among power women marriage rates fell from 48 to 47 percent and among low-power women they fell from 66 to 65 percent. Because we do not know metropolitan area of residence from the 1970 census five years ago, we only present results for 1980 to 1990.

VI. Colocation

The major pieces of evidence suggesting that colocation is an important explanation for the rise in power couple concentration are the double and triple differences based upon coincidental power couple comparisons. The double differences suggest that colocation explains up to 65 percent of the trend in power couple concentration in large cities and all of the trend in low-power couple concentration in large cities. The triple difference suggests that 19 to 36 percent of the trend in power couple concentration is attributable to the unique colocation problems faced by the college educated and 29 to 46 percent to the colocation problems faced by all couples.

Second, consider the prediction that power couples should be concentrating in large metropolitan areas faster than part- or low-power couples and that the increase in power couple concentration in large cities should mainly be among couples in which the wife works. As previously discussed, Table VIII shows that the differential trend in power couples being in large cities compared with low- and part-power couples was 0.060 and 0.049. Table VII shows that between 1970 and 1990 the predicted proportion of working power couples located in large cities rose by 0.202, whereas the proportion of power couples in which the wife does not work fell by 0.099. Note that the predicted proportion of working power couples in major cities grew relative to working part-power and low-power couples. The respective differential trends were 0.032 and 0.085 (see Table VII). In contrast, when the wife does not work, the differential trend in the predicted locational choice of power couples and part-power and low-power couples is smaller (0.017 and −0.026, respectively).

Finally, colocation also predicted that the trend in power couple concentration in large cities should be most pronounced among those couples in which the wife is working full-time or is in a nontraditional occupation and among power couples in which the husband and wife were in different professional occupations.[16] In the largest metropolitan areas the predicted proportion of

16. Although the choice of city size is likely to affect hours of work, full-time work may be an indicator of attachment to the labor force, particularly among the college educated. City size could affect occupation as well, but a wife who has at least a college education and is in an occupation that was traditionally male, say law or medicine, is more likely to need the diversified labor market of a large city than a wife who is in such a traditionally female occupation as that of schoolteacher. Husbands and wives in the same occupation may not need the diversified labor market offered by a large city.

power couples in which the wife was in a nontraditional occupation rose by 0.167 between 1970 and 1990. The increase among power couples in which the wife was in a traditional occupation was only 0.055. The predicted proportion of power couples in which the wife works full-time and who were in a large metropolitan area rose by 0.166 between these years, whereas the increase among couples in which the wife works part-time was only 0.053. Power couples in which the wife is in the same occupation increased their concentration in metropolitan areas by only 0.025 between 1970 and 1990, whereas those in which the wife is in a different occupation increased their concentration by 0.197.

The in-migration of power couples to large cities could reduce power couples' incentive to stay in or move to large cities. But, Table IX shows that wages are providing a continued incentive for power couples to continue to move to large cities. Increasing returns to scale models (such as Acemoglu [1996]) provide a microfoundation for why the demand for highly skilled workers increases with their numbers.[17] As returns to education increase the financial sacrifice of being in a small city rises, particularly for dual career households.

While wages provide an incentive for power couples to move to large cities, rents are a disincentive.[18] Because power, part-power, and low-power couples face the same rents but the wage incentives to power couples of being in a large city have increased, our results suggest that small cities have become relatively less attractive to power than to part-power or low-power couples.

VII. Implications

Our finding that since 1940 power couples have been increasingly likely to locate in large metropolitan areas and that the growth of the colocation problem accounts for a large proportion of this trend has implications for city growth. As the probability that power couples choose a large metropolitan area rises, mean educational levels in the city will rise. Educational levels in a city are in turn positively related to city wages [Rauch 1993] and city growth [Glaeser, Scheinkman, and Shleifer 1995].

17. Acemoglu's [1996] search model shows that ex ante investment and bilateral search in the labor market will make the rate of return on human capital increasing in the average human capital of the workforce. In Becker and Murphy's [1992] model the greater density of urban areas lowers the costs of coordinating specialists.

18. For evidence, see Rauch [1993] or Gyourko and Tracy [1991].

As the share of power couples among all the college educated rises, firms in smaller cities may find that it is becoming harder and harder to attract highly skilled individuals. We illustrate the difficulties faced by firms in small cities with suggestive evidence on a particular type of firm—the university. One advantage of examining universities is that their capital-to-labor ratio is fairly fixed. Another is that universities, unlike firms, rarely move. We therefore examine whether the relative quality of graduate research doctorate programs in small cities in the United States has fallen since 1970 to learn whether a firm that employs highly skilled workers is now less likely to locate to a small city.

We use the National Research Council's data set, *Research Doctorate Programs in the United States,* to obtain rankings of 1142 graduate programs of 100 universities in 1993, 1983, and 1970, and we link these data to metropolitan area population. (We use the same metropolitan areas as in our previous empirical work.) We classify all programs into quintiles in every year: distinguished, strong, good, adequate, and marginal. The relative proportion of programs in each category is therefore constant across years, but between 1970 and 1993 58 percent of programs changed categories. We then estimate an ordered probit model in which the dependent variable consists of a categorical variable for our five groups and in which the independent variables are the logarithm of metropolitan area population, dummy variables for broad program field (arts and humanities, biological sciences, engineering, physical sciences and mathematics, and social and behavioral sciences), and a dummy variable equal to one if the university was a public institution.

Table X presents the derivatives with respect to the logarithm of metropolitan area population from the ordered probit model.[19] Note that the relationship between graduate program ranking and population size is stronger in 1993 than in 1970. In 1970 an increase of one in the logarithm of population increased the probability that a program would be ranked distinguished by 0.007 and decreased the probability that it would be ranked marginal by 0.010. Both the increase and decrease in these respective probabilities for 1993 was 0.027. The relative decline in quality of universities in small cities suggests that, if there are spillover effects from universities, larger rather than smaller cities are more likely to reap these benefits.

19. The derivatives for the ordered probit model were calculated by taking the derivative for every observation and then taking the mean over all derivatives.

TABLE X
DERIVATIVES OF PROBABILITY THAT GRADUATE SCHOOL PROGRAM IS DISTINGUISHED STRONG, GOOD, ADEQUATE, AND MARGINAL WITH RESPECT TO LOGARITHM OF CITY POPULATION, 1993, 1983, AND 1970

	Derivative wrt logarithm of city population		
	1970	1983	1993
Mean of logarithm of population	7.075	7.547	7.673
Probability			
Distinguished (top quintile)	0.007	0.024	0.027
	(0.007)	(0.008)	(0.009)
Strong	0.007	0.013	0.007
	(0.006)	(0.004)	(0.003)
Good	−0.000	−0.006	−0.011
	(0.001)	(0.003)	(0.004)
Adequate	−0.005	−0.016	−0.017
	(0.005)	(0.006)	(0.006)
Marginal (bottom quintile)	−0.010	−0.027	−0.027
	(0.013)	(0.019)	(0.020)

1142 observations in all years. Population is in the 1000s. The categorical outcome variable for the ordered probit model is the quintile ranking, and the independent variables are the logarithm of population, dummy variables for broad program field, and a dummy variable equal to one if the university was a public institution. Derivatives are mean derivatives. Standard errors are in parentheses. We rejected the hypothesis that 1970 and 1993 and 1970 and 1983 should be pooled. Estimated from *Research Doctorate Programs in the United States*.

VIII. CONCLUSION

This paper has documented the rising concentration of power couples in larger over smaller metropolitan areas and over nonmetropolitan areas relative to other household types and to that which would have been predicted for two observationally identical single individuals. We argued that up to 65 percent of the increased concentration of power couples in larger metropolitan areas could be explained by the colocation problem. Of this 65 percent, 19 to 36 percent was accounted for by the unique colocation problems faced by the college educated and 29 to 46 percent by the colocation problems faced by all couples. The remaining 35 percent could be explained by the increasing urbanization of the college educated because of rising returns to city size by education.

The increased concentration of power couples in large metropolitan areas may have implications for the dynamics of city growth. Economic growth depends upon the ability to absorb existing knowledge and to create new knowledge, both of which are directly related to the existing stock of human capital. Smaller markets have always exported the highly skilled to larger markets and, as this paper has documented, this phenomenon has been magnified by the increased bundling of the highly skilled with other highly skilled spouses. Cities, especially low amenity cities, may face a greater net "brain drain" than in the absence of power couple bundling. The colocation problem may also affect a small city's adjustment to local labor market shocks. Regional adjustment to local labor market shocks is primarily driven by labor mobility [Blanchard and Katz 1992]. But, because of bundling a small city may only slowly attract high skilled talent despite a local boom. Foreseeing this, firms may be unwilling to locate in smaller cities. Universities provide suggestive evidence. We have shown that although the quality of graduate doctoral programs was positively related to city size in both 1970 and in 1993, the relationship between program ranking and city size has become stronger.

This paper has sketched a 50-year trend in power couple locational choice, but will information technology affect future locational choice? It is possible that the growth of information technology that permits highly skilled workers to telecommute may solve the colocation problem for some couples by permitting at least one spouse to live far from where their employer is located. This could allow smaller cities to attract a highly skilled couple. But, as more couples become true dual career households, an increasing proportion will be faced with a colocation problem. Both the 50-year trend and the increase in returns to city size by education suggest that power couples will turn to large cities. Furthermore, information technologies may be a complement, not a substitute, for living in a large city if they facilitate making new business contacts [Gaspar and Glaeser 1998]. Power couples are likely to have a comparative advantage in making new contacts relative to two highly educated single people. Although this paper has not explicitly explored the couple "synergies" of two highly educated people being married, a power couple may work as a "team" to maximize household income. They will therefore both seek potential business contacts who can work with them or their spouse, and such contacts are more likely to be found in large cities.

DATA APPENDIX

We use the 1940 and 1970–1990 censuses of population and housing.[20] For each person we observe marital status, age, sex, race, education, labor force status, occupation, and metropolitan area. Our couples are all married and living in the same household, and our singles are either never married, divorced, or widowed. We treat cohabitating couples (whom we can only identify in 1990) as singles. All estimates use the population weights for 1940 and 1990. With the exception of 1970 we observe metropolitan area five years ago.

We construct the following variables.

1. Metropolitan area size classifications.
   Although the concept of a metropolitan area has remained essentially the same throughout the years, the boundaries of metropolitan areas have grown, new metropolitan areas have emerged, and there were slight variations in how the concept was defined from census to census and in the confidentiality criteria that had to be met for a metropolitan area identified. We use metropolitan area size classifications that allow for comparability across all census years.
   Our first step in creating metropolitan area size classifications is to classify the suburbs of central cities as part of the labor market of the central city (e.g., Westchester county is classified as part of the New York City labor market). We allow for the expansion of metropolitan areas into farmland at the periphery. For example, the 1940 and 1970 censuses did not include Santa Rosa as part of the San Francisco Bay Area, whereas those of 1980 and 1990 did. Our definition of the San Francisco Bay Area excluded Santa Rosa in 1970 (when it was still a small, rural town) but included it in 1980 and 1990 (when it had become a suburb). We have experimented with consistent definitions of metropolitan area across census years and our results are not affected by the definition that we used.[21]
   Our final step is to create three city size categories: large

20. We use the integrated public use micro samples available at http://www.ipums.umn.edu/. Earlier censuses did not identify education. We cannot use the 1950 census because education is known only for the sample line person. We cannot use the 1960 census because metropolitan area is not identified.

21. Jaeger et al. [1998] show how to construct consistent definitions of metropolitan areas from 1970 to 1990.

metropolitan areas (those with populations of at least 2 million), midsize metropolitan areas (those with populations of between 2 million and 250,000), and small and nonmetropolitan areas (metropolitan areas with a population of less than 250,000 and nonmetropolitan areas). The 1940 census identified metropolitan areas if the population in these areas was at least 100,000 in 1980 and the 1980 and 1990 censuses identified metropolitan areas with populations of at least 100,000 in the census year. The 1970 census identified metropolitan areas with populations of at least 250,000 in 1970. Our definition of small and nonmetropolitan areas is therefore consistent across time.

2. Educational level
The definition of education differed across census years. We use the highest grade of school or year of college completed for 1940, 1970, and 1980. Education is overstated in 1940 [Goldin 1998]. In 1990 the education variable gives the respondent's highest grade of school completed through the eleventh grade, but classifies high school graduates according to their highest diploma or degree earned. We therefore define our categories of less than high school as grade 11 or less, high school as grade 12 in 1940, 1970, and 1980 and as twelfth grade, high school diploma, or GED in 1990, college as four or more years in 1940, 1970, and 1980 and as a bachelor's or graduate degree in 1990. We classify those who did not complete college (less than four years in 1940, 1970, and 1980 and some college but no degree or occupational/academic associate degree in 1990) together with the high school graduates.

3. Hourly Wage
Our hourly wage variable is constructed from annual wage and salary divided by annual hours worked (current weekly hours multiplied by weeks worked in the past year). We examine wage and salary income only because self-employment income is unavailable in 1940. We adjust all income numbers to 1997 dollars. We multiply the topcode by 1.45. In 1980 a larger proportion of the population was covered by topcoding than in 1970 or 1990. However, our results remain unchanged when we impose a new topcode in 1970 and in 1990.

The 1940, 1980, and 1990 censuses provide actual hours worked during the reference week and actual weeks worked in the past year. The 1970 census only provides intervals. We therefore take the midpoint of these intervals.

MASSACHUSETTS INSTITUTE OF TECHNOLOGY AND NATIONAL BUREAU OF ECONOMIC RESEARCH
COLUMBIA UNIVERSITY

REFERENCES

Acemoglu, Daron, "A Microfoundation for Social Increasing Returns in Human Capital Accumulation," *Quarterly Journal of Economics,* CXI (1996), 779–804.

Baumgardner, James R., "Physicians' Services and the Division of Labor across Markets," *Journal of Political Economy,* XCVI (1988), 948–982.

Becker, Gary S., and Kevin M. Murphy, "The Division of Labor, Coordination Costs, and Knowledge," *Quarterly Journal of Economics,* CVII (1992), 1137–1160.

Blanchard, Olivier Jean, and Lawrence F. Katz, "Regional Evolutions," *Brookings Papers on Economic Activity* (1992), 1–61.

Flyer, Frederick, and Sherwin Rosen, "The New Economics of Teachers and Education," *Journal of Labor Economics,* XV (1997, Part 2), S104–139.

Gaspar, Jess, and Edward L. Glaeser, "Information Technology and the Future of Cities," *Journal of Urban Economics,* XLIII (1998), 136–156.

Glaeser, Edward L., "Are Cities Dying?" *Journal of Economic Perspectives,* XII (1998), 139–160.

Glaeser, Edward L., and David C. Maré, "Cities and Skills," *Journal of Labor Economics,* forthcoming.

Glaeser, Edward L., José A. Scheinkman, and Andrei Shleifer, "Economic Growth in a Cross-Section of Cities," *Journal of Monetary Economics,* XXXVI (1995), 117–143.

Goldin, Claudia, *Understanding the Gender Gap: An Economic History of American Women* (New York, Oxford: Oxford University Press, 1990).

——, "The Meaning of College in the Lives of American Women: The Past One-Hundred Years," National Bureau of Economic Research Working Paper No. 4099, June 1992.

——, "Career and Family: College Women Look to the Past," in *Gender and Family Issues in the Workplace,* Francine Blau and Ronald Ehrenberg, eds. (New York: Russell Sage, 1997).

——, "America's Graduation from High School: The Evolution and Spread of Secondary Schooling in the Twentieth Century." *Journal of Economic History,* LVIII (1998), 345–374.

Gyourko, Joseph, and Joseph Tracy, "The Structure of Local Public Finance and the Quality of Life," *Journal of Political Economy,* XCIX (1991), 774–806.

Heckman, James, Anne Layne-Farrar, and Petra Todd, "Human Capital Pricing Equations with an Application to Estimating the Effect of Schooling Quality on Earnings," *Review of Economics and Statistics,* LXXVIII (1996), 562–610.

Jaeger, David A., Susanna Loeb, Sarah E. Turner, and John Bound, "Coding Geographic Areas across Census Years: Creating Consistent Definitions of Metropolitan Areas," National Bureau of Economic Research Working Paper No. 6772, October 1998.

Kahn, Matthew E., "Particulate Pollution Trends in the United States," *Regional Science and Urban Economics,* XXVII (1997), 87–107.

Katz, Lawrence F., and Kevin M. Murphy, "Change in Relative Wages, 1963–1987: Supply and Demand Factors," *Quarterly Journal of Economics,* CVII (1992), 35–78.

Kim, Sunwoong, "Labor Specialization and the Extent of the Market," *Journal of Political Economy,* XCVII (1989), 692–705.

Lucas, Robert E., Jr., "On the Mechanics of Economic Development," *Journal of Monetary Economics,* XXII (1988), 3–42.
Mare, Robert D., "Five Decades of Educational Assortative Mating," *American Sociological Review,* LVI (1991), 15–32.
Mincer, Jacob, "Family Migration Decisions," *Journal of Political Economy,* LXXXVI (1978), 749–773.
Rauch, James E., "Productivity Gains from Geographic Concentration of Human Capital: Evidence from the Cities," *Journal of Urban Economics,* XXXIV (1993), 380–400.
Ruggles, Steven, and Matthew Sobek, *Integrated Public Use Microdata Series, IPUMS-98 Version 2.0* (Social History Research Laboratory. Minneapolis, MN: Department of History, University of Minnesota, 1997), http://www.ipums-.umn.edu/.
Simon, Curtis, "Human Capital and Metropolitan Employment Growth," *Journal of Urban Economics,* XLIII (1998), 223–243.
Topel, Robert H., and Michael P. Ward, "Job Mobility and the Careers of Young Men," *Quarterly Journal of Economics,* CVII (1992), 439–479.

Part IV
The Empirics of Agglomeration and Growth

[14]

Productivity and the Density of Economic Activity

By ANTONIO CICCONE AND ROBERT E. HALL *

To explain the large differences in labor productivity across U.S. states we estimate two models—one based on local geographical externalities and the other on the diversity of local intermediate services—where spatial density results in aggregate increasing returns. Both models lead to a relation between county employment density and productivity at the state level. Using data on gross state output we find that a doubling of employment density increases average labor productivity by around 6 percent. More than half of the variance of output per worker across states can be explained by differences in the density of economic activity. (*JEL* R10)

Differences in average labor productivity across U.S. states are large: in 1988, output per worker in the most productive state was two thirds larger than in the least productive state, and output per worker in the top ten productive states was one third larger than in the ten states which ranked at the bottom. Our purpose in this paper is to look at data on the spatial dimension of externalities and increasing returns to examine how they relate to these differences in average labor productivity. To do so we develop two different models—one based on local geographical externalities and the other on the variety of local intermediate services—where the spatial density of economic activity is the source of aggregate increasing returns.

By density we mean simply the intensity of labor, human, and physical capital relative to physical space. Density is high when there is a large amount of labor and capital per square foot. Density affects productivity in several ways. If technologies have constant returns themselves, but the transportation of products from one stage of production to the next involves costs that rise with distance, then the technology for the production of all goods within a particular geographical area will have increasing returns—the ratio of output to input will rise with density. If there are externalities associated with the physical proximity of production, then density will contribute to productivity for this reason as well. A third source of density effects is the higher degree of beneficial specialization possible in areas of dense activity. Although the idea that denser economic activity had advantages from agglomeration was implicit in a large earlier literature, there does not appear to be any earlier work in which density was an explicit element of the theory, nor has there been empirical work based on measures of density.

The finest level of geographical detail in the United States for which reliable data on value added have been assembled appears to be the state level. Thus the observations on output are for the 50 states and the District of Columbia. But the average density of activity for a state is a meaningless concept. Most of the area of the United States supports essentially no economic activity at all. To get a meaningful measure of density, as well as a sensible specification for the geographical extent of the spillovers, we use much more detailed data by county. This work views the unit of production to be the labor, capital, and land present in a county. Estimation involves dealing with the aggregation from the county to the state level. In effect, we create an index of inputs for each

* Ciccone: Department of Economics, Universitat Pompeu Fabra, Balmes 132, 08008 Barcelona, Spain, and University of California, Berkeley; and Hall: Hoover Institution, Stanford University, Stanford CA, 94305-6072, and National Bureau of Economic Research. This research was supported in part by the National Science Foundation and is part of the Economic Fluctuations Program of the National Bureau of Economic Research. We would like to thank Steve Davis for generously providing data, Chris Wilkins for outstanding research assistance, and the editor and two anonymous referees for comments.

state, adjusted for density at the county level. The index depends on the extent of increasing returns. The estimate of increasing returns is the one that generates a cross-sectional pattern of the input index that most closely matches the pattern of value added across states.

To summarize our results briefly: capital accounts for some of the differences in productivity across U.S. states but leaves most of the variation unexplained. Estimation of our model of locally increasing returns reveals that accounting for the density of economic activity at the county level is crucial for explaining the variation of productivity at the state level. According to our estimates, a doubling of employment density in a county results in a 6-percent increase of average labor productivity. This degree of locally increasing returns can explain more than half of the variation of output per worker across states.

The paper starts by discussing the related literature. We develop the two models and the corresponding method of aggregating the county employment data to state levels. We then describe how differences in density and productivity can persist in equilibrium. Following a description of the county employment data and state value-added data, we discuss identification and estimation. The main results are summarized in Section VI. Section VII extends the models to account for differences in the availability of public capital, externalities from density at the state level, and externalities from output at the county level.

I. Related Literature

The economics of agglomeration began with Alfred Marshall (1920), who emphasized technological spillovers from one firm to another one nearby. J. Vernon Henderson (1974) formalized Marshall's ideas and demonstrated—building on work by Edwin S. Mills (1967)—that, in an equilibrium, disamenities from agglomeration on the side of households may offset the productivity advantages on the side of firms. A second branch of the literature on agglomeration hypothesizes economies of scale internal to firms. Mills was an early contributor. An essential task with internal increasing returns is to offer a coherent theory of the firm and its market. Mills assumed that all goods are produced by monopolists. More recent papers use a monopolistically competitive market structure to study agglomeration with internal increasing returns to scale. H. M. Abdel-Rahman (1988), Masahisa Fujita (1988, 1989) and Francisco L. Rivera-Batiz (1988) employ the well known formalization of monopolistic competition of A. Michael Spence (1976) and Avinash Dixit and Joseph E. Stiglitz (1977) to demonstrate that nontransportable intermediate inputs produced with increasing returns imply agglomeration. In related models, Paul R. Krugman (1991) demonstrates that agglomeration will result even when transportation costs are small, if most workers are mobile, and Ciccone (1992) argues that patterns of agglomeration are reinforced by endogenous technology adoption. The essence of these models is that when local markets are more active, a larger number of producers of the differentiated intermediate inputs break even. The production of final goods is more productive when a greater variety of intermediate inputs is available.

Empirical studies of agglomeration have focused on city and industry size as determinants of productivity and on technological spillovers as a source of agglomeration economies. Leo A. Sveikauskas (1975), David Segal (1976) and Ronald L. Moomaw (1981, 1985) estimated the effect of city population on productivity. Henderson (1986) found that the productivity of firms increases with the size of the industry as measured by industry employment. But all of these studies are seriously flawed by their reliance on unsatisfactory measures of output from the Census of Manufactures. In addition—following past theoretical and empirical work—they focus on the return to city size. We are not aware of any studies that have examined spatial density directly. We believe that density rather than size is a more accurate determinant. Close calls, such as whether San Francisco and Oakland are the same or different cities, have an important effect in empirical work based on city size, but none at all in our approach based on density. Finally, there appears to be little empirical work investigating the role of geographically localized externalities and increasing returns for explaining the differences in labor productivity across U.S. states. The most closely related work is by Gerald A. Carlino and Richard Voith (1992) who find that total factor productivity across U.S. states increases with urbanization.

An important branch of the empirical literature on agglomeration has studied geographic wage differentials. Wages are higher in cities and other dense areas. No study of wage differentials, though (so far as we know), has considered spatial density directly. We do not attempt to summarize this literature. Edward L. Glaeser and David C. Mare (1994) is an important recent contribution which looks at the wages in many cities. U.S. data on the noncash component wages and salaries are not available by state or other geographic breakdown, as far as we know; differences in cash wages may therefore reflect differences in state taxes and other policies that would affect the split between cash and noncash compensation. Still, exploitation of the rich geographic detail available for cash compensation may be a promising area for future research.

II. Models

A. *Increasing Returns from Externalities*

The ideas of this paper are easiest to understand in models without capital, with land and labor are the factors of production. We begin with a model based on externalities developed to show how density affects productivity and how to aggregate across productive units. The model says nothing new about the sources of agglomeration effects. Let $f(n, q, a)$ be the production function describing the output produced in an acre of space by employing n workers (all space is considered equivalent). The acre is embedded in a larger area (a county, in our empirical work) with total output q and total acreage a. The last two variables describe the density externality in a very general way. We make the assumptions that the externality depends multiplicatively on a particular measure of density, namely output per acre, the elasticity of output with respect to density is a constant, $(\lambda - 1)/\lambda$, and the elasticity of output with respect to employment is also a constant, α:

$$(1) \qquad f(n, q, a) = n^{\alpha}\left(\frac{q}{a}\right)^{(\lambda-1)/\lambda}.$$

The labor employed in a county, n_c, is distributed equally among all the acres in the county. Thus total output in county c is $q_c = a_c(n_c/a_c)^{\alpha}(q_c/a_c)^{(\lambda-1)/\lambda}$. The county-wide joint technology is described by the production function obtained by solving this equation for output:

$$(2) \qquad \frac{q_c}{a_c} = \left(\frac{n_c}{a_c}\right)^{\gamma}.$$

Here γ is the product of the production elasticity, α, and the elasticity of the externality, λ: $\gamma = \alpha\lambda$; α measures the effect of congestion and λ measures the effect of agglomeration. Only the product, γ, is identified in our data. Our empirical results show that the net effect favors agglomeration.

We turn now to aggregating to the state level. Let C_s be the set of counties covering state s. Output in state s is $Q_s = \Sigma_{c \in C_s} n_c^{\gamma} a_c^{-(\gamma-1)}$ and hence average labor productivity in the state is

$$(3) \qquad \frac{Q_s}{N_s} = \frac{\sum_{c \in C_s} n_c^{\gamma} a_c^{-(\gamma-1)}}{N_s},$$

where N_s is the number of workers in state s, and we define the factor density index, $D_s(\gamma)$:

$$(4) \qquad D_s(\gamma) = \frac{\sum_{c \in C_s} n_c^{\gamma} a_c^{-(\gamma-1)}}{N_s}.$$

Letting d_c be employment per acre in county c, D_s be employment per acre in state s, and D be employment per acre in the United States, we can decompose the density index into three components:

$$(5) \qquad D_s(\gamma) = D^{\gamma-1}\left(\frac{D_s}{D}\right)^{\gamma-1} \frac{\sum_{c \in C_s} n_c\left(\frac{d_c}{D_s}\right)^{\gamma-1}}{N_s}.$$

That is, the state density effect is the product of a national effect, a state effect—which depends on the relation of average state density to national density—and a factor that depends on the inequality of density across counties within the state. The last factor is the sum of county density relative to state density raised to the power $\gamma - 1$, weighted by county employment. If, for example, average density in state s is identical to average density in the nation, $D_s = D$, then, relative to the nation, productivity in the state depends on the distribution of employment within the state only.

Under neoclassical conditions, with γ less than one, the density factors would predict lower productivity in states with higher average density, and even lower productivity in states with some particularly dense, congested areas. But if agglomeration effects outweigh congestion effects, density has the opposite effect. States with higher average density and higher inequality of density will have higher levels of productivity.

B. *Increasing Returns from a Greater Variety of Intermediate Products in Denser Areas*

The second model hypothesizes increasing returns in the production of local intermediate goods, as in Abdel-Rahman (1988), Fujita (1988, 1989), and Rivera-Batiz (1988). Our development of this model gives density an explicit role. Let the production function for making the final good on an acre of land be

$$f(m, i) = [m^{\beta} i^{(1-\beta)}]^{\alpha}; \tag{6}$$

here m is the amount of labor used directly in making the final good, i is the amount of a composite service input which cannot be transported outside the acre, α describes decreasing returns to the two variable inputs on the acre (congestion effect), and β is a distribution parameter (agglomeration effect). The service composite, i, is produced from individual differentiated services, $x(t)$, indexed by type t, according to the constant elasticity of substitution production function,

$$i = \left(\int_0^z x(t)^{1/\mu}\, dt\right)^{\mu}. \tag{7}$$

Here z describes the variety of intermediate products produced—types 0 through z are available. The parameter $\mu > 1$ controls the substitutability of the intermediate products. The higher μ is, the less one product substitutes for others and the more monopoly power the producer of that product has. Under the standard Spence-Dixit-Stiglitz assumptions of Bertrand competition that, μ is the markup of price as a ratio to marginal cost that the producer will set in order to maximize profit.

We further assume that it takes $x + v$ units of labor to produce x. With labor paid w, the intermediate product maker will charge a price of μw and make a profit of $(\mu - 1)wx - wv$. With free entry to the intermediate product business, this profit will be pushed down to zero—the fixed cost will just offset the operating profit from market power. The level of output at the zero-profit point is

$$x = \frac{v}{\mu - 1}. \tag{8}$$

Putting this common value for all the service inputs into the production function for the service composite, equation (7), we have

$$i = z^{\mu} x. \tag{9}$$

Production of i uses zx units of intermediate inputs, so the productivity of the i-making process is $z^{\mu-1}$. Because $\mu > 1$, productivity rises with the available variety of intermediate goods. Denser acres have greater variety, because more intermediate services producers can break even. The result is a positive relation between density and productivity.

The Cobb-Douglas specification of the final output technology implies that the share of final output paid to labor employed directly is $\alpha\beta$; hence, $wm = \alpha\beta f(m, i)$. The share paid to land is $(1 - \alpha)$. In a free entry equilibrium all output not paid to land accrues to labor, either directly or indirectly through the intermediate service business. Therefore, $wn = \alpha f(m, i)$, where n, as before, is total labor employed in the acre. Combined, these relationships imply that the equilibrium allocation of labor to direct employment in final goods production is governed by the share parameter,

$$m = \beta n. \tag{10}$$

The remaining share $(1 - \beta)n$ of the labor makes intermediate services. Because we know the total amount of labor devoted to intermediate services and the amount of each one produced, we can solve for the variety of those services:

$$(11) \qquad z = (1 - \beta)\frac{\mu - 1}{\mu}\frac{n}{v}.$$

Intermediate product variety, as measured by z, is proportional to density, as measured by the number of workers, n, working on the acre.

Now we can insert the equilibrium value of z into equation (9) to determine i, and then put m and i into the production function for final goods to get the consolidated production function,

$$(12) \qquad \phi n^{\gamma}.$$

Here ϕ is a complicated function of the other constants and the elasticity of the production function is

$$(13) \qquad \gamma = \alpha[1 + (1 - \beta)(\mu - 1)].$$

Again, the parameter α describes congestion effects—lower productivity resulting from crowding more workers onto the same acre. To the extent that the differentiated intermediate goods are important ($\beta < 1$) and they are not good substitutes for each other ($\mu > 1$), there is a countervailing effect favoring higher density, because it makes possible a greater variety of the intermediate products. With a high enough μ and a low enough β, the production function could have increasing returns, where the favorable effect of density outweighs the congestion effect.

In this equilibrium the market provision of intermediate inputs is inefficient due to distortions from monopoly pricing. We have worked out the alternative where the quantity and variety of intermediate services is optimal, either because of government intervention or vertical integration. The resulting elasticity of output with respect to total labor is the same as for the monopolistic competition case.

If we normalize the measurement of the quantities to make $\phi = 1$ and assume, as before, that labor is distributed uniformly across the acres of a county, we have the county production function,

$$(14) \qquad \frac{q_c}{a_c} = \left(\frac{n_c}{a_c}\right)^{\gamma}.$$

Aggregation to the state level proceeds exactly as before. There are no observational distinctions between the externalities model and the intermediate product variety model. Both provide a theoretical foundation for the same estimation procedure in state data.

C. *Capital and Total Factor Productivity*

Now let the production function describing output produced in an acre of space in county c by employing n_c workers and k_c machines be

$$(15) \qquad A_s[(e_c n_c)^{\beta} k_c^{1-\beta}]^{\alpha}\left(\frac{q_c}{a_c}\right)^{(\lambda-1)/\lambda},$$

where A_s is a Hicks-neutral technology multiplier for state s and e_c is a measure of the efficiency of labor at the county level. As before, the elasticity α is less than one by the amount of the share of land in factor payments. The quantities of labor and capital employed in a county, n_c and k_c, are distributed equally among all the acres in the county. Thus total output in county c is

$$(16) \qquad q_c = a_c A_s\left[\left(\frac{e_c n_c}{a_c}\right)^{\beta}\left(\frac{k_c}{a_c}\right)^{1-\beta}\right]^{\alpha} \times \left[\frac{q_c}{a_c}\right]^{(\lambda-1)/\lambda}.$$

Solving for output per acre, we get

$$(17) \qquad \frac{q_c}{a_c} = A_s^{\lambda}\left[\left(\frac{e_c n_c}{a_c}\right)^{\beta}\left(\frac{k_c}{a_c}\right)^{1-\beta}\right]^{\gamma}.$$

Again, γ is the product of the production elasticity, α, which is less than one, and the elasticity from the externality, λ, which is greater than one. If γ exceeds one, agglomeration effects dominate congestion.

To deal with capital, we make the assumption that the rental price of capital, r, is the same everywhere. Then we use the factor demand function to substitute the factor price for the factor quantity. That is,

$$(18)\qquad \frac{k_c}{a_c} = \frac{\alpha(1-\beta)}{r}\frac{q_c}{a_c}.$$

Thus the county technology becomes

$$(19)\qquad \frac{q_c}{a_c} = \phi A_s^{\omega}\left(\frac{e_c n_c}{a_c}\right)^{\theta}$$

where ϕ is a constant that depends on the interest rate, and the elasticities for the technology multiplier for the state, ω, and for labor input for the county, θ, are:

$$(20)\qquad \theta \equiv \frac{\gamma\beta}{1-\gamma(1-\beta)}$$

and

$$(21)\qquad \omega \equiv \frac{\theta}{\alpha\beta}.$$

We assume that labor efficiency depends log-linearly on workers' average years of education h_c, $e_c = h_c^{\eta}$, where η is the elasticity of education. Using this relationship in equation (19) and aggregating to the state level, we obtain

$$(22)\qquad \frac{Q_s}{N_s} = \phi A_s^{\omega} D_s(\theta, \eta)$$

where

$$(23)\qquad D_s(\theta, \eta) = \frac{\sum_{c \in C_s} (n_c h_c^{\eta})^{\theta} a_c^{1-\theta}}{N_s}.$$

Under these alternative assumptions, the index of density has the same functional form as before with the elasticity θ in place of γ and efficiency units of labor instead of raw labor. The underlying value of γ can be calculated from equation (20). The relation between γ and θ for $\beta = .7$ is such that for values close to 1, as found in our empirical work, the overstatement of γ associated with the treatment of capital is small. The extension of the intermediate product variety model is analogous.

Regarding the stochastic specification in equation (22), we assume that state productivity A_s is distributed log-normally around an underlying nationwide level. We also allow for mismeasurement in state productivity, assuming that the measurement error has a log-normal distribution with zero mean. Using this stochastic specification in equation (22) and taking logarithms yields

$$(24)\qquad \log\frac{Q_s}{N_s} = \log\phi + \log D_s(\theta, \eta) + u_s.$$

Here u_s is the sum of the measurement error, and it is ω times the deviation of state productivity from the underlying level in the nation. We assume that the errors of different states are uncorrelated.

III. Equilibrium

How can states or counties be in equilibrium with different densities? This question arises if θ exceeds 1. Under neoclassical assumptions, density should be equal everywhere. The marginal product of labor is lower in a denser area, and there are arbitrage profits or a higher standard of living available by moving a worker from a dense area to a less dense one. On the other hand, with θ greater than one, the worker is more productive when moved to a denser area. Absent other considerations, the only equilibrium is for employment to concentrate in a single county.

The simplest answer, and a realistic one, is that some workers prefer to live in areas that turn out to be less dense. These workers are willing to accept the lower wages in those locations. The preference could be, but need not be, a preference for lower density itself. The preference could also take the form of devotion to a location that is not an agglomeration point. Furthermore, as households value land, its price drives a wedge between the product wage and the consumption wage. In equilibrium, there are no incentives to move for either firms or households. The marginal cost of production is equalized across all counties as the decrease in marginal cost associated with higher density is offset by higher product efficiency wages and higher land prices. Households find that differing product wages are counterbalanced by any of the considerations described above.

IV. Data

The data needed for estimation are available for the year 1988. The data cover the private nonproprietary economy. That is, data on labor input at the county level includes only employees, not the self-employed. The corresponding measure of output at the state level is gross state product (GSP) less Proprietors' Income (U.S. Bureau of Economic Analysis, 1985). We use GSP at sellers' prices; Indirect Business Taxes are excluded from the output measure. Data on employment by county are compiled by the Regional Economic Measurement Division (U.S. Bureau of Economic Analysis, 1991). Data on the area of each county are from U.S. Bureau of the Census (1989).

Data on GSP are conceptually far superior to those used in previous work on spatial differences in productivity. Moomaw (1985), Sveikauskas (1975), and Segal (1976) all measure output as the concept of value added or total value of production used in the Census of Manufactures. This concept omits all services either purchased in the market or obtained from corporate headquarters. It is hard to see how the Census of Manufactures value added could be used for any purpose in production economics, but it is a particularly unusable concept for agglomeration issues. Because there is likely to be less vertical integration in big cities or in dense areas, firms in those places are likely to purchase more services than do their counterparts in less dense areas. Moreover, a plant in a dense area is more likely to be close to its corporate headquarters and therefore more dependent on it for transferred services. For both reasons, studies using Census of Manufactures value added will overstate the productivity advantage of cities or dense areas. The research of Henderson (1986) uses total value of production, also from the Census of Manufacturers. Compared to the value-added data this concept has the added disadvantage of double-counting inputs traded within an industry. Our data are based on a careful allocation of purchased and transferred services by industry at the state level. Gross state output is a much more satisfactory measure of output than is the Census of Manufactures concept of value added. Our theoretical formulation assumes that all land is equivalent. Therefore, we use data on state output and county employment which exclude the agricultural and the mining sector. In some states, natural resources are sufficiently important for local economic activity to make our output measure unrealistic—despite our adjustment for mining output at the state level and mining employment at the county level. On this basis, we excluded all states where the mining contributes more than 15 percent of our output measure. These states are Alaska, Louisiana, West Virginia and Wyoming; on average mining stands at 21 percent of our output measure in these states compared to 1 percent in all other states.

Our data on education comes from two sources. At the state level, we have data from the Annual Demographic File of the Current Population Survey (U.S. Bureau of the Census, 1988) for 1988. Our education measure at the state level weighs the workers' years of education by the number of hours worked in 1988. At the county level, we have data from the 1990 Census of Population (U.S. Bureau of the Census, 1992). Our education measure at the county level is average years of education.

V. Identification and Estimation

We make two alternative identifying assumptions. First we assume that the random element of output per worker is uncorrelated with density and average education levels. This assumption amounts to saying that density and education are measured with little error and do not respond to the random element of productivity. Because it appears that much of the noise in productivity across states comes from measurement error, this assumption is not as strong as it may seem at first. Under this identifying assumption, we estimate the returns-to-scale parameter, θ, and the elasticity of average product with respect to education, η, by nonlinear least squares.

If there are true differences in the determinants of productivity across states, it is not realistic to assume that density is uncorrelated with those differences. States with natural features that make them more productive (for example, climate or geographic features suited to transportation) will attract workers because wages will be higher. Our alternative identifying assumption is that there is an exogenous characteristic of states that can function as an instrumental variable for the density index. The corresponding estimator is nonlinear instrumental variables. All of our candidate instruments rest on the hypothesis that the original sources of agglomeration in the United States have remaining influences only on the preferences of workers about where to live; they are not related to modern differences in productivity not explained by our model. The characteristics we use are:

1. Presence or absence of a railroad in the state in 1860, from John F. Stover (1961).
2. Population of the state in 1850, from U.S. Bureau of the Census (1975).
3. Population density of the state in 1880, from U.S. Bureau of Census (1975).
4. Distance from the eastern seaboard of the U.S., from Rand McNally (1993).

The direct measures of agglomeration—population and population density—are eligible as instruments if the main sources of agglomeration in the 18th and 19th centuries are not related to the residuals in our equation. Thus our hypothesis is that the early patterns of agglomeration in the United States did not reflect factors which significantly contribute to productivity today but have a remaining influence mainly through the legacy of agglomeration. Railroads became an important historical factor in agglomeration in the second half of the 19th century. Our hypothesis is that the development of railroads was not driven by modern productivity differences not accounted for by our model. Finally, we include distance from the eastern seaboard as an exogenous determinant of agglomeration in the 18th and 19th centuries.

The nonlinear instrumental variables estimator is discussed by Takeshi Amemiya (1983). The nonlinear model is

$$y_s = f_s(\beta) + u_s \quad (25)$$

where y is productivity, f describes our nonlinear specification, and β is the vector of parameters. Z is a matrix of values of the instrumental variables. The nonlinear instrumental variables estimator minimizes

$$[y - f(\beta)]'Z(Z'Z)^{-1}Z'[y - f(\beta)]. \quad (26)$$

When the number of instruments is the same as the number of parameters, the estimator is just the solution to the orthogonality condition,

$$[y - f(\beta)]'Z = 0. \quad (27)$$

When the instrument is a dummy variable, the estimator is based on grouping. For example, with our instrument for the presence of a railroad in 1860, the estimator of the density parameter is the value that explains the difference in the average level of productivity in states that did have railroads compared to states that did not.

The estimated covariance matrix of β is

$$\hat{\sigma}^2[F'Z(Z'Z)^{-1}Z'F]^{-1} \quad (28)$$

where $\hat{\sigma}$ is the standard error of the residuals and F is the matrix of derivatives of the model with respect to the parameters.

VI. Results

Table 1 gives the results using the county level education data. The least squares estimate of θ is 1.052 with a standard error of .008.[1] The elasticity of labor efficiency with respect to education, η, is .41 with a standard error of .40. The R^2 of the regression is 55 percent. Steven J. Davis (1992), using data on individuals, estimates the elasticity of earnings with respect to education to lie between .80 and 1.35. Our estimate is one standard error away from Davis's lower estimate. The

[1] Some readers have been surprised at the small size of the standard error. It is much smaller, for example, than the standard error of the OLS regression of state productivity on our density index. The reason is that θ predicts zero slope at $\theta = 1$. Small changes in θ correspond to large changes in the density index, so the parameter is correspondingly well estimated.

TABLE 1—ESTIMATION RESULTS

Instrument	Density elasticity, θ (standard error)	Education elasticity, η (standard error)	R^2
None (NLLS)	1.052	0.410	0.551
	(0.008)	(0.396)	
Eastern seaboard	1.055	0.460	0.548
	(0.017)	(0.51)	
Railroad in 1860	1.061	0.330	0.537
	(0.011)	(0.450)	
Population in 1850	1.060	0.350	0.539
	(0.015)	(0.510)	
Population density in 1880	1.051	0.530	0.549
	(0.019)	(0.550)	
All	1.06	0.060	0.536
	(0.01)	(0.82)	

Notes: The equation estimated is (24). The data are value added for 46 states and Washington DC. For the 46 states we have used data on employment and average years of education at the county level.

instrumental variable estimates for θ is 1.06 making joint use of all instruments. This estimate implies that doubling the employment density in a county increases labor productivity by 6 percent. The estimated value for γ is about 1.04 which implies that doubling employment density in a county results in a 4-percent increase of total factor productivity. Using the education data available at the state level, the estimating equation in (24) simplifies to

$$\text{(29)} \qquad \log \frac{Q_s}{N_s} = \log \phi + \eta \log h_s + \log D_s(\theta) + u_s$$

where $D_s(\theta)$ is defined in equation (4). The nonlinear least squares estimate of θ and η in equation (25) are 1.051 and .51, with standard errors of .008 and .45 respectively. Using instrumental variables, the estimates are 1.058 and .36 and the standard errors .011 and .49.

Table 2 shows the factor density index $D_s(\theta)$ evaluated at $\theta = 1.058$, average years of education of workers at the state level, and the private gross state product per worker in all sectors except farming and mining. The states are ranked in declining order of density. The densest area for which reliable output data is available is Washington, DC. Not surprisingly, New York ranks second. It is the extreme concentration of employment in New York City that gives the high value of the density measure. In fact, New York City comprises the densest county in the United States, New York county (with a factor density index of 1.94), and three of the 10 next densest counties (Bronx county, Kings county, and Queens county).

Our estimated density index for New York county implies, for example, that workers in New York county are 22 percent more productive than workers in New York state, the state with the highest average productivity in our sample. The other dense states are the highly urbanized states of the northeast plus Illinois and California. The least dense states are the thinly populated states of northern New England, the south, and the southwest. It is important to note that density is not just a measure of the inequality of distribution of the work force across counties—it is also dependent on the actual density in the counties where employment is significant. The third column of Table 2 shows output (in 1988 dollars) per worker by state. Output per worker in New Jersey ($44,488), the most productive state, is two-thirds higher than in South Dakota ($26,196), the least productive state. Average output per worker in the ten most productive states ($38,782) is one-quarter higher than in the ten least productive states ($31,578). The positive partial correlation of density and productivity is immediately apparent from Table 2

TABLE 2—DENSITY, EDUCATION, AND PRODUCTIVITY FOR $\theta = 1.058$

State	Density index	Years of education	Productivity (1988 $)
District of Columbia	1.67	14.0	43,164
New York	1.59	13.3	41,921
New Jersey	1.48	13.4	44,488
Massachusetts	1.47	13.4	37,296
Illinois	1.46	13.2	39,150
Maryland	1.45	13.6	34,439
Rhode Island	1.43	12.7	30,055
Connecticut	1.42	13.5	41,927
California	1.42	12.9	40,723
Pennsylvania	1.40	13.2	34,661
Top 10 average	1.48	13.3	38,782
Ohio	1.40	13.1	36,553
Virginia	1.40	13.2	35,986
Delaware	1.40	13.3	35,223
Michigan	1.39	13.2	39,001
Missouri	1.38	13.1	34,520
Hawaii	1.38	13.3	34,485
Minnesota	1.37	13.2	35,494
Florida	1.36	13.1	30,808
Georgia	1.36	12.7	35,407
Texas	1.36	12.6	36,798
Colorado	1.35	13.6	33,342
Indiana	1.34	12.9	34,721
Wisconsin	1.34	13.2	33,495
Tennessee	1.33	12.6	33,169
North Carolina	1.32	12.8	32,677
Kentucky	1.32	12.7	34,406
Utah	1.31	13.6	32,160
Washington	1.31	13.6	32,661
Nebraska	1.30	13.2	30,323
New Hampshire	1.30	13.4	33,668
Oklahoma	1.29	13.0	33,567
Oregon	1.29	13.3	32,713
South Carolina	1.28	12.8	29,623
Kansas	1.27	13.4	36,223
Alabama	1.27	12.4	32,980
Arizona	1.25	13.2	33,579
Iowa	1.25	13.1	32,318
Average	1.33	13.1	34,071
Maine	1.24	13.1	33,097
Vermont	1.23	13.4	33,733
Arkansas	1.23	12.5	32,150
Mississippi	1.21	12.8	32,707
New Mexico	1.21	12.6	31,249
Nevada	1.20	12.9	36,234
Idaho	1.17	12.7	29,861
South Dakota	1.15	13.0	26,196
North Dakota	1.12	13.3	30,248
Montana	1.10	13.3	30,302
Bottom 10 average	1.19	13.0	31,578

Note: Education is at the state level. The density index as defined in equation (4), uses raw employment at the county level, evaluated at $\theta = 1.058$.

and Figure 1. There are a number of outliers that call for further investigation: most conspicuous is Rhode Island, which is just as dense as its neighbors but has a productivity level of the least dense state. Nevada, on the other hand, has a much higher productivity

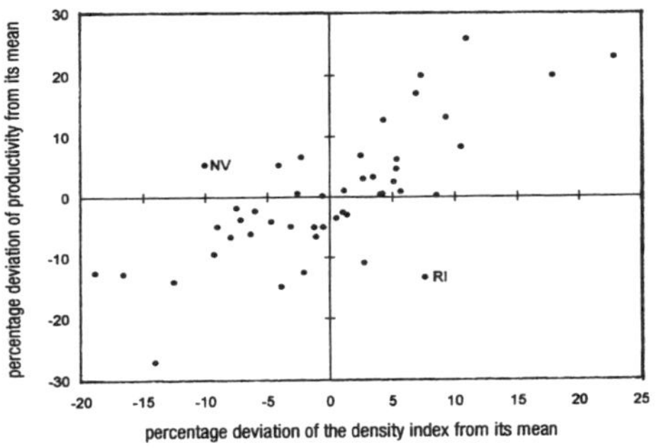

FIGURE 1. DENSITY AND PRODUCTIVITY BY STATE FOR $\theta = 1.058$

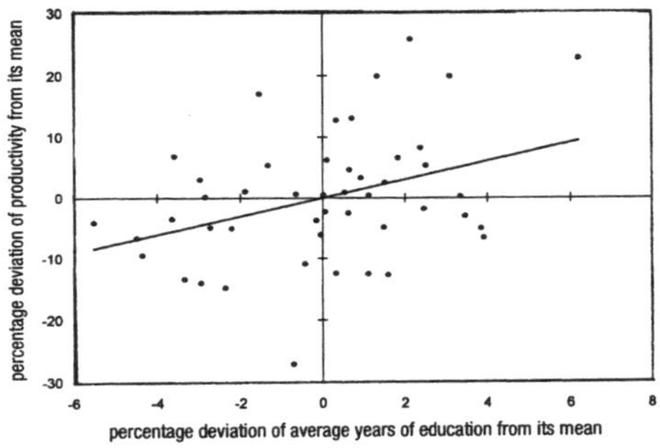

FIGURE 2. EDUCATION AND PRODUCTIVITY BY STATE

level than its low densities would predict. Among the counties with the smallest density indices are Garfield county (Montana), Kimball county (Nebraska), Newton county (Arkansas) and La Paz county (Arizona). We estimate that workers in the 15 counties with lowest density produce on average less than half the output of a worker in New York City.

Figure 2 plots average years of education against productivity at the state level. We have estimated equation (29) without density effects ($\theta = 1$). Using the education data at the state level, we find the elasticity of output per worker with respect to average education in equation (29) is 1.5 with a standard error of .5. The R^2 of the regression is .09. Using the education data at the county level to estimate equation (24) under the same hypothesis, $\theta = 1$, results in an elasticity of labor efficiency with respect to education of 1.2 with a standard error of .6 and a R^2 of .1. Education is a significant determinant of productivity in both cases and the estimate using data at the county level is within the range estimated by Davis (1992).

Figure 3 summarizes the results of our instrumental variables regression of equation (25). It plots estimated output per efficiency unit of labor at the state level against estimated density for $\theta = 1.058$. It is seen that Rhode Island remains an outlier despite the fact that its workers are significantly less educated than workers in neighboring states.

Table 3 decomposes the estimated density index $D_s(1.058)$ as defined in equation (4) into a state effect and a distribution effect along the lines described in equation (5). The column headed *state effect* gives the part of the state effect arising from the average density of the entire state. For example, if the density of employment in Massachusetts fell to the national level, while the distribution of employment over the counties remained unchanged, then this would result in a 15-percent drop in average product. The *distribution effect* measures the part of the state productivity effect attributable to an unequal distribution of employment over counties. For example, productivity in New York would fall by 19 percent if employment were to be allocated uniformly across the area of the state. Colorado, Nebraska, Missouri, Texas and Utah are examples of states with great inequality across counties but low overall density, because their major metropolitan areas have relatively high levels of employment per acre.

VII. Extensions

A. *Public Capital*

Some of the differences in average labor productivity across U.S. states may be due to differences in the amount of public capital that is available. To consider this possibility, we extend the basic model to account for public capital. We assume that the services from the public capital available in state s, g_s, enter county level production with constant elasticity, δ. Then, the county level production function in equation (1) becomes

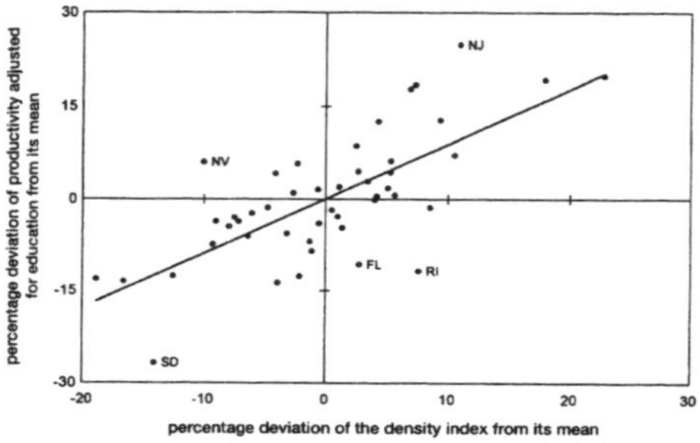

FIGURE 3. DENSITY AND PRODUCTIVITY ADJUSTED FOR EDUCATION, $\theta = 1.058$

$$(30) \quad f(n, q, a) = n^{\alpha}\left(\frac{q_c}{a_c}\right)^{(\lambda-1)/\lambda} g_s^{\delta}.$$

Solving for state level productivity we get that

$$(31) \quad \frac{Q_s}{N_s} = g_s^{\lambda\delta} D_s(\gamma),$$

where $D_s(\gamma)$ is defined in equation (4). Extending the model for exogenous differences in total factor productivity and differences in human and physical capital along the lines of Section II, we get the following estimating equation:

$$(32) \quad \log\frac{Q_s}{N_s} = \psi + \omega\delta \log g_s + \log D_s(\theta, \eta) + u_s$$

where $D(\theta, \eta)$ and ω are defined in equations (23) and (21) above, and ψ is a constant. Table 4 shows the results of estimating equation (32) using the value of public capital in streets and highways in 1988 at the state level from Douglas Holtz-Eakin (1993). The density elasticity falls somewhat, but public capital does not affect productivity at the state level significantly. We have also used other, more inclusive measures of public capital with the same results. Our negative results on public capital are in line with Teresa Garcia-Mila et al. (1994).

B. *State versus Distribution Effects*

As a further exploration of the role played by the state and distribution effects in Table 3 for agglomeration in the United States, we consider an extension of the basic model which allows for influences from density at the state level as well as at the county. The extended model provides a specification test for our earlier model. If there were important state effects not captured by our earlier model it would suggest that we need to consider externalities that cross county boundaries. In the extended model, the production function in equation (1) for output produced in an acre of space becomes

$$(33) \quad f(n, q, a) = n^{\alpha}\left(\frac{q_c}{a_c}\right)^{(\lambda-1)/\lambda}\left(\frac{Q_s}{A_s}\right)^{\kappa},$$

where κ denotes the elasticity with respect to average output per acre in the state, Q_s/A_s. Solving for state productivity along the lines of equations (2) and (3) yields

$$(34) \quad \frac{Q_s}{N_s} = D_s^{\lambda\kappa/(1-\lambda\kappa)} D_s(\gamma)^{1/(1-\lambda\kappa)}.$$

State productivity is determined by average employment density in the state, D_s, and the density index, $D_s(\gamma)$, as defined in equation (4). For $\kappa = 0$ the model reduces to the one discussed at the beginning of Section II.

Extending the model along the lines in Section II results in the following estimating equation:

$$(35) \quad \log\frac{Q_s}{N_s} = \delta + \xi \log D_s + (\xi + 1)\log D_s(\theta, \eta) + u_s,$$

where δ is a common constant across states and ξ is the elasticity of productivity with respect to state density,

$$(36) \quad \xi \equiv \frac{\kappa\omega}{1 - \kappa\omega}.$$

Table 5 shows the results of estimating equation (35). With nonlinear least squares, we obtain an estimate for ξ of 0.005 with a standard

TABLE 3—PRODUCTIVITY, STATE AND DISTRIBUTION EFFECTS FOR $\theta = 1.058$

State	State effect (percent)	Distribution effect (percent)	Productivity (1988 $)
District of Columbia	36	0	43,164
New York	9	19	41,921
New Jersey	16	4	44,488
Massachusetts	15	5	37,296
Illinois	6	13	39,150
Maryland	11	7	34,439
Rhode Island	16	1	30,055
Connecticut	14	2	41,927
California	5	11	40,723
Pennsylvania	7	8	34,661
Top 10 average	8	12	38,782
Ohio	7	7	36,553
Virginia	4	11	35,986
Delaware	10	4	35,223
Michigan	4	10	39,001
Missouri	−1	14	34,520
Hawaii	4	9	34,485
Minnesota	−2	15	35,494
Florida	6	6	30,808
Georgia	2	10	35,407
Texas	−2	14	36,798
Colorado	−6	17	33,342
Indiana	4	6	34,721
Wisconsin	1	9	33,495
Tennessee	2	7	33,169
North Carolina	3	5	32,677
Kentucky	−1	9	34,406
Utah	−9	18	32,160
Washington	−1	9	32,661
Nebraska	−8	16	30,323
New Hampshire	3	3	36,688
Oklahoma	−5	12	34,567
Oregon	−6	12	32,713
South Carolina	1	3	29,623
Kansas	−6	11	36,223
Alabama	−1	5	32,980
Arizona	−6	9	33,579
Iowa	−3	6	32,318
Average	−1	11	34,071
Maine	−4	6	33,097
Vermont	−2	2	33,733
Arkansas	−5	5	32,150
Mississippi	−4	4	32,707
New Mexico	−12	13	31,249
Nevada	−11	10	36,234
Idaho	−12	9	29,861
South Dakota	−13	9	26,196
North Dakota	−13	6	30,248
Montana	−16	7	30,302
Bottom 10 average	−10	9	31,578

Note: The density index as defined in equation (4), uses raw employment at the county level, evaluated at $\theta = 1.058$ decomposed into a state effect and a distribution effect as described in equation (5).

TABLE 4—ESTIMATION RESULTS WITH PUBLIC CAPITAL

Instrument	Density elasticity, θ (standard error)	Education elasticity, η (standard error)	Public capital elasticity, $\omega\delta$ (standard error)
None (NLLS)	1.046 (0.010)	0.570 (0.430)	0.021 (0.015)
All	1.056 (0.012)	0.480 (1.040)	0.017 (0.023)

Notes: The equation estimated is (32). The data are value added for 46 states and Washington, DC. For the 46 states we have used data on employment and education at the county level. The data for public capital at the state level is the capital in streets and highways for 1988 from Holtz-Eakin (1993).

error of .015 and an estimate for θ of 1.047 with a standard error of .018. With nonlinear instrumental variables, the estimates for ξ and θ are $-.019$ and 1.084 respectively with standard errors of .023 and .028. Both estimates suggest rather precisely that there is no state effect at all once the county effects are considered. Although we believe that a specification with some cross-county effects would be an improvement over our model, the absence of incremental state density effects indicates that our current specification captures most density effects. This issue is investigated further in Christopher J. Wilkins (1994) who considers different specifications for the geographical extent of externalities.

C. *Size versus Density Effects*

Finally, our framework allows us to consider size versus density effects at the county level. To do so we consider a further extension of the basic model, where the production function (1) accounts for both an externality from output density in the county and output in the county. We assume that the elasticity of firm level output with respect to county output also enters as a constant, ν:

$$(37) \quad f(n, q, a) = n^{\alpha}\left(\frac{q_c}{a_c}\right)^{(\lambda-1)/\lambda} q_c^{\nu}.$$

Solving for state level productivity, we obtain

$$(38) \quad \frac{Q_s}{N_s} = \frac{\sum_{c \in C_s} (n_c^{\gamma} a_c^{-(\gamma-1)})^{1/(1-\nu\lambda)}}{N_s}.$$

When $\nu = 0$, the framework reduces to the basic model with no size externalities at the county level. When $\gamma = 1$, the framework displays no density effects but only size effects. Extending the model for differences in physical and human capital and exogenous total factor productivity, we obtain

$$(39) \quad \log \frac{Q_s}{N_s} = \delta + \log D_s(\theta, \eta, \sigma) + u_s,$$

where $D_s(\theta, \eta, \sigma)$ is defined analogous to equation (38) with efficiency units of labor, $n_c h_c^{\eta}$, in place of raw labor, n_c,

$$(40) \quad D_s(\theta, \eta, \sigma) = \frac{\sum_{c \in C_s} ((n_c h_c^{\eta})^{\theta} a_c^{-(\theta-1)})^{\sigma}}{N_s},$$

where

$$(41) \quad \sigma = \frac{1}{1 - \nu\omega}.$$

Table 6 shows the results of estimating equation (40). The nonlinear least squares estimate of θ is 1.035 with a standard error of 0.013. The county size parameter σ is estimated to be 1.029 with a standard error of 0.019. The R^2 of the regression is 0.58. The nonlinear instrumental variables estimate of the density parameter is 1.046 with a standard error of 0.023 and the county size parameter is 1.026 with a standard error of 0.039. These estimates suggest that density externalities are more important than size externalities at the

TABLE 5—ESTIMATION RESULTS WITH STATE DENSITY EFFECTS

Instrument	County density elasticity, θ (standard error)	Education elasticity, η (standard error)	State density elasticity, ξ (standard error)
None (NLLS)	1.047 (0.018)	0.450 (0.420)	0.005 (0.015)
All	1.084 (0.028)	0.235 (0.498)	(0.019) (0.023)

Notes: The equation estimated is (35). The data are value added for 46 states and Washington, DC. For the 46 states we have used data on employment and education at the county level for the density index $D_s(\theta, \eta)$. Average density D_s is total employment in the state over its area.

TABLE 6—ESTIMATION RESULTS WITH SIZE EFFECTS

Instrument	County density elasticity, θ (standard error)	Education elasticity, η (standard error)	County size elasticity, σ (standard error)
None (NLLS)	1.035 (0.013)	0.259 (0.398)	1.029 (0.019)
All	1.046 (0.023)	0.140 (0.82)	1.026 (0.039)

Notes: The equation estimated is (39). The data used is value added for 46 states and Washington, DC. For the 46 states we have used data on employment and education at the county level.

county level. This issue is investigated further in Wilkins (1994) for size externalities at the level of metropolitan statistical areas and standard metropolitan statistical areas.

VIII. Concluding Remarks

Increasing returns to density play a crucial role for explaining the large differences in average labor productivity across U.S. states. We estimate that doubling employment density in a county increases average labor productivity by 6 percent. This degree of locally increasing returns can explain more than half of the variation in labor productivity across U.S. states. Our instrumental variables estimates rest on the hypothesis that the patterns of agglomeration in the 18th and the middle of the 19th century did not reflect factors which significantly contribute to productivity today but have a remaining influence mainly through the legacy of agglomeration. Our estimates control for labor quality at the county level and for differences in the available public capital at the state level. We also compare increasing returns to density with increasing returns to size at the county level and find that increasing returns to density describes the data better than increasing returns to size.

Our work can be extended in several directions. Because our data are available by industry it would be possible to distinguish between economies from localization—which arise from the collocation of firms in the same industry—and economies from urbanization—where favorable effects arise from the general diversity and scale of urban areas. Our approach can also be used to examine dynamic externalities. Work by Edward L. Glaeser et al. (1992) and Henderson (1994) quantifies dynamic externalities by looking at the behavior of industry employment. But small productive externalities may have large employment effects. This makes it difficult to infer the significance of spatial externalities for productivity from data on the spatial concentration of industry employment. Because our data are available since 1962 our approach could be extended to examine the effect of dynamic spillovers on productivity. Our empirical work also suggests that rising density over time may be an important factor in growth. Large U.S. cities are denser now than in earlier centuries, and a much larger fraction of the population is employed in cities or other dense areas. Our estimates could be applied to historical data on the distribution of employment by county to measure the part of total growth that can be associated with rising density.

REFERENCES

Abdel-Rahman, H. M. "Product Differentiation, Monopolistic Competition and City Size." *Regional Science and Urban Economics*, February 1988, *18*(1), pp. 69–86.

Amemiya, Takeshi. "Nonlinear Regression Models," in Zvi Griliches and Michael D. Intrilligator, eds., *Handbook of econometrics*. New York: North-Holland, 1983, pp. 333–89.

Carlino, Gerald A. and Voith, Richard. "Accounting for Differences in Aggregate State Productivity." *Regional Science and Urban Economics*, November 1992, *22*(4), pp. 597–617.

Ciccone, Antonio. "Cities and the Economy: Aggregate Production, Urban Productivity and the Distribution of Economic Activity." Mimeo, Stanford University, 1992.

Davis, Steven J. "Cross-Country Patterns of Change in Relative Wages." National Bureau of Economic Research (Cambridge, MA) Working Paper No. 4085, 1992.

Dixit, Avinash and Stiglitz, Joseph E. "Monopolistic Competition and Optimum Product Diversity." *American Economic Review*, June 1977, *67*(3), pp. 297–308.

Fujita, Masahisa. "A Monopolistic Competition Model of Spatial Agglomeration: Differentiated Product Approach." *Regional Science and Urban Economics*, February 1988, *18*(1), pp. 87–124.

——. *Urban economic theory: Land use and city size*. Cambridge: Cambridge University Press, 1989.

Garcia-Mila, Teresa; McGuire, Therese J. and Porter, Richard. "The Effect of Public Capital in State-Level Production Functions Reconsidered." *Review of Economics and Statistics*, 1995, *77* (forthcoming).

Glaeser, Edward L.; Kallal, Hedi D.; Scheinkman, Jose A. and Shleifer, Andrei. "Growth in Cities." *Journal of Political Economy*, December 1992, *100*(6), pp. 1126–52.

Glaeser, Edward L. and Mare, David C. "Cities and Skills." Working Paper in Economics E-94-11, Hoover Institution, Stanford University, 1994.

Henderson, J. Vernon. "The Sizes and Types of Cities." *American Economic Review*, September 1974, *64*(4), pp. 640–56.

——. "Efficiency of Resource Usage and City Size." *Journal of Urban Economics*, January 1986, *19*(1), pp. 47–70.

——. "Externalities and Industrial Development." Manuscript, Brown University, 1994.

Holtz-Eakin, Douglas. "State-Specific Estimates of State and Local Government Capital." *Journal of Regional Science and Urban Economics*, April 1993, *23*(2), pp. 185–209.

Krugman, Paul R. *Geography and trade*. Cambridge, MA: MIT Press, 1991.

Marshall, Alfred. *Principles of economics*, 8th Ed. London: MacMillan, 1920.

Mills, Edwin S. "An Aggregative Model of Resource Allocation in a Metropolitan Area." *American Economic Review* May 1967 (Papers and Proceedings), *57*(2), pp. 197–210.

Moomaw, Ronald L. "Productivity and City Size: A Critique of the Evidence." *Quarterly Journal of Economics*, November 1981, *96*(4), pp. 675–88.

——. "Firm Location and City Size: Reduced Productivity Advantages as a Factor in the Decline of Manufacturing in Urban Areas." *Journal of Urban Economics*, January 1985, *17*(1), pp. 73–89.

Rand McNally and Company. *The new international atlas*. Chicago: Rand McNally, 1993.

Rivera-Batiz, Francisco L. "Increasing Returns, Monopolistic Competition, and Agglomeration Economies in Consumption and Production." *Regional Science and Urban*

Economics, February 1988, *18*(1), pp. 125–53.

Segal, David. "Are there Returns to Scale in City Size?" *Review of Economics and Statistics*, August 1976, *58*(3), pp. 339–50.

Spence, A. Michael. "Product Selection, Fixed Costs and Monopolistic Competition." *Review of Economic Studies*, June 1976, *43*(2), pp. 217–35.

Stover, John F. *American railroads*. Chicago: University of Chicago Press, 1961.

Sveikauskas, Leo A. "The Productivity of Cities." *Quarterly Journal of Economics*, August 1975, *89*(3), pp. 393–413.

U.S. Bureau of Economic Analysis. "Experimental Estimates of Gross State Product by Industry," Staff Paper 42. Washington, DC: U.S. Department of Commerce, 1985.

______. Regional Economic Measurement Division. *REIS: regional economic information system*. Washington, DC: Economics and Statistical Administration, 1991 (CD-ROM computer file).

U.S. Bureau of the Census. "Historical Statistics of the U.S., Colonial Times to 1970." Washington, DC: U.S. Department of Commerce, 1975.

______. *Current population survey: Annual demographic file, 1988*. Ann Arbor, MI: Inter-University Consortium for Political and Social Research, 1988 (computer file).

______. Data User Services Division. *County and city data book*. Washington, DC: Department of Commerce 1989 (computer file).

______. "Educational Attainment in the U.S.: March 1989 and March 1988," Current Populations Reports, Series P-20, No. 451. Washington, DC: Government Printing Office, 1991.

______. Data User Services Division. *Census of population and housing (1990): Summary tape file 3A*. Washington, DC, 1992 (computer file).

Wilkins, Christopher J. "Estimating the Size of Geographical Externalities." Manuscript, Stanford University, 1994.

[15]

INDUSTRIAL CONCENTRATION AND REGIONAL GROWTH: EVIDENCE FROM THE PREFECTURES

Robert Dekle

Abstract—In this paper, we estimate the impact of dynamic externalities, using direct measures of total factor productivity (TFP) growth at the regional level. We find that, at the one-digit level, significant dynamic externalities exist for the finance, services, and wholesale and retail trade industries, but—contrary to the findings of most previous research—these externalities do not exist for the manufacturing industry.

I. Introduction

SEVERAL recent explanations of economic growth focus on increasing returns to scale external to the firm as a source of increasing productivity (Romer, 1986; Lucas, 1988). Because these externalities arise from the interaction of economic agents, these effects should be most pronounced when agents are in close physical proximity. Indeed, Lucas (1988) notes the similarity of his explanation of economic growth and the explanation for cities.

A growing body of research in recent years have tried to estimate the extent and type of dynamic externalities, using data for cities (Glaeser, Scheinkman, & Shleifer, 1992, 1995; Henderson, Kuncoro, & Turner, 1995; Kim, 1995; Simon, 1998; Glendon, 1998; Gordon, Richardson, & Yu, 1998). Despite the different data sources used, their methodologies are similar: this research has invariably examined the distributions of employment growth both over time and over different cities. From the dependence of these distributions on historical conditions, this research has also tried to infer the impact of dynamic externalities on productivity growth. This research has found that the kinds of externalities found in cities are generally important for employment and thereby productivity growth. However, as we explain later, this inference of productivity growth from employment growth can be problematic. For one thing, people may move to different cities for weather, schools, and other reasons unrelated to the productivities of those cities. As first noted by Glaeser et al. (1992), it is far better to have a direct measure of the productivity of cities, but the lack of output and capital at the city level has impeded this direct measurement in the United States.

In this paper, we estimate the impact of dynamic externalities, using direct measures of total factor productivity (TFP) growth at the regional level. To the best of our knowledge, this paper is the first to estimate dynamic externalities at the regional level, using direct measures of TFP growth. We obtain these direct measures of TFP growth using Japanese prefectural data, from which output data are available and the capital stock can be calculated. We can use Japanese prefectural data because Japanese prefectures have much higher densities than U.S. states and are more like U.S. cities. We find that, at the one-digit level, significant dynamic externalities exist for the finance, services, and wholesale and retail trade industries, but, contrary to the findings of most previous research, these externalities are nonexistent for the manufacturing industry. Finally, we show that our main results are robust to pooled (panel) data estimation.

Using the terminology of Glaeser et al. (1992), there are three types of dynamic externalities. The Marshall-Arrow-Romer (MAR) externality concerns knowledge spillovers among firms in an industry. This view says that the concentration of an industry in a region helps knowledge spillovers between firms, and therefore productivity growth of that industry. In contrast, Jacobs (1969) externalities derives from a buildup of knowledge or ideas associated with historical diversity. Jacobs's theory predicts that industries located in areas that are highly industrially diversified should grow faster. Finally, Porter (1990), like MAR, argues that industrial concentration stimulates growth, but that local competition (rather than local monopoly) fosters innovation and the dissemination of information.

In this paper, we find no dynamic externalities of any type in manufacturing; strong MAR externalities, but no Jacobs or Porter externalities for finance; and relatively strong MAR externalities, nonexistent Jacobs externalities, and some Porter externalities for the services industry and the wholesale and retail trade industry. When all nine one-digit industries are taken together (pooled results), there is some evidence of MAR and Porter externalities, but no evidence of Jacobs externalities.

This paper is organized as follows. In section II, we explain our methodology of calculating regional TFP growth and of estimating dynamic externalities. We show that inferring TFP from the value of marginal product equals wage equation (as done by previous researchers) can result in various biases. In section III, we explain our data and the construction of variables. In section IV, we depict the industry-by-industry and pooled-industry results of the paper. Section V concludes.

II. Dynamic Externalities

We examine TFP growth between 1975 and 1995 for nine Japanese one-digit industries: mining, manufacturing, construction, electricity/gas, wholesale and retail, finance/insurance, real estate, transportation, and services.

The starting point in the estimation of dynamic externalities is the measurement of TFP, A_{it}, from the usual growth-

Received for publication January 5, 2000. Revision accepted for publication April 2, 2001.

* University of Southern California–Los Angeles.

I thank Heijin Ryoo for excellent research assistance; the editor of this journal, John Campbell, and an anonymous referee for very helpful suggestions; and Peter Gordon, Mike Magill, and Bill Zame for very helpful comments.

The Review of Economics and Statistics, May 2002, 84(2): 310–315 accounting exercise. Assume a production function that is constant returns to scale (at the firm level) in capital and labor:

$$Y_{it} = A_{it}K_{it}^{\alpha_{it}}L_{it}^{1-\alpha_{it}}, \quad (1)$$

where K_{it} is the level of the capital stock of industry i in the region at time t,
L_{it} is the number of workers in industry i in the region at time t, and
A_{it} is the region-specific TFP level of industry i.

The growth in region-specific TFP between time t and $t - 1$ of industry i, $gr(A_{t-1,t})$, is measured in the usual way as (suppressing industry subscripts):

$$gr(A_{t-1,t}) = \ln\left(\frac{Y(t)}{Y(t-1)}\right) - \alpha \ln\left(\frac{K(t)}{K(t-1)}\right) - (1-\alpha)\ln\left(\frac{L(t)}{L(t-1)}\right). \quad (2)$$

To test for dynamic externalities, we model $gr(A_{t,t-1})$ as a function of historical (1975) conditions in regions. In particular, as arguments of $gr(A_{t-1,t})$, we include the following variables: the own industry concentration of output or employment, ρ_{i0}; an index of the diversity of other industries that may affect an industry's productivity, D_{i0}; and C_{i0}, an index of local competition of an industry. These variables are assumed to represent MAR, Jacobs, and Porter externalities, respectively. In addition, the log TFP level in 1975, $\ln(A_{1975})$, is included as an initial condition (IC), to capture the possibility of mean reversion. In sum, we obtain our estimating equation:

$$gr(A_{t-1,t}) = g(\rho_0, D_0, C_0, IC). \quad (3)$$

Because of the lack of capital stock and output data at the city level for the United States, earlier researchers (Glaeser et al., 1992; Henderson et al., 1995; Miracky, 1995; Kim, 1995; Glendon, 1998) could not perform the growth-accounting exercise of equation (2) to directly measure $gr(A_{t-1,t})$. Rather, these researchers indirectly attempted to infer the extent of dynamic externalities from the growth in city employment and wages, from the value of marginal product equals wage equation. From the production function (equation (1)), labor market equilibrium means that $p_t(1-\alpha)A_tK_t^{\alpha}L_t^{-\alpha} = w_t$.

Taking logarithms and rearranging provides

$$\ln\left(\frac{L(t)}{L(t-1)}\right) = -\frac{1}{\alpha}\ln\left(\frac{w(t)}{w(t-1)}\right) + \frac{1}{\alpha}gr(A_{t-1,t}) - \ln\left(\frac{K(t)}{K(t-1)}\right) + \frac{1}{\alpha}\ln\left(\frac{p(t)}{p(t-1)}\right).$$

If capital stock data are unavailable,

$$\ln\left(\frac{L(t)}{L(t-1)}\right) = -\frac{1}{\alpha}\ln\left(\frac{w(t)}{w(t-1)}\right) + \frac{1}{\alpha}g(\rho_0, D_0, C_0, IC) + \frac{1}{\alpha}\ln\left(\frac{p(t)}{p(t-1)}\right), \quad (4)$$

where equation (3) is used to substitute for $gr(A_{t,t-1})$.

At least three problems that do not arise in the estimation of externalities from equation (3) arise in the estimation of equation (4). First, unless the regional capital stock is constant, $\ln(K_t/K_{t-1} = 0)$, omitted-variables bias may plague the estimates. The constant regional capital stock assumption is unrealistic, even in relatively low-investment countries like the United States. Second, because the growth in regional prices $\ln(P_t/P_{t-1})$ by industry is usually unobserved, earlier researchers have had to assume some pattern for the growth in prices. For example, Glaeser et al. (1992) assume that the growth in prices is determined at the nationwide level and thus do not vary by city. To the extent that some goods are nontraded and that all manufactured goods include some nontraded component, the assumption of nationwide prices may be unrealistic. Third, it is well known that living costs such as housing rents and consumption amenities such as weather and local public goods affect migration decisions. Earlier research on dynamic externalities have usually not controlled for these amenities in the estimation of an equation like equation (4) (with the exception of Glaeser et al. (1995) and Glendon (1998) who explicitly control for local amenities). All of these difficult issues are avoided when TFP growth is estimated directly in equation (3). However, for comparability with earlier studies, we also show the results when the marginal-revenue-product-equals-wage-equation like equation (4) is estimated.

III. Construction of Data

The data pertain to 1975 and 1995 and are mainly from the 1998 edition of the *Japanese Annual Report on the Prefectural Accounts* (ARPA), published by the Economic Planning Agency. This publication is unique in that it includes at the regional level (47 Japanese prefectures) all of the data contained in conventional national income accounts.

To calculate TFP, we need output, the supplies of labor and capital, and the labor and capital shares, all by industry. As a measure of industry output, we use NNP at factor cost (GNP minus indirect business taxes minus depreciation). As a measure of industry labor supply, we take the number of employed persons by industry from the *Labor Force Survey* (published by the Ministry of Labor) and multiply this

TABLE 1.—REGIONAL MEANS OF VARIABLES BY INDUSTRY

Variable	Finance	Manufacturing	Services	Whole/ Retail	Mining	Construction	Electricity/ Gas	Real Estate	Transport
Growth of capital stock (in percentage)*	0.1	0.6	0.0	0.1	1.6	0.1	1.4	1.1	0.7
Growth of national capital stock (in percentage)***	1.3	0.7	2.0	0.6	1.0	1.0	1.2	4.9	0.2
Growth of employment (in percentage)***	−5.2	0.7	3.2	0.7	−11	2.3	−26	3.7	9.4
Total factor productivity growth (TFP) (in percentage)*	1.9	1.5	1.1	−2.1	1.2	1.1	6.3	2.2	−1.0
National TFP growth (in percentage)***	0.3	1.4	−3.8	1.8	−1.7	0.05	−0.2	−7.9	1.6
GDP per sq. km., 1975 (billions of 1995 Yen)	857	4684	1889	2835	94.3	1763	403	1185	1131
Employment per sq. km., 1975**	0.25	0.94	0.66	0.02	0.01	0.36	0.83	0.02	0.11

* Average annual growth over twenty years.
** Employment = (hours worked)*(number of people employed).
*** Average annual nationwide growth from 1984 to 1997 (from Japanese Ministry of Labor, 1997).

number by the average hours of worked by industry (from the *Basic Survey on the Wage Structure,* published by the Ministry of Labor). As a measure of the industry capital stock, we divide the amount of industry capital depreciation (from factor income tables) by the industry capital depreciation rate (from the *National Income Accounts,* published by the Economic Planning Agency) and, from this sum, subtract the amount of depreciation; that is, $K_t = \delta K_t/\delta - \delta K_t$. As a measure of the industry labor share, we take the share of employee compensation in NNP at factor cost. The industry capital share is simply 1 minus the estimated industry labor share. The industry output and capital stock are deflated by the industry GDP deflator for each prefecture (from ARPA).

As explanatory variables, we need base year (1975) levels of ρ_{i0}, D_{i0}, C_{i0}, and w_{it}. For base-year concentration, ρ_{i0} (MAR externalities), we take the ratio of own-industry output or own-industry employment to the total effective urban land area (in square kilometers). The effective urban land areas represent about 12% of the total land areas in Japan, and almost all industrial activity are concentrated in these areas. Output per square kilometers is preferable to employment per square kilometer as a measure of density because it better captures the intensity of labor, human, and physical capital combined relative to physical space. Also, we define the Hoover-type (1936) variable,

$$\rho_{i0} = \frac{\dfrac{y_{i0}}{y_0}}{\dfrac{y_{Ji}}{y_J}},$$

where y_{i0} is the industry output or employment in the region,
y_0 is the total output or employment in the region,
y_{iJ} is the industry output or employment in Japan, and
y_J is total output or employment in Japan.

As noted by Glaeser et al. (1992), this Hoover-type variable measures how specialized a city is in an industry relative to what one would expect if output or employment in that industry was scattered randomly across Japan.

For the index of diversity, D_{i0} (Jacobs externalities) we follow Henderson et al. (1995) and calculate the Herfindahl-Hirschman Index (HHI) for each region using all of our nine one-digit industries:

$$D_{i0} = HHI = \sum_{i=1}^{9} s_i^2$$

where s_i is the share of industry i output or employment in all other output or employment in the region.

As a measure of local competition, C_{i0} (Porter externalities), following Glaeser et al. (1992), we define

$$C_{i0} = \frac{\dfrac{y_0}{f_{i0}}}{\dfrac{y_J}{f_{iJ}}},$$

where f_{i0} is the number of firms in the region industry, and f_{iJ} is the number of firms in the industry in Japan. A value of C_{i0} greater than 1 means that the industry has fewer firms relative to its size in this region than it does in the rest of Japan; that is, the industry is less competitive. The number of establishments and the number of employees by establishment at the industry level are from the *Establishment Census,* published by the Management and Coordination Agency. Finally, as a measure for the industry wage, w_t, we divide employee compensation from the ARPA by our measure of industry labor supply. We then divide this industry wage by the industry GDP deflator.

Table 1 depicts the means over the 47 prefectures of several key variables. For most industries, the average growth rates of the prefectural capital stock and total factor productivity closely match the national growth rates (Ministry of Labor, 1997).

IV. Results

In this section, we show the results of our estimation of the nature and extent of external economies (MAR, Jacobs, and Porter). Although we have performed the estimation on all nine industries at the one-digit level, to save space and for comparability with earlier research our discussion here focuses on just four industries: finance, manufacturing, wholesale and retail, and services.

TABLE 2.—REGION-INDUSTRY TOTAL FACTOR PRODUCTIVITY GROWTH BETWEEN 1975 AND 1995 (ORDINARY LEAST SQUARES)

	Finance				Manufacturing				Services				Wholesale and Retail			
Specification	(1)	(2)	(3)	(4)	(1)	(2)	(3)	(4)	(1)	(2)	(3)	(4)	(1)	(2)	(3)	(4)
GDP per sq. km.	0.089	0.089		0.089	0.0022	0.0053		0.0049	0.04	0.04		0.05	0.041	0.041		0.022
(coefficient × 1000)	(3.3)	(3.5)		(2.6)	(0.2)	(0.5)		(0.5)	(2.4)	(2.4)		(1.88)	(5.4)	(5.3)		(0.37)
Herfindahl-Hirschman		−0.89				−0.58				−0.86				−0.17		
Index (output)		(−1.5)				(−0.7)				(−1.19)				(−0.3)		
GDP per establishment in			0.14	−0.19			0.027	0.044			0.29	−0.33			0.45	0.27
the region-industry relative to GDP per establishment in Japan			(1.4)	(−1.3)			(0.5)	(0.7)			(1.82)	(−1.53)			(4.2)	(1.7)

Initial conditions (IC): log (TFP) level in 1975.
47 observations (prefectures).

The main results, the impact of dynamic externalities on TFP growth (equation (3)) are shown in table 2. To control for mean reversion in the level of TFP, we include as an initial condition the level of log (TFP) in 1975 (not shown). The sign of log (TFP) is always negative and usually highly significant, suggesting the presence of mean reversion, which is a finding consistent with Glaeser et al. (1992) and Henderson et al. (1995). Although more than fifty different specifications were tried for each industry, table 2 depicts four specifications that are representative to save space. The coefficient signs and significance of the variables of interest were highly robust to the different specifications.

The most remarkable results in table 2 relate to the heterogeneity across industries in the type and extent of externalities. The finance industry is characterized by high own-industry agglomeration economies (MAR externalities): the initial level of the own-industry GDP density raises subsequent industry TFP growth. An increase of one standard deviation in finance GDP density raises TFP growth by 0.5% per year. However, the diversity of industries (Jacobs externalities) and the degree of local competition (Porter externalities) have no apparent effect on productivity growth in finance.

The presence of strong dynamic externalities in finance is consistent with Dekle and Eaton (1999), who find in Japanese regional data that agglomeration economies are far more geographically concentrated in finance than in manufacturing. The extent of human capital externalities may explain why agglomeration effects in finance are more localized. One can imagine that human interactions would be more important in raising productivity in financial services than in manufacturing. For one thing, financial services are more knowledge intensive: in Japan, 36% of workers in the financial sector have a university education, whereas in manufacturing the figure is only 15%.

In contrast, the manufacturing industry is characterized by the absence of external economies of any type. Besides the control variable, none of the coefficients are significant. This result goes against earlier research that estimated equation (4) and found significant MAR externalities for manufacturing industries at the two-digit level or lower. Taken together, the results from the earlier research and ours suggest that it may be problematic to infer productivity growth from employment growth, and that manufacturing as a whole is actually characterized by low or no dynamic externalities. Alternatively, if manufacturing dynamic externalities are present, they are MAR and are confined to rather narrow industry categories at the two-digit level or below (such as software or ball-bearing manufacturing), and that spillovers among these product categories (Jacobs externalities) are rather limited.

The services industry and the wholesale and retail trade industry are both characterized by relatively strong MAR externalities, nonexistent Jacobs externalities, and some Porter externalities. An increase of one standard deviation in own-industry GDP density raises TFP growth in services and in the wholesale and retail trade industries by 0.4% and 0.5% per year, respectively.

The presence of dynamic externalities in nonmanufacturers such as the services and the wholesale and retail industries is consistent with Glaeser et al. (1992), who find that dynamic externalities are, if anything, more pronounced in these industries than in manufacturing. Given that these industries produce mostly nontraded goods, for employees in these industries, opportunities for human interaction with people outside of the prefecture are probably quite limited (Losch, 1967). Thus, opportunities for human interaction within the prefecture, which is associated with own-industry concentration, may be more important in these industries. Also, in industries producing nontraded goods, the main source of competition is within the prefecture, which may explain the importance of Porter externalities for these industries. For manufacturing and finance, much of the source of competition that spurs innovation may come from outside the prefecture.

It may seem surprising that dynamic externalities are important in the wholesale and retail industry because employees in this industry are not typically thought of as well educated. However, employees in this industry actually are quite well educated. (More than 26% have a college degree, compared to only 15% in manufacturing.) Moreover, Koike (1984) and others have argued that, in Japan, much of human capital accumulation occurs not by formal education but by on-the-job training. To test for the importance of human capital acquired on-the-job in the wholesale and retail industry, we divided the workers in this industry into "full-time" and "part-time." Full-time workers have spent most of their careers in the industry, and their on-the-

TABLE 3.—REGION-INDUSTRY EMPLOYMENT GROWTH BETWEEN 1975 AND 1995 (ORDINARY LEAST SQUARES)

	Finance				Manufacturing				Services				Wholesale and Retail			
Specification	(1)	(2)	(3)	(4)	(1)	(2)	(3)	(4)	(1)	(2)	(3)	(4)	(1)	(2)	(3)	(4)
Labor per sq. km.	−0.17 (−0.5)			0.31 (1.1)	−0.26 (−4.5)			−0.27 (−4.8)	−0.12 (−0.9)			−0.0015 (−0.013)	−2.03 (−1.5)			1.97 (1.7)
Region-industry's share of region employment relative to industry's share of Japanese employment		−0.47 (−1.9)		−0.71 (−4.4)		−0.054 (−0.3)		0.078 (0.68)		−0.42 (−1.4)		−0.81 (−3.6)		−0.69 (−4.9)		−1.1 (−5.4)
Herfindahl-Hirschman Index (employment)		−0.48 (−0.2)				2.1 (0.8)				3.87 (1.4)				0.66 (0.51)		
Employment per establishment in the region-industry relative to employment per establishment in Japan			0.27 (2.3)	0.45 (4.2)			0.039 (0.6)	0.041 (1.2)			0.61 (2.2)	0.77 (3.1)			−0.28 (−2.3)	0.23 (1.7)

Initial conditions (IC): log (employment) level in 1975; log (change in wages) from 1975 to 1995.
47 observations (prefectures).

job human capital is much higher than those of part-time workers, who are mostly housewives, with intermittent work histories. We again ran equation (3) including two variables for ρ_{i0} (MAR externalities): "full-time" labor per squared kilometer and "part-time" labor per squared kilometer. The coefficient on full-time labor density was highly significant, but the coefficient on part-time labor density was small and insignificant (not shown), suggesting that dynamic externalities in the wholesale and retail trade industry are almost entirely due to the density of full-time, high-human capital labor.

Table 3 replicates, at the one-digit level, the marginal-revenue-product-equals-wage equation (4) that was estimated by most previous researchers at the two-digit level or below (Glaeser et al., 1992; Henderson et al., 1995; Miracky, 1995; Glendon, 1998). Consistent with the neoclassical theory of labor demand, the coefficient on the change in wages is negative and highly significant in all specifications (not shown). The coefficients on the MAR density variable (labor per squared kilometer) either are insignificant (finance, services, wholesale and retail) or are negative (manufacturing), implying the absence of MAR externalities. With the exception of the manufacturing industry, there is some evidence that competition raises the rate of productivity growth (Porter externalities). There is no evidence of Jacobs externalities for any industry. The negative coefficient on the MAR variable is consistent with Glaeser et al. (1992), who find that industry over representation hurts its employment growth. Our findings here of Porter externalities but weak Jacobs externalities are replicated in the earlier literature.

Our favored interpretation for the insignificant or negative MAR coefficients in these results (equation (4)) is omitted-variables bias. Suppose that higher density results in, and is positively correlated with, higher capital stock growth. Then, if equation (4) is estimated with capital stock growth omitted, the coefficient on the density variable will be biased downwards, by standard omitted-variable arguments (Goldberger, 1968).

A. *Panel Estimates*

By pooling all nine industries, we can estimate the coefficients on the externality measures using panel data techniques. Panel data estimation can improve the precision of the estimates by increasing the number of observations. Also, with panel data, we can control for unobserved prefectural fixed effects, which can bias the coefficient estimates.

Table 4 depicts the panel data estimation of equation (3). The GDP density variable is highly significant: an increase of one standard deviation in own-industry GDP density raises TFP growth by about 0.4% per year. The HHI has the wrong sign, but the local competition variable is significant. Thus, the pooled results show that Japanese industries, taken together, exhibit some evidence of MAR and Porter externalities, but no evidence of Jacobs externalities.

Table 4 also depicts the panel data estimates of the marginal-revenue-product-equals-wage equation (4). These results essentially reproduce with Japanese data the results found in Glaeser et al. (1992), who in fact pool their six industries over 170 U.S. cities. As in Glaeser et al., the Hoover-type concentration measure is strongly negative, and the variable measuring Jacobs externalities is highly positive and significant. However, as we have already pointed out, there are potential pitfalls in inferring agglomeration effects from an equation such as equation (4).

In sum, the panel data estimation supports our earlier findings that agglomeration effects, if present, are of the MAR and the Porter types. However, as shown in tables 2 and 3, there is substantial heterogeneity among the industries. As noted by Hsiao and Sun (1999) and others, when the data-generating process is heterogeneous, pooling the data can yield highly misleading inference. Thus, although the results presented in table 4 are informative, we should place more weight on the individual industry estimates presented earlier.

TABLE 4.—PANEL DATA ESTIMATES

	Region-Industry Total Factor Productivity Growth Between 1975 and 1995[a,b,c]				Region-Industry Employment Growth Between 1975 and 1995[b,c,d]			
Specification	(1)	(2)	(3)	(4)	(1)	(2)	(3)	(4)
GDP per sq. km. (coefficient × 1000)	0.025 (2.9)	0.02 (3.2)		0.021 (2.4)				
Labor per sq. km.					−0.097 (−1.8)			−0.12 (−2.5)
Region-industry's share of region employment relative to industry's share of Japanese employment						−0.24 (−8.2)		−0.26 (−8.1)
Herfindahl-Hirschman Index (output)		−0.85 (−1.9)						
Herfindahl-Hirschman Index (employment)						3.5 (4.4)		
GDP per establishment in the region-industry relative to GDP per establishment in Japan			0.069 (2.0)	0.042 (1.2)				
Employment per establishment in the region-industry relative to employment per establishment in Japan							−0.18 (−5.7)	−0.069 (−2.2)

[a] Initial conditions (IC): log (TFP) level in 1975.
[b] Including nine industry dummy variables.
[c] 423 observations (47 prefectures × 9 industries).
[d] Initial conditions (IC): log (employment level in 1975), log (change in wages from 1975 to 1995).

VI. Conclusion

We have shown that, at the prefectural level, there is considerable heterogeneity among industries in how dynamic externalities affect productivity growth. We have shown that specialization raises productivity growth in the finance, services, and wholesale and retail industries, and that competition helps growth in the services and wholesale and retail industries. At the one-digit level, the concentration of GDP or employment does not affect manufacturing productivity, suggesting that the benefits to concentration in manufacturing are small.

The evidence suggests that the cross-fertilization of ideas is especially important for nonmanufacturers, and that there will be a tendency of further geographic concentration in industries such as financial services. The manufacturing industry is characterized by low or no dynamic externalities. Thus, the manufacturing industry should continue to disperse geographically, both domestically and internationally.

REFERENCES

Dekle, R., and J. Eaton, "Agglomeration and Land Rents: Evidence from the Prefectures," *Journal of Urban Economics* 46:3 (1999), 200–214.

Economic Planning Agency, *Annual Report on the Prefectural Accounts* (Tokyo: Government of Japan Printing Office, 1998).

Economic Planning Agency, *National Income Accounts of Japan* (Tokyo: Government of Japan Printing Office, various years).

Glaeser, E., H. Kallal, J. Scheinkman, and A. Shleifer, "Growth in Cities," *Journal of Political Economy* 100:6 (1992) 1126–1152.

——— "Economic Growth in a Cross Section of Cities," *Journal of Monetary Economics* 36 (1995), 117–143.

Glendon, S., "Urban Life Cycles," Harvard University manuscript (1998).

Goldberger, A., *Topics in Regression Analysis* (New York: Macmillan, 1968).

Gordon, P., H. Richardson, and G. Yu, "Metropolitan and Non-metropolitan Employment Trends in the U.S.: Recent Evidence and Implications," *Urban Studies* 35:7 (1998), 1037–1057.

Henderson, V., A. Kuncoro, and M. Turner, "Industrial Development in Cities," *Journal of Political Economy* 103:51 (1995), 1067–1085.

Hoover, E., "The Measurement of Industrial Localization," this REVIEW 18 (1936), 162–171.

Hsiao, C., and B. H. Sun, "To Pool or Not to Pool Panel Data," University of Southern California mimeograph (1999).

Jacobs, J., *The Economy of Cities* (New York: Vintage, 1969).

Kim, S., "Expansion of Markets and the Geographic Distribution of Economic Activities: The Trends in U.S. Regional Manufacturing Structure, 1860–1987," *Quarterly Journal of Economics* 110:4 (1995), 881–908.

Koike, K., "Skill Formation Systems in the U.S. and Japan" (pp. 47–75), in M. Aoki (Ed.), *The Economic Analysis of the Japanese Firm* (Amsterdam: North-Holland, 1984).

Losch, A., *The Economics of Location* (New York: Wiley, 1967).

Lucas, R., "On the Mechanics of Economic Development," *Journal of Monetary Economics* 21:1 (1988), 3–42.

Management and Coordination Agency, *Establishment Census* (Tokyo: Government of Japan Printing Office, various years).

Management and Coordination Agency, *Labor Force Survey* (Tokyo: Government of Japan Printing Office, various years).

Ministry of Labor, *Basic Survey on the Wage Structure* (Tokyo: Government of Japan Printing Office, various years).

Ministry of Labor, "Productivity Growth in Japan" mimeograph (1997).

Miracky, W., "Economic Growth in Cities: The Role of Localization Externalities," unpublished doctoral dissertation, Massachusetts Institute of Technology (1995).

Porter, M., *The Competitive Advantage of Nations* (New York: Free Press, 1990).

Romer, P., "Increasing Returns and Long-run Growth," *Journal of Political Economy* 94:3 (1986), 1002–1037.

Simon, C., "Human Capital and Metropolitan Employment Growth," *Journal of Urban Economics* 43:2 (1998), 223–243.

[16]

Journal of Urban Economics **47**, 329–355 (2000)
doi:10.1006/juec.1999.2143, available online at http://www.idealibrary.com on IDEAL®

Economic Structure and Local Growth: France, 1984–1993

Pierre-Philippe Combes[1]

CNRS and CERAS-Ecole Nationale des Ponts et Chaussées, 28, Rue des Saints-Pères, 75 007 Paris, France
E-mail: combes@enpc.fr

Received October 5, 1998; revised June 28, 1999

For 52 industry sectors and 42 services sectors, this paper tests how the local economic structure (local sectoral specialization and diversity, competition, average size of plants, and total employment density) affects the 1984–1993 employment growth of 341 local areas. These areas entirely and continuously cover the French territory. The impact of the local economic structure differs in industry and services. In industrial sectors, local total employment density, competition, and plant size always reduce local growth. Sectoral specialization and diversity have a negative impact on growth, but also increase the growth of a few sectors. Service sectors always exhibit negative specialization effects and positive diversity effects. Competition and plant size have a negative impact and density a positive one, but exceptions are observed for some sectors.

1. INTRODUCTION

There is an ongoing debate about the relative impact of urbanization and localization economies in the process of local economic development. When sectoral diversity matters for local growth, urbanization economies are prevalent, as suggested by Glaeser et al. [19] in their study of the U.S. cities between 1956 and 1987. By contrast, Henderson et al. [22] show evidence of a positive effect of specialization on urban growth, thus reflecting localization economies, between 1970 and 1987. They find evidence of urbanization economies only in new high-tech sectors. This paper contributes to this debate by studying the growth of French local areas. Further, it shows how additional variables characterizing the local eco-

[1] I greatly thank Jan Brueckner, Gilles Duranton, Gilles Saint-Paul, Bernard Salanié, Jacques-François Thisse, Mickaël Visser, Yves Zenou, two anonymous referees, and participants at the CEPR-NBER International Seminar in International Trade (Paris, May 1997) and the Western Regional Science Association annual meeting (Monterey, February 1998) for very useful comments. I also thank Emmanuel Duguet, Sylvie Lagarde, and Françoise Maurel for their critical help concerning data and econometrics. My Web site is at http://www.enpc.fr/ceras/combes.

0094-1190/00 $35.00

nomic structure also contribute to the explanation of development. Finally, some methodological points are clarified.

More precisely, local employment growth by sector is regressed on five variables. The first two are specialization and diversity as in Glaeser et al. [19] and Henderson et al. [22]. However, it is argued that other local economic variables have a significant impact on local growth. First, the size of the local economy, sometimes considered as part of urbanization economies, as, for instance, in Ó hUallacháin and Satterthwaite [28], determines the size of local markets as well as the supply of local public goods. However, it may also be the origin of negative externalities such as pollution or high land rents. Second, as suggested in industrial organization and recalled by Glaeser et al. [19], the location and growth of firms also depend on the intensity of competition on both local input and output markets. Lastly, the size of plants, a variable also considered by Glaeser et al. [19] and Ó hUallacháin and Satterthwaite [28], is used here as a surrogate to test whether local economies of scale are internal or external to plants. Unlike previous works, we simultaneously consider all these variables. This allows us to provide a broader perspective of the issues by comparing the impact of each of these variables.

Previous comparable papers have mainly concentrated on manufacturing sectors. However, it is well known that the share of industry in modern economies is declining. In this paper, we consider both industry and services; our dataset includes 52 industrial and 42 service sectors. One should keep in mind that the intensity of agglomeration forces may differ across industrial and service sectors. For instance, some of the latter are nontradable as they must be consumed where they are produced. Moreover, they might be also less subject to economies of scale. To the extent that services are also more diversified in their input consumption and in the sectors they sell to, it is reasonable to believe that they benefit more from diversity. More generally, we may expect the economic structure to have a different impact on local growth, depending on the sector. Our analysis confirms this assumption.

It is worth stressing that the results obtained in this paper may not be identical to those derived for the American economy. Indeed, economic geography models show the importance of factor mobility in agglomeration processes. Unlike the U.S., labor mobility is very low in European countries. Furthermore, the existence of substantial unemployment within the European Union might have a significant impact on firms' location strategies. All of these suggest that the agglomeration process, and, in particular, the role of the local economic environment, may vastly differ in Europe from what it is in the U.S. In this respect, the present paper is a first attempt to compare a European country (France) with the U.S. In addition, whereas American studies often focus on metropolitan areas, we use a set of 341 spatial entities (*zones d'emploi* "employment areas") that covers the whole territory of France. As a result, the possible econometric problem due to the selection of particular entities partially vanishes, while the scope of the study is enlarged to cope with nonmetropolitan areas. Finally, we propose some methodological innovations that, hopefully, help to clarify the debate on the causes of local development. These include the replacement of the sectoral local employment level by the total local employment level in the explanatory variables, the use of a Herfindhal index of competition, and the use of a generalized Tobit model in estimation.

A last point is worth mentioning. Previous studies often argue that the impact of the local economy on growth mainly goes through information spillovers. In Section 2, we show that alternative interpretations are also consistent with the tested reduced form. Section 3 presents the dataset and the econometric method. The results are given and interpreted in Section 4, while Section 5 concludes.

2. ECONOMIC STRUCTURE AND AGGLOMERATION FORCES

Let us begin by justifying the reduced form we estimate as

$$y_{z,s} = I + \alpha_1 \log(\text{spe}_{z,s}) + \alpha_2 \log(\text{div}_{z,s}) + \alpha_3 \log(\text{size}_{z,s})$$
$$\alpha_4 \log(\text{comp}_{z,s}) + \alpha_5 \log(\text{den}_z), \qquad (1)$$

where $y_{z,s}$ is the local employment growth of sector s in zone z, I is an intercept, and $\text{spe}_{z,s}$, $\text{div}_{z,s}$, $\text{size}_{z,s}$, $\text{comp}_{z,s}$, and den_z are the explanatory variables corresponding respectively to specialization, diversity, average size of plants, competition, and total employment density. In this section, our first aim is to briefly present the two main families of agglomeration forces (information spillovers and market-based forces) that have been recently put forward to explain local development. We then provide a justification for using specification (1) by showing that all explanatory variables have an impact not only on information spillovers but also on market-based forces.

2.1. *Agglomeration Forces*

Fujita and Thisse [17] and Glaeser [18] provide recent surveys on agglomeration and dispersion forces.

Information Spillovers

Information spillovers arise when the following conditions are met. First, firms have different pieces of information, which they are able to exchange through the turnover of skilled labor and/or through face-to-face contacts.

These pieces of information bear on firms' organization, product demand (desired qualities, market locations), and input and/or output innovations. The expression "technological externality" is used in this last case. Second, distance is an impediment to the transmission of information. Indeed, even though communication technologies have been greatly improved, several recent studies, such as Jaffe [24], Acs et al. [3], Jaffe et al. [25], Audretsch and Feldman [5], or Anselin et al. [4], show that the diffusion of information and tacit knowledge across locations is far from being free. Consequently, local information spillovers are still relevant, and firms benefit from locating in the same place.

Market-based Forces

Whereas information spillovers correspond to pure externalities, other agglomeration forces operate directly through markets. Because of the coexistence of transportation costs and increasing returns, it is profitable for firms to be located close to large input and output markets. However, a high degree of competition for these products in these markets, by lowering output prices and increasing input prices, is a strong dispersion force. But this is not the end of the story. More competition also gives more incentives to suppliers and consumers to locate in the large area, thus increasing the size of the corresponding markets. Three families of models describe such spatial configurations: urban economics models, as initiated by Fujita and Ogawa [16], spatial competition in the spirit of Hotelling [23], and new economic geography inspired by Krugman [26]. Differences arise from the modelling of the physical substratum, from the nature of competition (perfect or imperfect, with or without product differentiation and strategic interactions), and from the fact that the setting is partial or general. Empirical studies aimed at validating these models are rare. This is mainly due to the difficulty in collecting good data at the micro-spatial level.

2.2. *Impact of the Economic Structure on Agglomeration Forces*

Like in previous comparable studies, the dataset used in this paper does not allow one to discriminate between the two types of externalities. This is not a major drawback here since the purpose is to determine which kind of local economic structure fosters economic growth, whatever agglomeration forces. In this section, we show how the explanatory variables introduced in specification (1) affect the two types of agglomeration forces.

Sectoral Specialization and Diversity

Localization economies imply that firms benefit from clustering with other firms in the same sector, whereas urbanization externalities imply inter-sectoral positive effects of agglomeration (see, e.g., Quigley [30]).

Regarding information spillovers, the innovations of a given sector mainly originate and diffuse from this very sector but also from other sectors. For example, improvement in electronics components increases the power of software. Conversely, the need for higher memory and speed capacities by software engineers gives electronics firms incentives to discover new technologies. If there is some uncertainty about the sector that is at the origin of innovation in another sector, high global diversity increases the probability of such a cross-fertilization of ideas. These impacts of specialization and diversity on local technological spillovers are detailed in Glaeser et al. [19]. Feldman and Audretsch [14] make one of the first attempts to directly test the impact of diversity (which is strong) and of specialization on the local rate of innovation.

However, this debate is also relevant for market-based forces. Abdel-Rahman and Fujita [2] show that the relative degree of internal and of inter-sectoral scale economies conditions the degree of urban diversity. In models based on homogenous inputs and outputs (for instance, under perfect competition as in the traditional trade theory or under imperfect competition *à la* Cournot, as in Combes [9]), local growth is associated with specialization. On the contrary, the use of the Dixit and Stiglitz [11] monopolistic competition model in urban economics[2] and in economic geography[3] yields a preference for diversity, inducing agglomeration. Uncertainty, on the quality of goods for instance, reinforces these effects as shown by Schulz and Stahl [32], with high diversity improving the quality of matching.

Size of the Local Economy

If rural as well as urban areas are considered, the size of the local economy also influences the intensity of agglomeration forces. This is an important explanation of the uneven distribution of activities in the U.S., as shown by Ciccone and Hall [8], and may be interpreted as another form of urbanization economies, as in Ó hUallacháin and Satterthwaite [28]. First, the level and quality of information exchanges in spillovers are sufficiently important only when the number of firms, and thus the potential complementarities, is high enough.

Second, the size of local markets greatly affects the firms' locational choices if transportation costs are non-zero. The locations of input and output markets for each sector are rarely available in datasets. However, sectoral effects being controlled by the specialization and diversity variables, the size of local markets is conditioned by the global size of the local economy and is measured here by total employment density. Moreover,

[2] See Abdel-Rahman [11], Fujita [15], and Rivera-Batiz [31].
[3] See Krugman [26], Krugman and Venables [27], and Puga [29].

this variable is relevant for some non-specialized markets, such as land: high density implies high land rent, which constitutes a dispersion force. Some local pure externalities, positive (such as the presence of local public goods) or negative (such as transportation congestion or pollution), also depend on the total size of local economy.

Local Competition

The positive effects of the size of local markets depend on the degree of competition in these markets. Due to strategic interactions, firms have incentives to locate at the periphery where competition is lowered, even though a more central location would allow them to attract more consumers. Different frameworks (product differentiation, uncertainty on the quality of goods) allow firms to relax price competition, thus leading them to choose more central locations (see Fujita and Thisse [17]).

The impact of competition on information spillovers is ambiguous, a fact which is not related to the spatial dimension. Indeed, Sutton [33] shows that empirical studies do not succeed in establishing that competition has a positive impact on innovations. Schumpeterian models underline the trade-off: high competition gives firms incentives to make important R & D investment, but, if the succession of innovations is too fast, returns from R & D are low, which reduces the amount of R & D and has in turn a negative impact on innovations. Since competition generates opposite effects on the level of local R & D and innovations, its effect is also indeterminate on local technological spillovers.

Average Plant Size

If scale economies are internal to plants, for instance, in the monopolistic competition models, large plants have lower average costs and benefit more from locating close to large markets. If scale economies are external to plants, in the endogenous growth model spirit, only the city size determines the degree of scale economies, large plants being penalized if internal returns are decreasing. For instance, at the country level, Caballero and Lyons [7], by comparing firms' and aggregate production functions, find very little evidence of internal economies of scale, whereas external ones exist for the four countries they study.

Concerning information spillovers, arguments in both directions can be presented. The size of the R & D department clearly increases with the size of plants. However, first, some empirical studies show that the efficiency of R & D decreases with the size. Second, small plants, which may not have an R & D department, are the most interested in technological spillovers and can even base their development on them, for instance, by encouraging the turnover of skilled labor at other firms.

As we have shown, all considered elements of the local economic structure may affect information spillovers and market-based forces, possibly in opposite directions. For a given family of externalities, their effects depend on the characteristics of production (e.g., the levels of transportation costs and scale economies), the degree of product differentiation, and the presence or absence of uncertainty. Depending on the sector, empirical studies such as this one show what the dominant effects are.

3. DATA AND ESTIMATION METHODOLOGY

In France, as is more generally the case in Europe, local data are scarce. Our study is based on 341 geographic units defined by the French National Institute of Statistics and Economic Studies (INSEE) and called *zones d'emploi* (ZEs, "employment areas"). These ZEs entirely and continuously cover the French territory, and thus include both urban and rural places. Their average area is 1570 km^2, which is fairly small (equivalent to a 40×40 kms square) but the standard-deviation is high (987 km^2). A ZE's definition is based on the observation of workers' daily migrations. This makes them economically more homogenous than administrative units, and it lowers some border effects.

We use a dataset on plants (*Enquête Structure des Emplois*, collected by INSEE), which includes all plants located in France that have more than 20 workers. It gives each plant's employment level between 1984 and 1993, the ZE where the plant is located, and its four-digit sector. We use INSEE's sectoral nomenclature (NAP 100) that aggregates sectors into 52 industrial sectors and 42 service sectors.

Some of the effects described above have a direct influence on output, but others only affect productivity. Local employment should vary in the same direction, but, if better productivity in a given place does not induce market-share gains, or if the substitutability between labor and capital is high, employment may decrease in a few specific cases. As in previous comparable studies, we hope this does not too much perturb the interpretations, since data on local output levels and capital stocks do not exist.

First, regressions are performed by pooling different sectors, as in Glaeser et al. [19]. They are computed on all industrial sectors, on the one hand, and on all services sectors, on the other hand, and are called "global regressions." Second, as in Ó hUallacháin and Satterthwaite [28] and Henderson et al. [22], regressions are computed on each sector separately. In order to avoid introducing a selectivity bias, all geographic units are kept, contrary to Glaeser et al. [19]. Moreover, each variable is normalized by the value it takes at the national level for the considered sector: this allows comparisons between sectors. For the same reason, Ellison and Glaeser [12] correct the spatial concentration index by the sectoral productive concentration. Surprisingly, Glaeser et al. [19] only normalize their specialization and competition variables, but not others.

The dependent variable is the difference between the employment growth of sector s in ZE z between 1984 and 1993 and the national employment growth of this sector in France during the same period,

$$y_{z,s} = \log\left(\frac{\text{emp}_{z,s,1993}}{\text{emp}_{z,s,1984}}\right) - \log\left(\frac{\text{emp}_{s,1993}}{\text{emp}_{s,1984}}\right),$$

where $\text{emp}_{z,s,t}$ and $\text{emp}_{s,t}$ ($t = 1984, 1993$) are employment levels in sector s at date t in ZE z and France, respectively. We do not want to explain why the growth of a sector in a given place is $x\%$, but why it is $y\%$ higher (or lower) in this place compared to the national level. In regressions on each sector, this normalization only changes the intercept, but this makes important differences in global regressions. It is worth noting that this variable can be interpreted in terms of employment density growth and that all other variables are implicitly normalized by land area (which cancels in the ratio form), except the one controlling for the size of the local economy. It is consequently controlled for differences in the ZEs' areas.

All explanatory variables are considered at the initial date, 1984. This is consistent with the observed lag between the emergence of agglomeration forces and their real impact on firms' relocation and on regional growth. Adding 1993 variables to the specification, as in Henderson et al. [22], makes it more difficult to interpret. All variables are taken in logarithms: the estimated parameters are their elasticities with respect to each variable, which makes them easily comparable.

The specialization index we consider is the ratio of the employment share of sector s in ZE z divided by this ratio at the national level,

$$\text{spe}_{z,s} = \frac{\text{emp}_{z,s}/\text{emp}_z}{\text{emp}_s/\text{emp}},$$

where emp_z and emp are the total employment and $\text{emp}_{z,s}$ and emp_s are the sectoral employment in ZE z and France, respectively.

Concerning diversity, we use, as in Henderson et al. [22], the inverse of an Herfindahl index of sectoral concentration based on the share of all sectors, except the one considered.[4] As previously, this variable is normal-

[4] See Encaoua and Jacquemin [13] for a discussion on concentration indexes. Ellison and Glaeser [12] also use Herfindahl indexes to study spatial concentration.

ized by the same variable computed at the French level,

$$\mathrm{div}_{z,s} = \frac{1 \Big/ \sum_{\substack{s'=1 \\ s' \neq s}}^{S} (\mathrm{emp}_{z,s'}/(\mathrm{emp}_z - \mathrm{emp}_{z,s}))^2}{1 \Big/ \sum_{\substack{s'=1 \\ s' \neq s}}^{S} (\mathrm{emp}_{s'}/\mathrm{emp} - \mathrm{emp}_s)^2},$$

where S is the total number of sectors. The numerator is maximum when all sectors except the one considered have the same size in the ZE. This indicator reflects the sectoral diversity faced by sector s in this zone and is therefore not necessarily negatively linked with the own local specialization of sector s. Note that these notions of specialization and diversity are conditional on the aggregation level implicit in the sectoral nomenclature.

We now tackle the problem of competition indicators. Glaeser el al. [19] consider that the number of firms per worker is a good proxy for competition. However, as in Ó hUallacháin and Satterthwaite [28], we interpret the inverse of this variable as the average size of plants located in ZE z, in order to test for internal economies of scale. It is normalized by the average size of plants in the sector in France,

$$\mathrm{size}_{z,s} = \frac{\mathrm{emp}_{z,s}/\mathrm{nbr}_{z,s}}{\mathrm{emp}_s/\mathrm{nbr}_s},$$

where $\mathrm{nbr}_{z,s}$ and nbr_s are the number of plants belonging to sector s in ZE z and France, respectively.

Competition is captured by the inverse of a local Herfindahl index of productive concentration. It is computed on the employment shares of the plants in the given sector belonging to the same ZE. It is also divided by the same indicator computed at the national level,

$$\mathrm{comp}_{z,s} = \frac{1 \Big/ \sum_{i \in z} (\mathrm{emp}_{z,s,i}/\mathrm{emp}_{z,s})^2}{1 \Big/ \sum_{i} (\mathrm{emp}_{s,i}/\mathrm{emp}_s)^2},$$

where $\mathrm{emp}_{z,s,i}$ and $\mathrm{emp}_{s,i}$ are the employment of plant i belonging to sector s and located in ZE z and France, respectively.

Glaeser et al. [19], Ò hUallacháin and Satterthwaite [28], and Henderson, et al. [22] include in the explanatory variables the level of the local sectoral employment. However, Combes [10] shows that this strongly changes the interpretation of the specialization variable and leads to an overestimation of localization economies. Actually, the impact of the share of the sectoral employment in total employment, holding the level of the sectoral employment constant, is simply the inverse of the effect of the total employment. Thus, it cannot be interpreted as intrasectoral local externalities. The correct interpretation is obtained if the level of the sectoral employment is replaced by the level of the total employment in control variables. In this case, the specialization variable really captures the impact of the relative size of the sector in local employment. Moreover, the total employment variable, which reflects the size of the local economy, is easily interpreted, as described above. In order to simultaneously control for the differences in ZEs' areas, it is here more relevant to consider the total employment density of the ZE,

$$\text{den}_z = \frac{\text{emp}_z}{\text{area}_z},$$

where area_z is the area of ZE z.

Because plants that are smaller than 20 workers are not in the dataset, sectoral employment in ZEs where there are only small plants is not observed. Because of this truncation, OLS estimates are biased. Moreover, the selection rule depends on an unknown random variable: a generalized Tobit methodology must thus be used. The methodology proposed by Heckman [20] first estimates a Probit model of a dummy variable which takes a value of 1 if sectoral employment is observed, 0 if not, as a function of the variables available for all locations. These variables are here an intercept, geographical dummies (Paris, Méditerrannée, Ile de France, Nord, and Est), and total employment density. This regression leads to an estimation of the Mills ratio, which is simply introduced as an extra explanatory variable in the initial model. OLS estimation now gives consistent but inefficient estimates. Therefore, we use the maximum likelihood estimate, which is efficient, of this generalized Tobit model. The likelihood maximization algorithm is initialized by the Heckman [20] estimate.[5] Note that Henderson et al. [22] also use a Tobit method because U.S. data are censored, at a much higher level (250 employees per sector and city).

4. RESULTS

As a background for the results, observe that whereas employment strongly decreases between 1984 and 1993 in industry (-15.4% on average over the ZEs), it increases in services ($+10.1\%$) during the same period. Moreover, the spatial disparity of growth rates is high, with a standard

[5] More details are available on request.

error of 19.2% in industry and of 34.5% in services. In industry and services, respectively, the 10% deciles are −34.4% and −15.2% and the 90% deciles, 6.6% and 37.7%. Hence, local factors have a critical effect on growth in France.

Correlations between the explanatory variables are smaller than 0.2. Average size of plants and competition are not significantly correlated, which confirms that the first variable cannot be used as an inverse competition proxy. Specialization and diversity are only very slightly negatively correlated. Density is positively correlated with competition and diversity.

Exhaustive results are given in Table 1 (global regressions), Table 2 (industry), and Table 3 (services). Unless mentioned, we only focus on estimates that are significant at least at the 10% level. On the contrary, in Figs. 1 to 5, the elasticities are plotted, in white for industry and in black for services, according to whether they are significant or not, after having ranked the sectors from the lowest to the highest estimate.[6]

Density

Concerning global regressions, the elasticity is negative for industry and non-significant for services. No industrial sector presents a positive elasticity whereas it is negative for 15 of them, 11 elasticities being between −0.1 and −0.3. On the contrary, only 2 service sectors have a negative elasticity, and for 5 others, it is higher than 0.1. Many others are positive but non-significant. Figure 1 confirms the global opposition between the industry and service sectors, but also shows that elasticities can in some cases be positive for industry and negative for services, although non-significantly.

As mentioned above, because density favors information spillovers, the induced productivity gains can negatively affect employment. However, we think that the negative elasticities of density are obtained because congestion effects (high land-rent or congestion of local infrastructures) create negative externalities on employment growth in dense places. The positive effects of having an important local economy, due to either information spillovers or input and output markets size, are dominated in industry as in a few services sectors. This occurs in many traditional industrial sectors such as primary processing of steel, smelting works, metalworking, manufacture of machine tools, production of industrial equipment, or the automobile industry. A complementary effect works through some inputs that are fairly expensive to transport and are produced in non-dense and non-congested places: firms such as wood working and the furniture industry have an advantage in locating close to them. A similar explanation

[6] We only keep sectors which are observed in more than 25 ZEs.

TABLE 1
Global Regressions

	Industry	Services
Number of observations	17,732	14,322
Non-zero observations	6664	5842
Probit variables		
Intercept	0.444	0.724
	(0.027)	(0.033)
Dummy Paris	−1.579	−0.471
	(0.184)	(0.427)
Dummy Ile-de-France	−0.351	−0.350
	(0.038)	(0.054)
Dummy Méditerrannée	−0.276	0.146
	(0.030)	(0.040)
Dummy Nord and Est	−0.115	−0.249
	(0.024)	(0.033)
Density	0.302	0.387
	(0.009)	(0.012)
Tobit variables		
Intercept	0.185	−0.018
	(0.048)	(0.054)
Density	−0.161	−0.040
	(0.010)	(0.019)
Specialization	−0.088	−0.211
	(0.012)	(0.013)
Diversity	−0.051	0.058
	(0.015)	(0.017)
Competition	−0.030	−0.011
	(0.011)	(0.009)
Size	−0.154	−0.110
	(0.017)	(0.022)
Likelihood	−17,502.72	−14,576.87

Note. Logarithm is taken for all variables.

Standard-errors in brakets.

All variables significant at the 5% level, for Student or Wald tests, except for services, the dummy Paris, density, and competition.

Likelihood for the model with only the intercept: −18637.68 for industry, −15736.09 for services can be given for the working of grain and the manufacture of miscellaneous food products, although the transportation costs of inputs seem to be lower in these cases.

On the contrary, the positive effects of the size of the local economy significantly dominate in five services sectors: they are either non-tradable or susceptible to present fairly high transportation costs, such as the food and the industrial wholesale trades, hotel and restaurant services, road transport, and consulting. In high density places, the size of the markets where these goods are sold is larger. The need for direct contact in transactions may also be high in these services, as well as search and matching effects under imperfect information. These last results are consistent with those obtained by Ó hUallacháin and Satterthwaite [28].

Specialization

In most cases, no localization economies are found. In fact, a negative effect of specialization is often observed. In the global regressions, specialization negatively affects growth, slightly for industry and more for services. This is confirmed by the regressions on each sector: for 10 industrial sectors, the elasticities are lower than -0.1, whereas they are lower than -0.5 for 4 sectors of services and between -0.5 and -0.1 for 14 others. The minimum estimate for industry is reached by distribution of water and urban heating, which is comparable to a service activity. Figure 2 confirms that a wide majority of elasticities are negative, although not always significantly.

Explanations of the negative effect of specialization can hardly be found in the agglomeration forces presented above. However, the study of sectoral cycles at the national level may give some answers. Two groups of sectors emerge. In the first one, sectoral employment expands at the national level. This concerns the services of retail trade (food and specialized non-food), consulting, the services auxiliary to finance and insurance, and, lastly, education and social work market services. Three industrial sectors are also in this situation but they are related to growing services: the distribution of water and urban heating, the bakery industry, and the pharmaceutical industry. The negative specialization effect can be interpreted in terms of a product's life-cycle: products, and here more particularly services, first develop in a few places and then diffuse across space, which would correspond to the observed period.

On the contrary, in the second group of sectors, both more numerous and more traditional, sectoral employment decreases at the national level. An interpretation may be that high specialization implies lower flexibility and worse adaptability of products, technologies, and infrastructures when the sector declines, whereas low specialized ZEs are more able to reconvert their activities. In this group, many traditional industrial sectors can

TABLE 2

Sectoral Regressions—Industry

Sector	Dens.	Spe.	Div.	Comp.	Size	Obs.	Gro.
Gas and oil production	−0.038	−0.114*	−0.093	−0.012	0.066	39	−21.3
Distribution services of water and urban heating	−0.129**	−0.452***	0.237***	−0.080	−0.123	103	70.4
Metallurgy of iron and steel	0.144	−0.092	−0.170	−0.082	0.041	37	−49.7
Primary processing of steel	−0.078**	0.021	0.183	0.042	−0.217***	92	−38.9
Metallurgy, primary processing of non-ferrous metals	0.011	−0.021	−0.159	−0.331**	−0.119	88	−28.9
Production of miscellaneous ores	−0.001	−0.101	0.095	−0.517**	−0.107	45	−25.0
Production of construction and ceramic materials	0.067*	0.078	0.068	−0.214***	−0.254***	276	−28.2
Glass industry	0.090	0.166**	0.198*	−0.372***	−0.327***	103	−10.4
Basic chemical industry	−0.024	−0.140*	−0.088	0.010	−0.029	143	−14.2
Parachemical industry	−0.016	−0.063	0.156	−0.258**	−0.236**	161	−1.6
Pharmaceutical industry	0.040	−0.205**	0.037	−0.076	0.070	93	15.8
Smelting works	−0.094***	−0.017	0.031	−0.005	−0.105**	124	−24.7
Metalworking	−0.079**	−0.156***	−0.065	−0.047	−0.112	309	−8.5
Manufacture of agricultural machinery	−0.080	−0.230**	−0.287**	−0.098	−0.100	97	−46.1
Manufacture of machine tools	−0.224***	−0.103	−0.128	−0.266***	−0.267***	127	−30.3
Production of industrial equipment	−0.118***	−0.266***	−0.070	−0.016	0.070	260	−10.8
Manufacture of civil-engineering equipment	−0.106	0.036	0.120	−0.500***	−0.453***	148	−31.7
Manufacture of office machinery and computers	0.145	0.482**	0.386*	−0.779***	−0.949***	50	−5.7
Manufacture of electrical equipment	0.001	0.066	0.103	−0.184*	−0.354***	195	−18.0
Manufacture of electronic equipment	0.012	−0.095	0.100	−0.168	−0.330***	179	−19.1
Manufacture of household equipment	0.006	−0.006	−0.066	0.014	−0.074	58	−22.8

continued over

Automotive and other land transport industry	−0.159***	−0.091	0.023	−0.282***	−0.095	216	−25.0
Aeronautics	0.100	0.115	0.183	−0.467***	−0.271***	63	−12.0
Manufacture of precision equipment	0.072	0.039	−0.185	−0.304**	−0.437***	119	−13.6
Meat products industry	−0.087	0.031	−0.037	−0.162	−0.312***	222	7.0
Milk products industry	−0.005	−0.033	−0.109	−0.285***	−0.074	205	−23.8
Canned foods industry	−0.013	−0.180	−0.229	0.007	−0.170	99	9.9
Bakery industry	−0.096	−0.203***	−0.056	−0.341***	−0.045	120	6.4
Working of grain	−0.166***	−0.112	−0.233***	−0.179*	−0.178*	197	−15.8
Manufacture of miscellaneous food products	−0.126***	−0.123***	−0.168***	−0.065***	−0.019	132	−23.4
Manufacture of beverages and alcohol	−0.080	−0.088*	−0.066	−0.186*	−0.022	113	−18.4
Industry of textile	−0.129***	−0.007	0.114	−0.128	−0.268***	182	−37.5
Industry of leather	−0.050	−0.026	−0.013	−0.346***	−0.246*	99	−28.6
Industry of shoes	−0.031***	−0.040	−0.084	0.053**	−0.063	81	−41.6
Manufacture of wearing apparel and dressing	−0.017	0.001	−0.124*	−0.269***	−0.294***	232	−40.0
Working of wood	−0.110***	−0.123***	−0.180***	−0.075***	−0.002	261	−19.3
Industry of furniture	−0.164***	−0.128	−0.054	−0.262***	−0.131	208	−22.2
Industry of paper and pulp	−0.036	−0.130***	0.004	−0.117	0.014	207	−3.9
Printing, press, and publishing	0.059	0.030	0.009	−0.151***	−0.266***	223	−8.5
Rubber industry	−0.300***	−0.137	−0.264**	−0.241	−0.053	118	−22.5
Working of plastic	−0.231***	−0.085	0.081	−0.170**	−0.365***	232	24.2
Miscellaneous industries	0.044	0.159**	−0.106	−0.449***	−0.415***	179	−27.1
Construction	0.015	−0.238***	0.088***	0.022	−0.031	340	−13.7

Note. The number of observations and the sectoral national growth rate are given in columns "Obs." and "Gro."
***, **, *: significant at the 5%, 10%, and 15% levels, respectively.

TABLE 3
Sectoral Regressions—Services

Sector	Dens.	Spe.	Div.	Comp.	Size	Obs.	Gro.
Reprocessing	−0.116	−0.191*	0.039	−0.186	−0.120	75	−15.3
Food wholesale trade	0.008	−0.048	0.146**	−0.160***	−0.291***	275	−17.6
Non-food wholesale trade	0.130***	−0.184**	0.047	−0.105	−0.167	224	−7.4
Inter-industrial wholesale trade	0.158***	−0.243***	−0.019	−0.100*	0.022	285	−12.3
Middleman's business	0.090	−0.273**	0.313*	−0.381**	−0.139	82	−5.6
Food retail trade	−0.033	−0.422***	0.114***	−0.194***	−0.070	330	62.7
Specialized food retail trade	−0.048	−0.337***	0.009	−0.069***	−0.082	138	−75.0
Non-specialized non-food retail trade	0.085	−0.115	0.171	−0.211	0.015	208	−28.6
Specialized non-food retail trade	0.053	−0.772***	0.314***	0.076	0.640***	207	12.4
Repair and trade of motor vehicles	−0.018	−0.284***	0.003	−0.041	0.180**	313	−17.2
Miscellaneous repair	0.030	−0.039	0.170	−0.386**	−0.674***	39	3.7
Hotel and restaurant services	0.157***	−0.099	0.098	−0.104	−0.547***	223	10.5
Rail transport	0.011	−0.039	0.070	−0.035	0.114**	251	−23.6
Road transport	0.104***	−0.238***	0.068	−0.078	−0.464***	313	23.8
Supporting transport services and warehouses	0.024	−0.075	−0.184	−0.408	−0.581***	74	71.1
Auxiliary transport and travel agency services	0.059	−0.435***	0.050	0.119	−0.088	149	−8.9
Holdings	−0.065	−0.074	0.186	0.143***	0.382***	33	184.7

continued over

Consulting	0.134***	−0.370***	−0.061	0.113	0.014	267	14.2
Services auxiliary to finance and insurance	−0.027	−0.464	0.220	0.002	−0.013	33	48.3
Property developpers	0.136	0.039	0.312*	−0.169	−0.432*	72	−7.6
Renting of personal goods	0.134	0.035	−0.079	−0.398***	−0.535***	65	0.5
Property renting	−0.101	−0.429***	0.095	−0.004	0.261*	101	−0.9
Education services (market)	−0.100	−0.765***	0.034	0.390**	0.246	52	184.2
Research (market)	0.024	−0.124	0.631*	−0.483	−0.471**	52	158.0
Health services (market)	−0.055**	−0.221***	0.059	0.093**	0.048	296	−2.0
Social work services (market)	−0.231***	−0.638***	0.112*	0.143**	0.100	265	99.3
Cultural and sporting services (market)	0.078	−0.036	0.218	−0.104	−0.327*	91	30.4
Miscellaneous services (market)	−0.029	−0.632***	0.098	0.138**	0.337***	204	37.7
Insurance	0.073	−0.110	0.308***	−0.255**	−0.371***	112	−0.7
Financial services	0.033	−0.172***	0.207***	−0.029	0.076	244	−18.6
Pension funding and social security services	−0.006	−0.215***	0.127***	0.074	0.117*	161	−5.7
Education services (non-market)	0.017	−0.085	0.153***	−0.217***	−0.470***	233	−18.0
Social work services (non-market)	0.054	−0.195**	0.155*	−0.147*	−0.509***	221	−4.4
Cultural and sporting services (non-market)	0.057	−0.070	0.125	−0.241	−0.611***	40	85.3
Miscellaneous services (non-market)	0.003	−0.010	0.047	−0.511***	−0.721***	127	−44.8

Note. The number of observations and the sectoral national growth rate are given in columns "Obs." and "Gro."
***, **, *: significant at the 5%, 10%, and 15% levels, respectively.

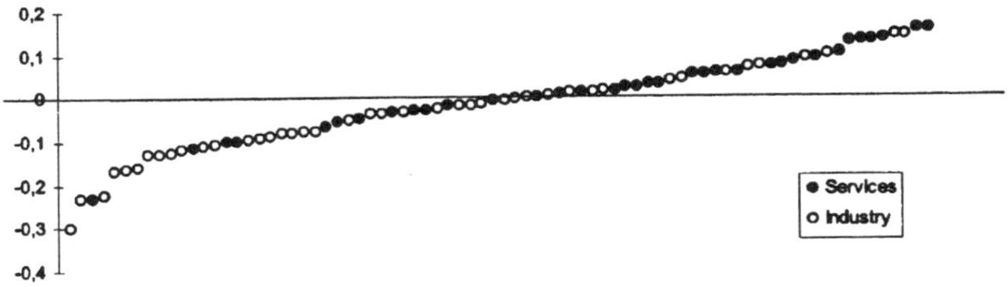

FIG. 1. Density elasticities.

FIG. 2. Specialization elasticities.

FIG. 3. Diversity elasticities.

FIG. 4. Competition elasticities.

FIG. 5. Size elasticities.

be found, such as metalworking, the manufacture of agricultural machinery, the production of industrial equipment or the industries linked to wood (the wood, furniture, and paper and pulp industries), as well as some services, such as wholesale trade (non-food and inter-industrial), specialized food retail trade, the repair and trade of motor vehicles, financial services, and pension funding and social security services.

Thirteen sectors experience a positive effect of specialization, but no service sector has a significant positive elasticity for specialization, and the contrary is only observed in three industrial sectors. These economies of localization can be the result either of market-based effects (for instance, due to the sharing of specialized inputs) or information spillovers. Both of these interpretations seem to be particularly relevant for the glass industry, the manufacture of office machinery and computers, and, although the effect is strong but non-significant, aeronautics. The case of miscellaneous industry is harder to interpret, because it covers many different activities.

These results globally confirm for French industry and services the absence of intra-sectoral local externalities stated by Glaeser et al. [19] for the U.S. industry. On the contrary, all industrial sectors studied by Henderson et al. [22], traditional as well as high-tech, present this type of externality, whereas it is the case only for a few of ours. However, these authors simultaneously control for the sectoral employment level, which increases the probability of obtaining a positive elasticity for specialization, as shown by Combes [10] and recalled above. Lastly, the decrease in France of the spatial concentration may lead to the following conjecture: localization economies could be linked to the business cycle and would work asymmetrically, positive in growing periods but negative in recessions. A longer period of observation would be necessary to precisely test this conjecture.

Diversity

Urbanization economies are observed in global regressions for services whereas industry experiences a negative effect of diversity. Figure 3 confirms this contrast between the industrial and service sectors. Moreover, the diversity impact is lower, in absolute value and on average, than the specialization effect.

Diversity elasticity is higher than 0.3 for two service sectors (plus three others but non-significantly) and is between 0.1 and 0.3 for five others. This validates the intuitions of the monopolistic competition models with differentiated inputs and outputs. Indeed, in services, inputs are fairly diversified and outputs are not specific to given sectors or given types of consumers. Firms consequently benefit from facing a great variety of sectors located in the same place, because of both supply and demand linkages. This is confirmed by the frequent simultaneous positive effects of diversity and density. Such an interpretation may apply to five sectors of trade, although the effect is not always significant, and also to finance, insurance, and pension funding and social security services.[7] The distribution of water and urban heating, already compared above to a service, and construction are the only industrial sectors that present a significant positive elasticity. Urbanization economies due to knowledge spillovers between different sectors may also explain the positive, and fairly high although non-significant, effect of diversity for the manufacture of office machinery and computers, the manufacture of electrical equipment and the manufacture of electronic equipment, and for aeronautics.

No service sector has a significant negative elasticity for diversity, whereas it is lower than -0.1 for five industrial sectors. They also present a negative elasticity for density and are often linked to agriculture, for instance, the working of grain and wood, the manufacture of miscellaneous food products and agricultural machinery, and the rubber industry. Moreover, many traditional industries experience a negative but non-significant effect. In these cases, inputs are simultaneously highly specialized and costly to transport: they consequently do not benefit from diversity.

Thus, some evidence of urbanization externalities is found for services, and there is a presumption that they exist for a few high-tech industrial sectors. While these externalities emerge on average for all industries in Glaeser et al. [19], our results are consistent with Henderson et al. [22], who find urbanization economies for new industries but not for mature ones.

[7] As well as services auxiliary to finance and insurance, and to property developers, although the effect is strong but not significant.

Competition

Global regressions show that local competition has a negative effect on growth in industry and is not significant in services. The elasticity is lower than −0.3 for 10 industrial and 4 services sectors and between −0.3 and −0.1 for 9 industrial and 4 services sectors. This reflects the dispersive effect of price competition on outputs, provided that markets are sufficiently local and segmented, which is often the case in services. Good examples can be found in different wholesale and retail trades, the middleman's business, the renting of personal goods, and insurance. Moreover, this effect can be reinforced if some congestion on inputs also emerges. Higher competition between firms means higher land-rent or wages of skilled labor, which is not very mobile in France. In particular, if the sector declines, as in many traditional industrial sectors, this decreases the local firms' survival rate. The production of construction and ceramic materials, the manufacture of machine tools, civil-engineering equipment, and wearing apparel and dressing, the automobile industry, the milk products industry, and the working of plastic simultaneously experience a negative competitive effect and a decrease in national employment higher than 20%.

Competition has a positive effect in only five service sectors, which is never observed for industry. A first explanation may be the positive impact of competition on information spillovers. Uncertainty about the quality of goods may also generate high demand in highly competitive places due to improved matching: this certainly plays an important role in the holdings, health, social work, and education market services.[8]

Size

The plants' average size has a negative impact on growth in global regressions for both industry and services. Nine industrial and 12 services sectors present an elasticity lower than −0.3, and for 8 industrial and 1 services sectors, it is between −0.1 and −0.3. No industrial sector presents a positive elasticity, whereas this happens in 5 services sectors. Figure 5 shows that elasticities are lower in absolute value in industrial sectors than in services, these ones presenting either high or low elasticities.

The fact that size positively affects growth in very few sectors cannot be strictly interpreted as an absence of internal economies of scale since production functions are not really estimated. However, one could think that larger plants would grow faster in more sectors, in particular, in traditional industries. Sectors such as gas and oil production, the metallurgy of iron and steel, the basic chemical industry, the production of

[8] And in consulting and auxiliary transport and travel agency services: the effect is greater than 0.1, although not significant.

industrial equipment, or the manufacture of household equipment do not present a negative impact of size either. Internal economies of scale may not only explain the lower employment decrease of large plants in declining sectors, such as rail transport or repair and trade of motor vehicles, but also their faster growth in expanding sectors, such as miscellaneous services, specialized non-food retail trade, and holdings.[9]

The negative elasticities of size may simply reflect a firm's life-cycle effect: new firms are in general of small size and are able to grow faster, whereas, once they have reached their optimal size, their employment stops expanding. This is intuitive in services, such as hotel and restaurant services, road transport, supporting transport services and warehouses, and the research market services, which experience the lowest effects and which are simultaneously growing and diffusing across space. Another conclusion would be that information spillovers are more important for small firms: in industry, high-tech sectors such as the manufacture of office machinery, computers, electrical equipment, electronic equipment, and precision equipment are among the ones which experience the strongest effect. Moreover, adaptability and flexibility can be higher in small firms. This benefits the sectors in which technologies change very quickly and it saves employment in declining sectors, such as most industrial ones.

Glaeser et al. [19] interpret the negative elasticity of size as a positive effect of competition. However, the previous results show that competition has mostly a negative effect on employment. Recall also that no correlation exists between size and competition in the dataset. These results are globally consistent with those of Glaeser et al. [19] and Caballero and Lyons [7], but the interpretations, in the first case, and methodology, in the second one, completely differ. Ó hUallacháin and Satterthwaite [28] obtain a positive effect of plants' size in a greater number of sectors.

Short-Run Effects

Another interesting question is related to the delay with which the economic structure affects growth. Using panel data, Henderson [21] shows that the strongest effect of localization externalities arises after three or four years, whereas urbanization externalities show a lag of up to eight years. Since the number of years of our panel is too small, we cannot perform such a study. However, we now regress the annual growth rate (between years t and $t + 1$) on the current economic structure (at date t). We pool all years between 1984 and 1992, and perform global regressions for industry and services, respectively. This reflects possible short-run

[9] To which could be added education services and social work services, although the effect is not significant.

effects, the previous regressions being interpreted as middle-run ones. The results are presented in Table 4.

It turns out that these effects are significantly smaller than the middle-run ones. Both for industry and services, no estimate which is significant in the short- and middle-run has a different sign in both cases. In this situation, the middle-run effect is roughly the sum of the short-run ones, and the economic structure influences growth in the same direction, whatever the horizon. Concerning services, the diversity effect, which is positive but small in the middle-run, is non-significant in the short-run. On the contrary, density and competition, which were non-significant in the middle-run in global regressions, now affect growth positively, as they do for some sectors in the middle-run. This confirms that these variables influence growth in a different way depending on the sector.

5. CONCLUSIONS

This study shows that the local economic structure significantly affects local employment growth. The separate regressions show that there are sharp differences between industrial and service sectors. Our interpretations include not only arguments based on information spillovers and market-based effects, but also the national evolution of the sector.

Industrial and services sectors react to density and diversity in an opposite way. In most cases, these factors favor local services employment growth, probably due to market-based effects arising from the local presence of large and diversified input and output markets and to possible inter-sectoral information spillovers. Thus, urbanization economies emerge in many services sectors. Density and diversity mainly slow down employment growth in industry, probably due to congestion effects increasing the costs of local inputs, such as land and local transportation.

In industry as in services, very few localization economies are found. This may be explained by the presence of an asymmetric effect, which remains to be tested: specialization would enhance local growth during expansion periods, but it would also favor employment decline during recessions, inducing adaptability problems. Concerning competition, the direct dispersive price effect dominates, in almost all sectors, except in a few services, possibly reflecting in this case positive agglomeration effects due to imperfect information. Lastly, this study shows that local externalities are generally external to plants.

For some sectors, our results differ from those observed in the U.S. It should, however, be recalled that our methodology concerning localization economies is more restrictive. Agglomeration mechanisms may differently work in the U.S. and France, which can be explained by differences in factor mobility. The period of study and the global evolution of the sector

TABLE 4
Annual Global Regressions

	Industry	Services
Number of observation	92,284	81,938
Non-zero observations	66,646	58,219
Probit variables		
Intercept	1.152	1.220
	(0.012)	(0.014)
Dummy Paris	−0.928	0.127
	(0.079)	(0.250)
Dummy Ile-de-France	−0.365	−0.350
	(0.019)	(0.020)
Dummy Méditerrannée	−0.254	−0.105
	(0.015)	(0.015)
Dummy Nord and Est	−0.139	−0.154
	(0.012)	(0.013)
Density	0.223	0.276
	(0.004)	(0.005)
Tobit variables		
Intercept	−0.134	0.030
	(0.008)	(0.009)
Density	−0.021	0.014
	(0.002)	(0.002)
Specialization	−0.033	−0.062
	(0.002)	(0.003)
Diversity	−0.026	−0.002
	(0.001)	(0.001)
Competition	−0.031	0.018
	(0.002)	(0.002)
Size	−0.013	−0.033
	(0.003)	(0.005)
Likelihood	−75,012.04	−80,934.45

Note. Logarithm is taken for all variables.
Standard-errors in brakets.
All variables significant at the 5% level, for Student or Wald tests, except for services, the dummies Paris and Méditerranée, and density.
Likelihood for the model with only the intercept: −77,905.28 for industry, −83,759.28 for services.

also influence the results: the effects are possibly asymmetric, or local externalities may just less influence local growth during some periods, as Bostic et al. [6] shows for the late 19th century in the U.S.

Although it would be important to deduce from our study some advice in terms of economic policy, our conclusions show the complexity of the problem: a local economic structure that is profitable in the short-run or for some sectors is not necessarily good in the middle- or long-run or for other sectors. For instance, many industrial sectors are in the paradoxical situation where neither specialization nor diversity enhances growth. Moreover, the magnitude of elasticities also greatly differs between sectors: no variable which policymakers might control exercises a systematically strong effect. Some aspects of the evolution of the geographical employment distribution can, however, be derived from our results. For instance, during this period and on average, industrial sectors work in favor of geographical convergence of the ZEs' total employment density, by growing more (or declining less) in non-dense places, whereas services expand more in dense and diversified ZEs. The negative effect of specialization on growth, both in industry and services, induces a convergence of the ZEs' employment sectoral composition.

This type of study could be improved by using longer data series and panel methodology, as in Henderson [21], and by considering some spatial autocorrelation of the effects. Moreover, a structural econometrics method based on recent economic geography or endogenous growth models would clarify what is really tested. It would, for instance, help to distinguish between productivity and output effects and between market-based effects and information spillovers.

REFERENCES

1. H. M. Abdel-Rahman, Product differentiation, monopolistic competition and city size, *Regional Science and Urban Economics*, **18**, 69–86 (1988).
2. H. M. Abdel-Rahman and M. Fujita, Specialization and diversification in a system of cities, *Journal of Urban Economics*, **33**, 189–222 (1993).
3. Z. Acs, D. B. Audretsch, and M. P. Feldman, Real effects of academic research: A comment, *American Economic Review*, **82**, 363–367 (1992).
4. L. Anselin, A. Varga, and Z. Acs, Local geographic spillovers between university research and high technology innovations, *Journal of Urban Economics*, **42**, 422–448 (1997).
5. D. B. Audretsch and M. P. Feldman, R & D spillovers and the geography of innovation and production, *American Economic Review*, **86**, 630–640 (1996).
6. R. Bostic, J. Gans, and S. Stern, Urban productivity and factor growth in the late nineteenth century, *Journal of Urban Economics*, **41**, 38–55 (1997).

7. R. Caballero and R. Lyons, Internal versus external economies in European industry, *European Economic Review*, **34**, 805–830 (1990).
8. A. Ciccone and R. Hall, Productivity and the density of economic activity, *American Economic Review*, **86**, 54–70 (1996).
9. P.-Ph. Combes, Industrial agglomeration under Cournot competition, *Annales d'Economie et de Statistique*, **45**, 161–182 (1997).
10. P.-Ph. Combes, "Marshall–Arrow–Romer externalities and city growth: A methodological note," CERAS Working Paper No. 99-06 (1999).
11. A. Dixit and J. Stiglitz, Monopolistic competition, and optimum product diversity, *American Economic Review*, **67**, 297–308 (1977).
12. G. Ellison and E. L. Glaeser, Geographic concentration in U.S. manufacturing industries: a dartboard approach, *Journal of Political Economy*, **105**, 889–927 (1997).
13. D. Encaoua and A. Jacquemin, Degree of monopoly, indices of concentration and threat of entry, *International Economic Review*, **21**, 87–105 (1980).
14. M. P. Feldman and D. B. Audretsch, Innovation in cities: Science-based diversity, specialization and localized competition, *European Economic Review*, **43**, 409–430 (1999).
15. M. Fujita, A monopolistic competition model of spatial agglomeration in urban economics, *Regional Science and Urban Economics*, **18**, 87–124 (1988).
16. M. Fujita and H. Ogawa, Multiple equilibria and structural transition on non-monocentric urban configurations, *Regional Science and Urban Economics*, **12**, 161–196 (1982).
17. M. Fujita and J.-F. Thisse, Economics of agglomeration, *Journal of the Japanese and International Economics*, **10**, 339–379 (1996).
18. E. L. Glaeser, Are cities dying?, *Journal of Economic Perspectives*, **12**, 139–160 (1998).
19. E. L. Glaeser, H. Kallal, J. Sheinkman, and A. Schleifer, Growth in cities, *Journal of Political Economy*, **100**, 1126–1152 (1992).
20. J. Heckman, Sample selection bias as a specification error, *Econometrica*, **47**, 153–161 (1979).
21. J. V. Henderson, Externalities and industrial development, *Journal of Urban Economics*, **42**, 449–470 (1997).
22. J. V. Henderson, A. Kuncoro, and M. Turner, Industrial development in cities, *Journal of Political Economy*, **103**, 1067–1090 (1995).
23. H. Hotelling, Stability in competition, *Economic Journal*, **39**, 41–57 (1929).
24. A. B. Jaffe, Real effects of academic research, *American Economic Review*, **79**, 957–970 (1989).
25. A. B. Jaffe, M. Trajtenberg, and R. Henderson, Geographic localization of knowledge spillovers as evidenced by patent citations, *Quarterly Journal of Economics*, **108**, 577–598 (1993).
26. P. Krugman, Increasing returns and economic geography, *Journal of Political Economy*, **99**, 483–499 (1991).
27. P. Krugman and A. Venables, Globalization and the inequality of nations, *Quarterly Journal of Economics*, **110**, 857–880 (1995).
28. B. Ó hUallacháin and M. Satterthwaite, Sectoral growth patterns at the metropolitan level: an evaluation of economic development incentives, *Journal of Urban Economics*, **31**, 25–58 (1992).
29. D. Puga, The rise and fall of regional inequalities, *European Economic Review*, **43**, 303–334 (1999).

30. J. Quigley, Urban diversity and economic growth, *Journal of Economic Perspectives*, **12**, 127–138 (1998).
31. F. Rivera-Batiz, Increasing returns, monopolistic competition, and agglomeration economies in consumption and production, *Regional Science and Urban Economics*, **18**, 125–153 (1988).
32. N. Schulz and K. Stahl, Do consumers search for the highest price? Equilibrium and monopolistic optimum in a differentiated products markets, *Rand Journal of Economics*, **27**, 542–562 (1996).
33. J. Sutton, Technology and market structure, *European Economic Review*, **40**, 511–530 (1996).

[17]

OXFORD REVIEW OF ECONOMIC POLICY, VOL. 14, NO. 2

AGGLOMERATION AND THE LOCATION OF INNOVATIVE ACTIVITY

DAVID B. AUDRETSCH
Institute of Development Statistics, Indiana University, and the Centre for Economic Policy Research, London[1]

A paradox has been the emergence of the importance of local proximity and geographic clusters precisely at a time when globalization seems to dominate economic activity. The purpose of this paper is to resolve this paradox by explaining why and how geography matters for innovative activity and ultimately for the international comparative advantage. Globalization and the telecommunications revolution have triggered a shift in the comparative advantage of the leading developed countries towards an increased importance of innovative activity. This shift in comparative advantage has increased the value of knowledge-based economic activity. Since knowledge is generated and transmitted more efficiently via local proximity, economic activity based on new knowledge has a high propensity to cluster within a geographic region. This has triggered a fundamental shift in public policy towards business, away from policies constraining the freedom of firms to contract and towards a new set of enabling policies, implemented at the regional and local levels.

I. INTRODUCTION

That innovative activity has become more important is not surprising. What was perhaps less anticipated is that much of the innovative activity is less associated with footloose multinational corporations and more associated with high-tech innovative regional clusters, such as Silicon Valley, Research Triangle, and Route 122 around Boston. Only a few years ago the conventional wisdom predicted that globalization would lead to the demise of the region as a meaningful unit of economic analysis. Yet the obsession of policy-makers around the globe to 'create the next Silicon Valley' reveals the increased importance of geographic proximity and regional agglomerations. The purpose of this article is to explain why and how geography matters for innovative activity and ultimately for international comparative advantage.

The second section of this paper explains how globalization and the telecommunications revolution have triggered a shift in the comparative advantage of the leading developed countries towards an

[1] I would like to thank the editors of this journal and two anonymous referees.

increased importance of innovative activity. The importance of new knowledge as an input in generating innovative activity is explained in the third section, along with why knowledge is fundamentally different from the more traditional factors of production. These differences account for the propensity for knowledge to spill over from the source creating it to the firm commercializing it, which is explained in the fourth section. However, as is pointed out in the fifth section, there are important reasons why knowledge stops spilling over as it moves across geographic space, bestowing important economic benefits to geographic proximity and localization. In the sixth section the gains from agglomerations are explained by linking knowledge spillovers to innovative activity. In the seventh section, the black box of geographic space is penetrated to link the structure of economic activity within an agglomeration to the innovative performance of that region. Finally, policy implications are discussed in the concluding section. In particular, the increased importance of innovation has triggered a fundamental shift in public policy towards business, away from policies constraining the freedom of firms to contract and towards a new set of enabling policies, implemented at the regional and local levels.

II. INNOVATION AND COMPARATIVE ADVANTAGE

The traditional comparative advantage in mature, technologically moderate industries, such as metalworking, machine tools, and car production had provided an engine for growth, high employment, and economic stability throughout Western Europe for most of the post-war economic period. When the Berlin Wall fell in 1989, many people expected even greater levels of economic well-being resulting from the dramatic reduction of the economic burden in the West that had been imposed by four decades of Cold War. Thus, the substantial unemployment and general economic stagnation during the subsequent 8 years has come as a shock. Unemployment and relatively low growth are the twin economic problems confronting Europe. Over 11 per cent of the work-force in the European Union (EU) was unemployed in 1997, ranging from 6.1 per cent in the United Kingdom and 6.2 per cent in The Netherlands, to 11.1 per cent in Germany, 12.6 per cent in France, and over 20 per cent in Spain.[2]

The traditional comparative advantage has been lost in the high-cost countries of Europe and North America in the last decade for two reasons. The first has to do with globalization, or the advent of competition not just from the emerging economies in South-east Asia but also from the transforming economies of Central and Eastern Europe. The second factor has been the computer and telecommunications revolution. The new communications technologies have triggered a virtual spatial revolution in terms of the geography of production. According to *The Economist*, 'The death of distance as a determinant of the cost of communications will probably be the single most important economic force shaping society in the first half of the next century.'[3]

Much of the policy debate responding to the twin forces of the telecommunications revolution and increased globalization has revolved around a trade-off between maintaining higher wages but suffering greater unemployment, versus higher levels of employment but at the cost of lower wage rates. Globalization and the telecommunications revolution have rendered the comparative advantage in traditional moderate technology industries incompatible with high wage levels. At the same time, the emerging comparative advantage that is compatible with high wage levels is based on innovative activity. For example, employment has increased by 15 per cent in Silicon Valley between 1992 and 1996, even though the mean income is 50 per cent greater than in the rest of the country.[4]

The global demand for innovative products in knowledge-based industries is high and growing rapidly; yet the number of workers who can contribute to producing and commercializing new knowledge is limited to just a few areas in the world. Economic activity based on new knowledge generates higher wages and greater employment opportunities reflecting the exploding demand for new and improved products and services. There are many indicators reflecting the shift in the comparative

[2] OECD, *Employment Outlook* (1997).

[3] 'The Death of Distance', *The Economist* (30 September 1995).

[4] 'The Valley of Money's Delights', *The Economist* (29 March 1997, special section, p. 1).

OXFORD REVIEW OF ECONOMIC POLICY, VOL. 14, NO. 2

advantage of the high-wage countries towards an increased importance of innovative activity. For example, Kortum and Lerner (1997, p. 1) document an unprecedented jump in patenting in the United States, as evidenced by the explosion in applications for United States patents by American inventors since 1985. Throughout this century, patent applications fluctuated within a band between 40,000 and 80,000 per year. By contrast, in 1995 there were over 120,000 patent applications. Similarly, Berman *et al.* (1997) have shown that the demand for less skilled workers has decreased dramatically throughout the OECD, while at the same time the demand for skilled workers has exploded.

III. THE KNOWLEDGE PRODUCTION FUNCTION

The starting point for most theories of innovation is the firm. In such theories the firms are exogenous and their performance in generating technological change is endogenous (Arrow, 1962). For example, in the most prevalent model found in the literature of technological change, the model of the knowledge production function, formalized by Zvi Griliches (1979), firms exist exogenously and then engage in the pursuit of new economic knowledge as an input into the process of generating innovative activity. The most decisive input in the knowledge production function is new economic knowledge. Knowledge as an input in a production function is inherently different from the more traditional inputs of labour, capital, and land. While the economic value of the traditional inputs is relatively certain, knowledge is intrinsically uncertain and its potential value is asymmetric across economic agents. The most important, although not the only, source of new knowledge is considered to be research and development (R&D). Other key factors generating new economic knowledge include a high degree of human capital, a skilled labour-force, and a high presence of scientists and engineers.

There is considerable empirical evidence supporting the model of the knowledge production function. However, the empirical link between knowledge inputs and innovative output apparently becomes stronger as the unit of observation becomes increasingly aggregated. For example, at the unit of observation of countries, the relationship between R&D and patents is very strong. The most innovative countries, such as the United States, Japan, and Germany, also tend to undertake high investments in R&D. By contrast, little patent activity is associated with developing countries, which have very low R&D expenditures. Similarly, the link between R&D and innovative output, measured in terms of either patents or new product innovations, is also very strong when the unit of observation is the industry. The most innovative industries, such as computers, instruments, and pharmaceuticals, also tend to be the most R&D-intensive. Audretsch (1995) finds a simple correlation coefficient of 0.74 between R&D inputs and innovative output at the level of four-digit standard industrial classification (SIC) industries. However, when the knowledge production function is tested for the unit of observation of the firm, the link between knowledge inputs and innovative output becomes tenuous and only weakly positive in some studies, and even non-existent or negative in others. The model of the knowledge production function becomes particularly weak when small firms are included in the sample. This is not surprising, since formal R&D is concentrated among the largest corporations, but a series of studies (Acs and Audretsch, 1990) has clearly documented that small firms account for a disproportionate share of new product innovations, given their low R&D expenditures.

IV. KNOWLEDGE SPILLOVERS

The breakdown of the knowledge production function at the level of the firm raises the question: *Where do innovative firms with little or no R&D get the knowledge inputs?* This question becomes particularly relevant for small and new firms that undertake little R&D themselves, yet contribute considerable innovative activity in newly emerging industries such as biotechnology and computer software (Audretsch, 1995). One answer that has recently emerged in the economics literature is from other, third-party firms or research institutions, such as universities. Economic knowledge may spill over from the firm conducting the R&D or the research laboratory of a university (Baptista, 1997).

Why should knowledge spill over from the source of origin? At least two major channels or mechanisms for knowledge spillovers have been identified in the literature. Both of these spillover mechanisms revolve around the issue of appropriability of new knowledge. Cohen and Levinthal (1989) suggest that firms develop the capacity to adapt new technology and ideas developed in other firms and are therefore able to appropriate some of the returns accruing to investments in new knowledge made externally.

By contrast, Audretsch (1995) proposes shifting the unit of observation away from exogenously assumed firms to individuals, such as scientists, engineers, or other knowledge workers—agents with endowments of new economic knowledge. When the lens is shifted away from the firm to the individual as the relevant unit of observation, the appropriability issue remains, but the question becomes: *How can economic agents with a given endowment of new knowledge best appropriate the returns from that knowledge?* If the scientist or engineer can pursue the new idea within the organizational structure of the firm developing the knowledge and appropriate roughly the expected value of that knowledge, he or she has no reason to leave the firm. On the other hand, if he places a greater value on his ideas than does the decision-making bureaucracy of the incumbent firm, he may choose to start a new firm to appropriate the value of his knowledge. In the metaphor provided by Albert O. Hirschman (1970), if voice proves to be ineffective within incumbent organizations, and loyalty is sufficiently weak, a knowledge worker may resort to exiting the firm or university where the knowledge was created in order to form a new company. In this spillover channel the knowledge production function is actually reversed. The knowledge is exogenous and embodied in a worker. The firm is created endogenously in the worker's effort to appropriate the value of his or her knowledge through innovative activity.

V. THE IMPORTANCE OF LOCATION AND AGGLOMERATION

That knowledge spills over is barely disputed. In disputing the importance of knowledge externalities in explaining the geographic concentration of economic activity, Krugman (1991) and others do not question the existence or importance of such knowledge spillovers. In fact, they argue that such knowledge externalities are so important and forceful that there is no compelling reason for a geographic boundary to limit the spatial extent of the spillover. According to this line of thinking, the concern is not that knowledge does not spill over, but that it should stop spilling over just because it hits a geographic border, such as a city limit, state line, or national boundary. As illustrated by the title page of *The Economist* proclaiming 'The Death of Distance' (30 September 1995), the claim that geographic location is important to the process linking knowledge spillovers to innovative activity in a world of e-mail, fax machines, and cyberspace may seem surprising and even paradoxical. The resolution to the paradox posed by the localization of knowledge spillovers in an era where the telecommunications revolution has drastically reduced the cost of communication lies in a distinction between knowledge and information. *Information*, such as the price of gold on the New York Stock Exchange, or the value of the yen in London, can be easily codified and has a singular meaning and interpretation. By contrast, *knowledge* is vague, difficult to codify, and often only serendipitously recognized. While the marginal cost of transmitting information across geographic space has been rendered invariant by the telecommunications revolution, the marginal cost of transmitting knowledge, and especially tacit knowledge, rises with distance.

Von Hipple (1994) demonstrates that high context, uncertain knowledge, or what he terms 'sticky knowledge', is best transmitted via face-to-face interaction and through frequent and repeated contact. Geographic proximity matters in transmitting knowledge, because as Kenneth Arrow (1962) pointed out over three decades ago, such tacit knowledge is inherently non-rival in nature, and knowledge developed for any particular application can easily spill over and have economic value in very different applications. As Glaeser *et al.* (1992, p. 1126) have observed, 'intellectual breakthroughs must cross hallways and streets more easily than oceans and continents'.

The importance of local proximity for the transmission of knowledge spillovers has been observed in many different contexts. It has been pointed out that, 'business is a social activity, and you have to be

knowledge spill.

OXFORD REVIEW OF ECONOMIC POLICY, VOL. 14, NO. 2

where important work is taking place.'[5] A survey of nearly one thousand executives located in America's 60 largest metropolitan areas ranked Raleigh/Durham as the best city for knowledge workers and for innovative activity.[6] The reason is that

> A lot of brainy types who made their way to Raleigh/Durham were drawn by three top research universities. . . . US businesses, especially those whose success depends on staying at the top of new technologies and processes, increasingly want to be where hot new ideas are percolating. A presence in brain-power centres like Raleigh/Durham pays off in new products and new ways of doing business. Dozens of small biotechnology and software operations are starting up each year and growing like *kudzu* in the fertile climate.[7]

VI. THE SPATIAL LINK BETWEEN KNOWLEDGE AND INNOVATION

Not only did Krugman (1991, p. 53) doubt that knowledge spillovers are not geographically constrained, but he also argued that they were impossible to measure because 'knowledge flows are invisible, they leave no paper trail by which they may be measured and tracked'. However, an emerging literature has overcome data constraints to measure the extent of knowledge spillovers and link them to the geography of innovative activity. Jaffe (1989), Feldman (1994), and Audretsch and Feldman (1996) modified the model of the knowledge production function to include an explicit specification for both the spatial and product dimensions:

$$I_{si} = IRD^{\beta_1} * (UR_{si})^{\beta_2} * \left[UR_{si} * (GC_{si})^{\beta_3}\right] * \varepsilon_{si} \quad (1)$$

where I is innovative output, IRD is private corporate expenditures on R&D, UR is the research expenditures undertaken at universities, and GC measures the geographic coincidence between university and corporate research. The unit of observation for estimation is at the spatial level, s, a state, and industry level, i. Jaffe (1989) used the number of inventions registered with the United States patent office as a measure of innovative activity. By contrast, Audretsch and Feldman (1996) and Acs *et al.* (1992) developed a direct measure of innovative output consisting of new product introductions.

Estimation of equation (1) essentially shifts the model of the knowledge production function from the unit of observation of a firm to that of a geographic unit. The consistent empirical evidence that supports the notion knowledge spills over for third-party use from university research laboratories as well as industry R&D laboratories. This empirical evidence suggests that location and proximity clearly matter in exploiting knowledge spillovers. Not only have Jaffe *et al.* (1993) found that patent citations tend to occur more frequently within the state in which they were patented than outside of that state, but Audretsch and Feldman (1996) found that the propensity of innovative activity to cluster geographically tends to be greater in industries where new economic knowledge plays a more important role. Prevenzer (1997) and Zucker *et al.* (1994) show that in biotechnology, which is an industry based almost exclusively on new knowledge, the firms tend to cluster together in just a handful of locations. This finding is supported by Audretsch and Stephan (1996) who examine the geographic relationships of scientists working with biotechnology firms. The importance of geographic proximity is clearly shaped by the role played by the scientist. The scientist is more likely to be located in the same region as the firm when the relationship involves the transfer of new economic knowledge. However, when the scientist is providing a service to the company that does not involve knowledge transfer, local proximity becomes much less important.

The spatial link between knowledge inputs and innovative output can be seen in the Data Appendix which links knowledge inputs to innovative output. Since Krugman (1991, p. 57) has emphasized, 'States aren't really the right geographical units', the relevant geographic unit of observation is at the city level. The measure of innovative output is the number of patents registered by firms located within the city between 1988 and 1992. The Appendix also shows the education level, measured as the share of the labour-force in 1992 accounted for by workers

[5] 'The Best Cities for Knowledge Workers', *Fortune* (15 November 1993, p. 44).
[6] The survey was carried out in 1993 by the management consulting firm, Moran, Stahl & Boyer, of New York City.
[7] 'The Best Cities for Knowledge Workers', *Fortune* (15 November 1993, p. 44).

who have graduated from a 4-year college course (BA or higher). In addition, the number of research centres located in that city as of 1992 is listed. While the high number of patents issued to firms located at the heart of Silicon Valley in San José (10,138) and Los Angeles (9,598) is not particularly surprising, what is perhaps more striking is that the greatest number of patents (11,793) was issued to firms located in Chicago. One explanation may be that Chicago accounts for a greater number of research centres than any other city, with the exceptions of New York and Boston. Of course, Chicago is also a much larger city than San José. When patent rates, or the number of patents per 100,000 residents, are compared in the second column, San José emerges as the most innovative city in the United States. San José, in fact, has the second highest educational attainment level, where almost one-third of its work-force has a university degree or the equivalent. In general, a close relationship can be seen between the availability of knowledge resources in a city and its innovative performance.[8]

There is reason to believe that knowledge spillovers are not homogeneous across firms. In estimating equation (1) for large and small enterprises separately, Acs *et al.* (1994) provide some insight into the puzzle posed by the recent wave of studies identifying vigorous innovative activity emanating from small firms in certain industries. How are these small, and frequently new, firms able to generate innovative output while undertaking generally negligible amounts of investment into knowledge-generating inputs, such as R&D? The answer appears to be through exploiting knowledge created by expenditures on research in universities and on R&D in large corporations. Their findings suggest that the innovative output of all firms rises along with an increase in the amount of R&D inputs, both in private corporations as well as in university laboratories. However, R&D expenditures made by private companies play a particularly important role in providing knowledge inputs to the innovative activity of large firms, while expenditures on research made by universities serve as an especially key input for generating innovative activity in small enterprises. Apparently, large firms are more adept at exploiting knowledge created in their own laboratories, while their smaller counterparts have a comparative advantage at exploiting spillovers from university laboratories.

A conceptual problem arises with economies accruing to the knowledge transmission associated with agglomeration. Once a city, region, or state develops a viable cluster of production and innovative activity why should it ever lose the first-mover advantage? One answer, provided by Audretsch and Feldman (1996) is that the relative importance of local proximity and, therefore, agglomeration effects is shaped by the stage of the industry life cycle. A growing literature suggests that who innovates and how much innovative activity is undertaken is closely linked to the phase of the industry life cycle (Klepper, 1996). Audretsch and Feldman (1996) argue that an additional key aspect to the evolution of innovative activity over this life cycle is *where* that innovative activity takes place. The theory of knowledge spillovers, derived from the knowledge production function, suggests that the propensity for innovative activity to cluster spatially will be the greatest in industries where tacit knowledge plays an important role. As argued above, it is *tacit knowledge*, as opposed to *information*, which can only be transmitted informally, and typically demands direct and repeated contact. The role of tacit knowledge in generating innovative activity is presumably the greatest during the early stages of the industry life cycle, before product standards have been established and a dominant design has emerged. Audretsch and Feldman (1996) classify 210 industries into four different stages of the life cycle. The results provide considerable evidence suggesting that the propensity for innovative activity to cluster spatially is shaped by the stage of the cycle. On the one hand, new economic knowledge embodied in skilled workers tends to raise the propensity for innovative activity to cluster spatially throughout all phases of the industry life cycle. On the other hand, certain other sources of new economic knowledge, such as university research, tend to elevate the propensity for innovative activity to cluster during the introduction stage of the life cycle, but not during the growth stage, and then again during the stage of decline.

Perhaps most striking is the finding that greater geographic concentration of production actually

[8] The link between innovative output and knowledge inputs at the city level has been substantiated in an econometric model.

leads to more, and not less, dispersion of innovative activity. Apparently innovative activity is promoted by knowledge spillovers that occur within a distinct geographic region, particularly in the early stages of the industry life cycle, but, as the industry evolves towards maturity and decline, may be dispersed by additional increases in concentration of production that have been built up within that same region. The evidence suggests that what may serve as an agglomerating influence in triggering innovative activity to cluster spatially during the introduction and growth stages of the industry life cycle, may later result in a congestion effect, leading to greater dispersion in innovative activity. While the literature on economic geography has traditionally focused on factors such as rents, commuting time, and pollution as constituting congestion and dissipating agglomeration economies (Henderson, 1986), this type of congestion refers to lock-in with respect to new ideas. While there may have been agglomeration economies in automobiles in Detroit in the 1970 and computers in the Northeast Corridor in the 1980s, a type of intellectual lock-in made it difficult for Detroit to shift out of large-car production and for IBM and DEC to shift out of mainframe computers and into mini-computers. Perhaps it was this type of intellectual congestion that led to the emergence of the personal computer in California, about as far away from the geographic agglomeration of the mainframe computer as is feasible on the mainland of the United States. Even when IBM developed its own personal computer, the company located its fledgling PC facility in Boca Ratton, Florida, way outside of the mainframe agglomeration in the Northeast Corridor. Thus, there is at least some evidence suggesting that spatial agglomerations, just like other organizational units of economic activity, are vulnerable to technological lock-in, with the result being, in certain circumstances, that new ideas need new space.

VII. PENETRATING THE BLACK BOX OF GEOGRAPHIC SPACE

While a new literature has emerged identifying the important role that knowledge spillovers within a given geographic location play in stimulating innovative activity, there is little consensus as to how and why this occurs. The contribution of the new wave of studies described in the previous section was simply to shift the unit of observation away from firms to a geographic region. But does it make a difference how economic activity is organized within the black box of geographic space? Political scientists and sociologists have long argued that the differences in the culture of a region may contribute to differences in innovative performance across regions, even holding knowledge inputs such as R&D and human capital constant. For example, Saxenian (1990) argues that a culture of greater interdependence and exchange among individuals in the Silicon Valley region has contributed to a superior innovative performance than is found around Boston's Route 128, where firms and individuals tend to be more isolated and less interdependent.

In studying the networks located in California's Silicon Valley, Saxenian (1990, pp. 96–7) emphasizes that it is the communication between individuals that facilitates the transmission of knowledge across agents, firms, and even industries, and not just a high endowment of human capital and knowledge in the region:

> It is not simply the concentration of skilled labour, suppliers and information that distinguish the region. A variety of regional institutions—including Stanford University, several trade associations and local business organizations, and a myriad of specialized consulting, market research, public relations and venture capital firms—provide technical, financial, and networking services which the region's enterprises often cannot afford individually. These networks defy sectoral barriers: individuals move easily from semiconductor to disk drive firms or from computer to network makers. They move from established firms to start-ups (or vice versa) and even to market research or consulting firms, and from consulting firms back into start-ups. And they continue to meet at trade shows, industry conferences, and the scores of seminars, talks, and social activities organized by local business organizations and trade associations. In these forums, relationships are easily formed and maintained, technical and market information is exchanged, business contacts are established, and new enterprises are conceived. . . . This decentralized and fluid environment also promotes the diffusion of intangible technological capabilities and understandings.'[9]

[9] Saxenian (1990, pp. 97–8) claims that even the language and vocabulary used by technical specialists can be specific to a region: 'a distinct language has evolved in the region and certain technical terms used by semiconductor production engineers in Silicon Valley would not even be understood by their counterparts in Boston's Route 128'.

Such observations suggest a limitation inherent to the general knowledge production function approach described in the previous section. While economists tend to avoid attributing differences in economic performance to cultural differences, there has been a series of theoretical arguments suggesting that differences in the underlying structure between regions may account for differences in rates of growth and technological change. In fact, a heated debate has emerged in the literature about the manner in which the underlying economic structure within a geographic unit of observation might shape economic performance. This debate revolves around two key structural elements—the degree of diversity versus specialization and the degree of monopoly versus local competition.

One view, which Glaeser *et al.* (1992) attribute to the *Marshall–Arrow–Romer externality*, suggests that an increased concentration of a particular industry within a specific geographic region facilitates knowledge spillovers across firms. This model formalizes the insight that the concentration of an industry within a city promotes knowledge spillovers among firms and therefore facilitates innovative activity. To the degree that individuals in the population are identical and engaged in identical types of activities, the costs of communication and transactions are minimized. Lower costs of transaction in communication result in a higher probability of knowledge spilling over across individuals within the population. An important assumption of the model is that knowledge externalities with respect to firms exist, but only for firms within the same industry. Thus, the relevant unit of observation is extended from the firm to the region in the tradition of the Marshall–Arrow–Romer model, but the spillovers are limited to occur solely within the relevant industry.

By contrast, restricting knowledge externalities to occur only within the same industry may ignore an important source of new economic knowledge—inter-industry knowledge spillovers. After all, Griliches (1992, p. 29) has defined knowledge spillovers as, 'working on similar things and hence benefiting much from each other's research'. Jacobs (1969) argues that the most important sources of knowledge spillovers are external to the industry in which the firm operates and that cities are the source of considerable innovation because the diversity of these knowledge sources is greatest in cities. According to Jacobs, it is the exchange of complementary knowledge across diverse firms and economic agents which yields a greater return on new economic knowledge. She develops a theory that emphasizes that the variety of industries within a geographic region promotes knowledge externalities and ultimately innovative activity and economic growth.

The extent of regional specialization versus regional diversity in promoting knowledge spillovers is not the only dimension over which there has been a theoretical debate. A second controversy involves the degree of competition prevalent in the region, or the extent of local monopoly. The Marshall–Arrow–Romer model predicts that local monopoly is superior to local competition because it maximizes the ability of firms to appropriate the economic value accruing from their investments in new knowledge. By contrast, Jacobs (1969) and Porter (1990) argue the opposite—that competition is more conducive to knowledge externalities than is local monopoly.[10] It should be emphasized that by local competition Jacobs does not mean competition within product markets, as has traditionally been envisioned within the industrial organization literature. Rather, Jacobs is referring to the competition for the new ideas embodied in economic agents. Not only does an increased number of firms provide greater competition for new ideas, but, in addition, greater competition across firms facilitates the entry of a new firm specializing in some particular new product niche. This is because the necessary complementary inputs and services are likely to be available from small specialist niche firms but not necessarily from large, vertically integrated producers.

The first important test of the specialization versus diversity debate measured economic performance in terms of employment growth. Glaeser *et al.* (1992) employ a data set on the growth of large industries in 170 cities between 1956 and 1987 in order to identify the relative importance of the degree of regional specialization, diversity, and local competition in influencing industry growth rates. The authors find evidence that contradicts the

[10] Porter (1990) provides examples of Italian ceramics and gold jewellery as industries in which numerous firms are located within a bounded geographic region and compete intensively for new ideas.

Marshall–Arrow–Romer model, but is consistent with the theories of Jacobs. However, their study provided no direct evidence as to whether diversity is more important than specialization in generating innovative activity.

Feldman and Audretsch (forthcoming) identify the extent to which the organization of economic activity is either concentrated, or alternatively consists of diverse but complementary economic activities, and how the underlying structure of economic activity influences innovative output. They link the innovative output of product categories within a specific city to the extent to which the economic activity of that city is concentrated in that industry, or conversely, diversified in terms of complementary industries sharing a common science base. Their results indicate that diversity across complementary economic activities sharing a common science base is more conducive to innovation than is specialization. In addition, their results indicate that the degree of local competition for new ideas within a city is more conducive to innovative activity than is local monopoly. Perhaps the most important conclusion from these two studies, however, is that more than simply an endowment of knowledge inputs is required to generate innovative activity. The underlying economic and institutional structure matters, as do the microeconomic linkages across agents and firms.

VIII. CONCLUSIONS

Globalization combined with the telecommunications revolution has drastically reduced the cost of transporting not just material goods but also information across geographic space. High wages are increasingly incompatible with information-based economic activity, which can be easily transferred to a lower cost location. By contrast, the creation of new ideas based on tacit knowledge cannot easily be transferred across distance. Thus, the comparative advantage of the high-cost countries of North American and Western Europe is increasingly based on knowledge-driven innovative activity. The spillover of knowledge from the firm or university creating that knowledge to a third-party firm is essential to innovative activity. Such knowledge spillovers tend to be spatially restricted. Thus, an irony of globalization is that even as the relevant geographic market for most goods and services becomes increasingly global, the increased importance of innovative activity in the leading developed countries has triggered a resurgence in the importance of local regions as a key source of comparative advantage.

As the comparative advantage in Western Europe and North America has become increasingly based on new knowledge, public policy towards business has responded in two fundamental ways. The first has been to shift the policy focus away from the traditional triad of policy instruments essentially constraining the freedom of firms to contract—regulation, competition policy or antitrust in the USA, and public ownership of business. The policy approach of constraint was sensible as long as the major issue was how to restrain footloose multinational corporations in possession of considerable market power. This is reflected by the waves of deregulation and privatization along with the decreased emphasis of competition policy throughout the OECD. Instead, a new policy approach emerges which focuses on enabling the creation and commercialization of knowledge. Examples of such policies include encouraging R&D, venture capital and new-firm start-ups.

The second fundamental shift involves the locus of such enabling policies, which are increasingly at the state, regional, or even local level. The down-sizing of federal agencies charged with the regulation of business in the United States and Great Britain has been interpreted by many scholars as the eclipse of government intervention. But to interpret deregulation, privatization, and the increased irrelevance of competition policies as the end of government intervention in business ignores an important shift in the locus and target of public policy. The last decade has seen the emergence of a broad spectrum of enabling policy initiatives that fall outside the jurisdiction of the traditional regulatory agencies. Sternberg (1996) documents how the success of a number of different high-technology clusters spanning a number of developed countries is the direct result of enabling policies, such as the provision of venture capital or research support. For example, the Advanced Research Program in Texas has provided support for basic research and the strengthening of the infrastructure of the University of Texas, which has played a central role in developing a high-technology cluster around Austin (Feller, 1997). The Thomas Edison Centers in Ohio, the Advanced Technology Centers in New Jersey, and the Centers for Advanced Technology at Case Western Reserve University, Rutgers University, and the University of Rochester have supported generic, pre-competitive research. This support has generally provided diversified technology development involving a mix of activities encompassing a broad spectrum of industrial collaborators.

Such enabling policies, that are typically implemented at the local or regional level, are part of a silent policy revolution currently under way. The increased importance of innovative regional clusters as an engine of economic growth has led policy-makers to abandon the policy cry frequently heard two decades ago, 'Should we break up, regulate, or simply take over General Motors, IBM and US Steel?' for a very different contemporary version, 'How can we grow the next Silicon Valley?'

DATA APPENDIX: PATENT ACTIVITY OF MAJOR US CITIES

City	No. of patents	Patents/population	No. of research centres	Education level
Albany	3,086	350.33	115	23.60
Atlanta	2,776	86.80	205	26.10
Austin	2,121	231.01	174	30.70
Baltimore	2,400	98.14	225	23.10
Birmingham	223	25.81	72	19.70
Boston	9,013	179.05	650	28.80
Buffalo	1,498	124.98	23	18.80
Charlotte	953	77.13	25	19.60
Chicago	11,793	154.92	516	24.50
Cincinnati	2,353	149.73	141	19.90
Cleveland	3,871	174.21	118	18.50
Columbus	1,524	108.12	170	23.30
Dallas	4,557	159.65	126	26.90
Dayton	1,958	202.55	98	19.10
Denver	2,097	121.34	302	29.10
Detroit	8,652	200.46	361	17.70
Fort Lauderdale	1,395	105.58	108	18.80
Fort Worth	1,174	80.45	49	22.40
Grand Rapids	1,301	132.78	26	17.80
Greensboro	1,147	105.10	44	17.50
Hartford	1,925	165.45	62	26.00
Honolulu	250	28.63	115	24.60
Houston	5,765	163.00	199	25.00
Indianapolis	1,818	126.30	69	20.00
Jacksonville	323	33.59	20	18.60
Kansas City	883	53.92	140	23.20
Las Vegas	273	27.26	27	13.30
Los Angeles	9,598	104.99	515	22.30
Louisville	639	65.74	53	17.20
Memphis	473	45.19	85	18.70
Miami	1,011	50.07	108	18.80

City	No. of patents	Patents/population	No. of research centres	Education level
Milwaukee	2,685	182.80	106	21.30
Minneapolis	7,513	282.42	235	26.90
Nashville	417	40.18	117	21.40
New Orleans	647	49.69	73	19.30
New York	7,482	43.92	788	25.40
Norfolk	689	45.74	67	19.80
Oakland	4,445	205.66	283	29.90
Oklahoma	526	52.90	83	21.60
Orlando	957	71.56	33	20.40
Philadelphia	8,565	171.95	469	22.60
Phoenix	3,334	140.11	121	21.40
Pittsburgh	4,367	182.22	220	18.70
Portland	1,842	112.49	72	23.30
Raleigh-Durham	1,745	188.55	248	31.70
Richmond	940	103.80	41	23.80
Rochester	7,034	647.89	77	22.90
Sacramento	886	60.76	97	22.70
St Louis	2,473	97.57	136	17.70
Salt Lake City	1,398	122.29	109	22.90
San Antonio	517	37.20	56	19.30
San Diego	4,590	173.00	195	25.30
San Francisco	4,233	259.04	345	34.90
San José	10,138	665.14	91	32.60
Scranton	256	39.83	22	13.60
Seattle	3,424	157.67	153	29.50
Tampa	1,285	59.84	42	17.30
Tulsa	858	116.19	81	20.30
West Palm Beach	1,460	157.73	25	22.10

REFERENCES

Acs, Z., and Audretsch, D. (1990), *Innovation and Small Firms*, Cambridge, MA, MIT Press.

— — Feldman, M. (1992), 'Real Effects of Academic Research', *American Economic Review*, **82**(1), 363–70.

— — — (1994), 'R&D Spillovers and Recipient Firm Size', *Review of Economics and Statistics*, **100**(2), 336–40.

Arrow, K. (1962), 'Economic Welfare and the Allocation of Resources for Invention', in R. Nelson (ed.), *The Rate and Direction of Inventive Activity*, Princeton, NJ, Princeton University Press.

Audretsch, D. (1995), *Innovation and Industry Evolution*, Cambridge, MA, MIT Press.

— Feldman, M. (1996), 'R&D Spillovers and the Geography of Innovation and Production', *American Economic Review*, **86**(4), 253–73.

— Stephan, P. (1996), 'Company-Scientist Locational Links: The Case of Biotechnology', *American Economic Review*, **86**(4), 641–52.

Baptista, R. (1997), *An Empirical Study of Innovation, Entry and Diffusion in Industrial Clusters*, PhD dissertation, University of London (London Business School).

Berman, E., Bound, J., and Machin, S. (1997), 'Implications of Skill-Biased Technological Change: International Evidence', Working Paper No. 6166, National Bureau of Economic Research, Cambridge, MA.

Cohen, W., and Levinthal, D. (1989), 'Innovation and Learning: The Two Faces of R&D', *The Economic Journal*, **99**(3), 569–96.

D. B. Audretsch

Ellison, G., and Glaeser, E. (1997), 'Geographic Concentration in US Manufacturing Industries: A Dartboard Approach', *Journal of Political Economy*, (4), 889–927.

Feldman, M. (1994), 'Knowledge Complementarity and Innovation', *Small Business Economics*, **6**(3), 363–72.

— Audretsch, D. (forthcoming), 'Innovation in Cities: Science-Based Diversity, Specialization, and Localized Competition', special issue of the *European Economic Review*, edited by E. Helpman.

Feller, I. (1997), 'Federal and State Government Roles in Science and Technology', *Economic Development Quarterly*, **11**(4), 283–96.

Glaeser, E., Kallal, H., Scheinkman, J., and Shleifer, A. (1992), 'Growth of Cities', *Journal of Political Economy*, **100**, 1126–52.

Griliches, Z. (1979), 'Issues in Assessing the Contribution of R&D to Productivity Growth', *Bell Journal of Economics*, **10**, 92–116.

— (1992), 'The Search for R&D Spill-Overs', *Scandinavian Journal of Economics*, **94**, 29–47.

Henderson, V. (1986), 'Efficiency of Resource Usage and City Size', *Journal of Urban Economics*, **19**(1), 47–70.

Hirschman, A. O. (1970), *Exit, Voice, and Loyalty*, Cambridge, MA, Harvard University Press.

Jacobs, J. (1969), *The Economy of Cities*, New York, Random House.

Jaffe, A. (1989), 'Real Effects of Academic Research', *American Economic Review*, **79**, 957–70.

— Trajtenberg, M. L., and Henderson, R. (1993), 'Geographic Localization of Knowledge Spillovers as Evidenced by Patent Citations', *Quarterly Journal of Economics*, **63**, 577–98.

Klepper, S. (1996), 'Entry, Exit, Growth, and Innovation over the Product Life Cycle', *American Economic Review*, **86**(4), 562–83.

Kortum, S., and Lerner, J. (1997), 'Stronger Protection or Technological Revolution: What is Behind the Recent Surge in Patenting?', Working Paper No. 6204, National Bureau of Economic Research, Cambridge, MA.

Krugman, P. (1991), *Geography and Trade*, Cambridge, MA, MIT Press.

Porter, M. (1990), *The Comparative Advantage of Nations*, New York, Free Press.

Prevenzer, M. (1997), 'The Dynamics of Industrial Clustering in Biotechnology', *Small Business Economics*, **9**(3), 255–71.

Saxenian, A. (1990), 'Regional Networks and the Resurgence of Silicon Valley', *California Management Review*, **33**, 89–111.

Sternberg, R. (1996), 'Technology Policies and the Growth of Regions', *Small Business Economics*, **8**(2), 75–86.

Venables, A. J. (1996), 'Localization of Industry and Trade Performance', *Oxford Review of Economic Policy*, **12**(3), 52–60.

Von Hipple, E. (1994), 'Sticky Information and the Locus of Problem Solving: Implications for Innovation', *Management Science*, **40**, 429–39.

Zucker, L., Darby, M., and Armstrong, J. (1994), 'Intellectual Capital and the Firm: The Technology of Geographically Localized Knowledge Spillovers', Working Paper No. 9496, National Bureau of Economic Research, Cambridge MA.

[18]

Convergence across countries and regions: Theory and empirics

Angel de la Fuente

1. Introduction

In the last decade or so, growth has come to occupy an increasingly important place among the interests of macroeconomists, displacing to some extent their previous preoccupation with the business cycle. This change is largely due to two factors. The first one is the realisation that, in terms of medium and long-term welfare, the trend is more important than the cycle - provided the volatility of income remains as low as it has been during the last few decades (Lucas, 1987). The second factor is the increasing dissatisfaction with the traditional neo-classical models that summarised the pre-existing consensus on the determinants of growth - essentially because of their perceived inability to account for such key features of the data as the observed increase in international inequality or the absence of capital flows toward less developed countries.

Dissatisfaction with the received theory has motivated the search for alternatives to the traditional neo-classical model that has driven the recent literature on endogenous growth. At the theoretical level, numerous authors have developed models in which departures from traditional assumptions about the properties of the production technology or the determinants of technical progress generate predictions about the evolution of the international income distribution that stand in sharp contrast with those of neo-classical theory. Some of these models emphasise the role of growth factors that were ignored by previous theories and generate policy implications that are considerably more activist than those derived from the traditional models. At the empirical level, there is also a rich literature that attempts to test the validity of the different theoretical models that have been proposed, and to quantify the impact of various factors of interest on growth and on the evolution of international or interregional income disparities.

This essay provides an introduction to the theoretical and empirical literature on growth and convergence across countries and regions. It is organised as follows. Section 2 contains some general considerations on the convergence and divergence mechanisms identified in the growth literature. In Section 3 develops a simple descriptive model that attempts to capture the main immediate determinants of the growth of output and illustrates how some key properties of technology determine the evolution of the international or interregional income distribution. Section 4 focuses on the empirical implementation of growth models through convergence equations and illustrates their theoretical implications. Finally, Section 5 discusses some loose ends as well as recent empirical developments, and concludes with a brief summary.

2. Convergence and divergence in growth theory

As the reader will soon discover, the concept of convergence plays a crucial role in the literature we will survey. Although we will eventually provide a more precise definition of this term, we can provisionally interpret it as shorthand for the tendency towards the reduction over

Angel de la Fuente is with Instituto de Análisis Económico, Barcelona.

time of income disparities across countries or regions. Hence, we will say that there is convergence in a given sample when the poorer economies in it tend to grow faster than their richer neighbours, thereby reducing the income differential between them. When we observe the opposite pattern (i.e. when the rich grow faster and increase their lead) we will say that there is divergence in the sample.

Economic theory does not provide unambiguous predictions about the convergence of income levels across regions, but it does identify factors that may generate this.

Economic theory does not provide unambiguous predictions about the convergence or divergence of per capita income levels across countries or regions. It does, however, identify a series of factors or mechanisms that are capable in principle of generating either convergence or divergence. At some risk of oversimplifying, we can classify growth models into two families according to their convergence predictions.

According to those in the first group, being poor is, to some extent, an advantage. In these models, other things equal, poor countries grow faster than rich ones. This does not necessarily imply the eventual elimination of inequality (other things may not be equal), but it does mean that the distribution of relative income per capita across territories will tend to stabilise in the long run, provided some key "structural" characteristics of the different economies remain unchanged over time. In the second set of models, in contrast, rich countries grow faster and inequality increases without any bound.

The source of these contrasting predictions must be sought in very basic assumptions about the properties of the production technology at a given point in time and about the dynamics of technological progress. A first necessary condition for convergence is the existence of decreasing returns to scale in capital (or, more generally, in the various types of capital considered in the model). This assumption means that output grows less than proportionally with the stock of capital. This implies that marginal productivity will decrease with capital accumulation, reducing both the incentive to save and the contribution to growth of a given volume of investment, and creating a tendency for growth to slow down over time. The same mechanism generates a convergence prediction in the cross-section: poor countries (in which capital is scarcer) will grow faster than rich ones. Under the opposite assumption (of increasing returns in capital), the preceding neo-classical logic is inverted and we obtain a divergence prediction. In this case, the return on investment increases with the stock of capital per worker, favouring rich countries that tend to grow faster than poor ones, thereby increasing inequality further.

The second factor to consider has to do with the determinants of technological progress. If countries differ in the intensity of their efforts to generate or adopt new technologies, their long-term growth rates will be different. One possible objection is that the persistence of such differences is not plausible. For instance, it may be argued that the return on technological capital should decrease with its accumulation, just as we would expect to find for other types of capital. In this case, large differences across countries in rates of technological investment would not be sustainable, and there would be a tendency towards the gradual equalisation of technical efficiency levels. It is far from clear, however, that the accumulation of knowledge should be subject to the law of diminishing returns. If the cost of additional innovations falls with scientific or production experience, for instance, the return on technological investment may not be a decreasing function of the stock of accumulated knowledge, and cross-country differences in levels of technological effort could persist indefinitely.

Technical progress could be an important divergence factor, but there are also forces that point in the opposite direction.

Hence, technical progress could be an important divergence factor. But there are also forces that point in the opposite direction. As Abramovitz (1979, 1986) and other authors have pointed out, the public good properties of technical knowledge have an international dimension that tends to favour less advanced countries, provided they have the capability to absorb foreign technologies and adapt them to their own needs. The idea is simple: not having to reinvent each wheel, followers will be in a better position to grow quickly than the technological leader, who will have to assume the costs and lags associated with the development of new leading-edge technologies (1). The resulting process of technological catch up could contribute significantly to convergence, particularly within the group of industrialised countries that are in a position to exploit the advantages derived from technological imitation.

In addition to decreasing returns and technological diffusion, the literature identifies a third convergence mechanism that, although featured less prominently in theoretical models, is likely to be of great practical importance. This mechanism works through structural change, or the reallocation of productive factors across sectors. Poorer countries and regions tend to have relatively large agricultural sectors. Given that output per worker is typically much lower in agriculture than in manufacturing or in the service sector, the flow of resources out of agriculture and into these other activities tends to increase average productivity. Since this process, moreover, has generally been more intense in poor economies than in rich ones in the last few decades, it may have contributed significantly to the observed reduction in productivity differentials across territories.

In conclusion, economic theory identifies forces with contrasting implications for income dynamics. Convergence mechanisms feature prominently in the neo-classical and catch-up models that dominated the literature until recently. The perceived failure of the optimistic convergence predictions of these models, however, has motivated the search for alternatives and contributed to the development of new theories that incorporate various divergence factors. Some of the pioneers of the "endogenous growth" literature (especially Romer 1986, 1987a, b) focused on the possibility of non-decreasing returns to scale in capital alone, while other authors, such as Lucas (1988), Romer (1990) and Grossman and Helpman (1991), developed models in which the rate of technical progress was determined endogenously and could differ permanently across countries, reflecting differences in structural characteristics. In both cases, the theory allows for the possibility of a sustained increase in the level of international or interregional inequality. The Box, which draws on de la Fuente (1995), provides a formal framework that illustrates these two classes of growth theories.

---

1) The idea seems to be due originally to Gerschenkron (1952) and has been developed among others by Abramovitz (1979, 1986), Baumol (1986), Dowrick and Nguyen (1989), Nelson and Wright (1992) and Wolff (1991).

Box 1: A formal model

Immediate determinants of the rate of growth

Let us consider a world in which there are only two factors of production and one final good. Capital (K) and labour (L) are combined to produce a homogeneous output (Y) that can be consumed directly or used as capital in the production process. We will assume that the production technology can be adequately described by an aggregate production function of the form

$$(1)\quad Y = \Phi K^{a}(AL)^{1-a} = \Phi ALZ^{a}$$

where A is an index of labour-augmenting technical efficiency and K denotes a broad capital aggregate that includes both human and physical capital. The variable $Z = K/AL$ denotes the capital/labour ratio in efficiency units and the coefficients a and 1-a measure the elasticity of output with respect to factor stocks.

To allow the possibility of increasing returns in the simplest possible way, we will assume that the term Φ, although perceived as an exogenous constant by individual agents, is in fact a function of the form $\Phi = Z^{b}$ that captures the external effects associated with investment. This specification is basically the one proposed by Romer (1986) building on Arrow (1962) to capture the possibility that capital accumulation may generate positive spillovers. Under these assumptions, output per worker, Q, is given by

$$(2)\quad Q = AZ^{\alpha}$$

where $\alpha = a + b$ measures the degree of returns to scale in capital taking into account this factor's indirect contribution to productivity through possible externalities.

Given equation (2), the growth of output per worker must be the result of the accumulation of productive factors or the outcome of technical progress. Taking logarithms of (2) and differentiating with respect to time, we see that the rate of growth of output per capita $\dot{Q}/Q = g_Q$, where $\dot{Q} = dQ/dt$, can be written as the sum of two terms that reflect, respectively, the rate of technical progress and the accumulation of productive factors:

$$(3)\quad g_Q = g_a + \alpha g_Z.$$

Let us explore the immediate determinants of g_a and g_Z, starting with the second factor. Denoting by s the share of investment in GDP and by δ the rate of depreciation, the increase in the aggregate capital stock is given by the difference between investment and depreciation, i.e.

$$(4)\quad \dot{K} = sY - \delta K = sLQ - \delta K$$

where $\dot{K} = dK/dt$ is the instantaneous increase in the capital stock. Since $Z = K/AL$, the growth rate of the stock of capital per efficiency unit of labour, g_Z, is the difference between $g_k = \dot{K}/K$ and the sum of the rates of technical progress (g_a) and labour force growth (n). Using (2) and (4), it is easy to see that

$$(5)\quad g_Z = g_k - g_a - n = sZ^{\alpha-1} - (n + g_a + \delta),$$

where the term $Z^{\alpha-1}$ $(=Q/(K/L))$ is the average product of capital. Substituting this expression into (3), we have:

(6) $g_Q = (1-\alpha)g_a + \alpha s Z^{\alpha-1} - \alpha(n+\delta)$.

Finally, we have to specify the determinants of the rate of technical progress, g_a. We will assume that g_a is an increasing function of the fraction of GDP invested in R&D, θ, and of the opportunities for technological catch-up, measured by the log difference $(b = \ln X - \ln A)$ between a "technological frontier" denoted by X and the country's own technological index, A, or:

(7) $g_a = \gamma\theta + \varepsilon b$.

The parameters ε and γ measure, respectively, the speed of diffusion of new technologies across countries and the productivity of R&D. We will also assume that best-practice technology improves at a rate g_x which we will take as exogenous from the perspective of each given country and assume constant for simplicity.

Substituting (7) into (6) we finally arrive at an expression,

(8) $g_Q = (1-\alpha)(\gamma\theta + \varepsilon b) + \alpha s Z^{\alpha-1} - \alpha(n+\delta)$,

that gives the rate of growth of output per worker, g_Q, as a weighted sum of two terms that capture the immediate determinants of the rates of technical progress and capital accumulation.

Dynamics

To study the dynamics of the system, given by equation (5), it will be convenient to organise the analysis according to the impact on growth of two separate processes - capital accumulation and technical progress - for two countries (the "leader" and the "follower").

Assuming that the rate of technical progress, g_a, is an exogenous constant, we can draw both terms on the right-hand side of (5) as functions of Z. As shown in Figure 1, the rate of factor accumulation, g_z, is the difference between the product of the investment rate and the average product of capital, $sZ^{\alpha-1}$, and the constant $(n + g_a + \delta)$, and corresponds, therefore, to the vertical distance between the two lines, as shown in the figure.

Figure 1. Dynamics of capital accumulation

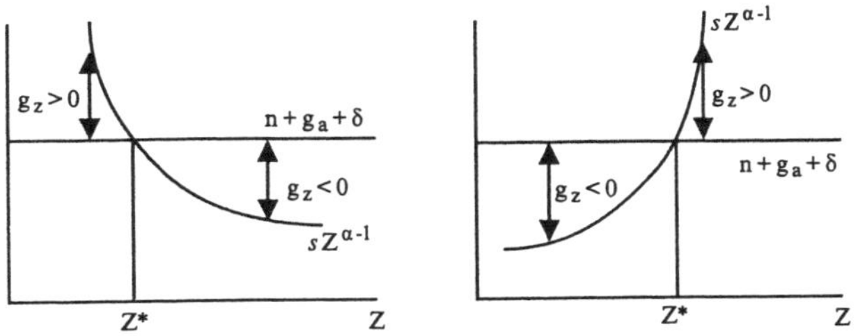

a.- Decreasing returns in capital ($\alpha < 1$)   b. - Increasing returns ($\alpha > 1$)

The two panels of Figure 1 show that the behaviour of the dynamical system depends crucially on the value of α. When $\alpha < 1$, that is, when the neo-classical assumption of decreasing returns holds, the return on investment decreases with the stock of capital. Hence, the term $Z^{\alpha-1}$, is a decreasing function of Z and cuts the horizontal line given by the constant $(n + g_a + \delta)$ at the point Z^* characterised by $g_z = 0$. This implies:

$$(9) \quad Z^* = \left[\frac{s}{n + g_a + \delta}\right]^{\frac{1}{1-\alpha}}$$

From a dynamic point of view, the key finding is that under the assumption of decreasing returns the curve $sZ^{\alpha-1}$ cuts the horizontal line from above, making the growth rate of Z a decreasing function of its level. This implies that the steady state or long-term equilibrium described by Z^* is stable. Notice that g_z is positive (that is, Z increases over time) when the stock of capital per worker is small (and therefore the return on investment is high), and negative (Z decreases over time) when Z is "large" (larger than Z^*), for in this case the volume of investment is not enough to cover depreciation and equip newborn workers with the average stock of capital. Hence, we can interpret the steady-state value of the stock of capital per unit of labour, Z^*, as the one corresponding to a long-term equilibrium to which the economy gradually converges for any given initial value of Z.

When the external effects associated with the accumulation of capital are sufficiently strong that $\alpha > 1$, the situation is very different, as shown in panel b of Figure 1. Since the return on investment, measured by $Z^{\alpha-1}$, is now an increasing function of the stock of capital per efficiency unit of labour, the rate of accumulation increases with Z instead of falling. Hence, Z grows when it is larger than Z^* and falls when it is smaller, moving farther and farther away from the steady state, which must now be interpreted as a threshold for growth rather than as a long-run equilibrium.

To analyse the impact of technical progress on growth and convergence it will be convenient to work explicitly with two countries, f and l, (follower and leader). Let us define the technological distance between leader and follower by:

$$b_{lf} = a_l - a_f = (a_l - x) - (a_f - x) = b_f - b_l$$

where b_l and b_f denote the technological distance between each of these countries and the best-practice frontier. Observe that the evolution of the technological gap between leader and follower, b_{lf}, satisfies the following equation:

$$(10) \quad \dot{b}_{lf} = \dot{a}_l - \dot{a}_f = \gamma(\theta_l - \theta_f) - \varepsilon(b_l - b_f) = \gamma(\theta_l - \theta_f) - \varepsilon b_{lf}$$

Figure 2 displays the dynamics of this equation under two assumptions on the value of ε. When there is no technological diffusion ($\varepsilon = 0$), the leading country (which by assumption invests more in R&D) always has a higher rate of productivity growth. As a result, $\dot{b}_{lf}$ is always positive and the technological distance between leader and follower, b_{lf}, grows without bound as shown in Figure 2a.

When $\varepsilon > 0$, on the other hand, the line εb_{lf} is positively-sloped and cuts the horizontal line $\gamma(\theta_l - \theta_f)$ at a finite value of b_{lf} we will denote by b_{lf}^*. Under this assumption, the model is stable: $\dot{b}_{lf}$ is positive (that is, the technological gap increases over time) when b_{lf} is below its stationary value, b_{lf}^*, and negative (b_{lf} decreases) otherwise (see Figure 2b). Hence, the technological gap converges to a finite value, b_{lf}^*, defined by $\dot{b}_{lf} = 0$, which reads:

$$(11) \quad b_{lf}^* = \frac{\gamma(\theta_l - \theta_f)}{\varepsilon}.$$

Figure 2. Evolution of the technological distance between leader and follower

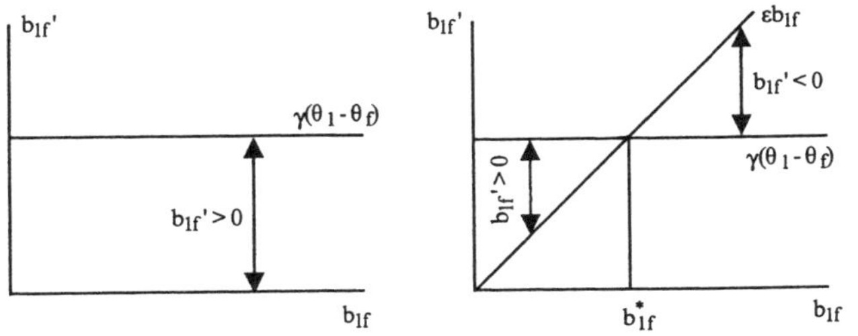

a.- No technological diffusion ($\varepsilon = 0$)   b. - Catch-up with technological diffusion ($\varepsilon > 0$)

In the long run, the (logarithm of the) ratio of the technical efficiency indices of the two countries converges to a constant value that is directly proportional to the difference between their rates of investment in R&D, and inversely proportional to the speed of technological diffusion.

Combining the results of the partial analyses undertaken so far, we can distinguish between two cases. When the technology exhibits increasing returns in capital ($\alpha > 1$) or there is no technological diffusion ($\varepsilon = 0$), the model is unstable and the growth paths of the two countries diverge. If there are decreasing returns and technological diffusion ($\alpha < 1$ and $\varepsilon > 0$), however, the model is stable. In the long run, the rates of growth of the two countries converge to the world rate of technical progress, g_x, and the ratio of their per capita incomes approaches a strictly positive constant value. Thus, long-run income disparities can be attributed to differences in levels of investment in physical and technological capital and in rates of population growth. Notice, however, that the extent to which such differences in "fundamentals" translate into long-term productivity differentials depends on the strength of the two convergence mechanisms present in the model. For given values of θ, s and n, the income differential across countries will be a decreasing function of the rate of technological diffusion (ε) and the degree of returns to scale in capital (α). Hence, both convergence mechanisms tend to mitigate the level of international inequality induced by cross-country differences in fundamentals, but do not eliminate it.

3. From theory to empirics: A framework for empirical analysis

When it comes to trying to distinguish empirically between these two families of models, set out above, a starting point is the observation that the main testable difference between them is the sign of the partial correlation between the growth rate and the initial level of income per capita. While this correlation should be negative according to standard neo-classical models (that is, other things equal poorer countries should grow faster), in some models of endogenous growth the expected sign would be the opposite one. This suggests that a natural way to try to determine which group of models provides a better explanation of the growth experience involves estimating a *convergence equation*, that is, a regression model in which the dependent variable is the growth rate of income per capita or output per worker and the explanatory variable is the initial value of the same income indicator.

The correct formulation of the empirical model, however, requires that we control for other variables that may affect the growth rate of the economies in the sample. As we have seen in a previous section, neo-classical and catch-up models predict that poor countries will grow faster than rich ones only under certain conditions. In Solow's (1956) neo-classical model, for instance, the long-term level of income is a function of the rates of investment and population growth and can, therefore, differ across countries. In a similar vein, Abramovitz (1979, 1986) emphasises that the process of technological catch-up is far from automatic. Although relative backwardness carries with it the potential for rapid growth, the degree to which this potential is realised in a given country depends on its "social capability" to adopt advanced foreign technologies (i.e. on factors such as the level of schooling of its population and the availability of qualified scientific and technical personnel) and on the existence of a political and macroeconomic environment conducive to investment and structural change.

Even in models where convergence forces prevail, long-term income levels can vary across territories, reflecting underlying differences in "fundamentals".

In short, even in models where convergence forces prevail, long-term income levels can vary across territories, reflecting underlying differences in "fundamentals". If we do not control for such differences, the estimated relationship between growth and initial income could be very misleading. Imagine, for instance, that the Solow model (with decreasing returns and access by all economies to a common technology) is the correct one, and that richer countries display on average higher rates of investment and lower rates of population growth than poorer countries (which is why they are richer in the first place). According to the model, these two factors would have a positive effect on the growth rate (during the transition to the long-run equilibrium) that could conceivably dominate the convergence effect that makes growth a decreasing function of income with other things constant. It is clear that if we do not include the rates of investment and population growth in the equation, we could find that the estimated coefficient of initial income is positive and conclude, erroneously, from this fact that the predictions of the Solow model fail to hold. To put it in a slightly different way, the problem would be that when we do not control for the determinants of the steady state, we are actually testing the hypothesis that all economies converge to the same long-run equilibrium. The rejection of this hypothesis, however, has no implications for the validity of the Solow model, since this model makes no such prediction except when the economies in the sample are exactly alike.

On the basis of the preceding discussion, we can conclude that a "minimal" model for the empirical analysis of convergence would be an equation of the form

$$(1)\quad \Delta y_{i,t} = \gamma x_{it} - \beta y_{i,t} + \varepsilon_{it},$$

where $y_{i,t}$ is income per capita or per worker in territory i at the beginning of period t, $\Delta y_{i,t}$ the growth rate of the same variable over the period, ε_{it} a random disturbance, and x_{it} a variable or set of variables that captures the "fundamentals" of economy i, that is, all those characteristics of this territory that have a permanent effect on its growth rate.

3.1 Structural convergence equations

Many empirical studies of growth and convergence have proceeded by estimating some variant of equation (1). In early studies the empirical specification was frequently *ad hoc* and only loosely tied with the theory (2). In recent years, however, researchers have increasingly focused on the estimation of "structural" convergence equations derived explicitly from formal models. One of the most popular specifications in the literature is the one derived by Mankiw, Romer and Weil (1992; henceforth MRW) from an extended neo-classical model à la Solow that would be equivalent to the one developed in the Box under the assumption that the rate of technical progress is an exogenous constant common to all countries (3). Working with a log-linear approximation to the model around its steady state, MRW show that the growth rate of output per worker in territory i during the period that starts at time t is given approximately by the following equation (4):

$$(2)\quad \Delta y_{i,t} = g + \beta(a_{io} + gt) + \beta\frac{\alpha}{1-\alpha}\ \ln \frac{s_{it}}{\delta+g+n_{it}} - \beta y_{i,t}$$

where

$$(3)\quad \beta = (1-\alpha)\,(\delta + g + n),$$

and where g is the rate of technical progress, δ the depreciation rate, α the coefficient of capital in the aggregate production function, t the time elapsed since the beginning of the sample period, a_{io} the logarithm of the index of technical efficiency at time zero, s the share of investment in GDP and n is the rate of growth of the labour force.

It is important to understand that the estimation of equation (2) does not imply that we are literally accepting the assumptions of the underlying Solow-type model (i.e. we do not need to assume that the investment rate is exogenous or constant over time). What we are doing is simply assigning to some of the parameters of the Solow model (in particular, to s and n) the observed average values of their empirical counterparts during a given period. During this period, the economy will behave approximately as if it were approaching the steady state of the Solow model that corresponds to the contemporaneous parameter values. In the next period, of course, we are likely to observe different values of the investment and population growth rates and therefore, a different steady state, but this poses no real difficulty. In essence, all we are doing is constructing a convenient approximation to the production function that allows us to recover its parameters using data on investment flows rather than factor stocks. This is very convenient because such data are easier to come by and can be expected to be both more reliable and more comparable over time and across countries than most existing estimates of factor stocks. It must be kept in mind, however, that the only information we can extract from the estimation of a convergence equation of the form (2)

2) See for instance Kormendi and McGuire (1985), Grier and Tullock (1989) and Barro (1991).

3) That is, the specification of the rate of technical progress as a function of R&D expenditure and the technological gap is abandoned, being replaced by the simple assumption that the rate of technological progress is an exogenous constant, g, equal for all countries. The part of the model that describes capital accumulation, on the other hand, would be exactly as developed in Section 2.

4) Barro and Sala-i-Martin (1990, 1992a) derive a similar expression from a variant of the optimal growth model of Cass (1965) and Koopmans (1965) with exogenous technical progress. The resulting equation is similar to (2) except that the investment rate (which is now endogenous) is replaced by the rate of time discount among the determinants of the steady state. The convergence coefficient, β, is now a more complicated function of the parameters of the model, but it still depends on the degree of decreasing returns to capital and on the rates of population growth, depreciation and technical progress. A second difference between the two models is that, whereas the MRW model can be easily extended to incorporate investment in human capital, Barro and Sala do not include this factor as an argument of the production function, although they do bring it into their empirical specification, in an ad hoc way, as a determinant of the steady state.

concerns the properties of the production technology. As Cohen (1992) emphasises, the estimated equation does not, in particular, tell us anything about the actual dynamics of the economy or the position of a hypothetical long-run equilibrium - although it does allow us to make predictions about long-term income levels conditional on assumptions about the future behaviour of investment and population growth rates.

The empirical implementation of equation (1) or (2) does not, in principle, raise special problems. Given time series data on income, population and investment for a sample of countries or regions, we can use (2) to recover estimates of the rate of convergence and the parameters of the production function. The convergence equation can be estimated using either cross-section or pooled data. Most of the earlier convergence studies took the first route, averaging the variables over the entire sample period and working with a single observation for each country or region. The second possibility, which has become increasingly popular, involves averaging over shorter sub-periods in order to obtain several observations per country.

In either case, one difficulty which immediately becomes apparent is that three of the variables on the right-hand side of the equation (g, δ and a_{io}) are not directly observable. In the first two cases, the problem is probably not very important. Although these coefficients can be estimated inside the equation (and this has been done occasionally), the usual procedure in the literature is to impose "reasonable" values of these parameters prior to estimation. The standard assumption is that $g = 0.02$ and $\delta = 0.03$, but researchers report that estimation results are not very sensitive to changes in these values.

The possibility that initial levels of technical efficiency may differ across countries raises a difficult problem that requires panel data techniques.

The possibility that initial levels of technical efficiency (a_{io}) may differ across countries does raise a more difficult problem. Although some authors have argued that it may be reasonable to assume a common value of a_{io} because most technical knowledge is in principle accessible from everywhere, casual observation suggests that levels of technological development differ widely across countries. If this is so, failure to control for such differences (or for any other omitted variables) will bias the estimates of the remaining parameters whenever the other regressors in the equation are correlated with the missing ones. In other words, we can only legitimately subsume technological differences across countries in the error term if they are uncorrelated with investment rates and population growth. This seems unlikely, however, as the level of total factor productivity is one of the key determinants of the rate of return on investment.

The standard solution for this problem is to turn to panel data techniques in order to control for unobserved national or regional fixed effects. The simplest procedure involves introducing country or regional dummies in order to estimate a different regression constant for each territory. It should be noted, however, that this is equivalent to estimating the equation with the dependent and independent variables measured in deviations from their average values (computed over time for each country or region in the sample). Hence, this procedure (as practically all panel techniques designed for removing fixed effects), ignores the information contained in observed cross-country differences and produces parameter estimates which are based only on the time variation of the data within each territory over relatively short periods. Since what we are trying to do is characterising the long-term dynamics of a sample of economies, this may be rather dangerous, particularly when the data contain an important cyclical component or other short-term noise.

The structural convergence equation methodology has some important advantages and limitations, both of which are derived from the close linkage between theory and empirics that characterise this approach. Its most attractive feature is that it allows us to use the relevant theory to explicitly guide the formulation of the empirical model - that is, the formal model is used to determine what variables must be included in the regression and how they must enter in order to obtain direct estimates of the structural parameters of the model. It is clear, however, that such guidance comes at a price, as our estimates will be, at best, only as good as the underlying theoretical model. Hence, an inadequate specification of this model can yield very misleading conclusions.

An inadequate specification of the model can yield very misleading conclusions.

Although this problem arises to some extent whenever we run a regression, there are reasons to think that it may be particularly important in the present context. In most of the recent empirical work on growth and convergence, the theoretical model of reference is some version of the one-sector neo-classical model with exogenous technical progress that underlies equation (2). Since the only convergence force present in this model is what we may call the neo-classical mechanism, the usual finding of a negative partial correlation between growth and initial income must be interpreted in this framework as evidence that the aggregate production function displays decreasing returns to scale in reproducible factors. In fact, this assumption is precisely what allows us to draw inferences about the degree of returns to scale from the estimated value of the convergence coefficient. The problem, of course, is that if there are any other operative convergence mechanisms, the inference will not be valid, as the estimated value of the convergence parameter will also capture their effects.

As we have seen, the literature identifies at least two factors other than decreasing returns that can generate a negative partial correlation between income levels and growth rates holding investment and population growth constant: technological diffusion and structural change. Although none of these convergence mechanisms is incompatible with the neo-classical story, the observation that this is not the only possible source of convergence suggests that it may be dangerous to accept without question an interpretation of the convergence coefficient based too literally on the preceding model. For instance, if income per capita is highly correlated with the level of technological development, the coefficient of initial income in a convergence regression could capture, at least in part, a technological catch-up effect. To avoid the danger of drawing the wrong conclusions about the properties of the technology, it may be preferable to interpret existing estimates of the convergence parameter, β, (particularly in the case of unconditional convergence equations) as summary measures of the joint effect of several possible convergence mechanisms. The value of this parameter (i.e. the partial correlation between the growth rate and initial income) will depend on the coefficient of capital in the production function, the speed of technological diffusion, the impact of sectoral change and on the response of investment rates to rising income), and will be positive (i.e. growth will be negatively correlated with initial income) whenever the forces making for convergence dominate those working in the opposite direction.

3.2 Some convergence concepts

Before we proceed to review the empirical evidence, it is convenient to introduce some concepts of convergence that will feature prominently in the discussion below. Perhaps the first question that arises concerning the evolution of the distribution of income per capita is whether the dispersion of this variable (measured for instance by the standard deviation of its logarithm) tends to decrease over time. The concept of convergence implicit in this question, called *σ-convergence* by Barro and Sala-i-Martin (1990, 1992a,b), is probably the one closest to the intuitive notion of convergence. It is not, however, the only possible one. We may also ask, for instance, whether poorer countries tend to catch up with richer ones, or whether the relative position of each country within the income distribution tends to stabilise over time. The concepts of *absolute* and conditional *β-convergence* proposed by Barro and Sala-i-Martin correspond roughly to these two questions.

To make more precise these two notions of convergence, we can use a variant of equation (1) in which we assume that each economy's fundamentals remain constant over time (that is, that $x_{it} = x_i$ for all t) and we interpret the variable y_{it} as relative income per capita, that is, income per capita normalised by the contemporaneous sample average. Omitting the disturbance term, the evolution of relative income in territory i is described by

$$\Delta y_{i,t} = \gamma x_i - \beta y_{i,t}.$$

Setting $\Delta y_{i,t}$ equal to zero in this expression, we can solve for the steady-state value of relative income,

$$y_i^* = \frac{\gamma x_i}{\beta}$$

It is easy to check that if β lies between zero and one, the system described by the above equation is stable. This implies that the relative income of territory i converges in the long run to the equilibrium value given by y_i^*. Notice that the equilibrium can differ across countries as a function of the "fundamentals" described by x_i.

In terms of this simple model, we will say that there is conditional β-convergence when β lies between zero and one, and absolute β-convergence when this is true and, in addition, y_i is the same for all economies - i.e. when all countries or regions in the sample converge to the same income per capita.

Even though they are closely related, the three concepts of convergence are far from being equivalent. Some type of β-convergence is a necessary condition for sustained σ-convergence, for the level of inequality will grow without bound when β is negative (i.e. when the rich grow faster than the poor). It is not sufficient, however, because a positive value of β is compatible with a transitory increase of income dispersion due either to random shocks or to the fact that the initial level of inequality is below its steady-state value (as determined by the dispersion of fundamentals and the variance of the disturbance). The two types of β-convergence, moreover, have very different implications. Absolute β convergence implies a tendency towards the equalisation of per capita incomes within the sample. Initially poor economies tend to grow faster until they catch up with the richer ones. In the long run, expected per capita income is the same for all members of the group, independently of its initial value. As we know, this does not mean that inequality will disappear completely, for there will be random shocks with uneven effects on the different territories. Such disturbances, however, will have only transitory effects, implying that, in the long run, we should observe a fluid distribution in which the relative positions of the different regions change rapidly.

With conditional β-convergence, on the other hand, each territory converges only to its own steady state but these can be very different from each other. Hence, a high degree of inequality could persist, even in the long run, and we would also observe high persistence in the relative positions of the different economies. In other words, rich economies will generally remain rich while the poor continue to lag behind.

It is important to observe that, although the difference between absolute and conditional convergence is very sharp in principle, things are often much less clear in practice. In empirical studies we generally find that a number of variables other than initial income enter significantly in convergence equations. This finding suggests that steady states differ across countries or regions and, therefore, that convergence is only conditional. It is typically the case, however, that these conditioning variables change over time and often tend to converge themselves across countries or regions. Hence, income may still converge unconditionally in the long run, and this convergence may reflect in part the gradual equalisation of the underlying fundamentals. In this situation, a conditional and an unconditional convergence equation will yield different estimates of the convergence rate. There is, however, no contradiction between these estimates once we recognise that they are measuring different things: while the unconditional parameter measures the overall intensity of a process of income convergence which may work in part through changes over time in various structural characteristics, the conditional parameter captures the speed at which the economy would be approaching a "pseudo steady state" whose location is determined by the current values of the conditioning variables.

4. Convergence across countries and regions: Empirical evidence and theoretical implications

The process of convergence seems to be extremely slow.

Having reviewed the theoretical and empirical framework used in the convergence literature, we are now in a position to examine the empirical evidence and discuss its implications. Contributions to the empirics of economic growth highlight three interesting empirical regularities. First, evidence of some sort of β-convergence is found in practically all available samples. While convergence is only conditional at the national level, in most regional samples a negative correlation between initial income and subsequent growth emerges without controlling for other variables. This second result is consistent with the existence of absolute convergence at the regional level - but most of the studies we have reviewed do not explicitly test this hypothesis (5). Secondly, the process of convergence seems to be extremely slow. Many of the existing estimates of the convergence parameter cluster around a value of 2 percent per year which implies that it takes around 35 years for a typical region to reduce its income gap with the national average by one half. Hence, the expected duration of the convergence process must be measured in decades. Finally, it is interesting to observe that the estimated convergence coefficient is remarkably stable across samples. This

5) Those that do test it by including different sets of conditioning variables generally reject it, as the significance of many of these variables implies important cross-regional differences in steady states. See for instance Dolado et al., (1994) and Mas et al., (1995) for the Spanish provinces, Herz and Röger (1996) for the German Raumordnungsregionen, Neven and Gouyette (1995) and Faberberg and Verspagen (1996) for various samples of European regions, Holtz-Eakin (1993) for the states of the US and Paci and Pigliaru (1995), and Fabiani and Pellegrini (1996). As we have noted in Section 3, however, this evidence does not conclusively reject the hypothesis of absolute convergence, as conditioning variables (and hence steady states) may themselves be converging over time. Note that the study by Vanhoudt et al., this volume, tackles this issue for Europe in more detail. The authors report strong support of conditional convergence within Europe - even at the regional level - with a speed of convergence of about half the size found for the United States.

stability suggests that the mechanisms that drive convergence in income per capita across different economies seem to operate in a regular fashion. Hence, we can at least hope to provide a unified structural explanation of the convergence process in terms of a "general" theoretical model.

A good candidate for a "general" model is a simple extension of the neo-classical one. All that is needed is to extend the concept of capital to intangibles.

Perhaps the dominant view in the literature is that a good candidate for this "general" model is a simple extension of the one-sector neo-classical model with exogenous technical progress. Just about the only departure from the traditional assumptions required in order to explain the empirical evidence is a broadening of the relevant concept of capital in order to include investment in intangibles such as human and technological capital. This conclusion is reached essentially by interpreting the results we have just reviewed within the framework of the growth model given in (2). According to our previous discussion, the finding of (at least conditional) β-convergence in most national or regional samples can be interpreted as evidence in favour of the neo-classical assumption of decreasing returns to capital, as this result would not be consistent with increasing returns models that predict an explosive behaviour of income and its distribution. On the other hand, the apparent slowness of the convergence process does suggest that we are not that far from having constant returns in reproducible factors - a result that seems considerably more plausible if we think in terms of a broad capital aggregate, rather than the rather restrictive concept of capital we find in old-fashioned neo-classical models.

Since this broader concept of capital is probably one of the most significant contributions of the recent literature to our understanding of the mechanics of growth, the issue deserves a fairly detailed discussion. The reader will recall that within the framework of the Solow model the convergence coefficient (β) depends on the degree of returns to scale, measured by α (the coefficient of capital in the aggregate production function with, as discussed in the Box, $\alpha = a + b$, where a is the coefficient of capital in the "private" production function and b captures the possible externalities), and on the rates of technical progress (g), population growth (n) and depreciation (δ). More specifically, we have seen that the relationship among these variables is given by equation (3): $\beta = (1 - a - b)(\delta + g + n)$.

Using this expression and making reasonable guesses about the values of some of the parameters, we can extract information about key properties of the production technology from empirical estimates of the convergence rate. To start, let us consider the expected value of β under conventional assumptions about the values of the remaining parameters. Within the framework of a traditional neo-classical model (with constant returns to scale in capital and labour, perfect competition and no externalities) we would have $b = 0$ and the coefficient a would be equal to capital's share of national income, which is around one third. The average rate of population growth in the industrial countries during the post-WWII period is approximately 1%. Available estimates of the rate of technical progress are around 2% per year. Finally, estimates of the rate of depreciation vary considerably. In the convergence literature it is commonly assumed that $\delta = 0.03$, but a higher value (around 5 or 6% per year) may be more reasonable. Given these assumptions, the expected value of β lies between 0.04 and 0.06.

The empirical results of Barro and Sala-i-Martin (1990, 1992a,b), Mankiw, Romer and Weil (1992) and other authors point towards a much lower convergence rate. Since the estimated value of the parameter is still positive, the evidence is consistent with decreasing returns to capital (i.e. $a + b < 1$). The low value of β, however, suggests that we are relatively close to having constant returns to capital. Maintaining our previous assumptions about the values of the remaining parameters, a convergence coefficient of 0.02 would imply a value of α between 0.67 and 0.78 - more than twice the share of capital in national income.

One possible explanation (Romer, 1987b) is that this result may reflect the existence of important externalities associated with the accumulation of physical capital. While these external effects would not be sufficiently strong to generate increasing returns in capital alone, they might still account for the apparent slowness of convergence. Other authors, however, argue that a more plausible explanation is that the omission of variables which are positively correlated with investment in physical capital may bias upward the coefficient of this variable. Barro and Sala-i-Martin (1990, 1992a) argue that a value of capital's coefficient around 0.7 only makes sense if we count accumulated educational investment as part of the stock of capital.

Mankiw, Romer and Weil (1992) advance the same hypothesis and test it explicitly by estimating a structural convergence equation similar to equation (2) that explicitly incorporates a proxy for the rate of investment in human capital as a regressor. Their results, and those obtained by other authors who estimate similar specifications, tend to confirm the hypothesis that investment in human (and technological) capital plays an important role in the growth process (6). As Mankiw (1995) points out, once human capital is included as an input in the production function, the resulting model is consistent with some of the key features of the data. Countries that invest more in physical capital and education tend to grow faster and therefore eventually attain high levels of relative income. Cross-country differences in rates of accumulation, moreover, are sufficiently high to explain the bulk of the observed dispersion of income levels and growth rates.

5. Loose ends and recent developments

It is probably fair to say that just a few years ago the extended neo-classical model we have just described summarised a consensus view on the mechanics of growth. In recent years, however, this consensus has been challenged by a series of papers that, relying on panel data techniques, obtain results that are difficult to reconcile with the prevailing theoretical framework. In this section we will summarise some of the key findings of these studies and discuss the theoretical difficulties they raise.

One of the key findings of the "classical" convergence studies is that convergence to the steady state is an extremely slow process. It has recently been argued, however, that this result may be due to a bias arising from the use of econometric specifications that do not adequately allow for unobserved differences across countries or regions. To get around this problem, a number of authors have proposed the use of panel techniques that allow for unobserved fixed effects. As we will see in this section, their results raise some puzzling questions.

For example, Marcet (1994), Raymond and García (1994), Canova and Marcet (1995), de la Fuente (1996a,b), Tondl (1997) and Gorostiaga (1998), estimate fixed-effects convergence models

6) See for instance Lichtenberg (1992), Holtz-Eakin (1993), Nonneman and Vanhoudt (1996) and de la Fuente, (1998b). de la Fuente (1997) provides a detailed review of this literature.

using panel data for a variety of regional samples. Their results suggest a view of the regional convergence process that stands in sharp contrast with the one advanced before: instead of slow convergence to a common income level, regional economies within a given country seem to be converging extremely fast (at rates of up to 20 percent per year) but to very different steady states. Cross-national studies provide a roughly similar picture: Knight *et al.*, (1993), Canova and Marcet (1995), Islam (1995) and Caselli *et al.*, (1996), among others, find evidence of rapid convergence across countries (at rates of up to 12% per annum) toward very different steady states whose dispersion can be explained only in part by observed cross-national differences in population growth and investment rates. In both cases, many of the standard conditioning variables (such as human capital indicators) lose their statistical significance, the estimated coefficient of physical capital adopts rather low values, and the size and significance of the regional or national fixed effects suggests that persistent differences in levels of technical efficiency play a crucial role in explaining the dispersion of income levels.

We can reject the assumption that increasing returns generate an explosive behaviour in the distribution of income across economies.

Should we take these results at face value? Before we do so and abandon the only workable models we have so far, it seems sensible to search for some way to reconcile these empirical findings with some kind of plausible theory. I believe that this can be done - at least to some extent. My argument is essentially that a more reasonable interpretation of the extremely high convergence rates obtained in recent studies is that, if we have correctly estimated the relevant parameter (and we may not), then convergence is much too fast to be simply the result of diminishing returns to scale. This observation points to two complementary lines of research. The first one asks whether panel specifications of growth equations do in fact yield estimates of the relevant parameter. The second proceeds by identifying plausible mechanisms that may help account for rapid convergence and incorporating them into theoretical and empirical models.

On the first issue, Shioji (1997a, b) and de la Fuente (1998a) provide some evidence that panel estimates of the convergence rate may tell us very little about the speed at which economies approach their steady states (and therefore about the degree of returns to scale in reproducible factors) - essentially because these estimates are likely to capture short-term adjustments around trend rather than the long-term growth dynamics we are really interested in. Both authors show that correcting for the resulting bias in various ways brings us back to convergence rates that are broadly compatible with sensible theoretical models.

On the second issue, de la Fuente (1995, 1996b) and de la Fuente and Doménech (2000) estimate a further extension of the neo-classical model that allows for cross-country differences in total factor productivity and for a process of technological catch-up and show that technological diffusion can go a long way towards explaining rapid convergence across countries and regions (7). It follows that fast convergence does not require us to abandon the broad concept of capital we have so laboriously developed over the last decades. In fact, the parameters of the aggregate production functions estimated by these authors at the regional and national level are not far from those

7) Dowrick and Nguyen (1989) also investigate the quantitative importance of technological catch-up as a convergence factor, but their empirical specification makes it difficult to disentangle this effect from the neo-classical convergence mechanism. Helliwell (1992), Coe and Helpman (1995) and Engelbrecht (1997) provide additional evidence on technological diffusion. There is also some evidence that a significant part of what appears to be TFP convergence at the aggregate level is in fact due to factor reallocation across sectors. See for instance Paci and Pigliaru (1995), de la Fuente (1996b), Caselli and Coleman (1999) and de la Fuente and Freire (1999).

obtained by Mankiw, Romer and Weil (1992) and suggest, in particular that educational investment plays a crucial role in growth that may not be apparent in previous studies in part because of data deficiencies. On the other hand, these studies do show that total factor productivity (TFP) differences across countries and regions are substantial and account for around half of observed productivity differences in the OECD in recent years, a result that is broadly consistent with the findings of Klenow and Rodríguez (1997) on the explanatory power of the extended neo-classical model. These results highlight the importance TFP dynamics as a crucial determinant of the evolution of productivity, a subject brought up recently by Prescott (1998), while retaining a significant role for differences in factor stocks as sources of income differentials across economies.

Recent results have still been useful in shaking-up an exaggerated confidence in our ability to explain why some countries are richer than others.

If we try to summarise, the key points that stand out in the theory and empirics on economic growth are as follows. In the current state of the literature, the conclusions we can draw must necessarily remain rather tentative. Practically all existing studies on the subject find clear evidence of some sort of long-run convergence both across countries and across regions over the post-war period. These findings allow us to reject with a fair degree of confidence a series of recent models in which the assumption of increasing returns generates an explosive behaviour of the distribution of income across economies that cannot be found in the data. Many of the results we have reviewed are consistent with an extended neo-classical model built around an aggregate production function that includes human capital as a productive input.

Recently, results using panel data techniques have suggested that educational investment was not productive and that the bulk of productivity differences across countries or regions has little to do with differences in stocks of productive factors. In my opinion, this has been largely a false alarm, but it has been useful in shaking up what was probably an exaggerated confidence in our ability to explain why some countries or regions are richer than others with an extremely simple model, and in directing researchers' attention to the determinants of technological progress and to some of the difficult econometric issues involved in the estimation of growth models.

References

Abramovitz, M. (1979). "Rapid Growth Potential and its Realization," in *Thinking About Growth and Other Essays on Economic Growth and Welfare*. Cambridge U. Press, 1989, pp. 187-219.

Abramovitz, M. (1986). "Catching Up, Forging Ahead and Falling Behind," in *Thinking About Growth and Other Essays on Economic Growth and Welfare*. Cambridge U. Press, 1989, pp. 220-44.

Arrow, K. J. (1962) "The Economic Implications of Learning by Doing," in *Collected Papers of Kenneth J. Arrow, vol. 5: Production and Capital*. Harvard U. Press, 1985, pp. 157-80.

Barro, R. (1991). "Economic Growth in a Cross Section of Countries. "*Quarterly Journal of Economics*, CVI (2), pp. 407-43.

Barro, R. and Sala-i-Martin, X. (1990). "Economic Growth and Convergence Across the United States." NBER Working Paper no. 3419, Aug. 1990.

Barro, R. and Sala-i-Martin, X. (1992a). "Convergence." *Journal of Political Economy*, 100(2), pp. 223-51.

Barro, R. and Sala-i-Martin, X. (1992b). "Regional Growth and Migration: A Japan-United States Comparison." *Journal of the Japanese and International Economies*, 6, pp. 312-46.

Baumol, W. (1986). "Productivity Growth, Convergence and Welfare: What the Long-Run Data Show." *American Economic Review*, 76(5), pp. 1072-85.

Canova, F. and Marcet, A. (1995). "The Poor Stay Poor: Non-convergence across Countries and Regions." CEPR Discussion Paper no. 1265.

Caselli, F. and Coleman, W. (1999). "How regions converge." CEPR Discussion Paper no. 2191.

Caselli, F., Esquivel, G. and Lefort, F. (1996). "Reopening the convergence debate: a new look at cross-country growth empirics." *Journal of Economic Growth*, 1(3), pp. 363-89.

Cass, D. (1965). "Optimum Growth in an Aggregative Model of Capital Accumulation." *Review of Economic Studies*, XXXII, July, pp. 223-40.

Coe, D. and Helpman, E. (1995). "International R&D spillovers." *European Economic Review*, 39, pp. 859-87.

Cohen, D. (1992). "Tests of the 'convergence hypothesis':a critical note." CEPR Discussion Paper no. 691.

de la Fuente, A. (1995). "Catch-up, Growth and Convergence in the OECD." CEPR Discussion Paper no. 1274.

de la Fuente, A. (1996a). "Convergencia y otras historias: economía regional desde una perspectiva neoclásica. "*Revista de Economía Aplicada*, IV(10), Primavera, pp. 5-64.

de la Fuente, A. (1996b). "On the sources of convergence: A close look at the Spanish regions." CEPR Discussion Paper No. 1543.

de la Fuente, A. (1997) "The empirics of growth and convergence: a selective review." *Journal of Economic Dynamics and Control*, 21(1), pp. 23-74.

de la Fuente, A. (1998a). "What kind of regional convergence?" CEPR Discussion Paper no. 1924.

de la Fuente, A. (1998b). "Convergence equations and income dynamics: The sources of OECD Convergence, 1970-95." CEPR Discussion Paper no. 1794.

de la Fuente, A. and Freire, M. J. (1999). "Estructura sectorial y convergencia regional." Mimeo, Instituto de Análisis Económico, Barcelona.

de la Fuente, A. and Doménech, R. (2000). "Human capital in growth regressions: how much difference does data quality make?" Mimeo, Instituto de Análisis Económico, Barcelona.

Dolado, J., González-Páramo, J. M. and Roldán, J. M. (1994). "Convergencia Económica entre las Provincias Españolas: Evidencia Empírica (1955-1989)." *Moneda y Crédito* 198, pp. 81-131.

Dowrick, S. and Nguyen, D. T. (1989). "OECD Comparative Economic Growth 1950-85: Catch-up and Convergence." *American Economic Review* 79(5), pp. 1010-1030.

Engelbrecht, H.-J. (1997). "International R&D spillovers, human capital and productivity in the OECD economies: an empirical investigation." *European Economic Review*, 41, pp. 1479-88.

Faberberg, J. and Verspagen, B. (1996). "Heading for divergence? Regional growth in Europe reconsidered. *Journal of Common Market Studies*, 34(3), pp. 431-48.

Gerschenkron, A. "Economic Backwardness in Historical Perspective," in B. Hosilitz, editor, *The Progress of Underdeveloped Areas*. Chicago University Press, 1952.

Grier, K. and Tullock, G. (1989). "An Empirical Analysis of Cross-National Economic Growth, 1951-80." *Journal of Monetary Economics*, 24, pp. 259-276.

Grossman, G. and Helpman, E. (1991). *Innovation and Growth in the Global Economy*. MIT Press, Cambridge, Mass.

Helliwell, J. (1992). "Trade and Technical Progress." NBER Working Paper no. 4226.

Herz, B. and Röger, W. (1996). "Economic growth and convergence in Germany," *Weltwirtschaftliches Archiv*, 1/1996, pp. 133-43.

Holtz-Eakin, D. (1993). "Solow and the states: Capital accumulation, productivity, and economic growth." *National Tax Journal*, XLVI, pp. 425-39.

Islam, N. (1995). "Growth Empirics: A Panel Data Approach". *Quarterly Journal of Economics*, CX(4), pp. 1127-70.

Klenow, P. and Rodríguez-Clare, A. (1997). "The neo-classical revival in growth economics: has it gone too far?" Mimeo, U. of Chicago.

Knight, M., Loayza, N. and Villanueva, D. (1993). "Testing the neo-classical theory of economic growth: a panel data approach." *IMF Staff Papers*, 40, pp. 512-41.

Koopmans, T. (1965). "On the Concept of Optimal Economic Growth," in *The Econometric Approach to Development Planning*. North-Holland, Amsterdam.

Kormendi, R. and Meguire, P. G. (1985). "Macroeconomic Determinants of Growth: Cross-Country Evidence." *Journal of Monetary Economics*, 16, pp. 141-63.

Lichtenberg, F. (1992). "R&D Investment and International Productivity Differences." NBER Working Paper no. 4161.

Lucas, R. (1987). *Models of Business Cycles*. Basil Blackwell, Oxford.

Lucas, R. (1988). "On the Mechanics of Economic Development." *Journal of Monetary Economics* 22(1), pp. 3-42.

Lucas, R. (1990). "Why Doesn't Capital Flow from Rich to Poor Nations?" *American Economic Review Papers and Proceedings*, 80, pp. 92-6.

Mankiw, G. (1995). "The Growth of Nations." *Brookings Papers on Economic Activity* I, pp. 275-326.

Mankiw, G., Romer, D. and Weil, D. (1992). "A Contribution to the Empirics of Economic Growth." *Quarterly Journal of Economics*, CVII(2), pp. 407-37.

Marcet, A. (1994). "Los pobres siguen siendo pobres: Convergencia entre regiones y países, un análisis bayesiano de datos de panel," en *Crecimiento y convergencia regional en España y Europa, Vol. II*. Instituto de Análisis Económico, Barcelona.

Nelson, R. and Wright, G. (1992). "The Rise and Fall of American Technological Leadership: the Post-war Era in Historical Perspective." *Journal of Economic Literature*, Vol. XXX, pp. 1931-64.

Neven, D and Gouyette, C. (1995). "Regional convergence in the European Community." *Journal of Common Market Studies*, 33, pp. 47-65.

Nonneman, W. and Vanhoudt, P. (1996). "A further augmentation of the Solow model and the empirics of economic growth for OECD countries," *Quarterly Journal of Economics*, CXI (3), pp. 943-53.

Paci, R. and Pigliaru, F. (1995). "β convergence and/or structural change? Evidence from the Italian regions." Nota di Lavoro 72.95, Fondazione Eni Enrico Mattei.

Prescott, E. (1998). "Needed: A theory of total factor productivity." *International Economic Review*, 39(3), pp. 525-51.

Romer, P. (1986). "Increasing Returns and Long-Run Growth." *Journal of Political Economy*, 94(5), pp. 1002-37.

Romer, P. (1987a). "Growth Based on Increasing Returns due to Specialization." *American Economic Review Papers and Proceedings* 77(2), pp. 56-62.

Romer, P. (1987b). "Crazy Explanations for the Productivity Slowdown." *NBER Macroeconomics Annual* 2, pp. 163-210.

Romer, P. (1990). "Endogenous Technical Change." *Journal of Political Economy*, 98, pp. S71-S102

Shioji, E. (1997a). "Convergence in panel data: evidence from the skipping estimation." Mimeo, Universitat Pompeu Fabra, Barcelona.

Shioji, E. (1997b). "It's still 2%. Evidence of convergence from 116 years of the US states panel data." Mimeo, Universitat Pompeu Fabra, Barcelona.

Solow, R. (1956). "A Contribution to the Theory of Economic Growth. "*Quarterly Journal of Economics*, LXX(1), pp. 65-94.

Wolff, E. (1991). "Capital Formation and Productivity Convergence Over the Long Term." *American Economic Review*, 81(3), pp. 565-79.

[19]

The Economic Journal, **106** (*July*), 1045–1055. Published by Blackwell Publishers, 108 Cowley Road, Oxford OX4 1JF, UK and 238 Main Street, Cambridge, MA 02142, USA.

TWIN PEAKS: GROWTH AND CONVERGENCE IN MODELS OF DISTRIBUTION DYNAMICS

Danny T. Quah

Convergence concerns poor economies catching up with rich ones. At issue is what happens to the cross sectional distribution of economies, not whether a single economy tends towards its own steady state. It is the latter, however, that has preoccupied the traditional approach to convergence analysis. This paper describes a body of research that overcomes this shortcoming in the traditional approach. The new findings – on persistence and stratification; on the formation of convergence clubs; and on the distribution polarising into twin peaks of rich and poor – suggest the relevance of a class of theoretical ideas, different from the production-function accounting traditionally favoured.

Conventional analyses of economic growth and convergence address one natural set of questions. What is the contribution of physical capital to output? Knowing this allows us to understand or explain patterns of growth by pointing to rates of capital accumulation. How quickly can poor countries catch up with richer ones? What factors aid this convergence? Appreciating these gives us perspective on the relative levels of development that we observe across different countries, and insight into how poor countries can improve their circumstances.

There is a traditional approach to answering such questions: estimate a cross-section regression of growth rates on income levels, possibly including other variables on the right hand side of that regression. In this reasoning, the levels coefficient informs on both capital's contribution to output and the rate at which poor economies catch up with those richer. (Whether this catch up occurs is known as the *convergence hypothesis*.) Such an equation relating growth rates and levels takes on added significance when we recall that it can be derived from theoretical growth models. This traditional approach thus seems doubly blessed. It sheds light on important economic questions; it dovetails neatly with theoretical reasoning. This is the standard that all empirical analysis strives for; what, in this traditional approach, could be controversial?

This paper argues that conventional analyses miss altogether key aspects of economic growth and convergence. The reason is the following. One dimension of growth is the mechanism by which agents in an economy push back technological and capacity constraints; this increases aggregate output. When the mechanism works spectacularly well, we consider the economy a growth success. Such economic progress is germane to rich countries, just as it is to poor ones – there need be no distinction between them. A different dimension of growth, however, is the mechanism that determines the relative performance of rich and poor economies: does growth in poorer economies lead to their catching up with the richer ones? Here, one wants to know if economic progress occurs differently in poorer economies than it does in richer ones.

The two mechanisms – pushing back and catching up – are related, but logically distinct: one can occur without the other. For brevity, I will refer to the first as a *growth* mechanism, and the second as a *convergence* mechanism. As with all such taxonomies, the distinction is imperfect, but, we will see, is better than nothing. Taking the distinction seriously means, temporarily, divorcing the convergence hypothesis from issues of any one country's productivity performance. What is important for convergence is how economies perform relative to each other, not how a single economy performs relative to its own history. Obviously, both growth and convergence mechanisms matter: to make progress in understanding, however, the details of one are usefully abstracted away to focus on the other.

This paper argues that a key shortcoming of the traditional approach is that it fails to distinguish these two dimensions of economic growth. Theoretical and empirical statements made about one are taken, inappropriately, to apply to the other. Consequently, theoretical insights recognising the distinction are unavailable in the standard approach.

I will describe below a body of newer empirical research that repairs this shortcoming. This work models directly the dynamics of the cross-section distribution of countries. In doing so, it uncovers regularities fundamentally different from those in conventional analyses. This research provides evidence on persistence and stratification; on the formation of convergence clubs; and on the cross section distribution polarising into twin peaks of rich and poor.

Such regularities raise intriguing questions. What economic structures produce these dynamics? What mechanisms determine club formation and membership? Is it only those already-rich economies that converge towards each other, leaving the poor to form a different convergence club? What features of cross-country interaction generate polarisation and stratification? When physical capital flows more freely from one part of the world to another, does that lead to a spreading out of the distribution – so that the rich get richer and the poor, poorer? Or, does the opposite happen, and the poor have opportunity to become richer than those previously rich? In addressing these questions, the researcher is led to draw on fresh theoretical ideas, in ways hidden to the traditional approach. Thus, these distribution dynamics empirics not only repair the failure in the traditional approach to represent reality accurately, they also generate new theories on economic growth and convergence.

The discussion below concentrates on income distributions across countries. It directly applies, however, to convergence and growth in other economic units as well. Thus, the criticisms of the traditional approach extend readily. They imply that the traditional approach cannot at all address the concerns of policy-makers interested in regional development, economic and geographical redistribution, and comparative economic performance. Instead, revealing analysis must be found elsewhere – possibly in extensions of the models of distribution dynamics described below.

The goal of the rest of this paper is to flesh out the points just made. The paper is not intended as a broad survey of all possible criticisms of the traditional approach. Rather, the coverage is selective. Section I highlights those aspects of conventional analyses relevant to the current discussion.

Section II describes that class of newer empirical findings that use distribution dynamics, and indicates the theoretical issues raised in such work. Section III concludes.

I. THE TRADITIONAL APPROACH

Traditional empirical analyses of growth and convergence derive from an elegant theoretical insight. This is that, in many growth models, equilibrium growth rates can be shown to be related to income levels through physical capital's relative contribution to national income (Barro and Sala-i-Martin, 1992; Romer, 1994; Sala-i-Martin, 1995; 1996). Developed explicitly, this insight gives a 'convergence equation' with growth on the left-hand side, explained by – among other things – income levels on the right.

In this reasoning, the cross-country correlation between growth rates and income levels is doubly interesting. It sheds light on the rate at which poor economies catch up with rich ones. Simultaneously, it informs on physical capital's importance for growth. Estimated on a wide range of data, this correlation implies a stable uniform rate of convergence equal to 2% a year. Thus, while the poor do eventually catch up with the rich, the speed with which this happens is low: only half the gap between rich and poor is closed in 35 years. Moreover, the implied contribution of physical capital to aggregate output is high – much higher than suggested by factor income shares in national income accounts.

The second of these implications raises a puzzle: if it is physical capital that is driving growth, why is it not being properly compensated by the market? This basic question has motivated research on externalities and endogenous technological progress (Romer, 1990). Such research seeks to explain the observed empirical regularities on convergence rates and capital's factor income share. At the same time, it resolves deep theoretical subtleties in the theory of economic equilibrium with non-rival commodities.

In the taxonomy given earlier, such analyses provide powerful insights on the growth mechanism. However, whether they help us understand the convergence mechanisms hinges on auxiliary assumptions. What is the nature of interaction across different countries? Are currently leading economies always the first to push back technology frontiers, and does new technology then always filter passively to poorer economies? Are there costs of adoption that lead to leap-frogging, where it is the temporarily follower economies that jump to being leader, because they find it easier to exploit new discoveries? Or, do persistent advantages accrue to the leader, richer countries, simply by virtue of their already being leader and richer? Do poorer economies need to overcome poverty-trap barriers before they can hope to catch up with richer ones?

Traditional cross-section regressions on the 'convergence equation' can address none of these issues. That they are revealing to the coefficient of physical capital in a production function is just that, no more and no less. Such exercises, while using dynamic information creatively, are part of a time-honoured practice in production-function accounting, and might be usefully compared to empirical analyses like those in Griliches and Ringstad (1971).

However, in the absence of auxiliary assumptions, they give no insight on whether poor countries are catching up with rich ones.

I show below that all the different possibilities relating rich and poor, described two paragraphs above, are consistent with a 'stable uniform 2% rate of convergence' – as estimated from the traditional convergence equation. Thus, a negative correlation between growth rates and levels says nothing about the poor catching up with the rich.[1] Contrary to claims made elsewhere, traditional empirics are completely silent on the important convergence dimension in economic growth.

To see this, I need to make explicit some ideas – empirical and theoretical – on the dynamics of large cross sections. We turn to this next.

II. DISTRIBUTION DYNAMICS

This section develops models of distribution dynamics to study the convergence hypothesis.[2]

Fix a year – say t – and consider the then-extant empirical distribution of *per capita* incomes across countries. Suppose that the density of that distribution is as plotted, at time t, in Fig. 1. That density shows some rich countries in the upper part of the distribution; a majority of middle-income countries in the middle part of the distribution; and some poor countries, in the lower.

There is a density for each year: Fig. 1 plots, at $t+s$, the density at some date in the future from t. As drawn, two suggestive classes of features of Fig. 1 should be noted. The first class constitutes the *location*, *shape*, and other external characteristics of the distributions at different times: these can, in general, fluctuate. The second comprises the *intra-distribution* dynamics, or churning-like behaviour – indicated by arrows in Fig. 1 – when individual economies transit from one part of the distribution to another. We consider these different features in turn.

Fig. 1 has drawn the income distribution at $t+s$ to be bimodal or twin-peaked: in the picture, there is a group of the rich, collecting together; a group of the poor, collecting together; and a middle-income class, vanishing.[3] There is no *a priori* reason for this. The $t+s$ distribution might well have been unimodal, and tightly concentrated at a single point: then, the researcher could, with some confidence, say the originally poor at t had, by $t+s$, attained equal footing with the originally rich. The researcher might even want to call that catching up.[4]

[1] Sometimes, evidence on that negative correlation comes only with additional conditioning, hence the term '*conditional convergence*.' Sometimes, in the traditional approach, that evidence is buttressed also with evidence on cross-sectional standard deviations. While this last is marginally helpful, it remains potentially misleading: the next section shows why. As for conditional convergence, even in the best of all possible scenarios, all it could show is whether each country converges to its own steady state, different from that of other countries. It is a complete puzzle to me how this can be interesting for whether the poor are catching up with the rich.

[2] Emphases on the empirics of distribution characteristics and dynamics appeared earlier in the personal income distribution literature, e.g., Atkinson (1970) and Shorrocks (1978).

[3] Why say 'twin peaks' rather than just 'bimodal', or make up the word 'twin-peakedness' rather than simply use 'bimodality'? Despite having more letters, the former contain fewer syllables.

[4] Something like this must be what European Commission policy makers have in mind when they talk about achieving cohesion or equity across rich and poor regions in Europe.

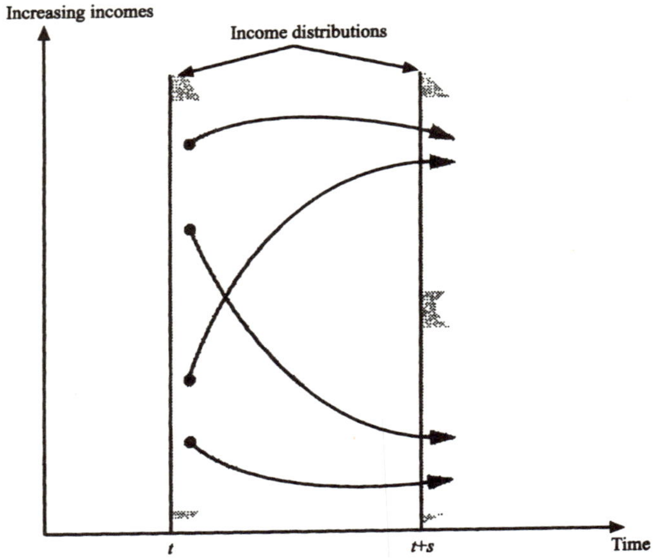

Fig. 1. Twin-peaks distribution dynamics.

If time $t+s$ is within the researcher's data sample, then a hypothesised tendency towards twin-peakedness can be examined directly from observed data. If, however, time $t+s$ is beyond the available sample, then a model is needed before the researcher can reach a conclusion on this.

Is the twin-peakedness drawn in Fig. 1 more than just whimsy and artistic licence? Below, I describe empirical techniques to study this. The quick answer is that the world cross-section of countries does show such tendencies. There is even evidence that twin-peakedness can already be observed for $t+s$ within current data samples. However, twin-peakedness will certainly not be seen if all the researcher does is calculate means, standard deviations, third moments, and so on, of the cross-section distributions.

Turn now to intra-distribution dynamics. It does not take a high-tech econometrician to note that, in the world, there are some rich countries that have remained rich for long periods of time, and, similarly, that there are some poor countries that have remained poor. Casual observation also readily comes up with examples of rich countries that have transited to being relatively poor; poor countries, to relatively rich; and groups of countries, beginning at similar levels of development, eventually diverging, with some becoming richer, and others, poorer. (Korea and the Philippines are the usual examples for the last.) Put briefly, one sees a broad range of intra-distribution dynamics.

Next consider the intra-distribution arrows drawn in Fig. 1. Just as cross-sectional standard deviations give no insight on potential twin-peakedness in the distribution, they say nothing either about churning within the cross section. Understanding these intra-distribution dynamics, however, would inform on the dynamics of the poor catching up with the rich. It would inform on the poor stagnating within poverty traps; on the poor overtaking those previously rich; and on convergence club dynamics – sub-groups or clubs forming, with member countries converging towards each other, and diverging away from different clubs. It would shed light on possibilities for the poorest 5 % of the cross section catching up with the richest 5 %; and on whether global development takes multi-tier forms. Intra-distribution dynamics include information on switches in ranks – the leading country falling to seventeenth position, or *vice versa* – but, more than that, they also include information on the distance traversed when such switches happen.

I have just described some characteristics of (cross-country income) distribution dynamics that will be of interest in discussing convergence. Formalising this description offers two payoffs: first, precise statistical quantification; second, theoretical analysis based on economic ideas.

The simplest useful model of distribution dynamics is one where a stochastic difference equation describes the evolution of the sequence of distributions. Let F_t denote the time t cross-country income distribution. Associated with each F_t is a probability measure λ_t, where

$$\forall y \in \mathbb{R}: \lambda_t((-\infty, y]) = F_t(y).$$

A stochastic difference equation describing distribution dynamics is then

$$\lambda_t = T^*(\lambda_{t-1}, u_t), \quad \text{integer } t, \tag{1}$$

where $\{u_t : \text{integer } t\}$ is a sequence of disturbances, and T^* is an operator mapping the Cartesian product of probability measures with disturbances to probability measures. (Needless to say, the first-order specification in (1) is just a convenience for the discussion. Nothing substantive hinges on it, and the model easily generalises to higher-order dynamics.)

Since our concerns include intra-distribution dynamics, (1) has to record more than just means and standard deviations – or more generally – of a finite set of moments of the distribution sequence $\{F_0, F_1, \ldots\}$. Equation (1) takes values that are measures, rather than just scalars or finite-dimensioned vectors, and thus differs from the typical time-series model.

The structure of T^* reveals if dynamics like those in Fig. 1 occur. Estimated from observed data, T^* allows empirical quantification of those dynamics. Economic hypotheses restrict T^* in particular ways: they therefore provide predictions on how λ_t, and thus the distributions F_t, can evolve over time.

Just as in time-series analysis, the researcher might seek to understand T^* by its 'impulse response function': set the disturbances u to zero, and run the difference equation forwards.

$$\begin{aligned} T^*(\lambda_{t+s-1}, 0) &= T^*(T^*(\lambda_{t+s-2}, 0), 0) \\ &\vdots \\ &= T^*(T^*(T \ldots (T^*(\lambda_t, 0), 0) \ldots 0), 0), \end{aligned} \tag{2}$$

with the result being a proxy for λ_{t+s}. Then, convergence in country incomes to equality might be represented by (2) tending, as $s \to \infty$, towards a degenerate point mass. Alternatively, the world polarising into rich and poor might be represented by (2) tending towards a two-point measure: the implied limit distribution F_{t+s}, $s \to \infty$, would then be bimodal or twin-peaked. More generally, stratification into different convergence clubs might manifest in (2) tending towards a multi-point, discrete measure, or equivalently, a multi-modal distribution. How quickly a given initial distribution, F_0, evolves into the limiting distribution, F_{t+s}, $s \to \infty$, can be read off T^*'s (spectral) structure.

Finally, T^* also contains information on intra-distribution dynamics. Exploiting that structure, one can quantify the likelihood of the poor catching up with the rich, and characterise the (random) occurrence times for such events.

In summary, studying T^* informs on all the interesting issues in convergence analysis. What then does empirical evidence – the Summers–Heston (1991) data – tell us about T^* and Fig. 1? Desdoigts (1994), Lamo (1995), Paap and van Dijk (1994), and Quah (1993*a*, *b*; 1996*a*) take the approach of estimating – in some form – the operator T^*. Some of this work views estimating T^* as an exercise in nonparametric analysis, others, in semi-parametrics; yet others take discretisations of λ, whereupon T^* becomes just a stochastic matrix. The important insight driving these methods is not a technical one, say, of greater flexibility in estimating a 'convergence equation' regression. Rather, it is that all these methods provide a global, entire picture of what happens with incomes across countries. For cross-country data, all the research just mentioned find T^* having features that imply 'twin-peaks' dynamics.[5] Estimated T^*'s indicate that clustering or clumping together of country incomes – convergence club behaviour – occurs eventually, Estimated T^*'s reveal precise descriptions of events where economies, initially starting out close together, diverge over time towards either of the twin peaks. Thus, the empirical evidence shows all the features hypothesised in Fig. 1.

Durlauf and Johnson (1995) side-step analysing T^* directly. Instead, they estimate cross section regressions, but allow the regression to 'adapt' subsamples, depending on data realisations. This innovative empirical technique permits consistently uncovering local basins of convergence. Durlauf and Johnson find evidence for the kind of multi-modal behaviour depicted in Fig. 1. They interpret their findings as multiple regimes; in the distribution-dynamics framework here, multiple regimes and multi-modality are in-distinguishable.

Bianchi (1995) takes yet a third approach to studying twin-peakedness. As in Durlauf and Jonson (1995), Bianchi eschews dealing directly with T^*. Actually, he goes even further, and considers each distribution F_t, in isolation, ignoring dynamic information. Bianchi estimates each F_t non-parametrically, and then applies to each a bootstrap test for multi-modality. He finds that in the early part of the sample (the early 1960s), the data show unimodality. However, by the end of the sample (the late 1980s) the data reject unimodality in favour of bimodality. Since Bianchi imposes less structure in his analysis –

[5] Ben-David (1994) takes a different approach, but with end results that have the same interpretation.

nowhere does he consider T^* dynamics – one can reasonably guess that his findings are more robust to possible misspecification. Here again, twin-peakedness manifests.

It is obvious that calculating standard deviations or any other moment of the cross section distribution can show nothing about twin-peaks dynamics. The cross-section correlation between growth rates and income levels reveals even less, its interpretation plagued by a version of Galton's Fallacy.[6] However, operator T^* *can* shed light on that seductive intuition – the poor growing faster and thereby catching up with the rich – that growth-on-levels regressions wish to exploit. Quah (1996*a*) calculates, from an estimated T^*, the probability density of passage times from poor parts of the income distribution to rich parts.[7] He finds that although growth miracles – the Hong Kongs, the South Koreas, and the Singapores – can happen with reasonable positive probability, the passage time from the bottom 5% percentile to the top, given the magnitude of the gap extant, averages in the hundreds of years. Thus, persistence and immobility characterise the world cross section of country incomes.

(Although their being stated with T^*-induced preciseness is new with the body of research that I have just summarised, all such empirical facts have long been used informally in work such as Lucas (1988, 1993)).

What new economic ideas do these distribution dynamics suggest? These dynamics draw attention towards the nature of cross-country interactions – although, to be clear, not entirely away from production function accounting. They suggest that an appropriate test of economic ideas about the convergence hypothesis will come from looking at implications on how the entire cross section distribution evolves, not from studying the behaviour of a single, representative economy.

A theoretical model of distribution dynamics – in generational earnings – was developed by Loury (1981). Many of those technical modelling ideas apply here as well, although the current emphasis on clustering and coalition formation across individual elements of the distribution is novel. This focus on cross-sectional grouping does, however, mesh with recent econometric research (Brock and Durlauf, 1995; Manski, 1993).

That particular economic features – threshold externalities, capital market imperfection, heterogeneity, country size, club formation – might produce 'twin peaks' dynamics across countries can be seen in theoretical models in Azariadis and Drazen (1990), Galor and Zeira (1993), Quah (1995b, 1996a), and Tamura (1992). Quah (1995*b*, 1996*a*) most closely relates the theoretical message in these papers to empirical analysis.

The theoretical model in Quah (1995*b*) describes economic forces that determine coalition or convergence club formation. That model shows why

[6] This connection is made in Friedman (1992) and Quah (1993*b*, 1996*b*). Quah (1996*b*) also details why no combination of β-convergence and σ-convergence (in the terminology of Barro and Sala-i-Martin (1992) and Sala-i-Martin (1995, 1996)) can provide a satisfactory work-around.

[7] Durlauf and Johnson (1994) have studied similar phenomena in the dynamics of personal income distribution.

'conditional convergence' in the traditional approach can be misleading: when different convergence clubs form, factor inputs (e.g. human capital) and social characteristics (e.g., democracy) will endogenously align around values determined by each country's convergence club. Conditioning on such 'explanatory variables' leads the researcher using the traditional approach to conclude, erroneously, that it is those variables that determine a country's economic position. By contrast, in the model, it is the factors deciding club membership that determine everything. The traditional researcher never finds those, and incorrectly attributes growth and convergence to factor inputs and social characteristics. Moreover, because in that traditional approach, the researcher only estimates a cross-section regression, he sees only the behaviour of the (conditional) representative economy. He will never detect the multi-peakedness that arises in the cross-country distribution.

Similar lessons manifest in the model in Quah (1996*a*). Here, it is varying degrees of capital market imperfection that lead to twin-peaks dynamics in the model. In the traditional approach, the researcher might simply proxy the capital market imperfectness by interest rates, say. However, in the model, all countries eventually have equal rates of return for borrowing and investment. The traditional researcher, therefore, never finds out the reason why twin-peaks dynamics occur – not that he ever even realises their presence. Moreover, the model predicts that every country converges (in a univariate sense) to its own steady state at an identical rate shared by all other countries. The traditional researcher then finds exactly a globally stable, constant rate of 'convergence' in the traditional conditional convergence regression. Such a finding, however, sheds no light on the actual distribution dynamics occurring.

III. CONCLUSION

With hindsight, the key point in this paper is obvious. Convergence concerns poor economies catching up with rich ones. What one wants to know here is, what happens to the entire cross sectional distribution of economies, *not* whether a single economy is tending towards its own, individual steady state. However, it is the latter that has preoccupied the traditional approach. Proposed fixes to that approach (e.g., the increased emphasis on σ-convergence in Sala-i-Martin (1995)) continue to miss the principal important features of economic growth and convergence.

Such criticisms would be merely idle if there were no alternative empirics that appropriately address the key issues relevant to convergence analysis. This paper has described a rich and growing body of research that does exactly that. The new findings reported here – on persistence and stratification; on the formation of convergence clubs; on the distribution polarising into twin peaks of rich and poor – suggest the relevance of a class of theoretical ideas, different from the production-function accounting favoured by the traditional approach. It might, ultimately, be those factors that are important for growth, not just crudely boosting the inputs in a neoclassical production function.

Many issues remain to be researched in this alternative approach. The empirical analyses of distribution dynamics can be substantially refined: Quah (1995*a*, *c*) explore some ways to do this. Theoretical models for cross-country, or more general social, interaction (e.g., Benabou (1995); Brock and Durlauf (1995); Quah (1995*b*), among many others) provide new insights on how economies evolve – and, in turn, generate intriguing new predictions to be studied empirically.

London School of Economics

References

Atkinson, Anthony B. (1970). 'On the measurement of inequality.' *Journal of Economic Theory*, vol. 2 (3), pp. 244–63 (September).

Azariadis, Costas and Drazen, Allan (1990). 'Threshold externalities in economic development.' *Quarterly Journal of Economics*, vol. 105 (2), pp. 501–26 (May).

Barro, Robert J. and Sala-i-Martin, Xavier (1990). 'Convergence.' *Journal of Political Economy*, vol. 100 (2), pp. 223–51 (April).

Ben-David, Dan (1994). 'Convergence clubs and diverging economies.' Working paper 922, Centre for Economic Policy Research, London (February).

Bénabou, Roland (1995). 'Heterogeneity, stratification, and growth: macroeconomic implications of community structure and school finance.' Working paper, Economics Department, New York University (March).

Bianchi, Marco (1995). 'Testing for convergence: a bootstrap test for multimodality.' Working paper, Bank of England (May).

Brock, William A. and Durlauf, Steven N. (1995). 'Discrete choice with social interactions.' Working paper, University of Wisconsin, Madison (April).

Desdoigts, Alan (1994). 'Changes in the world income distribution: a nonparametric approach to challenge the neoclassical convergence argument. PhD thesis, European University Institute, Florence (June).

Durlauf, Steven N. and Johnson, Paul (1994). 'Nonlinearities in intergenerational income mobility.' Working paper, University of Wisconsin, Economics Department.

Durlauf, Steven N. and Johnson, Paul (1995). 'Multiple regimes and cross-country growth behavior.' *Journal of Applied Econometrics*, vol. 10. (Forthcoming).

Friedman, Milton (1992). 'Do old fallacies ever die?'. *Journal of Economic Literature*, vol. 30 (4), pp. 2129–32 (December).

Galor, Oded and Zeira, Joseph (1993). 'Income distribution and macroeconomics.' *Review of Economic Studies*, vol. 60 (1), pp. 35–52 (January).

Griliches, Zvi and Ringstad, Vidar (1971). *Economies of Scale and the Form of the Production Function*, Amsterdam: North-Holland.

Lamo, Ana R. (1995). 'Cross-section distribution dynamics.' Ph.D thesis, London School of Economics, London. (In progress).

Loury, Glenn C. (1981). 'Intergenerational transfers and the distribution of earnings.' *Econometrica*, vol. 49 (4), pp. 843–67 (July).

Lucas, Robert E. Jr. (1988). 'On the mechanics of economic development.' *Journal of Monetary Economics*, vol. 22 (3), pp. 3–42 (June).

Lucas, Robert E. Jr. (1993). 'Making a miracle.' *Econometrica*, vol. 61 (2), pp. 251–71 (March).

Manski, Charles F. (1993). 'Identification of endogenous social effects: the reflection problem.' *Review of Economic Studies*, vol. 60 (3), pp. 531–42 (July).

Paap, Richard and van Dijk, Herman K. (1994). 'Distribution and mobility of wealth of nations.' Working paper, Tinbergen Institute, Erasmus University (October).

Quah, Danny (1993). 'Empirical cross-section dynamics in economic growth.' *European Economic Review*, vol. 37 (2/3), pp. 426–34 (April).

Quah, Danny (1993*b*). 'Galton's fallacy and tests of the convergence hypothesis.' *The Scandinavian Journal of Economics*, vol. 95 (4), pp. 427–43 (December).

Quah, Danny (1995*a*). 'Coarse distribution dynamics for convergence, divergence, and polarization.' Working paper, Economics Department, London School of Economics (July).

Quah, Danny (1995*b*). 'Ideas determining convergence clubs.' Working paper, Economics Department. London School of Economics (August).

Quah, Danny (1995*c*). 'International patterns of growth: II. Persistence, path dependence, and sustained take-off in growth transition.' Working paper, Economics Department, London School of Economics (June).

Quah, Danny (1996*a*). 'Convergence empirics across economies with (some) capital mobility.' *Journal of Economic Growth*, vol. 1 (1), pp. 95–124 (March).

Quah, Danny (1996*b*). 'Empirics for economic growth and convergence.' *European Economic Review*. (Forthcoming).

Romer, Paul M. (1990). 'Endogenous technological change.' *Journal of Political Economy* vol. 98 (5, Part 2), pp. S71–102 (October).

Romer, Paul M. (1994). 'The origins of endogenous growth.' *Journal of Economic Perspectives* vol. 8 (1), pp. 3–22 (Winter).

Sala-i-Martin, Xavier (1995). 'The classical approach to convergence analysis.' Working Paper 117, Universitat Pompeu Fabra, Barcelona (June).

Sala-i-Martin, Xavier (1996). 'Regional cohesion: evidence and theories of regional growth and convergence.' *European Economic Review* (Forthcoming).

Shorrocks, Anthony F. (1978). 'The measurement of mobility.' *Econometrica*, vol. 46 (5), pp. 1013–24 (September).

Summers, Robert and Heston, Alan (1991). 'The Penn World Table (Mark 5): an expanded set of international comparisons, 1950–1988.' *Quarterly Journal of Economics*, vol. 106 (2), pp. 327–68 (May).

Tamura, Robert (1992). 'Efficient equilibrium convergence: heterogeneity and growth.' *Journal of Economic Theory*, vol. 58 (2), pp. 355–76 (December).

[20]

Regional Studies, Vol. 33.2, pp. 143–156

US Regional Income Convergence: A Spatial Econometric Perspective

SERGIO J. REY and BRETT D. MONTOURI
Department of Geography, San Diego State University, San Diego, CA 92182, USA

(Received January 1997; in revised form August 1998)

REY S. J. and MONTOURI B. D. (1999) US regional income convergence: a spatial econometric perspective, *Reg. Studies* 33, 143–156. This study reconsiders the question of US regional economic income convergence from a spatial econometric perspective. Recently developed methods of exploratory spatial data analysis provide new insights on the geographical dynamics of US regional income growth patterns over the 1929–94 period. Strong patterns of both global and local spatial autocorrelation are found throughout the study period, and the magnitude of global spatial autocorrelation is also found to exhibit strong temporal co-movement with regional income dispersion. A spatial econometric analysis of the familiar Baumol specification reveals strong evidence of misspecification due to ignored spatial error dependence. Because of this dependence, shocks originating in one state can spillover into surrounding states, potentially complicating the transitional dynamics of the convergence process.

Regional income convergence   Spatial econometrics   Exploratory spatial data analysis

REY S. J. et MONTOURI B. D. (1999) La convergence du revenu régional aux Etats-Unis: une perspective économétrique, spatiale, *Reg. Studies* 33, 143–156. Cette étude remet en cause la convergence du revenu économique régional à partir d'une perspective économétrique, spatiale. De nouvelles méthodes qui permettent une première analyse des données spatiales, fournissent un autre aperçu sur la dynamique géographique de la répartition de la croissance du revenu régional aux Etats-Unis de 1929 à 1994. Pendant toute la période étudiée, de fortes autocorrélations géographiques à la fois globales et locales sont à noter. Il s'avère aussi que l'ampleur de l'autocorrélation spatiale, globale va de pair dans le temps avec la dispersion du revenu régional. Une analyse économétrique, spatiale de la spécification bien connue de Baumol fait preuve de la mauvaise spécification due à la dépendance vis à vis des erreurs spatiales à laquelle on n'a pas fait attention. A cause de cette dépendance, des chocs qui proviennent d'un état particulier peuvent avoir des retombées sur les états limitrophes, ce qui risque de compliquer la dynamique transitoire du processus de convergence.

Convergence de revenu régional   Econométrie spatiale
Première analyse des données spatiales

REY S. J. und MONTOURI B. D. (1999) Konvergenz regionaler Einkommen in den Vereinigten Staaten: ein räumlich-ökonometrischer Ausblick, *Reg. Studies* 33, 143–156. Diese Studie behandelt noch einmal die Frage der Konvergenz regionaler Einkommen in den Vereinigten Staaten vom Standpunkt der räumlichen Ökonometrie aus. Kürzlich entwickelte Methoden einer Analyse räumlicher Untersuchungsdaten verschaffen neue Einsichten in die geographische Dynamik der Muster regionalen Wachstums von Einkommen in den Vereinigten Staaten im Zeitraum 1929–94. Für die genannte Untersuchungsperiode werden robuste Muster globaler wie auch örtlicher räumlicher Autokorrelationen festgestellt, wobei der Umfang letzterer sich zudem als in kräftigem zeitlichem Gleichschritt mit der Streuung regionaler Einkommen erweist. Eine räumliche ökonometrische Analyse der bekannten Baumol Spezifizierung liefert handfeste Beweise fehlerhafter Spezifizierungen infolge unbeachtet gebliebener Abhängigkeit von räumlichen Irrtümern. Dank dieser Abhängigkeit kann der Schock eines Staates in Nachbarstaaten Kreise ziehen, und die Übergangsdynamik des Konvergenzprozesses verkomplizieren.

Konvergenz regionaler Einkommen
Räumliche Ökonometrie
Analyse räumlicher Untersuchungsdaten

INTRODUCTION

A prominent theme in the recent macroeconomic literature has been the topic of economic convergence. As stated by ABRAMOVITZ, 1986, convergence implies a long-run tendency towards the equalization of *per capita* income or product levels. In other words, convergence addresses the important question of whether 'poor' countries, as measured by low per capita incomes, display faster growth rates in per capita income than 'rich' countries with higher per capita incomes? An important contribution by BAUMOL, 1986, has stimulated a large number of studies examining the convergence hypothesis at the international

0034-3404/99/020143-14

level. Because these studies have been informed by different theoretical perspectives (i.e. neo-classical models versus endogenous growth models) and have employed different empirical strategies (i.e. cross-sectional versus time-series versus panel data), the existing empirical evidence on convergence between nations is subject to much debate (see, for example, BAUMOL, 1986; DE LONG, 1988).

This interest has led to numerous studies of regional income convergence on intra-national scales. Many of these studies focus on the US experience (BARRO and SALA-I-MARTIN, 1991; CARLINO and MILLS, 1993, 1996a, 1996b; CROWN and WHEAT, 1995; BERNARD and JONES, 1996a; VOHRA, 1996; among others), where the consensus is that income convergence has been very strong. In addition to the US studies, regional convergence processes have been examined for: Canadian provinces (COULOMBE and LEE, 1995); Colombian departments (CARDENAS and PONTON, 1995); Mexican states (MALLICK and CARAYANNIS, 1994); British counties (CHATTERJI and DEWHURST, 1996); and other European regions (ARMSTRONG, 1995). By and large, the econometric methods employed to test the convergence hypothesis at the regional scale are virtually identical to those applied in the international studies. In this regard, the key methodological issues examined thus far include: temporal stability (CARLINO and MILLS, 1996b); sectoral composition/contribution (BERNARD and JONES, 1996b, 1996c); reconciliation of the evidence from time-series and cross-sectional studies (BERNARD and DURLAUF, 1996); and interpretation of convergence frameworks (QUAH, 1993a, 1993b).

Despite the fact that theoretical mechanisms of technology diffusion, factor mobility and transfer payments that are argued to drive the regional convergence phenomenon have explicit geographical components, the role of spatial effects in the regional studies has been virtually ignored. Exceptions include ARMSTRONG, 1995, and CHATTERJI and DEWHURST, 1996, where calls are made for a more explicit spatial econometric treatment in regional studies. To date these calls have yet to be answered and, consequently, it is unclear to what extent the current body of empirical evidence on regional income convergence is robust to ignored spatial effects and processes.

This study reconsiders the question of regional economic income convergence from a spatial econometric perspective and aims at two central objectives. The first is to provide new insights into the geographical dynamics of US regional income growth patterns using recently developed methods of exploratory spatial data analysis. The second objective is to suggest and apply a set of spatial econometric methods that extend existing econometric models used in the study of regional income convergence to more fully treat any ignored spatial effects.

In the remainder of the paper we first provide an overview of the recent research on regional income convergence and identify a number of outstanding methodological and substantive issues related to spatial effects. Next, we present an exploratory spatial analysis of US regional income dynamics over the period 1929–94. We then discuss the results of a confirmatory spatial econometric analysis of the regional income convergence hypothesis. The paper closes with a summary and concluding comments.

CONVERGENCE CONCEPTS AND SPATIAL EFFECTS

The recent explosion of interest in regional convergence has not followed a uniform path. Instead, several distinct types of convergence have been suggested in the literature, each being analysed by distinct groups of scholars employing different methods. In this section, we first review the alternative notions of income convergence and methods employed in previous studies. We follow this with a discussion of the role of spatial effects in the econometric analysis of regional income convergence.

Convergence concepts

The first convergence concept pertains to the decline in the cross-sectional dispersion of per capita incomes. Several different measures have been employed to examine this form of convergence including the (unweighted) standard deviation (CARLINO and MILLS, 1996a) and the coefficient of variation (BERNARD and JONES, 1996a) of the log of per capita income. This form of convergence has been referred to as σ-convergence and has attracted much attention in the regional science and economic geography literature (KUZNETS, 1955; EASTERLIN, 1960a, 1960b; WILLIAMSON, 1965; AMOS, 1988, 1989; COUGHLIN and MANDELBAUM, 1988; FAN and CASETTI, 1994).

A second form of convergence, which has primarily been the focus of macroeconomists, occurs when poor regions grow faster than rich regions, resulting in the former eventually catching up to the latter in per capita income levels. To test this form of convergence, numerous studies have employed a cross-sectional specification as follows:

$$\ln\left(\frac{y_{i,t+k}}{y_{i,t}}\right) = \alpha + \beta \ln(y_{i,t}) + \varepsilon_{it} \quad (1)$$

where: $y_{i,t}$ is per capita income in state i year t; α and β are parameters to be estimated; and ε_{it} is a stochastic error term. Following BAUMOL, 1986, the convention has been to interpret a negative estimate for β as support for the convergence hypothesis since such an estimate would suggest that the growth rates in per capita incomes over the k year period were negatively correlated with starting incomes. Thus, this second form of convergence has been labelled β-convergence.[1]

It is important to recognize that a finding of a negative convergence parameter does not necessarily imply declining cross-sectional variance in income levels (or σ-convergence). QUAH, 1993a, has demonstrated that it is possible for a negative cross-sectional relationship between initial income and growth to coexist with a stable cross-section variance in income levels. This arises from the presence of shocks to country-specific growth rates that can offset the negative β coefficient.[2]

A third perspective on convergence can be found in time-series studies by CARLINO and MILLS, 1996a, 1996b, and BERNARD and DURLAUF, 1995. Here convergence requires that the long run forecasts of income level differences between two economies goes to 0. As noted by BERNARD and DURLAUF, 1996, this definition is violated if shocks to individual economies persist into the indefinite future. In the presence of such shocks, the income series would contain unit roots and, because of this stationarity requirement, this concept of convergence has been referred to as *stochastic convergence.*

The results from the cross-sectional (β and σ-convergence) and time-series studies (stochastic convergence) seem to be at odds. Cross-sectional tests (BARRO and SALA-I-MARTIN, 1991, 1992; MANKIW *et al.*, 1992) generally find evidence of convergence, while the time series tests (QUAH, 1992; BERNARD and DURLAUF, 1995) have tended to fail to reject the no-convergence hypothesis. In an attempt to reconcile these findings, CARLINO and MILLS, 1996a, argue that, in the case of the US over the period 1929–90, there is evidence of unit roots in state income levels and persistent state-specific shocks which implies a lack of stochastic convergence. However, they demonstrate that, by allowing for a trend break in 1946, stationary state-specific shocks are found in the two sub-periods which are consistent with stochastic convergence. They also report strong evidence in support of the cross-sectional notion of β convergence.

Spatial effects in the analysis of regional income convergence

In all three notions of convergence, the unit of analysis has been an individual region observed either as part of a cross section or in a time-series. Implicitly, each region has been viewed as an independent entity and the potential for observational interactions across space has gone largely ignored. While technology spill-overs (e.g. KRUGMAN, 1987; and JONES, 1997) have been identified as key mechanisms that may lead to convergence, the geographical dimensions of these spill-overs have yet to be explored. At the same time, BERNARD and JONES, 1996b, suggest that comparative advantage leading to regional specialization in tradable goods sectors may result in a lack of convergence at the aggregate level. While theoretically intriguing, such arguments have not been formally incorporated in the empirical models used to examine the convergence hypothesis at the regional scale. However, by recognizing such forms of interaction as cases of *substantive spatial dependence* (ANSELIN and REY, 1991), a rich body of spatial process models becomes available to the study of regional income convergence.

In addition to the substantive form of spatial dependence, the geographical organization of the observations in regional convergence studies may give rise to a second type of spatial dependence. This can result from a mismatch between the spatial boundaries of the market processes under study and the administrative boundaries used to organize the data. Spatial dependence due to this form of boundary mismatch has been referred to as *nuisance dependence* (*ibid.*), since it is reflected in a spatially autocorrelated error term.

Both substantive and nuisance forms of spatial dependence can result in major model misspecification if they are ignored (ANSELIN, 1988). Recent developments in spatial econometrics offer procedures for testing for the potential presence of these misspecifications and suggests the proper estimators for models that treat the spatial dependence explicitly (for recent reviews, see ANSELIN and FLORAX, 1995; ANSELIN and BERA, 1997; and ANSELIN and REY, 1997). To date these methods have not been extensively applied in convergence studies. In a later section, we outline the application of these methods to the analysis of regional income convergence in the US.

A second type of spatial effect relevant to convergence studies is spatial heterogeneity which reflects a general instability of a behavioural relationship across the observational units. For example, CARLINO and MILLS, 1996a, argue that the traditional cross-sectional analysis of convergence assumes that all regions have an identical rate of convergence. Because of this, they eschew cross-sectional methods in favour of a time-series investigation.[3] In contrast, CHATTERJI and DEWHURST, 1996, provide an interesting framework that allows for spatial heterogeneity in the form of *convergence clubs.*[4] Therefore, we argue that, even in a pure cross-sectional analysis, an analysis of regional variations in rates of income convergence is not precluded.

Our empirical analysis focuses on the case of the US during the period 1929–94. We consider both σ and β-convergence over this period as well as investigate the spatial dimensions of US income dynamics. Attention is first directed towards σ-convergence and the related spatial patterns, followed by a spatial econometric analysis of β-convergence.[5]

EXPLORATORY SPATIAL DATA ANALYSIS OF US INCOME CONVERGENCE

σ-convergence and global spatial autocorrelation

While σ-convergence has attracted a good deal of attention, it is important to note that this measure is

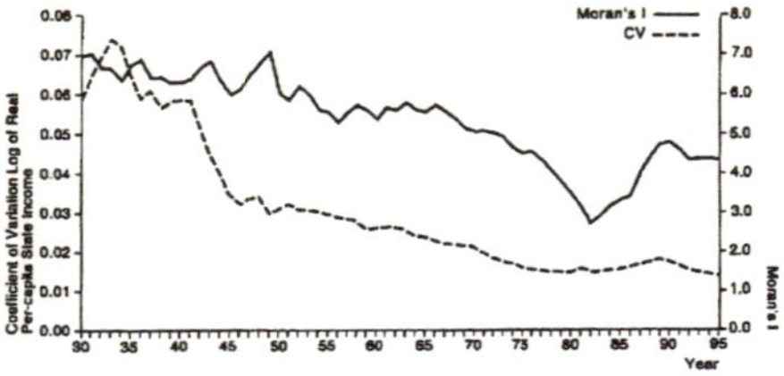

Fig. 1. US relative income convergence and spatial autocorrelation, 1929–94

only concerned with spread-dispersion (2nd moment) of the state income distribution. We argue that the current focus on the dispersion of the state income distributions may mask nontrivial geographical patterns that may also fluctuate over time. Therefore, in addition to analysing the dynamic behaviour of income dispersion for the 48 conterminous states over time, we will also explore the geographic dimensions of these distributions.

Fig. 1 displays the by now familiar pattern of declining per capita income dispersion in the US, as measured by the coefficient of variation for the natural log of real state per capita incomes. The long term trend appears to have been towards convergence with a few exceptions, most notably the depression years (1929–32) and the slight increase in dispersion over the 1979–89 period. The most rapid period of convergence was in the early 1940s.[6]

Fig. 1 also portrays the path of spatial autocorrelation for the state incomes over the same time period.[7] The measure is based on the Moran's I statistic expressed as:

$$I_t = \left(\frac{n}{s_o}\right) \frac{\sum_{i=1}^{n}\sum_{j=1}^{n} w_{ij} x_{i,t} x_{j,t}}{\sum_{i=1}^{n}\sum_{j=1}^{n} x_{i,t} x_{j,t}} \qquad (2)$$

where: $w_{ij,t}$ is an element of a binary spatial weights matrix **W** such that $w_{ij} = 1$ if states i and j share a border and zero otherwise; $x_{i,t}$ is the natural log of real per capita income in state i in year t (measured as a deviation from the mean value for that year); n is the number of states; and s_o is a scaling factor equal to the sum of all the elements of **W**.[8]

An analysis of the natural logarithms of the per capita income values revealed no evidence of departures from normality; thus we based the significance of the Moran's I statistics on the normality assumption.[9] There is very strong evidence of spatial dependence as the statistics are significant at $p = 0{\cdot}01$ for all years. Interestingly, the measure of spatial autocorrelation also tends to co-move with the measure of income dispersion. In fact, the simple correlation between the Moran's I statistic and the coefficient of variation for the incomes is 0·785 over the 66-year period. In particular, the spatial dependence tends to reach its minimum values in 1981–82, followed by rapid increases from 1983–88, coinciding with the period some have previously identified with a reversal of long term regional income convergence (AMOS, 1989; COUGHLIN and MANDELBAUM, 1988; BRAUN, 1991; ROWLEY *et al.*, 1991).

Several impressions may be taken away from Fig. 1. First, in any given year the state income distribution displays a high degree of spatial autocorrelation. Although the magnitude of the dependence seems to weaken as the income dispersion lessens, the dependence is still significant. This suggests that the evolution of the state income distribution appears to be clustered in nature. That is, the relatively high (low) income states tend to be located nearby other high (low) income states more often than would be expected due to random chance. If this is the case, then each state should not be viewed as an independent observation, as has been implicitly assumed in previous studies of regional income convergence.

The second impression is that the co-movement between income dispersion and spatial dependence may reflect a dynamic characteristic of the regional clustering. There are several intriguing questions that can be asked about this relationship. First, what is the nature of the weakening (strengthening) of the regional clustering in times of income convergence (divergence)? Two possibilities can be identified. On the one hand, an increase in spatial dependence could be due to the states in each cluster becoming more similar in their income levels. On the other hand, an increase in spatial dependence could also be due to newly formed clusters emerging during a period of increased income dispersion. The second question addresses the issue of spatial stationarity: to what extent does the global measure of spatial autocorrelation mask pockets of non-stationarity or so called 'hot-spots' that deviate from the overall pattern? Unfortunately, Moran's I, which is a global measure of spatial dependence, does not allow us to distinguish between these possibilities. For that we turn to a more disaggregated view of the structure of spatial dependence in US regional incomes.

σ-convergence and local spatial autocorrelation

Figs. 2 and 3 provide a more disaggregated view of the nature of the spatial autocorrelation for the initial (Fig. 2) and terminal (Fig. 3) years.[10] Each figure contains a Moran scatterplot, suggested by ANSELIN, 1993, which plots the standardized income of a state against its spatial lag (also standardized). A state's spatial lag is a weighted average of the incomes of its neighbouring states, with the weights being obtained from the simple contiguity matrix. The four different quadrants of the scatterplot identify four types of local spatial association between a state and its neighbours: (HH) a

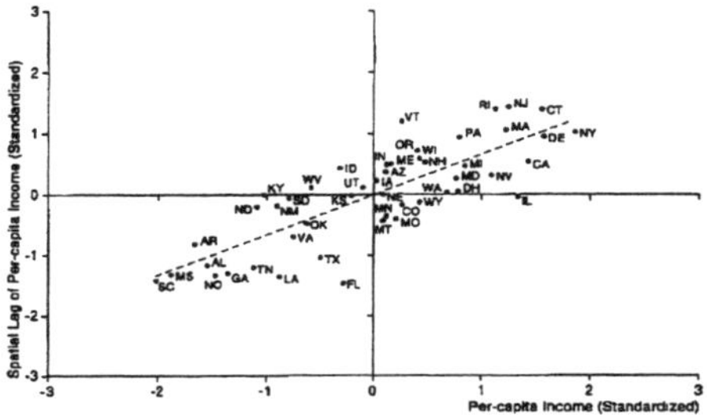

Fig. 2. Moran scatterplot real state per capita income, 1929

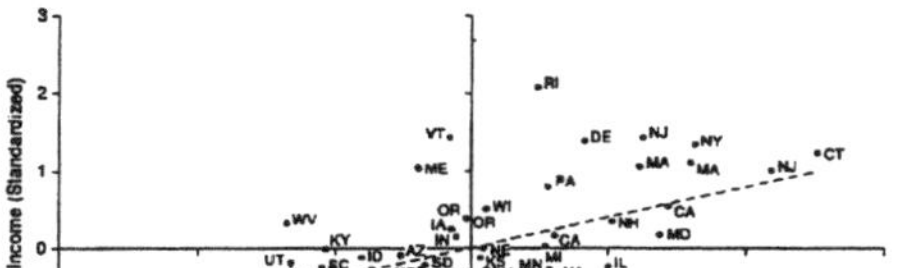

Fig. 3. Moran scatterplot real state per capita income, 1994

high income state with high income neighbours (quadrant I); (LH) a low income state surrounded by high income neighbours (quadrant II); (LL) a low income state surrounded by low income neighbours (quadrant III); and (HL) a high income state with low income neighbours (quadrant IV). Quadrants I and III pertain to positive forms of spatial dependence while the remaining two represent negative spatial dependence. Used in conjunction with the global measures of spatial dependence (underlying Fig. 1), the scatterplot provides a visual impression on the overall stability of the global pattern of dependence, as well as the ability to identify local regimes of spatial dependence that may depart from the overall pattern.

A slightly different perspective from the scatterplot is found in Figs. 4 and 5, where the local Moran statistics (ANSELIN, 1995) are mapped for each state at the initial and terminal years of our sample. The local Moran for state i takes the following form:

$$I_{i,t} = \left(\frac{x_i}{m_o}\right)\sum_{j=1}^{n} w_{ij}x_{j,t} \tag{3}$$

with:

$$m_o = \sum_i^n x_{i,t}^2$$

Viewing Figs. 2–5 together suggests that there has been a slight modification of the overall structure of spatial dependence between the two years. More specifically, membership in quadrant I of the scatterplot declines (Fig. 3 vs. Fig. 2) and the states demonstrating this change tend to be located on the border of a cluster, while the core members remain (Fig. 5 vs. Fig. 4). For example, Virginia, found in quadrant III and on the northern border of the LL cluster of south-eastern states in 1929, moved into quadrant IV (HL) by the end of the study period. Nevada, in quadrant I in 1929 and on the eastern border of the HH cluster on the west, moves to quadrant IV in 1994, a relatively high income state bordering poorer states.[11]

The results from the application of the local Moran statistics to the income values in each of the years in the sample are summarized in Table 1. Reported in the third column is the number of years, out of the 66, for which the local statistic provides indications of clustering using a pseudo-significance level of $p = 0{\cdot}05$. The significance level is based on a conditional randomization approach involving 1,000 random permutations of the neighbouring states for each observation. Also reported is the number of years the significant local Moran value falls in each of the four quadrants of the Moran's scatterplot.

The results in Table 1 illustrate several points. The first thing to note is that the local pattern of spatial association tends to reflect the global trend of positive spatial association reported earlier. More specifically, over 95% of the local indicators that are significant fall in either quadrants I or III of the scatterplot, reflecting HH and LL clustering respectively. At the same time the remaining significant indicators revealing negative spatial association are roughly divided between HL (i.e. 'diamond in the rough') and LH (i.e. 'doughnut') forms of clustering. This suggests that these deviations from the global trend are not dominated by a particular form of negative spatial association.

The second thing to note is that two strong regional clusters seem to be persistent throughout the 66 years. The first is the Northeast–Mid Atlantic cluster of high income states including Massachusetts, New York, Pennsylvania, Connecticut, Rhode Island and Delaware, each of which appears in quadrant I when its local Moran is significant. The second cluster is in the Southeast consisting of the relatively low income states of North Carolina, Tennessee, Alabama, Mississippi, Georgia, South Carolina, Arkansas and Louisiana, each of which falls in quadrant III the vast majority of years. The results in column three provide fairly strong evidence that the clustering in these two regions is not due to chance alone. It appears, therefore, that the positive correlation between the global Moran's I and the measure of income dispersion, depicted in Fig. 1, is due to a strengthening of the regional clusters during periods of income divergence, rather than the appearance of newly formed clusters.

While the exploratory analysis of income levels has

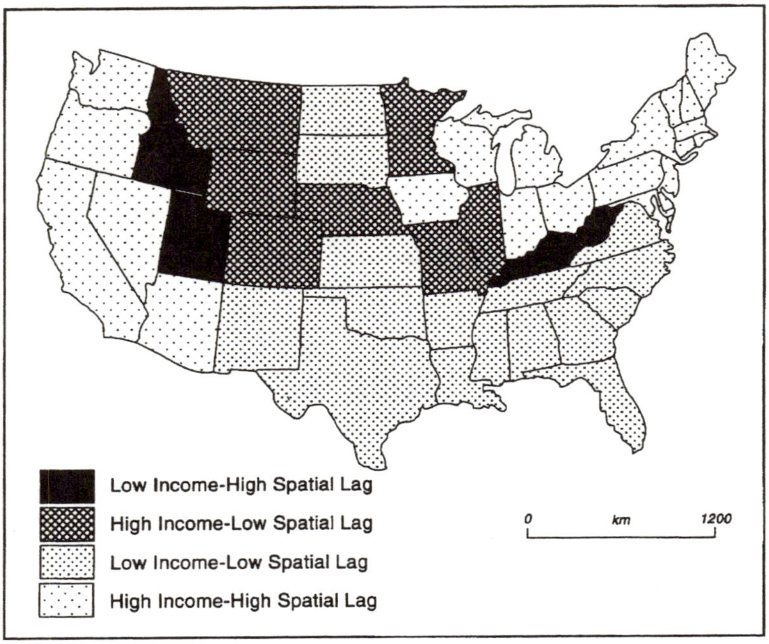

Fig. 4. Local Moran statistics per capita income, 1929

revealed very strong evidence of spatial autocorrelation over the sample period, the convergence hypothesis is concerned with the relationship between the growth rate in the incomes and their starting levels. A spatial analysis of the growth rates between 1929–94 indicates that these rates are also highly spatially autocorrelated as the z-value associated with Moran's I using the simple contiguity matrix is 7·01 which is significant at $p = 0{\cdot}001$. Fig. 6 contains the Moran scatterplot for the growth rates over the period. The overall pattern of the local measures of spatial association is positive as reflected by the slope of the trend line which is driven by the majority of the states falling in quadrants I and III.

Interestingly, a comparison of the pattern of spatial association of the growth rates in Fig. 6 with the pattern of spatial association in the initial incomes in Fig. 2 suggests an inverse relationship. More specifically, it appears that the states that had high initial incomes and were surrounded by high income states, also had growth rates that were below average as did their neighbours. A similar finding holds for states displaying negative spatial associations in their initial incomes that were in quadrant II (IV) in Fig. 2, and display negative spatial associations in their growth rates that are in quadrant IV (II) in Fig. 6.

These patterns raise an important question: what is the extent to which the similarity of the spatial patterns in the growth rates and the starting income levels may be due solely to the convergence process? If the unconditional convergence model was correct, then the *a priori* expectation would be for the spatial pattern in the growth rates to be the inverse of the pattern for the initial incomes. On the other hand it remains to be seen if any spatial structure remains in the unexplained variation of the growth rates after conditioning on the starting levels. We now turn to a confirmatory spatial econometric analysis of the convergence hypothesis in order to provide insights to this question.

CONFIRMATORY SPATIAL ANALYSIS OF β-CONVERGENCE

Our point of departure for the confirmatory analysis of regional income convergence is the unconditional model of equation (1) which is rewritten here in vector notation:

$$\ln\left(\frac{y_{t+k}}{y_t}\right) = \alpha + \beta \ln(y_t) + \varepsilon_t \qquad (4)$$

where the vector y_t now contains the observations on real per capita income from all states in a given year.

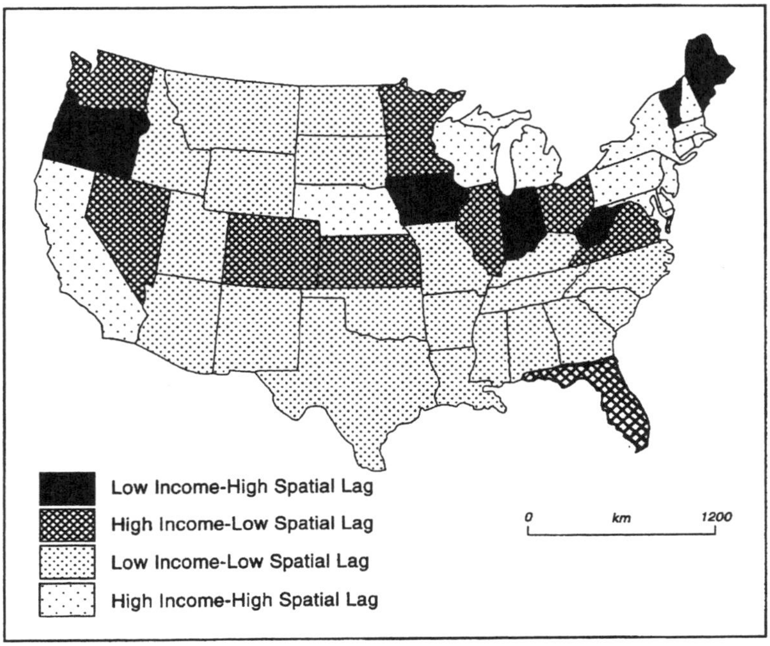

Fig. 5. Local Moran statistics per capita income, 1994

We extend this specification to deal with the presence of spatial dependence in the US income data.[12]

Spatial dependence models

In most applications of the Baumol framework to the US, an implicit assumption is that the error terms from different states are independent:

$$E\left[\varepsilon_t \varepsilon_t'\right] = \sigma_t^2 I \qquad (5)$$

However, in such a cross-sectional context in which the observational units are spatially organized, this assumption may be overly restrictive. In particular, the possibility exists for spatial spill-overs across state boundaries leading to forms of spatial dependence that would violate these assumptions. Below we outline alternative specifications that are appropriate for these different forms of spatial dependence.

Spatial error model. This specification is relevant when the dependence works through the error process in that the errors from different states may display spatial covariance. Using vector notation, the error term would be expressed as:

$$\begin{aligned} \varepsilon_t &= \zeta W \varepsilon_t + u_t \\ \varepsilon_t &= (I - \zeta W)^{-1} u_t \end{aligned} \qquad (6)$$

where: ζ is a scalar spatial error coefficient; and $u \sim N(0, \sigma^2 I)$. In this case the original error term has the following non-spherical covariance matrix:

$$E[\varepsilon_t \varepsilon_t'] = (I - \zeta W)^{-1} \sigma^2 I (I - \zeta W)^{-1'} \qquad (7)$$

As is well known, use of ordinary least squares (OLS) in the presence of non-spherical errors would yield unbiased estimates for the convergence (and intercept) parameter, but a biased estimate of the parameter's variance. Thus, inferences based on the OLS estimates may be misleading. Instead, inferences about the convergence process should be based on the spatial error model estimated via maximum likelihood or general methods of moments.

From a spatial process perspective, the spatial error specification has an interesting interpretation when applied to the convergence hypothesis. This can be seen by substituting equation (6) into equation (4):

$$\ln\left(\frac{y_{t+k}}{y_t}\right) = \alpha + \beta \ln(y_t) + (I - \zeta W)^{-1} u_t \qquad (8)$$

Table 1. Summary of local measures of spatial association: real per capita income, 1929–94

	State	$p < 0{\cdot}05$	Q1	Q2	Q3	Q4
AL	Alabama	55	0	0	55	0
AZ	Arizona	0	0	0	0	0
AR	Arkansas	62	0	0	62	0
CA	California	5	5	0	0	0
CO	Colorado	1	0	0	0	1
CT	Connecticut	55	55	0	0	0
DE	Delaware	59	59	0	0	0
FL	Florida	25	0	0	19	6
GA	Georgia	56	0	0	56	0
ID	Idaho	15	9	6	0	0
IL	Illinois	0	0	0	0	0
IN	Indiana	0	0	0	0	0
IA	Iowa	1	1	0	0	0
KS	Kansas	0	0	0	0	0
KY	Kentucky	0	0	0	0	0
LA	Louisiana	66	0	0	66	0
ME	Maine	0	0	0	0	0
MD	Maryland	0	0	0	0	0
MA	Massachusetts	46	46	0	0	0
MI	Michigan	0	0	0	0	0
MN	Minnesota	2	0	0	0	2
MS	Mississippi	66	0	0	66	0
MO	Missouri	11	0	0	2	9
MT	Montana	6	0	0	6	0
NE	Nebraska	0	0	0	0	0
NV	Nevada	2	2	0	0	0
NH	New Hampshire	0	0	0	0	0
NJ	New Jersey	55	55	0	0	0
NM	New Mexico	0	0	0	0	0
NY	New York	61	61	0	0	0
NC	North Carolina	52	0	0	52	0
ND	North Dakota	0	0	0	0	0
OH	Ohio	0	0	0	0	0
OK	Oklahoma	0	0	0	0	0
OR	Oregon	46	46	0	0	0
PA	Pennsylvania	64	64	0	0	0
RI	Rhode Island	64	62	2	0	0
SC	South Carolina	15	0	0	15	0
SD	South Dakota	1	1	0	0	0
TN	Tennessee	66	0	0	66	0
TX	Texas	61	0	0	54	7
UT	Utah	0	0	0	0	0
VT	Vermont	34	15	19	0	0
VA	Virginia	21	0	0	21	0
WA	Washington	0	0	0	0	0
WV	West Virginia	0	0	0	0	0
WI	Wisconsin	6	6	0	0	0
WY	Wyoming	4	0	0	3	1

Notes: $p < 0{\cdot}05$, number of years local statistic is significant at 0·05. Q1, number of years local statistic is in quadrant 1 of Moran's scatterplot; Q2, number of years local statistic is in quadrant 2 of Moran's scatterplot; Q3, number of years local statistic is in quadrant 3 of Moran's scatterplot; Q4, number of years local statistic is in quadrant 4 of Moran's scatterplot.

From equation (8) it is evident that a random shock introduced into a specific state will not only affect the growth rate in that state but, through the spatial transformation $(I - \zeta W)^{-1}$, will impact the growth rates of other states. Moreover, while any state has a limited number of neighbours, as is expressed by the sparseness of the spatial weights matrix, the inverse operator in the transformation defines an error covariance structure that diffuses state-specific shocks not only to that state's neighbours but throughout the system.

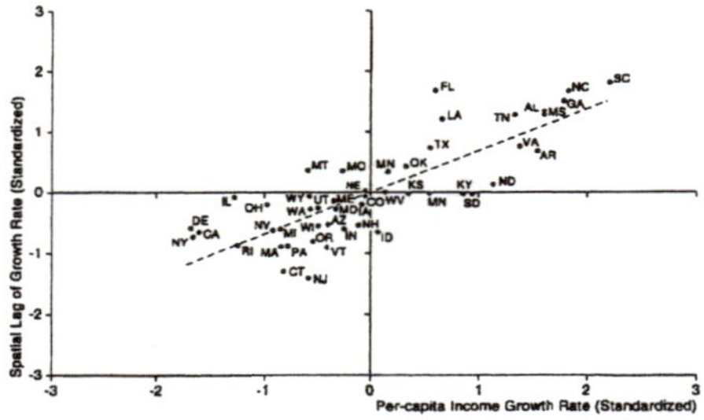

Fig. 6. Moran scatterplot state income growth rates, 1929–94

Spatial lag model. Spatial dependence can also take on several substantive forms which may be relevant to the convergence hypothesis. The first form of substantive dependence we consider is incorporated into the unconditional specification through a spatial lag:

$$\ln\left(\frac{y_{t+k}}{y_t}\right) = \alpha + \beta \ln(y_t) + \rho W \ln\left(\frac{y_{t+k}}{y_t}\right) + \varepsilon_t \quad (9)$$

where: ρ is the scalar spatial autoregressive parameter and all other terms are as previously defined. This specification can be interpreted in a number of ways (Anselin and Bera, 1997). From a filtering perspective (Getis, 1990, 1995), the focus is on the nature of the convergence relationship after the spatial effect has been controlled for:

$$(I - \rho W)\ln\left(\frac{y_{t+k}}{y_t}\right) = \alpha + \beta \ln(y_t) + \varepsilon_t \quad (10)$$

Alternatively, when the interest centres on the spatial dependence in the dependent variable, the question arises as to how the growth rate in a state may relate to those in its surrounding states after conditioning on the starting year levels of income. This perspective is important because it addresses the question of whether the indications of spatial dependence in the growth rates, reported in the univariate tests of spatial dependence in the previous section, may be an artifact of the convergence process operating on initial incomes that were spatially autocorrelated.

Finally, from the perspective of the data generating

process for the lag specification, the expected value of the income growth rates can be expressed as follows:

$$E\left[\ln\left(\frac{y_{t+k}}{y_t}\right)\right] = E[(I-\rho W)^{-1}(\alpha+\beta\ln(y_t))] + E[(I-\rho W)^{-1}\varepsilon_t] \quad (11)$$

This reveals how the expected value of the growth rate of each state's income is related not only to its own starting level of income, but to those in other states as well. While the expected value of the error term is 0, a non-zero realization of a shock to a particular state will impact not only on that state but, through the spatial transformation, will also affect other states (in the same fashion as for the error model).

OLS applied to the lag specification is inconsistent due to the simultaneity introduced through the spatial lag. Instead a number of alternative estimators based on maximum likelihood and instrumental variables have been suggested (ANSELIN, 1988).

Spatial cross-regressive model. A second possibility for dealing with substantive spatial spill-over effects is the cross-regressive model in which the spatial lag of starting per capita incomes is added to the original specification:

$$\ln\left(\frac{y_{t+k}}{y_t}\right) = \alpha+\beta\ln(y_t)+\tau W\ln(y_t)+\varepsilon_t \quad (12)$$

In contrast to the lag model, where the spatial dependence in the variation unaccounted for by the unconditional model is reflected in the growth rates in per capita income over the period under consideration, in the cross-regressive model the remaining spatial dependence is with respect to the starting levels of income. Because the latter variable and its spatial lag are exogenous, estimation of the cross-regressive model can be based on OLS. We consider this specification in the analysis that follows because the erroneous omission of the cross-lag term would lead to spatially autocorrelated errors. Since each of these three spatial income convergence models hold different interpretations for the nature of the convergence process, it becomes important to discriminate between these three as well as the original aspatial convergence model of equation (4).

Table 2. Unconditional model OLS estimation

	R^2 (σ^2)	AIC[1]	β (p-value)[2]	Convergence rate (θ)[3]
1929–94	0·913	− 101·956	− 0·708	0·019
	(0·007)		(0·000)	
1929–45	0·823	− 111·662	− 0·427	0·035
	(0·005)		(0·000)	
1946–94	0·703	− 97·570	− 0·555	0·017
	(0·007)		(0·000)	

	Robust LM (error)[4] p-value	Robust LM (lag)[5] p-value	Moran's I (error)[6] MI/p-value
Diagnostics for spatial dependence			
1929–94	0·318	0·273	0·162/0·037
1929–45	0·020	0·144	0·388/0·000
1946–94	0·109	0·165	0·354/0·000

	Breusch-Pagan test p-value
Diagnostics for heteroscedasticity	
1929–94	0·857
1929–45	0·155
1946–94	0·142

Notes: 1. Value of the Akaike Information Criterion.
2. Estimate for β and its p-value.
3. The convergence rate θ is obtained using $\theta = \ln(\beta+1)/-k$, where k is the number of years in the period.
4. P-value for the robust Lagrange Multiplier test for error dependence.
5. P-value for the robust Lagrange Multiplier test for lag dependence.
6. Value of Moran's I for the error term, along with its probability.

Empirical results: unconditional convergence models

In Table 2, we present the results of the estimation of a cross-sectional regression of the unconditional convergence model for the 48 conterminous states. To allow for the trend break identified by CARLINO and MILLS, 1996a, we estimate models for three different sample periods: 1929–94, 1929–45 and 1946–94. The results provide much support for β-convergence as the overall fit of the simple specification is generally high, with an adjusted R^2 above 0·70 in all three samples. Additionally, the regressions from each sample yield highly significant and negative coefficients for the starting income levels, confirming the consensus result of β-convergence for the US states.

In column 5 of Table 2, the implied annual rate of convergence over the entire study period is reported to be 1·9% which is in general agreement with previous findings of BARRO and SALA-I-MARTIN, 1991. However, it appears that the rate of convergence was not stable over the entire period, as the implied rate in the earlier years (1929–45) is roughly twice that of the later years (1946–94). This instability of the convergence rate also concurs with the findings of CARLINO and MILLS, 1996a, who report more rapid cross-sectional convergence in the earlier period. We return to this issue below.

The bottom portion of Table 2 reports a number of diagnostics for the presence of spatial effects. Three different tests for spatial dependence are included: a Moran's I test; and two robust Lagrange multiplier tests. As reported in ANSELIN and REY, 1991, the first test is very powerful against both forms of spatial dependence, the spatial lag and spatial error autocorrelation; unfortunately, it does not allow for the discrimination between these two forms of misspecification. In contrast, the robust tests have displayed good power against a specific alternative in an extensive set of Monte Carlo experiments (ANSELIN *et al.*, 1996). These properties are reflected here, as Moran's I provides very strong evidence of spatial dependence in each sample. However, following the strategy suggested by ANSELIN and REY, 1991, the robust tests point to the presence of spatial error autocorrelation rather than the spatial lag. While there is very strong evidence of spatial dependence, a spatially adjusted Breusch–Pagan test for heteroscedasticity is not significant in any of the sub-samples. Thus, in the remainder of the empirical analysis we limit attention to the spatial dependence models and omit further consideration of the spatial heterogeneity models.

Table 3 reports the estimation results for the different spatial dependence models over the three periods. Based on the value of the Akaike Information Criterion (AIC), the fit of each of the three spatial models is superior to that of the original unconditional model from Table 2.[13] As expected from the findings of the diagnostic tests in Table 2, the spatial error model achieves the best fit for each of the periods. This suggests that the original unconditional model, which has been the work-horse of much previous research, suffers from a misspecification due to omitted spatial dependence. It also implies that the finding of significant spatial autocorrelation in the growth rates reported above is not explained entirely by the convergence hypothesis coupled with the spatial dependence of the starting income levels.

The fourth column of the table reports the asymptotic p-values for the coefficient on the spatial variable for each model and period. The coefficients on the error and lag terms are significant in both of the sub-periods, while only marginally so for the lag and not for the error term when the entire period is considered. In contrast, the coefficient on the spatial lag of the initial income levels in the cross regressive model is never significant. In fact, the diagnostics indicate that there is significant spatial dependence remaining in the cross-regressive model.

The bottom of Table 3 reports the implied convergence rates based on the estimates from the spatial error model. In each case, explicitly taking the error dependence into account results in a slower estimated annual rate of convergence than that based on the ordinary least squares estimate in Table 2. The pattern of a faster rate in the first relative to the second period is, however, repeated in the spatial error estimates.

Table 3. Spatial dependence models

Model specification	AIC[1]	β (p-value)[2]	β, λ, ζ,[3] p-value	LM test,[4,5] p-value
1929–94				
Spatial error (ML)	− 104·014	− 0·695 (0·000)	0·158	0·287
Spatial lag (ML)	− 102·777	− 0·641 (0·000)	0·087	0·454
Cross regressive (OLS)	− 101·173	− 0·661 (0·000)	0·288	0·029
1929–45				
Spatial error (ML)	− 124·740	− 0·399 (0·000)	0·000	0·665
Spatial lag (ML)	− 119·505	− 0·338 (0·000)	0·002	0·146
Cross regressive (OLS)	− 111·847	− 0·370 (0·000)	0·155	0·000
1946–94				
Spatial error (ML)	− 106·038	− 0·499 (0·000)	0·004	0·483
Spatial lag (ML)	− 105·395	− 0·414 (0·000)	0·002	0·916
Cross regressive (OLS)	− 97·542	− 0·465 (0·000)	0·176	0·000

Convergence rates based on spatial error (ML) estimates

	Convergence rate (θ)
1929–94	0·018
1929–45	0·032
1946–94	0·014

Notes: 1. Value of the Akaike Information Criterion.
2. Estimate for β and its p-value.
3. P-value for the spatial coefficient.
4. P-value for the Lagrange Multiplier test for the alternative model (spatial error or spatial lag).
5. Moran's I test of spatial dependence for the cross regressive model.
6. The convergence rate θ is obtained using $\theta = \ln(\beta + 1)/-k$, where k is the number of years in the period.

Structural change and spatial dependence

While the results in Tables 2 and 3 provide indications of different convergence rates in the two sub-periods, the extent to which formal inference regarding this structural change is sensitive to the presence of spatial error autocorrelation has been ignored in the previous literature. In Table 4, a seemingly unrelated regression (SUR) specification is estimated with each of the two sub-periods treated as a separate equation with allowance for cross-equation error covariance. Based on maximum likelihood estimation of the SUR (ML-SUR), several findings emerge. First, the ML-SUR estimates of the convergence parameters in each period are larger than the OLS estimates reported in Table 2. This implies a lower rate of convergence for the ML-SUR estimates for both periods. At the same time, a Wald test on the stability of the convergence parameter across these equations is rejected at $p = 0{\cdot}10$, which is in agreement with the casual interpretation behind the OLS results in Table 2, namely, more rapid convergence in the first period. However, there is also very strong evidence of spatial error dependence in the two equations as is indicated by the Lagrange Multiplier test at the bottom of Table 4. Again, the diagnostics point to the error model as the more appropriate specification.

Table 5 reports the results from the estimation of a spatial SUR (ANSELIN, 1988) which extends the traditional SUR to allow for spatial autocorrelation in

Table 4. Seemingly unrelated regression tests of structural change

Variable	SUR-ML	Standard deviation	t
Constant2945	4·233	0.243	17·436
Income29	− 0·425	0·029	− 14·888
Constant4694	5·709	0·471	12·122
Income46	− 0·534	0·052	− 10·283

R^2 0·8354

Cross-equation error covariance matrix

0·526*10-2	− 0.122*10-2
− 0.122*10-2	0·708*10-2

Wald test on coefficient homogeneity across equations

$\chi^2_{(1)}$	2·294	p-value	0·086

Spatial dependence tests

Lagrange Multiplier Error	$\chi^2_{(1)}$	19·361	p-value	6·2*10-5
Lagrange Multiplier Lag	$\chi^2_{(1)}$	18·906	p-value	7·8*10-5

Table 5. Spatial seemingly unrelated regression tests of structural change

Variable	SUR-ML error	Standard deviation	t
Constant2945	4·020	0·451	8·934
Income29	− 0·400	0·053	− 7·587
ζ	0·606	0·122	4·966
Constant4694	5·471	1·217	4·496
Income46	− 0·508	0·134	− 3·792
ζ	0·465	0·149	3·120

R^2 Buse 0·766

Cross-equation error covariance matrix

0·36*10-2	0·04*10-2
0·04*10-2	0·056*10-2

Wald test on coefficient homogeneity across equations

$\chi^2_{(1)}$	0·687	p-value	0·407

the errors of each sub-period equation, while at the same time permitting cross-temporal covariance between the errors from the two equations. The spatial SUR estimates of the parameters on starting income are significant and larger than the respective ML-SUR estimates in both periods, implying a slower rate of convergence than both the ML-SUR and OLS estimates. In addition, the spatial error coefficients are significant in both periods, while the Wald test on the stability of the starting income coefficient is no longer significant. This suggests that the indications of structural change in the rate of convergence based on the traditional SUR approach are misleading due to the presence of spatial autocorrelation in both sub-periods.

Spillover effects in the convergence process

Overall, the results in Tables 2–5 provide strong evidence of spatial effects in the unconditional convergence model widely applied in the literature. Specifically, the spatial error model appears to be the more appropriate specification, over the entire sample period as well as for the two sub-samples. There are several implications of the spatial error specification for the convergence hypothesis. The first concerns a comparison of the implied rates of convergence from the original unconditional model of Table 2 against the implied rates from the spatial error models reported at the bottom of Table 3. In the longer period, the estimated convergence rates are virtually identical between the original and error specifications while, in the two sub-samples, the effect of explicitly taking the error dependence into account is to slightly lower the estimated rate of convergence. While this seems to suggest only a modest role for spatial effects in the convergence process, consideration of the second implication reveals otherwise.

The second implication follows from the properties of the spatial error model as a data generating process detailed above. The presence of significant spatial error dependence results in the random shocks to a specific state being propagated throughout the nation. This is illustrated in Fig. 7 where we introduce a shock to the error term for the state of Missouri and substitute the maximum likelihood estimates of the spatial error model coefficients into equation (8) to estimate the degree of spatial spill-over.[14] As expected, the introduction of the shock has the largest relative impact on Missouri where the estimated growth rate over the 1929–45 period is 22·2% higher relative to the estimate without the shock. However, there is a clear spatial pattern to the propagation of this shock to the other states. The immediate neighbouring states have their predicted growth rates increased by between 1% and 5% due to the spill-over from the Missouri shock, while the magnitude of the shock spill-over dampens as the focus moves away from these central states.

The presence of spatial error dependence as depicted in Fig. 7 implies that movements away from some steady state equilibrium may not be a function of state-specific shocks alone, but instead the possibility now exists for a complex set of shock spill-overs. Given the prominent role of temporal shocks in the recent convergence literature, we feel that our results warrant that similar attention be given to the geographical nature of these shocks. Examination of the interaction between the temporal and spatial dimensions of shocks to individual states remains an important area for future study.

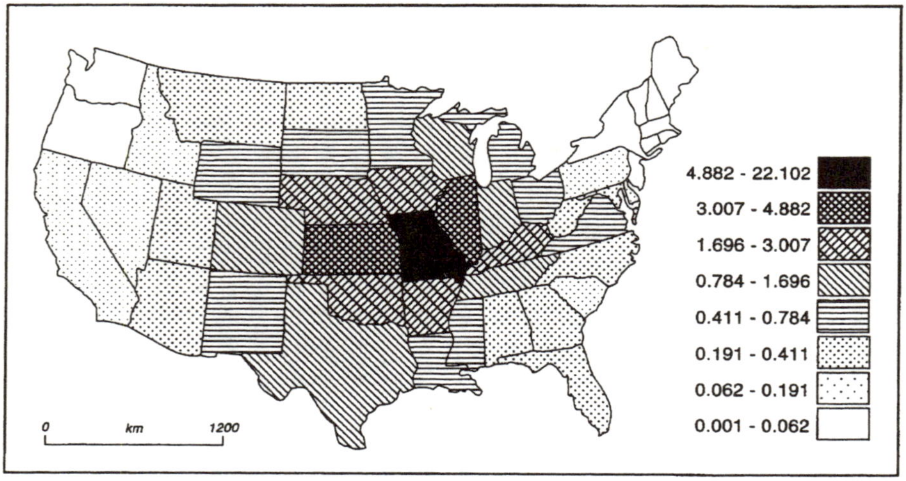

Fig. 7. Percentage change in income growth rate due to spillover of shock to Missouri, 1929–45

CONCLUSION

In this paper, we have provided new insights as to the nature of regional income convergence patterns in the US over the post 1929 era. Our empirical strategy was based on recent developments in exploratory spatial data analysis as well as an explicit spatial econometric perspective. While our results corroborate previous findings on the general pattern of regional income convergence for the US, we are able to provide precise insights as to the geographical dimensions of state income growth as well as new evidence on the role of spatial effects in the formal econometric analysis of regional income convergence.

The application of exploratory spatial data analysis methods revealed strong evidence of spatial autocorrelation in the levels of state per capita incomes over the sample period. We showed that the strength of the spatial autocorrelation in the state incomes was strongly associated with the dispersion of state incomes. We found that the state income growth rates also displayed a great deal of spatial autocorrelation. This suggests that, while states may be converging in relative incomes, they do not do so independently but rather tend to display movements similar to their regional neighbours.

Our confirmatory analysis revealed that the traditional Baumol specification is misspecified due to the presence of strong spatial error dependence. This implies that the finding of spatial autocorrelation in the growth rates based on the univariate tests is not an artifact of the convergence relationship since there remains strong spatial dependence after conditioning on the initial incomes. The presence of spatial error autocorrelation also provides an avenue for random shocks to individual states to not only move that state away from its steady state equilibrium, but to propagate throughout the system of states, thereby complicating the transitional dynamics of the overall convergence process. We also find evidence that previous econometric results indicating the presence of structural change in the rate of regional income convergence for the US had ignored spatial error autocorrelation. When we take the spatial dependence into account, there is no longer any evidence of a structural break in the convergence process over the sample period.

Our results are important in that they represent the first detailed evidence on the role of spatial effects in a regional income convergence study. We have also outlined an initial set of explicit spatial econometric models that can be applied to studies of regional income convergence in other contexts. We hope that this will stimulate others to pursue extensions of these models, perhaps to more fully integrate the spatial and temporal dimensions of the data underlying regional convergence studies.

Acknowledgements – We thank Luc Anselin, Roger Bolton, Jim Gerber, Art Getis, Michael Greenwood, Geoffrey Hewings, Mike Jerrett, the editor and an anonymous referee for very helpful comments. Any errors or omissions remain our responsibility.

NOTES

1. The literature makes a distinction between conditional and absolute (unconditional) convergence, with the former pertaining to the partial correlation of the growth

rate and initial level after controlling for a number of additional variables reflecting differences in equilibrium wages and technologies. Because differences in these variables are likely to be minor across US states (BARRO and SALA-I-MARTIN, 1992) our study focuses on absolute or unconditional convergence.

2. CHATTERJI, 1992, raises similar criticisms of β-convergence.
3. Although CARLINO and MILLS, 1996a, argue that both time-series and cross-sectional tests are necessary for convergence, their approach is based on a largely time-series perspective.
4. Because this framework requires a 'leader' in the sense of an economy with the highest income throughout the study period, it is not applicable to the US system.
5. The source for our data is US BUREAU OF ECONOMIC ANALYSIS, 1996.
6. A similar pattern of σ-convergence is reported for regional per-capita earnings in CARLINO and MILLS, 1996a.
7. All computations were carried out using the SpaceStat software packages (ANSELIN, 1995).
8. The role of the spatial weights matrix is to introduce the notion of a neighbourhood set for each state. Because the determination of a set of neighbours is not without some arbitrariness, we also utilized three alternative definitions to define our weights matrices, which generated results that were very similar to those based on the simple contiguity matrix. These include two other binary matrices and were obtained from using a distance threshold to define a state's neighbourhood set. DC1 uses the first quartile of all state-to-state distances to define states as neighbours, while DC2 uses the second-quartile distance to define the neighbours. Finally, ID1 is a general weights matrix where, for pairs of states separated by less than the first quartile distance, the elements are set equal to the inverse of the squared distances between the states, and for all other pairs the elements are set to zero. For a detailed discussion of the impacts of the choice of a spatial weights matrix in econometric analyses, see FLORAX and REY, 1995.
9. For details on the assumptions underlying the Moran's I statistic, see CLIFF and ORD, 1973, 1981; UPTON and FINGLETON, 1985.
10. The state abbreviations used in Figs. 2, 3 and 6 are defined in Table 1.
11. For further discussion of the properties of local spatial autocorrelation statistics and their application, see GETIS and ORD, 1996.
12. We also implemented and tested a number of models to deal with spatial heterogeneity. However, these models performed poorly relative to the spatial dependence models.
13. The Akaike Information Criterion (AIC) corrects the log likelihood function for overfitting and is a valid measure for comparisons of models with different numbers of explanatory variables (as is the case here). Formally: $AIC = -2L + 2K$, where L is the value of the log likelihood function and K is the number of variables. The best fitting model is the one with the lowest value for the AIC. For further discussion see ANSELIN, 1995.
14. The shock is set equal to twice the standard error of the estimated spatial error specification. We introduce the shock to Missouri because it is close to the centre of the nation and allows for a complete view of the spill-over pattern.

REFERENCES

ABRAMOVITZ M. (1986) Catching up, forging ahead, and falling behind, *J. Econ. Hist.* 46, 385–406.

AMOS O. M. JR (1988) Unbalanced regional growth and regional income inequality in the latter stages of development, *Reg. Sci. Urban Econ.* 18, 554–66.

AMOS O. M. JR (1989) An inquiry into the causes of increasing regional income inequality in the United States, *Rev. Reg. Studies* 19, 1–12.

ANSELIN L. (1988) *Spatial Econometrics: Methods and Models.* Kluwer, Dordrecht.

ANSELIN L. (1993) The Moran scatterplot as an ESDA tool to assess local instability in spatial association, GISDATA Specialist Meeting on GIS and Spatial Analysis, Amsterdam.

ANSELIN L. (1995) Local indicators of spatial association-LISA, *Geogr. Analysis* 27, 93–115.

ANSELIN L. and BERA A. (1997) Spatial dependence in linear regression models, in ULLAH A. and GILES D. (Eds) *Handbook of Applied Economic Statistics.* Marcel Dekker, New York.

ANSELIN L., BERA A., FLORAX R. J. G. M. and YOON M. (1996) Simple diagnostic tests for spatial dependence, *Reg. Sci. Urban Econ.* 26, 77–104.

ANSELIN L. and FLORAX R. J. G. M. (Eds) (1995) *New Directions in Spatial Econometrics*, Springer, Berlin.

ANSELIN L. and REY S. J. (1991) Properties of tests for spatial dependence in linear regression models, *Geogr. Analysis* 23, 112–31.

ANSELIN L. and REY S. J. (1997) Introduction to the special issue on spatial econometrics, *Int. Reg. Sci. Rev.* 20, 1–7.

ARMSTRONG H. W. (1995) Convergence among regions of the European Union, 1950–1990, *Pap. Reg. Sci.* 74, 143–52.

BARRO R. J. and SALA-I-MARTIN X. (1991) Convergence across states and regions, *Brookings Pap. Econ. Activity*, no. 1, pp. 107–82.

BARRO R. J. and SALA-I-MARTIN X. (1992) Convergence, *J. Pol. Econ.* 100, 223–51.

BAUMOL W. (1986) Productivity growth, convergence and welfare: what the long run data show, *Am. Econ. Rev.* 76, 1,072–85.

BERNARD A. and DURLAUF S. (1995) Convergence in international output, *J. Appl. Econ.* 10, 1,072–85.

BERNARD A. and DURLAUF S. (1996) Interpreting tests of the convergence hypothesis, *J. Econometrics* 71, 161–73.

BERNARD A. and JONES C. (1996a) Productivity and convergence across US states and industries, *Empirical Econ.* 21, 113–35.

BERNARD A. and JONES C. (1996b) Productivity across industries and countries: time series theory and evidence, *Rev. Econ. Statist.* 78, 135–46.

BERNARD A. and JONES C. (1996c) Comparing apples to oranges: productivity convergence and measurement across industries and countries, *Am. Econ. Rev.* 86, 1,216–38.

BRAUN D. (1991) Income inequality and economic development, *Soc. Sci. Quart.* 72, 520–36.

CARDENAS M. and PONTON A. (1995) Growth and convergence in Colombia: 1950–1990 *J. Develop. Econ.* 47, 5–37.

CARLINO G. and MILLS L. (1993) Are US regional incomes converging?, *J. Monetary Econ.* 32, 335–46.

CARLINO G. and MILLS L. (1996a) Testing neoclassical convergence in regional incomes and earnings, *Reg. Sci. Urban Econ.* 26, 565–90.

CARLINO G. and MILLS L. (1996b) Convergence and the US states: a time-series analysis, *J. Reg. Sci.* 36, 597–616.

CASETTI E. (1972) Generating models by the expansion method, *Geogr. Analysis* 4, 81–91.

CHATTERJI M. (1992) Convergence clubs and endogenous growth, *Oxf. Rev. Econ. Policy* 8, 57–69.

CHATTERJI M. and DEWHURST J. H. LL (1996) Convergence clubs and relative economic performance in Great Britain: 1977–1991, *Reg. Studies* 30, 31–40.

CLIFF A. and ORD J. (1973) *Spatial Autocorrelation*. Pion, London.

CLIFF A. and ORD J. *Spatial Processes, Models and Applications.* Pion, London.

COUGHLIN C. C. and MANDELBAUM T. B. (1988) Why have state per-capita incomes diverged recently?, *Rev. Fed. Res. Bank of St Louis* 70, 24–36.

COULOMBE S. and LEE F. C. (1995) Convergence across Canadian provinces, 1969 to 1991, *Can. J. Econ.* 28, 886–98.

CROWN W. H. and WHEAT L. F. (1995) State per capita income convergence since 1950: sharecropping's demise and other influences, *J. Reg. Sci.* 35, 527–52.

DE LONG B. (1988) Productivity growth, convergence, and welfare: comment, *Am. Econ. Rev.* 78, 1,138–59.

EASTERLIN R. (1960a) Interregional differences in per capita income, population and total income, 1840–1950, in NATIONAL BUREAU OF ECONOMIC RESEARCH *Trends in the American Economy in the Nineteenth Century.* Princeton University Press, Princeton, NJ.

EASTERLIN R. (1960b) Regional growth of income, in KUZNETS S., MILLER A. and EASTERLIN R. (Eds) *Population Redistribution and Economic Growth in the United States, 1870–1950.* American Philosophical Society, Philadelphia.

FAN C. C. and CASETTI E. (1994) The spatial and temporal dynamics of US regional income inequality, 1950–1989, *Ann Reg. Sci.* 28, 177–96.

FLORAX R. J. G. M. and REY S. J. (1995) The impacts of misspecified spatial interaction in linear regression models, in ANSELIN L. and FLORAX R. J. G. M. (Eds) *New Directions in Spatial Econometrics.* Springer, Berlin.

GETIS A. (1990) Screening for spatial dependence in regression analysis, *Pap. Reg. Sci.* 69, 69–81.

GETIS A. (1995) Spatial filtering in a regression framework, in ANSELIN L. and FLORAX R. J. G. M. (Eds) *New Directions in Spatial Econometrics.* Springer, Berlin.

GETIS A. and ORD J. (1996) Local spatial statistics: an overview, in LONGLEY P. and BATTY M. (Eds) *Spatial Analysis: Modeling in a GIS Environment.* GeoInformation International, Cambridge, MA.

JONES C. (1997) On the evolution of the world income distribution, *J. Econ. Perspectives* 11, 19–36.

KRUGMAN P. (1987) The narrow moving band, the Dutch disease, and the competitive consequences of Mrs Thatcher, *J. Develop. Econ.* 45, 1–28.

KUZNETS S. (1955) Economic growth and income inequality, *Am. Econ. Rev.* 45, 1–28.

MALLICK R. and CARAYANNIS E. (1994) Regional economic convergence in Mexico, *Growth & Change* 25, 325–34.

MANKIW N., ROMER D. and WEIL D. (1992) A contribution to the empirics of economic growth, *Quart. J. Econ.* 107, 407–37.

QUAH D. (1992) International patterns of growth: I, persistence in cross-country disparities, London School of Economics.

QUAH D. (1993a) Galton's fallacy and tests of the convergence hypothesis, *Scand. J. Econ.* 95, 427–43.

QUAH D. (1993b) Empirical cross-section dynamics in economic growth, *Europ. Econ. Rev.* 37, 426–34.

ROWLEY T., REDMAN J. and ANGEL J. (1991) *The Rapid Rise in State Per Capita Income Inequality in the 1980s: Sources and Prospects.* US Department of Agriculture, Washington, DC.

UPTON G. and FINGLETON B. (1985) *Spatial Data Analysis by Example,* Vol. 1. Wiley, New York.

US BUREAU OF ECONOMIC ANALYSIS (1996) *Regional Economic Information System, 1964–94* (CD-ROM). US Department of Commerce, Washington, DC.

VOHRA R. (1996) How fast do we grow?, *Growth & Change* 27, 47–54.

WILLIAMSON J. (1965) Regional inequality and the process of national development, *Econ. Develop. & Cultural Change* 4, 3–47.

Part V
The New Economic Geography

[21]

Increasing Returns and Economic Geography

Paul Krugman

Massachusetts Institute of Technology

This paper develops a simple model that shows how a country can endogenously become differentiated into an industrialized "core" and an agricultural "periphery." In order to realize scale economies while minimizing transport costs, manufacturing firms tend to locate in the region with larger demand, but the location of demand itself depends on the distribution of manufacturing. Emergence of a core-periphery pattern depends on transportation costs, economies of scale, and the share of manufacturing in national income.

The study of economic geography—of the location of factors of production in space—occupies a relatively small part of standard economic analysis. International trade theory, in particular, conventionally treats nations as dimensionless points (and frequently assumes zero transportation costs between countries as well). Admittedly, models descended from von Thünen (1826) play an important role in urban studies, while Hotelling-type models of locational competition get a reasonable degree of attention in industrial organization. On the whole, however, it seems fair to say that the study of economic geography plays at best a marginal role in economic theory.

On the face of it, this neglect is surprising. The facts of economic geography are surely among the most striking features of real-world economies, at least to laymen. For example, one of the most remarkable things about the United States is that in a generally sparsely populated country, much of whose land is fertile, the bulk of the population resides in a few clusters of metropolitan areas; a quarter of the inhabitants are crowded into a not especially inviting section of the East Coast. It has often been noted that nighttime satellite

[*Journal of Political Economy*, 1991, vol. 99, no. 3]

photos of Europe reveal little of political boundaries but clearly suggest a center-periphery pattern whose hub is somewhere in or near Belgium. A layman might have expected that these facts would play a key role in economic modeling. Yet the study of economic geography, at least within the economics profession, has lain largely dormant for the past generation (with a few notable exceptions, particularly Arthur [1989, 1990] and David [in press]).

The purpose of this paper is to suggest that application of models and techniques derived from theoretical industrial organization now allows a reconsideration of economic geography, that it is now time to attempt to incorporate the insights of the long but informal tradition in this area into formal models. In order to make the point, the paper develops a simple illustrative model designed to shed light on one of the key questions of location: Why and when does manufacturing become concentrated in a few regions, leaving others relatively undeveloped?

What we shall see is that it is possible to develop a very simple model of geographical concentration of manufacturing based on the interaction of economies of scale with transportation costs. This is perhaps not too surprising, given the kinds of results that have been emerging in recent literature (with Murphy, Shleifer, and Vishny [1989*a*, 1989*b*] perhaps the closest parallel). More interesting is the fact that this concentration of manufacturing in one location need not always happen and that whether it does depends in an interesting way on a few key parameters.

The paper is divided into four sections. Section I sets the stage with an informal discussion of the problem. Section II then sets out the analytical model. In Section III, I analyze the determination of short-run equilibrium and dynamics. Section IV analyzes the conditions under which concentration of manufacturing production does and does not occur.

I. Bases for Regional Divergence

There has been fairly extensive discussion over time of the nature of the externalities that lead to localization of particular industries. Indeed, Alfred Marshall's original exposition of the concept of external economies was illustrated with the example of industry localization. Most of the literature in this area follows Marshall in identifying three reasons for localization. First, the concentration of several firms in a single location offers a pooled market for workers with industry-specific skills, ensuring both a lower probability of unemployment and a lower probability of labor shortage. Second, localized industries can support the production of nontradable specialized inputs. Third, informational spillovers can give clustered firms a better production function than isolated producers. (Hoover [1948] gives a particularly clear discussion of agglomeration economies.)

These accounts of industry localization surely have considerable validity. In this paper, however, I shall offer a somewhat different approach aimed at answering a somewhat different question. Instead of asking why a particular industry is concentrated in a particular area—for example, carpets in Dalton, Georgia—I shall ask why manufacturing in general might end up concentrated in one or a few regions of a country, with the remaining regions playing the "peripheral" role of agricultural suppliers to the manufacturing "core." The proposed explanation correspondingly focuses on generalized external economies rather than those specific to a particular industry.

I shall also adopt the working assumption that the externalities that sometimes lead to emergence of a core-periphery pattern are *pecuniary* externalities associated with either demand or supply linkages rather than purely technological spillovers. In competitive general equilibrium, of course, pecuniary externalities have no welfare significance and could not lead to the kind of interesting dynamics we shall derive later. Over the past decade, however, it has become a familiar point that in the presence of imperfect competition and increasing returns, pecuniary externalities matter; for example, if one firm's actions affect the demand for the product of another firm whose price exceeds marginal cost, this is as much a "real" externality as if one firm's research and development spills over into the general knowledge pool. At the same time, by focusing on pecuniary externalities, we are able to make the analysis much more concrete than if we allowed external economies to arise in some invisible form. (This is particularly true when location is at issue: how far does a technological spillover spill?)

To understand the nature of the postulated pecuniary externalities, imagine a country in which there are two kinds of production, agriculture and manufacturing. Agricultural production is characterized both by constant returns to scale and by intensive use of immobile land. The geographical distribution of this production will therefore be determined largely by the exogenous distribution of suitable land. Manufactures, on the other hand, we may suppose to be characterized by increasing returns to scale and modest use of land.

Where will manufactures production take place? Because of economies of scale, production of each manufactured good will take place at only a limited number of sites. Other things equal, the preferred sites will be those with relatively large nearby demand, since producing near one's main market minimizes transportation costs. Other locations will then be served from these centrally located sites.

But where will demand be large? Some of the demand for manufactured goods will come from the agricultural sector; if that were the whole story, the distribution of manufacturing production would essentially form a lattice whose form was dictated by the distribution of agricultural land, as in the classic schemes of Christaller (1933) and Lösch (1940). But it is not the whole story: some of the demand for manufactures will come not from the agricultural sector but from the manufacturing sector itself.

This creates an obvious possibility for what Myrdal (1957) called "circular causation" and Arthur (1990) has called "positive feedback": manufactures production will tend to concentrate where there is a large market, but the market will be large where manufactures production is concentrated.

The circularity created by this Hirschman (1958)–type "backward linkage" may be reinforced by a "forward linkage": other things equal, it will be more desirable to live and produce near a concentration of manufacturing production because it will then be less expensive to buy the goods this central place provides.

This is not an original story; indeed, a story along roughly these lines has long been familiar to economic geographers, who emphasize the role of circular processes in the emergence of the U.S. manufacturing belt in the second half of the nineteenth century (see in particular Pred [1966] and Meyer [1983]). The main goal of this paper is to show that this story can be embodied in a simple yet rigorous model. However, before we move on to this model, it may be worth pursuing the intuitive story a little further to ask two questions: How far will the tendency toward geographical concentration proceed, and where will manufacturing production actually end up?

The answer to the first question is that it depends on the underlying parameters of the economy. The circularity that can generate manufacturing concentration will not matter too much if manufacturing employs only a small fraction of the population and hence generates only a small fraction of demand, or if a combination of weak economies of scale and high transportation costs induces suppliers of goods and services to the agricultural sector to locate very close to their markets. These criteria would have been satisfied in a prerailroad, preindustrial society, such as that of early nineteenth-century America. In such a society the bulk of the population would have been engaged in agriculture, the small manufacturing and commercial sector would not have been marked by very substantial economies of scale, and the costs of transportation would have ensured that most of the needs that could not be satisfied by rural production would be satisfied by small towns serving local market areas.

But now let the society spend a higher fraction of income on nonagricultural goods and services; let the factory system and eventually mass production emerge, and with them economies of large-scale production; and let canals, railroads, and finally automobiles lower transportation costs. Then the tie of production to the distribution of land will be broken. A region with a relatively large nonrural population will be an attractive place to produce both because of the large local market and because of the availability of the goods and services produced there. This will attract still more population, at the expense of regions with smaller initial production, and the process will feed on itself until the whole of the nonrural population is concentrated in a few regions.

This not entirely imaginary history suggests that small changes in the parameters of the economy may have large effects on its qualitative behavior. That is, when some index that takes into account transportation costs, economies of scale, and the share of nonagricultural goods in expenditure crosses a critical threshold, population will start to concentrate and regions to diverge; once started, this process will feed on itself.

The story also suggests that the details of the geography that emerges—which regions end up with the population—depend sensitively on initial conditions. If one region has slightly more population than another when, say, transportation costs fall below some critical level, that region ends up gaining population at the other's expense; had the distribution of population at that critical moment been only slightly different, the roles of the regions might have been reversed.

This is about as far as an informal story can take us. The next step is to develop as simple a formal model as possible to see whether the story just told can be given a more rigorous formulation.

II. A Two-Region Model

We consider a model of two regions. In this model there are assumed to be two kinds of production: agriculture, which is a constant-returns sector tied to the land, and manufactures, an increasing-returns sector that can be located in either region.

The model, like many of the models in both the new trade and the new growth literature, is a variant on the monopolistic competition framework initially proposed by Dixit and Stiglitz (1977). This framework, while admittedly special, is remarkably powerful in its ability to yield simple intuition-building treatments of seemingly intractable issues.

All individuals in this economy, then, are assumed to share a utility function of the form

$$U = C_M^{\mu} C_A^{1-\mu}, \tag{1}$$

where C_A is consumption of the agricultural good and C_M is consumption of a manufactures aggregate. Given equation (1), of course, manufactures will always receive a share μ of expenditure; this share is one of the key parameters that will determine whether regions converge or diverge.

The manufactures aggregate C_M is defined by

$$C_M = \left[\sum_{i=1}^{N} c_i^{(\sigma-1)/\sigma}\right]^{\sigma/(\sigma-1)}, \tag{2}$$

where N is the large number of potential products and $\sigma > 1$ is the elasticity of substitution among the products. The elasticity σ is the second parameter determining the character of equilibrium in the model.

There are two regions in the economy and two factors of production in each region. Following the simplification suggested in Krugman (1981), each factor is assumed specific to one sector. Peasants produce agricultural goods; without loss of generality we suppose that the unit labor requirement is one. The peasant population is assumed completely immobile between regions, with a given peasant supply $(1 - \mu)/2$ in each region. Workers may move between the regions; we let L_1 and L_2 be the worker supply in regions 1 and 2, respectively, and require only that the total add up to the overall number of workers μ:[1]

$$L_1 + L_2 = \mu. \tag{3}$$

The production of an individual manufactured good i involves a fixed cost and a constant marginal cost, giving rise to economies of scale:

$$L_{Mi} = \alpha + \beta x_i, \tag{4}$$

where L_{Mi} is the labor used in producing i and x_i is the good's output.

We turn next to the structure of transportation costs between the two regions. Two strong assumptions will be made for tractability. First, *transportation of agricultural output will be assumed to be costless.*[2]

[1] This choice of units ensures that the wage rate of workers equals that of peasants in long-run equilibrium.

[2] The reason for this assumption is that since agricultural products are assumed to be homogeneous, each region is either exporting or importing them, never both. But

The effect of this assumption is to ensure that the price of agricultural output and, hence, the earnings of each peasant are the same in both regions. We shall use this common agricultural price/wage rate as numeraire. Second, transportation costs for manufactured goods will be assumed to take Samuelson's "iceberg" form, in which transport costs are incurred in the good transported. Specifically, of each unit of manufactures shipped from one region to the other, only a fraction $\tau < 1$ arrives. This fraction τ, which is an inverse index of transportation costs, is the final parameter determining whether regions converge or diverge.

We can now turn to the behavior of firms. Suppose that there are a large number of manufacturing firms, each producing a single product. Then given the definition of the manufacturing aggregate (2) and the assumption of iceberg transport costs, the elasticity of demand facing any individual firm is σ (see Krugman 1980). The profit-maximizing pricing behavior of a representative firm in region 1 is therefore to set a price equal to

$$p_1 = \left(\frac{\sigma}{\sigma - 1}\right)\beta w_1, \tag{5}$$

where w_1 is the wage rate of workers in region 1; a similar equation applies in region 2. Comparing the prices of representative products, we have

$$\frac{p_1}{p_2} = \frac{w_1}{w_2}. \tag{6}$$

If there is free entry of firms into manufacturing, profits must be driven to zero. Thus it must be true that

$$(p_1 - \beta w_1)x_1 = \alpha w_1, \tag{7}$$

which implies

$$x_1 = x_2 = \frac{\alpha(\sigma - 1)}{\beta}. \tag{8}$$

That is, output per firm is the same in each region, irrespective of wage rates, relative demand, and so forth. This has the useful implication that the number of manufactured goods produced in each region

if agricultural goods are costly to transport, this would introduce a "cliff" at the point at which the two regions have equal numbers of workers and thus at which neither had to import food. This is evidently an artifact of the two-region case: if peasants were spread uniformly across a featureless plain, there would be no discontinuity.

is proportional to the number of workers, so that

$$\frac{n_1}{n_2} = \frac{L_1}{L_2}. \tag{9}$$

It should be noted that in zero-profit equilibrium, $\sigma/(\sigma - 1)$ is the ratio of the marginal product of labor to its average product, that is, the degree of economies of scale. Thus although σ is a parameter of tastes rather than technology, it can be interpreted as an inverse index of equilibrium economies of scale.

I have now laid out the basic structure of the model. The next step is to turn to the determination of equilibrium.

III. Short-Run and Long-Run Equilibrium

This model lacks any explicit dynamics. However, it is useful to have a concept of short-run equilibrium before we turn to full equilibrium. Short-run equilibrium will be defined in a Marshallian way, as an equilibrium in which the allocation of workers between regions may be taken as given. We then suppose that workers move toward the region that offers them higher real wages, leading to either convergence between regions as they move toward equality of worker/peasant ratios or divergence as the workers all congregate in one region.

To analyze short-run equilibrium, we begin by looking at the demand within each region for products of the two regions. Let c_{11} be the consumption in region 1 of a representative region 1 product, and c_{12} be the consumption in region 1 of a representative region 2 product. The price of a local product is simply its free on board price p_1; the price of a product from the other region, however, is its transport cost–inclusive price p_2/τ. Thus the relative demand for representative products is

$$\frac{c_{11}}{c_{12}} = \left(\frac{p_1\tau}{p_2}\right)^{-\sigma} = \left(\frac{w_1\tau}{w_2}\right)^{-\sigma}. \tag{10}$$

Define z_{11} as the ratio of region 1 *expenditure* on local manufactures to that on manufactures from the other region. Two points should be noted about z. First, a 1 percent rise in the relative price of region 1 goods, while reducing the relative *quantity* sold by σ percent, will reduce the *value* by only $\sigma - 1$ percent because of the valuation effect. Second, the more goods produced in region 1, the higher their share of expenditure for any given relative price. Thus

$$z_{11} = \left(\frac{n_1}{n_2}\right)\left(\frac{p_1\tau}{p_2}\right)\left(\frac{c_{11}}{c_{12}}\right) = \left(\frac{L_1}{L_2}\right)\left(\frac{w_1\tau}{w_2}\right)^{-(\sigma-1)}. \tag{11}$$

Similarly, the ratio of region 2 spending on region 1 products to spending on local products is

$$z_{12} = \left(\frac{L_1}{L_2}\right)\left(\frac{w_1}{w_2\tau}\right)^{-(\sigma-1)}. \tag{12}$$

The total income of region 1 workers is equal to the total spending on these products in both regions. (Transportation costs are included because they are assumed to be incurred in the goods themselves.) Let Y_1 and Y_2 be the regional incomes (including the wages of peasants). Then the income of region 1 workers is

$$w_1L_1 = \mu\left[\left(\frac{z_{11}}{1+z_{11}}\right)Y_1 + \left(\frac{z_{12}}{1+z_{12}}\right)Y_2\right], \tag{13}$$

and the income of region 2 workers is

$$w_2L_2 = \mu\left[\left(\frac{1}{1+z_{11}}\right)Y_1 + \left(\frac{1}{1+z_{12}}\right)Y_2\right]. \tag{14}$$

The incomes of the two regions, however, depend on the distribution of workers and their wages. Recalling that the wage rate of peasants is the numeraire, we have

$$Y_1 = \frac{1-\mu}{2} + w_1L_1 \tag{15}$$

and

$$Y_2 = \frac{1-\mu}{2} + w_2L_2. \tag{16}$$

The set of equations (11)–(16) may be regarded as a system that determines w_1 and w_2 (as well as four other variables) given the distribution of labor between regions 1 and 2. By inspection, one can see that if $L_1 = L_2$, $w_1 = w_2$. If labor is then shifted to region 1, however, the relative wage rate w_1/w_2 can move either way. The reason is that there are two opposing effects. On one side, there is the "home market effect": other things equal, the wage rate will tend to be higher in the larger market (see Krugman 1980). On the other side, there is the extent of competition: workers in the region with the smaller manufacturing labor force will face less competition for the local peasant market than those in the more populous region. In other words, there is a trade-off between proximity to the larger market and lack of competition for the local market.

As we move from short-run to long-run equilibrium, however, a third consideration enters the picture. Workers are interested not in nominal wages but in real wages, and workers in the region with the larger population will face a lower price for manufactured goods. Let $f = L_1/\mu$, the share of the manufacturing labor force in region 1. Then the true price index of manufactured goods for consumers residing in region 1 is

$$P_1 = \left[f w_1^{-(\sigma-1)} + (1-f)\left(\frac{w_2}{\tau}\right)^{-(\sigma-1)} \right]^{-1/(\sigma-1)}; \qquad (17)$$

that for consumers residing in region 2 is

$$P_2 = \left[f\left(\frac{w_1}{\tau}\right)^{-(\sigma-1)} + (1-f) w_2^{-(\sigma-1)} \right]^{-1/(\sigma-1)}. \qquad (18)$$

The real wages of workers in each region are

$$\omega_1 = w_1 P_1^{-\mu} \qquad (19)$$

and

$$\omega_2 = w_2 P_2^{-\mu}. \qquad (20)$$

From (17) and (18), it is apparent that if wage rates in the two regions are equal, a shift of workers from region 2 to region 1 will lower the price index in region 1 and raise it in region 2 and, thus, raise real wages in region 1 relative to those in region 2. This therefore adds an additional reason for divergence.

We may now ask the crucial question: How does ω_1/ω_2 vary with f? We know by symmetry that when $f = \frac{1}{2}$, that is, when the two regions have equal numbers of workers, they offer equal real wage rates. But is this a stable equilibrium? It will be if ω_1/ω_2 decreases with f, for in that case whenever one region has a larger work force than the other, workers will tend to migrate out of that region. In this case we shall get regional convergence. On the other hand, if ω_1/ω_2 *increases* with f, workers will tend to migrate *into* the region that already has more workers, and we shall get regional divergence.[3] As we have seen, there are two forces working toward

[3] This description of dynamics actually oversimplifies in two ways. First, it implicitly assumes that ω_1/ω_2 is a monotonic function of f, or at least that it crosses one only once. In principle, this need not be the case, and there could be several stable equilibria in which both regions have nonzero manufacturing production. I have not been able to rule this out analytically, although it turns out not to be true for the numerical example considered below. The analytical discussion in the next section simply bypasses the question. Second, a dynamic story should take expectations into account. It is possible that workers may migrate into the region that initially has fewer workers because they expect other workers to do the same. This kind of self-fulfilling prophecy can occur, however, only if adjustment is rapid and discount rates are not too high. See Krugman (1991) for an analysis.

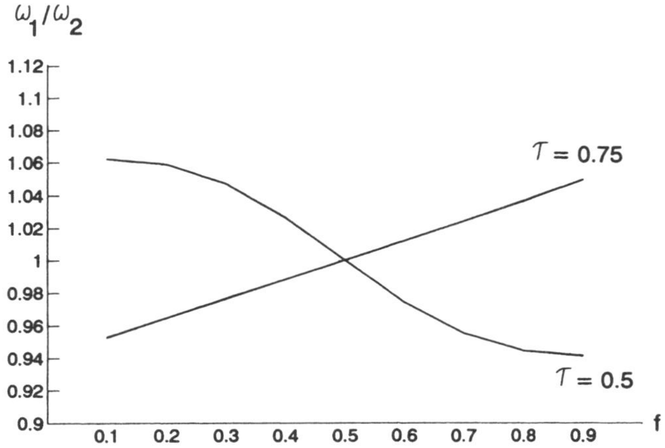

FIG. 1

divergence—the home market effect and the price index effect—and one working toward convergence, the degree of competition for the local peasant market. The question is which forces dominate.

In principle, it is possible simply to solve our model for real wages as a function of f. This is, however, difficult to do analytically. In the next section an alternative approach is used to characterize the model's behavior. For now, however, let us simply note that there are only three parameters in this model that cannot be eliminated by choice of units: the share of expenditure on manufactured goods, μ; the elasticity of substitution among products, σ; and the fraction of a good shipped that arrives, τ. The model can be quite easily solved numerically for a variety of parameters. Thus it is straightforward to show that depending on the parameter values we may have either regional convergence or regional divergence.

Figure 1 makes the point. It shows computed values of ω_1/ω_2 as a function of f in two different cases. In both cases we assume $\sigma = 4$ and $\mu = .3$. In one case, however, $\tau = .5$ (high transportation costs); in the other, $\tau = .75$ (low transportation costs). In the high-transport-cost case, the relative real wage declines as f rises. Thus in this case we would expect to see regional convergence, with the geographical distribution of the manufacturing following that of agriculture. In the low-transport-cost case, however, the slope is reversed; thus we would expect to see regional divergence.

It is possible to proceed entirely numerically from this point. If we take a somewhat different approach, however, it is possible to characterize the properties of the model analytically.

IV. Necessary Conditions for Manufacturing Concentration

Instead of asking whether an equilibrium in which workers are distributed equally between the regions is stable, this section asks whether a situation in which all workers are concentrated in one region is an equilibrium. This is not exactly the same question: as noted above, it is possible both that regional divergence might not lead to complete concentration and that there may exist stable interior equilibria even if concentration is also an equilibrium. The questions are, however, closely related, and this one is easier to answer.

Consider a situation in which all workers are concentrated in region 1 (the choice of region of course is arbitrary). Region 1 will then constitute a larger market than region 2. Since a share of total income μ is spent on manufactures and all this income goes to region 1, we have

$$\frac{Y_2}{Y_1} = \frac{1 - \mu}{1 + \mu}. \tag{21}$$

Let n be the total number of manufacturing firms; then each firm will have a *value* of sales equal to

$$V_1 = \left(\frac{\mu}{n}\right)(Y_1 + Y_2), \tag{22}$$

which is just enough to allow each firm to make zero profits.

Now we ask: Is it possible for an individual firm to commence production profitably in region 2? (I shall refer to such a hypothetical firm as a "defecting" firm.) If not, then concentration of production in region 1 is an equilibrium; if so, it is not.

In order to produce in region 2, a firm must be able to attract workers. To do so, it must compensate them for the fact that all manufactures (except its own infinitesimal contribution) must be imported; thus we must have

$$\frac{w_2}{w_1} = \left(\frac{1}{\tau}\right)^{\mu}. \tag{23}$$

Given this higher wage, the firm will charge a profit-maximizing price that is higher than that of other firms in the same proportion. We can use this fact to derive the value of the firm's sales. In region 1, the defecting firm's value of sales will be the value of sales of a representative firm times $(w_2/w_1\tau)^{-(\sigma-1)}$. In region 2, its value of sales will be that of a representative firm times $(w_2\tau/w_1)^{-(\sigma-1)}$, so the total value of the defecting firm's sales will be

$$V_2 = \left(\frac{\mu}{n}\right)\left[\left(\frac{w_2}{w_1\tau}\right)^{-(\sigma-1)} Y_1 + \left(\frac{w_2\tau}{w_1}\right)^{-(\sigma-1)} Y_2\right]. \tag{24}$$

Notice that transportation costs work to the firm's disadvantage in its sales to region 1 consumers but work to its advantage in sales to region 2 consumers (because other firms must pay them but it does not).

From (22), (23), and (24) we can (after some manipulation) derive the ratio of the value of sales by this defecting firm to the sales of firms in region 1:

$$\frac{V_2}{V_1} = \tfrac{1}{2}\tau^{\mu(\sigma-1)}[(1+\mu)\tau^{\sigma-1} + (1-\mu)\tau^{-(\sigma-1)}]. \tag{25}$$

One might think that it is profitable for a firm to defect as long as $V_2/V_1 > 1$, since firms will collect a constant fraction of any sales as a markup over marginal costs. This is not quite right, however, because fixed costs are also higher in region 2 because of the higher wage rate. So we must have $V_2/V_1 > w_2/w_1 = \tau^{-\mu}$. We must therefore define a new variable,

$$\nu = \tfrac{1}{2}\tau^{\mu\sigma}[(1+\mu)\tau^{\sigma-1} + (1-\mu)\tau^{-(\sigma-1)}]. \tag{26}$$

When $\nu < 1$, it is unprofitable for a firm to begin production in region 2 if all other manufacturing production is concentrated in region 1. Thus in this case concentration of manufactures production in one region is an equilibrium; if $\nu > 1$, it is not.

Equation (26) at first appears to be a fairly unpromising subject for analytical results. However, it yields to careful analysis.

First note what we want to do with (26). It defines a *boundary:* a set of critical parameter values that mark the division between concentration and nonconcentration. So we need to evaluate it only in the vicinity of $\nu = 1$, asking how each of the three parameters must change in order to offset a change in either of the others.

Let us begin, then, with the most straightforward of the parameters, μ. We find that

$$\frac{\partial \nu}{\partial \mu} = \nu\sigma(\ln \tau) + \tfrac{1}{2}\tau^{\sigma\mu}[\tau^{\sigma-1} - \tau^{-(\sigma-1)}] < 0. \tag{27}$$

That is, the larger the share of income spent on manufactured goods, the lower the relative sales of the defecting firm. This takes place for two reasons. First, workers demand a larger wage premium in order to move to the second region; this "forward linkage" effect is reflected

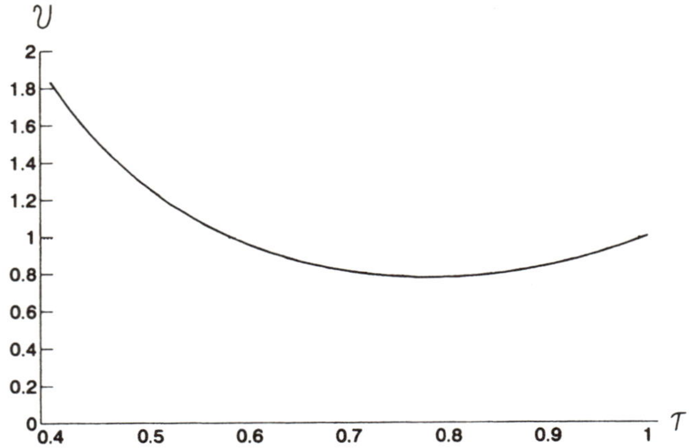

FIG. 2

in the first term. Second, the larger the share of expenditure on manufactures, the larger the relative size of the region 1 market and hence the stronger the home market effect. This "backward linkage" is reflected in the second term in (27).

Next we turn to transportation costs. From inspection of (26), we first note that when $\tau = 1$, $\nu = 1$; that is, when transport costs are zero, location is irrelevant (no surprise!). Second, we note that when τ is small, ν approaches $(1 - \mu)\tau^{1-\sigma(1-\mu)}$. Unless σ is very small or μ very large, this must exceed one for sufficiently small τ (the economics of the alternative case will be apparent shortly). Finally, we evaluate $\partial\nu/\partial\tau$:

$$\frac{\partial \nu}{\partial \tau} = \frac{\mu\sigma\nu}{\tau} + \frac{\tau^{\mu\sigma}(\sigma - 1)[(1 + \mu)\tau^{\sigma-1} - (1 - \mu)\tau^{-(\sigma-1)}]}{2\tau}. \qquad (28)$$

For τ close to one, the second term in (28) approaches $\mu(\sigma - 1) > 0$; since the first term is always positive, $\partial\nu/\partial\tau > 0$ for τ near one.

Taken together, these observations indicate a shape for ν as a function of τ that looks like figure 2 (which represents an actual calculation for $\mu = .3$, $\sigma = 4$): at low levels of τ (i.e., high transportation costs), ν exceeds one and it is profitable to defect. At some critical value of τ, ν falls below one and concentrated manufacturing is an equilibrium, and the relative value of sales then approaches one from below.

The important point from this picture is that at the critical value of τ that corresponds to the boundary between concentration and nonconcentration, $\partial\nu/\partial\tau$ is negative. That is, higher transportation costs militate against regional divergence.

We can also now interpret the case in which $\sigma(1 - \mu) < 1$, so that $\nu < 1$ even at arbitrarily low τ. This is a case in which economies of scale are so large (small σ) or the share of manufacturing in expenditure is so high (high μ) that it is unprofitable to start a firm in region 2 no matter how high transport costs are.

Finally, we calculate $\partial\nu/\partial\sigma$:

$$\begin{aligned}\frac{\partial\nu}{\partial\sigma} &= \ln(\tau)\{\mu\nu + \tfrac{1}{2}\tau^{\mu\sigma}[(1+\mu)\tau^{\sigma-1} - (1-\mu)\tau^{-(\sigma-1)}]\} \\ &= \ln(\tau)\left(\frac{\tau}{\sigma}\right)\left(\frac{\partial\nu}{\partial\tau}\right).\end{aligned} \tag{29}$$

Since we have just seen that $\partial\nu/\partial\tau$ is negative at the relevant point, this implies that $\partial\nu/\partial\sigma$ is positive. That is, a higher elasticity of substitution (which also implies smaller economies of scale in equilibrium) works against regional divergence.

The implications of these results can be seen diagrammatically. Holding σ constant, we can draw a boundary in μ, τ space. This boundary marks parameter values at which firms are just indifferent between staying in a region 1 concentration and defecting. An economy that lies inside this boundary will not develop concentrations of industry in one or the other region; an economy that lies outside the boundary will. The slope of the boundary is

$$\frac{\partial\tau}{\partial\mu} = -\frac{\partial\nu/\partial\mu}{\partial\nu/\partial\tau} < 0.$$

If we instead hold μ constant and consider changing σ, we find

$$\frac{\partial\tau}{\partial\sigma} = -\frac{\partial\nu/\partial\sigma}{\partial\nu/\partial\tau} > 0.$$

Thus an increase in σ will shift the boundary in μ, τ space outward.

Figure 3 shows calculated boundaries in μ, τ space for two values of σ, 4 and 10. The figure tells a simple story that is precisely the intuitive story given in Section I. In an economy characterized by high transportation costs, a small share of footloose manufacturing, or weak economies of scale, the distribution of manufacturing production will be determined by the distribution of the "primary stratum" of peasants. With lower transportation costs, a higher manufacturing share, or stronger economies of scale, circular causation sets in, and manufacturing will concentrate in whichever region gets a head start.

What is particularly nice about this result is that it requires no appeal to elusive concepts such as pure technological externalities: the external economies are pecuniary, arising from the desirability of selling to and buying from a region in which other producers are

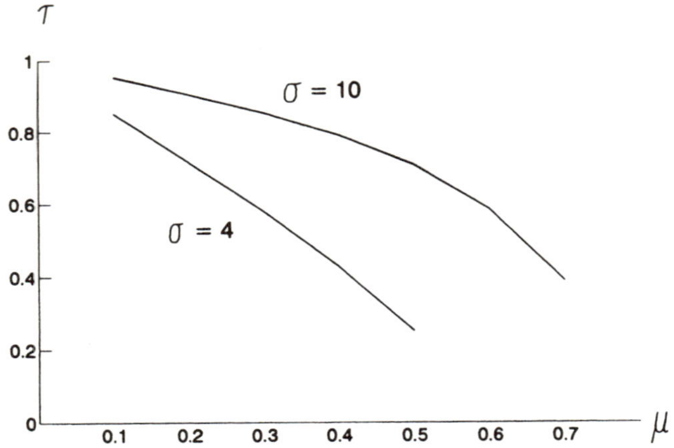

FIG. 3

concentrated. It also involves no arbitrary assumptions about the geographical extent of external economies: distance enters naturally via transportation costs, and in no other way. The behavior of the model depends on "observable" features of the tastes of individuals and the technology of firms; the interesting dynamics arise from interaction effects.

Obviously this is a vastly oversimplified model even of the core-periphery issue, and it says nothing about the localization of particular industries. The model does illustrate, however, how tools drawn from industrial organization theory can help to formalize and sharpen the insights of a much-neglected field. Thus I hope that this paper will be a stimulus to a revival of research into regional economics and economic geography.

References

Arthur, W. Brian. "Competing Technologies, Increasing Returns, and Lock-in by Historical Events." *Econ. J.* 99 (March 1989): 116–31.

———. "Positive Feedbacks in the Economy." *Scientific American* 262 (February 1990): 92–99.

Christaller, Walter. *Central Places in Southern Germany.* Jena: Fischer, 1933. English translation by Carlisle W. Baskin. London: Prentice-Hall, 1966.

David, Paul. "The Marshallian Dynamics of Industrialization: Chicago, 1850–1890." *J. Urban Econ.* (in press).

Dixit, Avinash K., and Stiglitz, Joseph E. "Monopolistic Competition and Optimum Product Diversity." *A.E.R.* 67 (June 1977): 297–308.

Hirschman, Albert O. *The Strategy of Economic Development.* New Haven, Conn.: Yale Univ. Press, 1958.

Hoover, Edgar M. *The Location of Economic Activity.* New York: McGraw-Hill, 1948.

Krugman, Paul. "Scale Economies, Product Differentiation, and the Pattern of Trade." *A.E.R.* 70 (December 1980): 950–59.

———. "Intraindustry Specialization and the Gains from Trade." *J.P.E* 89 (October 1981): 959–73.

———. "History versus Expectations." *Q.J.E.* 106 (May 1991).

Lösch, August. *The Economics of Location.* Jena: Fischer, 1940. English translation. New Haven, Conn.: Yale Univ. Press, 1954.

Murphy, Kevin M.; Shleifer, Andrei; and Vishny, Robert W. "Income Distribution, Market Size, and Industrialization." *Q.J.E.* 104 (August 1989): 537–64. (*a*)

———. "Industrialization and the Big Push." *J.P.E* 97 (October 1989): 1003–26. (*b*)

Meyer, David R. "Emergence of the American Manufacturing Belt: An Interpretation." *J. Hist. Geography* 9, no. 2 (1983): 145–74.

Myrdal, Gunnar. *Economic Theory and Under-developed Regions.* London: Duckworth, 1957.

Pred, Allan R. *The Spatial Dynamics of U.S. Urban-Industrial Growth, 1800–1914: Interpretive and Theoretical Essays.* Cambridge, Mass.: MIT Press, 1966.

von Thünen, Johann Heinrich. *The Isolated State.* Hamburg: Perthes, 1826. English translation. Oxford: Pergamon, 1966.

[22]

Journal of Economic Literature
Vol. XXXIX (June 2001) pp. 536–561

Of Hype and Hyperbolas: Introducing the New Economic Geography[1]

J. PETER NEARY[2]

1. *Introduction*

NEW ECONOMIC geography has come of age. Launched by Paul Krugman in a 1991 *JPE* paper, extended in a series of articles by Krugman, Masahisa Fujita, Tony Venables and a growing band of associates, recently institutionalized with the appearance of a new journal, it has now been comprehensively synthesized between hard covers[3] in *The Spatial Economy* by Fujita, Krugman, and Venables (henceforward "FKV").

Such rapid progress would make anyone dizzy, and at times the authors risk getting carried away with their heady prose style. They find the predictions of one model so plausible that they call it "History of the World, Part I" (p. 253); they describe the pattern of world industrialization implied by another as "a story of breathtaking scope" (p. 277); and on his website Krugman expresses the hope that economic geography will one day become as important a field as international trade. This sort of hype, even if tongue-in-cheek, is not to everyone's taste, especially when the results rely on special functional forms and all too often can only be derived by numerical methods. What next, the unconvinced reader may be tempted to ask. The tee-shirt? The movie?

In this paper I argue that, despite the hype, there is interesting work here which deserves to be better known. The key contribution of the new economic geography is a framework in which standard building blocks of mainstream economics (especially rational decision making and simple general equilibrium models) are used to model the trade-off between dispersal and agglomeration, or centrifugal and centripetal forces. The approach thus gives a choice-theoretic basis for a "propensity to agglomerate"—only a propensity, since agglomeration is a possible outcome but not an inevitable one.

[1] Masahisa Fujita, Paul Krugman, and Anthony J. Venables (1999): *The Spatial Economy: Cities, Regions, and International Trade*. Cambridge Mass.: MIT Press, pp. xiii + 367. ISBN 0-262-06204-6.

[2] University College Dublin and CEPR. Some of the ideas below were presented at a seminar in Leuven and at conferences in Bergen, Geneva, and Royaumont. I am very grateful to participants on these occasions and to Mary Amiti, Richard Baldwin, Frédéric Robert-Nicoud, Gianmarco Ottaviano, Jacques Thisse, Tony Venables, the editor and two anonymous referees for comments. This paper was written while I was visiting the Laboratoire d'Econometrie of the Ecole Polytechnique, Paris, and it forms part of the Globalisation Programme of the Centre for Economic Performance at LSE, funded by the UK ESRC.

[3] The first issue of the *Journal of Economic Geography*, published by Oxford University Press, and with an editorial board representing both "old" and "new" approaches, appeared in January 2001. Ottaviano and Diego Puga (1998) and Fujita and Thisse (2000) provide overviews of the field.

I begin with exposition. In section 2, I try to show that the basic new economic geography model is much simpler than most presentations suggest. I use a simple diagram to illustrate how the model works, and give a self-contained algebraic derivation of the main results (with technical details in appendices). But that in turn suggests that for some purposes the model may be too simple. In section 4, I argue that it is, and try to disentangle which lessons are wedded to the special functional forms typically used and which are of more generality. In between, section 3 highlights some of the novel insights that come from applying the model to topics in regional economics, urban economics, and international trade. In section 5, I discuss how much is new in the new economic geography, and finally, in section 6, I comment on policy implications and empirical tests.

2. *The Core of the Core-Periphery Model*

Like so much recent work in a variety of fields, the underlying model in most of the new economic geography is one of Chamberlinian monopolistic competition, parameterized using the symmetric constant-elasticity-of-substitution utility function of Avinash Dixit and Joseph Stiglitz (1977). As the authors disarmingly admit, the book "sometimes looks as if it should be entitled *Games You Can Play with CES Functions*"! But these are not everyone's idea of games. The authors have made a huge effort to expound the model clearly, but even they cannot prevent the calculations from degenerating at times into a near-impenetrable soup of CES algebra. All the more reason then to try and present the main ideas in a simple diagram. In this section, I first illustrate equilibrium in a closed economy, and then extend it to take account of transport costs, factor mobility, and intermediate inputs.

2.1 *Equilibrium à la Chamberlin-Dixit-Stiglitz*

Start with a closed economy, or, more in the spirit of the book, a world in which all economic activity is concentrated at a single point. There are two sectors. Agriculture is perfectly competitive and produces a homogeneous good under constant returns to scale. Manufacturing is monopolistically competitive and produces many varieties under increasing returns to scale. Each sector uses a single factor specific to it: farmers in agriculture, workers in manufacturing. Aggregate utility is a Cobb-Douglas function of agricultural output A and of a CES sub-utility function M derived from consuming manufactures:

$$U = M^{\mu}A^{1-\mu}, \quad M^{\frac{\sigma-1}{\sigma}} = \sum_{i}^{n} m_i^{\frac{\sigma-1}{\sigma}} \qquad (1)$$

where m_i is the amount of each variety of the manufactured good demanded and σ (which must exceed one) is the elasticity of substitution between varieties.[4] From (1), μ is the share of nominal income Y spent on manufactures. This in turn is allocated between individual varieties according to demand functions which are log-linear in own price p_i and in total spending on manufactures μY, both deflated by a manufacturing price index P:[5]

[4] I follow FKV's notation for the most part, though with some simplifications. Here I assume a finite number of firms, which makes the equations a bit neater at the cost of some hand-waving: I need to assume that the number of firms is sufficiently large that the integer constraint is not binding. This seems reasonable, and is standard in the literature, though see some intriguing speculative comments on the role of integer constraints on page 223.

[5] P is the unit expenditure function dual to the sub-utility function M. Note that it is defined in terms of *negative* exponents (since σ must exceed one): a frequent source of confusion.

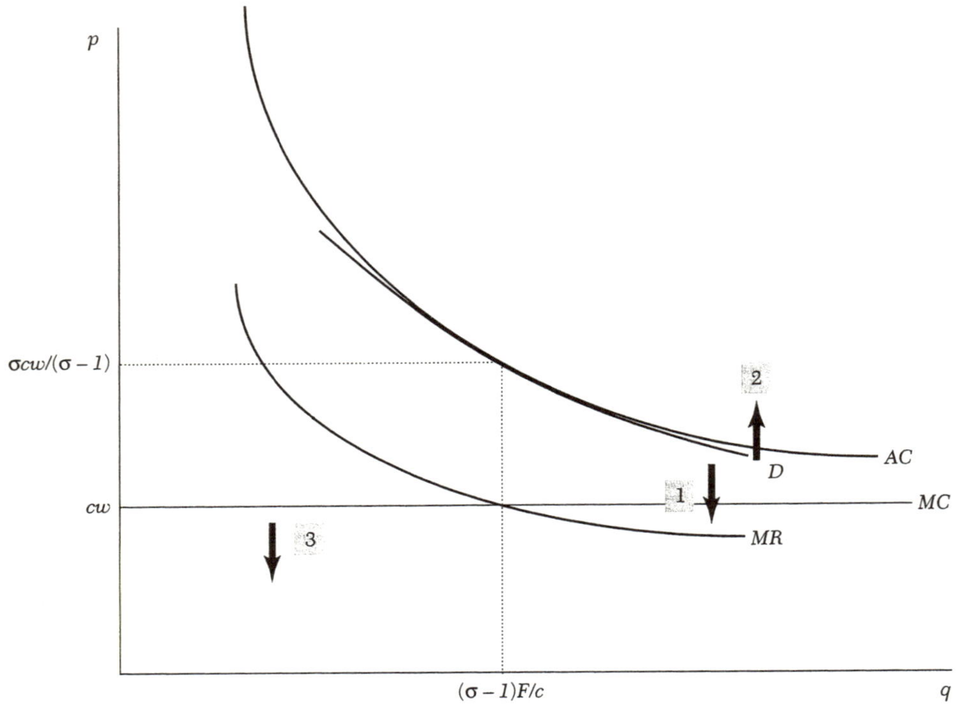

Figure 1. Chamberlin-Dixit-Stiglitz Equilibrium and Effects of Entry by a New Firm

$$m_i = \mu \left(\frac{P_i}{P}\right)^{-\sigma} \frac{Y}{P} \quad \text{where:} \quad P^{1-\sigma} = \sum_j^n p_j^{1-\sigma} \qquad (2)$$

Turn next to manufacturing firms. Because the manufacturing sub-utility function embodies a preference for diversity, and there are increasing returns to scale, each firm produces a distinct variety. Hence the number of firms, n, is also the number of varieties consumed, and firm output q_i equals the demand for that variety m_i. The typical firm therefore faces the demand function 2. However, a key feature of the Dixit-Stiglitz approach is that firms ignore the effects of their actions on income Y and on the industry price index P. Hence the demand curve perceived by the typical firm is not 2 but rather:

$$q = \phi p^{-\sigma} \quad \text{where:} \quad \phi = \mu Y P^{\sigma - 1} \qquad (3)$$

with the intercept ϕ assumed to be taken as given by the firm. Since all firms are identical, the subscript i can be suppressed. Marginal revenue $(d(pq)/dq)$ is then easily shown to be:

$$MR = \frac{\sigma - 1}{\sigma} p \qquad (4)$$

Equations (3) and (4) define two constant-elasticity curves in $\{p,q\}$ space, labelled D and MR respectively in figure 1. (Ignore the numbered arrows in the figure for now.)

The cost structure of a typical firm is even simpler. Workers are hired at a given wage w, fixed costs are Fw and variable costs per unit output are cw. Hence total costs are:

$$C = (F + cq)w \tag{5}$$

This implies a horizontal marginal cost curve at the level cw, and an average cost curve which is a rectangular hyperbola with respect to the vertical axis and the marginal cost curve. These curves are also illustrated in figure 1, labelled MC and AC respectively.

Equilibrium for the firm exhibits Chamberlin's tangency condition, as figure 1 shows. Moreover, the special functional forms imply very simple expressions for equilibrium price and output. From profit maximization, marginal revenue equals marginal cost:

$$\frac{\sigma - 1}{\sigma} p = cw \tag{6}$$

So the price-marginal-cost mark-up depends only on σ; while free entry drives profits to zero: $\pi = pq - (F + cq)w = 0$, which simplifies, using (6), to give the level of output:

$$q = (\sigma - 1)\frac{F}{c} \tag{7}$$

So the equilibrium output of each firm is totally independent of developments outside the industry: it depends only on the cost parameters F and c and on the elasticity of substitution σ. Changes in any other parameters or variables (including income Y and the wage rate w) lead to adjustments in industry output via changes in the number of firms only.[6]

[6] This adjustment mechanism can be written $\dot{n} = f(\pi)$, $f(0) = 0, f' > 0$. To test for local stability, totally differentiate π in the neighborhood of equilibrium: $d\pi = (pq/\sigma)\hat{q}$, where $\hat{q} \equiv dq/q$. Hence profits are monotonic in demand. When Y and w are given, q (and hence π) is decreasing in n from 3, so equilibrium is stable. Matters are different when Y and w are endogenous, as in section 2.3.

2.2 *Transport Costs and the Home-Market Effect*

So far, I have interpreted the model as a closed economy. However, everything said until now applies also to a multi-regional or multinational economy, provided we make the strong assumptions (not shocking to trade theorists, though possibly so to others) of identical tastes, identical technology, and no barriers to goods trade. Of these three assumptions the first and second are maintained throughout the book. The next step is to relax the third by introducing transport costs, modelled using the so-called "iceberg" assumption, that a constant fraction of output is lost in transportation. This seemingly innocuous change takes us from a world with equalized factor prices, whether under Ricardian (one-factor) assumptions as in Krugman (1979), or Heckscher-Ohlin (two-factor) assumptions as in Dixit and Victor Norman (1980, section 9.3), and Elhanan Helpman and Krugman (1985); and transports us to a world with international differences in goods and factor prices as in Krugman (1980).

So, switch to two countries, labelled "1" and "2" respectively. (In the relevant sections of the book they are called "regions"; more on this in section 4.) Assume that the cost of transporting a unit of manufactures in either direction is $T - 1$ times the producer price (which is also the price paid by consumers in the country of production); this amounts to assuming that, for every T units shipped, only one unit arrives. Agricultural goods by contrast incur no transport costs. (I return to this assumption in section 4.) How much of the preceding model must be changed? Perhaps surprisingly, the answer is that, apart from adding country subscripts to utility, wages and so on, only two equations need to be altered. First, the demand function 3 facing a typical firm located in country 1 must be extended to incorporate exports. A little manipulation gives:[7]

$$q_1 = \phi_1 p_1^{-\sigma} \quad \text{where:} \quad \phi_1 = \mu[Y_1 P_1^{\sigma-1} + Y_2 P_2^{\sigma-1} T^{1-\sigma}] \tag{8}$$

Total demand depends positively on the industry price index (P_1 and P_2) and on the level of manufacturing expenditure (μY_1 and μY_2) in both markets, and negatively on the level of trade costs T. Note, however, that firms are oblivious to all these complications: the perceived demand function is identical to 3. Herein lies the simplicity of iceberg transport costs. CES preferences yield log-linear demand functions. Adding log-linear transport costs changes the level but not the elasticity of the perceived demand functions.

The second equation that must be changed is that for the price index. In a closed-economy equilibrium, with all varieties selling for the same price, 2 simplifies to $P^{1-\sigma} = np^{1-\sigma}$. Matters are more complicated with two countries and transport costs, because the consumer prices of goods from different countries are not the same: the n_1 domestic varieties cost p_1, while the n_2 imported varieties cost p_2T. Hence the price index becomes:

$$P_1^{1-\sigma} = n_1 p_1^{1-\sigma} + n_2(p_2T)^{1-\sigma} \tag{9}$$

Since every firm sells in both markets, the price index is decreasing in the number of firms in both markets (because greater variety benefits consumers) and is increasing in trade costs.

[7] Since each firm produces a distinct variety, the demand which a typical country-1 firm faces in market s is identical to 2: $q_{1s} = \mu(p_{1s}/P_s)^{-\sigma}Y_s/P_s$, though with the proviso that p_{1s} equals the price paid by *consumers* in market s. This matters for exports, since $p_{12} = p_1T$ (where p_1 is the producer or mill price). In addition, this demand function gives the level of export *sales*, whereas we must gross up by transport costs to get export *shipments*: so total demand equals $q_1 = q_{11} + Tq_{12}$. Combining these expressions gives (8).

Equations (8) and (9), with the corresponding equations for country 2, define a sub-system that, for given demands Y_1 and Y_2 and given wages w_1 and w_2 (so from 6 prices are also given), determines the size of the manufacturing sector in both countries, n_1 and n_2, and the price indices P_1 and P_2. Inspecting the equations shows they share an important feature: provided transport costs are strictly positive ($T > 1$), the left-hand sides are more responsive to home than to foreign variables. This asymmetry has two useful implications, which are most easily seen by linearizing the model around the symmetric equilibrium (where $Y_1 = Y_2$, $n_1 = n_2$, etc.) and considering a small increase in the size of country 1 (so country subscripts can be dropped: $\hat{Y} = \hat{Y}_1 = -\hat{Y}_2$, $\hat{n} = \hat{n}_1 = -\hat{n}_2$, etc., where a circumflex denotes a proportional rate of change). Differentiating first equation (9) gives:

$$\hat{P} = -\frac{Z}{\sigma-1}\hat{n} + Z\hat{p}, \quad \text{where:} \quad Z \equiv \frac{1-T^{1-\sigma}}{1+T^{1-\sigma}} \tag{10}$$

Here Z is an index of transport costs, which ranges from zero to one. With wages and hence p fixed, equation (10) gives what FKV call the "price index effect": because imports incur transport costs but home-produced varieties do not, the cost of living is lower the larger the market. Next, differentiating (8) gives:

$$\hat{q} = Z[\hat{Y} + (\sigma-1)\hat{P}] - \sigma\hat{p} \tag{11}$$

If firm output and the price of each individual variety are fixed, an increase in demand can only be accommodated by a fall in the industry price index. From (10), this in turn requires an increase in the number of varieties: eliminating $\hat{P}$ from (10) and (11) gives:

$$\hat{n} = \frac{1}{Z}\hat{Y} \tag{12}$$

This gives what Krugman (1980) calls the "home-market effect": the country with higher demand has (since $Z < 1$) a proportionately larger share of manufacturing.

2.3 *Migration and Agglomeration*

The home-market effect is of independent interest since it predicts that countries with a larger home market tend to export manufactures.[8] This can be given a core-periphery interpretation, as in Krugman and Venables (1990): larger countries have a disproportionately larger share of manufacturing. However, by itself the home-market effect is only a prelude to a complete theory of economic geography. It assumes rather than explains international differences in incomes, since as yet there is no force pushing toward agglomeration in the model. Two such forces are considered in the book, international labor mobility (following Krugman 1991) and intermediate inputs (pioneered by Venables 1996 and developed by Krugman and Venables 1995). In this subsection, I concentrate on the former.

Assume therefore that the farmers who produce agricultural goods are country- as well as sector-specific, with equal numbers in each country. Hence (with no agricultural transport costs) the wage and the price of agricultural output can be set equal to unity everywhere. By contrast, the workers employed in manufacturing move internationally in response to differences in real wages (ω_s in country s, equal to nominal wages w_s deflated by the consumer price index P_s^μ). Note that the relevant price index is the local one: workers consume only in the country where they are employed.

We are finally ready to address the central theoretical question in the new economic geography: when will the equilibrium exhibit diversification, with manufacturing produced in both countries, and when will it exhibit agglomeration in one country, or a "core-periphery" pattern? These are actually two distinct questions, since it turns out that equilibrium is not unique for all parameter values. To answer them, consider in turn the local stability of diversified and agglomerated equilibria. Assume that workers migrate rapidly between countries in response to differences in real wages and that manufacturing firms enter or leave the industry sluggishly in response to profits or losses.[9]

[8] The effect has also been shown to hold in some though not all other models. See Head, Mayer, and Ries (1999).

[9] A digression on dynamics. Following Krugman (1991), FKV test equilibria for stability by asking how migration by a single worker affects relative real wages. If they end up higher in the host country, then further migration is encouraged and the initial equilibrium is unstable. This heuristic argument is equivalent to testing for local stability a dynamic adjustment mechanism, whereby migration is driven by the real-wage ratio. Two comments are in order. First, this adjustment mechanism assumes that firms are always in equilibrium; i.e., that entry and exit of firms occurs infinitely faster than migration. Reversing these assumptions, as in Puga (1999), does not affect the stability conclusions. I follow Puga's approach here since it can be more easily related to figure 1 and since (unlike FKV's approach) it applies with minimal modifications to the intermediate-goods model of section 2.4. Second, both these dynamic adjustment mechanisms are myopic: migrating workers or newly entering firms consider only current returns (relative real wages or relative profits) in making their decisions. FKV justify such nonrational expectations by appealing, rather unsatisfactorily, to the "replicator dynamics" of evolutionary game theory. (See pp. 7–8 and p. 77, footnote 2: "our model can, if one likes, be regarded as an evolutionary game.") I prefer a more robust defense. Just as in the comparison between Neary (1978) and Michael Mussa (1978), replacing *ad hoc* with forward-looking dynamics leads to greater elegance and a more satisfactory basis for normative analysis. However, it makes no difference to positive comparative-statics predictions. This has been demonstrated formally for the internationally mobile labor variant of the core-periphery model by Richard Baldwin (1999b).

Take first the case where the world economy is in a symmetric diversified equilibrium, and go through the following thought experiment. Assume that a single new manufacturing firm enters in country 1 (and, for symmetry, a single firm exits in country 2) and ask how this affects the incentives for further entry or exit. If profits in country 1 (which are initially zero) fall relative to country 2, the diversified equilibrium is stable: the new firm is encouraged to exit and the initial equilibrium is restored. However, if relative profits in country 1 rise, the initial equilibrium is unstable. More firms are encouraged to enter and the world economy moves towards an equilibrium with agglomeration: more than half of world manufacturing locates in country 1.

There are three effects of entry, indicated by the numbered arrows in figure 1. The first arises from the price-index effect: an extra firm lowers the industry price index, which reduces the demand facing each existing firm. In figure 1, the demand and marginal revenue curves shift downward, as indicated by the arrow numbered "1." This competition effect reduces profits and so encourages stability of the diversified equilibrium. By contrast, the two other effects raise profits and so encourage instability and a tendency towards agglomeration.

The second effect is a *demand* or *backward* linkage. An extra firm raises the demand for labor in country 1. This puts incipient upward pressure on local wages, which encourages foreign workers to migrate. The new workers in turn raise demand for local varieties. The demand and marginal revenue curves shift upwards in figure 1, as indicated by the arrow numbered "2," and this tends to *raise* profitability.

It is easy to see which of these two effects dominates, if we assume provisionally that nominal wages do not change. From (10) and (11), the stabilizing competition effect depends on Z: when transport costs are higher, a reallocation of firms has a greater impact in lowering the price level and raising competition in the expanding country. As for the demand linkage, consider the effects of entry on country 1's labor market. Supply is L, and demand is $n(F + cq)$, so from (7) the labor-market equilibrium condition is:

$$L = n\sigma F \tag{13}$$

(Once again, country subscripts can be dropped since we are linearizing around a symmetric equilibrium: whatever goes up in country 1 must come down in country 2.) If equilibrium is to be maintained, entry of new firms must be matched by an equi-proportionate increase in the labor force. To see how this affects demand, consider its effect on national income. With the number of farmers fixed and their wage constant by choice of numeraire, the proportional change in national income equals the changes in the manufacturing wage and labor force, times the share of the sector in GNP, μ:[10]

$$\hat{Y} = \mu(\hat{w} + \hat{L}) \tag{14}$$

Hence, with w fixed, the magnitude of the demand linkage depends on μ. Returning to 11, the demand linkage dominates the competition effect at the initial wage, so entry by a new firm raises the demand facing all existing firms, if and only if μ is greater than Z. When this condition holds the initial diversified

[10] Since the initial equilibrium is symmetric, there is no inter-industry trade. Hence the share of manufacturing in each country's GNP equals its share in consumption, μ. Note that this has nothing to do with choice of units. Following Krugman (1991), FKV choose units such that the world labor force equals μ and the world supply of farmers equals $1-\mu$. But this is not needed to prove any of the results that follow, and I find it distracting. I comment on other choices of units in section 4.

equilibrium is unstable: agglomeration is more likely when the share of manufacturing in national income is high and when transport costs are low.

However, this condition ($\mu > Z$) underestimates the pressure towards agglomeration, because migration is driven by differentials in *real* rather than nominal wages. As we have seen, entry by a new firm lowers the price index in country 1. But this induces a third effect, since it reduces the cost of living for workers and so tends to raise real wages in country 1. The resulting migration restores international equality of real wages, which means that the nominal wage must fall. The result is a *cost* or *forward* linkage which shifts the average and marginal cost curves downwards in figure 1, as indicated by the arrow numbered "3," and so *raises* profitability further.

Deriving a necessary and sufficient condition for stability of the diversified equilibrium requires combining the three effects explicitly, and is best left to the appendix. However, it is fairly easy to see how stability is affected by changes in the three key parameters, T, μ, and σ. Higher transport costs T always encourage stability. For sufficiently high T, imports are so expensive that home production is always profitable;[11] while for sufficiently low T, diversification is always unstable since the countries are *ex ante* identical (neither has a comparative advantage). Somewhere in between is a threshold level of trade costs T^B, the "break" point, at which the diversified equilibrium is on the brink of instability. (Such a threshold must exist provided there is some incentive for agglomeration, which means, provided μ is strictly positive.) A convenient way to summarize the results is to consider how T^B varies with the other parameters. As shown in the appendix:

Proposition 1: T^B is increasing in μ and decreasing in σ.

The threshold value T^B must be increasing in μ since both potentially destabilizing effects are more important the greater is μ. First, the greater the share of manufactures in national income, the greater the demand linkage whereby entry by a new firm induces migration which raises demand and hence encourages further entry (in older times this would have been called a "bootstraps" effect) hence the larger the range of trade costs at which diversification is not an equilibrium. Second, the greater the budget share of manufactures, the greater is the cost linkage whereby entry by a new firm lowers the cost of living and so encourages further migration and entry. Finally, the threshold value of T is negatively related to σ, the elasticity of substitution in demand. Higher σ means that consumers view different varieties as closer substitutes. Such a reduced preference for diversity leads to an equilibrium with fewer varieties and a higher output of each. (Recall equation 7.) As a result, both countries are more likely to hold on to some production at low trade costs.

Transport costs lower than the break level T^B are sufficient for the existence of an agglomerated equilibrium. Are they necessary? To show that the answer is "no," consider a different thought experiment. Assume that the world economy initially exhibits a core-periphery

[11] Actually, this is an assumption rather than an intrinsic property of the model. When Z equals one, the numerator of equation (22) in the appendix equals $-(\sigma - 1 - \sigma\mu)(1 - \mu)$. Hence, if $\sigma - 1 < \sigma\mu$, the diversified equilibrium is unstable even when Z is one (transport costs are infinite, so the economies are closed). It makes sense to rule out this possibility, where the propensity to agglomerate is always one. So we assume that the preference for diversity and/or the budget share of manufactures are sufficiently low to ensure that $\sigma - 1 > \sigma\mu$. FKV call this the "no-black-hole" condition.

pattern and ask whether there are incentives for a firm to deviate from it. Assuming (arbitrarily) that manufacturing is agglomerated in country 1, can a firm earn positive profits by entering in country 2?

We can answer this question heuristically by referring again to figure 1, this time with all three arrows *reversed*. Assume that the initial equilibrium illustrated is that in the core (country 1) and ask what are the incentives for a potential firm to enter in the periphery. The first incentive is that it faces less competition from country-1 firms in serving country-2 consumers. Hence the demand and marginal revenue curves are higher (represented by the arrow numbered "1" in reverse). On the other hand, a periphery firm has worse market access to consumers in the core: this demand linkage is represented by the arrow numbered "2" in reverse. Finally, because the periphery has fewer firms to begin with, the bulk of manufactures consumed there must be imported, incurring transport costs. The cost of living is therefore higher in the periphery, so, to induce workers to migrate, a new firm in the periphery must pay higher nominal wages. This cost linkage is represented by the arrow numbered "3" in reverse.

In the light of this intuitive discussion it is not surprising that there is once again a threshold level of trade costs, T^S, the "sustain" point, at which agglomeration ceases to be an equilibrium. This new threshold has the same relationship to the underlying parameters as T^B, and for similar reasons:

> *Proposition 2:* T^S is increasing in μ and decreasing in σ.

Finally, a key result is that the two thresholds can be unambiguously ranked:

> *Proposition 3:* T^S is higher than T^B provided only that μ is strictly positive.

There is always some range of trade costs at which half the world's manufacturing firms are content to locate in each country but a single firm on its own has no incentive to exit in the core or enter in the periphery. The appendix proves the result and shows that it is driven by the cost linkage: if workers cared only about nominal wages, perhaps because they consumed only in their home country, the break and sustain thresholds would coincide.[12]

In the light of propositions 1 to 3, figure 2 illustrates how the number and types of equilibria vary with the level of trade costs T. (FKV call this diagram evocatively a "tomahawk bifurcation.") The vertical axis measures λ, the share of the world manufacturing labor force located in country 1; solid and dotted lines denote stable and unstable equilibria respectively. Recall that the countries are *ex ante* identical, so at every level of trade costs there exists a symmetric diversified equilibrium. However, from proposition 1, it is unstable for trade costs below T^B. Similarly, from proposition 2, the core-periphery equilibrium cannot be sustained for trade costs above T^S. At or below T^S, there are *two* stable core-periphery configurations: manufacturing may agglomerate in either country. Finally, from proposition 3, there are three stable equilibria between T^B and T^S, one diversified and two agglomerated.[13] It is this gap between T^B and T^S which opens up the

[12] Hence international capital mobility, at least as normally modelled in trade theory, with capital reallocating internationally in response to differences in *nominal* rentals, would not give the same richness of results: T^B and T^S would coincide. See Baldwin (1999a).

[13] Could there be other stable equilibria? The inherent symmetry of the model makes it unlikely, but no analytic proof is provided in the book, so we have to rely on simulation results to be sure.

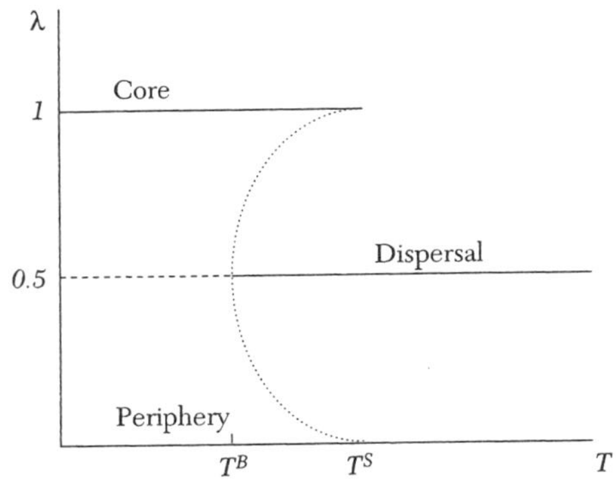

Figure 2. Agglomerated and Dispersed Equilibria as a Function of Trade Costs

possibilities of multiple equilibria and hysteresis that are the distinctive predictions of the economic geography literature and which are highlighted in the book. Within the range where $T^B < T < T^S$, *both* agglomeration and diversification are possible equilibria, so history and policy have a potential role in influencing which equilibrium prevails.

Now we are ready to apply the model. For example, falls in trade costs from initially high levels will lead to catastrophic agglomeration once T^B is reached; subsequent reversals of the trend in trade costs (as long as they remain below T^S) will not restore the diversified equilibrium; and whichever country is lucky enough to first acquire the manufacturing agglomeration will hold on to its initial advantage indefinitely. Complicating the model by adding other exogenous variables clearly opens the door to many more such "stories of breathtaking scope," or, if you prefer, interesting comparative-statics applications.

2.4 *Intermediate Inputs and Agglomeration*

We have seen that models that exhibit a propensity to agglomerate require increasing returns and transport costs. But we have also seen that these features are not enough: some mechanism that actually brings about agglomeration is also needed. So far, international labor mobility has been the mechanism assumed. An alternative route is to allow for inter-industry linkages. The potential importance of intermediate inputs in models of monopolistic competition, and the relative ease of incorporating them into the Dixit-Stiglitz model, have been clear since Wilfred Ethier (1982). It turns out that they provide another channel for agglomeration and lead to an analysis that is almost identical to that of labor mobility.

Assume that labor is now permanently country-specific, though it is used in both agriculture and industry. Manufacturing also uses an intermediate good, which is a CES aggregate of the output of all manufacturing firms (both domestic and foreign). For convenience, assume this aggregate has the same elasticity of substitution as the manufacturing sub-utility function M, so the price index for intermediates facing producers in country 1 is just P_1 (given as before by 9). Intermediates are then combined with labor to form a Cobb-Douglas composite input, with unit cost W_1 and intermediate cost share α :

$$W_1 = w_1^{1-\alpha} P_1^{\alpha} \qquad (15)$$

Hence, production costs depend positively on the local price index P_1.

The second way in which the model is altered is that the demand for each variety comes not only from consumers but also from firms. So, for example, the demand from country-1 consumers μY_1 which appears in every demand function must be replaced by total country-1 expenditure on manufactures E_1, given by:

$$E_1 = \mu Y_1 + \alpha n_1 p_1 q_1 \qquad (16)$$

Local consumers spend μY_1 as before; in addition the n_1 local firms spend a fraction α of their revenue $p_1 q_1$ on intermediates.

It is now straightforward to write down the full model. The cost of the composite input W_1 replaces the wage rate in the pricing equation 6; but otherwise the equations for individual firms derived in section 2.1 are unchanged. And total country s expenditure, E_s, replaces consumer expenditure μY_s in the demand function 8 (and in the corresponding demand function facing firms in country 2); but otherwise the equilibrium equations derived in section 2.2 are unchanged. (In particular, the price index equation 9 still holds.) The model can then be solved in exactly the same way as in section 2.3. Matters are particularly simple if we make the further assumption that the agricultural wage rate is always fixed. (The consequences of relaxing this are considered in section 3.) This in turn fixes the manufacturing wage and gives the model a partial equilibrium flavor, but the pay-off is considerable. FKV show that the results are very similar to those of the model with internationally mobile labor. In particular, the expressions for the break and sustain levels of transport costs are identical to (23) and (29), except that α, the cost share of intermediate goods, replaces μ, the budget share of manufactures. This is because, as equations (15) and (16) show, it is now α that determines the magnitude of the cost and demand linkages. Hence, the analysis of the model (whether diagrammatically or algebraically) proceeds essentially as in the internationally mobile labor case.

3. *Extending the Model*

Almost every chapter of the book relies on the basic model just outlined. From among many interesting extensions, let me highlight three.

Generalizing the model to many locations might seem impossible without resort to simulation. However, the authors succeed in deriving a local analytic result for a multi-location extension by borrowing a result from theoretical biology due to the mathematician Alan Turing. Assume a circular world in which a continuum of locations, each identical to one of the two countries in the last section, is spread evenly around the circumference. (FKV call this the "racetrack" economy.) Start from a uniform distribution of manufacturing (the "flat earth" equilibrium). Whether this symmetric equilibrium is broken depends on the stability of a dynamic labor-adjustment mechanism similar to that used to calculate the threshold T^B above. Turing's result can now be invoked to derive an analytic expression for the (algebraically) largest eigenvalue of the linearized dynamic system. If this is positive, the symmetric equilibrium will be broken and the economy will move towards a pattern of agglomeration. The agglomerated locations will be spread evenly around the circle in a pattern which can be represented by a sine curve, and the Turing result allows their frequency to be calculated. It turns out that exactly the same forces that apply at the two-country level determine this frequency: agglomerated equilibria will be fewer and located more sparsely around the circle the lower are transport costs, the higher the share of spending on manufacturing, and the lower the elasticity of substitution in demand. This shows that the forces found to be crucial in the two-country case apply much more generally.

A second extension retains the assumption of a continuum of locations but assumes that they are spread along an infinite line rather than around the circumference of a circle. Now, population and hence economic activity are not spread evenly along the line. Rather the population is initially large enough to support only a single location for manufacturing (which naturally can be called a "city"). A final difference is that the only variable factor, labor, is equally suited to both manufacturing and agriculture. Hence both sectors must pay the same wage in equilibrium. All this makes the set-up identical to that commonly used in formal models of urban economics. Now add a manufacturing sector such as that of section 2 potentially active at each point, and ask how the equilibrium pattern of manufacturing location changes as the population grows. It turns out that the details can only by solved by simulation, but they can be expressed in terms of a neat technical trick. This calculates a "market potential function" which gives as a function of distance from the city the *virtual* manufacturing wage at each location (i.e., the wage at which production there just breaks even) relative to the current equilibrium wage. This curve is always downward-sloping in the neighborhood of an existing city: increasing returns plus transport costs mean that every city casts a "shadow" within which it is not profitable for other manufacturing to locate. But it need not be monotonically decreasing and may hit unity at other locations, in which case manufacturing (and so cities) will be established there. Simulations show that, as population grows, the initially monocentric city system gives rise to increasing numbers of cities which emerge to produce for the hinterland. Finally, the model is extended to allow for many industries, differing in terms of their substitution elasticities and transport costs, following Fujita, Krugman, and Tomoya Mori (1999). Again, simulations show that the extended model implies a hierarchy of cities: a central city in which all industries are located, and an evolving series of subsidiary cities which attract "lower-order" industries (meaning those with higher transport costs and/or higher elasticities of substitution). This pattern of urban growth mimics real-world developments, and provides a theoretical rationale for a hierarchical or "central place" urban system of the kind described by location theorists such as Walter Christaller (1933) and August Lösch (1940).

A third extension takes the intermediate goods variant of the basic model and extends it to full general equilibrium by allowing wages to be endogenously determined (for example, by diminishing returns to labor in agriculture, because land is in scarce supply). Analytic results for this case are not available, but simulations reveal a common feature, independent of the details of different models. As before, industry is dispersed and wages are equalized internationally at high transport costs, and falls in transport costs lead to agglomeration. The new feature is that agglomeration drives up wages in the core country, which introduces a disincentive for industry to locate there. As transport costs fall further, this disincentive comes to dominate, so industry once again becomes dispersed and (when transport costs reach zero) wages are equalized internationally. This suggests a general phenomenon: there is likely to be a U-shaped relationship between the level of manufacturing transport costs and the propensity to agglomerate. Clearly many factors other than rises in agricultural wages (such as housing as in Helpman 1997) can cause diseconomies of agglomeration and so lead to dispersal of manufacturing and convergence of per capita incomes in what Krugman and Venables (1995) call the "globalization" phase of the world economy.

Following Puga and Venables (1996), this model is then extended to allow for many countries and industries, and to consider the effects of exogenous growth (uniform increases in the efficiency of all factors) rather than exogenous falls in transport costs. Simulations of the resulting pattern of industrialization show that manufacturing gradually spreads to other countries, with industries that are more labor-intensive and have weaker inter-industry linkages leading the way (since they benefit more from lower wages in countries that have not yet industrialized and benefit less from agglomeration in the initial core country).

4. *Limitations of the Model*

Models are unrealistic by definition. Simplifying assumptions are a virtue when the goal is to illustrate possibilities that previously could not be shown to hold. However, when it comes to applying a model to other questions, the assumptions may not be so helpful. In this section, I argue that the model used throughout the book has a number of special features that make it less suitable for addressing some issues. In particular, I want to single out the ways it treats increasing returns, firms' strategies, transport costs and, finally, space itself.

Increasing returns are intrinsic to the model, of course, and the cost function 5 is probably the most natural way of specifying such a technology in a simple tractable way. A quirk of the Dixit-Stiglitz model, however, is that standard measures of the degree of returns to scale turn out to depend not on the cost parameters F and c but rather on the elasticity of substitution. Though σ starts as a taste parameter, it ends up as an index of returns to scale. There is nothing wrong with this in principle, but it raises issues in interpreting the results and also highlights the shadowy role played by individual firms in the model.

Figure 3 illustrates how different values of σ affect the equilibrium. Consider first the case where σ is high. As an assumption this can be expressed in various equivalent ways: different varieties are closer substitutes; products are less differentiated; there is less preference for diversity. As a consequence, equilibrium is at a point such as A. From (7), firm output is relatively high, so fewer varieties are produced with higher output of each. From (6), price is close to marginal cost, so the demand and marginal revenue curves are flat and close together. By contrast, if σ is low, equilibrium is at a point such as B. Now there is a greater preference for diversity, so more varieties are produced with less output of each. To cover the fixed costs of shorter production runs, the price-marginal-cost margin must be high, with the demand and marginal revenue curves relatively convex and far apart.

Since the only underlying difference between the two cases is the value of σ, it can be interpreted as "an inverse index of equilibrium economies of scale" (Krugman 1991, p. 490). (In equilibrium, $\sigma/(\sigma-1)$ equals the ratio of the composite factor's marginal product to its average product, or one over the output elasticity of total costs.) But this terminology risks suggesting to the unwary that the theory of the firm embodied in the model is richer than in fact it is. It is not that industries with a higher value of σ have access to a different technology, rather that the pattern of demand encourages them to produce at a different scale. Better surely to say that returns to scale are more exploited at A than at B.

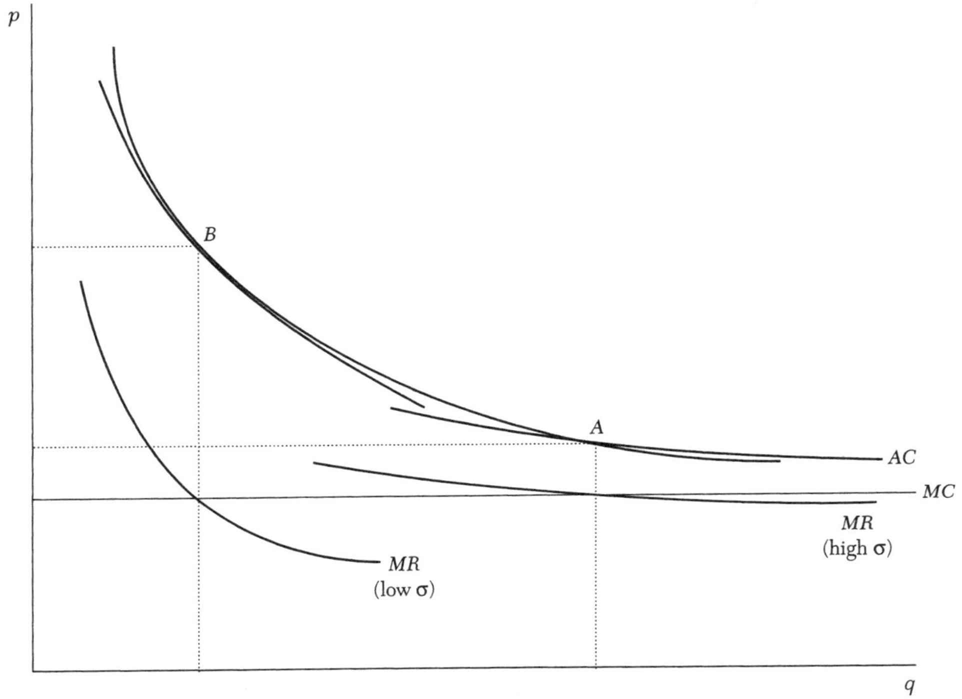

Figure 3. Effects of Changes in the Elasticity of Substitution

All of this is obscured by a particular normalization used for much of the book. Units are chosen to set the fixed and marginal cost parameters F and c equal to μ/σ and $(\sigma - 1)/\sigma$ respectively. This is harmless for local analysis, and may help in deriving analytical expressions for the break and sustain levels of transport costs, equations (23) and (29). (Though as I have shown in section 2, it can be dispensed with.) But in non-local comparisons it seems both unnecessary and undesirable. Unnecessary since one of the points of simulations is surely to avoid reducing the dimensionality of the parameter space. Undesirable because the effects of greater substitutability in demand (a rise in σ) cannot be distinguished from the effects of a higher ratio of variable to fixed costs. Changes in one are exactly offset by changes in the other such that (from 7) both firm output q and the unit input requirement $F + cq$ are always equal to μ. This in turn can lead to questionable interpretations. For example, bakery shops are given as an illustration of a high-σ industry (p. 193). Figure 3 shows that this makes little sense in the absence of normalization.

This discussion reflects a worrying fact: like the traditional competitive model, the Dixit-Stiglitz model has almost nothing to say about individual firms. Except for the fact that it incorporates increasing returns, the new economic geography has industrial organization underpinnings which are very rudimentary. In particular, the assumption of free entry—a perfectly elastic supply of firms at all locations—allows almost no role for strategic interactions between firms.[14] As a result, while costs may be fixed they are never sunk, so firms, industries, and even cities are always free to move. Footloose cities seem particularly odd. They might make sense in a long-run model, but even then not in the context of a growing economy with given technology such as that explored in Part 3 of the book. The authors note (p. 213) that introducing urban infrastructure would avoid the problem but that begs the question of exactly how to model it other than in an ad hoc way.

Completely footloose firms also sit oddly with the discussion of the emergence of industrial clusters or a "manufacturing base" in chapter 16, since the logic of the model is that such clusters are themselves footloose. At a superficial level the model is of course prejudiced in favor of a manufacturing base. The prior existence of other firms at one location lowers the costs of entry for a new firm there. Yet this feature alone does not seem to capture many of the issues that arise in discussions of industrial policy. Hysteresis or lock-in arises only from pecuniary (market-mediated) externalities in the new economic geography, not from technological externalities or local public goods (such as R&D spillovers). Further, the myopic Chamberlinian firms used throughout the book cannot engage in industrial strategies to shore up their position. They cannot make strategic commitments to create artificial barriers to entry, nor vertically integrate to internalize the externalities arising from the combination of intermediate inputs with increasing returns. And of course out-sourcing or cross-border horizontal mergers in response to changes in trade policy, technology, or market size are not allowed. The absence of these considerations makes the model less relevant to current debates on industrial location than it at first appears.

Transport costs are intrinsic to the model: if they are low enough, there are no barriers to agglomeration (though congestion effects may make it unprofitable); if they are high enough, there can be no departure from diversification. Such elementary insights should be robust to alternative specifications of transportation technology. But as we have seen, the detailed results in the book rely on the assumption of "iceberg" transport costs, usually attributed to Paul Samuelson. This amounts to assuming that the technology used to transport a good is identical to that used to produce it. This works for icebergs; also for grain if the main cost of transporting it is the grain consumed on the way by the horses pulling the wagon. (FKV note on p. 59 that von Thünen gave this example in 1826, so anticipating Samuelson by well over a century.) But it is obviously a very special case. An older literature in trade theory tried to model the transportation sector explicitly in a Heckscher-Ohlin framework, treating it just like any other industry, with an endogenous capital-labor ratio. (See Rodney Falvey 1976 for example.) That approach never led to simple or easily summarizable results, and is now largely forgotten. Perhaps it is due a revival. Even more

[14] There is only one mention of strategic behavior in the book: a brief reference (on page 52) to Alasdair Smith and Venables (1988), who show that an increase in market size has a pro-competitive effect if firms adopt either Cournot or Bertrand conjectures, so enhancing the home-market effect. This is an interesting point, but like Pierre-Philippe Combes (1997), it allows only for *post-entry, one-shot*, strategic behavior. When oligopolistic firm conjectures are combined with free entry and exit, it is the latter that drives most of the results.

important, in a field that emphasizes the importance of increasing returns, would be to allow for fixed costs in transportation. Of all industries, it seems to be characterized by very high ratios of fixed to variable costs, which is presumably why it is typically either publicly owned or highly concentrated. This is particularly important if transport costs are interpreted broadly to include the communications and other costs associated with trade, which are likely to exhibit network externalities. (See Richard Harris 1995.) Overall, the models in this book make interesting predictions about the effects of exogenous changes in per-unit transport costs. However, they are not well suited to examining positive questions such as the links between transportation, technology, and agglomeration (will what Danny Quah 1997 has called the increasing "weightlessness" of GNP facilitate backyard capitalism?) or normative questions such as the optimal level of provision of transport infrastructure.

A final point about transport costs is that, as noted earlier, the basic model assumes that they apply only to manufactures, and that agricultural goods (which really means goods produced under constant returns) are transported freely. Donald Davis (1998) criticizes this on two counts. He makes the empirical point that real-world transport costs appear to be at least as high for the latter, and he shows theoretically (in the model of section 2.2 above) that this neutralizes the home-market effect. Chapter 7 of the book derives similar results (without referring to Davis) but gives them a totally different spin. Whereas Davis concludes that there is "no compelling argument . . . that market size will matter for industrial structure, . . ." FKV note that a reduction of agricultural transport costs may trigger agglomeration. So, relatively low agricultural transport costs are either a necessary and implausible condition for agglomeration, or a source of yet more "stories of breathtaking scope": take your pick.

Geography is about space, and as the authors note (p. 325), a strength of the book is that it integrates the continuous approach to space of location theory with the discrete approach of trade theory. However, they never mention an offsetting drawback: space is almost always one-dimensional, whether along a line or (as in the "racetrack" economy) around a circle. (The sole exception is an interesting digression in chapter 13 showing how forks in a valley are natural locations for agglomeration). Perhaps it will prove possible to extend the Dixit-Stiglitz approach to a two-dimensional plain, though the complexities involved (such as the overlapping circular "shadows" cast by competing cities) suggest that the results may be long on trigonometry and short on elegance. Even if this can be done, the worry will remain that omitting strategic considerations misses much of importance. Strategic location issues in two dimensions are unresolved, but no references are given to the extensive literature on this topic. (Fujita and Thisse 1996 is a recent overview.)

Apart from dimensionality, it is also necessary to specify the spatial unit of analysis. The book deals in turn with regions, cities, and countries, but there is nothing intrinsic to the models that conclusively identifies these units. In particular, FKV assert, with little discussion, that the distinction between regions and countries coincides with the difference between factor mobility and intermediate inputs as the trigger for agglomeration. Ultimately, this is an empirical judgement and it is easy to think of counterexamples. (Labor mobility from some small to large European countries is considerable; and surely Silicon Valley, if it fits the new economic geography paradigm at all, reflects a regional concentration of intermediate supply rather than of migration-induced final demand for computer hardware and software?) More generally, the new economic geography, with its emphasis on pecuniary externalities, faces competition in the market for ideas from alternative theories at both ends of the spatial spectrum. At the local level, pure externalities such as knowledge spillovers may well prove to be the determining force behind most agglomerations. Krugman (1991) could dismiss technological externalities as a satisfactory basis for modelling spatial agglomeration with the quip "How far does a technological spillover spill?" But subsequent empirical work by David Audretsch and Maryann Feldman (1996), among others, has shown that their geographic reach can be measured, and that they are typically very localized. As for the national level, it is not obvious that agglomeration effects are nearly so crucial there. It is possible for example to give a factor-endowments-based explanation for the pattern of East Asian development, which is at least as plausible as Puga and Venables's agglomeration story. (See Jaime Ventura 1997.) And, as I note in Neary (1999), calibration studies tend to find that the extent of intermediate input usage is not sufficient to yield strong agglomeration effects at the national level. Only further theoretical and empirical work will tell at what level of spatial analysis, if any, the forces emphasized in this book are the dominant influences on agglomeration and economic development.

5. *Old versus New Economic Geography?*

"With friends like this, who needs enemies?" the authors may wonder if they have read this far. But in fact the new economic geography has real enemies out there; or, more prosaically, reputable academic critics who question the whole research program rather than just the details of its implementation. In particular, economic geographers of a more traditional kind, typically based in geography rather than economics departments, have not taken kindly to the self-proclaimed arrival of a new paradigm. Ron Martin (1999) summarizes their objections and concludes that what he calls the 'new geographical economics' "represents a case of mistaken identity: it is not that new, and it most certainly is not geography." No doubt this hostility is partly induced by Krugman's prose style: guaranteed to influence people but not necessarily to win friends, not at least from the ranks of those wedded to different approaches. But there are genuine issues at stake. Is this just a turf war, or have economists taken a bridge too far?

Martin's central objection to the new economic geography is that its mathematical formalism leads it to neglect "real places." Economic geographers of whom he approves avoid abstract theory, and focus instead on the contingency and particularity of real communities going about "the ordinary business of life." This methodological position reflects the "movement away from logical positivism" that took place in geography in the late 1970s. Though not averse to theory in general, even to economic theory provided it is "heterodox," economic geographers prefer to build explanations "'from below', often relying upon close dialogue with individual agents and organisations, and linking this 'local' knowledge with wider, larger stylized facts and conceptual frameworks."

Economists call these case studies, and regularly bemoan the fact that not enough get done. But the key issue is whether such studies can ever be "theory-free." Most economists would argue not, and would follow FKV in preferring an explicit model to inform (though not blindly predetermine) a case study rather than letting the facts speak for themselves. It is ironic that Krugman should be the target of such criticism, since he has shown unusual sympathy with heterodox traditions. In the same book (Krugman 1995) where he takes "old" economic geography to task, he also argues that increased formalism in economics as a whole held back progress in development and spatial economics, since pre-Dixit-Stiglitz no clean way of modelling imperfect competition was available. This may seem like trying to have it both ways, but it reflects the attitude of most working economists to what FKV call (p. 79) "aggressively unrealistic" models. They are, as the Roman poet Propertius said of his lover, difficult to live with, impossible to live without.

As for the "new" in "new economic geography," FKV make explicit their intellectual debt to location theory and regional science.[15] But they also make a persuasive case that they have extended their insights significantly by giving them behavioral underpinnings. It is one thing to make assertions about processes of cumulative causation leading to agglomeration, or to describe urban systems as central-place hierarchies. It is quite another to explain such patterns as the outcome of decentralized self-interested behavior.

Given mainstream economists' impatience with methodology, it is a fair bet that debates between old and new economic geographers will have little influence on the direction of future economic research. The genie is out of the bottle, and FKV are sure to inspire further theoretical developments.[16] Such work is important, but probably hard empirical work is even more so if nonbelievers are to be persuaded that the new approach represents a promising way forward. And, on a more hopeful note, perhaps there is potential common ground in the process of empirical implementation, scope for integrating the theoretical insights of the new economic geography with the detailed contingent knowledge of the old.

6. *From Theory to . . . What? Empirical and Policy Applications*

FKV do not present any empirical work of their own.[17] Nor do they discuss the policy implications of the new economic geography at length. But it is in these areas that the ultimate usefulness of the field will most likely be determined.

As far as empirics are concerned, the increasing availability of large data sets

[15] Mention could also be made of Hesham Abdel-Rahman (1988), who used the Dixit-Stiglitz specification to explain agglomeration at the city level, and with Ping Wang (Abdel-Rahman and Wang 1995) developed a model of a core-periphery urban system.

[16] Interesting recent contributions not already mentioned include Gianmarco Ottaviano, Takatoshi Tabuchi, and Jacques-François Thisse (1999), who develop an agglomeration model with linear rather than Dixit-Stiglitz preferences: they find that the basic insights remain intact, though incorporating transport costs enriches the model's outcomes; and Baldwin (1999a) and Philippe Martin and Ottaviano (1999), who embed economic geography in explicit growth models.

[17] The only empirical chapter in the book is a digression on the sizes of cities and the difficulties of accounting for the empirical regularity known as "Zipf's Law" or the "rank-size rule": to a remarkably close approximation, data on city size tend to show that the *r*th largest city has *1/r* of the total population. This pattern is not exhibited by the simulations of the authors' model discussed in section 3 above, although Xavier Gabaix (1999) has shown that it can be explained by assuming that both the growth rate and the variance of the growth rate of a city's population are independent of city size.

has encouraged a recent explosion of studies showing the relevance of location to many economic phenomena.[18] Among many examples, see the work of Audretsch and Feldman on local R&D spillovers mentioned above; John Gallup and Jeffrey Sachs (1998) who show the influence on living standards of geographical features such as latitude and length of coastline; and the revival of interest in the "gravity equation" which emphasizes the role of distance in explaining trade patterns. (See Alan Deardorff 1998 for a discussion of its theoretical underpinnings and further references.) While these studies have developed independently of the new economic geography, there is also a small but growing body of empirical work that builds directly on it. Most of the papers are unpublished, so a full evaluation is premature. Nevertheless some patterns can be identified.

One group of papers takes seriously the injunction of Edward Leamer and James Levinsohn (1995): "estimate do not test." Stephen Redding and Venables (2000) use cross-section data on 103 countries to estimate the intermediate-goods model of section 2.4, with incomes and firm numbers exogenous. They use the estimated coefficients from a gravity equation for trade flows to construct measures of demand and cost linkages;[19] these in turn are used to explain cross-country variations in incomes and in manufacturing wages and prices. Remarkably, they find that demand and cost linkages alone explain up to 70 percent of the cross-country variation in per capita income and up to 50 percent of the variation in manufacturing wages. Gordon Hanson (1998) uses Helpman's (1997) variant of the mobile-labor model of section 2.3 to estimate the determinants of ten-year changes in wages from 1970 to 1990 in all 3,075 counties of the continental United States. Including distance-weighted measures of housing stock and wages in adjacent states, as the theory suggests, improves the fit over an ad hoc specification (which only includes distance-weighted incomes). The estimated equation explains over 20 percent of the variation in the dependent variable and yields parameter estimates that are reasonably consistent with theory. Finally, whereas the other two papers use distance to proxy for transport costs, Pierre-Philippe Combes and Miren Lafourcade (2000) use a very detailed data set on actual transport costs in mainland France. They estimate a specification based on a model similar to FKV's to explain employment patterns in 64 sectors (including services as well as manufacturing) across 341 employment areas and find that, when allowance is made for intermediate inputs, transport costs have a significant impact on specialization patterns in nearly all sectors.

These papers show the usefulness of the economic geography model in guiding empirical work. However, they do not test the model against plausible alternatives, and the specifications they estimate are not necessarily inconsistent with other perspectives. A different set of papers attempts to discriminate between economic geography and alternative theories. Sukkoo Kim (1995) uses a long data set (from 1860 to 1987) on U.S. manufacturing employment to measure trends in regional specialization and industrial localization. He argues that the evidence is inconsistent

[18] This is not to mention the many empirical studies of regional growth and convergence. At the risk of descending into semantics, I am inclined to agree with Martin (1999) that these do not constitute economic geography proper (either old or new) since for the most part they merely take regions as units of analysis without specifically considering issues of relative location (such as transport costs, market access, etc.).

[19] This empirical technique, discussed further below, seems to originate with Leamer (1997).

with an important role for external economies, since industry localization patterns are negatively correlated with characteristics associated with external economies. In particular, high-tech sectors are less localized. Kim does not discuss the distinction between technological and pecuniary externalities, but his findings are also inconsistent with the latter provided we interpret high-tech sectors in the economic geography framework as sectors with higher shares of intermediate inputs and higher "equilibrium economies of scale," which the model predicts should be more agglomerated. By contrast, Kim finds that average plant size (his proxy for scale economies) explains industry localization patterns over time (recall that the new economic geography model relies on increasing returns but has nothing to say about firm or plant size); while raw material intensity (his proxy for Heckscher-Ohlin endowment effects) explains localization patterns across industries.

More encouraging results for the economic geography model come from a series of papers by Donald Davis and David Weinstein. They focus on the home-market effect, which as we have seen is a key building block of the model, though not sufficient for it. They note that this effect does not arise in models where trade is determined by comparative advantage. In such models, a positive shock to home demand for a good only affects home production if it raises price; but the price increase calls forth extra imports and so dampens the effect of demand on home production. By contrast, equation (12) shows that in a monopolistically competitive model with transport costs, a positive shock to home demand has a magnified effect on home production. This difference suggests a test that can discriminate between the two sets of models. In a first application to OECD data, Davis and Weinstein (1996), they found no evidence for home-market effects: above-average home demand for a sector was typically associated with a less-than-proportional excess of local production above the world average. However, in subsequent work, Davis and Weinstein (1998) interpret "home" demand more broadly: as in Redding and Venables, they use the estimated coefficients from a gravity equation for trade flows to measure *effective* home demand (including demand from trading partners, inversely weighted by distance). This time the home-market effect shows up as important for between one-half and two-thirds of manufacturing output (with comparative advantage determining trade patterns for the remainder). These results complement their finding in Davis and Weinstein (1999) that home-market effects are important in explaining the structure of production across Japanese regions.

To summarize, the overall thrust of these papers is support for Krugman (1980) from Davis and Weinstein, but rejection of Krugman (1991) by Kim. But much more work needs to be done. In particular, I am not aware of any cross-industry tests of the model's predictions about the effects of the "three T's": tastes, technology, and transport costs (all potentially measurable variables). As we saw in section 2, agglomeration is more likely in industries with higher demand (both final and intermediate), greater product diversity, and lower transport costs. Further work is needed to refine these implications and to devise plausible tests of them against real rather than straw alternatives. If the theory fails to find support from this process of empirical testing, it will not fade away but it will be much less persuasive. Of course, falsifiability at least in principle is a strength rather than a weakness of the model. The ultimate defense of the new economic geography is one that FKV themselves might prefer not to make: it could be wrong.

With the empirical verdict not yet in, is it too early to draw policy conclusions? The field's potential to throw light on policy is undoubtedly part of its appeal. This is especially true in Europe, where the development of the theory has coincided with debates on the effects of moves to deepen European union through greater economic and monetary integration, and to widen it through enlargement. Fears that these developments may deindustrialize the periphery have so far proved groundless: in the immediate aftermath of the January 1999 launch of European monetary union, the fastest-growing countries in the European Union have been small (the Netherlands), peripheral (Spain), or both (Finland and Ireland). Nevertheless, it is clear that Europe is at a different stage of economic-geographical evolution than the United States. Kim (1995) shows that U.S. interregional specialization reached its peak during the interwar years but (as of 1987) has fallen continuously and substantially since. By contrast, Karen Helene Midelfart-Knarvik, Henry Overman, and Venables (2000) show that international specialization in the EU increased from 1980–83 to 1994–97. In the light of this relevance to topical issues, it is hardly surprising that the new economic geography has stimulated more academic interest in Europe than in the United States, as a comparison of the recent CEPR and NBER trade programs shows. Moreover, the approach has already been used fruitfully as a background to policy discussions, as in Pontus Braunerhjelm, Riccardo Faini, Victor Norman, Frances Ruane, and Paul Seabright (2000). But using the models to evaluate policy options explicitly is surely premature.

The key problem is that the policy implications of the basic core-periphery model are just too stark to be true. The model turns Sartre's "Hell is other people" on its head: agglomeration is unambiguously good for you. Because the cost of living is lower in the core, it is always better to live there than in the periphery, with the level of utility in a diversified economy lying in between. Even when congestion costs are added to the model, utility is always at least as great in the core as in the periphery and is usually higher. Faced with multiple equilibria which have a clear welfare ranking, it is tempting to suggest a role for government in "picking equilibria." This in turn may encourage a new sub-field of "strategic location policy," perhaps drawing on fifteen years' work on strategic trade policy, which, as James Brander (1995) and Neary and Dermot Leahy (2000) argue, has produced much interesting theory but no simple robust rules to guide policy making. All these are temptations to be resisted, since they take too literally the neat structure of the model, and ignore the econometric difficulties in estimating the nonlinear, non-monotonic relations it predicts. In any case, greater industrial specialization, even if it takes the form of more agglomeration, is not the same as deindustrialization once we allow for many sectors. And, of course, the neglect of strategic issues which I discussed in section 4 is particularly relevant in this context. No harm then that FKV are mostly neutral on the applicability of the models to policy (except for some tentative interventionist thoughts in the chapter on industrial clustering).

7. *Conclusion*

In this paper, I have taken the appearance of FKV's book as an opportunity to review the "new" economic geography. It is not the only approach to location and agglomeration economists have taken. Many authors such as Brian Arthur (1986) and Robert Lucas (1988) have theorized about the role of regions and cities in economic development. But no other body of work does quite the same thing as the new economic geography: explain agglomeration in a theoretical framework that is tractable, has solid micro foundations, and makes testable empirical predictions. So, to paraphrase Robert Solow (1962), everyone should read this book, or at least encourage their students to do so!

Remember though that Solow's remark was made about the two-sector growth model, as emblematic of the 1960s as mini-skirts or the Beatles, though not as long-lasting. Will the new economic geography prove more durable? I suspect that it will, though maybe not as a distinct field. Instead, I am tempted to suggest that it will survive as "merely" another simple general equilibrium model, supplementing the trade theorist's tool kit; to quote Solow again, another "general equilibrium model of matchbox size" (since even a continuum of identical matchboxes arranged symmetrically around a circle is, well, just a matchbox).[20] Saying this risks sounding disparaging (and falls short of the authors' ambitions). But it is high praise in my view.

The new economic geography is firmly in the tradition of trade theory in at least two respects. First, it follows Ohlin in viewing interregional and international trade as different manifestations of the same influences. National boundaries are often coterminous with some economic forces, such as public policies, language, and institutions. But most influences on trade and industrial patterns operate similarly in large regions and small countries, and so the study of them should use the same analytic tools. Ohlin's view was not ignored—there are many examples of trade models applied to regional issues—but as long as trade theory remained tied to the competitive paradigm, its relevance was questionable. (Though, as Krugman 1999 notes, Ohlin himself gave an important role to increasing returns as a determinant of trade patterns.) In stressing the relevance to regional issues of models derived from trade theory, Krugman has not so much created a new subfield as extended the applicability of an old one.

Second, both the strengths and weaknesses of the new economic geography reflect the fact that it follows the tradition of focusing on a single cause of trade and location: technology in Ricardo, factor endowments in Heckscher-Ohlin, monopolistic competition in Krugman (1979), or oligopolistic competition in Brander (1981). Models such as these, which strip away the superfluous to focus on a single feature, are essential for understanding the world. Adding pecuniary externalities to the list and working out their implications is a significant achievement. But no one monocausal model can hope to capture the complexities of any applied problem, certainly not a model where space is one-dimensional, firms are identical and infinitesimal, and every function in sight is either constant-elasticity or a rectangular hyperbola. So, hold on the tee-shirt, skip the movie, but do read this book, possibly the best on interregional and international trade and location since Ohlin.

[20] Those who remember the lessons of Ronald Jones (1965) will have noted how the exposition in section 2 is simplified by using standard techniques for analyzing simple general equilibrium models: logarithmic differentiation, a focus on factor-market equilibrium conditions, etc.

Appendix: Proofs of Propositions[21]

Proof of Proposition 1: Totally differentiating the model at the symmetric equilibrium gives six equations in eight variables, $\hat{q}, \hat{Y}, \hat{P}, \hat{p}, \hat{n}, \hat{w}, \hat{L}$ and $\hat{\omega}$. Equation 10 gives the change in the home price index, and equation 11 gives the change in demand facing an individual home firm. Firms always maximize profits, so from (6) prices and wages move together:

$$\hat{p} = \hat{w} \tag{17}$$

The full-employment condition (13) implies that the labor force and the number of firms in the home country must always move together:

$$\hat{L} = \hat{n} \tag{18}$$

From the definition of the real wage ω:

$$\hat{\omega} = \hat{w} - \mu\hat{P} \tag{19}$$

Finally, equation (14) gives the change in GNP.

As noted in footnote 9, two alternative approaches can be taken to testing whether the symmetric equilibrium is stable. FKV assume that firms are always in equilibrium whereas migration takes time. In my notation, they set $\hat{q}$ equal to zero (since output is always at its equilibrium value, given by 7), take $\hat{L}$ as exogenous, and solve for $\hat{\omega}/\hat{L}$. Here, following Puga (1999), I assume instead that workers are always in equilibrium whereas entry and exit take time. Hence, I set $\hat{\omega}$ equal to zero (migration ensures that the real wage is the same in both countries) take $\hat{n}$ as exogenous, and solve for $\hat{q}/\hat{n}$. (From footnote 6, changes in profits are monotonic in changes in q.) Both approaches yield the same stability condition.

To solve for $\hat{q}/\hat{n}$, first use (10) and (14) to eliminate $\hat{P}$ and $\hat{Y}$ from (11), and then use (17) and (18) to replace $\hat{p}$ and $\hat{L}$ by $\hat{w}$ and $\hat{n}$ respectively. This yields:

$$\hat{q} = (\mu - Z)Z\hat{n} - [\sigma - \{\mu + (\sigma - 1)Z\}Z]\hat{w} \tag{20}$$

The first term on the right-hand side gives the first result quoted in the text: with equal nominal wages in the two countries ($\hat{w} = 0$), equilibrium is stable if and only if μ is less than Z. Next, to impose equality of *real* wages, I need to solve for the change in the price index from (10), setting $\hat{p} = \hat{w} = \mu\hat{P}$ (using (19) with $\hat{\omega}$ equal to zero):

$$\hat{P} = -\frac{Z}{(\sigma - 1)(1 - \mu Z)}\hat{n} \tag{21}$$

Note in passing that the coefficient of $\hat{w}$ in (20) is negative and that $\hat{P}$ itself is negative from (21). (This is just the price index effect with real rather than nominal wages fixed.) These results confirm the assertion made in the text: the condition $\mu > Z$ underestimates the pressure toward agglomeration, since the symmetric equilibrium can be unstable even when the condition is not met. To find the full stability condition, substitute from (21) into (20) (once again setting $\hat{w}$ equal to $\mu\hat{P}$):

$$\hat{q} = \frac{(2\sigma - 1)\mu - \{\sigma(1 + \mu^2) - 1\}Z}{(\sigma - 1)(1 - \mu Z)} Z\hat{n} \tag{22}$$

The denominator is positive since $\sigma > 1 > \mu$, Z. Hence the threshold value of Z is that which sets the numerator equal to zero. Using the definition of Z from (10), we can solve in turn for the threshold value of T :

$$\underset{+\ -}{T^B(\mu, \sigma)} = \left[\frac{\{\sigma(1 + \mu) - 1\}(1 + \mu)}{\{\sigma(1 - \mu) - 1\}(1 - \mu)}\right]^{\frac{1}{\sigma - 1}}. \tag{23}$$

The proposition follows by differentiating this expression with respect to μ and σ.

Proof of Proposition 2: Consider the initial agglomerated equilibrium. Since μ is the fraction of world income spent on manufactures, national income in country 1, Y_1, equals its agricultural output X_A plus world manufacturing output $\mu(Y_1 + Y_2)$. By contrast, country 2 has no manufacturing, so its income Y_2 is simply X_A. Combining these equations gives:

$$Y_2 = \frac{1 - \mu}{1 + \mu}Y_1 \tag{24}$$

Income is lower in the periphery, because there are no manufacturing workers there. Next, from equation (9) for the manufacturing price index, with n_2 initially zero:

$$P_2 = P_1 T \tag{25}$$

Manufacturing prices are higher in the periphery because all manufactures must be imported.

Now, consider whether there are incentives for firms to exit in the core and enter in the periphery. This will be profitable if a typical firm can sell more in the periphery than in the core. Assume to begin with that migration equalizes nominal wages. Then relative demands depend on the ratio of the demand intercepts. That in the core is given by (8), which simplifies, using (24) and (25), to:

$$\phi_1 = \frac{2\mu}{1 + \mu}Y_1 P_1^{\sigma - 1} \tag{26}$$

As for the demand intercept in the periphery, it is given by an equation symmetric to (8):

$$\phi_2 = \mu[Y_1 P_1^{\sigma - 1} T^{1 - \sigma} + Y_2 P_2^{\sigma - 1}] \tag{27}$$

Using (24), (25), and (26), potential demand in the periphery relative to the core is:

$$\phi_2 = H\phi_1 \quad \text{where:} \quad H \equiv \frac{1 + \mu}{2}T^{1 - \sigma} + \frac{1 - \mu}{2}T^{\sigma - 1} \tag{28}$$

[21] Propositions 1 and 2 first appear in Krugman and Venables (1995) and Krugman (1991) respectively; propositions 3 and 4 appear to be new.

Because of transport costs, a periphery firm is at a disadvantage ($T^{1-\sigma} < 1$) in serving the larger market, but has an advantage ($T^{\sigma-1} > 1$) in serving the smaller local market. The balance of advantage is ambiguous and depends on whether H is greater or less than one.

Finally, just as in the earlier discussion of the stability of the diversified equilibrium, migration equalizes *real* not nominal wages. This places potential periphery firms at a further disadvantage, since they must charge higher prices to cover the higher nominal wages needed to compensate workers for the higher cost of living: $p_2/p_1 = w_2/w_1 = \omega_2 P/\omega_1 P = T^{\mu}$ (from (25)). Hence, the full expression for relative demands, which must equal one when deviation from the agglomerated equilibrium is just profitable, is:

$$\frac{q_2}{q_1} = \frac{\phi_2 p_2^{-\sigma}}{\phi_1 p_1^{-\sigma}} = H\left(\frac{p_2}{p_1}\right)^{-\sigma} = HT^{-\sigma\mu} = 1 \qquad (29)$$

Since $T^{-\sigma\mu}$ is less than one, the level of trade costs sufficient to equalize nominal wages (i.e., just sufficient to set H equal to one) overestimates the incentives to deviate from the agglomerated equilibrium: at that level, real wages in the periphery are still lower than in the core. To equalize real wages requires a higher level of trade costs, defined by setting the left-hand side of (29) equal to one.

Equation (29) is trivially satisfied for $T = 1$: with no transport costs, firms are indifferent between locations. At $T = 1$ the left-hand side is decreasing in T, so q_2/q_1 must fall below one, but it must rise above it for high T (provided the "no-black-hole" condition is met). The second value of T at which (29) is satisfied defines a new threshold, T^S, at which agglomeration is just on the margin of being an equilibrium. The proposition is proved by totally differentiating (29) and evaluating in the neighborhood of T^S.

Proof of Proposition 3:[22] Direct comparison of the two thresholds T^B and T^S is not promising, since (29) only defines the latter implicitly. Instead, consider the left-hand side of (29), which gives the incentive to deviate from the agglomerated equilibrium, and evaluate it at the break threshold T^B. This defines a function h of μ:

$$h(\mu) \equiv H[T^B(\mu)] \cdot [T^B(\mu)]^{-\sigma\mu} \qquad (30)$$

By inspection, $h(0) = 1$: if there is no demand for manufactures, there is no propensity to agglomerate at any level of transport costs, so the break and sustain thresholds coincide. The proposition is proved by showing that, if there is any finite demand for manufactures (i.e., for any value of μ in the interior of the admissible region: $\mu \in (0,(\sigma - 1)/\sigma)$), there is no incentive to deviate from the agglomerated equilibrium (i.e., $h(\mu) < 1$), when $T = T^B$.

Begin with the first derivative of $\ln h$ (writing H^B as shorthand for $H[T^B(\mu)]$):

$$\frac{d\ln h}{d\mu} = \frac{d\ln H^B}{d\mu} - \sigma \ln T^B - \sigma\mu\frac{d\ln T^B}{d\mu} \qquad (31)$$

This is zero at $\mu = 0$ (obvious for the second and third terms; refer to (34) below for the first). To eliminate the term in $\ln T^B$, proceed to the second derivative:

$$\frac{d^2\ln h}{d\mu^2} = \frac{d^2\ln H^B}{d\mu^2} - 2\sigma\frac{d\ln T^B}{d\mu} - \sigma\mu\frac{d^2\ln T^B}{d\mu^2} \qquad (32)$$

Evaluating this requires explicit expressions for $\ln T^B$ and its derivatives:

$$(\sigma - 1)\ln T^B = \ln\alpha - \ln\beta + \ln(1 + \mu) - \ln(1 - \mu) \geq 0$$

$$(\sigma - 1)\frac{d\ln T^B}{d\mu} = \frac{\sigma}{\alpha} + \frac{\sigma}{\beta} + \frac{1}{1+\mu} + \frac{1}{1-\mu} > 0 \qquad (33)$$

$$(\sigma - 1)\frac{d^2\ln T^B}{d\mu^2} = -\frac{\sigma^2}{\alpha^2} + \frac{\sigma^2}{\beta^2} - \frac{1}{(1+\mu)^2} + \frac{1}{(1-\mu)^2} > 0$$

where $\alpha \equiv \sigma - 1 + \sigma\mu > 0$ and $\beta \equiv \sigma - 1 - \sigma\mu > 0$ (the latter is the no-black-hole condition). I also need explicit expressions for $\ln H^B$ and its derivatives:

$$\ln H^B = \ln\eta - \ln\alpha - \ln\beta \geq 0$$

$$\frac{d\ln H^B}{d\mu} = \frac{2\sigma(3\sigma-2)\mu}{\eta} - \frac{\sigma}{\alpha} + \frac{\sigma}{\beta} \geq 0 \qquad (34)$$

$$\frac{d^2\ln H^B}{d\mu^2} = \frac{2\sigma(3\sigma-2)}{\eta^2}[(\sigma - 1)^2 - \sigma(3\sigma - 2)\mu^2] + \frac{\sigma^2}{\alpha^2} + \frac{\sigma^2}{\beta^2}$$

where: $\eta \equiv (\sigma - 1)^2 + \sigma(3\sigma - 2)\mu^2 > 0$. Substituting into 32 and collecting terms gives:

$$\frac{d^2\ln h}{d\mu^2} = \frac{2\sigma(\sigma-1)^2(3\sigma-2)}{\eta^2} - \frac{2\sigma^2(3\sigma-2)^2\mu^2}{\eta^2} - \frac{2\sigma^2}{\alpha\beta} - \frac{4\sigma}{\sigma-1}\frac{1}{(1-\mu^2)^2} \qquad (35)$$

This is zero at $\mu = 0$ and approaches minus infinity as μ approaches the black-hole threshold ($\beta = 0$); its second term is zero at $\mu = 0$ and negative otherwise; and each of the other three terms is decreasing in μ.[23] Hence (35) is negative throughout the admissible region. To sum up, h equals unity and is stationary in μ at $\mu = 0$, and it is concave in μ throughout. It follows that $h(\mu) < 1$ for $\mu > 0$. Hence, at the break threshold of transport costs, there is no incentive to deviate from the agglomerated equilibrium, so $T^B < T^S$, as required.

To show that the cost linkage is crucial for proposition 3, consider two new thresholds, $T^{B'}$ and $T^{S'}$, defined respectively as the break and

[22] Many thanks to Frédéric Robert-Nicoud for spotting an error in my first proof and for pointing me in the direction of this one.

[23] This follows since η is increasing in μ and $\alpha\beta = (\sigma - 1)^2 - \sigma^2\mu^2$ is decreasing in μ.

sustain levels of trade costs that equalize *nominal* rather than real wages between countries. Then:

Proposition 4: $T^{B'}$ equals $T^{S'}$, and both are less than T^B and T^S, provided $\mu > 0$.

Proof of Proposition 4: From the discussion following (14), $T^{B'}$ is defined by the condition $Z = \mu$. Substituting for Z from (10) gives: $(T^{B'})^{\sigma-1} = (1+\mu)/(1-\mu)$. As for $T^{S'}$, it is evident from (28) that it is defined by the condition $H = 1$, or $(1 + \mu)T^{1-\sigma} + (1-\mu)T^{\sigma-1} = 2$. This is a quadratic in $T^{\sigma-1}$. Solving, and ignoring the trivial root $T = 1$, gives $(T^{S'})^{\sigma-1} = (1+\mu)/(1-\mu)$. This proves that $T^{B'} = T^{S'}$. But we have already seen that (provided μ is strictly positive) the level of trade costs just sufficient to yield equal nominal wages *under*estimates the incentives to deviate from the symmetric equilibrium, so $T^{B'} < T^B$; while it *over*estimates the incentives to deviate from the agglomerated equilibrium, so $T^{S'} < T^S$.

References

Abdel-Rahman, Hesham M. 1988. "Product Differentiation, Monopolistic Competition, and City Size," *Reg. Sci. Urban Econ.* 18:1, pp. 69–86.

Abdel-Rahman, Hesham M. and Ping Wang. 1988. "Toward a General Equilibrium Theory of a Core-Periphery System of Cities," *Reg. Sci. Urban Econ.* 25:4, pp. 529–46.

Arthur, W. Brian. 1986. "Industry Location Patterns and the Importance of History," in *Increasing Returns and Path Dependence in the Economy*. W. Brian Arthur, ed. Michigan U. Press, pp. 49–68.

Audretsch, David B. and Maryann P. Feldman. 1996. "R&D Spillovers and the Geography of Innovation and Production," *Amer. Econ. Rev.* 86:3, pp. 630–40.

Baldwin, Richard E. 1999a. "Agglomeration and Endogenous Capital," *Eur. Econ. Rev.* 43:2, pp. 253–80.

———. 1999b. "The Core-Periphery Model with Forward-Looking Expectations," CEPR Discussion Paper 2085.

Brakman, Steven; Harry Garretsen and Charles van Marrewijk. 2001. *An Introduction to Geographical Economics*. Cambridge: Cambridge U. Press, forthcoming.

Brander, James A. 1981. "Intra-Industry Trade in Identical Commodities," *J. Int. Econ.* 11:1, pp. 1–14.

———. 1995. "Strategic Trade Policy," in *Handbook of International Economics, Vol. 3*. Gene M. Grossman and Kenneth Rogoff, eds. Amsterdam: North-Holland, pp. 1395–455.

Braunerhjelm, Pontus; Riccardo Faini, Victor Norman, Frances Ruane and Paul Seabright. 2000. *Integration and the Regions of Europe: How the Right Policies Can Prevent Polarization*. London: CEPR.

Christaller, Walter. 1933. *Central Places of Southern Germany*. Jena, Germany: Fischer. (English translation, London: Prentice Hall, 1966.)

Combes, Pierre-Philippe. 1997. "Industrial Agglomeration under Cournot Competition," *Ann. Econ. Statist.* 45, pp. 161–82.

Combes, Pierre-Philippe and Miren Lafourcade. 2000. "Transportation Costs and Regional Employment Inequalities: Evidence from France, 1993," mimeo, CERAS.

Davis, Donald R. 1998. "The Home Market, Trade and Industrial Structure," *Amer. Econ. Rev.* 88:5, pp. 1264–76.

Davis, Donald R. and David E. Weinstein. 1996. "Does Economic Geography Matter for International Specialization?" NBER Working Paper 5706.

———. 1998. "Market Access, Economic Geography and Comparative Advantage: An Empirical Assessment," NBER Working Paper 6787.

———. 1999. "Economic Geography and Regional Production Structure: An Empirical Investigation," *Eur. Econ. Rev.* 43:2, pp. 379–407.

Deardorff, Alan V. 1998. "Determinants of Bilateral Trade: Does Gravity Work in a Neoclassical World?" in *The Regionalization of the World Economy*. Jeffrey A. Frankel, ed. Chicago: U. Chicago Press, pp. 7–22.

Dixit, Avinash K. and Victor Norman. 1980. *Theory of International Trade: A Dual, General Equilibrium Approach*. London: Cambridge U. Press.

Dixit, Avinash K. and Joseph E. Stiglitz. 1977. "Monopolistic Competition and Optimum Product Diversity," *Amer. Econ. Rev.* 67:3, pp. 297–308.

Ethier, Wilfred J. 1982. "National and International Returns to Scale in the Theory of International Trade," *Amer. Econ. Rev.* 72:3, pp. 389–405.

Falvey, Rodney E. 1976. "Transport Costs in the Pure Theory of International Trade," *Econ. J.* 86:343, pp. 536–50.

Fujita, Masahisa; Paul Krugman and Tomoya Mori. 1999. "On the Evolution of Hierarchical Urban Systems," *Eur. Econ. Rev.* 43:2, pp. 209–51.

Fujita, Masahisa and Jacques-François Thisse. 1996. "Economics of Agglomeration," *J. Japanese Int. Econ.* 10:4, pp. 339–78.

———. 2000. "Agglomeration and Market Interaction," presented to the World Congress of the Econometric Society, Seattle.

Gabaix, Xavier. 1999. "Zipf's Law for Cities: An Explanation," *Quart. J. Econ.* 114, pp. 739–67.

Gallup, John Luke and Jeffrey D. Sachs with Andrew D. Mellinger. 1998. "Geography and Economic Development," in *Annual World Bank Conference on Development Economics*. Boris Pleskovic and Joseph E. Stiglitz, eds. Washington DC: World Bank, pp. 127–78.

Hanson, Gordon H. 1998. "Market Potential, Increasing Returns, and Geographic Concentration," NBER Working Paper 6429.

Harris, Richard. 1995. "Trade and Communication Costs," *Can. J. Econ.* 28, pp. 46–75.

Head, K.; T. Mayer and J. Ries. 1999. "On the

Pervasiveness of Home Market Effects," mimeo, U. British Columbia.
Helpman, Elhanan. 1997. "The Size of Regions," in *Topics in Public Economics: Theoretical and Applied Analysis*. David Pines, Efraim Sadka and Itzhak Zilcha, eds. Cambridge: Cambridge U. Press.
Helpman, Elhanan and Paul R. Krugman. 1985. *Market Structure and Foreign Trade*. Cambridge, MA: MIT Press.
Jones, Ronald W. 1965. "The Structure of Simple General Equilibrium Models," *J. Polit. Econ.* 73, pp. 557–72.
Kim, Sukkoo. 1995. "Expansion of Markets and the Geographic Distribution of Economic Activities: The Trends in U.S. Regional Manufacturing Structure, 1860–1987," *Quart. J. Econ.* 110:4, pp. 881–908.
Krugman, Paul R. 1979. "Increasing Returns, Monopolistic Competition and International Trade," *J. Int. Econ.* 9:4, pp. 469–79.
———. 1980. "Scale Economies, Product Differentiation and the Pattern of Trade," *Amer. Econ. Rev.* 70, pp. 950–59.
———. 1991. "Increasing Returns and Economic Geography," *J. Polit. Econ.* 99:3, pp. 483–99.
———. 1995. *Development, Geography and Economic Theory*. Cambridge, MA: MIT Press.
———. 1999. "Was It All in Ohlin?" at http://web.mit.edu/krugman/www/ ohlin.html.
Krugman, Paul R. and Anthony J. Venables. 1990. "Integration and the Competitiveness of Peripheral Industry," in *Unity with Diversity in the European Community*. Christopher Bliss and Jorge Braga de Macedo, eds. Cambridge: Cambridge U. Press, pp. 56–75.
———. 1995. "Globalization and the Inequality of Nations," *Quart. J. Econ.* 110:4, pp. 857–80.
Leamer, Edward E. 1997. "Access to Western Markets and Eastern Effort," in *Lessons from the Economic Transition: Central and Eastern Europe in the 1990s*. Salvatore Zecchini, ed. Dordrecht: Kluwer Academic, pp. 503–26.
Leamer, Edward E. and James Levinsohn. 1995. "International Trade Theory: The Evidence," in *Handbook of International Economics, Vol. 3*. Gene M. Grossman and Kenneth Rogoff, eds. Amsterdam: North-Holland, pp. 1339–94.
Lösch, August. 1940. *The Economics of Location*, Jena, Germany: Fischer. (English translation, New Haven: Yale U. Press, 1954.)
Lucas, Robert E., Jr. 1988. "On the Mechanics of Economic Development," *J. Mon. Econ.* 22:1, pp. 3–42.
Martin, Philippe P. and Gianmarco I. P. Ottaviano. 1999. "Growing Locations: Industry Location in a Model of Endogenous Growth," *Eur. Econ. Rev.* 43:2, pp. 281–302.
Martin, Ron. 1999. "The New 'Geographical Turn' in Economics: Some Critical Reflections," *Cambridge J. Econ.* 23:1, pp. 65–91.
Midelfart-Knarvik, Karen Helene; Henry G. Overman and Anthony J. Venables. 2000. "Comparative Advantage and Economic Geography: Estimating the Location of Production in the EU," mimeo, LSE.
Mussa, Michael. 1978. "Dynamic Adjustment in the Heckscher-Ohlin-Samuelson Model," *J. Polit. Econ.* 86, pp. 775–92.
Neary, J. Peter. 1978. "Dynamic Stability and the Theory of Factor-Market Distortions," *Amer. Econ. Rev.* 68:4, pp. 671–82.
———. 1999. "Discussion" of "Economic Policy and the Manufacturing Base: Hysteresis in Location" (by Anthony J. Venables), in *Dynamic Issues in Commercial Policy Analysis*. Richard E. Baldwin and Joseph F. Francois, eds. Cambridge: Cambridge U. Press, pp. 196–201.
Neary, J. Peter and Dermot Leahy. 2000. "Strategic Trade and Industrial Policy Towards Dynamic Oligopolies," *Econ. J.* 110:463, pp. 484–508.
Ohlin, Bertil. 1933. *Interregional and International Trade*. Cambridge, MA: Harvard U. Press.
Ottaviano, Gianmarco and Diego Puga. 1998. "Agglomeration in the Global Economy: A Survey of the 'New Economic Geography'," *World Econ.* 21, pp. 707–31.
Ottaviano, Gianmarco; Takatoshi Tabuchi and Jacques-François Thisse. 2000. "Agglomeration and Trade Revisited," mimeo, CORE, U. Catholique de Louvain.
Puga, Diego. 1999. "The Rise and Fall of Regional Inequalities," *Eur. Econ. Rev.* 43:2, pp. 303–34.
Puga, Diego and Anthony J. Venables. 1996. "The Spread of Industry: Spatial Agglomeration and Economic Development," *J. Japanese Int. Econ.* 10:4, pp. 440–64.
Quah, Danny T. 1997. "Increasingly Weightless Economies," *Bank Engl. Quart. Bull.* 37, pp. 49–56.
Redding, Stephen and Anthony J. Venables. 2000. "Economic Geography and International Inequality," mimeo, LSE.
Smith, Alasdair and Anthony J. Venables. 1988. "Completing the Internal Market in the European Union: Some Industry Simulations," *Eur. Econ. Rev.* 32:7, pp. 1501–25.
Solow, Robert M. 1962. "Comment" on "On a Two-Sector Model of Economic Growth" (by Hirofumi Uzawa), *Rev. Econ. Stud.* 29, pp. 255–57.
Venables, Anthony J. 1996. "Equilibrium Locations of Vertically Linked Industries," *Int. Econ. Rev.* 37:2, pp. 341–59.
———. 1999. "Economic Policy and the Manufacturing Base: Hysteresis in Location," in *Dynamic Issues in Commercial Policy Analysis*. Richard E. Baldwin and Joseph F. Francois, eds. Cambridge: Cambridge U. Press, pp. 177–95.
Ventura, Jaume. 1997. "Growth and Interdependence," *Quart. J. Econ.* 112:1, pp. 57–84.

[23]

Localization Economies, Vertical Organization, and Trade

By GORDON H. HANSON*

The past decade has seen an unprecedented move toward free trade in the developing world. As expected, trade has reallocated resources toward labor-intensive activities (Michael Michaely et al., 1991). Within industries, trade has had some unexpected effects: in apparel, electronics, and other labor-intensive industries, developing countries are shifting from vertically integrated production for the domestic market to product assembly for foreign firms (Joseph Grunwald and Kenneth Flamm, 1985). In this arrangement, which I term a "regional production network," developed-country firms supply product designs, process technology, and marketing services and subcontract assembly services to branch plants in developing countries. Regional production networks account for a large portion of developing-country trade. In Mexico, assembly plants in 1992 accounted for 40 percent of total exports and 53 percent of manufacturing exports.

The distinguishing feature of a regional production network is that the services developed-country firms provide (design, engineering, and marketing) are skill-intensive. In Hanson (1994), I develop a model of regional production networks based on external economies. Consider a small country with an industry that has two production stages: design, which has location-specific external economies, and assembly, which has constant returns to scale. Localization economies arise endogenously from the fact that design involves many specialized subsidiary services, each produced under increasing returns to scale. By agglomerating in an industry center, firms share design capacity and expand the range of services available to them. Agglomeration, however, drives up wages in the industry center, pushing assembly into outlying regions. Now suppose the small country opens to trade with a large country. Trade recreates the regional production network on a global scale: the large country, by virtue of its size, captures the industry center, and the small country specializes in assembly.

In this paper, I apply my model of regional production networks to the Mexican apparel industry. Mexico provides a unique opportunity to study the effects of trade on industry location. In 1985, Mexico opened its economy to trade, bringing a sudden end to four decades of import-substitution industrialization. For Mexico, the proximity of the United States makes trade reform tantamount to economic integration with its northern neighbor. The North American Free Trade Agreement (NAFTA) only formalizes a de facto process of integration already underway. What makes apparel an interesting case is variation in factor intensity across production stages. Activities such as design and marketing are specialized tasks that require skilled labor. In the global apparel industry, these activities are concentrated in New York, Los Angeles, and Hong Kong. (The fact that New York City remains a major apparel producer is perhaps the most persuasive evidence one can find of localization economies.) Assembly, another major production task, requires relatively few skills and is done mostly by firms in low-wage countries.

Data for Mexico are consistent with the hypothesis of localization economies. Under the closed economy, high-skill apparel tasks clustered in Mexico City, while assembly took place in outlying regions. With the opening to trade, Mexican apparel producers are shifting from production for the domestic market to product assembly for U.S. firms. Estimation of Mexico's pre- and post-trade regional

* Department of Economics, University of Texas, Austin, TX 78712, and National Bureau of Economic Research. I thank Dan Hamermesh, Paul Krugman, Preston McAfee, Michael Piore, and two anonymous referees for helpful comments. Financial support from the MacArthur Foundation through the Center for International Studies at MIT is gratefully acknowledged.

wage structure supports the regional-production-network hypothesis. This suggests that NAFTA will not only shift apparel assembly jobs from the United States to Mexico, as many studies have predicted, but also will lead to a substantial relocation of production within Mexico, reducing wages in Mexico City relative to those along the Mexico–U.S. border.

I. Theory

In this section, I outline a model of regional production networks.[1] Consider a world with two countries: Foreign, which has a single region and represents the United States; and Home, which has two regions, North and South, and represents Mexico. Each country has two factors of production, land and labor. Labor is mobile between regions but not between countries; land is immobile. Foreign's labor force is large relative to that of Home.

A. *Production*

Suppose for simplicity that there is a single industry, which has a two-stage production process. Stage 1 involves many high-skill tasks, which are combined to produce a composite input (ready-to-assembly components); stage 2 involves a routine low-skill task (product assembly). I use apparel to motivate the model, but the features of production apply to many semi-durable consumer goods. Stage-1 tasks include designing the product, producing components (fabric pieces), and identifying buyers. Differences in skill intensity are captured by assuming that individual stage-1 tasks have increasing returns to scale and that stage-2 assembly has constant returns to scale. Suppose further that the individual inputs produced in stage 1 have sufficiently high transport costs that they are not traded across space (think of these costs as resulting from coordinating input production in different locations). The same need not be true for the composite stage-1 input. I assume that there are transport costs in the composite input (ready-to-assembly components), but that the costs are not sufficient to prevent it from being traded. This allows input production and assembly to occur in different locations.

The environment gives stage-1 input producers an incentive to agglomerate spatially. Given firm-level increasing returns, input producers prefer to concentrate production in one location. Naturally, an individual input producer will choose to locate where demand for her input is highest. The nontradability of individual inputs implies that input demand will be higher the larger is the concentration of other input producers in a region. Thus, the combination of increasing returns, nontradability, and multistage production creates location-specific external economies in stage-1 activities. There are costs to geographic concentration, however. The agglomeration of workers in one region drives up land prices relative to other regions. Real-wage equalization requires firms in high-land-price regions to pay workers relatively high wages.

B. *Autarky*

Consider autarky in Home; the Foreign case is analogous. Localization economies in stage-1 activities imply that the agglomeration of stage-1 firms in one region is an equilibrium. Either region may become the industry center. To motivate the Mexican case, consider the outcome in which stage-1 firms agglomerate in the South (imagine the South as Mexico City and the North as the U.S. border region). Costs in transporting the composite input imply that, all else equal, stage-2 (assembly) firms prefer to locate in the same region as stage-1 firms. The agglomeration of workers in the South bids up land prices relative to those in the North, requiring Southern firms to offer their workers relatively high wages. For sufficiently large wage differentials, some assembly firms will prefer to move to the North and incur the transport costs involved in importing the composite input from the South. In fact, transport costs fix the size of the regional nominal wage differential.

The aggregate result of individual firms' location decisions is the formation of a regional production network. The South becomes an industry center, with firms engaged in both stages of production; the North specializes in

[1] The model in Hanson (1994) extends work by Paul Krugman (1991) and Francisco L. Rivera-Batiz (1988).

assembly. Relative to the North, the South has high wages, high land prices, and high employment. The combination of location-specific external economies, land rents, and transport costs creates a regional wage contour: wages decline over space as one moves away from the industry center.

C. *Trade*

Now suppose that Home and Foreign open their economies to trade. Trade recreates the regional production network on a global scale. Given that Foreign is large relative to Home, Foreign is the low-cost producer of stage-1 inputs at the time the countries open to trade. An equilibrium outcome is for Foreign to specialize in stage-1 activities and for Home to specialize in assembly. Home imports the composite input from Foreign and exports the assembled final good. Foreign may or may not engage in assembly.

Conditional on the autarky equilibrium, trade has a dramatic effect on the location of activities in Home. Now that Home specializes in assembly, which has global constant returns, there is no benefit to agglomeration in the South. Since assembly firms in Home import the composite input from Foreign, there is a transport-cost advantage to locating in the region that has relatively good access to the Foreign market. Continuing the Mexican analogy, suppose the North is that region. Transport costs again fix a regional wage differential, but it is the inverse of the autarky case. Since the North has low-cost access to the Foreign market, assembly firms concentrate in that region. Relative to the South, the North now has high wages, high land prices, and high employment. The opening to trade causes labor to migrate from the South to the North and causes the closed-economy regional wage contour to break down.

II. The Data

This section presents evidence on the organization and location of apparel production in Mexico before and after trade reform. I use data from the Mexico *Industrial Census* (Instituto Nacional de Estadística, Geographía e Informática [INEGI], various years; Secretaría de Programación y Presupuesto, various years) and from 95 firm-level interviews I conducted in the Mexican apparel industry during 1990–1991 (see Hanson, 1994). The Mexican apparel industry exhibits the essential features of a regional production network. Prior to trade reform, high-skill apparel tasks were concentrated in Mexico City, and low-skill tasks were located in outlying areas. With the opening to trade, the Mexican apparel industry has shifted from vertically integrated production for the domestic market to product assembly for foreign manufacturers. This shift has involved the relocation of production activities from the center of the country to the Mexico–U.S. border region.

A. *Mexican Trade Policy*

Mexico began to construct a trade regime based on import substitution in the 1940's. Trade restrictions took the form of import licenses, tariffs, and export controls (Timothy King, 1970). In 1985, Mexico reversed its inward-oriented policy by liberalizing trade. Between 1985 and 1987, import-license requirements fell from 92.2 percent of national production to 23.2 percent, and the weighted-average tariff fell from 27.0 percent to 11.0 percent, with a 20.0-percent maximum. In apparel, the weighted-average tariff fell from 49.8 percent to 20.0 percent and import licenses fell from 100.0 percent to zero (Hanson, 1994).

Trade liberalization was not the apparel industry's first exposure to world markets. In the 1960's, the government began to allow off-shore assembly in free-trade zones along the Mexico–U.S. border (Grunwald and Flamm, 1985). Off-shore assembly is one component of a regional production network. A foreign firm, typically from the United States, establishes an assembly plant, known as a *maquiladora,* in Mexico. The maquiladora imports all inputs from the foreign firm, assembles the inputs in Mexico, and exports the final product to the foreign firm.[2] Figure 1 shows the value

[2] The U.S. tariff schedule gives tariff breaks to firms that engage in the off-shore assembly of U.S.-made components. In Mexico, off-shore assembly plants are exempt from import duties and value-added taxes.

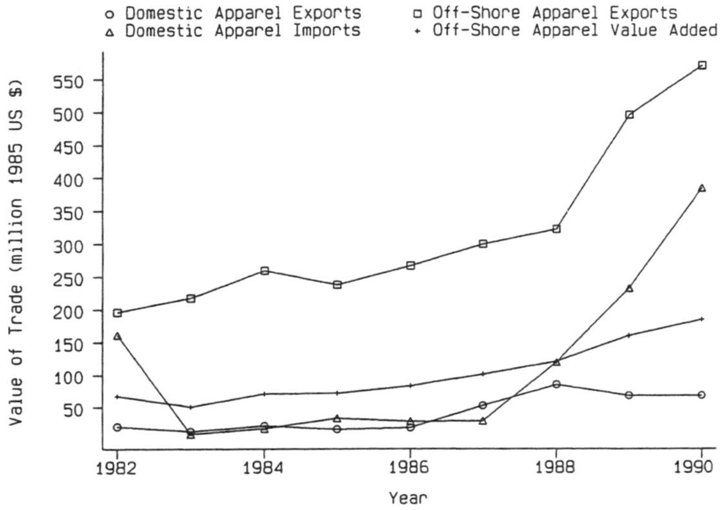

FIGURE 1. MEXICO FOREIGN APPAREL TRADE, 1982–1990

of imports and exports for the domestic and off-shore apparel industries from 1982 to 1990 (Secretariat of Trade and Industrial Promotion [Mexico], unpublished data).[3] Trade has increased dramatically since liberalization. The United States is Mexico's major trading partner in apparel. In 1990, 66.2 percent of non-maquiladora apparel exports went to the United States, and 52.9 percent of Mexican apparel imports came from the United States.[4]

B. *Apparel Production*

Apparel production is organized around assembly subcontracting. Manufacturers control product design and marketing, and divide assembly between their own shops and independent subcontractors. Under the closed economy, most domestic apparel manufacturers were located in Mexico City and subcontracted assembly to shops in outlying areas.[5] The Mexico *Industrial Census* shows indirect evidence of subcontracting. Table 1 reports the size distribution of apparel establishments in 1980. At one end of the distribution are a small number of large establishments, the manufacturers; 250 shops, about 2 percent of total establishments, employed 100 or more workers and accounted for 43.0 percent of total apparel employment. At the other end of the distribution are a large number of small establishments, the subcontractors; 9,233 shops, about 75 percent of total establishments, employed five or fewer workers.

Domestic manufacturers were not the only source of assembly subcontracting under the closed economy. Through the maquiladora arrangement, foreign manufacturers also subcontracted assembly activities to Mexican firms. Despite the similarities in domestic and offshore subcontracting, the two industries remain

[3] Value added in off-shore apparel exports is off-shore exports less imported inputs.

[4] Virtually all maquiladora exports go the United States.

[5] I use the term "closed economy" to refer to the import-substitution period in Mexico, even though the economy was not completely shut off from trade during this time.

TABLE 1—SIZE DISTRIBUTION OF APPAREL ESTABLISHMENTS, 1980

	Number of:		Share of total	
Establishment type	Establishments	Workers	Establishments	Workers
Establishments without paid labor[a]	7,047	10,515	0.578	0.073
Establishments with paid labor	5,152	133,831	0.422	0.927
1–5 workers	2,186	6,188	0.179	0.043
6–25 workers	1,842	22,468	0.151	0.156
26–100 workers	874	43,185	0.072	0.299
101+ workers	250	61,990	0.021	0.430
Total	12,199	144,346	—	—

Source: INEGI (1981).
[a] Establishments without paid labor include the self-employed and shops with only family labor.

entirely separate. Apparel maquiladoras have virtually no linkages with domestic industry. Foreign firms provide all inputs, including fabric, and the maquiladoras, as the law until recently stipulated, export all of their output.

C. *The Location of Production in the Closed Economy*

Figure 2 shows the location of apparel and overall manufacturing employment in Mexico from 1970 to 1988 (INEGI, 1981, 1989b). In 1970, 55.4 percent of national apparel employment was located in the Federal District, the federal entity in which Mexico City is located. In the 1970's manufacturers began to leave the capital; the share of apparel employment located in the Federal District declined to 33.2 percent in 1985. During the same period, the share of apparel jobs located in central states, which neighbor the capital, increased from 13.5 percent to 24.3 percent, and the share in north-central states increased from 12.5 percent to 21.6 percent. Interview material suggests that the activities that left the capital were those related to assembly, and that design and marketing activities remained concentrated in Mexico City. In 1980, 69.8 percent of wholesale trade in apparel and textiles was still conducted in the Federal District.

The relocation of apparel production followed the emergence of wage differentials between Mexico City and outlying states. Figure 3 shows the ratio of average nominal regional wages to average nominal national wages in apparel and all manufacturing from 1970 to 1988 (Secretaría de Programación y Presupuesto, 1971, 1976; INEGI, 1981, 1989b).[6] In 1970, average apparel wages in the Federal District ranged from 1.11 times those in central states to 2.97 times those in southern states. Apparel jobs did not move to regions with the lowest wages, but to regions nearest the capital, suggesting that the location of apparel production was conditioned by access to the industry center in Mexico City.

D. *The Location of Production in the Open Economy*

Since the opening to trade in 1985, there has been a substantial relocation of Mexican apparel production. Figure 2 shows that between 1980 and 1988 the share of apparel employment in border states increased from 15.0 percent to 21.8 percent, while the share of apparel employment in the Federal District and central states declined. Consistent with the predictions of the theory, there has also been a shift from domestic production toward off-shore assembly. Table 2 shows total employment in apparel, employment in off-shore apparel assembly (assembly for foreign firms), and a breakdown of off-shore assembly between

[6] The average wage is calculated as total remuneration per worker.

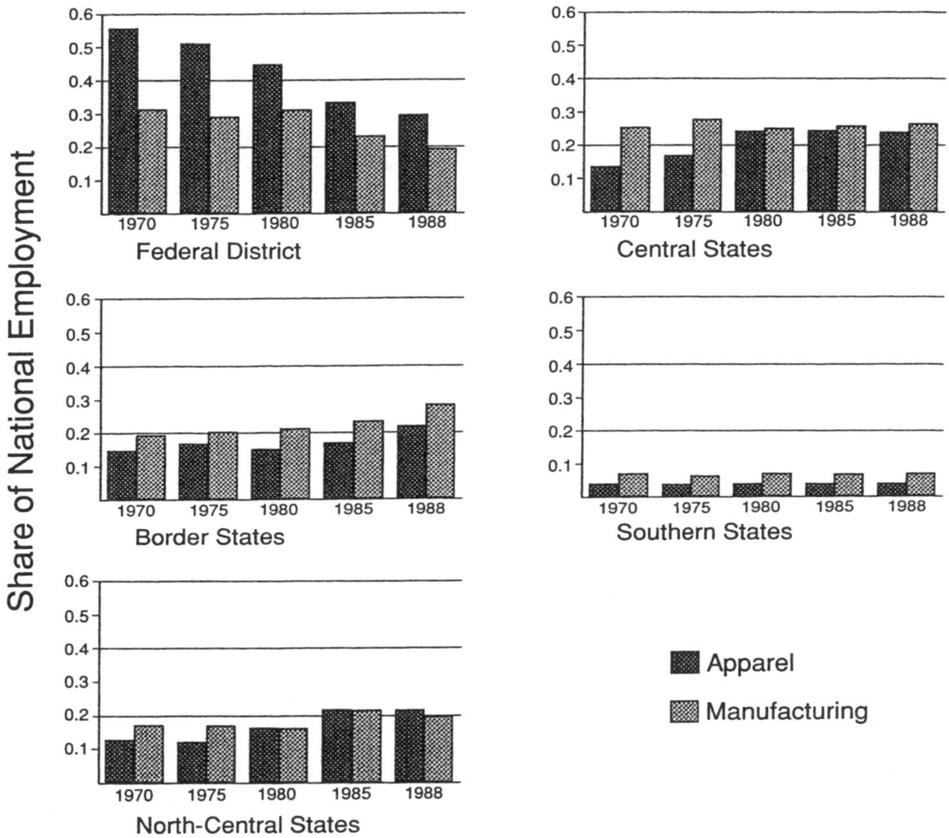

FIGURE 2. REGIONAL EMPLOYMENT SHARES, 1970–1988

border and interior states. Between 1981 and 1988, the share of national apparel employment in off-shore assembly increased from 12.9 percent to 20.0 percent. Most job growth in off-shore assembly has taken place in interior Mexico, as firms that used to produce for the domestic market have shifted to assembly for foreign firms.[7] Figure 1 shows that off-shore assembly exports have boomed since trade reform, increasing from $300.0 million in 1987 to $496.3 million in 1989. By contrast, domestic apparel exports rose from $52.7 million in 1987 to $68.3 million in 1989.[8]

[7] Even as interior firms have shifted from domestic production to off-shore assembly, the share of apparel employment in nonborder states has declined. Net job growth has been concentrated in border states.

[8] Before NAFTA, the United States maintained quotas on Mexican apparel exports under the Multi-Fiber Arrangement. Maquiladoras did have first access to quotas, but quotas were binding in only a few products. Between 1988 and 1990, average quota utilization rates were over 60 percent in just four product categories out of 61 (overalls, pants, pajamas, and shirts and blouses).

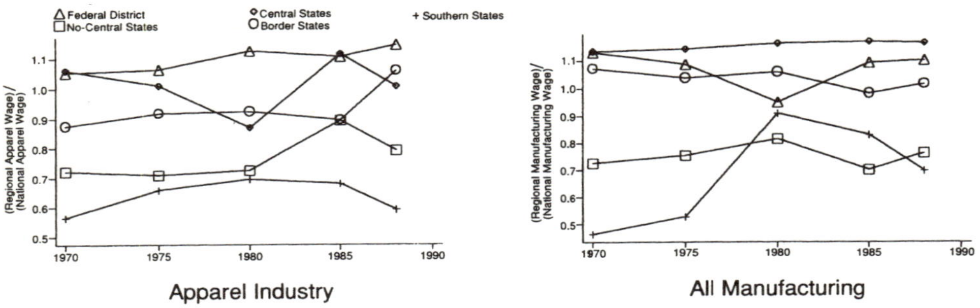

FIGURE 3. RATIO OF REGIONAL TO NATIONAL WAGE, 1970–1988

NAFTA will further integrate Mexico into the U.S. economy by eliminating apparel quotas in the United States and tariffs on both sides of the border. Adjustment to trade liberalization provides a preview of the changes to come. For Mexico, NAFTA implies the continued conversion to apparel assembly and the continued relocation of production activities to the north. The further reduction of trade barriers is only likely to reinforce the emerging structure of production and bilateral trade flows, holding constant changes in other industries.

III. Empirical Results

A. *Model Specification*

The model outlined in Section I predicts that in a closed economy regional wages are decreasing in transport costs to the industry center, but that in an open economy regional wages are determined by access to foreign markets. To test the predictions of the model, I specify a log-linear relationship between regional relative wages in the Mexican apparel industry and transport costs to the apparel industry center in Mexico City:

$$(1) \quad \log(w_{it}/w_{ct}) = \beta_0 + \beta_{1t}\log(d_i) + \mu_{it}$$

where w_i is the apparel wage in region i, w_c is the apparel wage in the industry center (Mexico City), d_i is unit transport costs between region i and Mexico City, which I measure in terms of distance, and μ_{it} is an error term, whose structure I discuss below.

Let T be the unanticipated date of trade liberalization. Theory predicts

$$(2) \quad \beta_{1t} < 0 \qquad t < T$$

$$\beta_{1t} = 0 \qquad t = T.$$

The existence of free-trade zones along the Mexico–U.S. border in effect liberalized trade for the border region before trade was liberalized for the rest of the country. This provides an additional testable hypothesis: given the access of border apparel producers to foreign markets, border apparel wages should be unrelated to distance from Mexico City.

Table 3 lists summary statistics on the regression variables. Wage data are from the Mexico *Industrial Census*. Mexico contains 32 states, including the Federal District. I measure the wage, w_{it}, as average annual remuneration per employee in the apparel industry of state i in year t. I divide w_{it} by the national average apparel wage, w_{nt}, rather than by the Mexico City average apparel wage, w_{ct}, to omit variation in the capital wage that is unrelated to the apparel industry. To isolate regional wage differentials that are specific to the apparel industry, I divide w_{it}/w_{nt} by the ratio of the average manufacturing wage in state i to the national average manufacturing wage, y_{it}/y_{nt}.[9] The estimating equation is

[9] Regression results with $\log(w_{it}/w_{nt})$ as the dependent variable are similar to those given here.

TABLE 2—APPAREL EMPLOYMENT IN MEXICO, 1981–1989

Year	Total employment[a]	Off-shore assembly	Border assembly		Interior assembly	
			Level	Percentage	Level	Percentage
1981	143,986	18,059	14,278	79.1	3,781	20.9
1982	—	15,002	11,891	79.3	3,111	20.7
1983	—	16,212	12,885	79.5	3,327	20.5
1984	—	19,888	15,161	76.2	4,727	23.8
1985	146,809	21,473	15,089	70.3	6,384	29.7
1986	—	25,311	16,883	66.7	8,428	33.3
1987	—	30,273	19,399	64.1	10,874	35.9
1988	173,263	34,707	20,289	58.5	14,418	41.5
1989	—	41,400	—		—	

Source: INEGI (1981, 1989a, b).
[a] Total apparel employment includes the domestic and off-shore apparel industries.

$$(3)\quad \log\left(\frac{w_{it}/w_{nt}}{y_{it}/y_{nt}}\right) = \beta_0 + \beta_{1t}\log(d_i) + \mu_{it}$$

where I allow β_{1t} to vary over time and between border states and the rest of the country.

Data are available for five years (1970, 1975, 1980, 1985, and 1988), providing 155 observations (5 years × 31 states, omitting the Federal District), of which four years (1970, 1975, 1980, and 1985) correspond to the closed economy, and one year (1988) corresponds to the open economy. To control for variation between states in transportation infrastructure, I measure distance as average hours required to travel by first-class passenger bus from the capital of state i to Mexico City.[10]

B. *Econometric Issues*

I have observations on relative apparel wages across states and over time. To control for idiosyncratic components in the error term, I assume that μ_{it} has the form

$$(4)\quad \mu_{it} = \omega_i + \nu_t + \eta_{it}$$

where ω_i is a fixed effect for state i, ν_t is a fixed effect for year t, and η_{it} is an independently and identically distributed random variable with mean zero and variance σ^2. I can control for fixed year effects by including year dummy variables in the regression. Given that the distance measure varies across states but not over time, I cannot control for fixed state effects by including dummy variables for states, as that would introduce perfect multicollinearity into the regression.

Instead, I estimate (3) in levels and in first differences. Estimating (3) in levels will generate coefficient estimates for the effects of distance on regional relative wages before and after trade reform. Without controlling for fixed state effects, however, coefficient estimates from a regression in levels may be subject to bias. First-differencing eliminates fixed state effects from the regression. Incorporating (4) into (3) and taking first differences, I obtain

$$(5)\quad \log\left(\frac{w_{it}/w_{nt}}{y_{it}/y_{nt}}\right) - \log\left(\frac{w_{i,t-1}/w_{n,t-1}}{y_{i,t-1}/y_{n,t-1}}\right) = [\beta_{1t} - \beta_{1,t-1}]\log(d_i) + \nu_t - \nu_{t-1} + \eta_{it} - \eta_{i,t-1}.$$

Under the hypothesis in (2), $\beta_{1t} - \beta_{1,t-1} = 0$ for $t < 1988$, and $\beta_{1t} - \beta_{1,t-1} = -\beta_{1,t-1} > 0$ for $t = 1988$. This implies that the pre-trade reform distance coefficient is identified in 1988. If the Mexican economy had not fully adjusted to trade reform by 1988, the effects of distance from Mexico City on regional relative apparel wages may not have been fully

[10] Bus hours are from Ben Box (1990).

TABLE 3—VARIABLE MEANS

Year	w_{it}/w_{nt}	$(w_{it}/w_{nt})/(y_{it}/y_{nt})$
1970	0.516	0.780
	(0.281)	(0.368)
1975	0.602	0.829
	(0.435)	(0.473)
1980	0.566	0.755
	(0.317)	(0.418)
1985	0.662	0.845
	(0.383)	(0.500)
1988	0.689	0.894
	(0.386)	(0.544)

Notes: Standard errors are given in parentheses. The number of observations is 31 (values are for all states except the Federal District, the federal entity that contains Mexico City). The mean distance to Mexico City (bus hours) is 14.25 (SE = 14.12).

eliminated between 1985 and 1988. The distance coefficient from a regression in first differences may underestimate the true value and should be considered a lower bound.

C. *Empirical Results*

Table 4 gives estimation results on regional relative apparel wages for 155 observations from 1970, 1975, 1980, 1985, and 1988. The (a) columns include year dummies; the (b) columns do not. I interact log distance to Mexico City ("Distance") with "Border," a dummy variable for border states, and with "yr1988," a dummy variable for the year 1988.[11]

The results show strong support for the hypothesis that regional relative apparel wages decrease with distance from Mexico City. In all regressions, Distance is negative and statistically significant at the 5-percent or 1-percent level. The quantitative effect of distance is moderate. From the results in column (iii-b) a one-standard-deviation increase in log distance (0.966) reduces the log of state relative apparel wages by 0.184, which is one-fourth of a standard deviation (0.679). It should be emphasized that the regional wage contour identified by the regression results exists holding constant overall manufacturing regional wage differentials.

The results for levels regressions show some support for the hypothesis that trade liberalization eliminates the distance effect. The coefficient on Distance × yr1988 is positive, and in regressions with year dummies it is similar in absolute value to the coefficient on Distance, but it is not statistically significant in any regression. However, I fail to reject the null hypothesis that the coefficient on Distance in 1988 (the sum of the coefficients on Distance and Distance × yr1988) is zero at the 5-percent level.

There is other evidence that trade matters for wages. The coefficient on Distance × Border is positive and statistically significant in all regressions. This is consistent with the hypothesis that under the closed economy the existence of free-trade zones in the border region separated border apparel producers from the domestic apparel-industry center in Mexico City. While it may not seem surprising to find that wages on the Mexico–U.S. border are high relative to other regions, this result holds even controlling for overall regional wage differentials.[12] What is surprising is that the estimated distance coefficient for border states (the sum of the coefficients for Distance and Distance × Border) is positive, implying that relative apparel wages in the border region are highest for states farthest from Mexico City. Among border states, distance to Mexico City increases as one moves from east to west, implying that apparel wages are highest for border states closest to California. Outside of New York, Los Angeles is the largest apparel-industry center in the United States. High relative apparel wages in states that are proximate to California may reflect the benefits

[11] I also include Border in the regression to capture the effects of time and distance-invariant factors specific to the border that matter for relative wages (such as possibilities for emigration to the United States). Since these factors may not be related to the apparel industry, I limit the hypothesis tests below to whether distance coefficients differ over time or between border and nonborder states. In unreported regressions, I found no evidence that the border intercept term varies over time.

[12] The intercept term for border states is negative, but the positive border distance coefficient is sufficiently large that predicted border relative apparel wages exceed those in all other regions except Mexico City.

TABLE 4—REGRESSION OF STATE RELATIVE APPAREL WAGES ON DISTANCE FROM MEXICO CITY

	Regression					
	(i)		(ii)		(iii)	
Variable	(a)	(b)	(a)	(b)	(a)	(b)
Constant	−0.195 (0.122)	−0.182 (0.155)	−0.195 (0.120)	−0.108 (0.158)	−0.195 (0.120)	−0.097 (0.160)
Distance	−0.150* (0.062)	−0.150* (0.062)	−0.162** (0.059)	−0.183** (0.061)	−0.165** (0.060)	−0.192** (0.064)
Distance × Border	0.506** (0.101)	0.506** (0.102)	0.506** (0.097)	0.506** (0.100)	0.514** (0.096)	0.520** (0.098)
Distance × yr1988			0.063 (0.056)	0.166 (0.125)	0.076 (0.080)	0.210 (0.160)
Distance × Border × yr1988					−0.041 (0.088)	−0.071 (0.095)
Border	−0.838** (0.273)	−0.838** (0.276)	−0.838** (0.261)	−0.838** (0.271)	−0.838** (0.262)	−0.838** (0.270)
F on H1 [d.f.]			1.50 [1, 150]	0.02 [1, 146]	0.89 [1, 149]	0.01 [1, 145]
F on H2 [d.f.]	19.70** [1, 151]	19.02** [1, 147]	20.43** [1, 150]	15.20** [1, 146]	21.83** [1, 149]	16.64** [1, 145]
F on H3 [d.f.]					4.53* [1, 149]	0.89 [1, 145]
Adjusted R^2:	0.138	0.121	0.140	0.125	0.135	0.121
N:	155	155	155	155	155	155
Year dummies:	no	yes	no	yes	no	yes

Notes: Heteroscedasticity-consistent standard errors are given in parentheses. Variable definitions: "Distance" is log (bus hours to Mexico City); "Border" is a dummy variable that indicates border states; yr1988 is a dummy variable that indicates the year is 1988. Hypothesis tests are as follows:

H1 indicates H_0: Distance = −Distance × yr1988

H2 indicates H_0: Distance = Distance × Border

H3 indicates H_0: Distance × yr1988 = (Distance × Border) + (Distance × Border × yr1988).

* Statistically significant at the 5-percent level.
** Statistically significant at the 1-percent level.

of relatively low-cost access to the apparel-industry center in Los Angeles.

Given that the time span of my sample only covers three years following trade reform, requiring that trade liberalization eliminates the effect of distance from Mexico City may be too strong a test of the trade-liberalization hypothesis. A weaker test would be to see whether distance effects for interior states in 1988 are converging to those of border states. In the final two columns of Table 4, I test the hypothesis that the distance coefficient for 1988 in interior states (the sum of the coefficients for Distance and Distance × yr1988) is equal to the distance coefficient for border states in 1988 (the sum of the coefficients for Distance, Distance × Border, and Distance × Border × yr1988). In the regression with year controls, I fail to reject the null hypothesis that the distance coefficients for border and interior states are equal in 1988 (while I reject the null hypothesis that they are equal in earlier

TABLE 5—REGRESSION OF FIRST DIFFERENCE OF STATE RELATIVE APPAREL WAGES ON DISTANCE FROM MEXICO CITY

	Regression					
	(i)		(ii)		(iii)	
Variable	(a)	(b)	(a)	(b)	(a)	(b)
Constant	−0.026 (0.031)	−0.031 (0.039)	−0.026 (0.030)	0.020 (0.039)	−0.026 (0.030)	0.030 (0.040)
Distance	0.016 (0.016)	0.016 (0.016)	0.009 (0.014)	−0.007 (0.015)	0.006 (0.014)	−0.015 (0.016)
Distance × Border	−0.003 (0.009)	−0.003 (0.027)	−0.003 (0.008)	−0.003 (0.008)	0.005 (0.007)	0.009 (0.008)
Distance × yr1988			0.028* (0.012)	0.090** (0.026)	0.038* (0.016)	0.121** (0.030)
Distance × Border × yr1988					−0.033 (0.021)	−0.051* (0.021)
F on H4	0.64	0.63	0.19	0.55	1.29	0.79
[d.f.]	[2, 121]	[2, 118]	[2, 120]	[2, 117]	[2, 119]	[2, 116]
Adjusted R^2:	−0.003	0.006	0.056	0.110	0.068	0.151
N:	124	124	124	124	124	124
Year dummies:	no	yes	no	yes	no	yes

Notes: Heteroscedasticity-consistent standard errors are given in parentheses. Variable definitions: "Distance" is log (bus hours to Mexico City); "Border" is a dummy variable that indicates border states; yr1988 is a dummy variable that indicates the year is 1988. The hypothesis test (H4) is

$$H_0\text{: Distance} = 0 \text{ and Distance} \times \text{Border} = 0.$$

* Statistically significant at the 5-percent level.
** Statistically significant at the 1-percent level.

years). This constitutes evidence for the trade-liberalization hypothesis: since trade reform, distance effects for border and interior states are converging to similar levels.

To control for fixed state effects, Table 5 presents estimation of equation (5), in which I regress the first difference of regional relative apparel wages on log distance. The first-differenced results show much stronger support for the trade-liberalization hypothesis than those from levels regressions. The hypothesis in (2) predicts that before 1988 the distance coefficient will be zero and that in 1988 it will equal the negative of the pre-trade reform distance coefficient.[13] The results show that distance coefficients are not statistically different from zero before 1988 and that in 1988 the distance coefficient is positive and statistically significant. This is consistent with the hypothesis that the distance coefficient prior to 1988 is negative and that there is a statistically significant decline in the magnitude of the distance coefficient between 1985 and 1988. Coefficient estimates increase when year dummies are included and when a separate distance coefficient for border states in 1988 is included. The largest distance coefficients in Table 5 are smaller than any of those in Table 4, but this may be due to the fact that the first-differenced results are lower-bound estimates.

Consistent with the results in Table 4, the first-differenced results show evidence of convergence in distance coefficients for border and interior states. The final two columns of Table 5 show that the change in the distance

[13] In unreported regressions I allowed distance coefficients to vary over all years and in all cases failed to reject the null hypothesis that distance coefficients are constant for the period 1970–1985.

coefficient is negative for border states in 1988; in column (iii-b), which includes year controls, this change is statistically significant. This is consistent with the hypothesis that between 1985 and 1988 the distance coefficient fell in absolute value in all regions, becoming less negative in interior states and less positive in border states.

Overall, the results show strong support for the existence of a regional wage contour in the Mexican apparel industry under the closed economy and for the partial breakdown of this contour in the transition to an open economy. The strength of the results is that, even controlling for overall manufacturing regional wage differentials, relative apparel wages are lower for interior states that are more distant from the capital. There is no indication that the open-economy wage contour will exhibit less dispersion in regional relative wages. Border states currently have relatively high wages. The relocation of apparel jobs to the north, which is only likely to continue under NAFTA, suggests that regional wage differentials will also be a feature of the open economy. Given the importance of access to U.S. apparel industry centers in an open economy, a new wage contour may be emerging in which regional relative wages are determined not by distance to Mexico City, but by access to the U.S. market.

IV. Concluding Remarks

This paper develops the concept of a regional production network in which localization economies arise endogenously from the provision of specialized inputs. Congestion costs created by agglomeration push low-skill activities into outlying regions. I apply the model to a study of the effects of trade liberalization on the Mexican apparel industry. Consistent with the model, closed-economy apparel production was geographically concentrated. Since trade reform, the domestic apparel industry is converting to product assembly for foreign firms. Concurrently, producers are relocating their activities to the Mexico–U.S. border region. Estimation results on regional apparel wages are consistent with the existence of localization economies.

For a developing economy, trade liberalization involves a transition from vertically integrated manufacturing to a specialized role of subcontracting for developed-country firms. In apparel, and other labor-intensive industries, this transition implies the conversion to off-shore assembly and possibly profound changes in the spatial location of production. Sectoral-level analyses miss these changes by focusing on resource movements across industries while ignoring the organizational and locational changes that occur within industries. This has been the case in most of the economy-wide models developed to study NAFTA (e.g., U.S. International Trade Commission, 1992). The effects of NAFTA on the pattern of regional specialization in Mexico are likely to be at least as profound as those on the pattern of industrial specialization.

REFERENCES

Box, Ben. *South American handbook 1990*. New York: Prentice-Hall, 1990.

Grunwald, Joseph and Flamm, Kenneth. *The global factory: Foreign assembly in international trade*. Washington, DC: Brookings Institution, 1985.

Hanson, Gordon H. "Localization Economies, Vertical Organization, and Trade." National Bureau of Economic Research (Cambridge, MA) Working Paper No. 4744, April 1994.

Instituto Nacional de Estadística, Geographía e Informática (INEGI). *XI censo industrial, 1981*. Mexico City: Instituto Nacional de Estadística, Geographía e Informática, 1981.

______. *Estadísticas de la industria maquiladora de exportación, 1978–1988*. Aguascalientes, Mexico: Instituto Nacional de Estadística, Geographía e Informática, 1989a.

______. *Resultados oportunos*. Aguascalientes, Mexico: Instituto Nacional de Estadística, Geographía e Informática, 1989b.

King, Timothy. *Mexico: Industrialization and trade policies since 1940*. London: Oxford University Press, 1970.

Krugman, Paul. "Increasing Returns and Economic Geography." *Journal of Polit-*

ical Economy, June 1991, *99*(3), pp. 483–99.

Michaely, Michael; Papageorgiou, Demetris and Choksi, Armeane M. *Liberalizing foreign trade: Lessons of experience in the developing world, Volume 7*. Cambridge, MA: Blackwell, 1991.

Rivera-Batiz, Francisco L. "Increasing Returns, Monopolistic Competition, and Agglomeration Economies in Consumption and Production." *Regional Science and Urban Economics*, February 1988, *18*(1), pp. 125–53.

Secretaría de Programación y Presupuesto. *IX censo industrial, 1971*. Mexico City: Secretaría de Programación y Presupuesto, 1971.

______. *X censo industrial, 1976*. Mexico City: Secretaría de Programación y Presupuesto, 1976.

U.S. International Trade Commission. "Economy-Wide Implications of a FTA with Mexico and a NAFTA with Canada and Mexico." U.S. International Trade Commission Publication No. 2508. Washington, DC: U.S. Government Printing Office, 1992.

[24]

ELSEVIER European Economic Review 43 (1999) 379–407

EUROPEAN ECONOMIC REVIEW

Economic geography and regional production structure: An empirical investigation

Donald R. Davis[a,c], David E. Weinstein[b,c,*]

[a] *Harvard University, Federal Reserve Bank of New York, New York, USA*
[b] *School of Business Administration, University of Michigan, Ann Arbor, MI 48109, USA*
[c] *NBER, Cambridge, MA 02138, USA*

Accepted 1 June 1998

Abstract

There are two principal theories of why countries or regions trade: comparative advantage and increasing returns to scale. Yet there is virtually no empirical work that assesses the relative importance of these two theories in accounting for production structure and trade. We use a framework that nests an increasing returns model of economic geography featuring 'home market effects' with that of Heckscher–Ohlin. We employ these trade models to account for the structure of regional production in Japan. We find support for the existence of economic geography effects in eight of nineteen manufacturing sectors, including such important ones as transportation equipment, iron and steel, electrical machinery, and chemicals. Moreover, we find that these effects are economically very significant. The latter contrasts with the results of Davis and Weinstein (1996, Does economic geography matter for interactional specialiazation?, NEBR # 5706), which found scant economic significance of economic geography for the structure of OECD production. We conclude that while economic geography may explain little about the international structure of production, it is very important for understanding the regional structure of production. © 1999 Elsevier Science B.V. All rights reserved.

JEL classification: F1; D5; E1

Keywords: Economic geography; Home market; Comparative advantage

* Corresponding author. Tel.: + 1 313 936-2866; e-mail: weinstei@umich.edu.

PII: S0021-2921(98)00063-4

1. Introduction

Why is there trade? This is a fundamental question for international economists. And it is equally so for those who consider trade across regions. Theory has provided two principal answers: comparative advantage and increasing returns. Comparative advantage holds that trade across geographical units arises to take advantage of inherent differences. Increasing returns says that trade arises to take advantage of scale and variety gains from specialization.

While theorists have devoted great energy to developing myriad models of comparative advantage and increasing returns, empirical research has had next to nothing to say about the relative importance of these two forces in driving world trade.[1] At one time, researchers might have pointed to the large volume of intra-industry trade or of North–North trade as confirming the importance of increasing returns. Yet closer examination has proven that these phenomena do not distinguish the increasing returns theory from that of comparative advantage.[2]

Renewed hope for distinguishing the theories arises if we restrict ourselves to the class of increasing returns models that Krugman (1991) has labeled 'economic geography'.[3] The defining characteristic of these theories is the interaction of increasing returns and costs of trade. As Krugman (1980) showed, this does allow one to identify a critical test distinguishing a world of comparative advantage from one with increasing returns. In a world of comparative advantage, unusually strong demand for a good, *ceteris paribus*, will make that good an import. In a world with increasing returns, typically each good will have only one site of production. When there are trade costs, a country with unusually strong demand for a good makes that an excellent site to locate production, hence makes that country the exporter of that good. These 'home market effects' of demand on trade patterns thus provide a key feature to distinguish a world of comparative advantage from one of increasing returns.

In Davis and Weinstein (1996), we made this search for home market effects the centerpiece of our effort to distinguish the two theories. We noted that the home market effect has an equivalent characterization as a 'magnification effect' from idiosyncratic components of demand to output. We then applied this to

[1] In reviewing the empirics of the new trade theory, Krugman (1994, p. 23) asks: 'How much of world trade is explained by increasing returns as opposed to comparative advantage? That may not be a question with a precise answer. What is quite clear is that if a precise answer is possible, we do not know it'.

[2] See Chipman (1992), Davis (1995, 1997), and Deardorff (1998).

[3] The reader should note that the usage of the term 'economic geography' in this paper refers specifically to the class of models deriving from Krugman (1980, 1991) that interact trade costs and increasing returns in a monopolistic competition framework. As Krugman acknowledges in the latter work, there is a long tradition of work in the more general field referred to by the same name.

explain the structure of OECD production. Our null hypothesis was that the conventional Heckscher–Ohlin model explains production structure at the four-digit ISIC level. The alternative hypothesis was that Heckscher–Ohlin explains only the broad industrial structure of production in these countries at the three-digit ISIC level, and that this must be augmented with a model of economic geography to account for the finer four-digit production structure. Within this overarching structure, we identify three possibilities: a frictionless world (comparative advantage or IRS); comparative advantage with positive trade costs; and economic geography.

Our results did not support the proposition that economic geography plays an important role in determining the structure of OECD production. The data strongly rejected a frictionless model, since in such a model demand would have no influence on the location of production. Yet the results also rejected the economic geography framework in favor of a model of comparative advantage with trade costs. Some specifications did indicate significant economic geography effects in a number of important industries. However, all specifications which allowed for inclusion of factor endowments as predictors of fine production structure show that the economic geography effects were not robust.

The same question that we ask of countries can be asked of sub-units of countries: Why do regions trade? This is an important and fascinating problem in its own right. Moreover it promises to yield insights of broader applicability. From a theoretical standpoint, we should expect that the same basic forces are at work in the regional and international cases. However, from an empirical standpoint, there is no necessary reason that the answers of their relative importance be the same. It is perfectly conceivable that economic geography could have little influence on the structure of production across countries, yet be very important in explaining the structure of production across regions within a country. This could arise, for example, due to lower interregional trade costs, which theory suggests should strengthen economic geography effects. Thus, an investigation that examines the trade of regions may provide the best hope for identifying such effects, and so also provide a favorable experiment to distinguish the microeconomic stories underlying the comparative advantage and economic geography approaches.

2. Theoretical framework

2.1. A regional approach

The seminal theoretical contribution underlying our work is Krugman's (1980) model of the 'home market effect'. In Davis and Weinstein (1996), we showed how to nest his model of economic geography with a model of comparative advantage, the aim being to identify and estimate the importance of such home market effects on OECD production structure. Since the basic theoretical framework in the present paper follows that developed in our earlier work, we will here provide a more compact presentation. However, there are some important issues that must be addressed in moving from an international to a regional setting before we turn to the specifics of our framework.

A conventional contrast between international and regional economics is the greater degree of factor mobility across regions within a country than across countries. This could in principle be very important. Large countries or regions have highly diversified products available without trade costs, so tend to have low price indices. Under certain conditions, large countries may be desirable locations for producers to locate, so they may tend to pay high wages. As well, if some of the differentiated goods themselves serve as inputs to production of differentiated goods, then labor may be more productive in large economies, again tending to raise wages there. All of these suggest that large countries or regions may also attract large numbers of immigrants, tending to empty national or international hinterlands. The greater mobility of factors across regions within a country tends to raise the salience of this issue (see Krugman, 1980, 1991; Krugman and Venables, 1995).

Of course, the extensive literature on economic geography has considered at length the tensions between these pressures for concentration and the counteracting pressures for dispersion of economic activity. We choose to sidestep these issues, even as we recognize their importance. We will assume that within the economic geography section of our model, there are in fact some countervailing forces at work that prevent all economic activity from locating on a single point without inquiring the nature of those forces.

We will assume that the economy is in equilibrium. If this is so, then imposing a further condition that factors are not allowed to move *ex post* will not disturb the nature of the equilibrium. In other words, we are going to treat the regional model as a special case of the international model in which the specific combination of centrifugal and centripetal forces are such that in equilibrium no one would migrate even if they could. The legitimacy of treating a model of regions as if it were a model of countries depends on the questions one addresses. Clearly, the comparative statics of the two models will not be the same. However, our interest is precisely in the static equilibrium, which we believe justifies this approach.

2.2. Previous empirical studies

The role that scale economies, internal or external, play in production has been an important topic in a wide range of contributions from the regional economics literature (e.g. Sveikauskas, 1975; Nakamura, 1985; Henderson, 1986; Sveikauskas et al., 1988; Henderson et al., 1995; Glaeser et al., 1992). These studies have typically searched for the existence of economies of scale or spillovers by estimating production functions or growth specifications with aggregate industry- or city-size variables on the right-hand side.

The present study differs from the regional contributions in two important respects. The first is that we articulate our empirical specification from a general equilibrium perspective. The second is that within our general equilibrium framework we are able to identify precise null and alternative hypotheses. The focus on general equilibrium is valuable because it allows us to draw on the wealth of analytic results from the international trade literature. In the present study, it allows us to focus on a particularly surprising result (discussed more fully below) known as the 'home market effect'.

The full specification of null and alternate hypotheses is valuable, since it allows us to be precise about which hypotheses may be distinguished by the evidence. This is particularly important when searching for evidence of scale economies, as these may easily be confounded with omitted factors in regressions of industry output on aggregate regional variables, such as city size or employment. This difficulty common to many of the regional studies is voiced, for example, in Ellison and Glaeser's conclusion (Ellison and Glaeser, 1997, p. 897) that their own 'analysis of the mean concentration of industries [the principle dependent variable in their study]... is compatible with a pure natural advantage model, a pure spillover model, or models with various combinations of the two factors'.

The combination of a general equilibrium perspective with the explicit specification of a null and alternative hypothesis is particularly important in comparing our study with related work in the regional literature. An example is the suggestive work of Justman (1994), which also considers a variant of the Linder hypothesis. Justman approached the problem by calculating industry correlations between supply and demand across regions, and then regressing these correlations on industry characteristics. Justman argued that in industries in which the Linder hypothesis is valid there should be strong correlations between supply and demand. Our study, focused on home market effects, imposes a more stringent test on the data – not only must supply and demand be correlated, but demand must move supply more than one-for-one.

One might reasonably ask whether our more stringent test is justified or whether one might want to settle for correlations as in the Justman study. To understand this, we must return to the distinguishing prediction of the Linder hypothesis. Virtually any model with trade costs will have the feature that (*ceteris paribus*) local demand and supply are correlated. The critical feature of the Linder hypothesis is that demand deviations cause more-than-proportional supply responses. Thus it can be problematic if one focuses simply on correlations instead of magnitudes. Suppose that a demand deviation of ten causes output to rise by one but that the observed data is very tightly distributed around a line of slope one-tenth. The Linder hypothesis is clearly not valid, but the correlation might be quite high. Similarly, if a demand deviation of one caused output to move by ten, but the data are very noisy, one would have a low correlation but clear evidence of the Linder hypothesis. In other words, in order to test for the home market effects characteristic of the Linder hypothesis, one cannot search simply for correlations between supply and demand. Rather one must focus on the magnitude of the relationship. This forms the intuition for our tests which we explain more formally in the next section.

2.3. Economic geography, comparative advantage, and the home market effect

This section outlines the key theoretical insight underlying our empirical work. Building on an insight from Linder (1961), Krugman (1980) posed a simple question: Can idiosyncratically high demand for a good in a country or region, *ceteris paribus*, make that good an export? It is worth considering his intuitive argument before developing the formal models:

> In a world characterized both by increasing returns and by transportation costs, there will obviously be an incentive to concentrate production of a good near its largest market, even if there is some demand for the good elsewhere. The reason is simply that by concentrating production in one place one can realize the scale economies, while by locating near the larger market, one minimizes transportation costs. This point – which is more often emphasized in location theory than in trade theory – is the basis for the common argument that countries will tend to export those kinds of product for which they have relatively large domestic demand. *Notice that this argument is wholly dependent on increasing returns; in a world of diminishing returns, strong domestic demand for a good will tend to make it an import rather than an export.* (1980, p. 955, italics added).

This role for idiosyncratically high demand to lead a good to be exported – the 'home market effect' – is our central focus. Its value from an empirical standpoint is that, conditional on costs of trade, it provides a clear contrast between the diminishing returns, comparative advantage theory, and that of increasing returns and economic geography.

Krugman develops a special case of the Dixit–Stiglitz model of monopolistic competition. The crucial departure from Krugman (1979) is the introduction of iceberg costs of trade between economies. The particular example that he works with assumes that there are two types of consumers in the world, each of which demands only one of the two classes of differentiated varieties available in the world. He further assumes that the two equal-sized economies have the consumers in mirror proportions. Symmetry insures nominal factor price equalization. Well-known properties of the Dixit–Stiglitz iso-elastic case insure that output per variety is the same for all varieties of both types in each country. The only thing to be determined is how many of each variety are produced in each country. Assume that the majority-type consumers in each country exist in relative proportion $\lambda \geq 1$. Because of trade costs, consumers will demand smaller quantities of imported than of locally produced varieties. Let the ratio of the typical consumption of an imported to a local variety be given by $\sigma < 1$. Finally, let the number of varieties produced in a country tailored to the tastes of the majority be given by μ. Krugman (1980) shows that for the range of incomplete specialization,

$$\mu = \frac{\lambda - \sigma}{1 - \lambda\sigma}.$$

If there were no idiosyncratic component to demand, i.e. $\lambda = 1$, then each country would produce the same number of varieties of each of the two classes of goods, i.e. $\mu = 1$. This is important, since it suggests that the 'baseline' composition of production will be similar across countries, absent idiosyncratic demand. However, when there are idiosyncratic elements of demand, $\lambda > 1$, then it is easily verified that a country produces a larger number of the varieties preferred by its majority-type consumers, so $\mu > 1$.

The home market effect, though, requires a yet stronger result. As noted above, Krugman (1980) asked if idiosyncratically high demand could lead a good to be exported. If high demand is to lead the good to be exported, then production must rise by even more than demand. That is, the home market effect requires that idiosyncratically high demand have a *magnified* impact on production of the relevant good. These are equivalent statements. From above, and again for the range of incomplete specialization, we see that

$$\frac{\partial \mu}{\partial \lambda} = \frac{1 - \sigma^2}{(1 - \sigma\lambda)^2} > 1$$

That is, Krugman has shown that precisely this kind of 'magnification effect' from idiosyncratic demand to production holds in this model. When we turn to the empirical work, this will provide the foundation for deviations from the 'baseline' composition of production.

Weder extends this result to the case in which countries differ in size. His principal result is contained in his Proposition 3: 'In the open-economy equilibrium, each country is a net exporter of that group of differentiated goods where it has a comparative home-market advantage'. And a country has a comparative home-market advantage when it has a higher *proportion* of demanders of one type relative to the other. The insight is simple but powerful. Producers of varieties of the different classes of goods must compete for resources within a market. Absolute market size alone leads all producers to want to locate in the larger market. But the aggregate resource constraint in the large market forces an ordering of priorities. It is intuitively pleasing that it is the relative strength of demand that is in fact the deciding factor in determining the pattern of exports. It is straightforward to derive simple extensions considering separately more countries and more goods, indicating some robustness for the basic home market relation (cf. Davis and Weinstein, 1996).

We have seen that in the world of economic geography, unusually strong demand for a good leads that good to be an export, reflecting the home market effect. This contrasts with the results in a comparative advantage world. As noted above, Krugman (1980) argued that '... in a world of diminishing returns, strong domestic demand for a good will tend to make it an import rather than an export'. Let us think about the underlying logic in a simple import-demand export-supply framework. Consider a small idiosyncratic component of demand in a country. In a competitive world with rising marginal opportunity costs, this will be met with additional local supply only if the price rises. Will a home market effect arise? Note that with a fixed trade-cost wedge, the local price can rise in equilibrium only if the foreign price rises as well. But if the foreign export supply curve has the conventional slope, then this must also imply larger foreign net exports of this good. Hence the local idiosyncratic demand is met in part by a rise in local supply and in part by greater imports – hence local supply rises less than one-for-one with idiosyncratic demand. If the good in question were non-traded both before and after the demand perturbation, then local supply would rise exactly one-for-one. But unless the foreign export supply curve has a perverse slope, local supply will never rise more than one-for-one with idiosyncratic local demand. That is, in the comparative advantage world, home market effects will not arise.

2.4. Empirical specification

We turn now to translating this theory to an implementable empirical specification. The model of Krugman (1980) cannot be taken directly to data. The one-factor model that he develops is entirely appropriate for theory. But it can be rejected without recourse to data if the suggestion is that endowment differences are not important for the structure of production. Thus, if we are to give Krugman's theory a chance, we will need to build into it a structure in which endowments are allowed to matter at one level of aggregation, and economic geography to matter at a finer level of disaggregation. Such an approach is suggested by the work of Helpman (1981), and this is broadly the course that we take. However, we caution that the literature has not developed the economic geography model in sufficient generality to deal simultaneously with differences in the size of regions, goods, and industries, as well as to allow for differences in input composition and demand structure. We cannot fully remedy this shortcoming, but we do believe that the framework we develop presents a highly structured and sensible interpretation of Krugman (1980) that focuses on a central feature of the theory.[4]

In the discussion that follows, it will prove useful to distinguish three levels of production. The broadest level is what we term industries, with each industry composed of many goods. In the empirical section, we will have six industries covering the 19 goods that form the basis of our analysis. For the case of monopolistic competition, each good will feature many varieties. While the varieties play an important theoretical role as the locus of increasing returns, they are never directly observed.

Let us begin with the comparative advantage theory. Our representative of this class for the purpose of our empirical work is the square Heckscher–Ohlin model. Assume that all regions r of Japan share identical constant returns to scale technologies. Assume as well that these technologies are Leontief. Let there be F factors of production. Let there be N industries with G_n goods in industry n. Assume that the total number of goods is the same as the number of primary factors, so $\sum_{n=1}^{N} G_n = F$. Assume that the $F \times F$ technology matrix mapping output into factors is invertible, where the inverse is given by Ω. Assume that all regions are diversified in production. Letting the vector of goods output for region r and good g in industry n be X_g^{nr} the vector of factor endowments be V^r, and Ω_g^n be the corresponding row of Ω, there is an exact relation:

$$X_g^{nr} = \Omega_g^n V^r. \tag{1}$$

In this framework, endowments fully suffice to determine the structure of goods production (i.e. for our most disaggregated observations).

The alternative that we develop is in the spirit of Helpman's (1981) nesting of the Heckscher–Ohlin and simple monopolistic competition models. There endowments served to determine the broad industrial structure of a country while monopolistic competition led to intra-industry specialization. We follow the same division, assuming that Heckscher–Ohlin determines the output by regions of industries, while economic geography determines the output of goods within industries. Let A be a technology matrix, with A_n a column reflecting input usage within industry n. Within industry n, there are G_n goods. We assume that demand arises from Dixit–Stiglitz (1977) iso-elastic preferences, and that the elasticity of substitution between varieties of a good is common for all varieties of all goods within an industry. This implies that the equilibrium scale of

[4] To insist on a fully general model is to condemn the theory never to be considered empirically from a general equilibrium perspective. It will remain, as Krugman (1994, p. 9) noted in reviewing the new trade theory, 'an enormous theoretical enterprise with very little empirical confirmation'. Hence, in our empirical specification we will take what we see to be the robust core of these results, and make strong identifying assumptions as required to implement the theory.

production of each variety of each good within an industry is common (see Krugman, 1980). If we further assume that both fixed and marginal costs are in scalar proportion to A_n, then we can take that column as the total input coefficients for a variety of any good in industry n. We assume that the coefficients of A are fixed.

Here, as in Helpman (1981), endowments serve to determine the exact structure of production by industry. This can be expressed as

$$X^{nr} = \sum_{g=1}^{G_n} X_g^{nr} = \bar{\Omega}^n V^r, \tag{2}$$

where $\bar{\Omega}$ is an $N \times N$ matrix. However endowments provide no information about a region's production structure within an industry – viz. the goods composition of production within the industry. For example, they tell us which regions have a large textile industry, but not whether this will be occupied producing carpets, rugs, etc.

We now need to specify how the location of goods production within industries is determined for the economic geography specification. Absent idiosyncratic components of demand, regions will divide production across goods within an industry in the same proportion as all other regions. Hence regions with a large industry n will produce absolutely large amounts of all goods within n, but *ceteris paribus* will have the same composition across goods as regions with a smaller industry n. This base level of production of a particular good for a region, which depends on that region's overall commitment to the encompassing industry and to the importance of that good in the aggregate within that industry, is what we will refer to as SHARE.

However, in the spirit of Krugman (1980), we posit that this base level of production of a good must be adjusted to reflect the influences of idiosyncratically high demand. Our specification is influenced by Weder (1995) to focus on differences in the *relative* importance of a good for the specific region relative to all the regions taken together. The magnitude of this influence is, of course, also influenced by that region's total commitment of resources to the industry of interest. This will give rise to a variable that we term IDIODEM. This will play a key role when we turn to hypothesis testing, since the economic geography framework predicts that the responsiveness of goods production to movements in IDIODEM will be more than one-to-one.

We can state this hypothesis first in a general form. Let $\gamma_g^{nr} \equiv X_g^{nr}/X^{nr}$, $\delta_g^{nr} \equiv D_g^{nr}/D^{nr}$, and ROJ stand for the rest of Japan (except region r). Then goods production is modeled as

$$X_g^{nr} = f(\gamma_g^{nROJ} X^{nr}, (\delta_g^{nr} - \delta_g^{nROJ}) X^{nr}), \tag{3}$$

where D denotes absorption in either the region, r, or Japan as a whole, J, and the first derivatives are expected to be non-negative. The first term in f captures the tendency for each region to produce the same relative shares of each good as other regions. Specifically, we postulate that a region's output of any good, X_g^{nr}, is going to be centered around the product of: (a) the share of that good in that industry's output for the rest of Japan; and (b) a scale term reflecting that industry's total size within the region, X^{nr}. The second term in f measures the demand deviation. If all regions demanded the same share of each good, this term would equal zero. If a good comprises a greater (smaller) share of demand within an industry, however, this term will be positive (negative) indicating that the region is an idiosyncratically high (low) demander of that good. Again this is scaled by region r's output in industry n.

We will estimate a linear of version of Eq. (4) presented below:

$$X_g^{nr} = \alpha_g^n + \beta_1 \gamma_g^{nROJ} X^{nr} + \beta_2 (\delta_g^{nr} - \delta_g^{nROJ}) X^{nr} + \varepsilon_g^{nr} \tag{4}$$

or equivalently

$$X_g^{nr} = \alpha_g^n + \beta_1\, SHARE_g^{nr} + \beta_2\, IDIODEM_g^{nr} + \varepsilon_g^{nr}. \tag{4a}$$

While we believe this exercise is informative, we do not want to stop with estimation of Eq. (4a). The reason is that such a specification may suffer from an omitted variables bias, as it assumes that endowments play no role in the location of goods production once we know the level of industry output. Thus we estimate a nested model:

$$X_g^{nr} = \alpha_g^n + \beta_1\, SHARE_g^{nr} + \beta_2\, IDIODEM_g^{nr} + \Omega_g^n V^r + \varepsilon_g^{nr}. \tag{4b}$$

We want to verify that the conclusions derived from our earlier tests are robust to allowing endowments to matter for output at a finer level of production. The structure that we have placed on the analysis enables us to directly test the hypothesis of whether economic geography can improve our understanding of production patterns at the goods level relative to the hypothesis that all production is determined by endowments.

A few more words are in order about the specification. If the production of goods within a region is proportional to production of these goods in the rest of Japan, then SHARE will equal the expected level of production of a good given output at the industry level. In the specification without endowments, one should expect the coefficient on SHARE to be unity.

Our main interest is in testing a null that Heckscher–Ohlin predicts the level of goods output against an alternative that an augmented economic geography model does so. However, it will prove informative to postpone this test and first consider directly several hypotheses concerning Eq. (4b). The key is the interpretation of the coefficient β_2, for which we distinguish three hypotheses. In a frictionless world (comparative advantage or IRS), the geographical structure of demand should have no influence of production patterns, so $\beta_2 = 0$.[5] In a comparative advantage world with trade costs, the geographical location of demand does matter. But so long as import demand and export supply curves have the conventional slopes, the response of local supply to idiosyncratic components of demand should be at most one-to-one. Finally, as discussed previously, in the presence of economic geography, we expect the response of local production to idiosyncratic components of demand to be more than one-to-one. Summarizing:

Interpretation of β_2

(1) $\beta_2 = 0$: frictionless world (comparative advantage or IRS),
(2) $\beta_2 \in (0, 1]$: comparative advantage with trade costs,
(3) $\beta_2 > 1$: economic geography.

3. Empirics

3.1. Econometric issues

Eqs. (2) and (4a) can be estimated at various levels of aggregation, separately or as a system of seemingly unrelated regressions. The latter yields maximum power to discern the average impact of economic geography in our sample. Alternatively, we can allow the coefficients on the parameters to vary at the goods or industry level.

Direct estimation of Eq. (4a) is not possible because of a simultaneity problem. Because X_g^{nr} is an element of X^{nr} one cannot treat them as independent observations. Davis and Weinstein (1996) show however, that if we assume that factor endowments drive aggregate production, then we will have a theoretically consistent set of instruments: factor endowments. In what follows, we therefore always instrument X^{nr} on factor endowments.

Second, there are two types of heteroskedasticity in these data. Errors are likely to be correlated with the size of both regions and industries. These two types of heteroskedasticity can be corrected for by postulating that for each good the error process is of the form given below:

$$\mathrm{var}(\varepsilon_g^{nr}) = \phi_g^n GDP_r^{\theta_i} \tag{5}$$

[5] The fact that the home market effect distinguishes the theory only when there exist costs of trade is of little practical import. It is true that, for simplicity, the theoretical literature in both frameworks has traditionally ignored costs of trade. This is relatively innocuous in the case of comparative advantage, much less so for increasing returns. In any case, we will see that our data strongly reject the zero-trade-cost model, as is consistent with the recent work of McCallum (1995) and Engel and Rogers (1996).

where ϕ_g^n and θ_g^n are parameters. We corrected for heteroskedasticity by first estimating the system and generating the squared residuals. Following Leamer (1984), we then regressed the log of this series on the log of regional GDP and then used the fitted values to form our weighting series for the heteroskedasticity correction.

3.2. Data issues

In this section we provide an overview of the data used in the paper (details on the construction of variables are in the appendix). Our data set contains output, endowment, and absorption data for the 47 prefectures/cities of Japan. However, we were concerned that people in the cities of Tokyo and Osaka might be working in the city but living and consuming in an adjacent prefecture, so we were forced to aggregate some of the data. We formed two aggregates: *Kanto*, out of the city of Tokyo and the prefectures of Yamanashi, Kanagawa, Chiba, and Saitama; and *Kinki*, out of the prefectures/cities of Hyogo, Kyoto, Nara, and Osaka. This reduced our sample to 40 observations, but enabled us to significantly increase the probability that anyone within a region consumed largely within that region.

Our next problem was how to define industries and goods. Ideally, we would like to rely on industry classifications based on technological criteria rather than substitutability in demand. Unfortunately, industry classification schemes are typically based upon the latter more than the former. There is some evidence that standard industry definitions do contain information about production technologies (Maskus, 1991). However, since we had access to the Japanese technology matrix, we decided that we could provide more theoretically sensible classifications than those typically found in statistical annuals.

In earlier work (Davis et al., 1997) we had constructed a technology matrix for Japan. This matrix enabled us to have direct information on college, non-college, and capital usage for 30 sectors. Of these 30 sectors, we dropped eight non-tradable goods sectors and two agricultural sectors (agriculture, forest, and fishery products and processed foods). We felt it necessary to drop the agricultural sectors because large-scale Japanese industrial policy interventions, such as price supports, marketing boards, tax breaks, subsidies, zoning laws, etc., significantly distort demand and supply in these sectors. Indeed, this accounts for the fact that in our data 13% of private land in the *city* of Tokyo (i.e. not the greater Tokyo metropolitan area) is farmland. Finally, we also dropped mining since it is obviously an endowment-based sector.

The 19 sectors that we eventually used are reported in Table 1. Davis and Weinstein (1996) argued that in international data one can reject the economic geography specification in favor of the Heckscher–Ohlin specification for these industry categories. However, as we have suggested earlier, there is reason to be more optimistic that we can identify home market effects in Japanese data.

Table 1

	Aggregation scheme		
Sector	C/NC	K/NC	K/C
Textiles	1	1	4
Apparel	1	1	2
Lumber and wood	1	1	5
Furniture	1	1	3
Ceramics, stone, clay, glass	2	3	5
Iron and steel	2	5	6
Paper and pulp	3	4	5
Rubber	3	3	4
Fabricated metal products	3	2	3
Transportation equipment	4	4	5
Other manufacturing	4	3	4
Leather and leather products	5	1	1
Non-ferrous metals	5	4	5
General machinery	5	3	3
Electrical machinery	5	3	3
Precision instruments	5	2	2
Printing and publishing	6	2	2
Chemicals	6	5	4
Petroleum and coal products	6	6	6

Note: C, college employment; NC, non-college employment; *K*, capital.

Bernstein and Weinstein (1997) argue that the reason for the good fits in international data is the interaction between transaction costs and Heckscher–Ohlin effects. These authors demonstrate that on Japanese data, where transactions costs are small, there is substantial production indeterminacy at this level of aggregation. This has two important implications for our work. First, since endowments do not predict output as well on regional data as on international data, there is more latitude for other factors, such as economic geography, to determine regional production. Second, the fact that transportation costs are substantially smaller between regions means that the observed economic geography effects will be stronger (cf. Krugman, 1991). Both of these reasons suggest that we should be more optimistic about finding a role for economic geography in determining regional production.

In some of the exercises that we will carry out, aggregation of goods into industries may in principle matter a great deal. The theory literally holds that all varieties of all goods within an industry use common input coefficients. Obviously, this is too much to hope for with real data. So we are required to aggregate the goods into industries in a way that respects the underlying theoretical requirement that goods within an industry use similar input

Table 2

Variable	Obs	Mean	Std. dev.	Min	Max
SHARE/X^{nr}	760	0.3158	0.2113	0.0108	0.7746
IDIODEM/X^{nr}	760	0.0000	0.0824	− 0.4037	0.4037
Non-college	40	1 585 633	2 500 886	372 125	14 500 000
College	40	426 592	1 063 285	62 628	6 443 185
Capital	40	7 559 625	13 400 000	1 469 625	79 100 000
Land	40	2034	2570	555	16487

coefficients. Unfortunately, in a world with more than two inputs, there is no theoretically compelling manner for performing this aggregation. Hence we took a pragmatic approach of considering aggregation based on factor-intensity ratios, taking two factors at a time. Unfortunately, although ranking sectors by college to non-college ratios and capital to non-college ratios yields similar orderings, one obtains radically different orderings if one looks at capital to college ratios. Ultimately, we decided to form industry aggregates on the basis of college to non-college factor ratios, because this scheme yielded the most plausible aggregates. The other aggregations schemes, especially the capital to college scheme, had enormous outliers and produced very odd mixes of industries.

We calculated the ratio of college to non-college workers in each sector and then divided the 19 goods into six industry aggregates based on the similarity of these ratios. The last columns of Table 1 present these aggregates. Larger numbers indicate an industry composed of goods with higher factor-intensity ratios. The commodity groupings for the college/non-college aggregation scheme seem quite sensible, although there are a few anomalies, e.g. leather in industry 5.

Table 2 presents sample statistics for our data set using the college/non-college aggregation scheme. These reveal that the typical good constitutes about one-third of the typical industry and that there is substantial variation in idiosyncratic demand, which is important because we need variation in the latter to drive the home market effects.

3.3. Estimating the Heckscher–Ohlin production model

Since our theoretical framework requires us to find a level of aggregation for which factor endowments drive aggregate production, it is reasonable to ask whether our aggregation scheme enables us to explain much of the variance at the three-digit level. Table 3 presents results of estimating Eq. (1) for our sample of 40 regions. What is striking in our results is the fact that fits of the regressions are quite high. Indeed, our results indicate that, on average, factor endowments can explain almost 80 per cent (0.786) of the variation of our aggregates.

Table 3
Aggregated production on factor endowments (40 regions, heteroskedasticity corrected estimates)

	t-statistics					$F_{0.01,5,35} = 3.6$	
	Constant	College	Non-college	Capital	Land	F-statistic	Adjusted R^2
Aggregate 1	− 0.343	− 3.389	1.29	1.715	− 3.823	14.77	0.5854
Aggregate 2	− 1.208	− 2.413	− 0.085	2.432	− 3.522	24.02	0.7024
Aggregate 3	− 3.317	− 2.286	3.255	0.266	− 3.503	78.45	0.8882
Aggregate 4	− 2.702	− 1.758	1.213	1.209	− 3.422	11.86	0.5268
Aggregate 5	− 2.086	0.396	3.182	− 0.946	− 2.621	70.19	0.8765
Aggregate 6	0.467	4.994	1.323	− 1.098	− 0.534	1192.63	0.9919

It is worth remembering, however, that there are two sources of variation in these data. One source is pure size-based variation: larger regions produce more output. If all of our explanatory power came from this source of variation, it would be somewhat disturbing, since one would like to believe that endowments should tell us something about the relative sizes of industries within regions. In other words, we would like endowments to also tell us about cross-sectional variation within regions of similar size. One way to eliminate this size-based variation and examine the cross-sectional variation is to force the exponent on GDP to equal two in our heteroskedasticity correction. This is equivalent to estimating a version of Eq. (2) in which both sides have been deflated by GDP. When we estimated this version of the equation we obtained an average R^2 of 0.4. This suggests that even after controlling for size based variation, endowments explain almost half of the variance of aggregate output. Furthermore, our data revealed that endowments had a more difficult time explaining more disaggregated output levels. Using the same specification, we obtained an average R^2 of only 0.3 when we ran the same specification on the most disaggregated data. This is consistent with the theoretical notion that the Heckscher–Ohlin framework performs better using aggregates of industries with similar factor intensities than using disaggregated data.

Overall, our results suggest that endowments and output are highly correlated on regional data, and we have therefore established that the idea that endowments matter in determining the location of production is a credible null hypothesis.

3.4. *Testing for home market effects*

Before presenting our regression evidence, we begin by plotting our data. Our formulation of the theory, given in Eq. (4b), suggests that we have a multivariate relationship between the variables. If, however, we impose that β_1 equals 1, divide through by industry level output, and carry the SHARE variable over to the left-hand side, we obtain

$$\gamma_g^{nr} - \gamma_g^{nJ} = \frac{\alpha_g^n}{X^{nr}} + \beta_2(\delta_g^{nr} - \delta_g^{nJ}) + \tilde{\varepsilon}_g^{nr}.$$

The left-hand side of this equation measures how the share of industry output within a prefecture deviates from that share for the rest of Japan, while the term in parentheses indicates the deviation in absorption. In Fig. 1 we refer to these two variables as the 'Production Deviation' and the 'Absorption Deviation'.

If economic geography has some role to play in these data one should expect to see absorption deviations produce more than one-for-one movements in output. This would result in a line with a slope of more than one. On the other hand if comparative advantage determined production, then one would expect to see a line with a slope of less than one. As we see in Fig. 1, the slope of the fitted line is 1.7. This suggests economic geography effects. Based on the slope of the fitted line in this figure, a rise in a prefecture of idiosyncratic demand leads net *exports* to rise by 70 per cent of the increment to local demand.

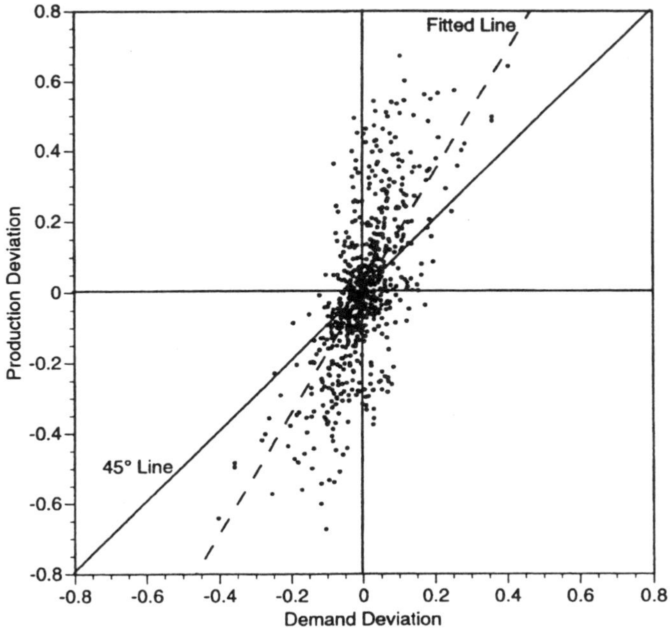

Fig. 1. Production deviation vs. Absorption deviation.

Table 4
Seemingly unrelated regression results. Dependent variable is production (standard errors are below estimates)

IDIODEM	1.416 0.025	0.888 0.070
Share	1.033 0.007	– 1.7441 0.211
Factors	No	Yes
Observations	760	760

These results are surprising in light of our earlier work on international data. We conducted a similar experiment for the OECD using two- and three-digit ISIC classifications (which approximately correspond to the level of aggregation here). In the international data, the fitted line was significantly below the diagonal at this level of aggregation, with a slope of only 0.66. In other words, international data revealed no economic geography effect at this level of aggregation, and only a very weak relationship at greater levels of disaggregation.

Although this graph is quite suggestive that economic geography might matter for regional specialization, regression analysis will allow us to examine these relations more precisely. We begin by estimating Eq. (4a). The results from this exercise are presented in Table 4. When we do not include factor endowments in the specification, our econometric results confirm the general impression of the data that we obtained in Fig. 1. Although the coefficient is slightly smaller, its value of 1.42 is clearly in the range of economic geography.

The results presented thus far have examined economic geography against a very weak null hypothesis: viz. that factor endowments do not matter at all at the goods level. Davis and Weinstein (1996), however, show that factor endowments play an important role in determining production at this level of aggregation on international data. This suggests that by leaving out factor endowments from our estimating equations we may be creating an omitted-variables bias. Consider the following possibility. We know that an important component of absorption is demand for intermediate goods. Demand for intermediates is determined by the production of final goods, but, if one believes in Eq. (1), production of the latter is driven by endowments. This implies that demand for intermediates may be driven by endowments. In other words, if one believes that endowments determine production, then it would not be surprising to find that there is a correlation between production and absorption because both are driven by endowments.

The obvious solution is to estimate Eq. (4b) since it includes factor endowments on the right-hand side. The results of this exercise are presented in the second column of Table 4. Interestingly, this causes the coefficient on IDIODEM to decline to 0.9.[6] This implies that once we account for factor endowments, it no longer is the case that movements in demand produce more than proportionate movements in production. In other words, this specification rejects economic geography.

This result is troubling, especially in light of our earlier work. On international data, we also rejected the economic geography specification, but when we did so in the specification with factor endowments, we obtained a coefficient on IDIODEM of 0.3. This implies that in international data, on average less than one-third of any deviation in demand was met by higher domestic production, the rest being met by imports. This result makes sense in light of the existence of international transaction costs which theoretically can cause demand and production to covary. What is more puzzling is that if one believes that comparative advantage drives production then one should also believe that in regional data, where transportation costs are presumably lower, one should obtain an *even smaller* coefficient on IDIODEM. Instead we have a coefficient that is too large to plausibly be generated by comparative advantage and transport costs, but too small to signal economic geography.

One explanation for these results is that not all sectors are composed of monopolistically-competitive industries. Suppose that only a few of our aggregates actually contain sectors exhibiting increasing returns. Then our system of equations would be pooling together industries in which the coefficient on IDIODEM is greater than unity with sectors in which the coefficient is less than unity. This pooling could be the explanation for a coefficient that is too high to plausibly describe a comparative advantage world, but too low to lead us to believe that economic geography matters.

Fortunately, it is straightforward to modify our theory to address this problem. Assume that some of our aggregates are composed entirely of constant returns to scale sectors and others of increasing returns to scale sectors. Then the correct test would be to run Eq. (4b) separately for each aggregate. This should result in aggregates without monopolistically-competitive sectors exhibiting low coefficients on IDIODEM, but sectors with increasing returns producing coefficients over unity. The results from this exercise are presented in Table 5. In the three least skill-intensive aggregates, we detect no significant economic geography effect. However, in the more skill-intensive aggregates 4 and 5 we find

[6] The coefficient on SHARE typically was negative in specifications with endowments. This is largely due to the high degree of multicollinearity between this variable and the endowments. Since SHARE simply picks up industry size effects that can easily be captured by endowments, we experimented with omitting the variable and constraining it to equal one. These experiments did not qualitatively alter our results.

Table 5
Estimation by aggregate. Dependent variable is output (standard errors below estimates)

Aggregate	IDIODEM	SHARE	Obs
1	0.1052	– 2.864	160
	0.1628	0.9320	
2	1.0320	– 1.6958	80
	0.3328	2.2646	
3	0.4272	– 10.681	120
	0.1480	1.6466	
4	1.4757	2.6239	80
	0.2521	0.7825	
5	1.3575	– 3.1882	200
	0.1430	0.8202	
6	0.8808	– 0.2538	80
	0.2230	0.2766	

a coefficient that is larger than unity and significant at the 10 and 5 per cent levels, respectively. The fact that these sectors contain such plausible economic geography candidates as general machinery, electrical machinery, transportation equipment, and precision instruments makes it even more believable that economic geography effects may be present in these data.

However, it is also important to focus on economic, not only statistical, significance. While we have been able to detect the presence of economic geography effects, it remains to be seen whether it matters much for production. To assess the latter we consider β-coefficients. These statistics tell us how sensitive production is to movements in idiosyncratic demand. Formally, a β-coefficient tells us how many standard deviations the dependent variable is predicted to move if the independent variable moves one standard deviation. As discussed by Leamer (1984), these statistics are useful in answering questions regarding which independent variables are important in determining movements in the dependent variable. In earlier work on international data, we found that often even when we could detect economic geography in the sample, this impact was economically small. While we find larger effects in the regional data, they nonetheless remain modest. A one-standard-deviation movement in idiosyncratic demand moves production by 0.22 standard deviations in aggregate 4, and by 0.09 standard deviations in aggregate 5. In other words, knowing the variation in idiosyncratic demand does not provide much information about the variation in production. Indeed, these numbers are not that different than what we found on international data, suggesting that even in the sectors where economic geography matters, the effects are relatively modest.

These results, however, are obviously very sensitive to the aggregation scheme. For example, the inclusion of an unlikely economic geography candidate, leather, in aggregate 5 may dilute the overall impact of economic geography in these data. In fact, while we found that changing the basis of our aggregation scheme had little impact on estimates obtained in the full system, changing the mix of goods within our industry definitions could cause different groups of industries to be labeled as sectors with significant economic geography effects.

One solution to this theoretical and empirical mire is to foreswear aggregation altogether, and allow all coefficients to vary at the goods level. This might be appropriate if, contrary to our initial theoretical specification, the elasticity of substitution between varieties of a good is different for the various goods within an industry. The results from this exercise are presented in Table 6. The coefficient on IDIODEM is significantly larger than unity for eight of the 19 sectors: textiles, paper and pulp, iron and steel, chemicals, transportation equipment, precision instruments, non-ferrous metals, and electrical machinery. With perhaps the exception of paper and pulp, all of these seem like plausible candidates for monopolistic competition, with textiles, transportation equipment, iron and steel, and electrical machinery providing canonical examples of the power of the economic geography framework (see Krugman, 1991). Furthermore, our results are robust to whichever aggregation scheme we choose. The variables SHARE and IDIODEM will vary depending on whether we group industries on the basis of college to non-college, capital to non-college ratios, or capital to college ratios. However, we found that all of these sectors except paper and pulp were identified as exhibiting economic geography effects regardless of the aggregation scheme.

We can run an additional robustness check to confirm that we are identifying economic geography effects here. We posit that the R&D-intensity of an industry may be used as a proxy for the increasing returns and monopolistic competition that underlie the economic geography theory. Fig. 2 plots our estimated coefficients against sectoral R&D expenses divided by sales. The correlation is 0.62, indicating that high R&D is associated with identification of economic geography sectors. In fact, the four most R&D-intensive sectors are also the four sectors for which we obtain the highest coefficients on IDIODEM.

Once again we confront the issue of economic significance. We repeat our experiment with beta-coefficients, only this time we use the disaggregated results presented in Table 6. Table 7 reports the β-coefficients for the eight sectors for which we obtained statistically significant economic geography coefficients. For these sectors, economic geography seems quite important. A one standard deviation movement in idiosyncratic demand on average moves production by half a standard deviation. In other words, observed fluctuations in idiosyncratic demand seem to provide a lot of information about production patterns. Furthermore, in the important sector of transportation equipment, these effects

Table 6
Disaggregated estimation. Dependent variable is output (standard errors below estimates)

Industry	Economic geography	IDIODEM	SHARE	Factors	Adjusted R^2	Observations
Textile	**	3.9532	0.5932	Yes	0.8468	40
		0.4570	3.2302			
Apparel		– 1.5866	– 24.3909	Yes	0.5725	40
		0.2843	4.3741			
Lumber		1.0622	4.1937	Yes	0.8106	40
		0.4440	1.8351			
Furniture		– 0.5538	– 5.1598	Yes	0.988	40
		0.2765	1.4389			
Pulp, paper	**	1.9913	– 8.9731	Yes	0.8917	40
		0.3150	1.7861			
Printing		0.7269	– 0.3423	Yes	0.9979	40
		0.2296	0.2876			
Chemicals	**	6.6781	0.9248	Yes	0.9928	40
		1.2454	1.1038			
Petrol,		– 0.4655	– 6.3220	Yes	0.9934	40
coal products		2.3048	4.2047			
Rubber		– 0.1081	– 24.5223	Yes	0.8454	40
		0.1763	5.78042			
Leather,		0.1643	– 7.1330	Yes	0.9412	40
leather products		0.4053	1.7866			
Stone, clay,		– 0.6454	– 5.0674	Yes	0.7681	40
glass		0.4148	2.4824			
Iron, steel	**	3.9294	– 3.9582	Yes	0.7663	40
		0.5613	6.2968			
Non-ferrous	**	1.5932	2.5509	Yes	0.962	40
metals		0.1741	3.1334			
Fabricated		– 0.8197	– 14.0257	Yes	0.5972	40
metal		1.0820	7.0734			
General		– 0.4219	– 4.4744	Yes	0.7802	40
machinery		0.9524	2.6163			
Electrical	**	6.2713	5.6614	Yes	0.9002	40
machinery		1.3552	3.7628			
Transport	**	6.7060	1.2685	Yes	0.8826	40
equipment		0.5024	0.9336			
Precision	**	4.32139	– 3.9460	Yes	0.7477	40
instruments		0.8115	1.8107			
Other		0.0655	1.1179	Yes	0.5307	40
manufacturing		0.3824	1.4888			

Note: Asterisks indicate that the coefficients on IDIODEM are significantly large than one at the 5% level.

are very strong. Although economic geography may not be that important for international specialization, there appears to be strong evidence that it matters for certain sectors on a regional level.

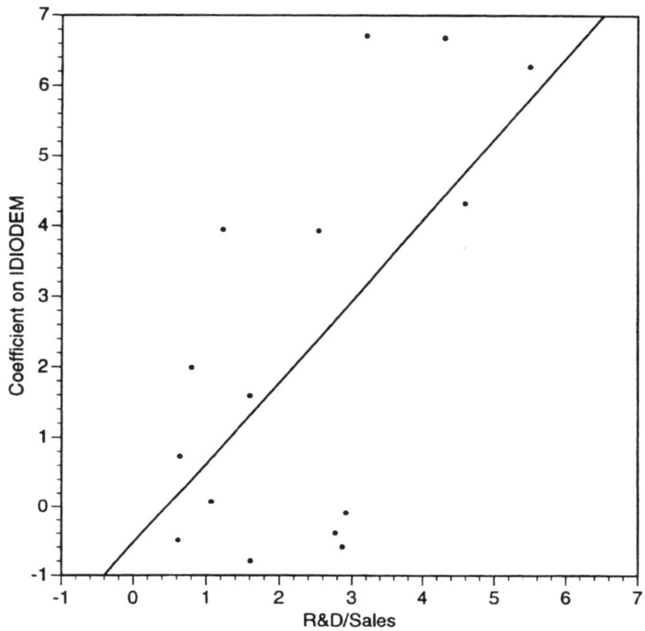

Fig. 2. Coefficient on IDIODEM vs. R&D Intensity.

Table 7
Beta coefficients for goods with significant coefficients on IDIODEM

Sector	Beta coefficient
Textiles	0.82
Iron and steel	0.40
Paper and pulp	0.51
Transportation equipment	0.74
Non-ferrous metals	0.42
Electrical machinery	0.37
Precision instruments	0.42
Chemicals	0.53

4. Conclusion

This paper investigates the existence and importance of economic geography effects in determining production structure for a sample of regions of Japan.

Results from this regional work both complement and contrast with those of Davis and Weinstein (1996) based on a sample of OECD countries. Within the hypothesis testing framework developed, the earlier work found scant support for the economic geography framework in the international sample. Moreover, even insofar as it was possible to statistically identify such effects, their economic significance was very minimal.

The regional data prove much more supportive of the economic geography hypothesis. We find statistically significant effects of economic geography for eight of nineteen manufacturing sectors: transportation equipment, iron and steel, electrical machinery, chemicals, precision instruments, nonferrous metals, textiles, and paper and pulp. Moreover, for many of these sectors, the economic geography effects are likewise very significant in economic terms.

Why are the regional effects of economic geography so strong, while the international effects are so weak? We suspect two principal reasons. The first is trade costs: both transport costs and myriad barriers to trade must surely be lower for trade between regions of a country than between countries. In the economic geography framework, lower (but strictly positive) trade costs lead to stronger effects, as this reflects lower implicit protection for production in the relatively smaller markets. The second likely reason is the greater mobility of factors across regions than countries. The suggestion is that such mobility will tend to reinforce the economic geography effects, relieving scarcities in regions favorable on economic geography grounds for production of particular goods.

How do these new results affect the conclusions of our earlier work regarding the significance of economic geography in determining production specialization within the OECD? They bring our earlier work into sharper focus in two respects. First, our earlier work had found weak evidence of economic geography effects in as many as one-third of the goods that comprise our sample. Since the microeconomic story that one tells at the regional and international level is by and large the same, this strengthens our confidence that we had in fact identified economic geography effects in the international data. The fact that we find the economic significance of economic geography to be greater in the regional data is exactly what one would expect. This likewise gives us greater confidence that our methodology is not inherently biased against finding important economic geography effects. Hence, it tends to strengthen our confidence in our earlier finding that economic geography does not matter a great deal in understanding the structure of international production.

The sharp contrast in the *economic* significance of economic geography effects across regions versus internationally is a strong caution against accepting the view that the boundary between international and interregional economics is on the verge of vanishing due to reductions in border barriers. As such, this reinforces the perspective offered in McCallum (1995) and Engel and Rogers (1996) that national borders continue to matter a great deal. Moreover, the strength of the economic geography effects on the regional data suggest that if the future holds a time when international trade costs truly do fall to the level of interregional trade costs, then quite substantial international restructuring of industry may be in the offing.

The empirical approach to identifying economic geography effects that we employ in this paper is novel. In order to keep our framework simple, we have set to the side a large number of important analytic and empirical questions. These include the roles of absolute market size, forward- and backward-linkages, and 'real-world' geography. Naturally, the results reported here should be interpreted with an understanding that many issues in this area remain to be explored.

In sum, economic geography appears to be very important in determining the structure of production across regions of Japan for eight of nineteen manufacturing sector. In contrast to Davis and Weinstein (1996), which in exactly the same framework had shown scant economic significance of economic geography for the structure of OECD production, here we find that it is very important for the structure of regional production.

Acknowledgements

The first author is grateful to the Harvard Institute for International Development for funding for this project. Trevor Reeve once again provided first-rate research assistance. The views expressed in this paper are those of the authors, and not those of supporting institutions, the Federal Reserve Bank of New York or the Federal Reserve System.

Appendix A: Data

Prefectural endowments

The numbers of workers by educational attainment were entered by prefecture directly from the *Employment Status Survey* of 1987 (*Shugyo Kozo Kihon Chosa Hokoku*). The capital stocks were imputed from prefectural investment data. Japan's yearly *Annual Report on Prefectural Accounts* (*Kenmin Keizai Keisan Nempo*) give investment flows for each prefecture from 1975 to 1985. These flows were used to impute capital stock levels for each prefecture in 1985, using capital goods price deflators from the *Annual Report on National Accounts* (*Kokumin Keizai Keisan Nempo*) and a rate of depreciation of 0.133 (This was the same rate of depreciation used by Bowen et al. (1987)). Each year's flow was deflated using a capital deflator from the *National Accounts*.

Prefectural production

Shipment data for 20 manufacturing sectors in each prefecture were taken from the Japanese *Census of Manufactures* for 1985. The gross output of 9 non-manufacturing sectors in each prefecture was taken from the *Prefectural Accounts* for 1985. Finally, these totals were scaled so that the 47-prefectural total for each sector exactly matched the total Japanese output as reported in the 1985 *Input–Output Table of Japan*. Thus, in effect, the data from the *Census of Manufactures* and from the *Prefectural Accounts* was used in order to distribute total Japanese output for each sector across the 47 prefectures as accurately as possible.

Technology

Each element of the 3×29 technology matrix $\boldsymbol{B}$ was calculated by dividing Japanese total output for the 29 sectors into the number of each factor present in each sector. Most of the data on college and non-college workers in each sector came from the 1988 *Wage Census* (*Chingin Sensasu*). There were some gaps in this data as follows: (1) There was no data for college and non-college workers for agriculture, forestry, and fisheries or for government. These numbers were taken from the 1987 *Employment Status Survey* (*Showa* 63 *Nen Shugyo Kozo Kihon Chosa Hokoku Chiiki Hen I II*). (2) There was also no data for the petroleum/coal and leather industries. Total employment for each of these sectors was taken from the 1985 *Census of Manufactures*. The number of college workers per unit output for each was then imputed by assuming that petroleum/coal has the same fraction of college workers as the chemicals sector and that leather has the same fraction as manufacturing overall. The capital stocks in each of the 30 sectors were imputed from investment numbers, using the *Annual Report of the Corporation Survey* for non-manufacturing and the *Census of Manufactures* for manufacturing.

Absorption

Intermediate input use in each region was calculated using the Japan 30×30 IO matrix for 1985. Thus, $\boldsymbol{INPUT}^r = \boldsymbol{AX}^r$, where $\boldsymbol{INPUT}^r$ is intermediate consumption in region r, $\boldsymbol{A}$ is the IO matrix, and $\boldsymbol{X}^r$ is gross output in region r. Both $\boldsymbol{INPUT}^r$ and $\boldsymbol{X}^r$, therefore, are 30×1 vectors. The 47 $\boldsymbol{INPUT}^r$ vectors together form a 30×10 intermediate consumption matrix. It is important to note that one of our sectors in both $\boldsymbol{A}$ and $\boldsymbol{X}^r$ is producers of government services. Government absorption is therefore included in $\boldsymbol{INPUT}^r$.

The construction of the consumption data was quite complex. In 1984, the Japanese government performed a detailed survey of Japanese consumption on the prefectural level, the *National Survey of Income and Expenditure*, that broke Japanese household consumption up into 65 categories. Unfortunately this data cannot be easily concorded into the 30 industrial categories that we use in the paper. However the Economic Planning Agency does provide a 30 × 42 bridging matrix which map the 42 consumption commodities that can easily be formed from the 56 consumption categories in the *Family Income and Expenditure Survey* for 1987 into 30 core sectors corresponding to the Japanese IO table. Unfortunately this second source of data only reports information for ten Japanese regions. Since the 65 categories of the *National Survey of Income and Expenditure* did not always correspond to the 56 categories of the *Family Income and Expenditure Survey*, we used the following procedure to develop consistent series. First, for most categories there was a perfect match between the two sources, so we used the *National Survey of Income and Expenditure* for entries wherever possible. We then used regional totals scaled by household income shares to fill in the gaps. Since we were using both 1984 and 1987 data all prefectural entries were scaled so that they matched the regional totals.

These data were then aggregated up to 42 categories, producing a 42 × 47 matrix of final consumption by region. The survey data was based, of course, on consumer prices, so the bridge matrix was specially constructed to translate the consumption expenditure into producer prices. Most of the difference between consumer and producer prices results from wholesale and retail markups and from transportation costs, so the mapping shifted portions of spending on each final good into the wholesale/retail trade and transportation sectors, reflecting the fact that to consume anything bought retail is to consume the wholesaling, retailing, and transportation services which brought the product to the store. Without this adjustment, the data would have greatly underestimated final consumption of wholesale/retail and transportation services and would have shown each region exporting far more of these services than is plausible.

There are no investment figures broken down for 30 sectors and 47 prefectures, so these numbers were imputed using IO Table investment data. The IO Table breaks down investment into the 30 sectors for Japan as a whole. This vector was then distributed across regions, using as weights each region's share in total investment for Japan as a whole. Thus, $\boldsymbol{INV}^r = (TI^r/TI^J)\boldsymbol{INV}^J$, where $\boldsymbol{INV}^r$ is a 30 × 1 investment vector for region r, TI^r is the total investment for that region in 1985 (taken from the prefectural accounts), TI^J is Japan's total investment for 1985, and $\boldsymbol{INV}^r$ is the 30 × 1 investment vector taken from the IO Table. These 10 $\boldsymbol{INV}$'s therefore formed a 30 × 10 investment matrix. Business consumption was added to the data in a similar fashion. The data for all prefectures was then aggregated into 29 sectors to make it compatible with our $\boldsymbol{B}$ matrix.

R&D Data

Research and Development data was taken from the *Report on the Survey of Research and Development*.

References

Bernstein, J., Weinstein, D., 1997. Do endowments predict the location of production? Evidence from national and international data. Mimeo., University of Michigan, East Lansin.

Bowen, H.P., Leamer, E., Sveikauskas L., 1987. Multicountry, multifactor tests of the factor abundance theory. American Economic Review 77.

Chipman, J.S., 1992. Intra-industry trade, factor proportions and aggregation. Economic Theory and International Trade: Essays in Memoriam of J. Trout Rader. Springer, New York.

Davis, D.R., 1995. Intra-industry trade: A Heckscher–Ohlin–Ricardo approach. Journal of International Economics 39.

Davis, D.R., 1997. Critical evidence on comparative advantage? North–North trade in a multilateral world. Journal of Political Economy 97, Oct.

Davis, D.R., Weinstein, D.E., 1996. Does economic geography matter for international specialization. Working paper no. 5706, NBER, Cambridge, MA.

Davis, D.R., Weinstein, D.E., Bradford, S.C., Shimpo, K., 1997. Using international and Japanese regional data to determine when the factor abundance theory of trade works. American Economic Review 87, June.

Deardorff, A.V., 1998. Determinants of bilateral trade: does gravity work in a neoclassical world? In: Jeffrey, F. (Ed.), Regionalization of the World Economy. U. of Chicago and NBER, Chicago.

Dixit, A.K., Stiglitz, J.E., 1977. Monopolistic competition and optimum product diversity. American Economic Review 67 (3), 297–308.

Ellison, G., Glaeser, E.L., 1997. Geographic concentration in U.S. manufacturing industries: A dartboard approach. Journal of Political Economy 105 (5), 889–927.

Engel, C., Rogers, J.H., 1996. How wide is the border? American Economic Review 86.

Glaeser, E.L. et al., 1992. Growth in cities. Journal of Political Economy 100 (6), 1126–1152.

Helpman, E., 1981. International trade in the presence of product differentiation, economies of scale and monopolistic competition: A Chamberlin–Heckscher–Ohlin approach. Journal of International Economics 11 (3).

Henderson, J.V., 1986. Efficiency of resources usage and city size. Journal of Urban Economics 19 (1), 47–70.

Henderson, J.V., Kuncoro, A., Turner, M., 1995. Industrial development in cities. Journal of Political Economy 103 (5), 1067–1090.

Justman, M., 1994. The effect of local demand on industry location. Review of Economics and Statistics 76 (4), 742–753.

Krugman, P., 1979. Increasing returns, monopolistic competition, and trade. Journal of International Economics 9 (4).

Krugman, P.R., 1980. Scale economies, product differentiation, and the pattern of trade. American Economic Review 70, 950–959.

Krugman, P.R., 1991. Geography and Trade. MIT Press, Cambridge, MA.

Krugman, P.R., 1994. Empirical evidence on the new trade theories: The current state of play. In: New Trade Theories: A Look at the Empirical Evidence. Center for Economic Policy Research, London.

Krugman, Venables, 1995. Globalization and the inequality of nations. Quarterly Journal of Economics CX (4).

Leamer, E., 1984. Sources of International Comparative Advantage: Theory and Evidence. MIT Press, Cambridge, MA.

Linder, S.B., 1961. An Essay on Trade and Transformation. Wiley, New York.

McCallum, J., 1995. National borders matter: Canada–US regional trade patterns. American Economic Review 85 (3).

Nakamura, R., 1985. Agglomeration economies in urban manufacturing industries: A case of Japanese cities. Journal of Urban Economics 17 (1), 108–124.

Sveikauskas, L.A., 1975. The productivity of cities. Quarterly Journal of Economics 89 (3), 393–413.

Sveikauskas, L.A., Gowdy, J., Funke, M., 1988. Urban productivity: City size or Industry size? Journal of Regional Science 28 (2) 185–202.

Weder, R., 1995. Linking absolute and comparative advantage to intra-industry trade theory. Review of International Economics 3 (3).

Part VI
Public Finance and Policy

[25]

Journal of Economic Literature
Vol. XXXVII (September 1999) pp. 1120–1149

An Essay on Fiscal Federalism

WALLACE E. OATES[1]

1. *Introduction*

FISCAL DECENTRALIZATION is in vogue. Both in the industrialized and in the developing world, nations are turning to devolution to improve the performance of their public sectors. In the United States, the central government has turned back significant portions of federal authority to the states for a wide range of major programs, including welfare, Medicaid, legal services, housing, and job training. The hope is that state and local governments, being closer to the people, will be more responsive to the particular preferences of their constituencies and will be able to find new and better ways to provide these services. In the United Kingdom, both Scotland and Wales have opted under the Blair government for their own regional parliaments. And in Italy the movement toward decentralization has gone so far as to encompass a serious proposal for the separation of the nation into two independent countries. In the developing world, we likewise see widespread interest in fiscal decentralization with the objective of breaking the grip of central planning that, in the view of many, has failed to bring these nations onto a path of self-sustaining growth.

But the proper goal of restructuring the public sector cannot simply be decentralization. The public sector in nearly all countries consists of several different levels. The basic issue is one of aligning responsibilities and fiscal instruments with the proper levels of government. As Alexis de Toqueville observed more than a century ago, "The federal system was created with the intention of combining the different advantages which result from the magnitude and the littleness of nations" (1980, v. I, p. 163). But to realize these "different advantages," we need to understand which functions and instruments are best centralized and which are best placed in the sphere of decentralized levels of government. This is the subject matter of fiscal federalism. As a subfield of public finance, fiscal federalism addresses the vertical structure of the public sector. It explores, both in normative and positive terms, the roles of the different levels of government and the ways in which they relate to one another through such instruments as intergovernmental grants.[2]

[1] Professor of Economics, University of Maryland, and University Fellow, Resources for the Future. I am most grateful for a host of helpful comments on an earlier draft from Robert Inman, Ronald McKinnon, Daniel Rubinfeld, Robert Schwab, John Wallis, Barry Weingast, and three anonymous referees; for research assistance from Tugrul Gurgur; and for the splendid editorial guidance of John Pencavel and John McMillan.

[2] This economic use of the term "federalism" is somewhat different from its standard use in political science, where it refers to a political system with a constitution that guarantees some range of autonomy and power to both central and

My purpose in this essay is not to provide a comprehensive survey of fiscal federalism. I begin with a brief review and some reflections on the traditional theory of fiscal federalism: the assignment of functions to levels of government, the welfare gains from fiscal decentralization, and the use of fiscal instruments. I then turn to some of the new directions in recent work in the field and explore a series of current topics: laboratory federalism, interjurisdictional competition and environmental federalism, the political economy of fiscal federalism, market-preserving federalism, and fiscal decentralization in the developing and transitional economies. Some of this research is expanding the scope of the traditional analyses in important and interesting ways. This will provide an opportunity both to comment on this new work and to suggest some potentially fruitful avenues for further research.

2. *The Basic Theory of Fiscal Federalism: Some Comments*

The traditional theory of fiscal federalism lays out a general normative framework for the assignment of functions to different levels of government and the appropriate fiscal instruments for carrying out these functions (e.g., Richard Musgrave 1959; Oates 1972). At the most general level, this theory contends that the central government should have the basic responsibility for the macroeconomic stabilization function and for income redistribution in the form of assistance to the poor. In both cases, the basic argument stems from some fundamental constraints on lower level governments. In the absence of monetary and exchange-rate prerogatives and with highly open economies that cannot contain much of the expansionary impact of fiscal stimuli, provincial, state, and local governments simply have very limited means for traditional macroeconomic control of their economies. Similarly, the mobility of economic units can seriously constrain attempts to redistribute income. An aggressive local program for the support of low-income households, for example, is likely to induce an influx of the poor and encourage an exodus of those with higher income who must bear the tax burden.[3] In addition to these functions, the central government must provide certain "national" public goods (like national defense) that provide services to the entire population of the country.

Decentralized levels of government have their raison d'etre in the provision of goods and services whose consumption is limited to their own jurisdictions. By tailoring outputs of such goods and services to the particular preferences and circumstances of their

decentralized levels of government. For an economist, nearly all public sectors are more or less federal in the sense of having different levels of government that provide public services and have some scope for *de facto* decision-making authority (irrespective of the formal constitution). In retrospect, it seems to me that the choice of the term "fiscal federalism" was probably an unfortunate one, since it suggests a narrow concern with budgetary matters. The subject of fiscal federalism, as I suggest above, encompasses much more, namely the whole range of issues relating to the vertical structure of the public sector.

[3] It is straightforward to show that a system of decentralized poor relief is characterized by a garden-variety externality that results in suboptimal levels of support for the poor. More specifically, increases in support payments in one jurisdiction confer external benefits in the form of a reduced number of poor households elsewhere. On this, see Charles Brown and Oates (1985). There is, moreover, evidence for the U.S. that state-level decisions on levels of welfare support are interdependent; Luz Amparo Saavedra (1998), among others, finds that states have responded to decreases (increases) in benefit levels in other states by reducing (raising) their own benefits to welfare recipients. For an excellent survey of this whole issue, see Jan Brueckner (1998).

constituencies, decentralized provision increases economic welfare above that which results from the more uniform levels of such services that are likely under national provision. The basic point here is simply that the efficient level of output of a "local" public good (i.e., that for which the sum of residents' marginal benefits equals marginal cost) is likely to vary across jurisdictions as a result of both differences in preferences and cost differentials. To maximize overall social welfare thus requires that local outputs vary accordingly.

These precepts, however, should be regarded more as general "guidelines" than firm "principles." As has been pointed out in the literature, there is certainly some limited scope for decentralized macroeconomic efforts (Edward Gramlich 1987) and for assistance to the poor. In particular, there is a theoretical case for some poor relief at local levels (Mark Pauly 1973), and the fact is that state and local governments undertake a significant amount of redistributive activity.[4]

Moreover, this prescription is a quite general one. It does not offer a precise delineation of the specific goods and services to be provided at each level of government. And indeed the spatial pattern of consumption of certain goods and services like education and health is open to some debate. As a result, we find in cross-country comparisons some divergence in just what is considered, say, "local" in its incidence. The specific pattern of goods and services provided by different levels of government will thus differ to some extent in time and place.[5] This is to be expected. Nonetheless, there remains much to be said for the basic principle of fiscal decentralization: the presumption that the provision of public services should be located at the lowest level of government encompassing, in a spatial sense, the relevant benefits and costs.[6]

Let me offer three observations on the general theory. First, the foundations of the Decentralization Theorem need some elaboration. The theorem is itself a straightforward normative proposition that states simply that " . . . in the absence of cost-savings from the centralized provision of a [local public] good and of interjurisdictional externalities, the level of welfare will always be at least as high (and typically higher) if Pareto-efficient levels of consumption are provided in each jurisdiction than if *any* single, uniform level of consumption is maintained across all jurisdictions" (Oates 1972, p. 54). The theorem thus establishes, on grounds of economic efficiency, a presumption in favor of the decentralized provision of public goods with localized effects. While the proposition may seem almost trivially obvious, it is of some interest both in terms of setting forth the conditions needed for its validity and, with

[4] However, Martin Feldstein and Marian Vaillant Wrobel (1998) present some recent evidence suggesting that state government attempts to redistribute income are largely unsuccessful. They find that progressive state income taxes in the U.S. have had little impact on the net-of-tax relative wage rates of skilled versus nonskilled workers. Their claim is that the mobility of workers across state borders undoes efforts at redistribution—and does so very quickly. The result is no redistribution, only deadweight losses from inefficient locational decisions.

[5] For two useful treatments of the assignment of specific public services to the appropriate level of government, see Anwar Shah (1994, ch. 1) and Ronald McKinnon and Thomas Nechyba (1997).

[6] In Europe, proponents of fiscal decentralization refer to the "principle of subsidiarity." The precept here is that public policy and its implementation should be assigned to the lowest level of government with the capacity to achieve the objectives. This principle has been formally adopted as part of the Maastrict Treaty for European Union. Its intellectual roots, interestingly, are found in twentieth-century Catholic social philosophy. On this see Robert Inman and Daniel Rubinfeld (forthcoming).

some further analysis, for providing some insights into the determinants of the magnitude of the welfare gains from fiscal decentralization (Oates 1998).

But there is more to the story. The presumption in favor of decentralized finance is established by simply assuming that centralized provision will entail a uniform level of output across all jurisdictions. In a setting of perfect information, it would obviously be possible for a benevolent central planner to prescribe the set of differentiated local outputs that maximizes overall social welfare; there would be no need for fiscal decentralization (although one might wish to describe such an outcome as decentralized in spirit!). The response to this observation has been twofold. First, one can realistically introduce some basic imperfections (or asymmetries) in information. More specifically, individual local governments are presumably much closer to the people and geography of their respective jurisdictions; they possess knowledge of both local preferences and cost conditions that a central agency is unlikely to have. And, second, there are typically political pressures (or perhaps even constitutional constraints) that limit the capacity of central governments to provide higher levels of public services in some jurisdictions than others. These constraints tend to require a certain degree of uniformity in central directives. There are thus important informational and political constraints that are likely to prevent central programs from generating an optimal pattern of local outputs.

My second observation concerns the magnitude of the welfare gains from fiscal decentralization. We can, in principle, measure the gains from the decentralized provision of public goods relative to a more uniform, centrally determined level of output. The theory suggests that the magnitude of these gains depends both on the extent of the heterogeneity in demands across jurisdictions and any interjurisdictional differences in costs. In particular, we find that the potential gains from decentralization stemming from interjurisdictional differences in demand vary inversely with the price elasticity of demand. If the costs of provision are the same across jurisdictions, but demands differ, then the extent of the welfare loss from a centrally imposed, uniform level of output increases, other things equal, with the price inelasticity of demand.[7] There is a large body of econometric evidence that finds that the demand for local public goods is typically highly price inelastic. This suggests that the potential welfare gains from decentralized finance may well be quite large.[8]

Pursuing this point into the realm of positive economics, we might expect the magnitude of the potential gains from fiscal decentralization to have some explanatory power. Where these gains are large, we would expect to find that the public sector is more decentralized. In exploring this issue some years ago, I found some (perhaps vague) evidence in its support: in a sample of countries, the fiscal share of the central government varied inversely with an

[7] In tax analysis, we are accustomed to a quite different result: the deadweight loss varies directly with the price elasticity of demand. Here it is just the reverse, since the distortion takes place on the quantity, rather than the price, axis. But interestingly, if the source of the difference in efficient local outputs is cost differentials, then the gains from fiscal decentralization bear the opposite relationship to the case where their source is differences in levels of demand: these gains then vary directly with the price elasticity of demand (Oates 1998).

[8] For surveys of this econometric literature, see Rubinfeld (1987) and Oates (1996a). For an attempt actually to measure the welfare gains from decentralization, see David Bradford and Oates (1974); they find large gains.

index of "sectionalism," a measure of the extent to which people in geographical subareas of a country identify "self-consciously and distinctively with that area" (Oates 1972, pp. 207–208). More recently, Koleman Strumpf and Felix Oberholzer-Gee (1998), in a more sharply focused study of states and counties in the United States, find that the decision to allow counties a local option to legalize the consumption of alcoholic beverages depends significantly on a measure of the heterogeneity in preferences across counties within each state. There is, I think, some interesting work to be done in exploring the extent to which the potential gains from decentralization can explain the observed variation in actual governmental structure and policies.[9]

Third, I sense a widespread impression, suggested in some of the literature, that the gains from decentralization have their source in the famous Tiebout model (Charles Tiebout 1956). In this model, highly mobile households "vote with their feet": they choose as a jurisdiction of residence that locality that provides the fiscal package best suited to their tastes. In the limiting case, the Tiebout solution does indeed generate a first-best outcome that mimics the outcome in a competitive market. But the gains from decentralization, although typically enhanced by such mobility, are by no means wholly dependent upon them.[10] In fact, if there were absolutely nothing mobile—households, factors, or whatever—there would still exist, in general, gains from decentralization. The point here is simply that even in the absence of mobility, the efficient level of output of a "local" public good, as determined by the Samuelson condition that the sum of the marginal rates of substitution equals marginal cost, will typically vary from one jurisdiction to another. To take one example, the efficient level of air quality in Los Angeles is surely much different from that in, say, Chicago.

This point is of importance, because the Tiebout model is often viewed as a peculiarly U.S. construction. The relatively footloose households that it envisions, responding to such things as local schools and taxes, seem to characterize the U.S. much better than, say, most European countries. As a result, observers outside the U.S. tend to believe that this strand of the theory of local finance is of limited relevance in their settings. While there may well be some truth to this, it most emphatically does not follow that there are no longer any significant welfare gains from the decentralized provision of public goods.

3. *Fiscal Instruments in a Federal System*

To carry out their functions, the various levels of government require specific fiscal instruments. On the revenue side, governments will typically have access to tax and debt instruments. But in a federal system there is a further method for allocating funds among the different levels of the public sector: intergovernmental grants. One level of government may generate tax revenues in excess of its expenditures and then transfer the surplus to another level of government to finance part of the latter's budget. I want to review and

[9] Another interesting case is the setting of federal standards for safe drinking water. After mandating a set of standards for the quality of drinking water to be met in all jurisdictions in the Safe Drinking Water Act of 1974, the federal government has backed off and now allows a range of exceptions in recognition of the large interjurisdictional differences in per-capita costs of meeting the standards (U.S. Congressional Budget Office 1997).

[10] In certain settings, mobility can itself be a source of distorted outcomes. See, for example, the seminal paper by Frank Flatters, Vernon Henderson, and Peter Mieszkowski (1974).

comment briefly on the use of these fiscal instruments in a federal fiscal system.

3.1 *Taxation in a Federal System*

The determination of the vertical structure of taxes is known in the literature as the "tax-assignment problem" (Charles McLure 1983). And the basic issue here is the normative question: Which taxes are best suited for use at the different levels of government? The question is typically posed in a setting in which there exists a nation state with a central government, where there is little or no mobility across national borders; at decentralized levels, in contrast, economic agents, goods, and resources have significant mobility across jurisdictional boundaries with the extent of this mobility increasing at successively lower levels of government. "Local" government, for analytical purposes, may sometimes be characterized as operating in a setting in which economic units can move costlessly among jurisdictions.

The difference in the mobility of taxed units at the central and decentralized levels has important implications for the design of the vertical structure of taxation. Taxes, as we know, can be the source of distortions in resource allocation, as buyers shift their purchases away from taxed goods. In a spatial setting, such distortions take the form of locational inefficiencies, as taxed units (or owners of taxed items) seek out jurisdictions where they can obtain relatively favorable tax treatment. High excise taxes in one jurisdiction, for example, may lead purchasers to bear unproductive travel costs in order to purchase the taxed items in jurisdictions with lower tax rates.

Such examples can suggest the conclusion that decentralized levels of government should avoid the taxation of highly mobile economic units (be they households, capital, or final goods). But this in itself is not correct. The real implication is that decentralized levels of government should avoid *nonbenefit* taxes on mobile units. Or, more accurately, the analysis shows that on efficiency grounds decentralized governments *should* tax mobile economic units with benefit levies (Oates and Robert Schwab 1991; Oates 1996b). Such economic units, in short, should pay for the benefits that they receive from the public services that local governments provide to them.

The most well-known case of this is the earlier-discussed Tiebout model in which local jurisdictions use benefit taxes that effectively communicate to households the cost of consuming different levels of local public goods; this results in an efficient pattern of consumption of these goods. But this is true not only for households. If local governments provide local inputs that increase the productivity of capital employed in their jurisdictions, then they should levy benefit taxes on capital in order to provide the set of signals needed for the efficient deployment of capital across localities (Oates and Schwab 1991). In sum, efficiency requires not only that decentralized jurisdictions refrain from nonbenefit taxation of mobile economic units, but that they actively engage in benefit taxation where the public sector provides services to these units.

The public sector must for various reasons rely to a substantial extent on nonbenefit taxes. Redistributive programs that provide assistance to the poor, for example, simply transfer income. But, as noted earlier, such programs are not well suited to use at decentralized levels of government, where the mobility of economic units across local boundaries can undermine the workings of such programs. It is for this reason that the literature suggests that nonbenefit taxes, to the extent they are needed, are best employed by higher levels of government.

But provincial, state, and local governments do, in fact, make use of some such levies.[11] In a seminal treatment of this issue making use of an optimal taxation framework, Roger Gordon (1983) has explored the ramifications of the decentralized use of a wide range of nonbenefit taxes. And Gordon finds several forms of potential distortion that result from an individual jurisdiction's ignoring the effects of its fiscal decisions elsewhere in the system; these include inefficiencies involving, for example, the "exporting" of tax burdens, external congestion effects, and impacts on levels of revenues in other jurisdictions, as well as certain equity issues associated with a generally regressive pattern of tax incidence.[12]

The analysis suggests, moreover, some guidelines for the use of such taxes. A reliance on *resident-based* taxes rather than *source-based* taxes, for example, can lessen tax-induced distortions by reducing the scope for tax-exporting (Inman and Rubinfeld 1996; McKinnon and Nechyba 1997).[13] The analysis, moreover, establishes a presumption for the taxation of relatively immobile economic units. A particularly attractive tax base is unimproved land, since a tax on a factor or good in perfectly inelastic supply will not be the source of any locational inefficiencies. Such taxes (and any associated benefits from spending programs) will simply be capitalized into local land values. Thus, fiscally hard-pressed city governments have at their disposal a tax base that cannot escape them through mobility. There is some evidence in this regard that the city of Pittsburgh, which has used a graded property tax under which land is taxed at five times the rate on structures, has experienced an expansion in building activity that might not have been forthcoming in the presence of a higher tax on mobile capital (Oates and Schwab 1997).

3.2 *Intergovernmental Grants and Revenue Sharing*

Intergovernmental grants constitute a distinctive and important policy instrument in fiscal federalism that can serve a number of different functions. The literature emphasizes three potential roles for such grants: the internalization of spillover benefits to other jurisdictions, fiscal equalization across jurisdictions, and an improved overall tax system.

Grants can take either of two general forms. They can be "conditional grants" that place any of various kinds of restrictions on their use by the recipient. Or they can be "unconditional," that is,

[11] There is a lively and important debate in the local finance literature over whether or not local property taxation, as employed in the U.S., constitutes benefit taxation. Bruce Hamilton (1975, 1976) and William Fischel (1992) make the case that local property taxes combined with local zoning ordinances produce what is effectively a system of benefit taxation. Peter Mieszkowski and George Zodrow (1989) take the opposite view.

[12] See Inman and Rubinfeld (1996) for an excellent restatement and extension of the Gordon analysis. David Wildasin (1998a) provides a valuable survey of the various implications of factor mobility both for economic efficiency and for the redistributive impact of public policy.

[13] Resident-based taxes (also called "destination-based taxes") are levies on factors of production (such as land, labor, and capital) based on the owner's residence and on goods and services based on the residence of the consumer. In contrast, source-based taxes (or "origin taxes") involve taxing factors where they are employed and goods and services where they are purchased. Under resident-based taxation, governments have much less capacity to export the incidence of their taxes onto economic units elsewhere. Source-based taxes, however, are often easier to administer and, in certain forms, tend to be more commonly used by state and local governments.

lump-sum transfers to be used in any way the recipient wishes. The theory prescribes that conditional grants in the form of matching grants (under which the grantor finances a specified share of the recipient's expenditure) be employed where the provision of local services generates benefits for residents of other jurisdictions. The rationale here is simply the usual Pigouvian one for subsidies that induce individuals (in this case policy-makers or the electorate) to incorporate spillover benefits into their decision-making calculus. The magnitude of the matching shares, in such instances, should reflect the extent of the spillovers.[14]

In contrast, unconditional grants are typically the appropriate vehicle for purposes of fiscal equalization. The purpose of these grants is to channel funds from relatively wealthy jurisdictions to poorer ones. Such transfers are often based on an equalization formula that measures the "fiscal need" and "fiscal capacity" of each province, state, or locality. These formulae result in a disproportionate share of the transfers going to those jurisdictions with the greatest fiscal need and the least fiscal capacity.[15]

Although widely used, equalizing intergovernmental grants are by no means a necessary feature of fiscal federalism (Dan Usher 1995; Robin Boadway 1996). Economists normally think of redistributive measures from rich to poor as those that transfer income from high- to low-income individuals. Intergovernmental equalizing transfers require a somewhat different justification based on social values.[16] In practice, such equalizing grants play a major role in many countries: in the fiscal systems of Australia, Canada, and Germany, for example, there are substantial transfers of income from wealthy provinces or states to poorer ones. In the United States, in contrast, equalizing grants from the federal to state governments have never amounted to much. Intergovernmental grants in the U.S. typically address specific functions or programs, but usually do not accomplish much in the way of fiscal equalization. At the levels of the states, however, there are many such programs under which states provide equalizing grants to local jurisdictions—notably school districts.

Fiscal equalization is a contentious issue from an efficiency perspective. Some observers see such grants as playing an important role in allowing poorer jurisdictions to compete effectively with fiscally stronger ones. This view holds that, in the absence of such grants, fiscally favored jurisdictions can exploit their position to promote continued economic growth, some of which comes

14 Matching grants (possibly negative) can, in principle, also serve to correct some of the distortions associated with the decentralized use of nonbenefit taxes (Gordon 1983).

15 Fiscal equalization can also make use of matching grants. If the objective of the equalization program is to equalize taxable capacity, the granting government may choose to supplement the revenue base of fiscally poorer jurisdictions by matching any revenues they collect by some specified percentage. Such a measure has the potential of allowing all jurisdictions to raise the same tax revenues per capita for a given tax rate (irrespective of the actual size of their tax base). This form of fiscal equalization is sometimes called "power-equalization" and has gotten some attention in the U.S. for state programs to achieve various equity goals—most notably in the area of school finance (e.g., Feldstein 1976; and Nechyba 1996).

16 The issue here is that from the perspective of redistributing income from rich to poor, equalizing intergovernmental grants are bound to have some perverse effects. For such grants, although transfering income from wealthy to poor *on average*, will inevitably result in some income transfers from poor individuals who reside in wealthy jurisdictions to rich persons in generally poor areas. In this sense, such equalizing measures are not as effective as programs that redistribute income from rich to poor *individuals*. But a society may well wish, for other reasons, to provide additional support for the provision of local public services (such as schools) in relatively low-income areas (e.g., Inman and Rubinfeld 1979).

at the expense of poorer ones. Fiscal equalization, from this perspective, helps to create a more level playing field for interjurisdictional competition.[17]

But the case is not entirely persuasive. Others have argued that fiscal equalization can stand in the way of needed regional adjustments that promote development in poorer regions. McKinnon (1997a), for example, contends that in the United States, the economic resurgence of the South following World War II resulted from relatively low levels of wages and other costs. It was this attraction of low wages and costs that ultimately induced economic movement to the South, bringing with it a new prosperity. Fiscal equalization, from this perspective, may actually hold back the development of poorer areas by impeding the needed interregional flow of resources (both emigration and immigration) in response to cost differentials.

But the primary justification for fiscal equalization must be on equity grounds. And it is as a redistributive issue that it continues to occupy a central place on the political stage. In some cases, as in Canada, it may provide the glue necessary to hold the federation together. In other instances, like Italy, it may become a divisive force, where regions, weary of large and longstanding transfers of funds to poorer areas, actually seek a dissolution of the union. Fiscal equalization is a complex economic and political issue.

The third potential role for intergovernmental grants is to sustain a more equitable and efficient overall tax system. For reasons we have discussed, centrally administered, nonbenefit taxes with a single rate applying to the national tax base will not generate the sorts of locational inefficiencies associated with varying rates across decentralized jurisdictions. Moreover, central taxes can be more progressive, again without establishing fiscal incentives for relocation. There is, in fact, considerable evidence to indicate that state and local systems of taxes are typically more regressive than central taxation (e.g., Howard Chernick 1992). There is thus some force in an argument for "revenue sharing" under which the central government effectively serves as a tax-collecting agent for decentralized levels of government.[18] The central government then transfers funds, in a presumably unconditional form, to provinces, states, and/or localities. It is certainly possible, where the polity wishes, to build equalizing elements into these transfers. While there is here a real case for the use of intergovernmental grants, a most important qualification is that such a system of grants must not be too large in the sense of undermining fiscal discipline at lower levels of government (more on this later).

The prescriptive theory of intergovernmental grants thus leads to a vision of a system in which there exists a set of open-ended matching grants, where the matching rates reflect the extent of benefit spillovers across jurisdictional boundaries, and a set of unconditional grants for revenue sharing and, perhaps, equalization purposes. Such a conception has, however, only modest

[17] As Boadway and Flatters (1982) have shown, equalizing grants may be required to offset distorting locational incentives where some jurisdictions offer pecuniary fiscal advantages to potential residents resulting, for example, from large, taxable natural resource endowments.

[18] This argument has even more force where, as in some developing countries and emerging democracies, provincial and local governments simply lack the capacity for effective tax administration. In this setting, central transfers and/or the piggybacking of supplementary rates on top of centrally administered taxes may be the only realistic options. See, for example, Inman (forthcoming).

explanatory power. We do, in fact, find federal matching programs that have supported a number of state and local activities with spillover effects, including, for example, grants for interstate highway construction. However, on closer examination, important anomalies appear. These grants are often closed, rather than open, ended. They thus do not provide incentives for expansion at the margin. Moreover, the federal matching shares are typically much larger than justifiable by any plausible level of spillover benefits. More generally, in a careful study of the intergovernmental grant system, Inman (1988) concludes that the economic theory of intergovernmental grants does not provide a very satisfactory explanation of the structure of U.S. grant programs; he finds that a political model can do a much better job of explaining U.S. grant programs.[19]

Some years ago, David Bradford and I (1971a,b) tried to lay the foundations for a positive theory of the response to intergovernmental grants by setting forth a framework in which the budgetary decisions of the recipients of such grants are treated explicitly in a collective-choice setting. In short, we treated these grants, not as grants to an individual decision-maker, but rather as grants to polities that make budgetary decisions by some collective algorithm (such as simple majority rule). This exercise produced some intriguing equivalence theorems. For example, it is straightforward to show that a lump-sum grant to a group of people is fully equivalent in all its effects, both allocative and distributive, to a set of grants directly to the individuals in the group. Moreover, this result applies to an important class of collective-choice procedures, encompassing several of the major models employed in the public-finance literature. These theorems, known as the "veil hypothesis," thus imply that a grant to a community is fully equivalent to a central tax rebate to the individuals in the community; intergovernmental grants, according to this view, are simply a "veil" for a federal tax cut.

The difficulty is that this hypothesis has not fared well in empirical testing. It implies that the budgetary response to an intergovernmental transfer should be (roughly) the same as the response to an equal increase in private income in the community. But empirical studies of the response to grants have rejected this equivalence time and again. Such studies invariably find that state and local government spending is much more responsive to increases in intergovernmental receipts than it is to increases in the community's private income. And this has come to be known as the "flypaper effect"—money sticks where it hits. While this finding may not be all that surprising, it is not so easy to reconcile with models of rational choice, for it suggests that the same budget constraint gives rise to different choices depending on what form the increment to the budget takes. There is now a large literature that tries in a variety of ways (some quite ingenious) to explain the flypaper effect.[20] James Hines and Richard Thaler (1995) have suggested recently that this is just one of a more general class of cases where having

[19] As Inman and Rubinfeld (1996) point out, the prescriptive theory of grants presumes a central planner or political process that "will select socially preferred policies" (p. 325). However, the public-choice literature makes clear the potential of central-government political mechanisms to make inefficient choices concerning policies that affect various groups differently. In addition, a grant-distributing agency may have its own objectives; for an excellent study of how such objectives can influence the pattern of grants, see Chernick (1979).

[20] For surveys and interpretations of this literature, see Gramlich (1977), Ronald Fisher (1982), Oates (1994), and Hines and Thaler (1995).

money on hand (e.g., from grants) has a much different effect on spending behavior than where the money must be raised (e.g., by taxation).

Much of the early empirical work on the expenditure response to intergovernmental grants studied the period from the 1950's through the 1970's, when these grants exhibited a continuing path of expansion. As a result, much of the interest focused on the budgetary response to increases in grants. However, in more recent times, efforts at fiscal retrenchment and devolution have led to large cuts in a wide range of federal grant programs. And this has raised the interesting and important question of whether the response to cuts in grants is similar in sign and magnitude to the response to increases in these grants. Gramlich (1987), for example, observed that during this period of retrenchment, state and local governments responded to the cutbacks in grants by picking up much of the slack: they increased their own taxes and replaced in large part the lost grant funds so as to maintain levels of existing programs. If Gramlich is right, then we should observe a basic asymmetry in response: the spending of recipients should be more responsive to increases in grant monies than to decreases in these revenues. This issue is of some importance if we are to understand the budgetary implications of the ongoing process of fiscal decentralization. In the first study of this issue, William Stine (1994), examining the response of county governments in Pennsylvania, found just the opposite of Gramlich's prediction: his estimates imply that these county governments not only failed to replace lost grant revenues, but that they reduced their spending from own-revenues on these programs as well, giving rise to a "super-flypaper effect." There are, however, some tricky and troublesome issues of measurement and interpretation in the Stine study. Subsequently, using national aggregate data on the state and local government sector, Shama Gamkhar and I (1996) were unable to reject the hypothesis that the expenditure response to increases and decreases in intergovernmental grants has the same absolute value per dollar of grants. Our findings are thus consistent with the proposition that the flypaper effect operates symmetrically in both directions. But much clearly remains to be done on this issue.

4. *A Note on Jurisdictional Boundaries*

The treatment to this point has implicitly taken as given a pattern of boundaries that divide the nation-state into a set of jurisdictions for decentralized governance. The existence and magnitude of spillover effects from localized public policies clearly depend on the geographical extent of the relevant jurisdiction. One way to deal with such spillovers is to increase the size of the jurisdiction, thereby internalizing all the benefits and costs. The problem, of course, is that such an extension may involve welfare losses from the reduced capacity to differentiate local outputs. There is clearly some kind of tradeoff here between internalizing spillover benefits (and costs) and allowing local differentiation.

In practice, much of the problem stems from a set of existing boundaries that are largely historically and culturally determined and that may make little sense in terms of the economic and geographical realities. Consider, for example, the United States. Suppose that we were to begin with a *tabula rasa*, a completely undefined set of boundaries for states and localities. And we set for ourselves the task of laying out both a rational set of levels of government and borders for the jurisdictions at each level of government. One thing seems clear: such a system of jurisdictions would bear little resemblance to our existing map. The states, in particular, are quite poorly designed to deal with the provision of certain important public goods, notably environmental resources. To take one example, rivers were used historically (for understandable reasons) to mark off one state from another. But from the perspective of effective management of a public good, this is the worst sort of border. It means that two independent and autonomous jurisdictions are making decisions that affect the public good whose output they jointly share. It seems clear that it would make much more sense to place such resources within a single jurisdiction. My own surmise is that a much more rational map would probably entail (1) some fairly sizeable regional governments that extend over watersheds, air sheds, and other environmental resources; (2) metropolitan governments that encompass center cities and the suburbs that house many city workers; and (3) smaller local governments that allow groups of residents to determine services of relevance mainly to themselves.

But political realities being what they are, we can expect to continue our collective life with much the same map in place. There does, however, remain some flexibility in terms of creating useful compacts or associations of jurisdictions to deal with particular issues. The management of the Chesapeake Bay, for example, is in important organizational ways now the joint enterprise of the relevant states (Delaware, Maryland, Pennsylvania, and Virginia), and Washington, D.C., with an important role also played by the federal government. Likewise, the recognition that the management of ground-level ozone involves pollutants that travel long distances across the midwestern and northeastern parts of the United States has led, under congressional legislation in 1990, to the formation of an Ozone Transport Region (OTR) for the coordination of efforts to manage air quality in eleven eastern states and the District of Columbia. Such regional organizations can be seen as the outcome of a kind of Coasian process in which interjurisdictional externalities are addressed through negotiation and coordinated decision-making. The history of such enterprises, however, attests to their difficulty. The fascinating study by Bruce Ackerman et al. (1974), for example, of the attempt to create a "model regional agency" in the form of the Delaware River Basin Commission reveals all the complexities and perverse incentives that can bedevil such joint enterprises. Nevertheless, such coordination does, in principle, offer an important avenue for addressing such interjurisdictional concerns.

5. *Laboratory Federalism and Welfare Reform*

It seems ironical in the light of the preceding treatment of principles (or guidelines) for fiscal federalism to find that welfare reform is in the vanguard of U.S. moves toward fiscal decentralization. The analysis suggests that the threat of mobility of both low and high income households will result in decentralized policies that provide too little assistance to the poor (sometimes described as a "race to the bottom"). Nevertheless, the decision has been made to shift the primary responsibility for poor relief back to the states. Under measures signed into law in 1996, the federal government has replaced the longstanding federal entitlement programs, which came with both detailed rules and generous matching grants to the states, by a system of block grants with few strings attached. The states now have broad scope to determine both the form and levels of assistance under their programs to assist poor households.[21]

How are we to understand this reform? Does it represent an outright rejection of the economic principles of fiscal federalism? My answer is a qualified no. There exists widespread recognition of, and concern with, the likely shortcomings of a decentralized system of poor relief. Policy makers are well aware of the threat of strategic cuts in state levels of welfare support. But, as I read it, we have decided to live with this threat in order to seek out superior policy alternatives. And this brings us to another dimension of fiscal federalism: laboratory federalism.

In a setting of imperfect information with learning-by-doing, there are potential gains from experimentation with a variety of policies for addressing social and economic problems. And a federal system may offer some real opportunities for encouraging such experimentation and thereby promoting "technical progress" in public policy. This point was made long ago by James Bryce (1888) who, in his insightful study of the U.S. system of government, observed that "Federalism enables a people to try experiments which could not safely be tried in a large centralized country" (Vol. I, p. 353). Better known is a later statement by Justice Louis Brandeis, who wrote in 1932 that

> There must be power in the States and the Nation to remould, through experimentation, our economic practices and institutions to meet changing social and economic needs . . . It is one of the happy incidents of the federal system that a single courageous State may, if its citizens choose, serve as a laboratory; and try novel social and economic experiments without risk to the rest of the country. (Osborne 1988)

It is my sense that this is the primary thrust behind the current welfare reform. There exists much disappointment and dissatisfaction with the operation and results under the traditional federal welfare programs. But we really don't have a clear sense of how to restructure them to achieve our societal goals of providing needed relief and, at the same time, establishing an effective set of incentives to move people off welfare and into jobs. The recent legislation that transfers the responsibility for these programs back to the states represents, I believe, a recognition of the failure of existing programs and an attempt to make use of the states as "laboratories" to try to find out what sorts of programs can work.[22]

There are, in fact, a number of important and intriguing examples of policies whose advent was at the state or local level and that later became fixtures of federal policy. Unemployment insurance, for example, was a state-level policy before the federal government made it effectively mandatory on a national scale in the 1930s. More recently, in the area of environmental policy, the experience in a number of states with their own forms of Emissions Trading was an important prelude to the adoption, in the 1990 Clean Air Act Amendments, of a national trading program in sulfur allowances to address the problem of acid rain. Without this experience in a number of states, I seriously doubt that policy-makers would have been willing to introduce such a new and unfamiliar policy measure as tradeable emissions rights on a national

[21] For an excellent and recent review of this whole debate in a historical context, see Therese McGuire (1997). Rebecca Blank (1997) provides a concise and insightful treatment of the new welfare legislation and its potential implications.

[22] For a concurring view, see Craig Volden (1997).

scale. More generally, since the dawn of the nation, programs successfully developed at the state level have often provided models for subsequent federal programs.

States, of course, may learn from others so that the diffusion of successful policy innovations may be horizontal as well as vertical. Both forms of diffusion have been the subject of study by a number of political scientists. Virginia Gray (1973) and Everett Rogers (1983), for example, have found that the cumulative distribution of states by date of adoption takes the S-curve shape, familiar from the study of the spread of other forms of innovation. Others, like Jack Walker (1969), James Lutz (1987), David Huff et al. (1988), and David Nice (1994), have explored the geographical and other determinants of the pattern of adoptions by states. Empirical studies of vertical diffusion are less numerous. Thomas Anton (1989), Keith Boeckelman (1992), and Michael Sparer and Lawrence Brown (1996) have examined the extent to which federal measures draw on the experience of the states. Some of this literature is relatively skeptical of the link. Sparer and Brown, for example, argue that (at least for health care) "These laboratory adoptions and adaptations are probably more the exception than the rule" (p. 196).

What are we to make of all this? A little reflection suggests first that there is nothing in principle to prevent the central government from undertaking limited experiments without committing the nation to an untested and risky policy measure. Indeed, there have been a number of such social experiments with, for example, income-maintenance and housing-allowance programs that have generated valuable information about how programs work and the response of participants to various values of the key parameters. We don't necessarily need states as the "laboratories" for experiments. At the same time, one might suspect that relatively independent efforts in a large number of states will generate a wider variety of approaches to public policy than a set of centrally designed experiments.

A basic problem here is that there has been little in the way of a real theory of laboratory federalism to organize our thought and to guide empirical studies. However, the beginnings of some theory are emerging, and they are quite illuminating. Susan Rose-Ackerman (1980) and, more recently, Strumpf (1997) have taken two quite different formal approaches to policy innovation in a federal system. One insight emerging from their analyses is an important, if familiar and unsurprising, one. There exists a basic "information externality" in that states that adopt new and experimental policies generate valuable information for others. And this creates a standard sort of incentive for free-riding. From this perspective, we might expect too little experimentation and policy innovation in a highly decentralized public sector. Indeed, as Strumpf shows, it is unclear whether a centralized or decentralized outcome will result in more policy innovation.[23]

The underprovision of experimentation at state and local levels can be addressed through a system of subsidies to encourage these activities. And this raises another point regarding existing welfare reform in the U.S. Under earlier programs, federal aid took a matching form such that the federal government effectively shared the costs and risks of new state-level programs. But

[23] The Rose-Ackerman and Strumpf analyses, incidentally, also produce a number of subtle and more surprising results. Strumpf finds, for example, that a state with a higher expected return from experimentation can have a lower propensity to experiment.

under the new welfare reform measures, matching aid has been replaced by block grants. This in itself serves to reduce incentives for experimentation. There are some conflicting incentives here. On the one hand, the new legislation gives the states broader scope for experimentation, but it places the full cost of any new measures on the state with no sharing from the center. The net outcome on the amount of experimentation is thus a priori unclear.

More generally, we need a lot more work on the implications of fiscal decentralization for both the amount and kinds of policy experimentation and innovation. As I have suggested, there are some clear and important cases where innovation and experimentation at state and local levels have led to new policy measures that have had broad national application. But it is much less clear how we are to understand this experience in terms of the overall effectiveness of a federal system in policy innovation.

6. *Interjurisdictional Competition and Environmental Federalism: A Challenge to the Basic View*

The preceding sections have set forth an economic conception of a federal system. It is one in which the central government plays the major role in macroeconomic stabilization policies, takes the lead in redistributive measures for support for the poor, and provides a set of national public goods. Decentralized levels of government focus their efforts on providing public goods whose consumption is limited primarily to their own constituencies. In this way, they can adapt outputs of such services to the particular tastes, costs, and other circumstances that characterize their own jurisdictions.

The general idea of decentralizing the provision of public services to the jurisdictions of concern has been widely recognized. It manifests itself clearly on both sides of the Atlantic. We see it in Europe under the nomenclature of the "principle of subsidiarity," where it is explicitly enshrined in the Maastrict Treaty as a fundamental principle for European union. In the U.S., it often appears more informally as an aversion to the "one size fits all" approach.

Somewhat paradoxically, however, this view is the subject of a widespread and fundamental challenge both at the theoretical and policy levels. The source of this challenge is the claim that interjurisdictional competition among decentralized levels of government introduces serious allocative distortions. In their eagerness to promote economic development with the creation of new jobs (so the argument goes), state and local officials tend to hold down tax rates and, consequently, outputs of public services so as to reduce the costs for existing and prospective business enterprise. This results in a "race to the bottom" with suboptimal outputs of public services.[24]

This argument has a substantial history. Some thirty years ago, for example, George Break (1967) made the case for the detrimental effects of interjurisdictional competition:

> The trouble is that state and local governments have been engaged for some time in an increasingly active competition among themselves for new business . . . In such an environment government officials do not lightly propose increases in their own tax rates that go much beyond those prevailing in nearby states or in any area with similar natural attractions for industry . . . Active tax competition, in short, tends to produce either a generally low level of state-local tax effort or a state-local tax structure with strong regressive elements. (Break 1967, pp. 23–24).

[24] Competition may also take place between different levels of government. On such "vertical competition" (as well as horizontal competition), see Albert Breton (1998).

Fear of losing local business and jobs thus leads to suboptimal levels of state and local public goods. Such competition can involve regulatory as well as purely fiscal policies. John Cumberland (1979, 1981) has extended the Break argument to encompass the setting of standards for local environmental quality. In the Break spirit, Cumberland contends that state and local governments engage in "destructive interregional competition." In order to attract new business and create jobs, public officials compete by reducing local environmental standards to lower the costs of pollution control for firms that locate within their borders. In this instance, interjurisdictional competition leads to excessive environmental degradation. The implication of the Cumberland view is that national standards for environmental quality are needed to prevent the excessive levels of pollution forthcoming under state and local standard setting.

More recently, Alice Rivlin (1992) has echoed these views in her "rethinking of U.S. federalism." Although advocating an extensive devolution of public-sector responsibilities to state and local government, Rivlin sees it as almost axiomatic that competition among the states results in inadequate levels of public services. Her remedy is a system of shared taxes under which the revenues from a new national value-added tax would be shared among the states. This, she argues, would free the states so that they would not have "to worry so much about losing businesses to neighboring states with lower tax rates" (p. 142).

This line of argument has proved quite powerful in the policy arena. There are strong forces for the "harmonization" of fiscal and environmental measures in Europe that draw heavily on this proposition. Likewise, the case for the "race to the bottom" has provided basic support for the centralization of environmental management in the United States.

What I want to stress here is the fundamental character of this challenge to the basic model of fiscal federalism. The claim is that the decentralized provision of public services is basically flawed; in the words of one recent U.S. observer, we need centralization in order to "Save the States from Themselves" (Peter Enrich 1996).[25]

But is this claim in fact true? This turns out to be a very complicated question both in theoretical and empirical terms. There is now a substantial theoretical literature that addresses this issue. In one set of papers, my colleague Robert Schwab and I have developed a series of models that explore the conditions under which horizontal competition among governments is efficiency-enhancing (Oates and Schwab 1988, 1991, 1996). It turns out that it is straightforward to develop an analogue to perfect competition in the private sector. In such a setting, governments compete with one another for a mobile capital stock that both generates income for local residents and provides a tax base for them—and such competition leads local officials to adopt efficient levels of outputs of public goods and tax rates. In these models, the invisible hand works in much the same way as in the private sector to channel policy decisions in individual jurisdictions into an efficient outcome from a national perspective.

These models, moreover, are quite rich in terms of the variety of policy instruments. Public officials provide not

[25] There is, incidentally, a very extensive, interesting, and lively debate on this matter among legal scholars. Recent issues of the law journals are full of papers on interjurisdictional competition and its consequences. See, for example, Richard Revesz (1992) and Daniel Esty (1996).

only outputs for local residents, but public inputs that enhance the productivity of locally employed capital, and environmental regulations that impose costs on local business and improve local environmental quality. They finance these public outputs with a set of taxes on local residents and capital. And there is no race to the bottom here. Instead, jurisdictions find it in their own interest to charge benefit taxes that lead to efficient decisions in both the public and private sectors.[26]

The problem is that these models make some strong assumptions. Let me note three of them here: jurisdictions behave as price-takers in national or international capital markets; public officials seek in their decisions to maximize the welfare of their constituencies; and these officials have access to the needed fiscal and regulatory policy instruments to carry out their programs efficiently. It is not hard to show (or surprising to find) that violations of any of these conditions can lead to distorted outcomes. Suppose, for example, that local policy makers are Niskanen-type agents that seek to maximize, not the well-being of their constituencies, but rather the size of the local public budget. It is then straightforward to show that they will set excessively lax environmental standards in order to encourage a larger inflow of capital so as to enlarge the local tax base (Oates and Schwab 1988).

The Oates-Schwab models provide a kind of baseline from which one can introduce a range of quite plausible and realistic modifications that can be the source of allocative distortions. A large number of papers explore outcomes either where jurisdictions are sufficiently large to have some influence over the price of capital or where local governments are restricted in their access to policy instruments and must, for example, tax business and household capital at the same rate. Many of these papers employ game-theoretic approaches in which there is strategic interaction among the jurisdictions (Wildasin 1988). In such settings, we find that outcomes can easily occur that involve suboptimal levels of public outputs.[27]

The theoretical literature thus generates some diverse findings on this issue. There seem to be some basic efficiency-enhancing aspects of interjurisdictional competition, but there are clearly a range of "imperfections" that can be the source of allocative distortions. The real issue here is the magnitude of these distortions. Are we dealing with minor deviations from efficient outcomes—or does such competition produce major welfare losses? The pure theory can't help us much in answering this question. Moreover, some of the terminology is not very helpful. In particular, the description of interjurisdictional competition as involving a "race to the bottom" seems quite misleading. Such a descriptive image may well be an effective rhetorical device: it conjures up a vision of one jurisdiction cutting its tax rates and lowering its environmental standards, only to be outdone by a neighboring jurisdiction, in a process that leads to a downward spiral to the "bottom" (suggesting a very bad

[26] I should emphasize here that all public outputs (including environmental quality) are entirely local in these models; there are no spillover effects into other jurisdictions. The analysis, incidentally, extends not only to fiscal instruments, but regulatory ones as well (such as environmental standards). The analysis of "regulatory federalism" is, in principle, analogous to that of fiscal federalism. The same general principles concerning decentralization apply to fiscal and regulatory instruments.

[27] See John Wilson (1996) for an excellent survey of this literature.

outcome indeed). However, the models that generate these results are nothing of the sort. They are often game-theoretic models that produce Nash equilibria with suboptimal public outputs as the outcome. What matters here is the extent of the suboptimality. And the race-to-the-bottom terminology tends to obscure this issue.

Unfortunately, we do not have many empirical studies to bring to bear on this matter. There is a substantial descriptive literature addressing economic competition among state and local governments in the U.S., with some interesting findings (Timothy Bartik 1991). But this body of work really does not shed much light on the normative question of whether such competition is efficiency-enhancing or not (Paul Courant 1994). In an interesting study that is of relevance, Anne Case, James Hines, and Harvey Rosen (1993) find evidence of strategic interaction in state-level fiscal policies. Using a similar methodology, Jan Brueckner (1998) finds empirical support for policy interdependence in the adoption of growth-control measures by local governments in California. But at this juncture, I think it is fair to say that the jury is still out on this matter. The welfare implications of interjurisdictional competition remain the subject of a lively ongoing debate with a real need for further empirical work to supplement the large theoretical literature. In my own view, the existing work is not sufficient to make a compelling case for the abandonment of (or basic amendment to) the principle of fiscal decentralization. The case remains strong, it seems to me, for leaving "local matters in local hands." Moreover, as we shall see shortly, there is another literature that takes a very different (and unambiguously positive) view of the role of interjurisdictional competition.

7. *Fiscal Federalism: Expanding the Scope of the Analysis*

The normative framework for most of the literature in fiscal federalism (and for my treatment in this essay as well) consists of the traditional principles of welfare economics. From this perspective, institutions are evaluated in terms of their impact on efficiency in resource allocation and the distribution of income. However, the choice of a system of governance involves other values as well: the extent of political participation, the protection of individual rights, and the development of various civic virtues. Political theorists throughout the ages have explored the ways in which different political systems address these various objectives of the polity. In addition, the vertical structure of government may have important implications for the way in which the public sector functions and its impact on the operation of a system of markets. In this section, I want to explore some of the new (and older) literature that addresses some broader implications of fiscal federalism.

7.1 *Economic and Political Objectives in a Federal System*

The first issue involves extending the conceptual horizon to encompass additional political objectives. What might this add to our more narrowly focused economic view of fiscal federalism? Inman and Rubinfeld, in one strand of their important new work on fiscal federalism, have (and are) exploring this issue in an attempt to redefine and extend the analytical framework to encompass some of these additional political and constitutional dimensions of public-sector structure.

The approach of Inman and Rubinfeld (1997a,b,c) incorporates explicitly certain political goals into a more extended objective function. In such a setting, we find ourselves examining tradeoffs between such goals as economic efficiency and political participation. In one such illustration, they present a "federalism frontier" in which (over the relevant range) increased political participation comes at the expense of economic efficiency (1997a, p. 1230).

The basic presumption here is that more decentralized political systems are conducive to increased citizen impact on political outcomes and political participation. The evidence on this issue, in truth, is somewhat mixed, but overall it suggests on balance "that both citizen influence and effort increase as the size of government declines" (1997a, p. 1215). The basic political objectives thus strengthen the case for increased decentralization; they point to a system that is more decentralized than one chosen simply on the grounds of an exercise in economic optimization.

While this is suggestive at a general level, it raises the more difficult question of how one addresses these tradeoffs in the actual design of fiscal institutions. How, for example, can we define and measure in a meaningful way the marginal rate of substitution between economic efficiency and political participation and incorporate this into the design of a political system? To approach this question in a substantive way requires the study of more specific issues. And here Inman and Rubinfeld (1997a) provide a provocative beginning with a careful study of "anti-trust state-action doctrine." This involves an intriguing series of Supreme Court decisions in which state programs, that—had they been designed and introduced by producers themselves, would have constituted a violation of anti-trust laws—were upheld on the basis of state legislative sovereignty. Although the history of this doctrine is a complicated one, it is interesting that the Court has seen fit to set aside, in certain instances, the presumed economic consequences of certain state regulations in favor of decentralized political choices, so long as they "were decided by an open, participatory political process, as evidenced by state legislative involvement" (1997a, p. 1252).

It seems unlikely that we can ever hope to quantify such tradeoffs in a formally satisfying way. But the Inman-Rubinfeld work does suggest that careful analysis can certainly help to clarify the nature of the tradeoffs involved in the vertical design of the political system and allow economics to play a broader role in the debate. It is interesting, moreover, that the political objectives seem, on the whole, to strengthen the case for fiscal decentralization.

7.2 *Public-Sector Institutions: Market-Preserving Federalism*

An alternative approach to federalism, related to the "new institutional economics," sees political decentralization in terms of its capacity to sustain a productive and growing market economy. From this perspective, Barry Weingast (1995), Ronald McKinnon (1997a), and their colleagues have explored the institutional structure of a system that promises to provide a stable framework for a market system (see also McKinnon and Nechyba 1997 and Qian and Weingast 1997). Weingast's point of departure is a "fundamental political dilemma of an economic system," namely that "a government strong enough to protect property rights and enforce contracts is also strong enough to confiscate the wealth of its citizens" (1995, p. 1).[28]

The attraction of federalism for Weingast is its potential for providing a

[28] However, as Martin McGuire and Mancur Olson (1996) have shown, even a self-aggrandizing autocrat (if secure) has powerful incentives for supporting an economically efficient system.

political system that can support an efficient system of markets. In a provocative treatment, Weingast lays out a set of three conditions for a federal system that characterize what he calls "market-preserving federalism." These conditions require that (1) decentralized governments have the primary regulatory responsibility over the economy; (2) the system constitutes a common market in which there are no barriers to trade; and (3) decentralized governments face "hard budget constraints." By this last condition, Weingast means that lower-level governments have neither the capacity to create money nor access to unlimited credit. And it implies further that the central government does not stand ready to bail them out in instances of fiscal distress.

Weingast goes on to argue in historical terms that eighteenth century England and the United States in the nineteenth century were effectively such systems of market-preserving federalism, and that this fostered in important and fundamental ways the process of economic growth. It proved critical, argues Weingast, to the industrial revolution in England and supported a system of "thriving markets" in the United States throughout the nineteenth century.

McKinnon (1997a) has explored in more detail the importance of Weingast's last condition of a hard budget constraint. Crucial to this view is the separation of monetary and fiscal powers. In a federal system, if the central government controls the common currency, then lower-level governments will be limited to fiscal instruments and will not have access to the "soft" option of monetized debt. As McKinnon points out, state and local governments in the United States engage in extensive debt finance for capital projects. This makes good economic sense in terms of spreading the payments for long-lived capital projects over their useful life. But they have no recourse to public sources for funding this debt; they operate in private credit markets just like private borrowers. These markets themselves, through the determination of credit ratings and other forms of monitoring fiscal performance, create an environment in which the fiscal authorities must behave in responsible ways.[29] These markets, by creating a hard budget constraint in terms of debt finance, have imposed a very useful discipline on decentralized fiscal behavior.[30]

More generally, a hard budget constraint implies that decentralized governments must place a basic reliance on their own sources of revenues. They must not be overly dependent on transfers from above. I discussed in an earlier section the potential role for intergovernmental grants, but Weingast and McKinnon (as well as others) remind us of the important discipline that stems from self-financing. It is especially important that intergovernmental grants not be expansible in the sense that recipients can turn to the grant system to bail them out of fiscal difficulties (Wildasin 1998b). In particular, public authorities need to fund their own expenditures at the margin.[31]

The institutional perspective reminds us that there is more to the design of a

[29] James Poterba and Kim Rueben (1997), for example, have found that those states with tighter anti-deficit rules, and more restrictive limitations on the authority of the state legislature to issue debt, pay lower rates of interest on their bonds.

[30] McKinnon (1997b) has gone on to argue that much of the impetus for European Monetary Union has as its source a collectively imposed budgetary retrenchment. His interesting argument is that European decision makers, realizing that they cannot achieve fiscal stability with continued access to monetary powers, are seeking through EMU to create the hard budget constraints that are the prerequisite for responsible fiscal management.

[31] This is subject to the qualification that matching grants may be needed to internalize interjurisdictional spillover benefits.

federal fiscal system than just the allocation of functions to the appropriate levels of government. In addition, we need sets of formal and informal institutions that embody the rights sorts of incentives for public decision makers (Olson 1990). These rules or procedures must make the costs of public programs as fully visible as their benefits in ways that make public officials accountable for their decisions (Shah 1998).

The treatment of fiscal structure in this section is not unrelated to Geoffrey Brennan and James Buchanan's (1980) view of fiscal decentralization as a mechanism for controlling the size of the public sector. Drawing by analogy on the conventional theory of monopoly in the private sector, they envision the government sector as a monolithic agent, a "Leviathan," that seeks its own aggrandizement through maximizing the extraction of tax revenues from the economy. From this perspective, the design of the constitution and associated institutions has as a major objective the placing of a set of constraints that limits Leviathan's access to tax and other fiscal instruments. Fiscal decentralization can, in their view, play a most important role in constraining public sector growth. Competition among decentralized governments for mobile economic units greatly limits the capacity of Leviathan to channel resources into the public sector. As Brennan and Buchanan put it, competition among governments in the context of the "interjurisdictional mobility of persons in pursuit of 'fiscal gains' can offer partial or possibly complete substitutes for explicit fiscal constraints on the taxing power" (1980, p. 184).[32]

[32] In a more formal treatment of this matter, Dennis Epple and Allan Zelenitz (1981) have shown that while competition among jurisdictions can constrain government rent-seeking behavior, it cannot altogether eliminate it.

The Brennan-Buchanan view suggests the hypothesis that the overall size of the public sector "should be smaller, ceteris paribus, the greater the extent to which taxes and expenditures are decentralized" (1980, p. 185). The evidence on this hypothesis is, however, at best mixed. For example, I was unable to find any systematic relationship between public-sector size and the extent of fiscal decentralization (Oates 1985). However, some later and more disaggregated studies have found some tendencies of this kind (See Oates 1989 for a survey of this work.).

More generally, there is not much evidence on the relationship between fiscal decentralization and economic performance. But there is some. Jeff Huther and Anwar Shah (1996) at the World Bank have assembled a large and diverse set of indices for eighty nations. These indices encompass a wide variety of measures of economic and political structure and performance: quality of governance, political freedom, political stability, debt-to-GNP ratios, measures of income, the degree of equality in the distribution of income, and many more. In examining the statistical associations among these various indices, they find in nearly every case a statistically significant and positive correlation between increased decentralization and improved performance (either in political or economic terms). There are obvious and important qualifications here. Such associations do not prove causation. In particular, the degree of fiscal decentralization is itself the outcome of a complex of political and economic forces. Nonetheless, the initial results are suggestive and invite further exploration. Elsewhere, Sang-Loh Kim (1995) in an intriguing econometric study making use of an international panel data set, has estimated a Barro-type growth model. In addition to the usual explanatory variables, he included a measure of fiscal decentralization that, in most of his estimated equations, has a significant and positive partial association with the rate of economic growth. Kim's findings thus support Shah's contention that fiscal decentralization enhances economic performance—in this case, more rapid economic growth. In contrast, Heng-fu Zou and his colleagues have found a negative relationship between economic growth and fiscal decentralization in two studies, one examining a sample of forty-six countries over the period 1970–89 (Davoodi and Zou 1998) and the other a study of the growth of provinces in China (Zhang and Zou 1998). Much obviously remains to be done at the empirical level in order to give us a better sense of the relationship of fiscal decentralization to economic and political performance.

There is also much more to do at the conceptual level. While Weingast's initial forays into market-preserving federalism are certainly provocative, they raise at least as many questions as they answer. It is fair, I think, to characterize the analysis as fairly "loose" at this stage. For example, are Weingast's conditions for market-preserving federalism to be regarded as necessary or sufficient (or both) for an effective political foundation for a private market economy? Jonathan Rodden and Susan Rose-Ackerman (1997) have raised a number of probing questions concerning the Weingast analysis. There is clearly much to chew on here. The next step, it seems to me, is to attempt to formalize these relationships more explicitly so as to get a better sense of how different political and budgetary institutions influence the functioning of a market system.

Finally, it is impossible to leave this section without noting an obvious irony that has no doubt occurred to the reader. In the earlier section on interjurisdictional competition, the central concern was that such competition leads to too little in the way of public outputs. There it was argued that competition for new firms and jobs may lead to public budgets that are too small, and to overly lax environmental standards. In contrast, the thrust of this section has been on the beneficial effects of competition as a disciplining force that restrains the tendencies in the public sector towards excessive spending and other forms of fiscal misbehavior. One's view of the role of intergovernmental competition clearly depends on how one views the operation of the public sector more generally!

8. *Fiscal Decentralization and Economic Development*

When examining international cross-sectional data on intergovernmental structure, one is immediately struck by the sharp contrast in the extent of fiscal decentralization in the industrialized and developing countries. In a study of my own involving a group of forty-three countries (Oates 1985), the sample statistics revealed an average share of central-government spending in total public expenditure of 65 percent in the subsample of eighteen industrialized countries, as contrasted to 89 percent in the subsample of twenty-five developing nations. In terms of total public revenues, the central-government share for this same subsample of developing countries was over 90 percent!

Although there are real concerns with the accuracy of some of these fiscal data (Richard Bird 1986), the general presumption that the developing countries are characterized by relatively high degrees of fiscal centralization seems firmly grounded. And this, moreover, is not something new. Writing over forty years ago, Alison Martin and W. Arthur Lewis (1956) noted that "the weakness of local government in relation to central government is one of the most striking phenomena of under-developed countries" (p. 231).

What are we to make of this? Some observers attribute the poor economic performance of many of the developing countries in large measure to the failure of central planning and make a strong case for the devolution of fiscal responsibilities. But the issue is clearly more complicated than this. In particular, the question arises as to whether fiscal decentralization is a cause or a result of economic development. Roy Bahl and Johannes Linn (1992), for example, argue that as economies grow and mature, economic gains from fiscal decentralization emerge. As they put it, "Decentralization more likely comes with the achievement of a higher stage of economic development" (p. 391); the "threshold level of economic development" at which fiscal decentralization becomes attractive "appears to be quite high" (p. 393). From this perspective, it is economic development that comes first; fiscal decentralization then follows. But not all would agree. More generally, it seems to me, we must regard intergovernmental structure as part of a larger political and economic system that both influences and is determined by the interplay of a variety of political and economic forces. It may well be that fiscal decentralization itself has a real contribution to make to improved economic and political performance at different stages of development.

To gain further insight into this issue, we might turn to the historical experience of the industrialized countries and examine the course of fiscal decentralization through extended periods of economic growth. This, in fact, does not prove to be very helpful. If we look at the United States, for example, we find that in the late nineteenth century the public sector was both very small and highly decentralized. At the turn of the century, the public sector accounted for only about 8 percent of GNP in the U.S., while the central-government share of total public expenditure was around 30–35 percent. By 1955, the central-government share of public spending had roughly doubled from one-third to two-thirds.[33] The fiscal records of other industrialized nations like Great Britain reveal roughly similar patterns.

The point is that the trend over this period of economic growth was *not* one of increasing fiscal decentralization; it was just the reverse! It is worth noting, however, that these centralizing tendencies seem to have played out around the middle of the century. For most of the industrialized countries, fiscal centralization ratios appear to have peaked in the decade of the 1950's, and since that time, they have actually declined slightly in most cases (Oates 1978; Werner Pommerehne 1977). What typically seems to be taking place is a complicated process of intergovernmental evolution. We see efforts at devolution in a number of OECD countries accompanied, at the same time, by the emergence of a new top layer of government in the European Community.

But all this may not have much relevance for the developing nations. This is because they have a very different starting point for the growth process. As Diana Conyers (1990) stresses, "Most less developed countries inherited relatively centralized systems of governments from their colonial powers, and in the first years of independence there

[33] See John Wallis and Oates (1997) for a description and analysis of the evolution of American federalism in the twentieth century.

was often a tendency to maintain—if not strengthen—central control and centralized systems of planning, in order to encourage a sense of national unity and reinforce the new government and its policies" (p. 16). Thus, many of these countries entered upon nationhood with highly centralized government sectors; they have not undergone anything like the process of public-sector evolution experienced in the industrialized countries.

The implication of all this is that the potential of fiscal decentralization for improving economic and political performance must be evaluated in terms of the specific circumstances that characterize the current state of a developing nation. There remains, in my view and that of some others (Shah 1994), a strong case on traditional grounds for a significant degree of decentralization in public-sector decision-making in the developing nations. This case, as we have discussed, rests both on the potential economic gains from adapting levels of public outputs to specific regional or local conditions and on the political appeal of increased participation in governance. The economic case has been made formally in purely static terms (as noted earlier in the treatment of the Decentralization Theorem), but it may well have some validity in a dynamic setting of economic growth. Development policies that are sensitive to particular regional or local needs for infrastructure and even human capital are likely to be more effective in promoting economic growth than are centrally determined policies that largely ignore these geographical differences. There exists, incidentally, no formal theory of fiscal decentralization and economic growth; it might be useful to set out such a theory, for a framework that incorporates jurisdiction-specific investment programs might provide some insights into the parameters on which improved growth performance depends.[34]

The prescriptive literature on fiscal structure for the developing countries harks back directly to several of the points made in the preceding sections. In particular, there is a heavy emphasis on reliance on own finance in order to create hard budget constraints. This can have special relevance in the developing-country context, where decentralized governments often have very limited access to their own major sources of tax and other revenues and are heavily dependent on transfers from above. In some instances, provincial or state governments may even have access to the public banking system to absorb their debt issues. This predictably leads to large budgetary deficits and both fiscal and monetary instability.

This literature makes reference to the problem of "vertical imbalance," meaning a disparity between different levels of government in their expenditure commitments and their access to revenues. Although the concept suffers from certain ambiguities, it does focus attention on the important issue of the widespread inadequacy of revenue sources at decentralized levels of government. The often heavy reliance of provincial, state, and local governments on transfers from above undercuts incentives for responsible fiscal decision-making; fiscal decisions become outcomes of politically driven negotiations between central and "local" authorities, not the result of weighing benefits and costs of prospective public programs.

The case for establishing adequate

[34] Some observers, like Remy Prud'homme (1997), argue that the case for fiscal decentralization has been much exaggerated. Prud'homme claims that many of the premises of the fiscal federalism vision are typically not satisfied in the developing-country setting; decentralized government bodies, he argues, are frequently unresponsive to the needs of their constituencies and manifest widespread corruption.

and effective tax systems at decentralized levels of government is one of the critical issues of fiscal federalism in the developing world. And it is a truly challenging problem (Bahl and Linn 1992; Bird 1992). The earlier section dealing with the tax-assignment problem set forth some of the properties of "good" taxes at decentralized levels of government. But provincial and local governments in developing countries often face serious obstacles to the use of these tax bases. The scope, for example, for using local property taxes is circumscribed in many instances by the absence of the requisite institutions for tax administration. As Bahl and Linn (1992) point out, there is typically more potential for such taxes in urban than in rural areas in most developing countries. The obstacles are real, but there are ongoing and extensive efforts to build up the administrative capacity for more effective revenue systems.

Fiscal reform efforts in the developing world thus must focus on (1) Restructuring systems of intergovernmental grants, in some instances to reduce the extent of financing that they provide to decentralized levels of government, and, more generally, to remove the perverse incentives that they often embody for fiscal behavior on the part of recipients; (2) Redesigning revenue systems so as to provide decentralized levels of government a much expanded access to own-revenues to finance their budgets and thereby reduce their dependence on transfers from above; and (3) Reviewing the use and restrictions on debt finance to ensure that debt issues are not a ready way to finance deficits on the current account. All three of these avenues of reform contribute in important ways to the establishment of a hard budget constraint, but one that permits decentralized levels of government to do their job. Finally, running through all these dimensions of fiscal reform is the crucial attention to fiscal decision-making institutions and procedures themselves to introduce mechanisms that provide incentives for public officials to act in the public interest; this means largely, as Shah (1998) stresses, establishing channels for accountability.[35] In the interim, provincial and local governments cannot be left to fend entirely for themselves; depending on the specific circumstances, there will often be a need for significant transfers from the center, especially to impoverished jurisdictions. But the general direction of needed reform seems clear.

The ongoing efforts to decentralize the public sectors of former socialist states encounter much the same set of issues. But the problems are in some ways even more complicated, inasmuch as the process of decentralization is going on alongside a process of privatization; the complicated and sometimes chaotic transition from a command economy to a market system does not provide a stable environment within which to restructure the public sector. Nevertheless, a comprehensive process of fiscal decentralization is underway in much of Central and Eastern Europe, and it involves the same issues of defining the fiscal responsibilities of the different levels of government and introducing the fiscal instruments and procedures needed both to support emerging private markets and to deliver needed public services (Bird, Ebel, and Wallich 1995).

9. *Some Concluding Observations*

The evolution of the vertical structure of the public sector continues in

[35] See Govinda Rao (1998) for an illuminating treatment in the Indian context of the wide range of mechanisms (or "subterranean transfers" as he calls them) through which central government subsidizes the states.

interesting and novel ways. As I noted earlier, the first half of the twentieth century was characterized by a strong trend toward increased fiscal centralization. Indeed, some acute political observers in the nineteenth century forecast this trend. Tocqueville, writing in the first half of the nineteenth century, predicted that "in the democratic ages which are opening upon us . . . centralization will be the natural government" (1945, Vol. II, p. 313). And nearer the end of the century, Lord Bryce reiterated this forecast (at least for the U.S.). After reviewing both the "centrifugal" and "centripetal" forces at work in American government, Bryce concluded that while the centrifugal forces were "likely, as far as we can see, to prove transitory . . . the centripetal forces are permanent and secular forces, working from age to age" (1901, Vol. II, p. 844). Bryce then proceeded to forecast that " . . . the importance of the States will decline as the majesty and authority of the National government increase" (1901, Vol. II, p. 844). Later, Edward McWhinney (1965) went on to generalize all this to what he calls "Bryce's Law," the proposition that " . . . federalism is simply a transitory step on the way to governmental unity" (p. 105).

But such forecasts have not been borne out. The second half of the twentieth century has seen the extent of centralization in most of the industrialized countries reach some sort of peak with a modest swing back in the direction of devolution of public sector activity. There are, as Bryce suggests, important forces working in both directions, and one can expect the net effect to move in different directions as nations evolve over time.

What does seem to be taking place is a growing complexity and specialization in the vertical structure of the public sector. Recent decades have seen the creation of special districts to provide particular public services and the formation of metropolitan area governments to bring center cities and their suburbs into a single jurisdiction (again for purposes of addressing specific needs such as transportation and housing). It is especially striking to witness in the European Community the moves toward devolution in many member countries, while, at the same time, the Community develops a set of supranational institutions for governance and economic management. Other countries, like South Africa and the former socialist states, are struggling with their own sets of pressing issues in their attempts to find effective mechanisms for political and fiscal decentralization.

While the existing literature in fiscal federalism can provide some general guidance on these issues, my sense is that most of us working in the field feel more than a little uneasy when proffering advice on many of the decisions that must be made on vertical fiscal and political structure. We have much to learn!

References

Ackerman, Bruce et al. 1974. *The Uncertain Search for Environmental Quality*. NY: Free Press.

Anton, Thomas J. 1989. *American Federalism and Public Policy*. Philadelphia: Temple U. Press.

Bahl, Roy W. and Johannes F. Linn. 1992. *Urban Public Finance in Developing Countries*. Oxford: Oxford U. Press.

Bartik, Timothy J. 1991. *Who Benefits from State and Local Development Policies?* Kalamazoo, MI: W.E. Upjohn Institute.

Bird, Richard M. 1986. "On Measuring Fiscal Centralization and Fiscal Balance in Federal States," *Gov. Pol.*, 4, pp. 384–404.

———. 1992. *Tax Policy and Economic Development*. Baltimore: Johns Hopkins Press.

Bird, Richard M.; Robert D. Ebel, and Christine I. Wallich, eds. 1995. *Decentralization of the Socialist State*. Washington, DC: World Bank.

Blank, Rebecca. 1997. "Policy Watch: The 1996 Welfare Reform," *J. Econ. Perspect.*, 11:1, pp. 169–78.

Boadway, Robin. 1996. "Review of 'The Uneasy Case for Equalization Payments' by Dan Usher," *Nat. Tax J.*, 49:4, pp. 677–86.

Boadway, Robin and Frank R. Flatters. 1982. "Efficiency and Equalization Payments in a Federal System of Government: A Synthesis and Extension of Recent Results," *Can. J. Econ.*, 15:4, pp. 613–33.

Boeckelman, Keith. 1992. "The Influence of States on Federal Policy Adoptions," *Pol. Stud. J.*, 20:3, pp. 365–75.

Bradford, David F. and Wallace E. Oates. 1971a. "Towards a Predictive Theory of Intergovernmental Grants," *Amer. Econ. Rev.*, 61:2, pp. 440–48.

———. 1971b. "The Analysis of Revenue Sharing in a New Approach to Collective Fiscal Decisions," *Quart. J. Econ.*, 85:3, pp. 416–39.

———. 1974. "Suburban Exploitation of Central Cities and Governmental Structure," in *Redistribution Through Public Choice*. Harold Hochman and George Peterson, eds. NY: Columbia U. Press, pp. 43–90.

Break, George F. 1967. *Intergovernmental Fiscal Relations in the United States*. Washington, DC: Brookings Institution.

Brennan, Geoffrey and James Buchanan. 1980. *The Power to Tax: Analytical Foundations of a Fiscal Constitution*. Cambridge: Cambridge U. Press.

Breton, Albert. 1998. *Competitive Governments: An Economic Theory of Politics and Public Finance*. Cambridge: Cambridge U. Press.

Brown, Charles C. and Wallace E. Oates. 1987. "Assistance to the Poor in a Federal System," *J. Pub. Econ.*, 32, pp. 307–30.

Brueckner, Jan E. 1998a. "Testing for Strategic Interaction Among Local Governments: The Case of Growth Controls," *J. Urban Econ.*, 44, pp. 438–67.

———. 1998b. "Welfare Reform and the Race to the Bottom: Theory and Evidence," Institute of Gov. and Public Affairs, U. Illinois, WP 64.

Bryce, James. 1901. *The American Commonwealth*. London: Macmillan [first published 1888].

Case, Anne; James R. Hines, Jr., and Harvey S. Rosen. 1993. "Budget Spillovers and Fiscal Policy Interdependence: Evidence from the States," *J. Pub. Econ.*, 52, pp. 285–307.

Chernick, Howard. 1979. "An Economic Model of the Distribution of Project Grants," in *Fiscal Federalism and Grants-in-Aid*. P. Mieszkowski and W. Oakland, eds. Washington DC: Urban Institute, pp. 81–103.

———. 1992. "A Model of the Distributional Incidence of State and Local Taxes," *Pub. Fin. Quart.*, Oct., pp. 572–85.

Conyers, Diana. 1990. "Centralization and Development Planning: A Comparative Perspective," in *Decentralizing for Participatory Planning*. P. de Valk and K. Wekwete, eds. Aldershot: Avebury.

Courant, Paul N. 1994. "How Would You Know a Good Economic Policy If You Tripped Over One?" *Nat. Tax J.*, 47, pp. 863–81.

Cumberland, John H. 1979. "Interregional Pollution Spillovers and Consistency of Environmental Policy," in *Regional Environmental Policy: The Economic Issues*. H. Siebert et al., eds. NY: NYU Press, pp. 255–81.

———. 1981. "Efficiency and Equity in Interregional Environmental Management," *Rev. Regional Stud.*, 2, pp. 1–9.

Davoodi, Hamid and Heng-fu Zou. 1998. "Fiscal Decentralization and Economic Growth," *J. Urban Econ.*, 43, pp. 244–57.

Enrich, Peter D. 1996. "Saving the States from Themselves: Commerce Clause Constraints on State Tax Incentives for Business," *Harvard Law Rev.*, 110, pp. 378–461.

Epple, Dennis and Allan Zelenitz. 1981. "The Implications of Competition Among Jurisdictions: Does Tiebout Need Politics?" *J. Polit. Econ.*, 89, pp. 1197–217.

Esty, Daniel C. 1996. "Revitalizing Environmental Federalism," *Mich. Law Rev.*, 95, pp. 570–653.

Feldstein, Martin S. 1975. "Wealth Neutrality and Local Choice in Public Education," *Amer. Econ. Rev.*, 65:1, pp. 75–89.

Feldstein, Martin and Marian Vaillant Wrobel. 1998. "Can State Taxes Redistribute Income?" *J. Pub. Econ.*, 68:3, pp. 369–96.

Fischel, William. 1992. "Property Taxation and the Tiebout Model: Evidence for the Benefit View from Zoning and Voting," *J. Econ. Lit.*, 30:1, pp. 171–77.

Fisher, Ronald C. 1982. "Income and Grant Effects on Local Expenditure: The Flypaper Effect and Other Difficulties," *J. Urban Econ.*, 12, pp. 324–45.

Flatters, Frank; Vernon Henderson, and Peter Mieszkowski. 1974. "Public Goods, Efficiency, and Regional Fiscal Equalization," *J. Pub. Econ.*, 3, pp. 99–112.

Gamkhar, Shama and Wallace Oates. 1966. "Asymmetries in the Response to Increases and Decreases in Intergovernmental Grants: Some Empirical Findings," *Nat. Tax J.*, 49, pp. 501–12.

Gordon, Roger. 1983. "An Optimal Tax Approach to Fiscal Federalism," *Quart. J. Econ.*, 97, pp. 567–86.

Gramlich, Edward M. 1977. "Intergovernmental Grants: A Review of the Empirical Literature," in *The Political Economy of Fiscal Federalism*. Wallace Oates, ed. Lexington, MA: Heath-Lexington, pp. 219–39.

———. 1987. "Federalism and Federal Deficit Reduction," *Nat. Tax. J.*, 40, pp. 299–313.

Gray, Virginia. 1973. "Innovation in the States: A Diffusion Study," *Amer. Polit. Sci. Rev.*, 67, pp. 1174–85.

Hamilton, Bruce W. 1975. "Zoning and Property Taxation in a System of Local Governments," *Urban Stud.*, 12:2, pp. 205–11.

———. 1976. "Capitalization of Intrajurisdictional Differences in Local Tax Prices," *Amer. Econ. Rev.*, 66:5, pp. 743–53.

Hines, James R. Jr., and Richard H. Thaler. 1995. "The Flypaper Effect," *J. Econ. Perspect.*, 9, pp. 217–26.

Huff, David L.; James M. Lutz, and Rajendra Srivastava. 1988. "A Geographical Analysis of the Innovativeness of States," *Econ. Geogr.*, 64, pp. 137–46.

Huther, Jeff and Anwar Shah. 1996. "A Simple Measure of Good Governance and Its Application to the Debate on the Appropriate Level of Fiscal Decentralization." Washington, DC: World Bank.

Inman, Robert P. 1988. "Federal Assistance and Local Services in the United States: The Evolution of a New Federalist Fiscal Order," in *Fiscal Federalism*. Harvey Rosen, ed. Chicago: U. Chicago Press, pp. 33–74.

———. Forthcoming. "On Designing Intergovernmental Transfers With an Application in the New South Africa," in *Environmental and Public Economics*. Arvind Panagariya, Paul Portney, and Robert Schwab, eds. Cheltenham, UK: Edward Elgar.

Inman, Robert P., and Daniel L. Rubinfeld. 1979. "The Judicial Pursuit of Local Fiscal Equity," *Harvard Law Rev.*, 92, pp. 1662–750.

———. 1996. "Designing Tax Policy in Federalist Economies: An Overview," *J. Pub. Econ.*, 60:3, pp. 307–34.

———. 1997a. "Making Sense of the Antitrust State-Action Doctrine: Balancing Political Participation and Economic Efficiency in Regulatory Federalism," *Texas Law Rev.*, 75, pp. 1203–99.

———. 1997b. "The Political Economy of Federalism," in *Perspectives on Public Choice: A Handbook*. D. Mueller, ed. Cambridge: Cambridge U. Press, pp. 73–105.

———. 1997c. "Rethinking Federalism," *J. Econ. Perspect.*, 11:4, pp. 43–64.

———. Forthcoming. "Subsidiarity and the European Union," in *The New Palgrave Dictionary of Economics and Law*.

Kim, Sang Loh. 1995. *Fiscal Decentralization, Fiscal Structure, and Economic Performance: Three Empirical Studies*. Unpublished Ph.D. Dissertation, U. Maryland.

Lutz, James M. 1987. "Regional Leadership Patterns in the Diffusion of Public Policies," *Amer. Polit. Quart.*, 15, pp. 387–98.

Martin, Alison and W. Arthur Lewis. 1956. "Patterns of Public Revenue and Expenditure," *Manchester Sch. Econ. Soc. Stud.*, 24, pp. 203–44.

McGuire, Martin C. and Mancur Olson, Jr. 1996. "The Economics of Autocracy and Majority Rule: The Invisible Hand and the Use of Force," *J. Econ. Lit.*, 34, pp. 72–96.

McGuire, Therese J. 1997. "Intergovernmental Fiscal Relations and Social Welfare Policy," in *Intergovernmental Fiscal Relations*. Ronald C. Fisher, ed. Boston: Kluwer, pp. 173–98.

McKinnon, Ronald I. 1997a. "Market-Preserving Fiscal Federalism in the American Monetary Union," in *Macroeconomic Dimensions of Public Finance: Essays in Honor of Vito Tanzi*. Mario Blejer and Teresa Ter-Minassian, eds. London: Routledge, pp. 73–93.

———. 1997b. "EMU as a Device for Collective Fiscal Retrenchment," *Amer. Econ. Rev.*, 87, pp. 227–29.

McKinnon, Ronald I. and Thomas Nechyba. 1997. "Competition in Federal Systems: The Role of Political and Financial Constraints," in *The New Federalism: Can the States be Trusted?* John Ferejohn and Barry Weingast, eds. Stanford: Hoover Institution Press, pp. 3–61.

McLure, Charles E., Jr. ed. 1983. *Tax Assignment in Federal Countries*. Canberra: Australian National U.

McWhinney, Edward. 1965. *Comparative Federalism*. 2nd ed. Toronto: U. Toronto Press.

Mieszkowski, Peter, and George R. Zodrow. 1989. "Taxation and the Tiebout Model: The Differential Effects of Head Taxes, Taxes on Land, Rents, and Property Taxes," *J. Econ. Lit.*, 27:3, pp. 1098–146.

Musgrave, Richard M. 1959. *The Theory of Public Finance*. NY: McGraw-Hill.

Nechyba, Thomas. 1996. "A Computable General Equilibrium Model of Intergovernmental Aid," *J. Pub. Econ.*, 62, pp. 363–99.

Nice, David C. 1994. *Policy Innovation in State Government*. IA: Iowa U. Press.

Oates, Wallace E. 1972. *Fiscal Federalism*. NY: Harcourt Brace Jovanovich.

———. 1978. "The Changing Structure of Intergovernmental Fiscal Relations," in *Secular Trends of the Public Sector*. H. Recktenwald, ed. Paris: Editions Cujas, pp. 151–60.

———. 1985. "Searching for Leviathan: An Empirical Study," *Amer. Econ. Rev.*, 75, pp. 748–57.

———. 1989. "Searching for Leviathan: A Reply and Some Further Reflections," *Amer. Econ. Rev.*, 79, pp. 578–83.

———. 1994. "Federalism and Government Finance," in *Modern Public Finance*. J. Quigley and E. Smolensky, eds. Cambridge, MA: Harvard U. Press, pp. 126–51.

———. 1996a. "Estimating the Demand for Public Goods: The Collective Choice and Contingent Valuation Approaches," in *The Contingent Valuation of Environmental Resources*. D. Bjornstad and J. Kahn, eds. Aldershot: Edward Elgar, pp. 211–30.

———. 1996b. "Taxation in a Federal System: The Tax-Assignment Problem." *Pub. Econ. Rev.*, 1, pp. 35–60.

———. 1998. "On the Welfare Gains from Fiscal Decentralization," U. Maryland Econ. Dept. WP 98–05.

Oates, Wallace E. and Robert M. Schwab. 1988. "Economic Competition Among Jurisdictions: Efficiency-Enhancing or Distortion-Inducing?" *J. Pub. Econ.*, 35, pp. 333–54.

———. 1991. "The Allocative and Distributive Implications of Local Fiscal Competition," in

Competition Among States and Local Governments. D. Kenyon and J. Kincaid, eds. Washington, DC: Urban Institute, pp. 127–45.

———. 1996. "The Theory of Regulatory Federalism: The Case of Environmental Management," in *The Economics of Environmental Regulation*. Wallace Oates. Aldershot: Edward Elgar, pp. 319–31.

———. 1997. "The Impact of Urban Land Taxation: The Pittsburgh Experience," *Nat. Tax J.*, 50, pp. 1–21.

Olson, Mancur Jr. 1990. "The IRIS Idea." IRIS, U. Maryland.

Osborne, David. 1988. *Laboratories of Democracy*. Boston: Harvard Business School Press.

Pauly, Mark V. 1973. "Income Redistribution as a Local Public Good," *J. Pub. Econ.*, 2, pp. 35–58.

Pommerehne, Werner W. 1977. "Quantitative Aspects of Federalism: A Study of Six Countries," in *The Political Economy of Fiscal Federalism*. Wallace Oates, ed. Lexington, MA: Heath-Lexington, pp. 275–355.

Poterba, James M. and Kim S. Rueben. 1997. "State Fiscal Institutions and the U.S. Municipal Bond Market," NBER WP 6237.

Prud'homme, Remy. 1995. "On the Dangers of Decentralization," *World Bank Res. Observer*, pp. 201–10.

Qian, Yingyi, and Barry R. Weingast. 1997. "Federalism as a Commitment to Preserving Market Incentives," *J. Econ. Perspect.*, 11:4, pp. 83–92.

Rao, M. Govinda. 1998. "Invisible Transfers in Indian Federalism," Australian National U. Econ. Dept. WP 98/1.

Revesz, Richard L. 1992. "Rehabilitating Interstate Competition: Rethinking the 'Race-to-the-Bottom' Rationale for Federal Environmental Regulation," *NYU Law Rev.*, 67, pp. 1210–54.

Rivlin, Alice. 1992. *Reviving the American Dream*. Washington, DC: The Brookings Institution.

Rodden, Jonathan, and Susan Rose-Ackerman. 1997. "Does Federalism Preserve Markets?" *U. Virginia Law Rev.*, 83, pp. 1521–72.

Rogers, Everett. 1983. *Diffusion of Innovations*. 3rd ed. NY: Free Press.

Rose-Ackerman, Susan. 1980. "Risk Taking and Reelection: Does Federalism Promote Innovation?" *J. Legal Stud.*, 9, pp. 593–616.

Rubinfeld, Daniel L. 1987. "The Economics of the Local Public Sector," in *Handbook of Public Economics*, Vol. II. Alan Auerbach and Martin Feldstein, eds. Amsterdam: North-Holland, pp. 571–645.

Saavedra, Luz Amparo. 1998. "A Model of Welfare Competition with Evidence from AFDC," Inst. Govt. and Public Affairs, U. Illinois, WP 63.

Shah, Anwar. 1994. *The Reform of Intergovernmental Fiscal Relations in Developing and Emerging Market Economies*. Washington, DC: World Bank.

———. 1998. "Fostering Fiscally Responsive and Accountable Governance: Lessons from Decentralization," in *Evaluation and Development: The Institutional Dimension*. Robert Picciotto and Eduardo Wiesner, eds. Washington, DC: World Bank, pp. 83–96.

Sparer, Michael S., and Lawrence D. Brown. 1996. "States and the Health Care Crisis: The Limits and Lessons of Laboratory Federalism," in *Health Policy, Federalism, and the American States*. Robert F. Rich and William D. White, eds. Washington, DC: Urban Institute Press, pp. 181–202.

Stine, William F. 1994. "Is Local Government Revenue Response to Federal Aid Symmetrical?" *Nat. Tax J.*, 47, pp. 799–816.

Strumpf, Koleman S. 1997. "Does Fiscal Decentralization Increase Policy Innovation?" unpublished paper.

Strumpf, Koleman S. and Felix Oberholzer-Gee. 1998. "Endogenous Institutions and Policy Decentralization: Local Liquor Control from 1934–1970": unpublished paper.

Tiebout, Charles. 1956. "A Pure Theory of Local Expenditures," *J. Polit. Econ.*, 64, pp. 416–24.

Tocqueville, Alexis de. 1945. *Democracy in America*. NY: Vintage Books Random House: first published 1838.

US Congressional Budget Office. 1997. *Federalism and Environmental Protection: Case Studies for Drinking Water and Ground-Level Ozone*. Washington, DC: US Govt. Printing Office.

Usher, Dan. 1995. *The Uneasy Case for Equalization Payments*. Vancouver, BC: The Fraser Institute.

Volden, Craig. 1997. "Entrusting the States with Welfare Reform," in *The New Federalism: Can the States Be Trusted*? John Ferejohn and Barry Weingast, eds. Stanford: Hoover Institution Press, pp. 65–96.

Walker, Jack L. 1969. "The Diffusion of Innovation Among the American States," *Amer. Polit. Sci. Rev.*, 63, pp. 880–99.

Wallis, John J. and Wallace E. Oates. 1998. "The Impact of the New Deal on American Federalism," in *The Defining Moment: The Great Depression and the American Economy in the 20th Century*. M. Bordo, C. Goldin, and E. White, eds. Chicago: U. Chicago Press, pp. 155–80.

Weingast, Barry R. 1995. "The Economic Role of Political Institutions: Market-Preserving Federalism and Economic Development," *J. Law Econ. Org., 11, pp. 1–31.*

Wildasin, David E. 1988. "Nash Equilibria in Models of Fiscal Competition," *J. Pub. Econ.*, 35, pp. 229–40.

———. 1998a. "Factor Mobility and Redistributive Policy: Local and International Perspectives," in *Public Finance in a Changing World*. Peter B. Sorensen, ed. London: MacMillan, pp. 151–92.

———. 1998b. "Externalities and Bailouts: Hard and Soft Budget Constraints in Intergovernmental Fiscal Relations," World Bank Policy Research WP 1843.

Wilson, John Douglas. 1996. "Capital Mobility and Environmental Standards: Is There a Theoretical Basis for a Race to the Bottom?" in *Fair Trade and Harmonization: Prerequisities for Free Trade*? Vol. I. Jagdish Bhagwati and Robert Hudec, eds. Cambridge, MA: MIT Press, pp. 393–427.

Zhang, Tao and Heng-fu Zou. 1998. "Fiscal Decentralization, Public Spending, and Economic Growth in China," *J. Pub. Econ.*, 67, pp. 221–40.

[26]

Jacques Crémer
Institut déconomie Industrielle
Université des sciences sociales de Toulouse

Antonio Estache
The World Bank and European Center for Applied Reseauch in Economics

Paul Seabright
Cambridge University

Decentralizing Public Services : what can we learn from the Theory of the Firm ?

Décentralisation des services publics : que nous enseigne la théorie de la firme ?

Decentralizing - Public Services - Firm
Décentralisation - Services publics - Entreprise

This is a revised version of « The Decentralization of Public Services Lessons from the Theory of the Firm », published in Decentralizing Infrastructure : Advantages and Limitations, Antonio ESTACHE, ed., *World Bank Discussion Paper* 290, The World Bank, Washington, D.C., 1995.

Summary. — This paper explores how the techniques used for the analysis of decentralization within firms can be used to analyze the decentralization of political systems. Section 2 reviews the Tiebout approach to decentralization and its shortcomings. We turn to a simple model of decentralization in section 3, while section 4 discusses different aspects of contract theory — the endogeneity of information acquisition the incompleteness of contacts, renegotiation and their implications for the theory of decentralization. Section 5 tries to refine the definition of a jurisdiction and the determinations of its boundaries. Section 6 applies the concepts developed in the first five sections to specific problems.

The large expansion of government powers in some of the Western countries in the post World War II period was given theoretical backing by the theory of market failure and the advances in the studies of externalities, public goods, and optimal taxation. Many of these studies have found their way into the analysis of economic development issues. During the 1980s, these theories, or at least their applications in the public debate, have been justly criticized for their lack of attention to government failures. Moreover, in recent years government intervention in the economy has come to be regarded with more suspicion than in the past, and an increasing number of policymakers in countries as different as Argentina, China or Hungary have adopted a more pragmatic approach to development favoring reliance on the market to allocate goods and service.

The theoretical intuition behind the superiority of market allocation is well known. Given the efficiency of market exchanges, agents should be left to make as many decisions for themselves as possible. When these decisions are transferred to the public sector, there are asymmetries of information and the associated opportunities for rent seeking activities, and the loss of efficiency may be large enough for even the poorest members, who are supposed to benefit from these policies, to lose out.

These insights have been applied to the organization of the public sector itself. If political economy teaches us that as many decisions as possible should be decentralized through the market, doesn't it follow that within the public sector decisions should also be decentralized as much as is feasible ? What one cannot leave to private initiative should be left to the lowest possible level of government.

Things are not that simple because these policy insights are based on a very unbalanced theoretical underpinning. Economists have a good theory of the functioning of markets, their benefits and their failures. Our understanding of governments and of public administration is much more imperfect, in great part because the topic is more difficult. When one compares markets to public provision, one compares something understood relatively well to something one does not understand very well at all. The situation is even more complex when one wants to compare two types of public provision, for instance a very centralized government with a federation that leaves much power to local units. One compares two situations of which neither is understood very well.

We believe that improvements in the analytical treatment of the internal functioning and of the optimal structure of government should be accessible through the transfer of the intuitions developed in the theory of the firm in the last twenty years. Some work has been done on this topic, but much more can be done. In particular, the very important advances of contract theory in the last ten years have not been adequately integrated into the discussion. The aim of this paper is to open channels of thoughts along these lines, with a special emphasis on the provision of infrastructure. This is not to imply that results from the theory of the firm can be directly imported. The public sector has very specific features, some of which will be discussed below. What can be imported are intuitions and techniques for the study of organizational problems. Furthermore, normative issues are of much greater importance in the choice of optimal policies than appears from the summary that follows, and we neglect them for the major part of the sequel.

The paper is organized as follows. In section 2, we describe a simple model that lies, at least implicitly, at the basis of much of recent policy discussion. In section 3, we enrich this model through the use of contract theory, as developed in the 1970's and the beginning of the 1980's. This enables us to discuss the problems of transfers among jurisdictions as well as aspects of financing. In section 4, we discuss the shortcomings of these approaches and show that recent developments in contract theory and the theory of organizations — incomplete contracts and renegotiation — provide a natural language to speak of some of these issues. Some of the themes of that section are also discussed at a more theoretical level in the paper by Caillaud, Jullien and Picard in this issue of the Revue d'Economie Politique. The sequel of the paper is used to develop applications of this methodology. In section 5 we try to provide some preliminary reflections on the concept of political jurisdictions, paralleling the famous nature of the firm debate in organization theory. Finally, section 6 provides a pot pourri of applications.

1. The received wisdom on decentralization

This section summarizes the received wisdom on decentralization of responsibilities for regulation and provision on goods and services in the standard public economics literature. It outlines the key assumptions underlying the main policy guidelines of the standard public finance literature on fiscal federalism, focusing in particular on those that can much more easily be addressed by relying on a contractual approach to the issues raised by the structure of government.

1.1. A Quick Survey

The standard public finance literature provides both ex-ante and ex-post arguments for decentralization. The classic ex-ante case for decentralization is provided by Oates in 1972. He points out that public goods can have spatial characteristics reflecting the specific boundaries-global, regional or local-of the benefits they provide to their consumers. Oates' decentralization theorem suggests that, for a given information structure about demands, each type of good should be provided by a level of government — say central, state and municipal — enjoying a comparative advantage in accounting for the diversity of preferences in its choice of service delivery. Club theory provides related arguments to make the case for an optimum size of local authorities.

Based on these demand elements and on the recognition that spillovers and other forms of externalities in production and consumption can matter, a « standard » list of desirable expenditure assignments — in terms of provision and/or responsibility — provides the basis of the policy guidelines for countries considering a decentralization of government structures. For instance, airways and railways should be a central concern in view of the national scope of their benefits and costs, while provision of services in highways could be national, state or local-reflecting the balance between spillovers and local preferences.

Where does the comparative advantage of the various government levels come from ? It reflects an assumed government failure. In one version, the failure stems from an information asymmetry between central and subnational governments. Central governments are assumed to have some institutional disadvantage in picking up local information on preferences. More decentralized governments have better knowledge of local preferences, either in the sense of having access to information denied to central government, or in the sense of observing preferences with less noise. In a second version of the government failure argument, the central government is assumed to be institutionally compelled to adopt a uniformity constraint in service delivery. Even if it were able to identify the diversity of demands across regions and municipalities, it could not diversify its supply accordingly. These failures reveal the second best nature of the decentralization argument.

The classic ex-post case for decentralization was made by Tiebout in 1956. Tiebout's point was that population mobility reinforces ex post the ex-ante case based on superior information or flexibility of local government. This mobility should eventually ensure a perfect match between public sector supply and consumer preferences. Consumers vote with their feet and move to the municipality or region which provides them with what they want both in terms of services and in terms of financing mix-taxes, user fees, etc. In sum, it explains how jurisdictions of optimal size come to be established or how individuals take membership in these « local clubs ».

1.2. Shortcomings of the Tiebout approach

Since most analysts of fiscal federalism have used generalized versions of the Tiebout model in which the incentives of the different districts are fundamentally linked to the ability to attract new inhabitants and/or new capital, it is worth focusing on some of its limitations as a model of political decentralization in practice :

1) The role of the national government is not endogenous, or rather it can only be considered as trying to circumvent the negative aspects of the competition between jurisdictions.

2) The governments' objectives in the Tiebout model are assumed to be profit maximization (see Bewley [1981]), without any discussion of how such objectives might arise from a realistic model of the political process. The latter issue is generally only addressed explicitly in public choice models.

3) Government failures (including corruption) can arise at the subnational level just as much as they arise at the central level.

4) The actual mobility of factors is generally much more limited than assumed by Tiebout and the effect of positive decisions by the government of one district will influence the competitive position of the district only in the long run. From an empirical point of view, as pointed out by Walsh [1992], the main relevance of the model is in a metropolitan setting — *i.e.* within suburbs located near other communities and hence with exit options than in communities with no or fewer exit options.

5) Mobility can give rise to externalities which are not accounted for in the design of the financing mode of the jurisdiction.

6) In practice, politicians often try to favor specific interest groups in their districts (for instance, US congressmen will try to introduce in the law tax breaks designated to favor specific firms whose headquarters are in their districts). Tiebout theory would predict more stress on favoring the transfer of factors of production to the district.

7) Responsibilities are actually often shared by various levels of government. For instance, governments must decide on aggregate road expenditures in a jurisdiction, and on the allocation of this expenditure among different types of roads. The first decision can be left to the federal government and the second to the local government. Similarly, the federal government can set pollution standards, and the local government can be in charge of monitoring their implementation (see Estache and Zheng [1992] and [1993] and Jack [1992]). The difficulty in the study of this responsibility sharing mechanism stems from the modeling of the incentives of the different levels of governments.

In addition to appreciating the particular shortcomings of the Tiebout framework, it is important to appreciate what the underlying approach can and cannot be expected to achieve. Tiebout's basic insight was that population mobility can enable governments to overcome the well-known problem of inducing citizens to reveal their preferences for public goods. This problem arises if governments have no way to exclude from consumption those citizens who state that they would prefer not to pay for the provision of a certain public good. If goods are « local », however, they can be provided only for the citizens of a given local jurisdiction (together with a local tax), thereby excluding from consumption all non-residents and allowing citizens in their choice of residence to select their preferred combination of public goods. In the limit, when mobility is costless and various other technical conditions are satisfied, the public goods problem disappears and the allocation of resources is efficient.

The Tiebout approach has nothing to say, however, about how the appropriate local bundles of public goods might come to be established. This might, of course, happen as the result of spirited competition between independent local governments (though to do so they would have to be profit maximizing, and it is far from clear how such a goal might emerge from any plausible political process). But there is no reason in principle why a central government could not also put the Tiebout insight to use, and differentiate its supply of public goods by locality in order to induce the revelation of preferences. In short, the Tiebout model describes the virtues of local differentiation of public goods supply, not the virtues of decentralization of power. In order to understand the pros and cons of decentralization as such, it therefore needs supplementing by an account of the respective abilities of central and local governments to undertake the kind of local differentiation whose virtues the Tiebout model has described.

Such an account would return us essentially to the ex ante approach to decentralization. Underlying many scholarly as well as popular accounts of decentralization is a view of the essential informational advantages of local government, and an implicit model with the following elements (1) :

1) A country is divided into n districts, and there are no other political divisions, either above the district or below it.

(1) A model with the some of the features discused below is presented in DE GROOT [1988].

2) Each district has a local government which has knowledge of the relevant characteristics of that district.

3) Each local government takes decisions in the interest of its own district, without taking into account the desires of other districts except if this is imposed by the federal government.

4) There is a central government that takes decisions in the interest of the country as a whole (whatever exactly this may mean).

5) The central government knows only the average of the characteristics of the districts. Consequently it can do no better than implement a uniform package of public goods for all districts (2).

For each issue, the power to take decisions is given either to the federal/central government (FG) or to the local governments (LGs). The types of issue that we have in mind are the levels of expenditure on elementary education, pollution control, the mileage of new roads to be built. Such a model yields results that are quite close to the « common » wisdom on decentralization : there is a fundamental trade-off between decisions that are more appropriate to local conditions and the internalization of externalities. There are of course other benefits from coordinated decisions than simply the internalization of externalities : those due to the exploitation of increasing returns, for instance.

The drawback of the model, however, is that it leaves the informational advantage of local government essentially unexplained. To explore this issue further we turn to a discussion of the implications of recent developments in contract theory.

2. A simple contract model of decentralization

In this section, we revisit the preceding model with the help of a simple contractual approach. This allows us to enrich the description of the communications between the FG and LGs. We begin by a brief exposition of revelation contracts, and apply the insights to the problem of decentralization.

2.1. Asymmetry of information and contracts

It is hard to overestimate the revolution that took place at the beginning of the 1970s in economic theory. For a long time, economists had talked informally about the strategic use of information (see for instance the famous

(2) This inference is not correct in a dynamic model in which the central government, while initially uninformed, experiments with differentiated public good supply and thereby learns about the different characteristics of the districts. This would be similar to a tatonnement process in Walrasian models. We are not aware of such a dynamic model explicitly developed in the public finance literature.

planning debate of the 1930's between Hayek and Lange [1938]), but it was not until over thirty years later that the strategic use of information was the first time formally integrated into our models. This revolution changed our understanding of markets (following the path breaking contributions of Akerlof [1970] and Spence [1973]) and of incentives in organizations (following the no less path breaking contributions of Groves [1973] and Weitzman [1974]).

The basic framework is very simple. A federal government wants a municipality to build a sewage system in a poor neighborhood. It has no administrative power to force it to do so, and must offer a cost sharing formula. Typically, this formula will be part of a contract that links the amount paid by the federal government to the characteristics of the sewage system that is built. If the costs of building the sewage system are better known to the local government than to the federal government, the former will be able to extract an informational rent. This informational rent is not only a transfer from one government level to another, it has efficiency costs : it order to reduce it the FG will build a cost sharing formula that will induce the local government to choose a system that is not optimally dimensioned.

It is possible to show that the FG of our example never loses anything by offering a contract of the following form : « Tell me everything you know that is relevant to the estimate of cost. As a function of what you tell me I will, according to a predetermined formula, transfer funds to you and order you to build a system of predetermined characteristics ».

Furthermore, it is possible to choose a contract such that the local government will truthfully reveal its information. The equivalence of any cost sharing formula to one of these « revelation mechanisms » in which the informed party is given incentives to announce its information truthfully — *i.e.* the revelation principle —, is supported by the following intuition. Given any initial contract, the FG can calculate under what circumstances the local government would have incentives to misreport its information. It can then modify the contract so as to increase the transfers to which the local government would be eligible under these circumstances, so as to leave it no worse off if it tells the truth. The increased transfers which it must therefore implement are a necessary cost of the initial asymmetry of information, and cannot be reduced by any strategic manipulation. The validity of the principle depends, however, on the assumption that the FG knows enough about the payoffs of the local government to calculate its incentives for lying ; even more importantly, it depends on the assumption that it has no difficulty committing itself to a truth-inducing contract. We shall discuss the limitations of these assumptions below, but shall concentrate for the moment on the theory's strengths. (For a formal statement and proof of the revelation principle see, for instance, Myerson [1979]).

Many variations on this theme are possible, of which one is specially relevant to our purposes. The revelation principle can easily be adapted to a situation where the construction of the sewage system extends over a long period of time and where the information becomes available to the local government progressively. Then, any contract between the two parties is equivalent to a contract in which the local government informs the FG as soon as information becomes available.

The fact that any contract is equivalent to a revelation mechanism is a useful technical tool. It also brings out clearly the limitations of the theory. The Constitution of the United States can be considered the founding contract of that country. Using contract theory to analyze the present, one would need to assume (implicitly) that the Founding Fathers had foreseen present conditions as one of the contingencies in the contract they drew up.

2.2. Implications for decentralization

In light of contract theory, the basic model sketched above can be substantially modified. There is no reason to assume that the FG will accept the fact that the information of the local government is not accessible. It can propose contracts (implicit or explicit) that ask the LGs to reveal their information and commit it to some actions as a function of this information. All the apparatus of contract theory can be used to study the end result.

A revelation mechanism need not only be interpreted as a contract signed between the FG and the LGs. It can also be thought of as a system of taxation, where the tax is levied according to the observable actions and characteristics of the district. The same fundamental trade-off will be involved : efficiency requires large informational rents to the more fortunate districts. This makes a very strong case for performance based grants, though it also underlines that such grants may conflict with considerations of equity. The informational rents will not necessarily be allocated according to any normatively justifiable formula.

In order to limit informational rents, the FG will find it desirable to accept inefficiencies. The service that the district provide will not be priced in such a way that marginal cost is equal to its social marginal value. It will only be for these districts who are the most efficient at providing the service that the equality will hold.

An example may help. In a country in which the FG subcontracts to the LGs maintenance of the roads, the latter would try to exploit their superior knowledge of local technical conditions and of the taste of the local population. They would have a tendency to overstate costs and benefits of additional maintenance. The theory tells us that they will be able to reap some advantage from this superior knowledge. Furthermore, in order to limit this advantage the FG will accept that some inefficiencies creep into the system, and the direction of these inefficiencies can be predicted : there will be too little maintenance.

The rigor and clarity of the theory of revelation mechanisms has an associated cost. By appearing to suggest that a central government can, if it wishes, overcome the informational advantages of local government, it undermines the entire basis of the trade-off between information-gathering and the internalization of externalities that constituted the conventional wisdom as we characterized it in section 2. The conclusion might appear to be that centralization is always to be preferred to decentralization, but in fact the subversion of the traditional approach goes further than that. For if a central government can sign contracts with LGs, what is to prevent LGs from signing contracts with each other without the intermediation of a central authority at all ?

2.3. Why do we need a central government in order to internalize externalities ?

The management of river basins represents a typical example of decisions that one should expect to leave to levels above the local level (assuming, of course, that, as is usually the case, the river flows through many localities). Indeed there are strong externalities with the upstream localities able literally to dump their trash on the downstream localities. If this is the case, why can't the externality be resolved through direct negotiations between the localities themselves ?

More generally, the conventional wisdom has generally assumed that we need an authority that can order subordinate units to limit negative externalities, or encourage them to produce more positive externalities. There is no explanation of why we cannot apply a version of the reasoning in the Coase theorem, which states that in the absence of negotiation costs, bargaining will lead to optimal outcomes. One may acknowledge that the Coase theorem is more seductive at the theoretical level than as guide to reality, and one cannot expect a totally satisfactory solution to this problem. However, without at least some thought given to the discrepancy between theoretical and practical intuition, it is difficult to provide guidelines on the circumstances in which it would be better to let districts negotiate between each other (see Gatsios & Seabright [1989] and Jack [1992] for discussions of this point).

So far, then, the application of contract theory to the analysis of decentralization has yielded a somewhat nihilistic conclusion. Not only has it shown that the supposed advantages of decentralization are not really advantages ; it has also shown that the supposed disadvantages of decentralization are not really disadvantages. In consequence, without further refinement it implicitly makes it impossible to discuss the allocation of responsibilities among the different levels of government at all. For example, the literature contains arguments for the decentralization of secondary schools to LGs as well as arguments why they should be run at a regional or national level. How would we use standard contract theory to study these two situations ? In both cases, contracts, implicit or explicit, would be signed, and some parties would benefit from informational rents due to their superior « time and place » knowledge. There would really be no reason to have very different outcomes in one case and the other. Even if the objectives of the regional and the local governments were different, they would presumably be drawn to bargain together in such a way that the terms of the contract would represent both of their objective functions. The main difference would be in the identification of the party responsible for paying the informational rents to the other.

The implication of this reasoning is that studying the imperfections of contractual bargaining is not just the result of a pedantic desire for a baroque modeling strategy. On the contrary, it is absolutely central to understanding the strengths and weaknesses of decentralization in government. If contractual bargaining worked perfectly, the extent of decentralization in government would be an irrelevance. In section 4, therefore, we discuss three important aspects of the imperfections of contractual bargaining that are of particular importance : the endogeneity of information acquisition, the incompleteness of contracts, and the possibility of renegotiation.

3. Contract theory with imperfections in bargaining

3.1. The endogeneity of information acquisition

Both the conventional wisdom on decentralization and first-generation contract theory treated the allocation of information as exogeneous to the model. In reality the information possessed by agents depends on the cost of acquiring it and the cost of processing it, and therefore on the incentives that they have to incur these costs. A good allocation of responsibilities should give the proper incentives to agents to incur these costs.

For instance, the control of politicians by the electorate depends crucially on the information that the electors have on the performance of the different government entities to which they belong. As we discuss below, the allocation of responsibilities among levels of government affects this acquisition of information, by increasing the value of the information to voters in their efforts to control politicians.

The neglect of this point can also lead to underestimation of the cost of citizen participation in the running of government and can lead to recommendations for the creation of overly complicated administrative structures, with each citizen belonging to a multiplicity of districts, one by each type of public good.

Closer attention to the endogeneity of information acquisition is the first step in understanding whether and to what extent local jurisdictions enjoy any kind of informational advantage over central ones. Let us begin with an example. Should a public transportation system in a provincial city be run by a local agency or by a branch of a national agency ? The received wisdom would answer that it should. Externalities between cities are negligible, and hence the informational advantages of proximity dominate. Upon reflection though, it is difficult to understand what these informational advantages are. A national transportation agency could and presumably would employ representatives living in the city, who would have access to the same sources of information as the representatives of a local agency.

There seem to be two common reasons why local authorities are assumed to be better informed about local conditions than national ones. First, there is direct observation. Because local politicians and civil servants live in the district, they have direct access to information (quality of service, traffic problems) which is not available to individuals who live far away. Furthermore, the information that they do not gather directly can easily be provided by acquaintances, family members, or simple citizens who have easy access to them. Second, there are formal mechanisms. Governments often put in place formal procedures through which they collect information from their constituents : consultative assemblies, public hearings, advisory boards.

If LGs indeed have better information than central governments, it must be either because some of these techniques are available to them and not to the central government, or because they have better incentives to use them. However, it is clear that there is no reason why central government cannot use any of the techniques available to local government. Central governments do name representatives to local areas who collect information on their behalf (for instance, the French préfets) ; and they do use mechanisms by which citizens of a local area can express their views and provide information.

If anything, the balance of advantage as far as the availability of information gathering techniques is concerned probably lies with central government. There are economies of scope in the collection of information : a central agency which runs many transportation systems can transfer techniques acquired in one of them to the others at low cost ; it can also afford to hire technicians in more specialized areas than can a local agency.

If central governments do not in fact use the techniques available to them as assiduously as LGs (a matter on which empirical evidence is unclear and which will differ according to the type of information in question), this must be because they have less incentive to use them (3). In the city transportation case, it will be because local politicians, who live among and are up for re-election by local citizens, have more incentive to listen to what those local citizens say. National politicians could find out if they wished to the views and opinions of local citizens ; but they will have less incentive to take them seriously. Understanding why this is so depends critically on appreciating the significance of the incompleteness of political contracts.

3.2. The incompleteness of contracts

3.2.1. The notion of incompleteness

Whether in economic or in political life, a contract allocating responsibility to various parties for the accomplishment of certain tasks can never cover all the eventualities that may occur. This may be because the parties simply do

(3) Note that the higher incentive of local politicians to use local information does not imply that corruption may be a lesser problem in decentralized governments. In fact, corruption may actually become a more serious problem if increased access to information is not matched by increased accountability of local authorities.

not foresee all relevant eventualities ; it will certainly be because the cost of writing contracts to cover them all would be prohibitive ; and more subtly, some eventualities, though foreseeable and describable, could not be verified by any agency capable of enforcing the contract. For example, suppose the national government tried to sign an undertaking with the citizens of the provincial city to indemnify them financially if the performance of their transportation system were inadequate. Even in circumstances where the citizens and the government both knew perfectly well that the performance of the system was inadequate, such a clause would be unenforceable.

Thanks to Coase's [1937] insight that a good theory of the firm had to be built on a precise description of the costs of transactions, theorists of the firm have long focused their attention on the difficulties of writing contracts. If one can write explicit contracts for the delivery of some goods and services, this transaction can be conducted between firms without any loss of efficiency. When explicit contracts have limitations, there might be a place for internal organization.

The first formal model of incomplete contracts is the model of the employment relationship due to Simon [1951] (4). Simon argued that an employer cannot predict accurately the tasks it would like a future employee to do ; it is even impossible to write down explicitly a list of which tasks have to be accomplished under which circumstances. Under these conditions an employment contract specifies a salary and a set of tasks that the employer is allowed to ask the employee to do. Williamson [1975], who provided an essential link between this literature and the modern formal contracting literature, conducts a careful and exhaustive study of the difficulties of contracting.

Following Grossman and Hart [1986], this has been the subject of much recent work. Even relatively simple transactions necessitate very complex contracts ; the sale of an airplane gives rise to a contract of several hundred pages. Redistribution of income among political districts necessitates formulae whose consequences are not always clearly anticipated by their designers. In practice, the complexity is reduced by writing contracts that do not discriminate as finely as ideally desirable between different circumstances. For instance, the proportion of the cost of a project to be paid by different levels of government will be dependent on the values of a subset of all the variables that economic theory would deem relevant. In practice it is important to discriminate between two types of variables :

1) Those variables that depend on the actions of the parties. For instance, redistribution of funds between different areas should in principle depend on all the effort they make to provide services to the poorest segments of the population.

2) Those variables that are exogeneous to the actions of the parties. For instance, redistribution should depend on the relative prices of a number of internationally traded goods which influence the economic well being of the poor or the cost of providing them with services.

(4) ALCHIAN and DEMSETZ [1973] present counterarguments to the thesis of SIMON.

In both cases we observe real-life arrangements that take into account only some of the many variables that are potentially relevant.

3.2.2. Implications for the theory of organizations

This renewal of contract theory has had powerful implications for the theory of organizations. If it is impossible to specify fully in a contract what actions should be taken by which party, the best the contract can do may be to decide which party has the discretion to take the relevant decision. In other words, contracts become less a matter of specifying particular actions and more a matter of allocating rights of control. By contrast, complete contracts would remove the need for discretion and thereby make redundant the notion of control.

The notion of control paves the way for decisions with a « 0-1 » or « yes-no » character in contract theory. This sheds light on issues of integration : organizations are or are not vertically integrated with each other. This type of sharp distinction is not easily available in standard contracting models.

The idea that parties to a contract will need to agree on allocations of control rights also helps to explain the power of incumbency in organizations. With a complete long term contract the only benefits of incumbency come from the accumulation of specific capital or other physical changes in the system. All the rents associated with these benefits can in general be extracted by the party who has the most bargaining power at the outset. With incomplete contracts, the situation changes. One must often leave some power ex-post to the agent, who may share in the rents associated with the contract even if there is no asymmetry of information.

3.2.3. Implications for the theory of decentralization

This insight can be applied to the problem of the difference between giving the right to control an agency to a local government or to a central government. The contract between the agency and its controlling body specifies certain actions that it must take, certain rights that it has, but also certain actions that the controlling government body is entitled to take. In order to understand the consequences of the contract, it is therefore crucial to understand the objectives of the controlling body, and hence to know its identity. So in the case of the city transportation authority, answering to a local controlling body will mean having its policy determined by strictly local considerations, which is desirable so long as spillover effects on and from other regions are small. Answering to a national controlling body would mean possibly benefiting from the national coordination of policy but also being run by those with many other priorities than the welfare of citizens of the city concerned. Centralization may be said therefore to improve coordination but reduce accountability.

Similarly, the contract between the electorate and a politician elected to office is very incomplete. The actions taken by the politician will depend on a number of factors, including the other tasks for which he is responsible. This is rather trite, but it is very difficult to integrate those considerations in a complete contract model, where the electorate can give sophisticated instructions to the politician and adjust precisely the reward to the action taken. Likewise, contracts between jurisdictions will be very incomplete, and there will consequently be limits to the extent to which externalities can be internalized purely by bargaining between jurisdictions.

A stylized model of political accountability that explicitly incorporates the incompleteness of contracts is presented in Seabright [1995]. In this model, voters seek to provide politicians with incentives to act in their interests. However, the performance of the politicians depends on factors that are not verifiable and cannot be made the subject of an explicit contract. Therefore the only way to provide politicians with the right incentives is to give voters the power to eject them if they are dissatisfied.

Centralization in this model involves two features. Its advantage is that by allowing the central government to control more levers of policy it internalizes any externalities between the regions. Its disadvantage is that any one region loses its ability to eject the government purely according to its own preferences ; it faces the risk that in some circumstances a government will be re-elected whom it would have wished to eject, because of the preferences of other regions.

3.3. Renegotiation of contracts

A FG promises support for the construction by a local government of an irrigation system if a certain number of conditions are met : a design made by a reputable engineering firm, a cost benefit analysis which proves the desirability of going ahead, and a public hearing of the users. The local government complies with the first two conditions, but not with the third, which it feels politically dangerous. If it has been smart enough to keep the design of the system within acceptable bounds it can, explicitly or implicitly, propose to the FG the following deal : « Why don't you accept to fund the project, even though some conditions have not been met ? You will be better off than if you did not fund it, and so would we ». Under the general principle that bygones are bygones, the FG should accept this deal (5). The original contract is not « renegotiation proof ». The awareness of this fact will weaken the incentives of the local government to respect the terms of the original agreement.

The general idea is straightforward : if during the execution of a contract it becomes clear that it can be modified to increase the utility of all the parties involved, the original contract will be modified at this point. Foreseeing this modification, the parties may modify their behavior in previous periods.

(5) We are ignoring some important real world considerations, such as the desirability for the federal government to appear « tough » in possible subsequent negotiations.

This has important policy consequences, and makes it possible to understand policy choices that seem mysterious. For instance, penalties for delays in large projects are often renegotiated away when the contractor is late. The expectation of this renegotiation encourages delay. However, this is often unavoidable. Once the project is late, the client will often prefer not to impose the penalty so as to keep carrots with which to encourage not too untimely completion.

For decentralization of public services, the main lesson is that the federal government might want to set rules that prevent it from renegotiating penalties or rewards. Going back to the public hearings discussed above, the law should clearly state that there will be no support without public hearing, and there should be no possibility of excusing its absence (or at least, this should be very difficult so that it can be made only in truly worthwhile cases). This introduces rigidity in contractual relationships between different levels of government, and might be a cost associated with decentralization, and especially with the sharing of responsibilities.

3.4. Unresolved issues

In the excitement of new discovery, it is easy to underestimate the number and importance of topics which are important on applied grounds and on which the literature has difficulty progressing. We mention four.

Dynamics and transitions : We do not understand well the dynamics of organizations. There is informal evidence that transitions between one line of activity and another, between one industry and another, between one organizational form and another are difficult and require time. Analytical treatment of these phenomena is very difficult.

The constitutional framework : The contracts, implicit or explicit, that govern the life of an organization have different status's. Some are more fundamental than others, rather as, in the legal realm, clauses of constitutions have a higher status and are more difficult to change than ordinary laws. This hierarchy of rules, important in private firms and even more so in governments, is poorly understood.

Multidimensional uncertainty : Most of current theory has been developed in settings where uncertainty bears on the value of one real variable. The extension to multidimensional uncertainty creates very difficult technical problems, and has been successfully completed only in very special cases. It is difficult to give precise advice on methods to circumvent the problem, but one should be aware of this fact when using the insights of the theory.

Networks of contracts : Recently a number of authors have stressed the fact that firms should be thought of as networks or nexuses of contracts or of treaties (see Crémer and Riordan [1987] ; Aoki, Gustafson & Williamson [1990]). However, very little formal work has been done on the interrelationships between different contracts signed by the same agent. For instance, a provincial government will be party to contracts signed with the FG, with the districts at a lower level, with the unions representing its employees, implicitly with the voters, etc. We do not understand very well how these contracts interact with each other.

4. What is a jurisdiction and where should its boundaries lie ?

Traditional micro economic theory takes the definition of the firm and its objectives as given. The theory of the firm began making substantial progress by asking the seemingly very abstract question : « what is a firm ? » Even though the answers we have are still imperfect, the work done to find them has yielded lessons that have very concrete policy implications. It is therefore a reasonable strategy to try to ask the question : « what is a political jurisdiction ? »

4.1. Coordination

One important aspect of the definition of the firm is that it groups together numerous types of activities. Similarly, if we are to develop a good understanding of political jurisdictions, we need to take seriously the notion that they integrate the power to make decisions in different domains. Indeed, jurisdictions can be thought of as organizations that group together the power to take political decisions, and we can ask what determines the grouping of activities by analogy with the grouping of activities within a firm.

Simon [1973] has argued that what determines the grouping of activities is the necessity of coordination of activities in the short run. Crémer [1981] has analyzed formally this coordination. The following example, drawn from this paper, provides the necessary intuition.

The allocation of responsibilities for transportation within a country is usually done by mode of transportation. This seems to neglect the fundamental nature of the good. From the point of view of consumers, a plane trip between Paris and Lyons has more similarity with a train trip between the same two cities than with a plane trip between Paris and Toulouse. Yet, it is the two train trips that are the responsibility of the same agency, not the two trips between Paris and Lyons. Why is that ? In the day to day management of the transportation system, the decisions to be taken are decisions that involve the planes and the crews that will flow between all towns. Very few short run decisions involve planes and trains at the same time. It is true that for planning purposes one should weigh carefully the options of plane and train transportation one against the other. These decisions are made in circumstances where time is not a crucial factor, and hence the extra difficulty of coordination between agencies is not very important.

For the management of infrastructure, this might have some important consequences. For instance, one could think that main irrigation channels could be, let us say, a provincial responsibility, whereas smaller branches could be a municipal responsibility. This can only be true in circumstances where there is no necessity to coordinate rapidly the management of the two parts of the system.

4.2. Control by voters

The theory of the firm has spent much energy trying to understand the mechanisms through which managers of corporations are controlled. Stockholders have bounded rationality, and both the acquisition of information and the exercise of the right to vote on corporate matters have relatively large costs. Furthermore, the benefits of any improvement in corporate performance generated by such activities are shared with all the other stockholders. It would seem therefore that corporations are undercontrolled. The mechanisms used to remedy this situation are of two kinds. First, the control of the day to day management of the firm can be delegated to specialists (*i.e.* the board of directors). Second, underperforming firms will be targets for takeovers if outsiders believe that they can run the firm in ways that increase its profits. There is general consensus that the question of control affects considerably the structure and the behavior of organizations.

Different forms of grouping together activities affect considerably the nature of the control that is exercised on political managers. First, relying on cooperation between layers of government often blurs responsibility for the execution of particular projects, and hence might have negative effects on efficiency. This is a common problem in water projects in some parts of Latin America for instance where coordination efforts become a highly time consuming part of project management. Second, even where responsibilities are separate it makes sense to divide them according to principles that are easy to remember. For example, allocating responsibility for different types of road to different levels of government sometimes results in difficulties in identifying who is in charge of what.

Because voters invest in information gathering about the performance of LGs, there is some organizational capital invested in the quality of participation in public life at different levels. For instance, in a system where municipal governments are powerful, voters will pay attention to the actions of the mayor, newspapers will develop sources in townhalls, and so on. Under these conditions there will be strong benefits to allocate new responsibilities to town halls, rather than to weaker, and therefore less controlled, political entities. One can expect a certain stability of the allocation of power in the system.

If these intuitions resist further analysis, and if they are as important in practical terms as we suspect that they are, the consequences for the organization of the public sector are striking. Because one cannot determine the optimal level of government for specific tasks in isolation, it does not make sense to study the decentralization of decisions about infrastructure in isolation from the allocation of other public responsibilities. For instance, landfill management will be assigned to the municipalities, because they are responsible for garbage collection, and they are responsible for garbage collection because they have better information about the use of land, having gathered this information in order to collect property taxes.

Note that there is a cost to pushing too much responsibility onto one level of government. If the central government, for instance, is responsible for too many activities each of them will have relatively little weight in the decisions of the voters, and hence it will be easier to run some of them for private rather than public benefits.

5. Some Applications

5.1. The optimal size of a jurisdiction

Decentralization below the national level is relatively systematically promoted in the literature. Very often, one sees lists stating that this decision is to be taken at the federal level, this other at the state level, and yet another at the local level. Why would the efficiency criterion be a certain number of levels below the national level ? Some countries have a smaller national population than states or municipalities in other countries. It would seem that population, or area, or some other measure of the services to be rendered would be a more logical criterion, and if this is the case, it does not make much sense to push decentralization on smaller countries.

On the other hand, the notion of control might help explain why the optimal number of levels might vary in such a way that the smaller district is larger in large countries than in smaller countries. The bounded rationality of voters prevents them from exercising adequate control over more than a certain number of governmental identities, a number which is independent of the size of the country.

5.2. Does decentralization promote democracy ?

It is often argued that decentralization will promote democracy : LGs are more sensitive to local needs, hence an individual has more possibilities to influence decisions that affect his life and his welfare under greater decentralization. This statement can be made more precise in two ways. First, under decentralization, there is a greater responsiveness of decisions with respect to the changes of preference of a single agent or group of similar agents. Second, under decentralization, there is a higher probability that a given agent or group of agents is pivotal, and hence determines the choice of a solution between two alternatives.

However, these generalizations will hold, if they do, only when all other factors are equal. In particular, it is important to notice that decentralization might lower the political power of the poorest citizens (see Seabright [1995], especially sections 2.4 and 3.1). Under decentralization, government will indeed be more sensitive to local needs, but it will still be local needs as perceived by the local political system. Hence, the groups that find it easier to organize political activity at the local level will be favored by decentralization. Organization of political forces is easier for groups where the benefits of influencing public policy is shared among a small number of agents. Groups that have more difficulty organizing will in general prefer larger political districts so that organizing is easier. Indeed, there is a fixed cost of organization of mass movements, in particular because the incentives for potential leaders are larger the larger the power they can obtain. It will therefore be easier to organize in larger circonscriptions. Some empirical backing for this theory comes from the fact that political forces that have favored income equality have generally favored centralized governments. (Of course, classical fiscal federalism type arguments yield the same result : decentralization makes it more costly to transfer income as governments compete for resources).

5.3. Why should decentralization lead to more experimentation ?

The argument is often made that decentralization promotes experimentation : free from the strictures of central administration, LGs can try out new ideas and methods. Decentralization of decisions in water supply matters for instance has led Fortaleza in the North East of Brazil to adopt cheaper technological solutions such as community water pumps not yet tried in the South of the country where traditional large utilities have typically been the norm. The diversity of experiences in urban transport in France or in India for instance also illustrates what municipalities can do when given the freedom to choose.

However, one must be careful with this argument. If the regions of the country are very different, it does indeed seem likely that local control will lead to more diversification. On the other hand, experimenting with a new technique creates positive externalities for other districts : they do not suffer the consequences of potential failures but benefit from the information generated.

It might seem that one could have the best of both worlds : use a decentralized system to benefit from local adaptation, and have the central government fund experimentation. But note that it is very difficult to write a contract that will indeed incite a district to experiment with a different institutional arrangements. It is difficult to define precisely what is the innovation ; typically, institutional innovations are refined during implementation. It is also difficult to check whether it has indeed been implemented.

5.4. Decentralizing education

Seventy percent of French people believe that regional governments should be given more power in the financing and the management of schools ; 60 % believe that they should be given more power in the recruiting of teachers. On the other hand, only 30 % call for a greater role of regions in the development of curricula and 12 % are willing to give them the responsibility for granting diplomas (6). It seems fair to summarize these results by saying that French people believe that programs and standards should be decided at the national level, but that schools should be managed locally. We should like to show that the desirability of such an allocation can be fruitfully analyzed using the conceptual framework sketched in this paper.

To consider the allocation of powers over the management of schools, we must first weigh externalities between localities and knowledge of local conditions. The externalities stem from migration : students trained in a district may go and spend their adult lives in another district, and therefore the social benefits of training are only partially enjoyed by the district of schooling. The national setting of the curriculum, and the verification through national exams that the curriculum is actually learned by the students, prevent free riding by districts. On the other hand, decentralizing the management of the schools allows for better adaptation to local tastes by a better setting of the dates of vacations, hiring of teachers who are sensitive to local culture, and so on.

This analysis, which draws entirely on the conventional wisdom on decentralization as we described it in section 2, has strong policy implications, some of which we do not believe would be generally accepted. For instance, below a certain degree of inter district migration, responsibility for curriculum and standards become the responsibility of regions. Above a certain degree of international migration, they become the responsibility of supranational bodies such as the European Union. The analysis is also based on assumptions which seem difficult to defend. For instance, if tastes are regionally differentiated for vacations and personality of teachers, why are they not regionally differentiated for curriculum and the organization of examinations ?

Of course, all the elements sketched above are important in reality. However, we believe that an essential element of reality is missed if we do not

(6) More precisely, 12 % agree with the statement that « ... les regions devraient pouvoir remplacer les diplômesnationaux par des diplômes regionaux ». These statistics are taken from *Le Monde de l'Education*, Octobre1993 (from poll conducted by SCP Communication of 858 persons, representative of the French population).

think in more contractual terms. To use a contractual approach, we must first identify the fundamental contracting difficulties between the public and the school system. As a first approximation, consumers of school services (parents and/or pupils) have good information about the pleasure that they derive from the school system (facilities, friendliness of teachers...) but on the other hand, they have poor information about the difficulty and the quality of the curriculum.

The separation of powers defined above provides a way to circumvent the second difficulty, while maintaining the advantages of control by consumers on the aspect they control best. On the aspects that the consumers understand best, power should be local because « voice » can be exercised more easily at that level. On the other hand, it is very costly for the citizens to judge the appropriateness of locally set standards. There exist strong incentives for the local government to hide low standards in order to improve the perception of the quality of the education that is provided.

By detaching the right of control over standards from the right of control over management of the school, one limits the incentives to tinker with standards. Comparison of the results in national exams between different districts provides the basis for a fast judgment by citizens of the quality of their school districts.

A complete analysis would include many other factors, namely discussions of :

1) the burden that changes of standards can impose on the districts and their non internalization by the national authority ;

2) the tension due to the fact that the consequences of neglect of the educational sector has consequences that may not be felt until after the next election ;

3) the reallocation of resources depending on the wealth of the districts.

Nevertheless, our analysis already has strong policy implications. In particular the desirability of the proposed organization does depend on a certain national homogeneity of tastes for curriculum, but not at all on the intensity of migration between districts.

*

*   *

This paper has done no more than scratch the surface of a literature rich in both theoretical and practical insights. Its key messages are the following :

1) The modern theory of the firm provides many insights into political organization, for political jurisdictions can be thought of as pseudo-firms that provide services and which group together decision-making activities of various kinds.

2) Questions about decentralization in government are questions about the allocation of rights of control. If contractual relations were complete it

would not matter whether power were decentralized or not, since contracts would specify everything to be done at each level of government and there would be no need for discretion.

3) The appropriate degree of decentralization depends upon which level of government will have the most incentive to act to bring about the desired outcomes. In particular, centralized governments can reap benefits of coordination, but tend to be less accountable than decentralized ones, though there are important exceptions to this general rule.

4) The organizational design of government affects not only incentives to take decisions but also incentives to gather the information on which those decisions will be based.

References

AKERLOF George A. [1970], « The Market for 'Lemons' : Quality Uncertainty and the Market Mechanism ». *The Quarterly Journal of Economics,* 84 : 3, 488-500.

AOKI MASAHIKO B., GUSTAFSOON and WILLIAMSON E. [1990], *The Firm as a Nexus of Treaties.* London : European Stage.

CAILLAUD Bernard, JELLIEN Bruno and PICARD Pierre [1996], « Information et organisation publique des processus de décision », *Revue d'Economie Politique.*

COASE Ronald [1937], « The Nature of the Firm ». *Economica,* 4, 386-405.

CRÉMER Jacques [1981], « A Partial Theory of the Optimal Organization of a Bureaucracy », *The Bell Journal of Economics,* 11 : 2, 683-93.

CRÉMER Jacques [1995], « Arm's Length Relationship », *The Quarterly Journal of Economics,* CX : 2, 275-296.

CRÉMER Jacques [1995], « A Theory of Vertical Integration Based on Monitoring Costs », mimeo, GREMAR and IDI.

CRÉMER Jacques and RIORDAN Michael H. [1987], « On Governing Multilateral Transactions with Bilateral Contracts », *Rand Journal of Economics,* 18 : 3, 436-51.

DE GROOT Hans [1988], « Decentralizing Decisions in Bureaucracies as a Principal-agent Problem », *Journal of Public Economics,* 37, 323-37.

ESTACHE Antonio and ZENG Kangbin [1992], « Managing Pollution Control in Brazil : The Potential Use of Taxes and Fines by Federal and State Governments ». World Bank Working Paper 929, Washington, D.C. : World Bank.

GROSSMAN Sandford J. and HART Oliver D. [1986], « The Costs and Benefits of Ownership : A Theory of Vertical and Lateral Integration », *Journal of Political Economy,* 94 : 4, 691-719.

GROVES Theodore [1973], « Incentives in Teams », *Econometrica,* 31 : 6, 617-63.

JACK William [1992], « Power Sharing and Pollution Control : Coordinating Policies among Levels of Governments ». World Bank Working Paper 887, Washington, D.C. : World Bank.

LANGE O. [1938], « On the Economic Theory of Socialism », in *On the Economic Theory of Socialism,* eds. O. Lange and F. M. Taylor, Minneapolis : University of Minnesota Press, 57-143.

MCCLEARY William [1991], « The Earmarking of Government Revenue : A Review of Some World Bank Experience », *World Bank Research Observer,* 6 : 1, 81-104.

MYERSON Roger B. [1979], « Incentive compatibility and the bargaining problem », *Econometrica,* 47 : 1, 61-73.

OATES Wallace F. [1969], « The Effects of Property Taxes and Local Public Spending on Property Values : An Empirical Study of Tax Capitalization and Tiebout Hypothesis », *Journal of Political Economy,* 77 : 6, 957-71.

SEABRIGHT Paul [1995], « Accountability and Decentralization in Government : An Incomplete Contracts Model », *European Economic Review,* forthcoming.

SIMON Herbert A. [1973], « Applying Information Technology to Organization Design », *Public Administration,* 33 : 3, 268-78.

SPENCE Michael [1973], « Job Market Signalling », *The Quarterly Journal of Economics,* 87 : 3, 561-72.

WEITZMAN Martin L. [1974], « Prices Versus Quantities », *The Review of Economic Studies,* 41 : 4, 477-91.

[27]

The Structure of Local Public Finance and the Quality of Life

Joseph Gyourko
University of Pennsylvania

Joseph Tracy
Yale University

Differences in local fiscal conditions generate compensating differentials across local land and labor markets just as we have long known amenities to do. Thus the fiscal climate affects the quality of life across metropolitan areas. We present new results showing that intercity fiscal differentials are nearly as important as amenity differentials in determining the quality of life across urban areas. The paper also investigates the sensitivity of the quality-of-life rankings with respect to assumptions about the nature of the marginal entrant. We estimate a random effects model to account for city-specific error components in the housing and wage regressions. Those results indicate that the standard errors of previous OLS-based quality-of-life rankings have been biased downward substantially. More encompassing data on city traits as well as superior controls for worker and housing quality are needed to increase the precision of quality-of-life estimates.

We are grateful to Glenn Blomquist for his help in supplying some of the data. The suggestions of the referee and the editor of the *Journal* materially improved the paper. We also benefited from the comments of Jim Heckman, Kevin M. Murphy, Jim Poterba, and Harvey Rosen as well as from participants in workshops at the University of Chicago, the Federal Reserve Bank of Philadelphia, the National Bureau of Economic Research's State and Local Finance Summer Institute, and the conference on Comparisons of Urban Economic Development in the United States and Western Europe, 1950–1987, in Bellagio, Italy. Financial support from the Wharton Real Estate Center to Gyourko is gratefully acknowledged. Robert Stoddard provided excellent research assistance. The usual caveat applies.

[*Journal of Political Economy*, 1991, vol. 99, no. 4]

I. Introduction

Urban quality-of-life rankings date back to work by Liu (1976). Rosen (1979) and Roback (1980, 1982) provided a theoretical foundation for these rankings by identifying market prices for amenities that can serve as weights in the construction of quality-of-life measures. These prices are implicitly generated by the capitalization of interurban amenity differences into local land rentals and wage rates.[1]

In this paper, we relax three important assumptions that traditionally are made in this literature. The first is that all city characteristics used to construct the quality-of-life measure are pure amenities. A pure amenity is a nonproduced public good such as weather quality that has no explicit price. In practice, previous empirical studies include some government services such as education or public safety, with their marginal valuations measured using implicit prices. However, government services are not pure amenities in that they are produced and have explicit tax prices. If a service is fully priced via local taxes, then independent of the actual marginal valuation of the service, no implicit price in terms of wage or land rent capitalization will exist for the service. Estimating the full price for services necessitates adding state and local taxes to the land rental and wage specifications. We find that intercity fiscal differentials have nearly as much influence on the quality-of-life index values and rankings as intercity amenity differentials do.

The second assumption relaxed is that all locational rents are capitalized into land rentals or private-sector wages. This assumption has been employed to ensure that the implicit prices fully reflect marginal valuations of the amenities. However, Ehrenberg and Schwarz's (1986) and Freeman's (1986) reviews of the increasing unionization of the local public sector over the last 30 years cast doubt on the validity of this assumption. Collective bargaining by local public unions may lead to sharing of locational rents between residents and local public workers. This can give rise to explicit tax prices even for pure amenities. Consider an extreme case in which all the locational rents derived from an amenity are captured by the local public union in the form of wage premia. There would be no capitalization of the amenity in either the land or (private-sector) labor markets. The value of the amenity would be reflected in the differential tax burdens the

[1] There has been a renewed interest in this topic, with Blomquist, Berger, and Hoehn (1988) extending the Rosen/Roback framework to include agglomeration economies. Other recent efforts at estimating compensating differentials arising from city attributes include Hoehn, Berger, and Blomquist (1987), Berger and Blomquist (1988), Roback (1988), Gyourko and Tracy (1989*a*, 1989*b*), Leven and Stover (1989), and Voith (1991).

residents must pay in order to finance the union wage premia. This provides a second rationale for including controls for local taxes in quality-of-life measures. Consistent with our earlier work (Gyourko and Tracy 1989*a*), we find that land prices are lower in cities with more highly organized public-sector work forces. However, with taxes and service measures held constant, the independent impact of local public unionization is very small on average.

The third assumption relaxed is that there are no uncontrolled for city-specific group effects present in the housing and wage expenditure hedonics. Our data strongly indicate that the error terms in these equations contain both city-specific and individual-specific components. The city-specific components reflect systematic influences of omitted attributes on land rentals and wages. An important question is whether these city-specific effects should be included in the calculation of the quality-of-life rankings. If they reflect unmeasured housing structure quality or worker human capital, then they should not be included in the rankings. However, if they reflect omitted amenity or fiscal variables that would have been included in the specifications if the data had been available, then they should be priced out and included in the rankings. Because we cannot clearly identify the source of these city-specific group effects, quality-of-life rankings with and without the group effects are reported. The fact that including the group effects materially alters the rankings highlights the need for better worker, housing, and city data in order to pin down more precisely the true urban quality of life.

Section II briefly outlines an expanded Rosen/Roback model incorporating locally provided services and taxes as well as a rent-seeking local public sector. Section III describes the data used in the empirical analysis. Section IV details the econometrics and reports results on trait prices and quality-of-life rankings. There is a short conclusion (Sec. V) and a Data Appendix.

II. An Expanded Rosen/Roback Model

Government services and taxes can easily be included in the Rosen/Roback model, as our two earlier papers show. Because the underlying Rosen/Roback model is now well known, this section reproduces only the essential equations from our previous work.

Workers and firms compete for scarce sites across jurisdictions. Let there be a representative worker-resident consuming a composite traded good Y, land services N, and a package of locally provided services and amenities (G_j, A_j) for each city j. The service/amenity package is taken as exogenous by all potential residents and firms. The service package (G) is financed using one or more of the following taxes: a sales tax of rate s on the composite good whose price is the numeraire, an income tax of rate z on gross wages W^g, and a property tax of rate t per local land rental n. There is endowment income of I. Firms use land services, labor, and intermediate goods in production. The latter are assumed to be subject to the sales tax.

Via the standard utility and profit maximizations, worker and firm evaluations of communities are given by an indirect utility function (V) and an indirect profit function (Π). With perfect mobility in the long run, both worker utility and firm profitability must be equalized across jurisdictions as follows:

$$V = \overline{V}\{(1 - z_j)W_j^g, (1 + t_j)n_j, (1 + s_j), I; A_j, G_j\} \quad \text{for all } j, \tag{1}$$

$$\Pi = \overline{\Pi}\{W^g, (1 + t_j)n_j, (1 + s_j); A_j, G_j\} \quad \text{for all } j. \tag{2}$$

Worker utility in jurisdiction j is determined by the net wage received, $(1 - z_j)W_j^g$; gross-of-tax land rentals, $(1 + t_j)n_j$; what is essentially the nonland cost of living, $1 + s_j$; and the amenity and public-service package, A_j and G_j. Firm profits are determined by similar factors, although firms care about the gross wage paid (W_j^g). We assume that the amenity/service package enters the firm's indirect profit function through its underlying effect on the firm's production function.

These equilibrium conditions can be solved implicitly for the reduced-form wage and land rental equations (with R_j defined as the gross-of-tax land rent):

$$W_j^g = W\{(1 + s_j), z_j, I, G_j, A_j\}, \tag{3}$$

$$R_j = (1 + t_j)n_j = N\{(1 + s_j), z_j, I, G_j, A_j\}. \tag{4}$$

The equilibrium wage and land rental price are given by the intersection of the level sets of (1) and (2) as illustrated in figure 1. The comparative statics for the reduced-form equations are straightforward and are derived in our earlier papers.

As Linneman (1978) implies, if (3) and (4) could be estimated with exact measures of all fiscal variables, then the full prices for amenities and services could be recovered even when rent sharing takes place between residents and local public unions. (However, the marginal impact of local public employee rent seeking could not be directly observed.) Because of the inevitably inexact natures of our tax and service variables, it is helpful to augment the land rent and wage equations with a direct measure of local public union rent seeking (U). That measure should reflect potential residents' perceptions of the union's ability to extract current and future rents. This requires some estimate of the union's long-run institutional strength. We use the extent of local public-sector union coverage in the empirical work

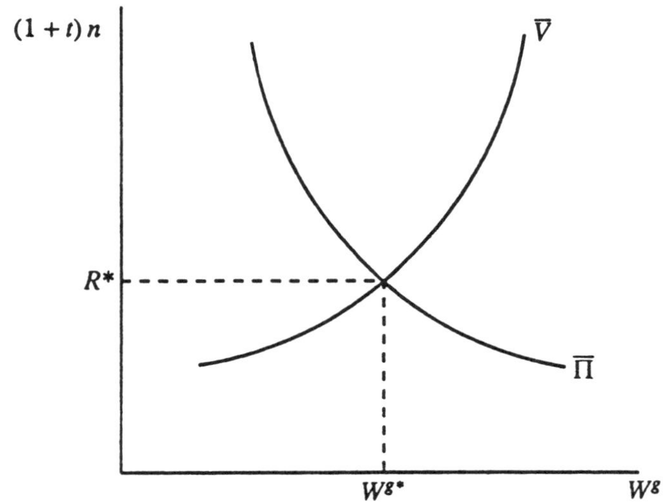

FIG. 1

below. Note that to the extent that the fiscal proxies already incorporate some impacts of rent-seeking activity, the measured influence of U on wages and land prices will not fully capture the costs (or benefits) to worker-residents of local public unionization.

III. Description of the Data

Data were collected for 130 cities throughout the United States. A house value measure is used to proxy for land prices (n_j) because there is no consistent land price series for our sample. Both the housing value and wage data (W^g) come from a 1 percent random subsample of the 1/1,000 public-use A sample of the 1980 *Census of Population and Housing* and pertain to the year 1979. There are 5,263 observations on housing units and 38,870 observations on individual workers.

The wage variable used is the worker's average weekly wage for 1979. To be included in the sample, the resident had to be a full-time labor market participant in the private sector. Public-sector workers are excluded because tax rates and service levels cannot be considered exogenous determinants of their wages, as Inman (1981, 1982) shows.

The housing expenditure variable is based on a reported interval of housing values in the census data. We use a two-step procedure to impute a specific housing value to each interval. First, we estimate the continuous distribution of housing values that best accords with the observed frequencies for each interval. This estimated distribution is then used to calculate expected housing values conditional on being in each interval. Those results are available on request. The imputed housing expenditure is the conditional expected housing value converted into an annual rent using the 7.85 percent discount rate from Peiser and Smith's (1985) user cost paper.

A variety of other selection criteria were also employed in generating the sample. First, the wage sample is restricted to individuals who live and work in the central city, while the housing sample is restricted to homes located in the central city. This is necessary for matching with city-specific fiscal data collected for central cities of major standard metropolitan statistical areas (SMSAs). Given the heterogeneity in fiscal conditions across any given urban area, it is important that the dependent variables pertain to the same jurisdiction as the right-hand-side fiscal measures. The housing sample is further restricted to units on lots of 1 acre or less in order to narrow the quality range of houses analyzed.

The model in Section II assumes a given quality worker and housing unit. To help control further for quality differences in housing structures, we included in the housing expenditure specification a variety of structural traits reported in the census. The wage specification includes the standard set of human capital proxies, which are also interacted with the worker's sex. Finally, a series of 22 major industry and occupation classifications are controlled for.

A host of city characteristics are merged with the census data. Appendix table A1 more fully describes these variables and their sources. The set of amenities includes the following weather and pollution variables: average annual precipitation, relative humidity, average wind speed, the percentage of days with sunshine, heating and cooling degree days, and an air pollution variable measuring mean total suspended particulates.[2] We also created a dichotomous variable indicating whether the city borders an ocean, the Gulf of Mexico, or one of the Great Lakes. Metro area size, measured by the population of the SMSA, is included as another amenity proxy. Intermediate

[2] Glenn Blomquist provided us with added pollution measures used in Blomquist et al. (1988). These included the number of effluent discharges, metric tons of landfill waste, and the number of treatment, storage, and disposal sites. Blomquist used county-level data, so we sometimes had trouble matching with individual cities. Including these added pollution measures reduced our sample size to under 90 cities. In order to have as much variation as possible in fiscal conditions, we decided to drop the added pollution measures in order to obtain the 130-city sample size that serves as the base for all results reported in the paper. On the smaller sample, we estimated wage and housing expenditure equations that included the added pollution variables. These variables are not statistically significant (individually or jointly) in the random effects specification. Further, the estimated group effects are only marginally smaller than those reported in table 1 below.

family metropolitan budget data from the Bureau of Labor Statistics (BLS), adjusted to remove housing costs, are used to approximate the nonland cost of living. Because of missing observations, this variable had to be imputed for many of the cities in the sample. All standard errors have been adjusted to reflect the imputation. (See the notes to Appendix table A1 for the details.) A final locational amenity controlled for is the percentage of workers in a city that work in another SMSA. This variable is intended to control for access to alternative labor markets. City size held constant, a Connecticut city near New York City is different from a similarly sized city in (say) Iowa because location near a large labor market makes the opportunity set of the Connecticut residents larger than that faced by the Iowa residents.

We collected data on seven fiscal variables. Each of these measures pertains to the central city only and is not a metropolitan area average. The income tax variable is the sum of state and local income tax rates. Data on state corporate tax rates are also included. The effective local property tax rate variable used is identical to that in Gyourko and Tracy (1989*a*) and is the product of the nominal rate times the assessment/sales ratio. We control for four government services: police, fire, health, and education. We attempted to construct output measures for each service since expenditures probably are very poor service proxies for many of the central cities in our sample. For police services, the per capita incidence of violent crimes is used. However, health services are proxied for by an input measure that is the number of hospital beds per thousand people.[3] The measure used for fire services is a rating scheme developed by insurance companies for setting premiums in a city. The ratings range from one to 10, with one being best. The last service controlled for is education. Data problems prevent us from employing standardized test scores as an output measure. Consequently, we use the student/teacher ratio.[4]

[3] In previous work, we experimented with both violent and property crime rates and found no significant effects of property crime, with violent crime held constant. We also investigated alternative input and output health measures including infant mortality rates, the number of physicians per capita, and the number of medical specialists per capita. These variables can be measured only at the county level. Consequently, we chose to employ the city-specific hospital beds measure.

[4] Even test score data have the potential defect of confounding the quality of educational services provided with the ability of students attending the schools. For example, the Scholastic Aptitude Test is taken only by those students applying to college, the fraction of which varies by city and state. Dynarski (1987) and Hanushek and Taylor (1988) demonstrate how to adjust statewide test scores for the selection bias. We were not successful in collecting district test score data via phone or letter surveys. Many districts claim not to have collected or saved data for 1979 or adjacent years. This made it impossible to implement those authors' selection correction procedure with the city district as the unit of observation. While there is little statistical evidence that class size affects student achievement (e.g., Hanushek 1986), Card and Krueger (1990) find a strong correlation between class size and subsequent labor market performance.

Our measure of the institutional strength of public-sector unions used to proxy for the perceived union rent-seeking potential (U) is the percentage of local public workers in the central city who are organized. By the late 1970s, public-sector unionization had leveled off. Differences in public-sector organization strength across cities in 1979 reasonably could be perceived by residents as reflecting long-run differences in union bargaining power.

IV. Econometric Specification and Results

To estimate the reduced-form wage equation given in (3), we assume that the wage for individual i in city j is represented as

$$\ln W_{ij} = \beta_0 + \mathbf{X}_i\beta_1 + \mathbf{Y}_i\beta_2 + \mathbf{Z}_j\beta_3 + u_{ij}, \quad u_{ij} = \alpha_j + \epsilon_i, \qquad (5)$$

where $\mathbf{X}_i$ is a vector of individual worker traits, $\mathbf{Y}_i$ is a vector of industry and occupation controls, $\mathbf{Z}_j$ is a vector of community amenity and fiscal attributes, $\alpha_j \sim N(0, \sigma^2_\alpha)$, and $\epsilon_i \sim N(0, \sigma^2_\epsilon)$. To estimate the reduced-form housing expenditure equation in (4), we assume that the housing expenditures for individual i in city j are represented as

$$\ln n_{ij} = \gamma_0 + \mathbf{H}_i\gamma_1 + \mathbf{Z}_j\gamma_2 + v_{ij}, \quad v_{ij} = \delta_j + \eta_i, \qquad (6)$$

where $\mathbf{H}_i$ is a vector of housing unit structural traits, $\mathbf{Z}_j$ is a vector of community amenity and fiscal attributes,[5] $\delta_j \sim N(0, \sigma^2_\delta)$, and $\eta_i \sim N(0, \sigma^2_\eta)$. In estimating (5) and (6), we allow the error terms to contain both an individual and a city component. The city component in each equation is common to all workers or housing units in a given city and is assumed uncorrelated across observations from different cities.

To test for the appropriateness of ordinary least squares (OLS) versus random effects in each specification, we calculated the one-sided Lagrange multiplier statistic for the null hypothesis that either $\sigma^2_\alpha = 0$ or $\sigma^2_\delta = 0$. In each case, the data strongly reject the null hypothesis of a zero group variance. We also tested for possible correlation between the city-specific error component and the included variables using the procedure described in Hausman and Taylor (1981). The data did not reject the null of zero correlation in either specification.

The results from the underlying wage and housing expenditure hedonics are presented in the first two columns of table 1. We report findings only for the city-specific traits. The results on the individual worker and housing unit traits yielded no surprises and are available

[5] Note that the effective property tax rate is included in the housing expenditure equation but not in the wage equation. The property tax is solved out of the reduced-form wage equation. The equilibrium model in Sec. II implies full capitalization into land prices. The results presented below do imply virtually full capitalization.

TABLE 1

Regression Results and Trait Prices: Random Effects Specification

City Trait	Annual Housing Expenditure Hedonic* (1)	Weekly Wage Hedonic† (2)	Annualized Trait Prices‡ Housing (3)	Wage (4)	Full (5)
Precipitation	−.0139	−.0027	−$22.82	−$21.59	−$1.22
	(.0030)	(.0009)	(4.98)	(6.83)	(8.45)
Cooling degree days (thousands)	−.1344	.0031	−7.97	.89	−8.86
	(.0562)	(.0157)	(3.33)	(4.49)	(5.59)
Heating degree days (thousands)	−.0277	.0172	−5.65	16.93	−22.58
	(.0248)	(.0069)	(5.06)	(6.82)	(8.49)
Relative humidity	.0145	.0033	36.53	40.14	−3.61
	(.0053)	(.0015)	(13.36)	(18.67)	(22.95)
Sunshine (percentage possible)	.0079	−.0005	21.84	−6.03	27.87
	(.0056)	(.0016)	(15.38)	(21.97)	(26.82)
Wind speed (mph)	−.0427	−.0192	−18.18	−39.57	21.39
	(.0179)	(.0055)	(7.62)	(11.31)	(13.64)
Particulate matter	−.0019	−.0003	−6.36	−4.34	−2.01
	(.0013)	(.0004)	(4.20)	(−5.79)	(7.15)
Coast	.1345	−.0201	654.15	−435.70	1,089.86
	(.0694)	(.0199)	(360.15)	(429.20)	(560.28)
Cost of living	.6496	.2633	28.89	56.58	−27.70
	(1.6197)	(.4208)	(71.94)	(90.42)	(115.55)
Violent crime	.0574	.0705	2.51	14.91	−12.40
	(.0425)	(.0109)	(1.86)	(2.31)	(2.97)

continued over

Student/teacher ratio	−.0107	−.0010	−6.84	−3.09	−3.76
	(.0096)	(.0027)	(6.14)	(8.31)	(10.33)
Fire rating	.0498	.0156	6.93	10.48	−3.55
	(.0255)	(.0078)	(3.55)	(5.28)	(6.36)
Hospital beds	.0031	−.0036	1.82	−10.03	11.85
	(.0037)	(.0010)	(2.12)	(2.82)	(3.53)
Property tax rate	−.1037	. . .	−6.14	. . .	−6.14
	(.0399)		(2.37)		(2.37)
State and local income tax rate	−.0287	.0020	−3.99	1.37	−5.36
	(.0101)	(.0029)	(1.41)	(1.95)	(2.41)
State corporate tax rate	.0208	−.0067	5.97	−9.33	15.30
	(.0100)	(.0029)	(2.88)	(3.98)	(4.91)
Percentage public union organized	−.1646	−.0041	−3.29	−.39	−2.89
	(.1302)	(.0385)	(2.60)	(3.72)	(4.54)
SMSA population (millions)	.0376	.0096	1.27	1.57	−.30
	(.0223)	(.0057)	(.76)	(.93)	(1.20)
Percentage working in other SMSA	1.4693	.1052	5.34	1.85	3.49
	(.6325)	(.1969)	(2.30)	(3.46)	(4.15)
Summary statistics:					
σ_α^2	.0434	. . .			
σ_ϵ^2	.1801	. . .			
σ_δ^2	. . .	.2905			
σ_η^2	. . .	.0023			
Number of observations	5,263	38,870			

* The housing hedonic contains 20 structural trait controls. All results are available on request. Estimated standard errors are in parentheses.

† The wage hedonic contains 11 worker quality variables and controls for 22 major industry and occupation groups. All results are available on request. Estimated standard errors are in parentheses.

‡ The calculations in cols. 3–5 are based on a 1 percent change about the mean of the variables except for the dichotomous coast variable. Its prices are based on a discrete change from noncoast to coastal status. All figures in these three columns are annualized. We assume 1.5 wage earners per household and 49 work weeks per year. These are the sample averages. Standard errors of the implicit prices are in parentheses. They are calculated via the "delta" method.

on request. As Roback (1980, 1982) showed, the compensating differentials estimated from (5) and (6) can be used to compute implicit prices of the amenities and fiscal conditions. The full implicit price of a given city trait is the sum of the land price differential and the negative of the wage differential.[6] Columns 3–5 of table 1 present the full implicit prices as well as the component prices in terms of housing expenditures and wages. Except for the dichotomous coast variable, the calculations are based on an assumed 1 percent change about the mean of each variable. All prices are stated in terms of annual housing expenditures or annual earnings (assuming 1.5 earners per household).

While there are anomalies, the full implicit prices generally have the expected signs in that beneficial traits have positive prices, with the converse being true for traits that are "bads." Consistent with Blomquist et al. (1988) and Gyourko and Tracy (1989*b*), we find that, for many city traits, the full price largely reflects capitalization in the labor rather than in the land market.

As a group, the 11 amenities are highly statistically significant (at better than the 1 percent level) in both the wage and housing hedonics. The same is true for the fiscal variables as a group (seven in the housing hedonic and six in the wage hedonic). Many of the amenity variables have been used in other hedonic estimations, and given this paper's interest in the influence of the fiscal climate, we focus on the taxes and services in our discussion.[7]

The full implicit price for each service proxy has the anticipated sign, with public safety and health services having the largest prices (in absolute value). Most of the impact of these two variables occurs via wage differentials. The property tax coefficient of −0.1037 in table 1 implies that property taxes are virtually fully capitalized into land prices. With services held constant, higher income taxes are viewed as a bad, with most of the compensation coming through the

[6] Roback's equation works with actual land prices. We use housing expenditures in which land rents are bundled with structural traits. As Blomquist et al. note, the problem is easily handled by putting housing instead of land into the utility function and incorporating a housing production function into the model. The full implicit price equation is essentially unchanged, with the quality of housing purchased replacing the quantity of land (see Blomquist et al. 1988, p. 92, eq. 6).

[7] However, two of the individual amenity findings are of unique interest. First, the influence of the size variable (SMSA population) is small. By way of comparison, Roback's (1982) OLS-based findings for the impact of SMSA population are approximately double the magnitude of our OLS and random effects findings. We also experimented with land area and population density measures at both the SMSA and central city levels. Those variables were not found to be influential or to affect other variables' coefficients. Second, there is a particularly strong influence for access to nearby labor markets as indicated by the coefficient on the percentage of residents working in another SMSA. For cities in the San Francisco Bay area and near New York City, where 30–40 percent of residents often work in another SMSA, the land rent coefficient on this variable implies that land prices are 15–30 percent higher, ceteris paribus.

land market. The effect on wages is small and positive, indicating that gross wages do not rise nearly enough to keep net wages constant. Entrants to cities with high corporate tax rates pay higher land rents and accept lower wages. This would be expected if the tax burden were being shifted to nonresidents. This seems unlikely given that many firms in the corporate sector produce for regional or national markets, making forward shifting to consumers difficult. It may be that this variable is picking up beneficial aspects of agglomeration that are being appropriated by the government through the tax. It is also possible that the variable might be proxying for the state's overall economic condition. Finally, cities with higher public-sector unionization rates do have somewhat lower land prices, but the partial correlation is not statistically significant.[8]

The underlying quality-of-life index value (QOL) is created as

$$QOL_j = \sum_k FP_k \times T_{kj}, \tag{7}$$

where FP_k is the full implicit price of city trait k and T_{kj} is the quantity of that trait in city j. We have standardized on a hypothetical city having the average values of all city traits. The index is measured in 1979 dollars and reflects the premium that individuals are willing to pay to live in city j relative to the hypothetical city with the sample average amenity, fiscal, and public-sector union conditions.

Information on the relative contributions of the amenity, fiscal, and public-sector union conditions to the quality of life is presented in columns 1 and 2 of table 2. The full range of quality-of-life values based on all city traits is $8,227. This band is wide because of a few extreme cities. The interquartile range is only $1,484. The separate impact of the 11 amenity variables (which include the weather and pollution variables, coastal status, cost of living, access to other labor markets, and size variables) can be seen in the second row of columns 1 and 2. All else constant, one would pay $3,979 more to live in the top-amenity city than in the city with the worst amenity set. Note that there is a particularly wide range for the impact of the seven tax/service variables ($6,582 [row 3]). However, restricting attention to the middle of the distribution shows that the fiscal vector makes approximately the same contribution as the amenity vector to the dispersion of quality-of-life index values ($1,188 vs. $1,372).

[8] We also experimented with a dichotomous union coverage variable. The variable was coded as a one if the city had a public-sector coverage rate that was at least one standard deviation above the sample mean (> 67 percent). As in Gyourko and Tracy (1989*b*), the transformed variable generated statistically significant lower land prices of about 10 percent. However, the full implicit price was little changed, as were the resulting quality-of-life rankings.

TABLE 2

AMENITY, FISCAL, AND PUBLIC-SECTOR UNION IMPACTS ON THE QUALITY OF LIFE AND INTERCITY HOUSING AND WAGE DIFFERENTIALS

			Housing		Wage	
Variable Set	Quality-of-Life Range (1)	Quality-of-Life Interquartile Range (2)	Maximum Partial R^{2*} (3)	Minimum Partial $R^{2\dagger}$ (4)	Maximum Partial R^2 (5)	Minimum Partial R^2 (6)
All city traits	$8,227	$1,484	.55	. . .	.44	. . .
Amenity component	3,979	1,372	.43	.39	.23	.20
Tax/service component	6,582	1,188	.16	.12	.21	.20
Public union component	571	193	.00	.00	.06	.00

* The maximum partial R^2 for the vector of traits in each row is defined to be the second-stage R^2 from the regression containing only the city traits listed in each row.

† The minimum partial R^2 for the vector of traits in each row is defined to be the difference between the R^2 obtained when including all city-specific variables (row 1) and the R^2 from the regression omitting the city traits listed in the relevant row.

For the typical city, the public-sector union coverage variable does not have an economically important independent impact on the overall quality-of-life index (row 4).

Columns 3–6 of table 2 summarize the relative importance of the amenity, fiscal, and public-sector union variables in explaining the variation in quality-adjusted housing prices and wages across cities. The minimum and maximum partial R^2's presented are calculated using a two-step procedure. In the first step, city fixed effects are estimated using OLS, controlling for housing or worker quality. The second step involves a generalized least squares regression of the fixed effects coefficients on the city-specific variables.[9] The city-specific variables explain 55 percent of the variation in quality-adjusted house prices and 44 percent of the variation in quality-adjusted wages across our 130 cities. The remaining rows in columns 3–6 document the relative importance of the amenity, fiscal, and union variables. Fiscal differentials clearly are empirically important in that they account for at least 21 percent of the explained variation in housing prices (.12/.55) and at least 47 percent of the explained variation in wages (.21/.44) across cities. However, variation in the degree of public-sector unionization has no ability to explain intercity wage or housing price differentials.

The quality-of-life index values and rankings based on the prices in table 1 are presented in the first two columns of table 3. Recall that the reason for estimating a random effects specification is to control for the influence of omitted traits common to a city-specific group of workers or housing units. If the group effects reflect omitted amenities or fiscal variables that would be included if observable, they should be priced and included in the quality-of-life computation. In contrast, if these traits reflect unmeasured heterogeneity in housing structure quality and worker human capital, then they should not be included in the quality-of-life computation. Unfortunately, it is not readily apparent how to discriminate between these sources.

The correlation between the errors of the two equations might allow some insight into the nature of the city-specific group effects, but only if we know much more about the underlying structure of the model than our reduced-form estimations afford. If both worker and housing quality were systematically underestimated (or overestimated) by city, a positive error correlation would result. However, a negative error correlation would ensue if quality was overestimated

[9] The variance-covariance matrix used in the generalized least squares estimation is the sum of the fixed effects variance-covariance matrix and a diagonal matrix with the estimated group error variance along the diagonal. This particular variance-covariance matrix reproduces the random effects coefficients and standard errors reported in table 1.

TABLE 3

QUALITY-OF-LIFE INDEX VALUES AND RANKINGS

	RANDOM EFFECTS		RANDOM EFFECTS, GROUP EFFECTS INCLUDED		OLS: ALL FISCAL VARIABLES		OLS: NO TAXES/NO UNION	
CITY	Ranking (1)	Index Value (2)	Ranking (3)	Index Value (4)	Ranking (5)	Index Value (6)	Ranking (7)	Index Value (8)
Norwalk, CT	1	3,986	23	2,132	1	5,192	1	4,335
	(4.1)	(1,135)	(20.9)	(2,226)	(.4)	(705)	(.8)	(685)
Pensacola, FL	2	2,963	6	3,812	4	3,145	5	2,588
	(4.0)	(714)	(3.8)	(1,601)	(1.5)	(401)	(2.9)	(347)
Gainesville, FL	3	2,819	46	1,019	5	3,115	3	3,026
	(7.3)	(890)	(23.5)	(2,408)	(2.2)	(533)	(2.6)	(512)
San Diego, CA	4	2,574	4	4,474	2	3,586	4	2,971
	(8.4)	(860)	(3.2)	(999)	(1.1)	(299)	(1.8)	(277)
Stamford, CT	5	2,497	38	1,339	17	1,668	58	137
	(9.4)	(875)	(20.6)	(1,808)	(7.4)	(462)	(15.3)	(354)
Columbia, SC	6	2,459	7	3,792	3	3,556	2	4,135
	(14.7)	(1,137)	(9.0)	(1,693)	(2.8)	(677)	(.9)	(653)
Santa Rosa, CA	7	1,955	45	1,024	6	2,443	10	2,309
	(11.4)	(744)	(18.8)	(1,462)	(2.7)	(324)	(2.6)	(284)
Bridgeport, CT	8	1,944	3	4,532	10	2,245	50	305
	(9.3)	(630)	(2.4)	(1,580)	(3.3)	(335)	(9.4)	(209)
Tucson, AZ	9	1,822	17	2,325	9	2,259	22	929
	(13.5)	(780)	(12.6)	(1,182)	(4.3)	(415)	(8.7)	(330)
Shreveport, LA	10	1,802	39	1,318	18	1,619	31	682
	(7.3)	(473)	(11.5)	(1,172)	(3.9)	(232)	(6.3)	(179)
Lancaster, PA	11	1,784	16	2,327	19	1,582	28	762
	(9.0)	(547)	(8.9)	(1,164)	(4.7)	(265)	(7.1)	(198)

continued over

Modesto, CA	12	1,678	62	517	11	2,053	12	2,141
	(9.4)	(550)	(15.6)	(1,485)	(3.2)	(249)	(2.5)	(217)
Asheville, NC	13	1,577	32	1,418	20	1,464	7	2,364
	(11.8)	(622)	(21.6)	(3,036)	(6.5)	(346)	(2.9)	(301)
New Orleans, LA	14	1,565	42	1,170	13	1,818	40	506
	(10.8)	(570)	(14.3)	(879)	(4.5)	(304)	(10.0)	(260)
Fall River, MA	15	1,549	85	−327	22	1,417	6	2,536
	(16.5)	(795)	(22.4)	(2,379)	(8.3)	(453)	(3.0)	(416)
Danbury, CT	16	1,498	1	6,662	33	826	9	2,329
	(22.1)	(1,009)	(1.9)	(3,658)	(15.9)	(587)	(4.5)	(540)
Amarillo, TX	17	1,475	59	680	24	1,232	37	551
	(16.9)	(795)	(20.9)	(1,612)	(9.3)	(472)	(15.7)	(418)
Jacksonville, FL	18	1,463	103	−992	27	1,113	30	694
	(13.1)	(630)	(13.1)	(1,003)	(6.4)	(322)	(9.7)	(291)
San Francisco, CA	19	1,416	29	1,578	8	2,296	13	2,046
	(16.4)	(796)	(16.1)	(884)	(2.8)	(291)	(3.0)	(279)
San Jose, CA	20	1,403	75	208	15	1,744	15	1,849
	(16.2)	(740)	(19.1)	(898)	(5.0)	(299)	(3.0)	(281)
New Britain, CT	21	1,389	35	1,395	7	2,335	8	2,345
	(23.1)	(1,003)	(22.8)	(1,931)	(6.2)	(592)	(4.9)	(569)
Lake Charles, LA	22	1,388	113	−1,636	25	1,177	36	588
	(15.9)	(725)	(11.4)	(1,800)	(7.6)	(365)	(9.7)	(252)
New Bedford, MA	23	1,316	51	791	54	179	34	652
	(17.9)	(765)	(20.2)	(1,692)	(14.2)	(387)	(12.1)	(344)
Tyler, TX	24	1,175	11	2,773	35	776	18	1,411
	(14.6)	(605)	(8.3)	(2,030)	(7.8)	(326)	(2.4)	(228)
Odessa, TX	25	1,118	61	577	30	960	42	478
	(17.1)	(671)	(19.4)	(2,953)	(8.9)	(393)	(14.3)	(366)
Erie, PA	26	1,103	18	2,299	23	1,250	64	−30
	(18.4)	(706)	(11.8)	(1,390)	(7.2)	(347)	(12.7)	(291)
Phoenix, AZ	27	1,097	78	59	31	932	20	993
	(26.5)	(1,038)	(24.8)	(1,158)	(10.4)	(424)	(10.4)	(408)
Knoxville, TN	28	1,071	83	−143	28	1,100	26	811
	(10.7)	(412)	(11.1)	(1,024)	(4.5)	(208)	(5.9)	(165)

TABLE 3 (*Continued*)

City	Random Effects		Random Effects, Group Effects Included		OLS: All Fiscal Variables		OLS: No Taxes/No Union	
	Ranking (1)	Index Value (2)	Ranking (3)	Index Value (4)	Ranking (5)	Index Value (6)	Ranking (7)	Index Value (8)
Lafayette, LA	29	930	13	2,615	26	1,164	78	−290
	(15.2)	(548)	(7.6)	(1,709)	(5.8)	(284)	(9.8)	(229)
Monroe, LA	30	905	19	2,287	42	524	60	82
	(11.1)	(404)	(7.3)	(1,740)	(5.9)	(194)	(6.9)	(169)
Wilmington, DE	31	898	72	363	16	1,675	19	1,146
	(19.2)	(666)	(17.9)	(1,141)	(5.4)	(309)	(4.4)	(244)
Waco, TX	32	880	21	2,162	32	870	24	859
	(21.4)	(745)	(13.1)	(1,560)	(10.7)	(430)	(10.9)	(379)
Springfield, MO	33	753	22	2,154	57	151	32	659
	(11.8)	(386)	(7.2)	(1,443)	(6.7)	(184)	(5.8)	(158)
Sacramento, CA	34	703	24	1,832	29	991	29	753
	(18.0)	(564)	(11.3)	(956)	(6.7)	(267)	(8.5)	(235)
Lubbock, TX	35	690	106	−1,107	34	796	46	410
	(20.3)	(650)	(12.7)	(1,400)	(9.5)	(378)	(13.5)	(330)
Los Angeles, CA	36	605	10	2,941	14	1,804	17	1,604
	(15.1)	(930)	(4.6)	(960)	(2.7)	(254)	(1.6)	(244)
Birmingham, AL	37	590	41	1,201	43	507	14	1,962
	(25.8)	(823)	(19.6)	(1,120)	(12.0)	(391)	(3.1)	(308)
Jersey City, NJ	38	573	95	−831	12	1,883	11	2,231
	(29.7)	(984)	(20.7)	(1,407)	(8.6)	(587)	(4.8)	(544)
Fresno, CA	39	542	60	604	21	1,446	16	1,668
	(24.6)	(773)	(20.3)	(1,265)	(7.0)	(365)	(3.9)	(344)
Roanoke, VA	40	518	87	−378	44	434	68	−79
	(16.7)	(490)	(13.4)	(1,415)	(7.7)	(238)	(7.0)	(158)

continued over

Columbia, MO	41	464	5	4,155	63	−108	25	844
	(22.5)	(667)	(3.7)	(2,299)	(12.4)	(292)	(8.5)	(261)
El Paso, TX	42	438	8	3,165	36	737	27	810
	(25.8)	(787)	(8.0)	(1,271)	(11.4)	(424)	(11.5)	(375)
Savannah, GA	43	428	52	787	51	294	23	899
	(20.8)	(600)	(16.6)	(1,477)	(9.8)	(288)	(6.8)	(249)
Richmond, VA	44	398	110	1,366	40	548	35	604
	(20.4)	(575)	(9.9)	(1,022)	(8.8)	(288)	(8.4)	(213)
Topeka, KS	45	383	64	478	41	532	44	450
	(14.4)	(392)	(12.1)	(1,508)	(6.2)	(200)	(7.3)	(164)
Baton Rouge, LA	46	376	93	−676	39	562	99	−756
	(18.9)	(540)	(12.2)	(1,176)	(8.1)	(268)	(8.1)	(237)
Albuquerque, NM	47	365	20	2,166	53	183	79	−290
	(23.4)	(673)	(11.9)	(1,197)	(14.4)	(381)	(15.5)	(351)
Memphis, TN	48	325	47	1,014	50	316	71	−156
	(20.2)	(576)	(14.8)	(945)	(10.0)	(296)	(9.8)	(225)
Orlando, FL	49	308	67	420	47	344	57	139
	(20.0)	(545)	(15.3)	(1,021)	(9.6)	(286)	(11.7)	(264)
Fort Wayne, IN	50	303	76	199	49	331	73	−216
	(16.1)	(437)	(12.3)	(1,073)	(7.8)	(215)	(7.7)	(164)
Evansville, IN	51	286	49	891	46	359	47	348
	(16.5)	(455)	(14.0)	(1,709)	(8.4)	(239)	(7.6)	(161)
Pittsburgh, PA	52	275	90	−647	38	589	85	−474
	(27.4)	(846)	(18.2)	(976)	(10.7)	(351)	(13.7)	(330)
Fayetteville, NC	53	274	37	1,357	37	675	55	206
	(19.8)	(543)	(14.2)	(1,727)	(7.5)	(264)	(6.7)	(147)
Mobile, AL	54	250	15	2,346	62	−91	51	299
	(24.7)	(712)	(11.3)	(1,345)	(14.8)	(363)	(13.1)	(314)
Wichita, KS	55	246	54	785	72	−286	74	−225
	(17.7)	(474)	(12.8)	(996)	(11.4)	(250)	(10.9)	(232)
Lynchburg, VA	56	241	30	1,548	69	−211	65	−30
	(16.3)	(439)	(10.6)	(1,505)	(10.5)	(234)	(8.8)	(201)
Worcester, MA	57	216	14	2,599	77	−379	21	969
	(21.6)	(599)	(8.4)	(1,386)	(14.2)	(315)	(7.6)	(278)

TABLE 3 (*Continued*)

City	Random Effects		Random Effects, Group Effects Included		OLS: All Fiscal Variables		OLS: No Taxes/No Union	
	Ranking (1)	Index Value (2)	Ranking (3)	Index Value (4)	Ranking (5)	Index Value (6)	Ranking (7)	Index Value (8)
Austin, TX	58	180	33	1,415	60	−24	41	479
	(23.7)	(666)	(15.6)	(1,124)	(14.2)	(357)	(12.7)	(321)
Lawton, OK	59	178	57	750	59	−20	49	308
	(21.0)	(578)	(22.5)	(2,940)	(12.2)	(308)	(12.7)	(290)
San Antonio, TX	60	110	9	3,069	56	173	45	444
	(25.7)	(740)	(7.7)	(1,025)	(14.1)	(389)	(15.0)	(372)
Waterbury, CT	61	107	73	311	107	−995	104	−914
	(24.1)	(684)	(20.9)	(1,868)	(11.3)	(353)	(8.1)	(303)
Springfield, OH	62	101	27	1,688	66	−184	101	−832
	(14.1)	(363)	(9.0)	(1,484)	(8.1)	(192)	(3.1)	(132)
Jackson, MS	63	18	40	1,237	61	−79	43	477
	(18.7)	(504)	(12.8)	(1,349)	(10.9)	(267)	(8.0)	(192)
Chattanooga, TN	64	−41	66	430	68	−202	89	−540
	(18.9)	(496)	(13.8)	(1,086)	(11.5)	(262)	(10.1)	(255)
St. Joseph, MO	65	−53	12	2,735	76	−374	38	523
	(17.9)	(479)	(7.3)	(1,985)	(10.5)	(237)	(8.1)	(176)
Pueblo, CO	66	−89	96	−861	52	185	39	513
	(21.0)	(564)	(13.1)	(1,935)	(11.3)	(303)	(11.6)	(279)
Manchester, NH	67	−100	53	786	64	−135	61	45
	(26.5)	(765)	(20.6)	(1,758)	(17.2)	(418)	(16.7)	(375)
Terre Haute, IN	68	−112	94	−677	80	−444	88	−491
	(15.4)	(404)	(9.9)	(1,659)	(8.1)	(187)	(6.4)	(176)
Bakersfield, CA	69	−120	112	−1,546	48	341	33	654
	(27.6)	(807)	(13.4)	(1,522)	(11.0)	(321)	(11.3)	(300)

continued over

Macon, GA	70	−140	65	463	86	−562	52	259
	(16.9)	(453)	(14.9)	(1,954)	(11.1)	(236)	(6.3)	(156)
Charleston, WV	71	−158	36	1,370	55	177	83	−466
	(23.5)	(647)	(16.1)	(1,598)	(11.7)	(314)	(10.8)	(248)
Decatur, IL	72	−161	107	−1,161	90	−635	72	−207
	(18.4)	(495)	(9.7)	(1,572)	(10.3)	(244)	(9.7)	(228)
Colorado Springs, CO	73	−165	70	384	65	−147	93	−605
	(22.0)	(598)	(16.7)	(1,479)	(13.7)	(329)	(11.9)	(305)
Lincoln, NE	74	−185	25	1,768	91	−638	95	−674
	(18.1)	(470)	(10.3)	(1,327)	(9.7)	(212)	(7.9)	(203)
Altoona, PA	75	−187	34	1,396	105	−963	97	−700
	(27.7)	(820)	(19.4)	(1,896)	(13.5)	(413)	(12.6)	(370)
Huntsville, AL	76	−199	26	1,732	104	−926	81	−411
	(19.1)	(519)	(11.0)	(1,271)	(9.5)	(271)	(9.6)	(231)
Anderson, IN	77	−234	124	−2,951	71	−268	56	170
	(18.2)	(458)	(3.5)	(1,585)	(11.3)	(247)	(11.5)	(238)
Oklahoma City, OK	78	−257	55	769	78	−384	70	−98
	(24.4)	(694)	(18.2)	(1,032)	(15.3)	(354)	(15.0)	(341)
Billings, MT	79	−285	114	−1,649	113	−1,375	109	−1,361
	(26.7)	(786)	(12.9)	(2,137)	(9.3)	(400)	(7.7)	(378)
Syracuse, NY	80	−301	44	1,062	67	−188	87	−478
	(24.8)	(707)	(18.1)	(1,168)	(14.2)	(337)	(11.3)	(272)
Columbus, GA	81	−305	50	808	111	−1,135	54	223
	(22.4)	(634)	(18.1)	(1,974)	(9.3)	(325)	(10.0)	(238)
Buffalo, NY	82	−314	102	−901	73	−287	59	86
	(27.1)	(806)	(16.3)	(1,055)	(15.7)	(368)	(13.7)	(309)
Canton, OH	83	−340	74	274	74	−296	84	−472
	(14.8)	(375)	(11.2)	(1,090)	(8.9)	(195)	(8.4)	(178)
Omaha, NE	84	−379	104	−1,051	94	−700	77	−283
	(12.8)	(337)	(6.7)	(994)	(7.4)	(173)	(7.1)	(150)
Springfield, IL	85	−409	58	747	87	−566	90	−551
	(14.0)	(362)	(12.1)	(1,703)	(8.1)	(162)	(7.1)	(158)
Miami, FL	86	−445	31	1,439	45	411	69	−86
	(29.1)	(925)	(20.7)	(1,114)	(14.5)	(435)	(17.8)	(410)

TABLE 3 (*Continued*)

City	Random Effects		Random Effects, Group Effects Included		OLS: All Fiscal Variables		OLS: No Taxes/No Union	
	Ranking (1)	Index Value (2)	Ranking (3)	Index Value (4)	Ranking (5)	Index Value (6)	Ranking (7)	Index Value (8)
South Bend, IN	87	-468	105	-1,079	92	-649	107	-1,116
	(15.6)	(430)	(8.8)	(1,357)	(9.5)	(222)	(3.2)	(187)
Salem, OR	88	-488	123	-2,898	110	-1,070	75	-260
	(21.1)	(604)	(4.6)	(1,704)	(8.6)	(288)	(11.3)	(257)
Tulsa, OK	89	-496	80	-31	85	-548	100	-792
	(13.7)	(377)	(10.1)	(807)	(8.9)	(182)	(5.4)	(151)
Portland, ME	90	-498	28	1,659	88	-597	62	15
	(26.5)	(812)	(17.6)	(1,568)	(17.0)	(419)	(16.4)	(381)
Akron,.OH	91	-520	77	173	75	-302	106	-1,036
	(15.8)	(438)	(12.2)	(944)	(9.2)	(205)	(3.7)	(164)
Harrisburg, PA	92	-537	111	-1,408	102	-904	53	253
	(24.3)	(724)	(12.2)	(1,194)	(13.9)	(388)	(15.4)	(352)
Cincinnati, OH	93	-544	56	759	58	68	82	-426
	(16.8)	(484)	(13.2)	(798)	(9.1)	(243)	(9.4)	(220)
Cedar Rapids, IA	94	-544	71	363	99	-823	94	-659
	(18.1)	(529)	(14.9)	(1,460)	(9.4)	(258)	(8.8)	(248)
Indianapolis, IN	95	-600	118	-2,147	106	-983	105	-935
	(16.3)	(477)	(5.1)	(715)	(7.6)	(242)	(4.3)	(188)
Reno, NV	96	-639	119	-2,186	97	-816	48	-315
	(29.1)	(977)	(11.7)	(1,551)	(19.2)	(542)	(17.0)	(412)
Sioux City, IA	97	-675	92	-653	93	-656	91	-582
	(17.9)	(553)	(14.1)	(2,041)	(10.8)	(270)	(9.7)	(262)
Dayton, OH	98	-699	89	-536	81	-484	102	-863
	(18.2)	(532)	(12.5)	(958)	(11.7)	(240)	(6.8)	(208)
Des Moines, IA	99	-700	81	-50	101	-884	98	-707
	(14.0)	(440)	(11.5)	(1,082)	(7.0)	(2,148)	(6.7)	(200)

continued over

Trenton, NJ	100	−715	68	415	120	−1,698	67	−68
	(21.7)	(679)	(18.4)	(1,337)	(4.8)	(3,089)	(12.3)	(266)
Philadelphia, PA	101	−736	117	−1,991	109	−1,043	108	−1,343
	(20.7)	(813)	(8.1)	(869)	(7.3)	(269)	(3.7)	(248)
Louisville, KY	102	−794	120	−2,248	79	−433	76	−264
	(13.3)	(429)	(4.4)	(851)	(9.5)	(205)	(8.0)	(181)
Columbus, OH	103	−811	101	−899	83	−514	115	−1,756
	(11.6)	(384)	(7.4)	(722)	(8.4)	(185)	(2.3)	(154)
Seattle, WA	104	−816	82	−58	70	−248	96	−690
	(25.1)	(848)	(20.9)	(969)	(14.9)	(346)	(11.0)	(312)
Rochester, NY	105	−842	122	−2,607	82	−495	80	−298
	(20.8)	(671)	(5.9)	(1,018)	(13.2)	(299)	(11.6)	(262)
Tacoma, WA	106	−846	97	−862	89	−599	66	−50
	(21.7)	(723)	(15.1)	(1,256)	(15.0)	(347)	(13.6)	(289)
Mansfield, OH	107	−965	48	934	103	−920	126	−2,443
	(20.4)	(710)	(19.1)	(1,861)	(12.0)	(349)	(2.2)	(312)
Boise, ID	108	−972	2	5,117	98	−822	92	−596
	(13.6)	(486)	(1.5)	(1,553)	(9.8)	(265)	(8.1)	(207)
Toledo, OH	109	−1,013	91	−647	95	−761	121	−1,974
	(12.9)	(479)	(10.5)	(847)	(9.0)	(237)	(2.6)	(168)
Boston, MA	110	−1,067	63	512	96	−764	103	−908
	(18.3)	(703)	(17.8)	(902)	(12.4)	(309)	(8.8)	(299)
Minneapolis, MN	111	−1,147	43	1,082	84	−520	122	−1,987
	(20.8)	(816)	(19.8)	(917)	(14.2)	(327)	(3.9)	(241)
Chicago, IL	112	−1,209	109	−1,337	112	−1,334	111	−1,486
	(17.3)	(1,031)	(12.2)	(1,061)	(3.5)	(249)	(2.8)	(240)
Tuscaloosa, AL	113	−1,259	99	−879	123	−1,981	86	−475
	(13.7)	(584)	(13.8)	(2,004)	(3.7)	(299)	(9.8)	(235)
Muncie, IN	114	−1,373	126	−3,290	124	−2,021	124	−2,122
	(12.9)	(595)	(3.7)	(2,113)	(3.0)	(306)	(3.5)	(281)
Ann Arbor, MI	115	−1,450	86	−376	126	−2,215	63	7
	(14.9)	(697)	(17.6)	(1,497)	(3.0)	(343)	(12.7)	(270)
Cleveland, OH	116	−1,492	108	−1,218	100	−851	116	−1,833
	(10.9)	(560)	(9.6)	(748)	(9.8)	(267)	(3.8)	(223)
Rockford, IL	117	−1,532	88	−431	122	−1,955	117	−1,845
	(7.0)	(399)	(10.0)	(1,200)	(2.8)	(211)	(3.2)	(176)

TABLE 3 (*Continued*)

City	Random Effects		Random Effects, Group Effects Included		OLS: All Fiscal Variables		OLS: No Taxes/No Union	
	Ranking (1)	Index Value (2)	Ranking (3)	Index Value (4)	Ranking (5)	Index Value (6)	Ranking (7)	Index Value (8)
Peoria, IL	118	−1,634	125	−3,052	121	−1,937	110	−1,396
	(6.5)	(411)	(2.6)	(1,150)	(2.4)	(203)	(2.2)	(175)
Spokane, WA	119	−1,815	84	−273	116	−1,544	114	−1,623
	(11.6)	(728)	(18.0)	(1,324)	(6.0)	(343)	(4.2)	(255)
Portland, OR	120	−1,874	69	388	119	−1,640	119	−1,890
	(8.7)	(607)	(16.3)	(807)	(3.9)	(264)	(3.9)	(249)
Kansas City, MO	121	−1,900	121	−2,523	118	−1,634	113	−1,600
	(5.4)	(441)	(3.7)	(682)	(3.4)	(230)	(3.1)	(203)
Atlanta, GA	122	−1,916	116	−1,980	114	−1,489	120	−1,939
	(9.7)	(671)	(8.1)	(841)	(5.5)	(285)	(4.2)	(251)
Hartford, CT	123	−1,931	79	0	117	−1,631	129	−2,839
	(13.9)	(871)	(22.4)	(1,377)	(7.5)	(434)	(1.5)	(347)
Baltimore, MD	124	−1,934	115	−1,843	115	−1,530	112	−1,524
	(9.4)	(662)	(8.4)	(806)	(5.1)	(274)	(3.8)	(223)
Newark, NJ	125	−2,477	100	−884	108	−1,002	125	−2,176
	(9.8)	(914)	(26.7)	(1,798)	(14.0)	(427)	(4.9)	(395)
Las Vegas, NV	126	−2,832	128	−4,198	125	−2,125	128	−2,637
	(9.0)	(1,027)	(3.4)	(1,403)	(6.1)	(553)	(4.2)	(523)
Grand Rapids, MI	127	−2,947	98	−865	127	−3,908	123	−1,991
	(2.6)	(589)	(12.3)	(1,009)	(.7)	(306)	(3.6)	(245)
Saginaw, MI	128	−3,668	129	−5,273	128	−3,939	118	−1,881
	(1.4)	(646)	(.6)	(1,423)	(.7)	(315)	(3.4)	(225)
Detroit, MI	129	−4,153	130	−5,273	129	−4,188	127	−2,544
	(1.1)	(751)	(.6)	(1,423)	(.6)	(267)	(1.5)	(288)
Flint, MI	130	−4,241	127	−3,537	130	−4,893	130	−2,917
	(1.2)	(786)	(3.5)	(1,251)	(.2)	(407)	(1.1)	(331)

Note.—The numbers in parentheses in cols. 1, 3, 5, and 7 are estimated standard errors of the rankings. The standard errors for the rankings were calculated using a sample of 100,000 simulated rankings. Housing and wage coefficient vectors were drawn from the relevant normal distributions implied by the appropriate regression analysis. Full implicit prices and associated quality-of-life rankings were calculated for each set of simulated coefficient vectors. The reported standard error for a city ranking is the standard deviation in the sample of the given city's simulated rankings. The numbers in parentheses in cols. 2, 4, 6, and 8 are estimated standard errors of the index values. They are calculated via the delta method.

continued over

in (say) the housing market and underestimated in (say) the labor market. If high-quality workers demand high-quality housing, then we would expect any systematic mismeasurement of quality to produce a positive error correlation. In contrast, if the group effects solely reflect an omitted amenity valued only by the workers, a negative error correlation across equations would be expected. The reason is that an omitted city trait that is beneficial to workers but not firms implies a negative wage residual and a positive land rent residual. However, if firms also value this trait, they might bid wages up, with the resulting error correlation across equations being of indeterminate sign. We simply cannot be certain that the impact from the worker side of the model is dominant, particularly for any omitted fiscal traits.[10] Consequently, the sign of the correlation does not reliably identify the source of the group effects without specific assumptions about the underlying model structure.[11]

Because we cannot be sure about the origin of the group effects, columns 3 and 4 of table 3 present the index values and rankings when the group error terms are included. There still is a fairly strong positive correlation between the rank orderings of the indexes with and without the group effects (ρ = .63). However, the rankings of many cities are materially affected by the inclusion of the group effect. The mean absolute change in rankings is 26.8 and the standard deviation of that change is 20.7. Norwalk, Connecticut, drops from being the top-ranked city to being number 23. Lake Charles, Louisiana, suffers the biggest decline, with its ranking falling from 22 to 113. Boise, Idaho, exhibits the biggest rise, increasing in rank from 108 to 2. For the cities exhibiting substantial decreases (increases) in ranks, it typically is the case that observed wages are much higher (lower) than predicted by the right-hand-side variables.[12]

The last four columns of table 3 present quality-of-life index values and rankings based on two OLS specifications, one with and the other without the fiscal/union variables. They provide a base for comparison with previous work that has not controlled for the tax side of local finance or estimated random effects specifications. The results indicate that the rankings are materially influenced not only by inclu-

[10] For example, we do not control for transportation service quality because such measures simply are not widely available. It is easy for us to imagine both the marginal worker and firm highly valuing that attribute.

[11] We do find slight positive correlations across the error terms, although neither is significantly different from zero at standard confidence levels. When the group error terms are weighted by the number of housing observations in the relevant city, ρ = .14. When the number of wage observations serves as the weight, ρ = .10.

[12] We generally have a reasonable number (well into double figures) of individual worker wage observations, making it unlikely that the large group effects found for some cities are the result of a few idiosyncratic worker observations.

sion of the tax and public-sector union variables but also by the econometric method used to estimate the prices. With the full set of amenity and fiscal variables included, the mean absolute change in rankings based on the random effects estimation (excluding group effects, cols. 1–2) versus the OLS-based results (cols. 5–6) is 10.2 with an associated standard deviation of 9.56. The mean absolute dollar change in index value is $391 with a standard deviation of $320.

The impact of including the tax and union vector can be seen by comparing the rankings based on the two OLS specifications (cols. 5–6 vs. cols. 7–8). The mean absolute change in rankings when these variables are added is 16.2 with a 15.2 standard deviation. The mean absolute dollar change in these index values is $603 with a standard deviation of $527.[13]

It is important to note that the influence of the fiscal variables does not appear to be the result of spurious correlation with broader regional forces. For example, when three region dummies are included in the specifications, the joint significance of the fiscal variables continues to hold at very high confidence levels (the same is true for the amenities). When group effects are controlled for, the only significant region effects occur for the West, where housing expenditures are substantially higher (by about 63 percent on average) and wages are slightly higher (by about 8 percent on average). Counting the regional effects as amenities does not materially change the relative aggregate effects of the amenity versus fiscal variables (cols. 1–2, table 2) or the rankings themselves (col. 2, table 3). In the random effects specification, the correlation between the sets of rankings with and without the region dummies included in the underlying hedonics is .97.

It is also noteworthy that our findings are robust with respect to some nonlinear specifications. We estimated a random effects specification in which those city traits with the highest coefficients of variation were entered in quadratic form. Trait prices changed only slightly over the range of city trait amounts found in the data, and rankings and index values were essentially unaltered. With only 130 cities, we opted to include only the linear terms. We also performed a Box-Cox analysis of the specification underlying the results in columns 5–6 of table 3. In addition, we estimated the housing hedonic using *only* the information on the interval of house values to which an observation belonged. While that analysis did reject the log speci-

[13] It should be noted that there is still a moderately strong positive correlation among the sets of rankings. The rankings based on random effects with group effects included (ranking 2 in cols. 3–4 of table 3) are the least strongly correlated with the other sets of rankings. Pairwise correlation coefficients between ranking 2 and the others range from .54 to .63. Pairwise correlations among the other three sets of rankings range from .85 to .94.

fication for both hedonics, this estimation procedure yielded results virtually identical to the OLS-based findings. The simple correlation between the Box-Cox and OLS rankings is .98. The mean absolute change in rankings was about 0.5 ranks. Estimating a random effects model in a nonlinear environment involves an order of magnitude increase in computing difficulty and cost, and our experimentation with this sample clearly shows modeling group effects to be far more important than incorporating nonlinearities.

While the pattern of results appears to be robust with respect to specification and functional form, we close with two important notes of caution about the general reliability of quality-of-life rankings. The reliability issue is starkly illustrated by the large standard errors about the quality-of-life rankings based on the random effects estimates. They are significantly higher than those calculated using the OLS estimates. This is not surprising since Moulton (1986, 1987) has shown that, when group effects exist in the data, the standard errors for the OLS coefficient estimates for variables having no within-group variation are downward biased. In our data, the random effects estimation typically results in a doubling in the standard error of a city's quality-of-life ranking. The average standard error of the rankings based on random effects (cols. 1–2 of table 3) is 16.9 versus an average of 8.6 for the rankings based on OLS (cols. 5–6 of table 3). At standard confidence levels, it becomes difficult to differentiate among many cities unless the comparison is between a very highly rated city and a very lowly rated city (e.g., top 20 vs. bottom 20).[14] The sharp drop in the precision of the full price estimates and the accompanying quality-of-life rankings points out the need for better data in order to reduce the magnitudes of the city-specific error components and to more precisely estimate a city's quality of life.

An added reliability concern arises from the fact that an arbitrary assumption typically is made about who the marginal entrant is. We assumed that the marginal entrant was the household with the sample average number of wage earners (1.5) and spending on housing per year ($4,524). The first four columns of table 4 illustrate how the top- and bottom-ranked cities change as the number of wage earners changes in the assumed marginal entrant household. (Of course, a similar point could be illustrated by varying the amount of housing expenditures.) Note that the rankings and quality-of-life index values do not change because the underlying hedonic coefficients change. Those coefficients are unaltered. However, the trait prices do change

[14] We should emphasize, however, that the random effects estimates of the model do make some progress toward differentiating among cities in our sample. If rankings were randomly assigned to each city, then the implied standard error for a city's rank would be 37.5. This is quite a bit larger than the average standard error of 16.9 produced from the random effects specification.

TABLE 4

RANKINGS FOR HOUSEHOLDS WITH DIFFERENT NUMBERS OF WAGE EARNERS

Rank	Households with 1.5 Earners (1)	Households with 0 Earners (2)	Households with 1 Earner (3)	Households with 2 Earners (4)	Net Subsidy for Retired Household with 0 Earners (5)
1	Norwalk, CT ($3,986)	San Francisco, CA ($4,232)	Norwalk, CT ($3,408)	Norwalk, CT ($4,564)	Gainesville, FL ($3,240)
2	Pensacola, FL (2,963)	San Diego, CA (4,075)	San Diego, CA (3,075)	Pensacola, FL (4,040)	Pensacola, FL (3,230)
3	Gainesville, FL (2,819)	Los Angeles, CA (3,709)	San Francisco, CA (2,355)	Gainesville, FL (3,899)	Columbia, SC (3,163)
4	San Diego, CA (2,574)	San Jose, CA (2,997)	Santa Rosa, CA (2,156)	Columbia, SC (3,513)	Tyler, TX (2,339)
5	Stamford, CT (2,497)	Santa Rosa, CA (2,557)	Stamford, CT (1,993)	Stamford, CT (3,001)	Lake Charles, LA (2,282)
6	Columbia, SC (2,459)	Norwalk, CT (2,253)	San Jose, CA (1,934)	Tucson, AZ (2,445)	New Bedford, MA (2,249)
7	Santa Rosa, CA (1,955)	Chicago, IL (1,762)	Pensacola, FL (1,886)	Shreveport, LA (2,300)	Amarillo, TX (1,950)
8	Bridgeport, CT (1,944)	Sacramento, CA (1,741)	Gainesville, FL (1,739)	Lancaster, PA (2,266)	Tucson, AZ (1,869)
⋮	⋮	⋮	⋮	⋮	⋮
123	Hartford, CT (−1,931)	Oklahoma City, OK (−1,070)	Tuscaloosa, AL (−1,448)	Portland, OR (−2,590)	Saginaw, MI (−2,593)
124	Baltimore, MD (−1,934)	Saginaw, MI (−1,075)	Atlanta, GA (−1,452)	Hartford, CT (−2,711)	Las Vegas, NV (−2,644)
125	Newark, NJ (−2,477)	Tyler, TX (−1,164)	Baltimore, MD (−1,503)	Grand Rapids, MI (−3,659)	San Francisco, CA (−2,816)
126	Las Vegas, NV (−2,832)	Louisville, KY (−1,181)	Las Vegas, NV (−1,951)	Las Vegas, NV (−3,714)	Chicago, IL (−2,971)
127	Grand Rapids, MI (−2,947)	Birmingham, AL (−1,221)	Grand Rapids, MI (−2,235)	Newark, NJ (−3,763)	Los Angeles, CA (−3,104)
128	Saginaw, MI (−3,668)	Mobile, AL (−1,399)	Saginaw, MI (−2,804)	Saginaw, MI (−4,532)	Detroit, MI (−3,320)
129	Detroit, MI (−4,153)	Altoona, PA (−1,478)	Flint, MI (−2,929)	Detroit, MI (−5,259)	Newark, NJ (−3,858)
130	Flint, MI (−4,241)	Tuscaloosa, AL (−1,826)	Detroit, MI (−3,406)	Flint, MI (−5,554)	Flint, MI (−3,939)

NOTE.—The numbers in parentheses in cols. 1–4 are quality-of-life index numbers assuming the marginal household is that listed at the top of the column. The net subsidy number in parentheses in col. 5 reflects the difference between the marginal valuation of a city's amenity, fiscal, and public union traits and the actual prices faced by a retired household with no wage earners. The marginal valuation calculation assumes identical preferences across household types and assumes that the 1.5-earner family is the true marginal entrant.

because they are based on some assumed degree of exposure to capitalization in the land and labor markets. The implicit assumption made here and in other quality-of-life studies is that the assumed wages and rents reflect the preferred degree of exposure based on the marginal entrant's utility function.

The rankings for households with one, one and a half, and two wage earners are highly correlated ($\rho > .87$ in all pairwise comparisons) as suggested by the fact that their top- and bottom-ranked cities tend to have substantial overlap. However, the rankings for the zero-earner household in column 2 are not nearly as strongly correlated with the other sets of rankings. The smallest correlation of $-.02$ occurs between the rankings for the zero-earner household and the two-earner household. The highest correlation of .38 is achieved with the rankings of the one-earner household.

Finally, it is worth noting that, even with identical preferences among households, the equilibrium prices typically will not make all households indifferent about location. This is a direct consequence of the observed differential capitalization of amenity and fiscal traits in the land and labor markets. As an example, assume that we have correctly identified the 1.5-earner household as the marginal entrant to all cities. In this case, our quality-of-life index values reported in table 3 would correctly measure the marginal valuations for all households. At these prices, a 1.5-earner household would be indifferent across cities. However, a retired-couple household would be inframarginal because the prices it faces are radically different because of its lack of exposure to labor market capitalization. Column 5 of table 4 lists the cities that provide the largest and smallest implied net subsidies to a retired-couple household. The net subsidy is defined to be the difference between the 1.5-earner household's marginal valuation of the city's amenity, fiscal, and public union package and the price the retired-couple household actually has to pay to consume that package. The highest-subsidy cities tend to be southern and western cities with high-value weather amenities whose full prices tend to contain large wage components (see table 1). The lowest-subsidy cities are a more diverse lot, including some northern cities as well as a few western cities with very high land values.[15]

[15] There is some evidence that retired-worker households are sorting into the highest net subsidy cities. Using the 1980 census tapes, we calculated for each city the ratio of retired residents to the sum of full-time labor market participants plus retired residents. Retired residents were defined to be people aged 50 or older who do not work and are not looking for work. We then computed the correlation between this ratio and the net subsidy figures listed in col. 5 of table 4. When the 130 observations are unweighted, $\rho = .15$ (the probability value is .08 for the null of $\rho = 0$). When the city observations are weighted by the total number of full-time labor market participants plus retired residents, the correlation rises to .35 (the probability value is .0001 for the null of $\rho = 0$).

Appendix

TABLE A1

VARIABLE DESCRIPTION AND SUMMARY STATISTICS

Variable	Description	Source	Mean*
Precipitation	Annual inches (multiyear average)	U.S. Dept. Commerce (1983)	36.17 (13.38)
Cooling degree days	Thousands per year (multiyear average)	U.S. Bur. Census (1985)	1.31 (.84)
Heating degree days	Thousands per year (multiyear average)	U.S. Bur. Census (1985)	4.49 (1.90)
Relative humidity	Percentage (multiyear average)	U.S. Dept. Commerce (1983)	55.58 (8.74)
Sunshine	Percentage possible (multiyear average)	U.S. Dept. Commerce (1983)	61.02 (8.31)
Wind speed	Miles per hour (multiyear average)	U.S. Dept. Commerce (1983)	9.36 (1.65)
Particulate matter	Micrograms per cubic meter (1979 data)	U.S. EPA (1980)	73.30 (21.71)
Coast	Dichotomous: 1 if on border of ocean, Great Lake, or Gulf of Mexico; 0 otherwise	Created by authors	.20 (.41)
Nonland cost of living	Logged index number†	U.S. Dept. Labor (1977)	.98 (.02)
SMSA population	Millions of persons (1979 data)	U.S. Bur. Census (1985)	.744 (1.122)
Percentage working in other SMSA	Percentage; variable entered as spline; cities with less than 16% of residents working in another SMSA (one standard deviation above sample mean) have a value of 0; all others are coded as their actual percentages minus .16 (16%)	U.S. Bur. Census (1983)	.013 (.042)
Violent crime rate	Per 100 people	U.S. Bur. Census (1985)	.96 (.64)

continued over

Student/teacher ratio	Ratio of students to full-time-equivalent instructional employees[‡]	*Census of Governments* (1982, vols. 2, 3)	14.07 (2.46)
Fire rating	Insurance company rating of fire department quality (1 = best; 10 = worst)	Internat. City Management Assoc. (1976)	3.07 (.90)
Hospital beds	Public beds per 1,000 people in the city	U.S. Bur. Census (1985)	12.73 (7.59)
Effective property tax rate	Nominal rate times assessment/sales ratio (1979 numbers)[§]	Assessment/sales and assessed base: *Census of Governments* (1982, vol. 2); city and special district property tax revenues: U.S. Bur. Census (1978–79; 1979)	1.31 (.79)
State and local income tax rate	State: average rate in 1979 after deductibility for person with $20,000 adjusted gross income	Feenberg and Rosen (1986, table 6.6)	3.61 (2.71)
	Local: flat rate typically; if not, highest rate applicable used	Tax Foundation (1978)	
State corporate income tax rate	Highest rate applicable as of 7/1/80 (for most states, the highest bracket began at a fairly low profit level)	Advisory Comm. Intergovernmental Relations (1981, table 89)	6.32 (3.05)
Percentage public union organized	Percentage of local public workers in the central city who are organized[‖]	U.S. Bur. Census (1979)[#]	.44 (.21)
Housing expenditures	Annual housing expenditures; converted using 7.85% discount rate	U.S. Bur. Census (1983)	$4,542 (3,904)
Wages	Weekly wages	U.S. Bur. Census (1983)	$299 (208)

* The summary statistics for all city-specific variables are unweighted (by housing or worker observations) means and standard deviations (in parentheses) over the 130 cities in the sample.

† In adjusting the cost-of-living data, we deleted the shelter component of the index except for costs associated with maintenance and furnishings. Property taxes and mortgage payments were also deleted. Because of the nature of the BLS data, we could not avoid deleting some costs such as utilities that are associated with normal upkeep. The remaining upkeep costs amount to 25 percent of the overall shelter budget on average. Social security and all income taxes were also deleted. Intercity variation in federal tax burdens reflects differences in income more than in the intrinsic cost of living. State and local taxes are controlled for separately except for sales taxes, which are reflected in the cost-of-living index. (It was not possible to obtain local sales tax data for many cities in our sample. Further, it is difficult to compute an effective sales tax rate because the base for the tax appears to differ widely across cities.) Finally, the BLS reports direct metropolitan area budget data for only 38 of the cities in our sample. We imputed a cost-of-living index for the other cities. This was done by regressing the adjusted budget data on region dummies and SMSA population density, with the resulting coefficients used to impute the missing index values. The R^2 for the regression was .51. Those results are available on request. All standard errors reported in the tables have been adjusted to account for the imputation of the missing cost-of-living index data (see Pagan [1984] and Murphy and Topel [1985] for the procedure).

‡ The data employed pertain to 1982. Similar data for many of our cities are also available for 1977. There is a very strong positive correlation between ratios across the two years.

§ The nominal rate is calculated by dividing total property tax revenues by the assessed base. It is noteworthy that our property tax revenue includes funds raised by the city municipal government as well as special districts within city boundaries. The nominal rate is then multiplied by the city's median aggregate assessment/sales ratio to obtain the effective rate.

‖ As with the property tax revenue data, these percentages are based on municipal workers as well as employees of special districts.

\# The *Survey of Governments* also provides information on the percentage of workers in bargaining units. That variable is a ratio in which the numerator and denominator come from different surveys conducted by the Bureau of the Census. Various cities were found to have nonsensical coverage ratios far in excess of one when the bargaining unit data were examined. The organization numbers do not suffer from this defect.

V. Conclusions

Differences in the local fiscal climate generate compensating differentials across local land and labor markets just as we have long known amenities to do. Thus they should affect the local quality of life. This paper presents new estimates of the quality of life that highlight the importance of local fiscal conditions. Unlike standard locational amenities, the fiscal climate is under the control of local authorities. Thus the quality of life may be more malleable than we have previously thought. Finally, accounting for city group effects through a random effects estimation is found to have a similarly strong impact on the rankings and their associated standard errors. The presence of strong group effects begs the question of whether they should be included in the quality-of-life index. Because it is not apparent what the proper procedure to follow is, we suggest that rankings with and without the group effects be presented to give the reader some idea of potential problems from omitted variables.

References

Advisory Commission on Intergovernmental Relations. *Significant Features of Fiscal Federalism, 1979–80*. Washington: Advisory Comm. Intergovernmental Relations, 1981.

Berger, Mark C., and Blomquist, Glenn C. "Income, Opportunities, and the Quality of Life of Urban Residents." In *Urban Change and Poverty*, edited by Michael G. H. McGeary and Laurence E. Lynn, Jr. Washington: Nat. Acad. Press, 1988.

Blomquist, Glenn C.; Berger, Mark C.; and Hoehn, John P. "New Estimates of Quality of Life in Urban Areas." *A.E.R.* 78 (March 1988): 89–107.

Card, David, and Krueger, Alan. "Does School Quality Matter? Returns to Education and the Characteristics of Public Schools in the United States." Working Paper no. 265. Princeton, N.J.: Princeton Univ., Indus. Relations Sec., April 1990.

Dynarski, Mark. "The Scholastic Aptitude Test: Participation and Performance." *Econ. Educ. Rev.* 6, no. 3 (1987): 263–73.

Ehrenberg, Ronald G., and Schwarz, Joshua L. "Public-Sector Labor Markets." In *Handbook of Labor Economics*, vol. 2, edited by Orley C. Ashenfelter and Richard Layard. Amsterdam: North-Holland, 1986.

Feenberg, Daniel R., and Rosen, Harvey S. "State Personal Income and Sales Taxes, 1977–1983." In *Studies in State and Local Public Finance*, edited by Harvey S. Rosen. Chicago: Univ. Chicago Press (for NBER), 1986.

Freeman, Richard B. "Unionism Comes to the Public Sector." *J. Econ. Literature* 24 (March 1986): 41–86.

Gyourko, Joseph, and Tracy, Joseph. "The Importance of Local Fiscal Conditions in Analyzing Local Labor Markets." *J.P.E.* 97 (October 1989): 1208–31. (*a*)

———. "Local Public Sector Rent-seeking and Its Impact on Local Land Values." *Regional Sci. and Urban Econ.* 19 (August 1989): 493–516. (*b*)

Hanushek, Eric A. "The Economics of Schooling: Production and Efficiency in Public Schools." *J. Econ. Literature* 24 (September 1986): 1141–77.

Hanushek, Eric A., and Taylor, Lori. "What Can Be Done with Bad School Performance Data?" Working Paper no. 126. Rochester, N.Y.: Univ. Rochester, March 1988.

Hausman, Jerry A., and Taylor, William E. "Panel Data and Unobservable Individual Effects." *Econometrica* 49 (November 1981): 1377–98.

Hoehn, John P.; Berger, Mark C.; and Blomquist, Glenn C. "A Hedonic Model of Interregional Wages, Rents, and Amenity Values." *J. Regional Sci.* 27 (November 1987): 605–20.

Inman, Robert P. "Wages, Pensions, and Employment in the Local Public Sector." In *Public Sector Labor Markets,* edited by Peter Mieszkowski and George E. Peterson. Washington: Urban Inst. Press, 1981.

———. "Public Employee Pensions and the Local Labor Budget." *J. Public Econ.* 19 (October 1982): 49–71.

International City Management Association. *The Municipal Year Book 1976.* Washington: Internat. City Management Assoc., 1976.

Leven, Charles, and Stover, Mark Edward. "Methodological Issues in the Determination of the Quality of Life in Urban Areas." Working paper. St. Louis: Washington Univ., September 1989.

Linneman, Peter. "The Capitalization of Local Taxes: A Note on Specification." *J.P.E.* 86 (June 1978): 535–38.

Liu, Ben-Cheih. *Quality of Life Indicators in U.S. Metropolitan Areas: A Statistical Analysis.* New York: Praeger, 1976.

Moulton, Brent R. "Random Group Effects and the Precision of Regression Estimates." *J. Econometrics* 32 (August 1986): 385–97.

———. "Diagnostics for Group Effects in Regression Analysis." *J. Bus. and Econ. Statis.* 5 (April 1987): 275–82.

Murphy, Kevin M., and Topel, Robert H. "Estimation and Inference in Two-Step Econometric Models." *J. Bus. and Econ. Statis.* 3 (October 1985): 370–79.

Pagan, Adrian R. "Econometric Issues in the Analysis of Regressions with Generated Regressors." *Internat. Econ. Rev.* 25 (February 1984): 221–47.

Peiser, Richard B., and Smith, Lawrence B. "Homeownership Returns, Tenure Choice and Inflation." *American Real Estate and Urban Econ. Assoc. J.* 13 (Winter 1985): 343–60.

Roback, Jennifer. "The Value of Local Urban Amenities: Theory and Measurement." Ph.D. dissertation, Univ. Rochester, 1980.

———. "Wages, Rents, and the Quality of Life." *J.P.E.* 90 (December 1982): 1257–78.

———. "Wages, Rents, and Amenities: Differences among Workers and Regions." *Econ. Inquiry* 26 (January 1988): 23–41.

Rosen, Sherwin. "Wage-based Indexes of Urban Quality of Life." In *Current Issues in Urban Economics,* edited by Peter Mieszkowski and Mahlon Straszheim. Baltimore: Johns Hopkins Univ. Press, 1979.

Tax Foundation. *Facts and Figures on Government Finances.* New York: Tax Found., 1978.

U.S. Bureau of the Census. *City Government Finance.* Washington: Government Printing Office, 1978–79.

———. *Survey of Governments.* Data tapes. Washington: Government Printing Office, 1979.

———. *Census of Population and Housing, 1980: Public Use Microdata Samples Technical Documentation.* Washington: Government Printing Office, 1983.

———. *County and City Data Book 1983*. Washington: Government Printing Office, 1985.

U.S. Department of Commerce. *Comparative Climatic Data*. Asheville, N.C.: Nat. Climatic Data Center, 1983.

U.S. Department of Labor. *Three Standards of Living for an Urban Family of Four Persons*. Washington: Bur. Labor Statis., 1977.

U.S. Environmental Protection Agency. *1979 Air Quality Data—Annual Statistics*. Washington: Government Printing Office, 1980.

Voith, Richard P. "Capitalization of Local and Regional Attributes into Wages and Rents: Differences across Residential, Commercial, and Mixed Use Communities." *J. Regional Sci.* 31 (May 1991).

[28]

Journal of Economic Literature
Vol. XXXII (September 1994), pp. 1176–1196

Infrastructure Investment: A Review Essay

By EDWARD M. GRAMLICH
The University of Michigan

I thank David Aschauer, Sheldon Danziger, Michael Deich, John Fernald, Charles Hulten, Alicia Munnell, Laura Rubin, Joel Slemrod, John Tatom, and two anonymous referees for helpful comments on earlier drafts.

ECONOMISTS TRY not to be faddists but they often cannot help themselves. While work on a topic should mirror the prospective importance of the topic, that situation seems to occur with disappointing frequency. Instead, the usual pattern is that some reasonably important topic will be totally ignored for the longest time, then recognized, and then the subject of a flurry of work all out of proportion to its likely long run importance.

Nowhere has this speculative bubble of economic research been more clearly illustrated than with infrastructure investment. Macroeconomists have long felt that the stock of public capital is an important factor input in the production of total output. Macroeconomists have known that U.S. productivity growth slowed dramatically in about 1973 and macroeconomists should have known that United States investment in public capital has been down since the late 1960s. Yet analysis of the U.S. productivity slowdown completely ignored infrastructure investment for the first fifteen years of this slowdown, concentrating instead on energy prices, social regulation, the composition of the work force, research and development, different rates of obsolescence of the private capital stock, and any number of other matters. The public capital stock was hardly ever even mentioned as a potential factor in the productivity slowdown.

Aschauer changed all that. He wrote a series of papers (1989a, 1989b, 1989c) that put these two movements together econometrically—infrastructure investment turned down and aggregate productivity turned down slightly later, both in the United States and in some other developed countries. His work hit the magic button. Those who had worried about the productivity puzzle for fifteen years welcomed a new suspect. Those who were worried about low rates of U.S. national saving welcomed a new way to make their argument even more forcefully than with official figures on saving and investment, which do not count infrastructure investment as investment. Political liberals and liberal politicians saw a way to rescue government spending and projects from the assaults of Reaganism, and even a way to avoid otherwise necessary budget cuts—just call the spending infrastructure investment. All of these planets came into proper alignment, and Aschauer's papers were followed by an unusual amount of attention, from politicians and economists. Beefing up infrastructure investment became simultaneously the liberals' political war cry of the early 1990s and one of the favorite topics for econometric research, by now the subject of at least forty other econometric studies using different data and techniques.

Now that the bubble has happened and may even be beginning to burst, it is useful to stand back and ask what has been learned from this discussion. It almost goes without saying that infrastructure investment was always more important than was indicated by its lack of attention up to 1989; never as important as the intense attention since 1989 would suggest. But in the process of debate, many other matters have been clarified—about how to identify a shortage of infrastructure investment, about whether there ever was an overall shortage, and about whether this possible shortage has been a factor in the aggregate productivity decline. In this essay I review all these questions. But I then go beyond this review to ask what I think is a much more fundamental question, the question that economists should have been focusing on all along. In a word, is the country doing something wrong, and if so, what? That is, what, if any, policies regarding infrastructure investment should be changed?

I. *Basic Facts About Infrastructure Capital*

There are many possible definitions of infrastructure capital. The definition that makes the most sense from an economics standpoint consists of large capital intensive natural monopolies such as highways, other transportation facilities, water and sewer lines, and communications systems. Most of these systems are owned publicly in the United States, but some are owned privately. An alternative version that focuses on ownership includes just the tangible capital stock owned by the public sector. Broader versions include successively human capital investment and/or research and development capital. Most econometric studies of the infrastructure problem have used the narrow public sector ownership version of infrastructure capital as their independent variable. This is in large part because it is very hard to measure anything else. It is difficult to measure privately owned infrastructure capital, and even if good measures were available, it would be difficult to distinguish private infrastructure capital from other private capital. It is difficult to distinguish human investment spending for health and education from consumption spending, difficult to know whether to count all research and development expenditures as investment, and difficult to know how to depreciate either of these types of spending in defining capital stocks. Hence for these purposes I follow others in using a relatively narrow public sector ownership definition of the stock of infsmstructure capital.

Bureau of Economic Analysis (BEA) estimates of this nonresidential stock in 1991 in current dollars are shown in Table 1. The net stock of infrastructure capital, structures plus equipment, military and domestic, was \$2755.8 billion, of which \$2034.1 billion (\$2755.8 − \$514.1 − \$207.6) was for nonmilitary structures and \$2241.7 billion (\$2755.8 − \$514.1) was for nonmilitary structures and equipment. Most of this nonmilitary capital, 88 percent of the structures and 71 percent of the equipment, is owned by state

1178 Journal of Economic Literature, Vol. XXXII (September 1994)

TABLE 1
PUBLIC INFRASTRUCTURE CAPITAL, 1991
(BILLIONS OF CURRENT DOLLARS)

Item	Federal	State and Local	Total
Nonmilitary structures	242.8	1791.3	2034.1
Highways	16.9	708.0	724.9
Education	1.2	318.8	320.0
Other buildings	33.7	224.3	258.0
Hospitals	11.7	50.0	61.7
Water and Sewers	—	295.5	295.5
Conservation	143.4	35.9	179.3
Industrial	25.7	—	25.7
Other	10.1	158.7	168.9
Nonmilitary equipment	61.0	146.6	207.6
Military	514.1	—	514.1
Total	**817.9**	**1937.9**	**2755.8**

Source: BEA, in Tatom (1993).

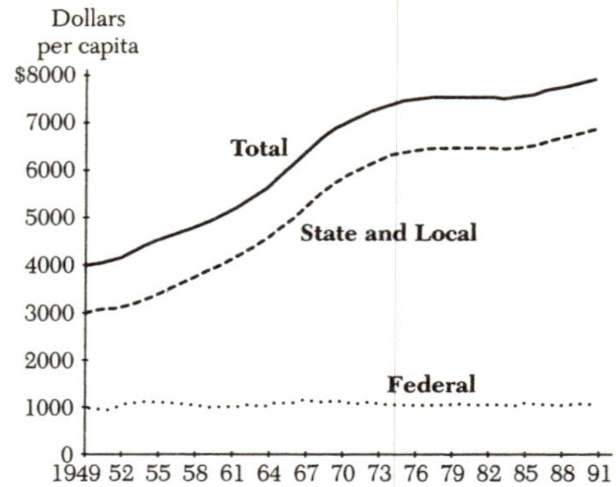

Figure 1. Real Nonmilitary Government Capital Stock per Person (1987 prices)

Source: Tatom (1993)

and local governments. While the infrastructure problem usually is described as a problem needing federal government attention, these figures indicate that, if infrastructure investment is a problem, it may be much more a state and local problem than a federal problem. This issue will be discussed in the policy section below.

The categories shown in Table 1 suggest why economists might have trouble analyzing infrastructure capital. The services of capital such as highways and schools are generally not sold on the market (though highway user fees could be used more extensively than now, and indeed user fees will be a big focus in the policy discussion below). While infrastructure capital is purchased on the market at the time of initial construction or installation, it is rarely sold, implying that economic rates of depreciation are almost never directly measured. Depreciation measures used in the construction of infrastructure stocks are physical measures based on service lives of different types of public structures. It would in principle be possible to measure rates of utilization of infrastructure capital—how many vehicles use roads, etc.—but in practice these measures are available only for some components of the public capital stock. And like other public goods, a large share of the benefits of infrastructure capital involve improved security, time saving, improved health, a cleaner environment, or improved outdoor recreation, magnitudes that are difficult to measure and that are not included in official measures of national output. Hence it will also be difficult to relate infrastructure investment to its goals, or changes in them. No wonder there are empirical controversies.

Measures of the stock of infrastructure capital are shown in Figures 1 and 2. Figure 1 shows total nonmilitary infrastructure capital ($2241.7 in Table 1) per capita, in 1987 dollars. The federal component of this capital, mainly for conservation structures and other buildings, has been close to $1000 per capita for more than four decades. Because this capital affects mainly the utility value of outdoor

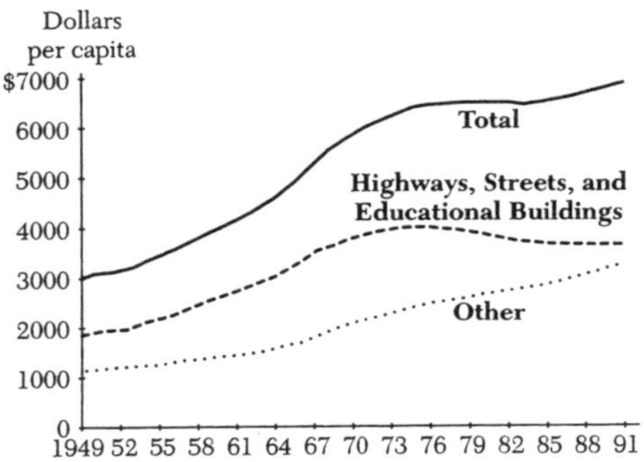

Figure 2. State & Local Net Capital Stock per Person (1987 prices)

Source: Tatom (1993)

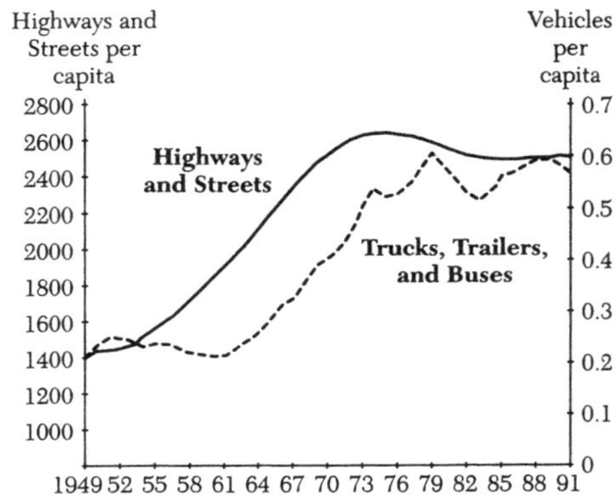

Figure 3. Business Trucks, Trailers, and Buses per Person and Highways and Streets per Person (1987 prices)

Source: Tatom (1993)

recreation, which is not counted in national output, and because it has been so constant for so long, not permitting serious time series inferences, it has generally been ignored in previous analyses of infrastructure investment and I will follow suit.

The stock of real state and local infrastructure capital per capita did grow steadily up to the early 1970s, but has leveled off since then. The implied investment numbers leading to this pattern for stocks have showed a decline in investment since the early 1970s, both absolutely and as a share of GDP (Clifford Winston and Barry Bosworth 1992; Hulten and Robert Schwab, forthcoming). Because 1973 was the watershed year beginning the overall national productivity decline, it is not surprising that simple time series analyses find a correlation between the stock of infrastructure capital and overall productivity. I will discuss a number of econometric issues in interpreting this correlation below; for now I continue just looking at the numbers to give the general patterns.

Figure 2 decomposes the total state and local capital stock into its biggest components: highways, educational buildings, and all other—water and sewer systems, hospitals, and miscellaneous other structures. The "other" component has not been constant but has grown at a relatively steady rate over four decades, so it would again be hard to make time series inferences about the causes of productivity movements on the basis of this series. The real action comes from the two biggest components of state and local infrastructure capital; highways, streets, and educational buildings, between them accounting for 53 percent of the state and local stock in 1991.

Figure 3 shows separately the highways and streets component of the state and local capital stock. This stock rose sharply from 1955 to 1975, the period when the U.S. interstate highway system was being built, and has since leveled off as interstate construction has slowed and the previously built highways have depreciated. An additional factor is the price of gasoline, which rose sharply in the mid 1970s and could have cut into the demand for highways, though over this time both the auto stock and the

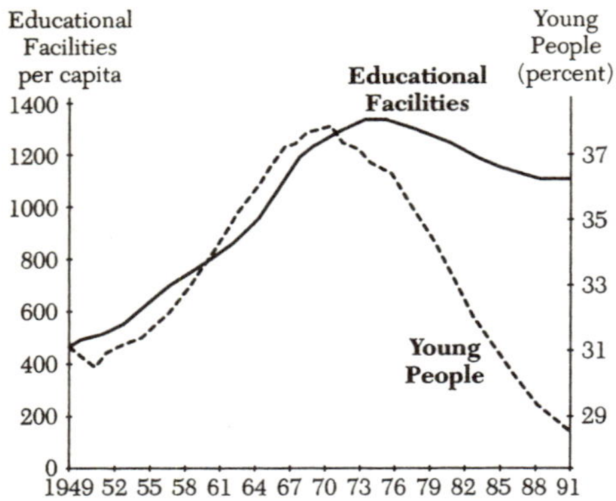

Figure 4. Stock of Educational Facilities per Person (1987 prices) and the Share of Young People in the Total Population

Source: Tatom (1993)

number of miles driven per capita has still increased. The price of gasoline apparently did cut into the number of trucks, trailers, and buses on the roads, also shown in the Figure. While one could get a shortage out of this pattern by extrapolating previous rates of investment spending, the rise in gasoline prices and the fall in numbers of heavy vehicles suggests that such an extrapolation may not be in order. It is certainly not obvious from these overall numbers that there is a highway shortage.

Figure 4 takes a similar look at public schools and other educational buildings, the second largest component of the state and local capital stock. Again the stock rose rapidly from 1950 to 1975, following by four years the rapid rise in the school and college age population also shown in the Figure. For the past two decades the school and college age population has plummeted, the share of pupils educated in public schools has been very stable, but the stock of public educational buildings has declined only gradually. If these numbers suggest one question, it is not whether there has been underinvestment in educational structures, but rather whether there is now too much educational capital stock—perhaps the value of educational structures should have declined even more rapidly as the publicly educated school and college age population declined. As for productivity studies, it is also clear that educational buildings should not be part of the independent variable, because while these structures may have a very important long run productivity impact, they certainly do not have a short run impact on aggregate supply. To the extent that the rise and fall of educational structures is responsible for a correlation with national productivity trends, the correlation is probably bogus.

These simple comparisons cannot resolve difficult policy questions by themselves, but they do suggest a number of pitfalls as one gets into more careful analysis. The net real stock of state and local structures per capita has risen sharply and then leveled off. But the rise was due in part to the building of the interstate highway system and in part to the building of educational structures to meet rapid increases in the school and college age population. Apart from these movements, the federal stock of infrastructure capital has been very stable and the other components of state and local capital have grown at stable rates. It is hard to find a great need for infrastructure capital based on these numbers alone, and one might be somewhat suspicious of correlations of these numbers and national productivity without some careful corrections.

II. *Is There a Shortage of Infrastructure Capital?*

I argue below that I think the most important question involving infrastructure investment is not whether there has been a shortage of infrastructure investment, but rather whether government policies regarding infrastructure investment should be changed. I get to the underlying policy issue below, but for now I lead up to it by focusing on the question that has been the focus of the vast majority of papers about infrastructure—whether there is or has been a shortage of infrastructure capital. There have been four ways of trying to determine if there is, or was, such a shortage:

- Engineering assessments of infrastructure needs.
- Political measures based on voting outcomes.
- Economic measures of rates of return.
- Econometric estimates of productivity impacts.

I review each in turn.

A. *Engineering Needs Assessments*

The first clarion calls regarding the infrastructure gap involved needs assessments (Associated General Contractors 1983; National Council on Public Works Improvement 1988). These assessments typically relied on engineering studies of the condition of and need for capital facilities. The studies specified some desired capital stock based on some arbitrary initial period when capital was presumed to be adequate, and then measured desired investment as the gap between this and the actual stock. There was almost no economic reasoning anywhere in the calculation—fixed proportions were assumed, there was no adjustment for excessive or underutilized initial capital, and there was no recognition that citizens may want to trade off the benefits of greater capital against the costs.

Many of these engineering-type studies involved highways, the largest and most volatile component of the infrastructure capital stock. Table 2, taken from George Peterson's (1991) analysis of the 1980s, shows that these physical needs studies suggested smaller highway infrastructure gaps as time passed and as they were done more carefully. Even though the Associated General Contractors study found actual highway investment to be less than a third of the desired level in the early 1980s (comparing actual investment, \$19.1 billion, with "needed" investment, \$65.4 billion), by 1987 there was no highway spending gap at all using the U.S. Congressional Budget Office (CBO) (1983) estimates and only a slight gap using the FHA (1989) estimates (comparing actual investment, \$29.0 billion, with either \$27.2 billion or \$34.5 billion).

TABLE 2
ENGINEERING ESTIMATES OF HIGHWAY AND BRIDGE INVESTMENT NEEDS
(ANNUAL COSTS, BILLIONS OF 1982 DOLLARS)

Study	Year	Period	Investment Need
Assoc. Gen. Contractors	1983	1983–2002	65.4
Cong. Budget Office	1983	1983–1990	27.2
Joint Economic Committee	1984	1982–2000	40.0
Fed. Highway Admin.*	1989	1987–2005	34.5
Fed. Highway Admin.**	1989	1987–2005	25.1
Capital expenditures	1982		19.1
Capital expenditures	1987		29.0

Source: Peterson (1991).
* Full constrained needs. Assumes that some urban needs for road widening cannot be met because of the difficulty of acquiring rights of way.
** Necessary to sustain current performance.

More up to date FHA numbers are shown in Table 3. The Table gives estimates of the percentage of pavement mileage needing improvement and the percentage of peak hour vehicle miles traveled under congested conditions. In each case the physical needs measure—

TABLE 3
PAVEMENT RATINGS AND PEAK HOUR CONGESTION
(PERCENTAGE OF PAVEMENT MILES OR VEHICLE MILES TRAVELED)

System and year	Needing improvement*	Congested**
Urban interstate		
1983	16.8	30.6
1987	11.1	42.0
1991	7.7	47.2
Urban and other arterials		
1983	10.0	28.5
1987	8.7	30.0
1991	6.8	28.7
Urban collectors		
1983	14.9	6.0
1987	13.6	6.0
1991	11.3	7.5
Rural interstates		
1983	13.3	3.0
1987	11.6	7.7
1991	7.6	8.8

Source: FHA (1993).
* Percent of pavement mileage rated in poor condition.
** Percent of vehicle miles travelled where the peak vehicle-capacity ratio exceeds a threshold set by FHA (0.8).

the percentage of highway miles in poor condition—declined steadily between 1983 and 1991. It is now at very low levels in all categories. The story is less clear for measures of highway congestion, which did all rise between 1983 and 1991, but congestion is still only at a high level for urban interstate and other arterials. There could be all kinds of pricing or other incentive policy changes that could reduce traffic congestion on these types of roads.

There are other needs assessments for water and sewer systems, aviation, and mass transit (Winston and Bosworth 1992). The story seems to be always the same—while one could make some case for a shortage of infrastructure capital, the shortages are not dramatic and it is far from clear that any step up in present rates of investment is in order.

Hence in the end these needs assessments do not make a compelling case for there being an overall shortage of infrastructure capital. They make a series of arbitrary, noneconomic assumptions, and even then do not give clear evidence that infrastructure capital is significantly out of balance. Perhaps the most convincing evidence in favor of a shortage involves urban highway congestion, and there could be many other explanations for, and ways of resolving, urban highway congestion.

B. *Political Voting Outcomes*

State and local officials themselves report that their biggest hurdle in building new infrastructure capital is in gaining the approval of voters. Roughly 20 percent of all new state and local construction must now be approved by referenda, which suggests that referenda voting might prove a good way to identify and measure infrastructure shortages.

Peterson (1991) also analyzed the results of referendum voting. He constructed a model explaining the results of voter referenda on capital investment projects. He reasoned that if public officials could guess the tastes of their voters right on average, they would submit spending proposals that reflected these tastes correctly on average, and roughly half of these proposals would be approved. But political officials might not be able to guess the tastes of their voters correctly on average, and they might fear the loss in credibility and public esteem should their bond proposals fail at the polls. Hence they might be expected to let infrastructure construction fall behind its true desired level so they could submit capital spending proposals that should capture large majorities, anticipating that more than half of these proposals would generally be approved.

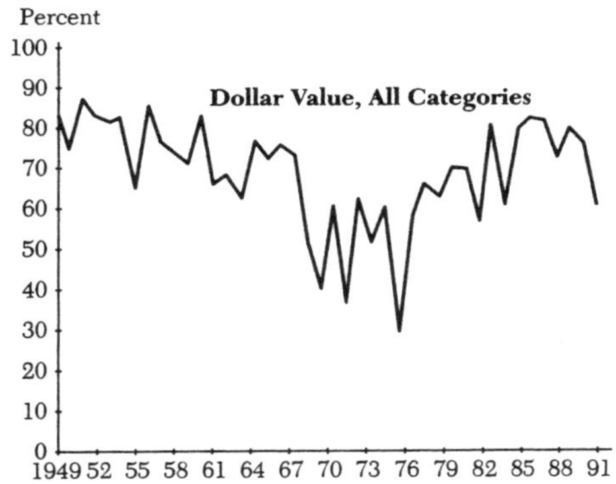

Figure 5. Local Bond Election Results, 1948–90 Percent Approved by Voters

Source: Peterson (1991)

There could be, in this political sense, a slight infrastructure shortage, but not one that policy measures should try to correct as long as there is no unhappiness with this general procedure for making infrastructure decisions. Moreover, apart from some lack of information or perception problems, there should never be a gross shortage of infrastructure capital because if this capital ever did fall far short of its desired level, vote-maximizing politicians could be expected to submit proposals to raise spending and utility-maximizing citizens could be expected to approve the proposals.

To determine whether a large gap in infrastructure investment opened up in the 1980s, Peterson analyzed the results of bond voting over time. The results, for overall capital projects for the 1948-90 period, are shown in Figure 5. Over the entire period the approval share averaged 70 percent, well above half as Peterson predicted. From 1968 to 1978, the share of construction dollars approved was below this average every single year, indicating either that voters were in an anti-public spending mood or that officials had overextended the public capital stock. Evidence in favor of the anti-spending explanation comes from the large number of state tax or spending limitation measures passed in this period. But from 1979 to 1989, the approval share was above the historical average in all years but 1981 and 1983. One could take these outcomes as evidence that the public capital stock had fallen below the level desired by voters. But by the very end of the period, the approval share seemed once again poised to fall below its historical average, suggesting that if there ever was any underinvestment, it might have already been corrected.

As with the needs assessments, there is no clear evidence of an infrastructure shortage from these voting data. There is evidence that voters were more unfavorable to infrastructure projects in the 1968-78 era and more favorable since. This could be because infrastructure capital fell behind voters' desire for it, or there could be other causes. But even if there was a persistent gap for a time, public officials and voters may have already corrected it.

C. *Economic Rates of Return*

The economic approach to infrastructure investment involves computing all the benefits and costs of projects and then their rate of return. If the effective real rate of return exceeds the going real interest rate, the investment is worthwhile. Alternatively, if the net present value of project benefits evaluated at the going real interest rate is positive, the investment is worthwhile.[1]

While the methodology for computing real rates of return, and the implied present value of net program benefits, has

[1] The latter statement assumes that the going real interest rate is the proper rate for evaluating project benefits. In an open economy, it is the proper measure of the opportunity cost of private capital; in a closed economy, the matter is more complicated but the going pre-tax real interest rate is at least a reasonable contender (Gramlich 1990).

TABLE 4
PERCENTAGE REAL RATES OF RETURN ON HIGHWAY INVESTMENT

Investment	Rate
Projects to maintain current highway conditions	35
New urban construction projects	15
Upgrading sections not meeting minimum standards	5
New rural construction projects	Low
Fix sections above minimum standards	Negative

Source: CBO (1988).

been around in one form or another for decades, it is surprising how few careful calculations of rates of return are available for infrastructure investment. The Army Corps of Engineers and the Tennessee Valley Association have made estimates of net benefits and rates of return for various canal and dam projects, but these estimates are suspect in a number of ways (CBO 1988; Gramlich 1990). Here the usual suspicion is that these agencies load the dice in favor of infrastructure spending that is pejoratively called pork barrel spending. For our standard highway category, the most complete and acceptable calculations of prospective rates of return have come from the FHA for various types of highway expenditures done in the early 1980s. These have been analyzed by the CBO and are shown in Table 4.

A mixed picture emerges from the Table. Figure 3 showed how it was hard to make an aggregate case that highway investment was too high or too low—this investment seemed to be more or less in balance with the number of heavy vehicles that might use highways. Table 4 now shows that some types of highway investment still seem highly desirable, such as plain old maintenance and to a lesser extent urban construction. Others do not seem as desirable, such as rural construction and improvements beyond minimum service standards. This distinction between maintenance and new construction will be important in the policy discussion below. The overall mixed picture is probably not surprising, and indeed it is the reason why economists generally prefer more disaggregated approaches in dealing with alleged capital shortages.

But even on their own terms, numbers like those shown in Table 4 may not ultimately be very informative. For one thing, rates of return were calculated in the early 1980s, when highway construction was much lower than it is now (see Table 2). By now, the pickup in highway construction could have lowered many rates of return substantially. For another, the numbers shown in the Table are not nearly disaggregated enough. There are growing and declining areas of the country, and surely infrastructure capital is more than adequate in some areas and quite inadequate in others. It is fine to disaggregate into particular categories of infrastructure capital, such as maintenance and new construction, but it would be far more useful to give particular rates of return—that on road maintenance in New York and Los Angeles, on new construction in San Francisco and Chicago, and so forth. With all the pages written on infrastructure investment, one is struck by how little there is of this sort of truly useful disaggregated information.

There are, of course, some problems even with this microeconomic approach. The most important in interpreting both the rate of return studies and the econometric studies (dealt with below) is benefit externalities. One argument for doing overall macroeconometric studies is that it is so difficult to deal with externalities in the micro studies. True, but it is also hard to know how serious the bias is.

Douglas Holtz-Eakin (1992) shows that it is unlikely that externalities would be a major problem because regional benefits do not seem to be any higher than state benefits in econometric studies. Gramlich (1990) reports data from license plate studies showing that even on major interstate highways most drivers are from within the state, and suggesting that the external benefits from highways for out-of-state drivers are not very large. Moreover, there are negative as well as positive externalities. The above estimates of high rates of return for urban road construction might be especially suspect in this regard, for often these projects impose significant external pollution and social costs on urban neighborhoods, costs that are difficult to quantify in rate of return studies.

While the picture is mixed, there are some categories of highway investment, maintenance, and possibly urban roads, that seem quite economic and where added infrastructure investment might make sense on average. There are other categories such as rural construction where added investment probably does not make sense on average. There are undoubtedly important regional differences in the value of added infrastructure investment. From this, it is hard to avoid the conclusion that while there may not be an aggregate shortage of infrastructure capital, at any time there could well be, or have been, shortages of particular types of infrastructure capital.

D. *Econometric Estimates of Productivity Impact*

Although macroeconometric studies might seem to be one of the least efficient approaches for determining infrastructure gaps, econometrics is what economists like to do, and these studies have commanded the most attention. Aschauer's initial papers have been followed by his own supporting work (1990, 1993) and that of Holtz-Eakin (1988, 1992), Munnell (1990a), Narayana Kocherlakota and Ke-Mu Yi (1992), Fernald (1993), and Rafael Flores de Frutos and Alfredo Pereira (1993). These papers have in turn generated a raft of criticisms from such authors as Henry Aaron (1990), Charles Schultze (1990), Hulten and Schwab (1991a, forthcoming), Rubin (1991), Dale Jorgenson (1991), and Tatom (1991a, 1991b, 1993, forthcoming).

The basic idea is simple—just expand an aggregate production function to include the public capital stock. The production function is written as:

$$Q = AF(K,L) \quad (1)$$

where K is the stock of private capital, L is the labor force, and A is an index representing total factor productivity. Aschauer and others then make A a function of the services provided by the government capital stock (G), rewriting (1) as:

$$Q = A^{*}F(K,L,G) \quad (2)$$

where A^{*} is total factor productivity purged of the influence of the government capital stock. Using the Cobb-Douglas form and writing (2) in logs gives:

$$\ln Q = \ln A^{*} + a\ln K + b\ln L + c\ln G. \quad (3)$$

Because government capital is not paid for its services, interpretation of the production elasticities, a, b, and c, is tricky. If one assumes that private capital and labor are paid their marginal products and finds c to be positive, $a + b = 1$ and $a + b + c > 1$, so that returns to scale are increasing. If one assumes returns to scale are constant and finds c to be positive, $a + b + c = 1$ and $a + b < 1$, so that labor and capital are paid more than their marginal products. When Aschauer did his macro time series regressions, he found c to be positive, from .38 to .56, forcing this choice between increasing returns and large factor rents.

It is also possible to use (3) to determine the rate of return on government capital. Differentiating the Cobb-Douglas form of (2) yields:

$$c = F_G G/Q \qquad (4)$$

where F_G is the marginal product of government capital. Given that G was \$1938 billion in 1991 (Table 1) and Q was about \$4800 billion (using private business output), estimates of production elasticity c from .38 to .56 result in pretty stratospheric estimates of the marginal product of government capital, 100 percent per annum or more.[2] That means that one unit of government capital pays for itself in terms of higher output in a year or less, which does strike one as implausible. When Holtz-Eakin (1988) and Munnell (1990a) followed similar procedures, they also got very high rates of return.

A number of logical criticisms have been made of this macro time series approach, and a number of econometric criticisms. On the logic side, a first question involves the definition of the variables. The usual version of public capital entered into these production regressions is the state and local stock, corresponding to the number that is \$1938 billion in Table 1.[3] As was seen in discussing Table 1, 37 percent of the total stock involves highways, which could influence overall national output if better highways lower the cost of trucking. But many of the benefits of highway investment will also involve the time saving of private individuals, which will generally not be reflected in national output. The 16 percent of the state and local stock representing education buildings, the 12 percent representing miscellaneous office buildings, the 3 percent representing hospitals, and the 2 percent representing conservation should not have much short term impact on the supply of aggregate output as it is now measured. Adding everything up, only about two-thirds of the existing state and local capital stock even purports to raise national output, so the stratospheric output rates of return for all public capital become all the more implausible.

This problem has been recognized and a number of authors have gone over to another concept called core infrastructure, defined as highways and water and sewer systems, about 60 percent of the state and local total. Both Aschauer (1989a) and Rubin (1991) have tried various definitions of the appropriate stock, and they do find that the core infrastructure component of the state and local stock has the highest production elasticity. But the rates of return for core infrastructure capital are still implausibly high, so this disaggregation is not the whole answer to the puzzle.

Another way to check on these results is used by Rubin and Fernald. If core infrastructure is to raise overall productivity, it ought to raise value added most in industries that directly benefit from the public capital stock, such as transportation. Rubin and Fernald do a number of tests of the impact of core infrastructure capital on productivity in various manufacturing industries. It is difficult to make an assessment here—Rubin does not find much pattern to the results but Fernald does.

[2] The implied marginal product of government capital is slightly less when evaluated for earlier years, but only slightly less. For example, the G/Q ratio is about .4 in 1991 and about .5 in 1970, roughly the midpoint of the time series estimation period for most authors. Had the calculations in the text been done in 1970, the marginal product of government capital would have been 75 percent or more, still pretty stratospheric.

[3] Some authors add the nonmilitary federal stock but the conclusions are little changed.

It would also be possible to check on the results by converting production functions to cost functions, as was originally suggested by Ann Friedlaender (1990). While nobody has estimated cost functions for the same data sets used in the productivity studies, Aschauer (1993) reports on a number of cost function studies that show positive social rates of return on infrastructure capital, for manufacturing industries in this and other developed countries.

Another logical problem involves the high rate of return. It is hard to see how the rate of return on public capital measured from output changes could ever lie above that of private capital. The private capital rate shows how private investors are making decisions at the margin, comparing marginal output benefits of their capital with the opportunity cost of their own funds. For public capital, these same investors would compare marginal output benefits with the opportunity cost of somebody else's funds. If public investment really were as profitable as claimed, would not private investors be clamoring to have the public sector impose taxes or float bonds to build roads, highways, and sewers to generate these high net benefits? The impact on business profits would be higher than for private capital and the cost to business far less. While it is hard to measure the clamor of private business investors, and even harder to determine whether inducing clamor is an efficient modus operandi for business investors, very little such pressure seems to have been observed, even when the implied econometric rates of return were allegedly very high. Most of the political arguments of private investors in the 1980s were that tax rates were too high, not that public investment was too low.

A final logical problem stressed by Hulten (forthcoming) might be described in various ways, either in terms of linkages or in terms of the old marginal-average problem. Simply saying that some capital has been productive in the past, which is all a production study can hope to say, does not mean that future investments will also be productive. It could be very beneficial to build up a network of highways and not very beneficial to expand this network. There could be many such examples for infrastructure investment, and there is a sense in which looking at past patterns might tell very little about future beneficial effects of public investment.

There are also a number of econometric problems with the macroeconomic time series method of estimating production functions. Perhaps the most serious involves common trends. We saw in Table 2 that the overall trend for state and local capital per capita mirrored the overall trend for national output per capita, rising rapidly up to the early 1970s and then much more slowly. There could be very different explanations for these trends—state and local capital could be influenced by the building of the interstate system and by the number of school and college age students; while overall productivity could have slowed for all the usual reasons—energy prices, environmental regulation, declining technology opportunities, and the like.

One way to deal with common trends is to use some form of differencing. When Hulten and Schwab (1991a) and Tatom (1991b) first difference macro time series observations, they get much lower estimates of the marginal product or rate of return of public capital, often not even positive and always statistically insignificant. Munnell (1992) feels that this correction may be too radical, because differencing could destroy the long term relationships in the data. Tatom (forthcoming) on the other hand tests the variables for stationarity and finds that differencing is required to make valid statistical estimates of the coefficients. Both authors agree that the proper approach is to test the variables for co-integration and adjust them before estimating the relationship. This is almost exactly what Tatom (1993) does, still finding essentially no productivity impact of infrastructure capital.

A second econometric problem involves missing variables, the obvious one being some measure of energy prices. These went up just when the stock of infrastructure capital and overall productivity stopped going up, and at a minimum one would think energy prices should be controlled for in aggregate production studies. When Tatom (1991b) makes such a control, in effect mixing production functions and cost functions, the estimated impact of infrastructure capital becomes weaker still. Tatom's approach can be criticized precisely because it does mix production functions and cost functions, and an obvious suggestion for future work is to try to pin this matter down by using measures of energy quantities in production functions.

A third econometric problem involves causality—does the levelling off of infrastructure capital reduce the growth of output, or does the reduced growth of output reduce the demand for infrastructure capital? Robert Eisner (1991) in particular has raised this question. Tatom (1993) does a series of lead-lag tests that indicate the causation may be more from output to infrastructure capital. Hulten (forthcoming) goes on to show that a plausible multi-equation growth model would make public capital an endogenous variable in the macro growth system, implying that its contribution to growth cannot be determined from a regression of output on public capital. To be sure, this type of criticism could be levelled at many production studies, many estimated production elasticities for private capital, and many lead-lag tests.

There is also another form of simultaneous bias. The idea of production studies is to relate the stock of infrastructure capital to aggregate supply, but when infrastructure investment rises, aggregate demand is what changes in the short run. Even if the true aggregate supply effect of core infrastructure were zero, a rise in infrastructure investment would raise aggregate demand and output in the short run, leading to an inappropriate inference of large productivity effects of infrastructure investment.

The idea of making public capital an endogenous variable in a macro growth system has been pursued by Flores de Frutos and Pereira (1993). They correct for both common trends and simultaneity and do find that public investment is clearly endogenous, driven positively by private output changes and negatively by private employment changes. But even with all these corrections, they still find very high rates of return on public capital, almost as high as those found by Aschauer.

Another way to correct for simultaneity was used by Fernald. He first disaggregated by industry, reasoning that individual industry productivity would not simultaneously determine the overall stock of public capital. He then focused only on roads, and he interacted this stock of roads with use of roads, as measured by industrial vehicle stocks. Again, even with all of these careful corrections, Fernald still found very high rates of return on public capital, as high as those found by Aschauer. These latest two studies destroy the notion that more careful econometrics leads inevitably to lower implied rates of return on public capital.

Some of these problems of econometric interpretation could be lessened by using pooled time series, cross section data across states, as Munnell (1990b), Jose Costa, Richard Ellson, and Randolph Martin (1987), Eisner (1991), Randall Eberts (1986, 1990), Kevin Duffy-Deno and Eberts (1991), Holtz-Eakin (1992), and Hulten and Schwab (forthcoming) have all done. This approach generally gives more sensible estimates of the implied rate of return on infrastructure investment: now that rate of return ranges from the implied rate of return on private capital on the high side to zero on the low side (see Munnell's summary, 1992). While this approach takes advantage of greater variation in the infrastructure (and other) independent variables, it may still overstate infrastructure impacts by confounding intrinsic state productivity differences with variation in infrastructure capital. It still is subject to the reverse causation criticism. It may also either understate or overstate infrastructure impacts by ignoring out-of-state benefit spillovers. Some of Ohio's capital has impacts in states other than Ohio, but some of the contribution to Ohio's output is from capital lying outside Ohio which may be correlated with that lying inside Ohio. It is very difficult to deal with problems of this sort.

If it makes sense to use data from different states, it also makes sense to use data from other countries, as Aschauer (1989b) did early on. As for the basic trends, Tatom (forthcoming) shows that infrastructure investment in Canada, Japan, and five advanced European countries has followed the same basic pattern as in the United States—as a share of GDP, public capital formation has dropped off since the 1960s and 1970s. As for the econometric relationships, there is by now a massive literature that attempts to use production function analysis to find the determinants of growth rates across countries. Ross Levine and David Renelt (1992) have in effect summarized this literature by trying to make fair comparisons of the whole list of variables suggested to influence growth rates across 119 countries. It turns out that most of the variables alleged to influence growth rates do not pass tests of statistical robustness. One of the variables that definitely does not pass their robustness test, indeed never gets significantly positive coefficients, is the government capital stock. But a similar analysis focusing just on transportation infrastructure for 96 countries by David Canning and Marianne Fay (1993) find normal to high rates of return in developed countries, high rates of return in industrializing countries, and moderate rates of return in underdeveloped countries.

Hence, while the business of estimating time series econometric relationships has preoccupied a large segment of the profession for the past five years, one cannot help but feel that there are two kinds of research bubbles here, time series and cross section. For time series, as was asserted above, public investment should never have been *totally* ignored up to 1989, and probably should not have been the focus of so much attention since 1989. On the cross-section side, compared to more detailed studies of referenda voting and benefit-cost analyses, the attention to macro time series seems way out of proportion to what ever could have been learned from inevitably low-powered comparisons of time series trends, even if buttressed by cross-sectional data.

III. *Policy Considerations*

Not only have previous studies not provided very convincing answers to whether there is or has been an infrastructure shortage, but they may not have even focused on the right question in the first place. Even if there were no doubt of an infrastructure shortage, it is not clear what infrastructure policy or policies should be changed. By the same token, finding no evidence of shortage would not mean that *no* policy should be changed. Hence rather than asking whether there is a shortage, it seems more helpful to ask what, if any, policies should be changed. In this section I switch the focus and analyze the infrastructure issue from this policy perspective.

A common way in which decisions about whether to invest in infrastructure capital are made is the one described above—states and localities propose bond issues and voters decide whether to build the structure. Because voters are deciding, it is hard to say there is a structural policy defect here. But voters are influenced by the financial and other terms of the deal, and these are set by governments and could be altered. The most important way in which this is done now is by federal grants, but other restrictions on whether and under what circumstances state and local governments can impose user charges can also be altered.

A. *Federal Grants*

Federal grants for construction purposes have followed a long swing process, ascending from less than 1 percent of GDP in the 1950s up to about 1.5 percent by 1978. At that point they began a long descent and grants are now back to close to the same percentage of GDP as in the 1950s.[4]

The standard argument for federal infrastructure grants is benefit spillovers: citizens outside of the jurisdiction receive some benefits from infrastructure projects, and if these citizens' votes are not reflected in decisions, too little infrastructure capital will be supplied. The most precise way to deal with the problem is by a series of Coasian bargains between governments, but given that there are something like 80,000 state and local governments in the United States, there would be very high transactions costs to arrive at such a set of bargains. It would be simpler, the argument goes, just to have the federal government provide matching grants for infrastructure projects, with the federal match in some general way representing the appropriate contribution of outsiders.

If this is the argument for federal grants, the actual terms of federal grant programs leave much to be desired. It is helpful to distinguish types of capital. One type is new capital with large costs and potentially enormous technological benefits, say as for the super-conductor, super-collider. For such capital technological spillovers are substantial, justifying federal support. Federal matching shares should reflect the benefits, technological and other, that flow beyond state lines. It is of course difficult to determine such benefits for these advanced technology projects, but present federal matching shares on this type of capital, generally about 90 percent, are probably way too high. Rather than keeping federal matching shares this high and having states lobby intensely for projects, as now happens, one quasi-market approach for determining proper federal matching shares would be to let states bid on projects. If the state of Massachusetts really wanted the super-conductor, super-collider, let it outbid Texas. Such an approach should save on federal tax dollars and improve the statewide allocation of government projects.

A second type of infrastructure capital, by far the most common, is capital like that already in place—widened or expanded roads, improved water and sewer plants, and on down the list. Studies have shown that for most infrastructure proj-

[4] In doing these calculations, it is important to distinguish federal grants for construction purposes from other federal grants, these days largely consisting of open-ended grants for medicaid and public welfare.

ects of this kind the majority of the benefits, 70 percent or so, are realized by those inside the state (Gramlich 1990). Given this, the proper federal matching grant would pay about 30 percent of the costs for the typical project. Instead, the typical federal infrastructure grant pays about 80 percent of the cost of a project up to some limit, then none of the costs. In the usual case where the grant limit is small relative to typical state spending on the project, the federal money provides no price subsidy at all at the margin, and much too large an inframarginal income subsidy. These capped grants then achieve the worst of both worlds—they cost the federal government too much, hence raising the federal deficit and probably lowering national saving, and they do nothing about external benefits at the margin. The correction is obvious—lower federal matching shares and remove the caps.

The problems with overly generous inframarginal matching could be even worse than they seem. Suppose state or local officials know that there is too little of some type of public infrastructure nationally, and they think that Congress will rise to the bait and pass a new grant program. Rather than simply building the facility in short supply, the generous federal matching gives these officials a powerful incentive to wait and see if they can get a federal grant, rather than just going ahead with their own project. Exactly this seems to have happened, first with a countercyclical public works grant program passed in the late 1970s (Gramlich 1978) and later with pollution-control grants (James Jondrow and Robert Levy 1984).

Another problem involves the distinction made earlier between new construction and maintenance. Basically, maintenance investment seems to have higher rates of return but new construction gets higher federal matching subsidies. In fact, often highway maintenance projects get little or no federal matching while new interstate construction projects get the generous treatment described above. The solution is obvious here too—while matching shares are lowered for new construction, they might actually be raised up to their proper low level for highway maintenance.

A further problem involves the financing of the federal grants. At the national level there are five dedicated trust funds—for airports, highways, aquatic resources, harbors, and inland waterways. The Department of Transportation (1990) has recently suggested creating others for the coast guard and railroads. Into each trust fund goes the dedicated revenue, such as that from the gas tax for highways, and out come the federal grants for the relevant projects. Many states have similar arrangements to finance their own infrastructure projects.

This trust fund arrangement can be useful in limiting federal subsidies by forcing the dedicated tax to pay for all or most of the spending in question. At the same time, if the arrangement is misapplied, it can lead to inefficient outcomes. One example of such a misapplication is the gas tax, which could also be rationalized as an energy conservation measure that should not have its returns sent to the highway trust fund and devoted to the construction of further highways. Recent budget bills have devoted much of the gas tax revenues to general federal revenues and not to the highway trust fund, but it was twenty years into America's energy crisis and fifteen years into America's budget crisis before this daring step was taken.

A second example of such a misapplication is that four of the trust funds, all but the one for aquatic resources, do not even limit federal subsidies by forcing trust fund revenues to cover all of the federal spending for the facilities in question (David Montgomery 1989). At a minimum they should do that. At present, whenever there is a hold-down on federal infrastructure grants for budget reasons, the revenues build up in the trust fund, again achieving the worst of both worlds—the funds are there, activating lobbyists in favor of increased spending, even though spending is already subsidized by federal general revenues. The solutions are obvious here too—finance all grants from the trust funds, and devote most gas tax revenues to general revenue.

B. *User Fees*

The above comments suggest some general reforms in federal grant programs for infrastructure investment. But if it were possible to impose user fees on infrastructure facilities, which it certainly is for highways and other transportation infrastructure, many higher education structures (the user fee is commonly known as tuition), hospitals, many water and sewer systems, some conservation structures, and some industrial structures, it would be possible to do even better than to have revamped federal grants finance the infrastructure investment.

Take the case of highway maintenance financing, perhaps the largest category of infrastructure investment where there are opportunities for desirable expansion. If these maintenance projects are eligible for federal grants, the federal government collects a gas tax, devotes a large share of it to the federal highway trust fund, and has the trust fund in turn provide grants with 80 percent federal matching to states, which probably match the federal money with revenues from their own gas tax. Suppose instead the gas tax were devoted to federal general revenues and budget deficit reduction, the federal highway trust fund were abolished, and the states were permitted to finance their own maintenance expenditures with revenues from tolls (which in general they cannot now levy if they have used federal money to build their interstate roads). The impressive list of advantages from such a change is as follows:

- Revenue. There would be a new source of revenue to pay for the highway maintenance, lessening budget problems at both the federal and state levels.
- Allocation. Over the long run the toll revenue from highway x could be devoted to restoring highway x, thus giving public officials a better quasi-market guide on how to allocate their maintenance (and other) funds (Wallace Oates 1991).
- Politics. The nasty political debate about excessive taxation could be moderated. At least in this area it would be very clear where the toll revenues were going.
- Taxation by Willingness to Pay. This has always been the public finance dream, to devise financing schemes that tax citizens according to their willingness to pay for the facility. How better to do that than to use user fees?
- Spillovers. Rather than have federal grants, even reformed federal grants, employ inevitably crude estimates of out-of-state marginal benefits in constructing matching ratios, toll user fee finance of highway maintenance would automatically be paid by out-of-state users in proportion to their use.
- Conservation. Highway engineers report that interstate roads depreciate according to the cubic power of vehicle axle weight (Kenneth Small, Winston, and Carol Evans 1989). Rather than letting all vehicles use the road for free, tolls could be based

on true damage imposed on the road, hence encouraging heavy truckers to lighten their axle weight and extend the life of the road. Or, states could build thicker roads and charge truckers for that. Part of the economic saving here would be that less road maintenance would need to be done if tolls were set efficiently.

- Congestion. Tolls could be varied by the time of day or week, hence lessening congestion.

With so many advantages, it is hard to say no. There are clear opportunities to have user fees finance much infrastructure investment, simultaneously financing the investment and extending the life of the capital. States could be allowed to finance their road maintenance and new construction projects by tolls (generally not possible now), airports could be allowed to use ticket taxes (recently made possible) and landing charges (still not possible), higher education could charge tuition rates nearer to marginal costs (giving more aid to needy students), hospital and other structures could finance themselves with fees. There are a number of technological innovations in the collection of these fees that could keep down administrative costs (Winston and Bosworth 1992; Martin Neil Baily, Gary Burtless, and Robert Litan 1993). The revenue from the fees could also be devoted to properly designed trust funds to keep revenues and spending in balance. One radical version of this proposal is that infrastructure capital could simply be privatized, with the private owners given both the permission and incentive to set up their own fee schedules.

There are, of course, economic objections to comprehensive user fee financing of all infrastructure capital. Present day federal matching grants could still be more efficient if it were costly to collect the user fees, if there were externalities, if there were natural monopolies with spillovers, or to complete a national network of roads and/or airports. While one can think of types of capital for which these types of objections are relevant, these exceptions to the general rule would seem to be of modest enough importance that a more extensive set of user fees should still bring about large efficiency gains. A more extensive set of user fees may in the end result in more or less infrastructure investment—that prediction is difficult to make. But the mechanism for making infrastructure decisions would be much improved. States would have a new and powerful incentive to find the optimal stock of infrastructure capital.

There could also be political objections to user fee financing of infrastructure capital. If user fees are so wonderful, why are they not used more widely? Space constraints prohibit a deep discussion of the politics of paying for government spending, a topic with many well-known subtleties. But one thing that can be said is that if the world gradually adjusts its institutions in the direction of the optimal approach, the use of user fees in the United States is growing dramatically (CBO 1993).

IV. *Conclusions*

As for the alleged infrastructure shortage, the evidence reviewed in the paper is decidedly mixed. The needs assessment approaches and macro time series approaches used to justify big increases in infrastructure spending are flawed in many ways. One might make some more headway by looking at more disaggregated time series, bond referenda voting, and rates of return, where there is some evidence that some types of infrastructure could have been in short supply, but even here the evidence is inconclusive and it is not clear that the overall shortage persists.

What should be done about any shortages? The best approach is not to try to analyze the numbers and tell how short the supply is and how much national or state spending or grants should be increased. A far more sensible approach is to set up institutional structures that permit state and local governments, the holders of almost all infrastructure capital, to find their own optimal stock. The way this might be done is to reform the present system of financing infrastructure investment. States could be forced to bid for costly, large-scale high technology projects. States could also be permitted or encouraged to impose user fees to finance their own capital and maintenance. And federal matching grants could be restructured and used much less intensively.

As for the contribution of economic researchers to this new understanding, there is some good news and some bad news. After years of ignoring the issue, economists led by Aschauer did finally find it, giving some more professional gloss to advocacy pieces that up to then were entirely from the infrastructure lobby. But the contributions of economists were not all they could have been—there seems to have been far too much attention to the details of macro production studies, which can never answer the relevant policy questions very well, and far too little attention to more disaggregated rate of return studies and studies of the impact of different types of policy changes.

While in some sense the problems outlined and discussed here are more at the state and local level than at the federal level, the federal government could help matters in various ways. The obvious way is to change policies to permit states to go on their own on infrastructure investment, cutting states loose from the federal grant system and giving states their own source of revenue and power to make key decisions. But there are some less obvious ways as well. Improved capital stock data would make it possible to conduct more disaggregated studies. Improved estimates of economic rates of depreciation of the infrastructure stock would also improve estimates of the size of this stock and the desirability of expansion. More importantly, the federal government might even give policy analysts something to study by doing experiments with policy changes of various sorts—permitting bidding for valued projects, permitting user fees, permitting privatization, permitting other sorts of incentive changes—to see how state and local governments and their voters will respond. Studying reactions of this sort can redirect the efforts of economists onto studies of just what policy changes are in order.

References

AARON, HENRY J. "Why Is Infrastructure Important? Discussion," in ALICIA H. MUNNELL, ed. 1990b, pp. 51–63.

ASCHAUER, DAVID A. "Is Public Expenditure Productive?" *J. Monet. Econ.*, Mar. 1989a, *23*(2), pp. 177–200.

———. "Public Investment and Productivity Growth in the Group of Seven," *Econ. Perspectives*, 1989b, *13*(5), pp. 17–25.

———. "Does Public Capital Crowd Out Private Capital?" *J. Monet. Econ.*, 1989c, *24*(2), pp. 171–88.

———. "Why Is Infrastructure Important?" in ALICIA H. MUNNELL, ed. 1990b, pp. 21–50.

———. "Genuine Economic Returns to Infrastructure Investment," *Policy Stud. J.*, 1993, *21*, pp. 380–90.

ASSOCIATION OF GENERAL CONTRACTORS. "America's Infrastructure: A Plan to Rebuild." May 1983.

BAILY, MARTIN NEIL; BURTLESS, GARY AND LITAN, ROBERT E. *Growth with equity: Economic policymaking for the next century*. Washington, DC: Brookings Institution, 1993.

CANNING, DAVID AND FAY, MARIANNE. "The Effect of Transportation Networks on Economic Growth." Columbia U., mimeo, May 1993.

DUFFY-DENO, KEVIN T. AND EBERTS, RANDALL W. "Public Infrastructure and Regional Economic Development: A Simultaneous Equations Approach," *J. Urban Econ.*, Nov. 1991, *30*(3), pp. 329–43.

EBERTS, RANDALL W. "Estimating the Contribution of Urban Public Infrastructure to Regional Economic Growth." Fed. Res. Bank of Cleveland Working Paper No. 8610, Dec. 1986.

______. "Public Infrastructure and Regional Economic Development," *Fed. Res. Bank of Cleveland Econ. Rev.*, 1990, *26*, pp. 15–27.

EISNER, ROBERT. "Infrastructure and Regional Economic Performance," *New Eng. Econ. Rev., Fed. Res. Bank of Boston*, Sept./Oct. 1991, pp. 47–58.

FEDERAL HIGHWAY ADMINISTRATION. *The status of the nation's highways, bridges, and transit: Conditions and performance.* Washington, DC: U.S. Department of Transportation, Federal Highway Adminstration, 1993.

FERNALD, JOHN. "How Productive is Infrastructure? Distinguishing Reality and Illusion with a Panel of U.S. Industries." Federal Reserve Board Discussion Paper, Aug. 1993.

FLORES DE FRUTOS, RAFAEL AND PEREIRA, ALFREDO. "Public Capital and Aggregate Growth in the United States: Is Public Capital Productive?" U. of California at San Diego Discussion Paper 93–31, July 1993.

FRIEDLAENDER, ANN F. "How Does Public Infrastructure Affect Regional Economic Performance? Discussion," in ALICIA H. MUNNELL, ed. 1990b, pp. 108–12.

GRAMLICH, EDWARD M. "State and Local Budgets the Day after It Rained? Why Is the Surplus So High?" *Brookings Pap. Econ. Act.*, 1978, *1*, pp. 191–214.

______. *A guide to benefit-cost analysis.* 2nd ed. Prentice-Hall, 1990.

HOLTZ-EAKIN, DOUGLAS. "Private Output, Government Capital, and the Infrastructure Crisis." Discussion Paper No. 394, Columbia U., May 1988.

______. "Public Sector Capital and the Productivity Puzzle, National Bureau of Economic Research Working Paper No. 4144, 1992.

HULTEN, CHARLES R. "Optimal Growth with Public Infrastructure Capital: Implications for Empirical Modeling." U. of Maryland Discussion Paper, 1993.

HULTEN, CHARLES R. AND SCHWAB, ROBERT M. "Is There Too Little Public Capital? Infrastructure and Economic Growth." American Enterprise Institute Discussion Paper, Feb. 1991a.

______. "Public Capital Formation and the Growth of Regional Manufacturing Industries," *Nat. Tax J.*, Dec. 1991b, *44*(4), pp. 121–34.

______. "Infrastructure Spending: Where Do We Go From Here?" in the National Tax Association Proceedings, forthcoming.

JOINT ECONOMIC COMMITTEE. "National Infrastructure Advisory Committee Report." Feb. 1984.

JONDROW, JAMES AND LEVY, ROBERT A. "The Displacement of Local Spending for Pollution Control By Federal Construction Grants," *Amer. Econ. Rev.*, May 1984, *74*(2) , pp. 174–78.

JORGENSON, DALE. "Fragile Statistical Foundations: The Macroeconomics of Public Infrastructure Investment." American Enterprise Institute Discussion Paper, Feb. 1991.

KOCHERLAKOTA, NARAYANA AND YI, KE-MU. "The Long Run Effects of Government Policy on Growth Rates in the United States." U. of Iowa/Rice U. mimeo, Sept. 1992.

LEVINE, ROSS AND RENELT, DAVID. "A Sensitivity Analysis of Cross-Country Growth Regressions," *Amer. Econ. Rev.*, Sept. 1992, *82*(5), pp. 942–63.

MONTGOMERY, W. DAVID. "Statement before the U.S. Senate Committee on Appropriations." May 11, 1989.

MUNNELL, ALICIA H. "Why Has Productivity Growth Declined? Productivity and Public Investment," *New Eng. Econ. Rev.*, Jan./Feb. 1990a, pp. 3–22.

______. *Is there a shortfall in public capital investment?* Ed.: ALICIA H. MUNNELL. Conference Series No. 34. Boston: Federal Reserve Bank of Boston, 1990b.

______."How Does Public Infrastructure Affect Regional Economic Performance?" in ALICIA H. MUNNELL, ed., 1990b, pp. 69–103.

______. "Infrastructure Investment and Economic Growth," *J. Econ. Perspectives*, Fall 1992, *6*(4), pp. 189–98.

NATIONAL COUNCIL ON PUBLIC WORKS IMPROVEMENT. "Fragile Foundations: A Report on America's Public Works." 1988.

OATES, WALLACE E. "Discussion." American Enterprise Institute Discussion Paper, Feb. 1991.

PETERSON, GEORGE E. "Is Public Infrastructure Undersupplied?" in ALICIA H. MUNNELL, ed. 1990b, pp. 113–30.

______. "Historical Perspective on Infrastructure Investment: How Did We Get Where We Are?" American Enterprise Institute Discussion Paper, Feb. 1991.

RUBIN, LAURA S. "Productivity and the Public Capital Stock: Another Look." Federal Reserve Board Discussion Paper, May 1991.

SCHULTZE, CHARLES L. "The Federal Budget and the Nation's Economic Health," in *Setting national priorities: Policies for the nineties.* Ed.: HENRY J. AARON. Washington, DC: Brookings Institution, 1990, pp. 19–64.

DA SILVA, JOSE COSTA; ELLSON, RICHARD W. AND MARTIN, RANDOLPH C. "Public Capital, Regional Output, and Development: Some Empirical Evidence," *J. Reg. Sci.*, Aug. 1987, *27*(3), pp. 419–37.

SMALL, KENNETH A.; WINSTON, CLIFFORD AND EVANS, CAROL A. *Road work: A new highway pricing and investment policy.* Washington, DC: Brookings Institution, 1989.

TATOM, JOHN A. "Should Government Spending on Capital Goods Be Raised?" *Fed. Res. Bank of St. Louis Rev.*, Mar./Apr., 1991a, pp. 3–15.

______. "Public Capital and Private Sector Performance," Fed. *Res. Bank of St. Louis Rev.*, May/June 1991b, *73*(3), pp. 3–15.

______. "Paved With Good Intentions: The Mythical National Infrastructure Crisis." Policy Analysis, Cato Institute, Aug. 12, 1993.

______. "Shifting Perspectives on the Role of Public Capital Formation," *Fed. Res. Bank of St. Louis Rev.*, forthcoming.

U.S. CONGRESSIONAL BUDGET OFFICE. *Public works infrastructure: Policy considerations for the 1980s*. Washington, DC: U.S. GPO, Apr. 1983.

______. *New directions for the nation's public works*. Washington, DC: U.S. GPO, Sept. 1988.

______. *The growth of federal user charges*. Washington, DC: U.S. GPO, Aug. 1993.

U.S. DEPARTMENT OF TRANSPORTATION. *Moving America: New directions, new opportunities*. Washington, DC: U.S. Department of Transportation, 1990.

WINSTON, CLIFFORD AND BOSWORTH, BARRY. "Public Infrastructure," in *Setting domestic priorities: What can government do*? Eds.: HENRY J. AARON AND CHARLES L. SCHULTZE. Washington, DC: Brookings Institution, 1992, pp. 267–93.

Name Index

The International Library of Critical Writings in Economics

1. Multinational Corporations
   Mark Casson
2. The Economics of Innovation
   Christopher Freeman
3. Entrepreneurship
   Mark Casson
4. International Investment
   Peter J. Buckley
5. Game Theory in Economics
   Ariel Rubinstein
6. The History of Economic Thought
   Mark Blaug
7. Monetary Theory
   Thomas Mayer
8. Joint Production of Commodities
   Neri Salvadori and Ian Steedman
9. Industrial Organization
   Oliver E. Williamson
10. Growth Theory
    (Volumes I, II and III)
    R. Becker and E. Burmeister
11. Microeconomics: Theoretical and Applied (Volumes I, II and III)
    Robert E. Kuenne
12. The Economics of Health
    (Volumes I and II)
    A.J. Culyer
13. Recent Developments in Macroeconomics
    (Volumes I, II and III)
    Edmund S. Phelps
14. Urban and Regional Economics
    Paul C. Cheshire and Alan W. Evans
15. Modern Public Finance
    (Volumes I and II)
    A.B. Atkinson
16. Exchange Rate Economics
    (Volumes I and II)
    Ronald MacDonald and Mark P. Taylor
17. The Economic Value of Education: Studies in the Economics of Education
    Mark Blaug
18. Development Economics
    (Volumes I, II, III and IV)
    Deepak Lal
19. The New Classical Macroeconomics
    (Volumes I, II and III)
    Kevin D. Hoover
20. The Economics of the Environment
    Wallace E. Oates
21. Post Keynesian Theory of Growth and Distribution
    Carlo Panico and Neri Salvadori
22. Dynamic Labor Demand and Adjustment Costs
    Giorgio Galeazzi and Daniel S. Hamermesh
23. The Philosophy and Methodology of Economics (Volumes I, II and III)
    Bruce J. Caldwell
24. Public Choice Theory
    (Volumes I, II and III)
    Charles K. Rowley
25. Evolutionary Economics
    Ulrich Witt
26. Economics and Psychology
    Shlomo Maital and Sharone L. Maital
27. Social Choice Theory
    (Volumes I, II and III)
    Charles K. Rowley
28. Non-Linear Dynamics in Economic Theory
    Marc Jarsulic
29. Recent Developments in Experimental Economics
    (Volumes I and II)
    John D. Hey and Graham Loomes

30. Monopoly and Competition Policy (Volumes I and II)
F.M. Scherer
31. The Economics of Technical Change
Edwin Mansfield and Elizabeth Mansfield
32. The Economics of Exhaustible Resources
Geoffrey Heal
33. The Economics of Institutions
Geoffrey M. Hodgson
34. The Economics of Transport (Volumes I and II)
Herbert Mohring
35. Implicit Contract Theory
Sherwin Rosen
36. Foundations of Analytical Marxism (Volumes I and II)
John E. Roemer
37. The Economics of Product Differentiation (Volumes I and II)
Jacques-François Thisse and George Norman
38. Economic Growth in Theory and Practice: A Kaldorian Perspective
John E. King
39. Markets and Socialism
Alec Nove and Ian D. Thatcher
40. Recent Developments in the Economics of Education
Elchanan Cohn and Geraint Johnes
41. The Theory of Inflation
Michael Parkin
42. The Economics of Location (Volumes I, II and III)
Melvin L. Greenhut and George Norman
43. Financial Intermediaries
Mervyn K. Lewis
44. The Political Economy of Privatization and Deregulation
Elizabeth E. Bailey and Janet Rothenberg Pack
45. Gender and Economics
Jane Humphries
46. Macroeconomics and Imperfect Competition
Jean-Pascal Bénassy
47. Labor Economics (Volumes I, II, III and IV)
Orley C. Ashenfelter and Kevin F. Hallock
48. The Economics of Altruism
Stefano Zamagni
49. The Economic Analysis of Rent Seeking
Robert D. Tollison and Roger D. Congleton
50. Economics and Biology
Geoffrey M. Hodgson
51. The Economics of Ageing
John Creedy
52. Fiscal and Monetary Policy (Volumes I and II)
Thomas Mayer and Steven M. Sheffrin
53. The Economics of Information (Volumes I and II)
David K. Levine and Steven A. Lippman
54. Transaction Cost Economics (Volumes I and II)
Oliver E. Williamson and Scott E. Masten
55. Agricultural Economics
George H. Peters
56. International Debt (Volumes I and II)
Graham Bird and P. Nicholas Snowden
57. Economics and Discrimination (Volumes I and II)
William A. Darity, Jr
58. Business Cycle Theory
Finn E. Kydland
59. International Trade (Volumes I and II)
J. Peter Neary
60. The Money Supply in the Economic Process
Marco Musella and Carlo Panico

61. Small Firms and Economic Growth (Volumes I and II)
Zoltan J. Acs
62. Producer Cooperatives and Labor-Managed Systems (Volumes I and II)
David L. Prychitko and Jaroslav Vanek
63. Ethics and Economics (Volumes I and II)
Alan P. Hamlin
64. The Economics of the Family
Nancy Folbre
65. The Economics of Training (Volumes I and II)
Orley C. Ashenfelter and Robert J. LaLonde
66. Chaos Theory in Economics: Methods, Models and Evidence
W. Davis Dechert
67. General Equilibrium Theory (Volumes I, II and III)
Gérard Debreu
68. Economic Growth: Theory and Evidence (Volumes I and II)
Gene M. Grossman
69. Long Wave Theory
Christopher Freeman
70. The Economics of Communication and Information
Donald M. Lamberton
71. The Foundations of Public Finance (Volumes I and II)
Peter Jackson
72. The Theory of the Firm
Mark Casson
73. The Economics of Uncertainty (Volumes I and II)
John D. Hey
74. The Economics of Global Warming
Tom Tietenberg
75. The Development of Ecological Economics
Robert Costanza, Charles Perrings and Cutler Cleveland
76. Economic Growth in the Long Run: A History of Empirical Evidence (Volumes I, II and III)
Bart van Ark
77. The Economics of Productivity (Volumes I and II)
Edward N. Wolff
78. The Economics of Population: Key Modern Writings (Volumes I and II)
Julian L. Simon
79. Political Business Cycles
Bruno S. Frey
80. Cultural Economics: The Arts, the Heritage and the Media Industries (Volumes I and II)
Ruth Towse
81. Law and Economics (Volumes I, II and III)
Richard A. Posner and Francesco Parisi
82. Independent Central Banks and Economic Performance
Sylvester Eijffinger
83. Culture, Social Norms and Economics (Volumes I and II)
Mark Casson
84. Industrial Policy and Competitive Advantage (Volumes I, II and III)
David B. Audretsch
85. The Economics of Housing (Volumes I and II)
John M. Quigley
86. Economic Demography (Volumes I and II)
T. Paul Schultz
87. Trade and the Environment: Economic, Legal and Policy Perspectives
Alan M. Rugman and John J. Kirton with Julie A. Soloway
88. The Economics of Fiscal Federalism and Local Finance
Wallace E. Oates
89. Price Theory and its Applications
Bernard Saffran and F.M. Scherer

90. Women in the Labor Market (Volumes I and II)
Marianne A. Ferber
91. Market Process Theories (Volumes I and II)
Peter Boettke and David Prychitko
92. Input–Output Analysis (Volumes I, II and III)
Heinz Kurz, Erik Dietzenbacher and Christian Lager
93. Mathematical Economics (Volumes I, II and III)
Graciela Chichilnisky
94. The Foundations of Regulatory Economics (Volumes I, II and III)
Robert B. Ekelund, Jr.
95. The Economics of Marketing
Martin Carter, Mark Casson and Vivek Suneja
96. Service Industries in the Global Economy (Volumes I and II)
J.R. Bryson and P.W. Daniels
97. Economic Justice (Volumes I and II)
Giorgio Brosio and Harold M. Hochman
98. Foreign Exchange Intervention: Objectives and Effectiveness
Sylvester C.W. Eijffinger
99. Economic Anthropology
Stephen Gudeman
100. Consumer Theory
Kelvin Lancaster
101. The Economics of Famine
Jean Drèze
102. Microeconomic Theories of Imperfect Competition
Jean J. Gabszewicz and Jacques-François Thisse
103. The Economics of Executive Compensation (Volumes I and II)
Kevin F. Hallock and Kevin J. Murphy
104. The Foundations of Long Wave Theory (Volumes I and II)
Francisco Louçã and Jan Reijnders
105. The Economics of Commodity Markets
David Greenaway and C.W. Morgan
106. Corporate Governance (Volumes I, II, III and IV)
Kevin Keasey, Steve Thompson and Mike Wright
107. Economic Welfare: Concepts and Measurement (Volumes I and II)
John Creedy
108. Economic Forecasting
Terence C. Mills
109. Recent Developments in Game Theory
Eric S. Maskin
110. The Economics of Increasing Returns
Geoffrey Heal
111. The Economics of Corruption and Illegal Markets (Volumes I, II and III)
Gianluca Fiorentini and Stefano Zamagni
112. The Economics of Price Discrimination
George Norman
113. The Economic Theory of Auctions (Volumes I and II)
Paul Klemperer
114. The Economics of Regional Policy
Harvey W. Armstrong and Jim Taylor
115. Economic Integration and International Trade
Carsten Kowalczyk
116. The Political Economy of Science, Technology and Innovation
Ben Martin and Paul Nightingale
117. The Economics of Science and Innovation (Volumes I and II)
Paula E. Stephan and David B. Audretsch
118. Innovation, Evolution of Industry and Economic Growth (Volumes I, II and III)
David B. Audretsch and Steven Klepper

119. The Economics of Energy
(Volumes I and II)
Paul Stevens
120. Privatisation in Developing Countries
(Volumes I and II)
Paul Cook and Colin Kirkpatrick
121. The Economics of Tourism
(Volumes I and II)
Clem Tisdell
122. The Economics of Unemployment
(Volumes I, II, III and IV)
P.N. Junankar
123. Privatisation and Corporate Performance
David Parker
124. Income Distribution
(Volumes I, II and III)
Michael Sattinger
125. International Finance
(Volumes I and II)
Robert Z. Aliber
126. Welfare Economics
(Volumes I, II and III)
William J. Baumol and Charles A. Wilson
127. The Theory of Trade Policy Reform
Carsten Kowalczyk
128. The Economics of Defence
(Volumes I, II and III)
Keith Hartley and Todd Sandler
129. The Economics of Property Rights
(Volumes I and II)
Svetozar Pejovich
130. Gender and Development: Theoretical, Empirical and Practical Approaches
(Volumes I and II)
Lourdes Benería with Savitri Bisnath
131. The Economics of Politics
(Volumes I and II)
Dennis C. Mueller
132. Economic Theory and the Welfare State (Volumes I, II and III)
Nicholas Barr
133. The Regulation and Supervision of Banks
(Volumes I, II, III and IV)
Maximilian J.B. Hall
134. The Political Economy of Monetary Union
Paul De Grauwe
135. The Economics of Sport
(Volumes I and II)
Andrew Zimbalist
136. The Economics of Advertising
Kyle Bagwell
137. Regulation, Economics and the Law
Anthony I. Ogus
138. The Economics of Barter and Countertrade
Rolf Mirus and Bernard Yeung
139. The Economics of Technology Transfer
Sanjaya Lall
140. The Political Economy of Development
(Volumes I, II and III)
Amitava Krishna Dutt
141. Macroeconomics and the Environment
Mohan Munasinghe
142. Happiness in Economics
Richard A. Easterlin
143. Speculation and Financial Markets
(Volumes I and II)
Liam Gallagher and Mark P. Taylor
144. Public Procurement
(Volumes I and II)
Sue Arrowsmith and Keith Hartley
145. The Economics of Intellectual Property
(Volumes I, II, III and IV)
Ruth Towse and R.W. Holzhauer
146. Forecasting Financial Markets
(Volumes I and II)
Terence C. Mills
147. The Economics of Labor Unions
(Volumes I and II)
Alison Booth

148. New Developments in Exchange Rate Economics
(Volumes I and II)
Lucio Sarno and Mark P. Taylor

149. Long Term Trends and Business Cycles
(Volumes I and II)
Terence C. Mills

150. The Economics of Language
Donald M. Lamberton

151. The Economics of Migration
(Volumes I, II, III and IV)
Klaus F. Zimmermann and Thomas Bauer

152. Cost–Benefit Analysis
Arnold C. Harberger and Glenn P. Jenkins

153. The Economics of Budget Deficits
(Volumes I and II)
Charles K. Rowley, William F. Shughart II and Robert D. Tollison

154. Alternative Theories of the Firm
(Volumes I, II and III)
Richard Langlois, Tony F. Yu and Paul Robertson

155. The Distribution of Tax Burdens
Don Fullerton and Gilbert E. Metcalf

156. International Financial Integration
(Volumes I and II)
Sylvester C.W. Eijffinger and Jan J.G. Lemmen

157. The Economics of Structural Change
(Volumes I, II and III)
Harald Hagemann, Michael Landesmann and Roberto Scazzieri

158. The Economics of Poverty and Inequality
(Volumes I and II)
Frank A. Cowell

159. The Economics of Schooling
(Volumes I and II)
Eric A. Hanushek

160. Intra-Industry Trade
Peter J. Lloyd and Herbert G. Grubel

161. Economic Analysis of Regional Trading Arrangements
Richard Pomfret

162. The Principal Agent Model: The Economic Theory of Incentives
Jean-Jacques Laffont

163. The Economics of Business Strategy
John Kay

164. Recent Developments in Transport Economics
Kenneth Button

165. The Economics of Higher Education
Clive R. Belfield and Henry M. Levin

166. Constitutional Political Economy
(Volumes I and II)
Stephan Voigt

167. Economics and Religion
(Volumes I and II)
Paul Oslington

168. The Economics of Conflict
(Volumes I, II and III)
Todd Sandler and Keith Hartley

169. Cognitive Economics
(Volumes I and II)
Massimo Egidi and Salvatore Rizzello

170. Comparative Law and Economics
(Volumes I, II and III)
Gerrit de Geest and Roger Van Den Bergh

171. Personnel Economics
(Volumes I and II)
Edward P. Lazear and Robert McNabb

172. Empirical Industrial Organization
(Volumes I and II)
Paul L. Joskow and Michael Waterson

173. Multinationals and Public Policy
(Volumes I and II)
Stephen Young

174. Complexity in Economics
(Volumes I, II and III)
J. Barkley Rosser, Jr.

175. Time in Economic Theory
(Volumes I, II and III)
Stefano Zamagni and Elettra Agliardi

176. The Economics of Affirmative Action
Harry J. Holzer and David Neumark

177. Recent Developments in Environmental Economics
(Volumes I and II)
Michael Hoel

178. The Economics of Natural Hazards
(Volumes I and II)
Howard Kunreuther and Adam Rose

179. Recent Developments in Growth Theory
(Volumes I and II)
K. Daron Acemoglu

180. The Political Economy of Environmental Regulation
Robert N. Stavins

181. The Economics of Nonprofit Enterprises
Richard S. Steinberg

182. Recent Developments in Urban and Regional Economics
Paul C. Cheshire and Gilles Duranton

Future titles will include:

The Economics of Public Private Partnerships
Darrin Grimsey and Mervyn K. Lewis

The Psychology of World Equity Markets
(Volumes I and II)
Werner De Bondt

The Economics of Crime
(Volumes I, II and III)
Isaac Ehrlich and Zhiqiang Liu

New Developments in Economic Sociology
(Volumes I and II)
Richard Swedberg

New Economic Geography
J. Vernon Henderson

The Economics of Deflation
(Volumes I and II)
Pierre L. Siklos

The Economics of Networks
Michael L. Katz and Carl Shapiro

The Economics of Contracts
Lars A. Stole

Spatial Economics
Masahisa Fujita

Recent Developments in Labour Economics
John T. Addison

Institutions and Economic Performance
Masahiko Aoki

Imperfect Competition, Nonclearing Markets and Business Cycles
Jean-Pascal Bénassy

The International Monetary Fund and the World Economy
Graham Bird and Dane Rowlands

International Taxation
Richard M. Bird and Michael Smart

The Economics of Knowledge
Robin A. Cowan

Path Dependence
Paul A. David

Recent Developments in Economic Methodology
John B. Davis

The Economics of the Mass Media
Gillian Doyle

The Economics of Gambling and National Lotteries
William R. Eadington

The Economics of Transfer Pricing
Lorraine Eden

Recent Developments in International Trade Theory
Rodney E. Falvey and Udo Kreickemeier

Financial Crises
Douglas Gale and Franklin Allen

The Economics of Association Football
Bill Gerrard

The Economics of Innovation Policy
Bronwyn Hall

Islamic Finance
M. Kabir Hassan and Mervyn K. Lewis

The Economics of Vouchers
Caroline M. Hoxby

The Economics of Free Trade
Douglas A. Irwin and Arvind Panagariya

The Economics of Organisation and Bureaucracy
Peter M. Jackson

Computational Economics
Kenneth L. Judd

Feminist Economics
Mary C. King, Ann Mari May and Diana L. Strassman

Cooperation, Competition and Collusion: The Economic Theory of Incentives
Jean-Jacques Laffont

The Phillips Curve
Richard G. Lipsey and Robert Leeson

The Economics of Biotechnology
Maureen McKelvey and Luigi Orsenigo

The Economic Role of the State
Steven G. Medema

Open Economy Macroeconomics
Norman C. Miller

Innovation and Economic Development
Lynn Mytelka

Forms of Capitalism: Comparative Institutional Analyses
Ugo Pagano and Ernesto Screpanti

The New Evolutionary Economics
Jason Potts and Kurt Dopfer

The Economics of Public Utilities
Ray Rees

The Economics of Modern Business Enterprise
Martin Ricketts

New Developments in Public Choice
Charles K. Rowley, Robert D. Tollison and William F. Shughart

Recent Developments in International Investment
Alan M. Rugman

Cartels
Stephen Salant and Margaret Levenstein

The Economics of the Hidden Economy
Vito Tanzi

The Economics of Leisure and Recreation
Clem Tisdell

Recent Developments in Evolutionary Economics
Ulrich Witt